DIGITAL LIBRARIES

DIGITAL LIBRARIES

(In 3 Volumes)

DIGITAL LIBRARY: PRINCIPLES AND PRACTICES

(Volume-1)

Editor

Dr. Vijay Lakshmi

Dr. S.C. Jindal

ISHA BOOKS

DELHI-110 033

Digital Libraries

Rs. 2500 (Set)
Rs. 835 (each volume)

ISBN: 81-8205-109-6 (Set)
ISBN: 81-8205-110-X (Vol.1)

Reprinted in 2011 in India by
Isha Publications
B-63, Ist Floor
New Gupta Colony
Near DDA Market
Delhi-110009

Printed at: G. Print Process, Delhi

Contents

Preface vii

1 **Digital Image Collections** 1

2 **Preservation of Digital Information** 15
Metadata for digital preservation; Role of Society; Challenges of Digital Information; Preserving E-Journals; Council on Library and Information Resources (CLIR): A Framework for E-journal Archiving; Preservation and Access.

3 **Strategy of Digital Preservation** 97
Digital Rosetta Stone Model; Role of Infrastructure; Preserving Access to Digital Information (PADI).

4 **Information Retrieval and Record Keeping** 124
Management of Electronic Records; Functional Requirements for Recordkeeping; Modern Information Retrieval; Preservation Policies and Procedures; Digital Migration.

5 **Metadata: The Foundations of Digital Record Keeping** 172
Growth of Internet; The NEDLIB project; SPIRT—Recordkeeping Metadata Research Project.

6 **Digital Collection Management System** **195**
Strategies for Digital Collection Management; Long-term Access to Digital Documents.

7 **Intellectual Property and Access Technolog** **228**
Intellectual Property Conservancies; Digital and Media Conversion Processes; Original Document; The Selection Process; The Preserved Copy; Usability of Digital Resources; The Open Archival Information System (OAIS); E-print and Long-term Services.

Bibliography 301

Index 303

Preface

The term 'intellectual property' can be defined as property from original thought protected by law: original creative work manifested in a tangible form that can be legally protected, for example, by a patent, trademark, or copyright. Intellectual property rights (IPRs) have become an area of international interest and controversy as the rate and cost of technological progress have increased, and as national borders have become ever more transparent. Disagreements have arisen not only over the mechanics of granting such rights, but even over the validity and merits of certain fundamental concepts concerning IPRs.

Since the internet has become a huge information outlet, the regulation of information passed along the Internet has become a central issue in protecting intellectual property—especially as hackers find more and more ways to download, swap, and burn multimedia works, and then pass those techniques onto others.

This book describes what intellectual property is, who owns ideas, how to distinguish between copyrights, trademarks, and patents, and the pros and cons of protecting intellectual property in today's high-tech world. It also deals with the debate surrounding the safeguarding of intellectual property, how people are affected by IP laws, and what is being done to protect ideas spread through various forms of media. It will be a highly informative reference tool for all concerned.

Editor

1

Digital Image Collections

Cultural institutions that are making digital image collections available via the Web consistently report large numbers of users. An essential effort of any digital initiative is to evaluate the effectiveness and usability of the delivery system, including its interface, ease of use, and the value of the information provided for users. Assessing the impact of digital image collections can be difficult due to the challenges of gathering, organizing, and sharing useful data.

Media and technology-rich environments, such as cultural Web sites, demand equally rich data collection and analysis tools that are capable of examining human-computer interactions. Evaluators can no longer consider technological devices in isolation, but must develop a functional understanding of how the technology is used within a particular context, such as the use of an image database in supporting a curriculum. Thus, current approaches to the evaluation of interactive systems are broadening to include multifaceted methods of data collection and analysis.

This approach requires considering the interactions among the various groups that are working to define and develop digital environments. The Social Construction of Technology (SCOT) model encourages evaluators to consider the interactions and complexities among the various groups that are working to define and develop digital environments. Simple measurements of technological performance (e.g., number of logins) are inadequate, especially when isolated from data about the social structure within which the systems are designed or for which they are planned.

Researchers and evaluators have experimented with and relied upon computers in evaluations of multimedia environments for many years. Early computer tracking systems allowed inquirers to record system usage, alert developers of problem areas, and save a record of the interaction for later use. Today's approaches have similar functions, in addition to the usefulness of intersecting multimedia, network, and participatory environments. They not only allow evaluators to gather data from Web sites as they are being used, but also make possible the integration of other data as well as observations, interviews, documents produced, and video and audio recordings. The technologies also support evaluators as they analyze the data and develop their interpretations.

There are also several Web annotation software packages, such as Hot Off the Web, that allow users to make annotations directly on Web-like documents. Any URL can be accessed via the custom browser. The program then presents the page as a single snapshot; hyperlinks and other HTML or Javascript codes become inactive. Reviewers are then able to post comments and other annotations using small "post-it" style notes, stickers, highlight pens, and drawing tools. The marked-up page can then be saved as HTML with all annotations saved in the same folder.

Asynchronous evaluations generally involve gathering user's opinions after-the-fact. Synchronous approaches employ extensive use of networked technologies both to collect data and to report findings. Users are able to provide feedback as they use the system, allowing designers to take their evaluations into account in an iterative design process. Synchronous efforts attempt to place evaluation in the context of actual usage. Consider, for example, having Web site evaluation activities a click or two away—or even open alongside—a Web product. Another advantage is that synchronous evaluations can improve response rates because of convenience, respondent motivation, and a greater sense of relevance and context.

In US, efforts to begin creating the national digital library—a concept that encompasses archival collections, texts, images, sound files, full-motion video, composite documents, and other document types—have led quickly to the need for new approaches to the bibliographic control of such items, at both the local and national level. RLG Digital Image Access Project (DIAP) suggest a new data model for the bibliographic control of and access to digital image collections, one based on current, standard cataloging practice but enlarged to incorporate the additional detail, hierarchy, and version information needed to adequately describe digital collections.

Though not addressed as part of DIAP, the same model may well be extensible to the cataloging of other types of digital items as well, especially digital reproductions of items created originally in non-digital form. The proposed data model could readily be "housed" in an SGML-encoded bibliographic (metadata) record that encapsulates both summary bibliographic information along with detailed hierarchical and version-related data, when such data is appropriate and considered useful to record.

The record would also include links to the actual digital items, to other related bibliographic records or, in fact, to diverse, related digital objects (such as external electronic publications, databases, numeric files, etc.) The working designation SGML Catalog Record (SCR) is proposed for this new type of record. The SCR would, by flexibly incorporating data-element "clusters," allow a more narrative approach to the recording and presentation of complex bibliographic information than is practical in the current AACR2/USMARC model, which requires the fragmentation of hierarchically- related components and version information into separate, discrete records.

That the current USMARC model serves libraries and users poorly—most notably in the cataloging of microfilm reproductions of printed texts and with complex serial publications--has been widely discussed. Attempts to rectify the situation have been unsuccessful, in large part because of the intrinsically flat structure of USMARC and the automated library systems that have been designed around it. The USMARC records would always contain pointers to local SCRs, where they exist, rather than pointers to individual electronic texts, images, etc.

Not only would the use of an SGML-based cataloging model better suit the description of digital collection and items, it would allow libraries to better take advantage of the many new non- library-based automated systems, standards and software tools, such as the World Wide Web, now becoming available. Without greater flexibility in the cataloging and encoding of digital documents, library-generated bibliographic data will not be easily integrated into the developing local and national information environment as effective inventories of and indexes to the electronic holdings of libraries.

This proposal is an outgrowth of the RLG Digital Image Access Project, though it should not necessarily be seen as a Project recommendation. It builds conceptually on the Berkeley Finding Aids Project (BFAP) data model and was refined in meetings and discussions with the Columbia DIAP project team. The DIAP participants made several working assumptions about the nature of the cataloging needed for digital image collections. One was that there was no way to anticipate—in system terms—the intellectual structure of a digital image collection or the number of hierarchically-related records that would be needed to describe it fully.

For example, an image collection at one institution might be cataloged with a collection level-record and several subcollection or series level records, with links to full records for selected individual items. Faced with the same type of collection, another institution might choose simply to create a collection level record and caption-level records for the individual items. This unpredictability of the content and structure of archival catalog records, well-understood among archivists and archival catalogers but somewhat less well appreciated by the mainstream of library automation and technical services, took on new significance in a project attempting to integrate cataloging data and linked digital images from multiple institutions into a single database search, retrieval and display system.

For example, although the project members initially specified that searching within Visual Photologue be able to be limited to specific hierarchical levels, it became clear that this was not only relatively useless but even confusing to the searcher because of the unpredictability of data content at the same hierarchical level. Another DIAP assumption was that there was no way to predict the level of cataloging detail that would be provided by an institution at any particular hierarchical level from one collection to another or even within a single collection.

The level of cataloging detail would always be subject to institutional practice, cost considerations, the character of particular collection, the importance of the collection within the owning institution s holdings, etc. Practically, this meant that all defined data elements would need to be repeatable at all levels of the model. Participants agreed that the model implied no prescriptive set of data elements at any level, except as required by national standards, network practice, etc., usually as applied to the highest-level information.

The DIAP data model implicitly allowed for description of multiple versions of images, i.e., original images (e.g., slides, photographic prints, maps), intermediate reproductions (e.g., 35mm film), and one or more purely digital versions of an image (e.g., a 600 x 300 dpi JPEG file). Although the project itself produced only a single, low resolution digital image for each image, at least one of the participant institutions also had items rescanned into the Kodak PhotoCD format, which normally provides five versions of the image at increasingly greater resolution; this resulted in up to six digital versions for each of Columbia's original images.

In addition to description of the original and one or more digital versions, participants also confirmed the desirability of including descriptive information about intermediate images. The lack of standards for the physical and in some cases intellectual description of the digital items themselves was noted by the participants. No systematic attempt to create a data dictionary or a prescribed set of elements was undertaken by the project, in part because of time constraints but also because of the awareness of other efforts to carry out this analysis nationally. The enormity of this task became clear, however, during DIAP-related discussions, where the need for various types of sets additional data elements was noted.

Another virtually inevitable set of issues raised by the project concerned the description of the original items from which the digital images were created. Consistent with other variable approaches to cataloging and description, participant institutions had different practices here, sometimes on a collection by collection basis. Participants agreed that, however desirable it might be to have piece-level description for their image holdings, it was in many cases a practical impossibility.

Under the best of circumstances, a full-set of descriptive and subject oriented data elements for each original image would be present in the record cluster. Intermediate, second- and subsequent-generation reproductions of the originals would be coded as hierarchical children of the originals, inheriting the description and access elements of the originals. While participants did decline to recommend universal piece-level cataloging as part of the project, there was a sense that the creation of digital image access techniques envisioned by this project did have certain implications for the cataloging of originals, however, namely that caption-level cataloging was highly desirable to enhance the display of individual digital images.

In some cases, however, the captions would necessarily be non-unique (e.g., in collections of closely related images), uninformative (e.g., a sequential ID number), or difficult to interpret without the inheritance of higher-level information. In short, the cataloging data model developed by DIAP may be described as follows:

— collection cataloging consists of a set of data element clusters

— clusters may be flexibly arranged into multiple hierarchical levels

— a full set of data elements is accommodated, though not required, at each hierarchical level

— descriptions of originals, intermediates, reproductions, versions, and components may be included

— within clusters, AACR2 and related cataloging guidelines and USMARC data element definitions are observed whenever feasible

— relationships between data element clusters may be implicit or explicit

— links to digital objects may be present at any level of hierarchy

An implicit assumption of the cataloging model developed by the Project was that an amalgam of existing cataloging standards and practices would provide an acceptable formula for the cataloging of digital image collections. The emphasis was on extrapolation from existing cataloging models and incremental modification of current practice.

One of the axiomatic assumptions of DIAP was that RLG image collections would continue to require some high-level cataloging or guide record in the national union databases (RLIN and OCLC) in addition to whatever was present at the local level. It was also assumed that local systems might well have more detailed information about collections and items and that links to the actual image files themselves would probably stored and managed at the local level. Participants agreed, and tested the assumption, that it should be possible to convert from USMARC into whatever format was used locally for the description of image collections.

The group did not feel, however, that it could impose "backward compatibility" by requiring that all descriptive and access data stored locally should necessarily be convertible directly back into USMARC. This decision was made, in part, so as not to constrain the exploration of access at the local level to what is currently supported in USMARC. It was also an acknowledgement that local, detailed information may inevitably reside in a variety of different local systems, some of which may simply not be capable of backward convertibility.

This issue naturally raised the important question the of whether it is acceptable bibliographic practice to store definitive descriptive information for collections and items at the local institution that is not only not present in national database systems, but is stored in a format incompatible with existing USMARC-based automated systems. The participants did seem comfortable with this principle so long as navigational tools would be implemented for moving seamlessly between national and local systems, e.g. using URLs stored in national bibliographic records to readily access locally stored data and the images themselves. This kind of national navigational system would, however, require that local data be stored in some recognized, standard format, if not USMARC.

SGML continued to be suggested as the likely possibility, in view of the work proceeding under the aegis of the Berkeley Finding Aids Project. It may be that SGML editing, display, and retrieval tools will become widespread enough in the near future to allow a consistent and standard approach to the creation of detailed local information. DIAP did not address the possibility of further extending USMARC or AACR2 to accommodate the type of data structure needed for local access to digital image collections.

Some project participants recognized the potential problems that multiple versions of digital and non-digital images (e.g., multiple intermediates, images at multiple resolutions, differently edited images, blow-ups, zooms, etc.) would immediately present to MARC, and were reluctant to pursue this issue in the MARC standards arena yet again, in light of earlier unsuccessful attempts to solve the multiple versions problem with respect to the much simpler problems presented by microform reproductions.

During the course of the Project, the RLIN local field 789 was in the process of being discussed at MARBI for possible inclusion in USMARC. This field was originally defined for providing linkage from online RLIN records to analog images stored on videodisc as for the Columbia University Libraries Aviador Project. Whether or not the use of this field becomes more widespread, it is clear that it cannot be used adequately to provide more than caption-level access to digital images at a single hierarchical level reflecting a simple parent-child relationship and a single image "generation."

This is because it lacks the full complement of descriptive and access-oriented data elements, the capability of reflecting hierarchies, and any technique to identify or distinguish multiple versions or unpredictable component part relationships. Beyond these, the considerations of record length mentioned above come into play. For these reasons and others, it was not considered a potential solution to the broad set of issues identified by DIAP.

A starting point for the DIAP project was the idea of modeling access and retrieval of image information within a local system. The Visual Photologue software, designed by staff at Stokes Imaging, provided an environment that allowed some prototyping work in interface design, indexing and retrieval. This approach had only limited success for a variety of reasons--chief among them the paradigm shift triggered by the sudden more general availability of technology to store images and image metadata locally in open systems and access them nationally and internationally through the Internet and World Wide Web.

This new model of distributed access and accompanying software "tool set" was seen as much more promising than the closed, proprietary Visual Photologue system and more in tune with the innovative and well-funded areas of information technology springing up around the Internet. Nonetheless, the data access architecture implied in both types of systems was that of locally stored detailed metadata and images, linked to (perhaps only summary) metadata in a national union database, and accessible broadly to authorized users via the Internet. Whether the images available on the Internet were to be considered index images and pointers to the locally held originals, or whether the images would be good enough quality to serve as surrogates for some range of uses, was a secondary and evolving consideration.

Unlike the Stokes model with which DIAP began, an expanded distributed access model requires that locally stored data, images, and linkage information be represented in a consistent way, following national and international standards to the extent feasible.

Standards for image file formats and for Uniform Resource Locators (URLs) and Uniform Resource Names (URNs) are being adequately addressed in the broader information community at this point. The remaining area, namely, content and format for locally created metadata, is the one most in need of standards work. Since USMARC is not an adequate tool to encode detailed information at the local level for digital image collections—for the reasons enumerated above—the obvious alternative candidate format is SGML, which is already increasingly being used not only for the encoding of texts but for the representation of metadata. The draft Document Type Definition (DTD) for a USMARC SGML record, prepared at U.C. Berkeley, is a clear starting point for current and future efforts to make USMARC functionally interoperable with the SGML and WWW worlds. In view of this, the approach proposed here entails the provision of:

— summary records for image (and other) collections in both online national union catalog and local USMARC-based online catalogs

— detailed SGML catalog records (SCRs) for the same collections stored and maintained by the local institution, optionally with thumbnail images incorporated

— multiple image sizes and resolutions stored at the local institution, linked to local SCRs

— pointers (URLs, URNs) from national online union catalog records to detailed SCRs

— local workstation access to summary USMARC data, local SCRs and local images using, for example, a World Wide Web browser that is both Z39.50- and SGML-capable

The proposal also has direct implications for the cataloging of non-collection digital items, particularly reproductions of existing monographic items. For example, a USMARC record for a printed text might well have a pointer to a local SCR for an electronic version of the text, which itself provides access to straight ASCII, TEI-encoded or bitmapped text files along with multiple image files including thumbnails and higher-resolution images. This model addresses both the multiple versions problem inherent in electronic reproductions of texts as well as the component part problem presented by multiple text and image files, all corresponding to a single original work.

The approach proposed here has the additional benefit of helping position research libraries to take advantage of the dramatic wave of innovation in access, display, indexing, retrieval and multimedia integration now washing over the Internet. Because library automation is such a small market and relatively poorly-funded, it is neither reasonable nor financially prudent to try to modify existing MARC-based systems to keep up with newer standards and technologies, at least in every case; nor, on the other hand, can we afford to shackle libraries to older MARC- based technology when events are moving so quickly in the world at large.

Existing MARC- based systems do their current jobs relatively well and will continue to be crucial as national and local guides to local holdings. In the developing research library information environment we can anticipate that users will come to access library-related information and documents through a variety of pathways: via RLIN or OCLC, the local OPAC, locally indexed WWW and SGML documents, courseware, electronic publications, remote links and references to local holdings, and many others. MARC- based systems, with their controlled vocabulary and powerful, if rudimentary, search capabilities may provide the most consistently high-quality access to information referenced in their files.

They are, however, only one means by which users will find out about digital collections and texts; in many cases users will be led from "courseware," from citations in other electronic documents, or from archival finding aids directly to electronic documents. Integration of local and remote resources will take place at the workstation, through browsers that support WWW, SGML, Z39.50 and other standards. Higher-level "metaindexes" and intelligent "agents" will be needed to navigate disparate information types.

2

Preservation of Digital Information

The preservation of digital information can be seen as one of the greatest challenges for the library and information professions at the end of the twentieth-century. It is easy to get caught-up in the general enthusiasm for digital libraries but more consideration needs to be given to the problem of making this information available to future generations. Libraries have traditionally understood at least one of their roles as the preservation of information for future use. This has been especially true of national libraries and selected institutions in the research library sector.

For example, in early 1996 the British Library proposed that legal deposit should be extended to include non-print materials, even allowing for the possibility of collecting networked (on-line) publications if this became technically and economically feasible. Most countries in Europe, North America and Australasia have either extended legal deposit to electronic publications or are considering doing so. This implies a commitment, by national libraries at least, to the long-term preservation of digital publications.

The main problem with digital preservation is that digital technology, in comparison to print, is an extremely fragile medium for the cultural memory of the world. The most commonly given example of this fragility is the 1960 United States Census, where raw data stored on magnetic tapes apparently became obsolete and, to all intents and purposes, unreadable by the late nineteen-seventies. Digital information has two main weaknesses:

1. *The storage medium* - digital storage media, whether magnetic or optical, are subject to relatively rapid decay: especially when compared with print.
2. *The hardware and software* - digital information is machine-dependent, and to be 'read' accurately it needs specific computer hardware and software. Unfortunately, hardware and software quickly become obsolescent or otherwise unusable.

Proposed solutions to these problems usually involve periodic 'refreshing' or recopying of the digital information onto new media and the occasional 'migration' of data into new formats. Assuming that some answer can be found to these problems, there remains the important issue of intellectual preservation. The archives community—especially in the United States - has been addressing these issues for some time now. This has partly been led by the need for electronic records to be accepted in legal evidence but the fact that electronic records are increasingly created in a variety of important situations: government; health-care; business-transactions, etc., has resulted in a renewed interest in authentication and validation issues.

Metadata for digital preservation

Michael Day suggests how the concept of metadata could

be extended to provide information in the specific field of digital preservation. When the library and information community discuss metadata, the most common analogy given is the library catalogue record. Priscilla Caplan, for example, has defined metadata as a neutral term for cataloguing without the "excess baggage" of the Anglo-American Cataloguing Rules or the MARC formats. The most well-known metadata initiative, the Dubin Core Metadata Element Set, has the specific aim of supporting resource discovery in a network environment.

The Internet has many virtues, but it—and in particular the World Wide Web—was not designed specifically for information retrieval. The search technologies that evolved - Archie for anonymous ftp sites, Veronica for gopher and search engines for the Web - were developed as a response to perceived needs rather than as an integral part of the original concept. Search engines like Digital Equipment Corporation's Alta Vista construct indexes by means of robots which 'crawl' through the Web collecting indexing information.

This is a less than perfect solution as Web sites typically do not contain all the relevant information for automated indexing and if they do it is unlikely to be in a form identifiable to most robots. It is possible that if Dublin Core metadata is attached to or embedded in a large number of Web documents, a new generation of Web robots or harvesters could collect this metadata and make it available through improved search services.

Search engines, however, are not the only solution to the Internet resource discovery problem. An alternative approach has been to get people to select resources according to agreed criteria and then make them available via a Web site, where they can be browsed or searched.

Metadata formats come in a variety of shapes and sizes. Dublin Core is intended to be a simple structured record which can, if required, be enhanced or mapped to more complex records.

Dublin Core may have a role as a minimal metadata set in order to allow for interoperability between other, more complex, metadata formats. Library and information professionals with an interest in the Internet should be interested in the development of metadata for resource discovery.

Clifford Lynch points out that if the Internet is to continue to thrive as a new means of communication, "something very much like traditional library services will be needed to organize, access and preserve networked information". Metadata does have an acknowledged role in the organisation of and access to networked information, but it could additionally be important in the general area of digital preservation.

Role of Society

Society has vital interest in preserving materials that document issues, concerns, ideas, discourse and events. Custodians of the cultural record have always had to manage the inherent conflict between letting people use manuscripts, books, recordings or videos, and being sure that they are preserved for future use. For works printed on acidic wood pulp paper, as most books have been since 1850, they measure the remaining lifetime of those materials in decades, not centuries.

In 1993, forty-five percent of U.S. workers were using a computer; the number is surely larger now. Virtually all printing and a rapidly increasing amount of writing is accomplished with computers. Professional sound recording is digital, and digital video is on the verge of moving from experimental to practical applications. As a means of recording and providing access to their cultural memory, digital technology has numerous advantages and may help relieve the traditional conflict between preservation and access. For materials stored digitally, users operate on exact images of the original works stored in their local computers.

Separating usage from the original in this way, digital technology affords multiple, simultaneous uses from a single original in ways that are simply not possible for materials stored in any other form. Digital technology also yields additional, effective means of access. In full text documents, a reader can retrieve needed information by searching for words, combinations of words, phrases or ideas. .

Readers can also manipulate the display of digital materials by choosing whether to view digital materials on a screen, store them on their computer or external media, or to print them. Digital technology, however, poses new threats and problems as well as new opportunities. Its functionality comes with complexity. Anyone with a compass (or a clear night to view the position of the stars in relation to true north) could theoretically set up or repair a sundial.

A digital watch is more useful and accurate for telling time than a sundial, but few people can repair it or even understand how it works. Reading and understanding information in digital form requires equipment and software, which is changing constantly and may not be available within a decade of its introduction. Who today has a punched card reader, a Dectape drive, or a working copy of FORTRAN II? Even newer technology such as 9-track tape is rapidly becoming obsolete. They cannot save the machines if there are no spare parts available, and they cannot save the software if no one is left who knows how to use it.

Rapid changes in the means of recording information, in the formats for storage, and in the technologies for use threaten to render the life of information in the digital age as, to borrow a phrase from Hobbes, "nasty, brutish and short." Some information no doubt deserves such a fate, but numerous examples illustrate the danger of losing valuable cultural memories that may appear in digital form.

In 1976, the US National Archives identified seven series of aggregated data from the 1960 Census files as having long-term historical value. A large portion of the selected records, however, resided on tapes that the Bureau could read only with a UNIVAC type II-A tape drive. By the mid-seventies, that particular tape drive was long obsolete, and the Census Bureau faced a significant engineering challenge in preserving the data from the UNIVAC type II-A tapes.

By 1979, the Bureau had successfully copied onto industry-standard tapes nearly all the data judged then to have long-term value. Though largely successful in the end, the data rescue effort was a signal event that helped move the Committee on the Records of Government six years later to proclaim that "the United States is in danger of losing its memory." The Committee did not bother to describe the actual details of the migration of the 1960 census records. Nor did it analyze the effects on the integrity of the constitutionally-mandated census of the nearly 10,000 (of approximately 1.5 million) records of aggregated data that the rescue effort did not successfully recover.

Instead, it chose to register its warning on the dangers of machine obsolescence in apocryphal terms. With more than a little hyperbole, it wrote that "when the computer tapes containing the raw data from the 1960 federal census came to the attention of NARS [the National Archives and Records Service], there were only two machines in the world capable of reading those tapes: one in Japan and the other already deposited in the Smithsonian as a relic".

In 1964, the first electronic mail message was sent from either the Massachusetts Institute of Technology, the Carnegie Institute of Technology or Cambridge University. The message does not survive, however, and so there is no documentary record to determine which group sent the pathbreaking message. Satellite observations of Brazil in the 1970s, critical for establishing a time-line of changes in the Amazon basin, are also lost on the now obsolete tapes to which they were written.

Similarly, in the late 1960s, the New York State Department of Commerce and Cornell University undertook the Land Use and Natural Resources Inventory Project (LUNR). The LUNR project produced a computerized map of New York State depicting patterns of land usage and identifying natural resources. It created a primitive geographic information system by superimposing a matrix over aerial photographs of the entire state and coding each cell according to its predominant features.

In the mid-1980s, the New York State Archives obtained copies of the tapes containing the data from the LUNR inventory along with the original aerial photographs and several thousand mylar transparencies.

Staff at the State Archives attempted to preserve the LUNR tapes, but the problems proved insurmountable. The LUNR project had depended on customized software programs to represent and analyze the data, and these programs were not saved with the data.

Even if the software had been retained, the hardware and operating system needed to run the software were no longer available. Today, information technologies that are increasingly powerful and easy to use, especially like those that support the World Wide Web, have unleashed the production and distribution of digital information. Such information is penetrating and transforming nearly every aspect of culture. If they are effectively to preserve for future generations the portion of this rapidly expanding corpus of information in digital form that represents their cultural record, they need to understand the costs of doing so and they need to commit ourselves technically, legally, economically and organizationally to the full dimensions of the task. Failure to look for trusted means and methods of digital preservation will certainly exact a stiff, long-term cultural penalty.

Challenges of Digital Information

Archivists responsible for governmental and corporate records have been acutely aware of the difficulties entailed in trying to ensure that digital information survives for future generations. Far more than their library colleagues, who have continued to collect and organize published materials primarily in paper form, archivists have observed the materials for which they are responsible shift rapidly from paper objects produced on typewriters and other analog devices to include files created in word processor, spreadsheet and many other digital forms.

Early attention to the difficulties in preserving digital information focused on the longevity of the physical media on which the information is stored. Even under the best storage conditions, however, digital media can be fragile and have limited shelf life. Moreover, new devices, processes and software are replacing the products and methods used to record, store, and retrieve digital information on breathtaking cycles of 2- to 5- years.

Given such rates of technological change, even the most fragile media may well outlive the continued availability of readers for those media. Efforts to preserve physical media thus provide only a short-term, partial solution to the general problem of preserving digital information. Indeed, technological obsolescence represents a far greater threat to information in digital form than the inherent physical fragility of many digital media.

In the face of rapid technological obsolescence and to overcome the problem of media fragility, archivists have adopted the technique of "refreshing" digital information by copying it onto new media. Refreshing digital information by copying will work as an effective preservation technique only as long as the information is encoded in a format that is independent of the particular hardware and software needed to use it and as long as there exists software to manipulate the format in current use.

Otherwise, copying depends either on the compatibility of present and past versions of software and generations of hardware or the ability of competing hardware and software product lines to interoperate. In respect of these factors—backward compatibility and interoperability—the rate of technological change exacts a serious toll on efforts to ensure the longevity of digital information.

Digital information today is produced in highly varying degrees of dependence on particular hardware and software. Moreover, it is costly and difficult for vendors to assure that their products are either "backwardly compatible" with previous versions or that they can interoperate with competing products. Refreshing thus cannot serve as a general solution for preserving digital information and this conclusion has prompted discussion of other kinds of solutions. Jeff Rothenberg, for example, has recently suggested that there may be sufficient demand for entrepreneurs to create and archive emulators of software and operating systems that would allow the contents of digital information to be carried forward and used in its original format.

Refreshing digital information by copying it from medium to medium and the possibility of maintaining a complex set of emulators describe two distinct points on a continuum of approaches to preserving digital information. However, neither refreshing nor emulation sufficiently describes the full range of options needed and available for digital preservation. Instead, a better and more general concept to describe these options is migration. Migration is the periodic transfer of digital materials from one hardware/software configuration to another, or from one generation of computer technology to a subsequent generation.

The purpose of migration is to preserve the integrity of digital objects and to retain the ability for clients to retrieve, display, and otherwise use them in the face of constantly changing technology. Migration includes refreshing as a means of digital preservation but differs from it in the sense that it is not always possible to make an exact digital copy or replica of a database or other information object as hardware and software change and still maintain the compatibility of the object with the new generation of technology.

Even for information that is encoded in a contemporary standard form, forward migration of the information to a new standard or application program is, as anyone knows who has witnessed or participated in such a process, time-consuming, costly and much more complex than simple refreshing.

Compounding the technical challenges of migrating digital information is the problem of managing the process in a legal and organizational environment that is in flux as it moves to accommodate rapidly changing digital technologies. Consider, for example, the barriers to decisive preservation action caused by widespread uncertainty about legal and organizational requirements for managing the intellectual property that digital information represents.

Addressing and resolving the legal and practical questions of migrating intellectual property in digital form necessarily involves a complex set of interested parties, including the creators and owners of intellectual property, managers of digital archives, representatives of the public interest, and actual and potential users of intellectual property. In addition, the parties who represent, for example, owners and users of different kinds of intellectual property (e.g., text and other document-like objects, photographs, film, software, multimedia objects) each operate under very different organizational regimes, with different experiences and expectations.

Adding to these complexities is the deep uncertainty that these groups face in confronting an increasingly digital world. Owners of intellectual property are unsure about how to price access to their information and worry, given the ease of copying, that the first digital copy of a work they sell may be the only copy they sell. Users of intellectual property are unsure about what rights are conveyed with the use of a particular digital information object and about how much such use is worth.

Government representatives seek in the public interest to manage the powerful changes that accompany digital technologies, but are unsure about what levels of influece are available to them and how to generate appropriate public policy. The state of the copyright law, which was generated and developed in an analog world but is applied in an increasingly digital universe, is itself confusing and uncertain. And all of these concerns are exacerbated by the fact that bits know no borders.

The costs and the technical, legal and organizational complexities of moving digital information forward into the future raise their greatest fear about the life of information in the digital future: namely, that owners or custodians who can no longer bear the expense and difficulty will deliberately or inadvertently, through a simple failure to act, destroy the objects without regard for future use.

Even after more than forty years of growth, the digital world of information technology and communication is still relatively young and immature in relation to the larger information universe, parts of which have been under development for centuries. Viewed developmentally, the problem of preserving digital information for the future is not only, or even primarily, a problem of fine tuning a narrow set of technical variables. It is not a clearly defined problem like preserving the embrittled books that are self-destructing from the acid in the paper on which they were printed.

Rather, it is a grander problem of organizing ourselves over time and as a society to maneuver effectively in a digital landscape. It is a problem of building—almost from scratch—the various systematic supports, or deep infrastructure. For digital preservation, the organizational effort -- the process of building deep infrastructure -- necessarily involves multiple, interrelated factors, many of which are either unknown or poorly defined.

One of the biggest unknowns is the full impact on traditional information handling functions of distributed computing over electronic networks. The effort to meet the cultural imperative of digital preservation thus requires a complex iteration and reiteration of exploration, development and solution as the relevant factors and their interrelationships emerge and become clearer and more tractable.

In US, the Commission on Preservation and Access and The Research Libraries Group (RLG) have joined together in charging the Task Force on Archiving of Digital Information to take this first essential step toward a national system of digital preservation. They have asked the Task Force to "consult broadly among librarians, archivists, curators, technologists, relevant government and private sector organizations, and other interested parties" in an effort to:

— "frame the key problems (organizational, technological, legal, economic etc.)" associated with digital preservation,

— "define the critical issues that inhibit resolution of each identified problem," and

— "recommend actions to remove the issue from the list."

The Task Force charge, however, itself frames the anticipated solutions in terms of the concept of "refreshing" In taking up this charge, the Task Force on Archiving of Digital Information starts from the premise, argued above, that migration is a broader and richer concept than "refreshing" for identifying the range of options for digital preservation. The Task Force defines digital archives strictly in functional terms as repositories of digital information that are collectively responsible for ensuring, through the exercise of various migration strategies, the integrity and long-term accessibility of the nation's social, economic, cultural and intellectual heritage instantiated in digital form.

Digital archives are distinct from digital libraries in the sense that digital libraries are repositories that collect and provide access to digital information, but may or may not provide for the long-term storage and access of that information. Digital libraries thus may or may not be, in functional terms, digital archives and, in fact, much of the recent work on digital libraries is notably silent on the archival issues of ensuring long-term storage and access. Conversely, digital archives necessarily embrace digital library functions to the extent that they must select, obtain, store, and provide access to digital information.

Many of the functional requirements for digital archives overlap those for digital libraries. The Task Force has deliberately taken a functional approach in these critical definitions and in its general treatment of digital preservation so as not to prejudge the question of institutional structure. Many traditional libraries, archives and museums, as institutions, have taken and may well continue to assume digital library and archival functions. However, the Task Force recognizes that, as the digital environment emerges and its requirements become clearer, traditional institutions may need to change in various structurally significant ways and new kinds of institutions and institutional structures may emerge to perform all or parts of key archival functions for digital information.

The Task Force sees repositories of digital information as held together in a national archival system primarily through the operation of two essential mechanisms. First, to ensure that no valued digital information is lost to future generations, repositories claiming to serve an archival function must be able to prove that they are who they say they are by meeting or exceeding the standards and criteria of an independently-administered program for archival certification. Second, certified digital archives will have available to them a critical fail-safe mechanism. Such a mechanism, supported by organizational will, economic means and legal right, would enable a certified archival repository to exercise an aggressive rescue function to save digital information that it judges to be culturally significant and which is endangered in its current repository.

The current repository may be a digital library, another digital archives, or some other individual, organizational, public or private source of digital information. Without the operation of a formal certification program and a fail-safe mechanism, preservation of the nation's cultural heritage in digital form will likely be overly dependent on marketplace forces, which may value information for too short a period and without applying broader, public interest criteria.

In order to lay out the framework for digital preservation that it has envisioned, the Task Force begins with an analysis of the digital landscape, focusing on features, including stakeholder interest, that affect the integrity of digital information objects and which determine the ability of digital archives to preserve such objects over the long term. The Task Force then introduces the principles that responsibility for archiving rests initially with the creator or owner of the information and that digital archives may invoke a fail-safe mechanism to protect culturally valuable information. Following are the roles and responsibilities associated with the critical functions of managing:

— the operating environment of digital archives;

— strategies for migration of digital information; and

— costs and financial matters.

Information Objects

Information objects in digital form, like those in other forms, move through life cycles. They are created, edited, described and indexed, disseminated, acquired, used, annotated, revised, re-created, modified and retained for future use or destroyed by a complex, interwoven community of creators and other owners, disseminators, value-added services, and institutional and individual users. The digital world is still too new for to describe fully the life cycle of the information objects that do now or will in the future reside there, but what surely unites the community of actors in their various information-based activities is their common purpose in support of the pursuit of knowledge. The pursuit of knowledge is a process in which the emergence of new knowledge builds on and reconstructs the old.

Knowledge cannot advance without consistent and reliable access to information sources, past and present. It is the archival function in the system of knowledge creation and use that serves to identify and retain important sources of information and to ensure continuing access to them. How reliable the archival process proves to be in the emerging digital environment hinges on the trustworthy operation of digital archives and on their ability to maintain the integrity of the objects they are charged to preserve .

For digital objects, no less than for objects of other kinds, knowing how operationally to preserve them depends, at least in part, on being able to discriminate the essential features of what needs to be preserved. In this section, the Task Force focuses on the integrity of information objects in the digital environment—on the kinds of attributes they acquire during the course of their lives to give them a distinct identity—and on the claims of various interested parties, or stakeholders, in the different kinds and attributes of digital information. In the next section, the Task Force explores the operational roles and responsibilities of digital archives.

The Integrity of Digital Information

Digital technologies increasingly serve to integrate information resources. Text, numeric data, images, voice, and video have heretofore resided in print or other analog media for storage and transmission. When they are encoded digitally, either by conversion or at the point of creation, these various kinds of resources share layers of technology—a common means of storage and transmission—that allows them to be brought together and used in both old and new ways.

Multimedia and hyperlinked objects on the World Wide Web represent some of the new kinds of information and new ways of knowing in the digital realm that bring together the traditional forms of information and transform their use. The application of computer hardware and software has also generated other new kinds of information objects, including the products of simulation, remote sensing, computer-aided design (CAD) and geographic information (GIS) systems. These objects come into being and exist as creatures of the digital environment; if nurtured well, digital technologies will certainly beget still other kinds of information objects, which they can now only anticipate.

The processes of preserving digital information will vary significantly with the different kinds of objects—textual, numeric, image, video, sound, multimedia, simulation and so on—being preserved. Whatever preservation method is applied, however, the central goal must be to preserve information integrity; that is, to define and preserve those features of an information object that distinguish it as a whole and singular work. In the digital environment, the features that determine information integrity and deserve special attention for archival purposes include the following: content, fixity, reference, provenance, and context.

Digital archives are trying to preserve after all is the intellectual substance contained in information objects. The notion of content, however, is itself a complex idea that operates at several different levels of abstraction. To preserve the integrity of objects in their charge, digital archives must decide at which level, or levels, of abstraction they are defining information content. At the lowest level of abstraction, all digital information objects consist of simple bitstreams of 0s and 1s. One can distinguish objects from one another merely by distinguishing the configuration of bits. Preserving the integrity of an information object in this sense means preserving the bit configuration that uniquely defines the object.

There are various well-established techniques, such as checksums and digests, for tracking the bit-level equivalence of digital objects and ensuring that a preserved object is identical to the original. Defining content as a collection of bits, however, is often too limited and simplistic to be useful. In the digital environment, as they have seen, ideas are typically embedded in particular formats and structures that are dependent on hardware and software technologies subject to rapid change.

Conceived at this higher level of abstraction—that is, in terms of format and structure -- the definition of content poses considerable difficulties for managing information integrity in an archival context, and they are just beginning to come to terms with the expression of these problems in the digital environment. Standard extensions exist for encoding diacritic characters in romance languages other than English and a new standard is slowly emerging to incorporate scripted languages under a new common encoding scheme (UNICODE). Alternative encoding methods, however, abound.

IBM maintains its own EBCDIC character encoding scheme and Apple and Intel-based personal computers differ in the ways that they support extended ASCII character sets. For documents in which any of these character codes can adequately represent the contents, the differences in encoding schemes may matter little and digital archives can manage object integrity by mapping character sets from one to the other. However, for works involving multiple languages or complex equations and formula, where character mapping is imperfect or not possible, character set format takes on considerably more significance over the long-term as a matter of content integrity.

In addition to character set issues, digital archives must also grapple with the means of representing and preserving textual content embedded in layout and structure. Markup systems, such as implementations of TeX and the Standard Generalized Markup Language (SGML), do exist as platform-independent mechanisms for identifying and tagging for subsequent layout and retrieval detailed structural elements of documents.

The use of TeX and its variants, for example, is relatively common among scholars in some scientific disciplines such as mathematics and computer science, and the federal government and scholarly publishers are increasingly employing the SGML standard in documents that they produce and distribute electronically. Beyond these relatively specialized segments, however, word processing and desktop publishing systems still dominate the market for the creation of documents with complex structure and layout, and the software for such use typically models and stores document structure and layout in proprietary terms.

Although software may provide mechanisms for converting documents to common interchange formats, use of such mechanisms often results in the loss or inadequate rendering of content such as page structures and the layout of headers, footers and section headings. The preservation of images comprises another example of the ways in which content, defined in terms of structure and format, poses integrity problems for digital archives. Image resolution, accuracy of color representation and compression for storage all require attention, but the interaction of these structural factors tends to pit judgments about the quality of content against the need for its efficient archival storage and use.

In general, one can express the tradeoffs as follows: the higher the resolution and the richer the color register, the larger the file size and more costly the storage. At the highest level of abstraction, digital archives define content in a way that transcends the limits of the hardware and software systems needed for reading and interpreting the bits of an information object and for rendering it for use in a specific format and structural representation; that is, they define content in terms of the knowledge or ideas the object contains.

Expressed in this way, the preservation challenge for digital archives is to migrate (or to enable the user to migrate) intellectual content using standard interchange algorithms and other appropriate migration strategies so that the ideas available in the end are identical to those contained in the original object. The measure of integrity in the preservation process thus turns, at least in part, on informed and skillful judgments about the appropriate definition of the content of an digital information object—about the extent to which content depends on its configuration of bits, on the structure and format of its representation, and on the ideas it contains—and for what purposes.

The process of identifying and preserving a digital information object as a whole and singular work goes well beyond considerations of content. It also depends,. for instance, on the way that the content is fixed as a discrete object. If an object is not fixed, and the content is subject to change or withdrawal without notice, then its integrity may be compromised and its value as a cultural record would be severely diminished. Outside the digital landscape, business practices, editorial policies, and legal constraints, have created disciplines for fixing information in discrete objects.

The acts of production and broadcast establish radio and television programs as discrete objects. And the act of publication marks a specific version or edition of a literary work. In each of these cases, it is virtually impossible to change or withdraw the cultural record that the release of an information object establishes.

On the digital landscape, by contrast, it is still relatively easy for a creator to alter or retract previously released information. Such actions can eliminate or overlay significant content and thereby corrupt the record. It is also relatively easy in an on-line environment—and equally confusing for purposes of preserving information integrity -- for an author (or user) to make available concurrently multiple representations of what he or she considers to be the same work, providing no definition of a canonical version and viewing all representations as having equal quality and validity.

To address these problems, a wide range of cryptographic techniques, such as watermarking, already exist for various kinds of digital information objects. These could serve well to mark and identify specific, canonical versions and editions of textual, audio and visual works, and to establish trusted, protected channels of distribution for those objects. However, the standards and infrastructure and the policies and practices for applying such techniques to the creation of fixed versions of digital information objects still need considerable development.

Absent such development and the fixity of information that would result, digital archives face considerable challenges in trying to preserve the integrity of digital objects. Some kinds of digital objects present the problem of fixity of information in yet another way. An increasing number of networked information resources are better modeled, not in terms of versions or editions of works, but as continuously updated databases.

The Human Genome Project supports such a database, which serves as a vehicle and record for a worldwide collaborative effort. The financial communities also depend on large, continuously updated databases. There is no natural way to fix these resources at the database level, no natural set of publication points for the objects as a whole. Their integrity, or singularity, as databases resides in the coherence of the database as a whole and in the continuousness of the updates. To preserve the integrity of such information resources, the complete record of changes has to be built into the design of the database and fixed at the record level.

Technology exists for constructing databases that maintain all previous versions of the records in the database as well as details about when new information is added or logically deleted. A database designed to a so-called time-travel specification, however, is expensive to construct and operate. In the absence of such a preservation-oriented design, digital archives may have no choice but to fix the database artificially in time and capture a series of snapshots of its state at periodic intervals as a way of preserving its integrity.

Another aspect of information integrity that bears crucially on the preservation process is that information objects must have a consistent means of reference.

Information objects come into being and acquire their distinctiveness in relation to various other objects in an information space. For an object to maintain its integrity, its wholeness and singularity, one must be able to locate it definitively and reliably over time among other objects.

Systems of citation, description and classification provide the necessary means of reference so that one can consistently discover, identify and retrieve relevant objects. Such systems traditionally include bibliographies, catalogs, indices, data dictionaries, directory systems, finding aids and the like, all of which collect, assemble and organize references to bodies of work. Creators of these resources are already extending them with such innovations, for example, as the use of the 856 field in bibliographic records, to incorporate reference to digital objects.

Moreover, in the electronic environment, there are also emerging sophisticated tools for automatically gathering and presenting in new kinds of products referential information from textual, image, sound, video and other kinds of digital objects. To meet the test of consistent reference, however, citations to digital objects from these various manually and autcmatically generated sources must over time reliably identify the works to which they refer.

One way of establishing confidence in a reference system is to generate citations in the first place—either manually or automatically—from the self-referential information that a work itself carries with it, perhaps in a header, a digital envelope or some other distinct part of the digital object. Unfortunately, except for documents marked up to the standard of the Text Encoding Initiative, few digital objects today contain self-referential information that meets conventional citation quality.

Matching citation and digital work to meet the test of consistent reference thus is difficult. Moreover, reliably identifying multiple versions and editions of works in electronic form remains a persistent reference problem. Part of the general problem of identifying and consistently referring to variant digital works is the specific problem of resolving names and locations for them. Coordinated by such groups as the Internet Engineering Task Force (IETF), active research and development has led to an emerging consensus that several factors contribute to the unique identification of digital information objects. Two of the most important factors are the Uniform Resource Name (URN) and the Uniform Resource Locator (URL).

Uniform Resource Name (URN)

The URL refers to the specific place where a digital object resides and is currently the dominant method of object location on the World Wide Web. The weakness of the URL, however, is that it may frequently change, especially as an object migrates from one machine to the next. By contrast, a name, the URN, is supposed to apply uniquely and permanently to a distinct object and to designate it independently of its particular location at any point in time.

URNs today exist more in concept than in practice. Thus, resolving the name and location for variant digital works and thereby providing consistent reference to them means moving from a conceptual design of the relation between names and locations to an operational reality through the implementation of naming authorities, which assign URNs, and and the development of digital services that translate names into currently valid URLs.

Uniform Resource Characteristics (URCs)

In order to provide a consistent means of reference for digital objects, systems of citation, description and classification will need to dispense more than name and location information. The IETF framework provides a general category for additional reference information in what it calls Uniform Resource Characteristics (URCs). Among the kinds of information that a reference system might provide under this general category is information about the intellectual property rights governing the use of a particular object and its cost. For archival purposes, however, there are two other qualities of digital information objects that a reference system must take into account. These are the features of provenance and context.

To preserve the integrity of an information object, digital archives must preserve a record of its origin and chain of custody. For some information objects, the formal process of publication creates a trusted channel of distribution and serves to establish a sophisticated record of provenance, at least from the creator through the point of release. In the digital environment, the problems of documenting provenance through a record of publication are bound up with the problems of fixity, and particularly with issues involved in tracing multiple versions and editions, as described above.

Outside the path of publication, however, there are several other channels of information creation and distribution, including tracing the path of migration within their own organization, that digital archives need to document in order to preserve the integrity of digital objects in their custody. First, there is a chain of provenance from individuals, a trail which has comprised a traditional concern of archivists. In the digital environment, as in other domains, individuals produce and accrete much information that relates to their private lives and to their public roles and responsibilities, including their means of livelihood.

Among the kinds of information objects that may count as personal records in digital form are electronic mail, notes, manuscripts, journals, photographs or videos, and databases of personal finances. For objects of these kinds, which make their way into digital archives and which the custodian deems worth keeping as part of the historical record, the archival responsibility in establishing provenance is to establish, as unambiguously as possible, the identity of the individuals who are the source of the objects and to trace the chain of custody to arrival in the archives.

A second kind of digital information flow that requires special attention with respect to provenance are those mediated or governed by corporate information systems. The digital products of such systems may include databases of employment and financial records, contracts and other legal records, planning documents, FDA filings, technical reports and so on. The distinctive feature of such objects is that they are all best viewed not as the result of individual works but as proceeding from the business, governmental or other social practices that the information system organizes and instantiates.

The archival challenge for establishing the provenance of such objects is to find ways to preserve an understanding of the corporate policies and processes and roles and responsibilities thus represented in the information system and its products. Third, there is the chain of provenance that traces information, particularly scientific data, to a source in electronic instrumentation.

In some cases, the instrumentation produces data in the service of individual experiments or of clinical practice; in other cases, remote sensors gather streams of observational data about physical systems in space or on earth. Of course, one ultimately accounts for the origin of the resulting data in the design and conduct of the experiment or clinical service, or in the character of the remote sensing program. However, the use of the instrumentation creates a special requirement to trace the provenance of the data to the design characteristics of the instrument itself.

Finally, a concern for provenance in preserving the integrity of digital information means that digital archives must document what happens to the information within their own organizations. They must keep a record of migration activity, and particularly of the transformations they make to keep information objects current with new technologies for use. Only by tracing such migratory activity, can a digital archives establish its own chain of custody back to the original object.

In the end, the investment that digital archives make in establishing the provenance of objects in their care serves to preserve the integrity of digital information in two distinct ways. First, a tracing of chain of custody from the point of creation helps to create the presumption that an object is authentic, that it is what it purports to be and that its content, however defined, has not been manipulated, altered or falsified . The second effect of establishing provenance through a chain of custody is to document, at least in part, the particular uses of the object by the custodians.

In thus creating a record of use, the archival concern with provenance is intimately related to the notion of context as a matter of information integrity. The context of digital information includes a technical dimension, a dimension of linkage to other objects, a communication dimension, and a wider social dimension. Digital archives must be attentive to the ways in which each of these contextual dimensions affects the integrity of the objects in their care.

First, to specify the technical context of digital information is to specify its hardware and software dependencies. Digital objects, by nature, require the use of computer hardware and software to create and use them. In some cases, an object may be closely dependent on a configuration of technology. For example, a particular digital document may require a particular word processing program running on a machine with a special kind of computer processing chip and operating system.

Other objects, such as an image file, may be readable using a variety of software programs, but may be stored on disk in a format that is readable only with a special computer. For still other objects, like World Wide Web documents marked-up in HTML, the hardware and software dependencies may be specified in very general terms because they are readable with a software browser that is available on almost any hardware platform.

The archival challenges for preserving the integrity of these various kinds of objects are, on the one hand, to represent faithfully the context of the objects in terms of their hardware and software dependencies and, on the other hand, to overcome, through appropriate migration efforts, those dependencies that threaten to hinder future use. A second dimension of the context of digital information objects is the linkages that may exist among them.

On the World Wide Web, for example, the HyperText Markup Language (HTML) provides a way to place in one object references to various other objects. A click of a mouse key then enables one to move quickly from one linked object to another. If the integrity of these objects is seen as residing in the network of linkages among them, rather than in the individual objects, or nodes, on the network, then the archival challenge would be to preserve both the objects and the linkages, a task that would today be exceedingly complex.

At present, there appears to be no good archiving solution; a possible stop-gap measure would be to treat the network in terms of its component parts and to take periodic snapshots of the individual WWW objects. The communications medium comprises a third dimension of the context of digital information. The character and integrity of digital information objects depends, in part, on their mode of distribution. Material distributed on CD-ROM, for example, has a set of file format and other characteristics that set it apart from material distributed in, say, networked form.

As digital materials increasingly come into being and subsist in an electronically networked environment, contextual features of the network, such as bandwidth and security, will account for characteristics of the digital objects. Increasing bandwidth, for example, will stimulate the production and dissemination of high-bandwidth digital materials such as full-motion video. Similarly, improved security on the network will encourage the conduct of a wide variety of confidential transactions.

As network-based objects, such as video and records of confidential transactions, make their way into digital repositories, an archival account of their integrity must include an account of the features of the network context that supports their existence. Finally, the wider social environment plays a significant contextual role that contributes to the integrity of digital information objects. Networked information, for example, depends on specific policy and implementation decisions that address the bandwidth, security and other qualities of the network and related technical infrastructure.

Electronic mail is subject to a variety of social distinctions when, in some contexts, it is used to convey highly personal messages among friends and, in other contexts, is a vehicle for formal communication among academic or business colleagues. One might account for digital business records, too, in the social context of the political and organizational regime in which they were generated.

Indeed, the social context of digital information objects is an expression of what one might characterize in other terms as the interests of stakeholders in those objects. Digital information objects acquire the qualities of content, fixity, reference, provenance and context—and thereby their integrity—as they move through a life cycle in a series of relationships with parties, or stakeholders, who have specific interests in their creation, management, dissemination, use or retention. The initial stakeholder in a digital information object is, of course, the creator of its content.

Following creation, a digital information object may pass through a series of gateways of increasingly public release and access. Some digital information objects may never be released beyond the initial creator; others will be limited to an immediate circle, which may or may not be physically co-located with the creator. Still other objects will be very widely disseminated. Once a creator fixes a digital information object by releasing it, for either personal or wider use, the object invites various other kinds of stakeholder interests. Depending on the extent of the release and the nature of the object, users and other stakeholders may refer to it, index it or cite it.

Still others may acquire, license or otherwise take custody of it to edit and publish it, to invoke it as evidence of a transaction or perhaps, as in the case of scientific data, to study, analyze and report it. They will all use it in the context of specific hardware and software applications and perhaps link it to related objects. And eventually during the course of its life, a digital information object may attract the interest of stakeholders, such as a digital libraries, which serve as collectors/disseminators of information objects.

What unites all these various stakeholders, of course, is their particular interest in adding to or making use of the value of digital information objects. However, the integrity of information objects in the digital environment is today so fragile that as stakeholders disseminate, use, reuse, recreate and re-disseminate various kinds of digital information, they can easily, even inadvertently, destroy valuable information, corrupt the cultural record, and ultimately thwart the pursuit of knowledge that is their common end. Against such a danger, a safety-net is needed to ensure that digital information objects with long-term cultural and intellectual value survive the expressions of stakeholder interest with their integrity intact.

Among the stakeholders serving as collector/disseminators, those who perform archival functions provide just such a safety-net. Digital archives build and maintain reliable collections of well-defined digital information objects and they preserve the features—content, fixity, reference, provenance and context—that give those objects their integrity and enduring value.

As the networked environment for digital information expands and matures, intense interactions among the parties with stakes in digital information are providing the opportunity and stimulus for new stakeholders to emerge and add value, and for the relationships and division of labor among existing stakeholders to assume new forms. For example, naming authorities for digital information objects are being organized, creators are assuming the role of publishers, publishers are contemplating the construction of digital archives, and collector/disseminators are facing the need to resolve the names and locations of digital objects.

Moreover, all of the stakeholders, including the new ones who are emerging, are exercising their various functions simultaneously in relation to particular digital information objects. That is, for example, the creator of an object may retain a financial or other stake in its dissemination and use for an extended period, just as a publisher/disseminator of the object exercises the same or similar interest.

Similarly, stakeholders acting as collectors/disseminators may retain an interest in the continuing use of the object, at the same time as they or other stakeholders acting as digital archives take steps to preserve it for future use. In a time of such sustained flux and change, during which these various divisions of labor are taking shape, the most effective and affordable strategy for developing a system of digital archives is to assume a distributed, rather than centralized, structure for collecting digital information objects, protecting their integrity over the long term, and retaining them for future use.

A distributed structure, built on a foundation of electronic networks, places archival responsibility with those who presumably care most about and have the greatest understanding of the value of particular digital information objects. Moreover, such a structure locates the economic and cultural incentives where they are most likely to prompt those preserving digital information to respond with the greatest agility to the changing digital landscape and to the shifting tides of technology.

Effective structures for digital archives in a distributed network will surely take various forms and will include corporations, federations and consortia, each of which may specialize in the archiving of digital information and range over regional and national boundaries. Both informal collaborations and formal partnerships among contractors and subcontractors, will also surely arise, in which responsibilities for archiving are allocated among various other interests in digital information.

Moreover, shared interests in, for example, intellectual discipline, in type of information, in function, such as storage or cataloging, and even interests in the output of information within national boundaries will all form a varied and rich basis for the kinds of formal and informal interactions that lead to the design of particular archival organizations. In the end, existing archival organizations may successfully adapt their current roles and responsibilities to changing needs, existing archival roles and responsibilities may be redistributed among other kinds of organizations with stakes in digital information, and focused attention on the division of labor in the digital information economy will lead to the emergence and growth of new kinds of archival structures.

Whatever the particular structural outcomes may be as stakeholders, new and old, interact and give shape to the distributed network of digital information, distributed responsibility for preserving that information requires commitment at least to the following set of organizing principles:

1. Information creators/providers/owners have initial responsibility for archiving their digital information objects and thereby ensuring the long-term preservation of those objects.

   — The creator/provider/owner may engage other parties, such as certified digital archives, to take over some or all of the archival responsibility.

   — Libraries and archival organizations may interact with creators/providers as subcontractors for maintaining digital archives during and after the active life of their information objects.

2. Certified digital archives have the right and duty to exercise an aggressive rescue function as a fail-safe mechanism to preserve information objects that become endangered because the creator/provider/owner does not accept responsibility for the preservation function and does not take steps formally to convey responsibility, or because there is no natural institutional home for the objects.

The conditions of creating digital information and giving it a useful life are essentially the same as those required for the information to persist over time. That is, it must be stored and maintained in an accessible form. It is not unreasonable, therefore, to assert, as the first principle does, that initial responsibility for preservation begins with creation of the information and rests with the creator, owner or provider of it. Individuals and public and private agencies already regard such a responsibility as a natural one for their critical internal records.

Creators of knowledge in other spheres depend on past knowledge and regularly acknowledge their responsibility to add to the enduring record when they publish their own ideas and findings. As the properties and usefulness of other kinds of information objects become more widely known, the ability in the digital environment to reuse and repackage these objects may generate revenue or other benefits.

Creators, owners or providers of these objects, including some publishers, who may not have otherwise counted long-term preservation among their key responsibilities, may thus be more inclined to do so and may either assume the responsibility themselves or find a qualified partner to do so. Among potential partners, they will likely find libraries, archives or similar agencies, which have specific collection agendas and will seek to take or share responsibility for preserving organized collections of digital materials.

The second organizing principle calls, in effect, for a fail-safe mechanism. A variety of factors—budgetary constraints, reorganization of priorities or focus, change of business, the need to go out of existence, or expiration of copyright—might prompt custodians to neglect, abandon or destroy their collections of digital information. No distributed system of digital archives will afford effective protection of electronic information unless it provides for a powerful rescue function allowing one agency, acting in the long-term public interest of protecting the cultural record, to override another's neglect of or active interest in abandoning or destroying parts of that record.

Digital archives operating normally and those operating in fail-safe mode differ mainly in the rights and obligations they have with respect to rescuing materials that have fallen in jeopardy because a custodian no longer accepts preservation responsibility. Section 108 of the 1976 Copyright Act of the United States defines the rights and obligations for libraries and archives operating normally to preserve copies of printed materials.

The proposed revision of the copyright law reserves to libraries and archives similar rights and duties for digital materials. However, neither in its present form nor in its proposed revision does the Copyright Act provide a legal foundation defining the rights and duties that must come into play to facilitate and encourage an aggressive rescue function. The Copyright Act, in fact, may not provide the best legal and institutional framework for establishing fail-safe mechanisms for digital archives.

However, such a framework is urgently needed because they know that one of the greatest dangers to the long life of digital information is the ease with which it can be abandoned and then deliberately or inadvertently destroyed. One appropriate foundation for an archival fail-safe mechanism against this danger might rest in articulating for the various domains of intellectual property—on analogy from the domain of real estate—a definition of the concept of abandonment and of the rights and duties that follow for digital archives operating in fail-safe mode when they can show that present custodians have abandoned, or are in the process of abandoning, culturally valuable objects. Other means of providing a fail-safe mechanism for digital archives also exist, however.

For example, a depository system might well serve the purpose. Under such a system, publishers could be legally bound to place with a certified digital archives a copy of their published digital works in a standard archival format. Given the principles articulated here, it follows that a commitment to preservation—collecting digital information objects, protecting their integrity over the long term, and retaining them in an accessible form for future use—is a defining feature of a digital archives, whether it is operating in normal or fail-safe mode. This commitment is fulfilled in practice in any digital archives by the exercise of three crucial functions: managing the operating environment of the archives, the migration of the archives as the operating environment changes, and the costs and finances of the operating environment and of periodic migrations.

For assuring the longevity of information, perhaps the most important role in the operation of a digital archives is managing the identity, integrity and quality of the archives itself as a trusted source of the cultural record. Users of archived information in electronic form and of archival services relating to that information need to have assurance that a digital archives is what it says that it is and that the information stored there is safe for the long term.

In the view of the Task Force, a formal process of certification, in which digital archives meet or exceed the standards and criteria of an independent certifying agency, would serve to establish an overall climate of value and trust about the prospects of preserving digital information. Appropriate organizations and individuals need to begin now developing such standards and criteria, including standard methods for a repository to declare its existence as a digital archives and therefore its intentions to preserve the contents over which it has custody, and for describing what the archives contains and what services it provides.

The certification process must also address the standards and best practices for other dimensions of archival operation, including selection and accessioning of material, its storage and access and the engineering of the systems environment. Archives cannot save all information objects; they must appraise and select for retention the most valuable items. Selection processes for archives of all kinds—paper and digital—are matters of intellectual judgment about what to include and save and what to exclude. Criteria for such judgments are largely tied to the intrinsic qualities of the material and many of the criteria that have proven useful in the paper world will no doubt translate to and prove equally effective in the digital environment.

In general, selection criteria include an appraisal of the content of the object—its subject and discipline—in relation to the collection goals of the digital archives, the quality and uniqueness of the object, its accessibility in terms of available hardware and software, its present value and its likely future value. Selection is also dependent on a number of extrinsic factors. For example, it is acutely dependent on search and retrieval mechanisms to help place and evaluate candidate objects in a larger universe of related materials.

Search and retrieval in large universes of diverse digital materials is the subject of very active computer science research, but search and retrieval today against a rapidly expanding universe of materials in all forms—digital, paper, microform—remains difficult, and the relatively primitive systems currently in operation may, in the short term at least, inhibit the effective selection of materials for digital archives. Redundancy of information is also important for effective selection. Selectors need to know before accepting an object where a copy of record is stored and if and where additional copies are distributed either as backup or for more efficient retrieval.

In addition, selectors ultimately need to have a rich understanding of the software and hardware dependencies of candidate digital information objects so that they can factor the carrying costs for an object into their overall assessment of its value. Such understandings remain in relatively short supply in some measure because the educational processes for wedding selection and technical skills still need to be devised and perfected. In larger measure, however, technical understandings are deficient because the digital environment is so immature that the dependencies of information objects on underlying hardware and software are still in many respects unknown.

Finally, selection for digital archives must be a continuing process. Given the need to migrate digital information regularly from its hardware and software environment, the stimulus and occasion will recur to reappraise the value of the material being migrated. Materials may lose value over time and may need to be withdrawn and discarded. Hard decisions may also be necessary about how and whether digital objects migrate if changes in a technical environment force alters what is preserved so that it differs in fundamental ways from what existed in the original object.

Once an information object is identified for inclusion in a digital archives, it needs to be accessioned, that is, prepared for the archives. The accession process involves both describing and cataloging selected objects, including their provenance and context, and securing them for storage and access. Standards for description are well developed for certain kinds of materials that are likely to appear in digital archives, such as monographs and serials. Because of the high degree of standardization, one might reasonably expect such descriptions eventually to accompany the digital object, thus simplifying the accessioning process.

For other kinds of materials, such as WWW pages, motion video and multimedia, relevant attributes are less well understood. Standards of description are less well practiced and one cannot reasonably expect satisfactory descriptive material to accompany the digital object. In all cases, special attention is needed in the accession process to creating, describing and tracking the versions of the object in the digital archives to satisfy the various requirements for display and other forms of access and for long-term storage. If material is to be deaccessioned then public declarations need to be made to that effect, particularly if it is the last known copy, so that rescue efforts by others can proceed if appropriate.

In the accession process, selected digital objects also need to be made secure for indefinite future use. A digital archives may need to establish access controls for its information objects and the means for authenticating them to future users. Establishing access controls involves setting terms and conditions for authorized use by specific users or classes of users. For certain extreme cases, such as rescued objects still under intellectual property protection, there may be no authorized uses for certain periods of time except for internal use within the digital archives to ensure that the object will be accessible in the future.

Authentication, which may make use of cryptography, provides verification that a digital object is what it purports to be and contains the contents that the author/creator or publisher originally intended. One of the characteristics of materials in digital archives may need to be that they contain a digital digest or signature that users can independently verify to assure themselves that the object is unchanged from its archival state.

The storage operation in digital archives attends primarily to the media level formatting of information objects. Primary considerations include levels of hierarchy and redundancy. In any digital archives, there may be multiple levels of storage graded to levels of expected use and needed performance in retrieval. Little used material may be stored most efficiently off-line, usually in tape format. For objects in high demand, where retrieval time is at a premium, on-line storage in magnetic media may serve best.

In a distributed network, they may need to be stored on-line in multiple locations. An intermediate solution is near-line storage, where information objects may be stored on optical or tape media and loaded in a jukebox. Retrieval time in near-line storage systems suffers by comparison to on-line storage, but is considerably more responsive to user demand than off-line storage.

Digital archives may use any or all of these methods. The most sophisticated systems combine the resources so that objects in use or recent use are stored on-line and, as they age from the time of most recent use, they move to near-line storage and then eventually off-line. Another important storage consideration is redundancy. In a system that is completely dependent on the interaction of various kinds and levels of hardware and software, failure in any one of the subsystems could mean the loss or corruption of the information object.

Effective storage management thus means providing for redundant copies of the archived objects as an insurance against loss. Depending on the copyright status of the objects, digital archives may choose to make backup copies on their own or to make arrangements for other sites, which hold the same object, in the network of digital archives to serve as backup, or they may choose to do both.

Providing access to digital information in a distributed network environment means above all that digital archives are connected to networks using appropriate protocols and with bandwidth suitable for delivering the information their control. Digital archives have an obligation to maintain the information in a form so that users over the network can find it with appropriate retrieval engines and view, print, listen to or otherwise use it with appropriate output devices. In the descriptions of the resources they hold, responsible digital archives must provide to their users what they know about the provenance and context of their digital objects so that users can make informed decisions about the reliability and quality of the evidence before them.

With respect to access, digital archives also have the responsibility to manage intellectual property rights by facilitating transactions between rights-holders in the information and users and by taking every reasonable precaution to prevent unauthorized use of the material. Because so many of the operational responsibilities of the digital archives—selection, accessioning, storage and access—are functionally identical to those of more traditional permanent repositories, they may successfully extend their scope to include digital materials.

Many traditional archives have already embraced digital materials, and libraries and museums are not far behind. Wherever digital archives may reside organizationally, their operation is highly distinctive in one crucial respect. That is, they need, at least now and for the foreseeable future, a high level of systems engineering skill to manage the interlocking requirements of media, data formats, and hardware and software on which the operation of the digital archives essentially depends.

As the digital environment matures, the role of systems engineer will serve to integrate new technical developments that promise to streamline and strengthen the operation of digital archives. Commercially available systems for user authorization, and document authentication, systems for using resource descriptions to automate the maintenance and delivery of archived information objects, and networked-based services that help manage the conventions for naming digital resources and provide means for conducting intellectual property transactions all will need the attention of systems engineers to ensure that they are effectively incorporated into the normal operation of digital archives.

In addition, the systems engineering function will serve an essential role in helping to determine when objects in digital archives should migrate to new hardware and software. As the operating environments of digital archives change, it becomes necessary to migrate their contents. There are a variety of migration strategies for transferring digital information from obsolete systems to current hardware and software systems so that the information remains accessible and usable. No single strategy applies to all formats of digital information and none of the current preservation methods is entirely satisfactory.

Migration strategies and their associated costs vary in different application environments, for different formats of digital materials, and for preserving different degrees of computation, display, and retrieval capabilities. Methods for migrating digital information in relatively simple files of data are quite well established, but the preservation community is only beginning to address migration of more complex digital objects. Additional research on migration is needed to test the technical feasibility of various approaches to migration, determine the costs associated with these approaches, and establish benchmarks and best practices.

Although migration should become more effective as the digital preservation community gains practical experience and learns how to select appropriate and effective methods, migration remains largely experimental and provides fertile ground for research and development efforts. Stewards of digital material have a range of options when faced with the need to preserve digital information. One might preserve an exact replica of a digital object with complete display, retrieval, and computational functionality, or a representation of it with only partial computation capabilities, or a surrogate such as an abstract, summary, or aggregation.

Detail or background noise might be dropped out intentionally through successive generations of migration, and custodians might change the form, format or media of the information. Enhancements are technologically possible through clean-up, mark-up, and linkage, or by adding indexing and other features. These technological possibilities in turn impose serious new responsibilities for presenting digital materials to users in a way that allows them to determine the authenticity of the information and its relationship to the original object.

One migration strategy is to transfer digital materials from less stable to more stable media. The most prevalent version of this strategy involves printing digital information on paper or recording it on microfilm. Paper and microfilm are more stable than most digital media, and no special hardware or software are needed to retrieve information from them. Retaining the information in digital form by copying it onto new digital storage media may be appropriate when the information exists in a "software-independent" format as ASCII text files or as flat files with simple, uniform structures.

Several data archives hold large collections of numerical data that were captured on punch cards in the 1950s or 1960s, migrated to two or three different magnetic tape formats, and now reside on optical media. As new media and storage formats were introduced, the data were migrated without any significant change in their logical structure. Copying from one medium to another has the distinct advantage of being universally available and easy to implement. It is a cost-effective strategy for preserving digital information in those cases where retaining the content is paramount, but display, indexing, and computational characteristics are not critical.

As long as the preservation community lacks more robust and cost-effective migration strategies, printing to paper or film and preserving flat files will remain the preferred method of storage for many institutions and for certain formats of digital information. Yet the simplicity and universality of copying as a migration strategy may come at the expense of great losses in the form or structure of digital information.

When the access method for some non-standard data changes, one must, in order to migrate them, often eliminate, or "flatten," the structure of documents, the data relationships embedded in databases, and the means of authentication which are managed and interpreted through software. Computation capabilities, graphic display, indexing, and other features may also be lost, leaving behind the skeletal remnant of the original object.

This strategy is not feasible, however, for preserving complex data objects from complex systems. It is not possible, for example to microfilm the equations embedded in a spreadsheet, to print out an interactive full motion video, or to preserve a multimedia document as a flat file. Another migration strategy for digital archives with large, complex, and diverse collections of digital materials is to migrate digital objects from the great multiplicity of formats used to create digital materials to a smaller, more manageable number of standard formats that can still encode the complexity of structure and form of the original.

A digital archives might accept textual documents in several commonly available commercial word processing formats or require that documents conform to standards like SGML. Databases might be stored in one of several common relational database management systems, while images would conform to a tagged image file format and standard compression algorithms. Changing format as a migration strategy has the advantage of preserving more of the display, dissemination, and computational characteristics of the original object, while reducing the large variety of customized transformations that would otherwise be necessary to migrate material to future generations of technology.

This strategy rests on the assumption that software products, which are either compliant with widely adopted standards or are widely dispersed in the marketplace, are less volatile than the software market as a whole. Also, most common commercial products provide utilities for upward migration and for swapping documents, databases, and more complex objects between software systems. Nevertheless, software and standards continue to evolve so this strategy simplifies but does not eliminate the need for periodic migration or the need for analysis of the potential effects of such migration on the integrity of the digital object.

Digital archives will benefit from the widespread adoption of data and communication standards that facilitate reference to digital information objects and enable their interchange among systems. Business needs in many institutions are driving the development and adoption of data standards. Organizations that create, use and maintain Geographic Information Systems (GIS), for example, are trying to reduce data conversion and maintenance costs by creating data that conform to widely accepted standards so that they can be exchanged, reused, or sold.

Standards initiatives that address business needs for the secure and reliable exchange of digital information among the current generation of systems will impose standardization and normalization of data that ultimately will facilitate migrations to new generations of technology. Digital archives must keep abreast of standards developments and make sure that their own technological infrastructure conforms to widely adopted standards. Planning for long-term preservation is a critical element of digital preservation.

To the extent that creators/providers/owners of digital information accept initial responsibility for archiving their objects, they may begin to see the wisdom of incorporating migration paths or other provisions for preservation as an integral part of the process or system that generates digital information. To assist in this educational process, digital archives might work one-on-one with potential donors to develop agreements early in their careers and establish arrangements for regular, on-line deposit of digital materials in a format acceptable to the repository.

In government, institutional, and corporate settings, archivists and librarians can issue guidelines and advice for digital preservation and encourage their parent institutions to adopt common usage rules, comply with data standards, and select applications software that supports migration. The preservation community as a whole needs to work with industry to create information systems and standards that build in archival considerations, such as backward compatibility from the point of initial design.

Backward compatibility or migration paths would enable new generations of software to "read" data from older systems without substantial reformatting. Although backward compatibility is increasingly common within software product lines, migration paths are not commonly provided between competing software products or for products that fail in the marketplace. Although standards and migration paths may become commonplace at some future date, a large body of digital material exists today in non-standard formats, and organizations and individuals continue to produce digital materials in formats that will require migration.

Developing "processing centers" that specialize in migration and reformatting of obsolete materials may provide a cost-effective method of digital preservation.

Processing centers might provide reformatting services for particular types of materials, such as text, certain database structures, geographic information systems (GIS), or multimedia products. Such centers might maintain older versions of hardware and software to support migration. They might provide a platform for reading and viewing digital information with the same "look and feel" as the original version by developing "software emulators" as suggested by Rothenberg.

Processing centers would take advantage of economies of scale and maximize the use of uncommon technical expertise. Migration/preservation services centers might resemble commercial firms that reformat old home movies and obsolete video formats or consortia of libraries and archives with distributed preservation programs. In US, a national laboratory for digital preservation, modeled after the National Media Laboratory, is another alternative. Feasibility studies and cost/benefit analyses would be necessary to determine the technological, economic, and commercial viability of such processing centers.

In addition to managing their operating environment and the migration of information through hardware and software platforms, a third function by which digital archives fulfill their commitment to preserve electronic information is in managing the costs of these activities. The principal cost factors of the operating environment are those associated with selection, accession, storage, use, migration, property rights transactions, and the systems engineering needed to manage migration and to maintain the digital archives within a distributed network infrastructure.

Some costs, like those for hardware and software as well as those for intellectual property if rights are purchased rather than leased, will appear as capital costs and will need to be amortized. Operating costs will vary by the form of the information, by usage and over time. Digital information in full text form will be relatively cheap to store and use compared to other forms, such as image, sound, video and multimedia information. Full-text takes up less space in storage and less bandwidth in transmission than other forms. The modes of usage for full-text are relatively well, though by no means completely, understood, and so the delivery and access software is relatively more stable and less subject to costly turnover than that for information in other forms.

Usage will also substantially affect operating costs. Healthy demand for particular information objects will push the digital archives that provide them to shift delivery to more costly on-line storage or to sophisticated and expensive systems of hierarchical storage. The costs of software and intellectual property may also be pegged to demand. Another usage factor affecting costs is the high variábility in the kinds of user access devices.

For many types of information objects, modes of access are still closely tied to the type of workstation available to the user. The tradeoff for the digital archives is either to limit access only to "approved" devices or to support multiple platforms and incur the added associated costs in hardware, software, intellectual property and systems engineering. Operating costs will also vary over time. Storage costs will likely continue to decline both absolutely and relative to other cost factors. The costs of access and of managing property rights transactions are relatively high today because the supporting systems are virtually non-existent; these systems are developing very rapidly and their relative costs will likely also fall.

The costs of the property rights transactions themselves, however, cannot be reasonably predicted at this stage and the danger is that costs will rise to the point that they become a barrier to access. In the long run, the cost factor that will most likely determine the success or failure of digital archives is the investment in the systems engineering and infrastructure needed to support highly distributed network-based functions. Migration costs will vary depending on the complexity of the original data objects, the frequency of migration, the extent to which the functionality for computation, display, indexing, and authentication must be maintained, and the need to compensate for acquisition of intellectual property rights.

Migration costs are much greater for complex objects, such as geographic information systems, where it is necessary to retain multiple formats of data, color display, and complex relations between the "layers" of a geographic information system than for flat files of data or ASCII characters. Computer models that drive artificial intelligence systems are of little long-term value if their computation capabilities are not retained; but migrating the models from one generation of software to the next involves complex and expensive transformations.

Some types of digital information may require frequent migration—as often as every three to five years—if they are stored in formats that are subject to frequent change. Digital archives may have to compensate for intellectual property rights and may be required to purchase software or site licenses in order to migrate digital information stored in proprietary formats. Planning for migration is difficult because there is limited experience with the types of migrations needed to maintain access to complex digital objects.

When a custodian assumes responsibility for preserving a digital object it may be difficult to predict when migration will be necessary, how much reformatting is needed, and how much migration will cost. There are no reliable or comprehensive data on costs associated with migrations, either for specific technologies and formats or for particular collections.

There is a large array of cost factors to understand for a panoply of differing kinds of digital information objects in which numerous parties have a variety of different kinds of interests. A multidimensional matrix—with present and future stakeholders mapped along one axis, kinds of digital information along a second, and cost factors against a third—might serve well as a framework for systematically assessing the value of digital information and the affordability of preserving it. There is much they need to know before they can fully elaborate an economic framework of this kind, and much to be learned from detailed studies of a wide variety of public and private institutional experiences with preserving digital materials.

In US, a number of organizations, including the National Aeronautics and Space Administration (NASA), the National Oceanic and Atmospheric Administration (NOAA), and the Inter-university Consortium for Political and Social Research (ICPSR), have relatively long and rich experiences in maintaining huge archives of certain kinds of digital information, and they are increasingly doing so in a distributed environment over electronic networks. Yet, despite these various experiences, little systematic understanding has yet emerged of the actual costs of digital archiving.

As a result, there is almost no sense of the detailed interplay of cost factors that might promote the kinds of specialization, division of labor and competition needed, in turn, to drive digital archives not just to manage costs against a standard of information quality and integrity, but to strive vigorously to lower those costs while maintaining and improving the standard of quality.

At the same time, many publishers, librarians and others contemplating the digital future express considerable fear that the digital world of information will not prove less expensive than the traditional paper environment, but in fact more expensive.

Components of storage costs in the digital archives include storage device costs—a jukebox, in this model—storage media costs, and the costs of operating and maintaining the storage equipment, and of periodically refreshing the media and migrating the data. The costs of providing access to the digital archives include providing a document server and software for the server that will support client machines on users' desks, maintaining the server and access software and of operating the server, and printing on demand a selected portion of volumes used and of delivering those printed copies to the user.

Systems engineering and management overhead costs are also included for both the storage and access services. The media are assumed to be refreshed and the data migrated as the technology changes on the same five year cycle. Hardware and software maintenance costs as well as equipment operations costs are estimated as a proportion of the original purchase price.

For example, tax incentives and accounting rules that favor the preservation of digital information in archives as investment in long-term capital stock might spur the growth of digital archives. Otherwise, solutions to cost questions are likely to be found in relation to specific bodies of digital materials and the communities that are interested in them. For some kinds of digital information direct charging for use will be entirely acceptable to the relevant user communities. One can imagine making an actuarial calculation of the lifetime cost of preserving a digital information object, finding creators/providers/owners with an economic interest in paying to preserve their information, and constructing an archival service that functions much like a safety deposit system for digital information objects.

The library of the future will not necessarily be an electronic library or even composed primarily of electronic materials. The place of electronic materials in the library of the future will depend on how well they measure up against the mission of the library of the future to generate, preserve and improve access to recorded knowledge.

The ideal model of digital imagery in the library posits an image document library that is created from multiple sources and with multiple uses. Digital image documents may be generated within the library from film and paper for preservation purposes as well as for other, more general reasons, such as the creation of reserve materials or customized books of course readings.

The library may also acquire image documents from external sources, such as service bureaus hired to reformat preservation materials or directly from publishers or vendors. After digitization, the library may opt to move the film and paper to remote storage. Users may then print documents from the image library, browse them at a workstation, or reformat them, say, by generating microfilm or by submitting them to a character recognition process.

The quality—measured primarily in terms of resolution—of the image documents that the library generates and maintains depends, at least in part, on the expected mix of these various uses in both the long and short term. For a variety of reasons, digital imagery is attractive as a reformatting tool for preserving access to deteriorating materials. One can duplicate a document in digital image form multiple times without a loss of quality. Standard imaging techniques can enhance the reproduction of an original by eliminating unsightly edges and the effects of yellowing and staining. Compared even to microfilm, digital image storage is relatively compact.

One can flexibly reproduce digital image documents in multiple formats, such as paper, microfilm, or CD-ROM. Multiple users can potentially gain simultaneous and remote access to documents in digital image form over electronic networks. And relatively easy remote access makes it possible to conceive of new and effective inter-library cooperative programs that have not before been possible. To achieve these potential advantages, however, we face numerous challenges. By creating documents in image form we impair physical access by disturbing collocation schemes and creating yet another source for scholars to look for relevant materials. It is not always easy to browse materials on a computer screen.

Compared to film, digital storage media has a relatively short life span and the life of the hardware and software needed to gain access to digital images is even shorter. And then there is the problem of administering the copyright of documents stored and used in digital image form. Like all capital assets, library holdings in all formats are subject to general notions of capital maintenance and renewal: the asset is acquired, it is then used, lost, or it otherwise depreciates—in the case of a book printed on acidic paper, the asset may simply disintegrate by sitting on a shelf—whereupon the library must either discard it or renew it by conserving it as an artifact or by preserving it in some other form. In this context, permanence of storage is not really an end in itself, but rather a measure of the length of the renewal period.

For information originally prepared in electronic form, we must now think deliberately in terms of a relatively short renewal period, because electronic media are not so durable as print and microfilm, and the hardware and software that we use to gain access to the electronic media are changing very rapidly. Otherwise, managing permanence in an access-oriented library is a capital maintenance exercise in which we must evaluate the use and accessibility of recorded knowledge against the durability of the medium in which it is stored and the cost to renew the medium.

The wholesale adoption of new and potentially revolutionary technologies is typically difficult to defend and justify in the large, established organizations that we manage. Rather, organizational and technical change tends to occur through a series of particular and incremental decisions and choices tailored to the mandate and needs of our specific institutions. An approach to digital image technology that is tailored to this kind of incremental economy is one in which development occurs in ordered phases with clear but relatively modest goals, measurable benchmarks, and a willingness to walk away from the process at any time.

The arenas for future action in digital preservation may be summarized in terms of four major goals. We need to verify and monitor the usefulness of digital imagery as a preservation tool. We need to define and promote shared methods and standards for image production, storage and distribution. We need to create and enlarge the base of materials preserved in digital image form. And we need to develop reliable and affordable mechanisms to gain access to digital image documents.

First, we need to verify and monitor the usefulness of digital imagery. To achieve this goal, we must confirm that libraries (or their agents in service bureaus) can, at high volume production levels, readily and economically convert digital images to microfilm for long-term storage and microfilm to digital images for ease of access and distribution. We need to foster projects designed to test the emerging technologies for capturing in digital form and at production levels specific subsets of special materials including oversize and bound volumes, color documents, grayscale images, maps, archival materials and so on.

We need to insure the longevity of digitized images by investigating and reporting the tradeoffs in the use of various storage media, the costs and benefits of storing images at various resolutions and in standard non-proprietary formats, and the requirements for backing up image databases and refreshing them to stay current with changing technology. In addition, we need to cultivate research on the application of character recognition technology to the collection of digital images, in part to guarantee that the quality of scanned images is sufficient to support character recognition.

Second, we need to define and promote shared methods and standards for the production, storage and distribution of digital images. In support of this goal, we need to sponsor forums to define production quality standards. Relevant quality-control issues include standards of image resolution, of image enhancement, image compression and of indexing levels and quality. We need to develop protocols for document structure and other interchange mechanisms.

The document structure file serves as an index and thus directly affects the ability of researchers to gain access to the digital image documents. It is the newest and perhaps the most critical component in the storage infrastructure that is emerging for digital preservation and access. In addition, through cooperative efforts, we need to create appropriate bibliographic control standards. We must help identify standard ways of describing location, accession number, processing statuses (analogous to preservation queues) and other key features of digital image documents, and must help insure that the bibliographic and holding record structures can accommodate these descriptions.

Although many materials in need of preservation are in the public domain, copyright still covers a large amount of deteriorating material. We need to address the legal and technical issues associated with copyright. Finally, to open as many access paths as possible to digital documents, we must organize specific projects to foster the interchange of documents in digital form.

The third arena for action is to enlarge the base of materials preserved in digital image form. The experiences of libraries in generating preservation microfilm suggests that service bureaus can generate economies of scale that individual libraries, each with their own conversion operations, cannot hope to achieve. We therefore need to involve service bureaus as partners in the creation of standards of performance and cost. The sooner libraries can hand off the conversion work to service bureaus, the greater the number of deteriorating materials they can expect to convert to digital form.

Collaborative efforts also need to focus on the conversion of thematically-related materials and, in particular, to mount a large-scale project designed to capture such documents from several different and geographically separated campuses. Such a project will both require and advance efforts to develop shared methods and standards of producing, storing and distributing digital images and to assist members of the research community in assimilating digital technology in their daily routines of work.

The last arena for action is to develop and maintain reliable and affordable mechanisms to gain access to digital image documents. We need to involve a broad base of constituents in technology development so that we can verify that image access products and services integrate well into the daily routines of scholarly work and that they meet the performance and other delivery requirements of the user community. We need to forge effective support structures for end users by making library and campus support staff informed and knowledgeable about digital image technology. Lastly, we need to determine the efficacy of access to digital materials in the context of traditional library collections.

Preserving E-Journals

For research libraries, the long-term preservation of digital collections may well be the most important issue in digital libraries. In certain ways, digital materials are incredibly fragile, dependent for their continued utility upon technologies that undergo rapid and continual change. In the world of physical research materials, a great number of valuable research resources have been saved passively: acquired by individuals or organizations and stored in little-visited recesses. These physical resources are still viable decades later. This is not the case with the digital equivalents.

Changes in computing technology will insure that, over relatively short timeframes, both the media and the technical format of old digital materials will become unusable. Keeping digital resources accessible for use by future generations will require conscious effort and continual investment. North American research libraries have been discussing the issues of digital preservation for some years now, but the number of active programs remains extremely small.

As the range of materials in collections available only in digital form grows, it will be increasingly important that libraries move from discussion to action. In the past two or three years, e-journals have become the largest and fastest growing segment of the digital collections for most libraries.

Collections that a few years ago numbered in the few hundreds of titles now number in the thousands, and the rate of growth continues to increase. In many ways, archiving and preserving e-journals will be dramatically different from what has been done for paper-based journals. In the paper era, there was large-scale redundancy in the storage of journals. Many different institutions collected the same titles.

The copies of journals being saved for future generations were the same copies being read by the current generation of users. Many of the things that helped maintain journals for the long term (binding, repair, sound handling and shelving practices, environmental control, reformatting when usability was threatened) were not differentiated from what a library did to provide current services. Other than in the case of preservation microfilming and the odd instance of shared book storage facilities, there was little conscious coordination of preservation activities, and in fact a level of redundancy was expected and thought useful.

Most e-journal access is through a single delivery system maintained either by the publisher or its agent. There is little replication, and only a few institutions actually hold copies of journals locally. Libraries can fulfill their current service requirements without facing the issues involved in the preservation of the resources. Further, in the digital realm the issues involved in day-to-day service are quite different from those involved in long-term preservation. The issue of long-term archiving and preservation of e-journal content has become one of increasing importance.

Specifically because of archiving concerns, many research libraries continue to collect paper copies at the same time they pay for access to the electronic versions. This dual expense is not likely to be sustainable over time. Publishers are finding that authors, editors, scholarly societies, and libraries frequently resist moving to electronic-only publication because of concern that long-term preservation and access to the electronic version is uncertain. Of perhaps even greater long-term concern, while libraries continue to rely on the paper copy as the archival version, from the viewpoint of publishers it is increasingly the electronic versions of titles that are the version of record, containing content not available in the print version.

Council on Library and Information Resources (CLIR): A Framework for E-journal Archiving

CLIR defined a framework for e-journal archiving. Based on this framework, the Mellon Foundation then invited a number of research libraries to apply for one-year planning grants to develop projects to create and operate experimental e-journal archives. The planning projects generally shared a number of key assumptions:

— Archives should be independent of publishers, and that archiving needs to be the responsibility of institutions for whom it is a core mission;

— Archiving should be based on active partnership with publishers, and that it will require a different kind of license agreement than the normal content usage license;

— Archives should address preservation over very long timeframes; long timeframes are likely to raise issues very different from those encountered in daily service provision;

— Archives will need to conform to standards and best practice guidelines as they evolve in the digital world and should be subject to auditing and certification;

— Archives should be based on the Open Archival Information System reference model, currently being vetted by the International Organization for Standardization (ISO).

Another key assumption of the Mellon initiative is that there will be relatively few archives holding any given set of e-journals, and that institutions operating archives will be doing so not just for their own users, but for the general community of subscribers and readers. In this environment, the design and operation of an archive therefore will be of concern not just to the publisher and the operating institution but to all who will rely on the archive.

There are many important technical and policy issues raised by archiving projects, and it is critical that these be discussed by the general community of libraries, publishers, and scholars, and not just left to the archive and publishers involved. An archive that keeps its content dark poses less of a threat of competition to the publishers with whom it is working.

A dark archive will also be relieved from having to maintain a current user interface, with all of the bells and whistles that users have come to expect, and from the complex task of maintaining information on who has access to what content. On the other hand, insuring that content that is never used remains sound and free from degradation will be challenging. Many archiving discussions revolve around the concept of "trigger" events, that is, conditions that change the access rule of the archive, for example:

— when a given journal is no longer accessible on-line;
— after a certain amount of time has passed since initial publication;
— when a title changes hands.

Keeping records of who has the right to access what and implementing appropriate access control mechanisms that recognize differential rights to various archived objects would be a major operational challenge. Most people assume that e-journal archiving is basically concerned with the content of journal articles. Indeed, while articles are the intellectual core of journals, in fact e-journals contain many other kinds of materials. Some examples of commonly found content are:

— Editorial boards

— Rights and usage terms

— Copyright statements

— Journal descriptions

— Advertisements

— Reprint information

— Editorials

— Events lists

— Errata

— Conference announcements

— Various sorts of digital files related to individual articles (datasets, images, tables, videos, models, etc.).

Some of these types of materials will pose issues for publishers. Not all of these items are controlled in publishers' asset management systems. Some are treated as ephemeral, "masthead" information and are simply handled as website content. When such information changes, the site is updated and earlier information is lost. For example, few if any e-journals provide a list of who was on the editorial board for an issue published a year or two ago. Another difficult content type is advertisements.

Advertisements are, of course, frequently not tied to any given issue, and they change over time with the business arrangements of the publisher. In some cases, advertisements are specific to certain populations, and what advertisements you see depend on who or where you are. Deciding what of all that is seen on e-journal sites today should be archived and maintained will require careful consideration by archives, publishers, and scholars.

The variety of formats of digital objects in an archive will affect the cost and complexity of operation. In order to control such complexity and cost, an archive might want to normalize deposited objects into a set of preferred formats whenever possible. Such normalization can happen at two levels:

— *File formats*: An archive might prefer to store all raster images in TIFF, for instance, and convert JPEG or GIF images into that format. Controlling the number of file formats will reduce the complexity of format monitoring and migration.

— *Document formats*: Many e-journal publishers encode article content in SGML or XML (or plan to do so soon). Most publishers create their own DTD (or modify an existing DTD) to suit their specific needs and delivery platforms. An archive might choose to normalize all such marked-up documents into a common DTD, reducing the complexity of documentation, migration, and interface software.

Normalization and translation always involve the risk of information loss. In archiving there may well be a difficult trade-off between information loss and reduced complexity and cost of operation. The OAIS model uses the concepts of "information packages," that is, bundles of data objects and metadata about the objects that are the unit of deposit, storage, and distribution by an archive.

A key element in digital preservation is maintaining the usability of digital objects in current delivery technology as the technical environment changes over time. This process is usually assumed to be one of "format migration," that is, the transformation of objects from obsolete to current formats, although it could also be carried out through emulation, that is, maintaining current programs capable of emulating older technology, thus rendering obsolete formats.

E-journals can contain a very wide range of technical formats, particularly as they begin to accept digital files created during the process of research that help validate, supplement, or further explain the basic content of articles. Whether it will be practical for archives to maintain current usability for such a diverse range of formats is far from clear. It is possible that archives will need to differentiate between formats where usability will be maintained and formats for which the archive will insure that the bits are maintained as deposited and that whatever documentation exists about them is kept useable for future "digital archeologists".

Archiving and preserving e-journal content will cost money. Perhaps the most important single financial issue is how archiving can be implemented to minimize the cost to the community. It is unlikely that archiving will be funded through a single source or even a single funding model. Over time, many different parties can be expected to contribute to the effort. Certainly for one-time or episodic expenses, sources such as foundations or government funding programs are likely sources of support. But archiving is a continual process, with expenses incurred on an on-going basis. So, a reasonably secure, continuous funding source is required.

It has been suggested by some that archives could support themselves through fees to users for access. However, if the purpose of an archive is to provide failsafe access rather than daily service, this model will not provide on-going operational funding. Archiving is a form of insurance, and as with insurance one experiences the expense on an on-going basis but experiences the benefit only occasionally.

Expecting to recover the cost of archiving only at the point at which access to the archived content is necessary is impractical. Such incidents will be rare and randomly timed, whereas the cost of archiving will occur from the first day of deposit. Another widely-discussed option is for archiving to be funded by governments through the agency of national libraries or similar bodies, particularly for materials subject to copyright deposit. This may indeed be a good model for support of some archiving, but it is unlikely to be sufficient. Not every country will be equipped or financially willing to assume archiving responsibilities.

More importantly, one archival agency for a work is insufficient. While digital archiving need not involve the scale of redundancy that we had in the paper era, some redundancy is highly desirable. There is too great a danger that a single incident, decision, or mistake can destroy what has been archived. A sound archiving model should involve multiple archival copies in the hands of different organizations, subject to different national laws and political influences, and dependent upon different technical infrastructures and preservation activities.

For archives lacking independent funding such as governments can provide, the most attractive funding model may well be one that involves the deposit of funds to maintain materials at the same time the materials themselves are deposited. Such a "dowry" would insure the growth of funds in proportion to the growth in responsibility. Dowry funding might come through the agency of the publisher, but its ultimate source is most likely to be the subscribers to the archived journals.

This funding could be made visible through the means of an "archiving surcharge" added to subscription fees, or it could be simply wrapped into the budgets of publishers and/or journal owners. The centralized e-journal delivery model pursued by many publishers does not account for the core function of archiving, and introducing it back into the model can be viewed as a natural cost element of electronic publishing. Of course, the general scholarly community is the key beneficiary of archiving. Subscribers and scholarly societies can serve as surrogates for that community in the realm of e-journals, and a cost model based on funding from such sources is not unreasonable.

Preservation and Access

The rapid growth and distribution of scholarly research in the mid and late twentieth century, the limited supply of old books and other paper-based materials. and the deterioration of items printed on acidic paper since the mid 1800s have meant that many libraries lack suitable copies of printed resources their users would like to read. For some time libraries have been converting books, journals and newspapers to forms that are more stable, easier and cheaper to copy, and more compact.

The most important such form has been microfilm which is a safe, durable and inexpensive preservation option. Digital imagery is now an attractive alternative, offering great long-term promise, and is rapidly becoming more accessible to libraries. It compares digital and microfilm imagery and emphasizes that making either kind of copy is preferable io leaving acidic paper to decay. The primary expense of salvaging a book is in the selection process and initial handling, while the cost of later conversion from one modern medium io another is comparatively small.

Two major problems confront a librarian seeking a pre-1900 book: durability and scarcity. A book printed from the mid-1800s on is probably made of acid paper, bound in a machine-made case. and very fragile. Even earlier books may be in bad shape since the chemical consequences of paper bleaching were not understood when it was first done around 1810, and by 1830 some paper was already deteriorating. Books made in the eighteenth century or before have more durable paper and binding, but the London stationers did not anticipate the number of U.S. libraries that would want copies of these books two hundred years later, and failed to order adequate press runs. Many nineteenth century books, of course, are also in short supply as well as falling apart.

Paper conservation deals only with the physically deteriorating item, not the supply of copies. Today, most bulk deacidification is in experimental or pilot stages, while page-by-page deacidification is expensive. The alternative of publishing facsimile reprints, such as those made by Arno and Scolar Presses, provides both durability and supply, but only the occasional title has an individual demand that will support a new press run. Thus, librarians have favored microfilming as a way of preserving books and other printed items.

Microfilming transforms one or more books into a roll of photographic film that is considerably smaller than the original, and that is easy to copy and thus to distribute to other libraries. Microfilm has a very long life, but needs controlled environments. A machine is needed to read it, and many users dislike it. Digital imagery, where books are scanned into computer storage, is a promising alternative process. Storing page images of books permits rapid transfer of books from library to library (much simpler and faster than copying microfilm).

The images can be displayed or printed, much as film images, although with greater cost today. Additionally, digital imagery permits considerable reprocessing: adjustment of contrast. removal of stains, adjustment of image size, and so on. At present the handling of these images still requires special skills and equipment few libraries possess, but there is rapid technological progress in the design of disk drives, displays, and printing devices. Imaging technology will be within the reach of most libraries within a decade. Digital imagery also may make possible instant reprints, and a new experiment at Cornell University employing very high speed and quality scanning/printing technology will be addressing the feasibility and cost of such an approach.

Microfilming deals with preservation, but not with access beyond the library. Digital transmission, combined with workstations in users' offices and nearby printers, offers an opportunity to deliver preserved material in better ways and to more people. Ideally, we might even be able to pay for preservation with revenues derived from improved access. The practical message for the librarian is that the most expensive parts of most preservation activities are:

(1) selecting the materials to preserve and

(2) turning the pages of the selected book for item-by-item chemical treatment, filming, or digitizing.

Whether what is done at each page is to spray alkaline buffering solution, make a microfilm image, or digitally scan, the major cost is the time required to gain access to each page. Thus, each book should be handled only once. Chemical paper preservation done sheet by sheet is expensive, must be done on each copy, and does not help alleviate any scarcity of the book. Bulk deacidification, which does not require page-turning, holds out the promise of lower-cost preservation, but also does not increase the number of copies, leaves the original item in its fragile state, and is not yet at a full production stage.

Microfilming and digital imagery, by contrast, make surrogates for the book that are inexpensive to copy. Moreover, conversion between microfilm and digital imagery is much less expensive than conversion to either form from paper. Bulk deacidification is promised for perhaps $5 to $10 per book. Unfortunately, most mass deacidification processes are currently in either experimental or pilot stages, and some processes involve potentially hazardous chemicals. With the possible exception of a new British Library experimental process, deacidification merely arrests deterioration for a while; if the book was already fragile, it remains so. From a collaborative perspective, if there are ten copies of an old book scattered around. In addition. microfilming creates a copying master and a bibliographic entry that provide broad access to the information.

Deacidification also can be done on an item-by-item basis at individual libraries. The cost of page-by-page paper treatment, by spraying a chemical fog on the page. is more than the cost of copying, even for one copy. The costs of these more elaborate preservation technique. which require disassembly and rebinding of each item, are basically prohibitive for books that do not have high value as artifacts.

Paper preservation and individual book conservation, however. are the only technologies that preserve the original book itself. For books with particular intrinsic value to scholars (e.g., those whose size or format is significant, or those whose readers are concerned with the manufacture of books, paper, or type), the original copies are important.

Process of Microfilming

The process of microfilming a book costs about 10-15 cents per page, not including the cost of choosing the book to microfilm or paying overhead charges to some central organization. Microfilming normally involves producing a roll film master, even if the final version of the book will be on fiche. Microfiche are not considered a preservation format, but can be produced from preservation roll film as an access medium.

Microfiche can provide random access to a particular frame faster than roll film, and fiche reading machines are cheaper than microfilm reading machines, which cost several hundred dollars. Fiche are clearly the medium of choice for a microform book catalog, for example. Unfortunately, many readers dislike both film and fiche. Microfilm, a photographic process, makes a faithful copy of original printed material, including foxing, waterstaining, dark (browning) pages, unsightly borders due to page edges, and faded ink. The use of high contrast film, which is standard, may help with the faded ink at the cost of aggravating discolorations, making it difficult to reproduce continuous-tone images.

The photographic materials used for microfilm are very fine-grain and can reproduce the print quality of the original without serious loss (1000 dots per inch). The process of preservation microfilming involves a series of quality control decisions and procedures that are executed throughout filming and developing of the exposed film. Quality monitoring, to determine the success of the quality control procedures, takes place during inspection of the film after it is developed. Both duplication of microfilm and conversion of microfilm to microfiche can be done fully automatically (as can the reprinting from microfilm to paper if desired).

Preservation microfilming (or other preservation techniques) must be done more carefully than work intended for only transitory use; thus costs for other kinds of filming or scanning may not be directly comparable. Roll microfilm comes in a variety of formats. The most common roll film formats are 16mm cartridge and 35mm roll. although preservation microfilming is done primarily in 35mm roll format. Many librarians prefer 35mm film, which provides a larger image readable with less expensive optics, and also offers a better quality source for reprinting.

The larger size 35mm film is also more resistant to damage from oxidation, scratching, abrasion, mold, or fungus, since the same amount of damage will obscure a smaller fraction of the page on the larger film. In general, 16mm cartridges can be handled faster automatically and take less space to store, but they also cost more. progress in photographic technology (such as the development of finer grain films) is improving the images we can make on 16mm film, however.

Although developments are occurring in the use of color microfilm for preservation purposes. nearly all filming or scanning currently is done in high contrast black and white. The practical limits of this large-scale preservation work mean that books with color content, shaded gray scale illustration, or extremely fine printed detail remain, until color filming or better digital technology is available, prime candidates for preservation in their original form.

Digital Imagery

The cost ot digitizing a set of images from a book is within a comparable range to microfilming. As in the case of microfilming, the primary cost is again handling. For example, a 30 page/minute 300 dots per inch (dpi) scanner itself costs $13,000; the major cost is obviously not the amortized scanner cost but the cost of the operator. This speed is for sheet-fed operation, with an 80 page stacker, so that attention is required every few minutes.

Unfortunately, for old books it is often impossible to process them quickly through a stacker, since the pages are delicate and must be turned carefully. This means substantially higher operator costs on old material or on material that cannot be cut into separate sheets. In US, the National Library of Medicine has estimated costs based on experiments with a prototype document conversion system developed in-house. This system is designed for bound volumes, fragile paper and face-up capture.

The experiments were conducted with a representative sample of the NLM's collection. The system is a distributed, networked, family of AT-based workstations that do document capture, enhancement, compression, quality control (QC) and final storage on WORM digital optical disks. Conversion costs were estimated for a variety of input conditions and in one typical configuration ranged between 13 and 28 cents per page.

Digital scanning can be done at a variety of scan densities. Roughly speaking, 150 dpi is the lowest scanning density that will yield basically acceptable pages for small print. More commonly, scanning is done at 200, 300 or 400 dpi; higher densities are becoming available. Three hundred dpi corresponds to the resolution of most laser printers and is basically able to produce quite acceptable copies, although not quite up to typographic quality. Higher definition is possible but adds considerably to storage cost, for example, doubling the number of dots per inch produces four times as many bits per page.

A 300 dpi 8.5 x 11 inch page is about I Mbyte uncompressed, and if filled with dense print as in some journal issues will compress to perhaps 0.2 Mbyte (remember I byte contains 8 bits). More normal books (e.g., 5 x 9 inch pages) would be 0.5 Mbyte uncompressed and would compress to under 0.1 Mbyte. Since a typical book is 300 pages long, if uncompressed, six books would fit in a gigabyte (one gigabyte, or Gbyte, is equal to 1,000 Mbytes). If compressed, perhaps 30 books would fit in a gigabyte. If 200 dpi rather than 300 dpi scanning were used, these numbers would become 12 books per gigabyte uncompressed and 45 books per gigabyte compressed (at higher scanning density, data compression is more efficient).

ASCII (non-image)

In contrast to all procedures that preserve the page or the

image of the page are techniques for obtaining a computer-readable version of the text. These produce an ASCII file of the characters on the pages. The words are preserved, but not their exact format and appearance. With an ASCII file, it is possible to search for names, specific terms, phrases or, with suitable software, to do various kinds of subject searches. Information can be located much more quickly using computer searches than by flipping through the book, and the thoroughness of a search using a complete text file can be much more complete than conventional indexes.

For much of the material considered for preservation, moreover, there is relatively little indexing available; few of our bibliographic secondary services existed in the nineteenth century. ASCII storage is also much more compact; a page of text that will use a few hundred Kbytes in image form will contain only one to two thousand bytes of ASCII, or 1/100th of the space. Other advantages of ASCII storage include the ability to reformat and reprint whole or partial documents easily; the ability to extract quotations or other subsections of the documents and include them in newer papers; and the ability to mechanically compare texts. Editing texts for later publication also needs ASCII rather than image storage.

ASCII text also can be displayed on a wider variety of equipment and on cheaper equipment, than can images. Even more important is that ASCII displays can be formatted for the particular screen size or program environment preferred by the user; there is less that can be done to rearrange images for display or printing on different devices. The image quality shown does not reflect any fading or discoloration of the original, but merely the quality of the display system.

Unfortunately, display systems using ASCII often provide lower quality than that of an image display system because typographic information is sometimes discarded as the material is converted. Various groups are working on standards for the representation of typographic markup, usually using the SGML format (standard generalized markup language), which will alleviate this problem once in common use. Saving the markup is also important for applications such as reprinting. Unfortunately, despite many advertisements of OCR (optical character recognition) programs, it is still rather difficult to go from image to character representation.

The programs now on the market are adequately fast (10-50 characters per second) for a job that is relatively easy to read (e.g., clear, uniform text), but they are not accurate or versatile enough to handle non-standard type and faded images that are characteristic of old books. Large text conversion projects are still often rekeying, finding this as economical as OCR followed by enough proofreading to maintain accuracy. OCR may well arrive first as a way of doing indexing, where recognizing half the words may well be useful.

Digital Storage Media

Although digital storage media are being improved, the length of time for safe storage remains well below that for microfilm when stored under appropriate conditions. Ten to 20 years are the figures quoted for most digital optical storage media, with some mention of 100 years. This compares with claims of 500 years of lifetime for microfilm. Even if digital storage media's lifetime is extended, the means of access to the stored information remains the most serious problem. This is because the technology to read the media often becomes obsolete. A librarian who commits to digital storage must expect to have to copy the data regularly ("refresh" the data) until the technology settles down. Fortunately, the cost of doing so is steadily declining.

In addition, digital storage at this time remains relatively expensive. The costs of some kinds of digital storage can be reduced by demounting"—or moving—them to less expensive storage. However, note that this requires an operator step to access the data. Computer media also have several other problems that are serious for librarians. For example, like books, they often require air-conditioned storage. In addition, it is not possible to tell by visual inspection whether computer media have been ruined.

The possibilities for digital storage, include:

1. Magnetic disk, usually of the Winchester variety. The current price is roughly $4000 per gigabyte. Access is fast and all material is online. Either software error or hardware error (such as a disk head crash when the reading head touches the disk surface) can destroy the information on a Winchester disk. Thus it is necessary to maintain a copy on some other medium, but the other medium is usually refreshed regularly and does not need to be permanent. The price of magnetic disks has been dropping by almost half each year or so, and the warranty periods doubling. Considerable advances in capacity are still expected: the advent of perpendicular magnetic recording is expected to increase capacity another factor of ten. The equipment is running continuously and some skilled attention is needed.

2. Optical WORM (write-once-read-many) disk. A typical drive costs $10,000 to $20,000 and holds two to six gigabytes per removable cartridge. The cartridge is bulky; typically 12-inch diameter platters are used, mounted in housings roughly an inch thick. They can be dismounted, cost about $200, and are reasonably permanent, with 30 to 100 year lifetimes quoted by the manufacturers. Several different manufacturers produce optical WORM drives, and their cartridge formats are not compatible. It is not clear who is going to win in the marketplace; among the vendors are Maxtor, LMSI and Sony. Technological obsolescence of any specific drive is likely to be far more rapid than physical deterioration. There are jukeboxes" available that can store more than 100 gigabytes, ranging up to more than 300 gigabytes in in one jukebox. The cost of a jukebox starts at $40,000, but larger ones are more likely to be $100,000 or more. These WORM jukeboxes are mechanically very complex devices, and it is not clear whether they will be successful in the long run.

3. Digital video tape. One vendor, Exabyte, has adapted 8mm videotape into a digital storage medium. The cartridges cost about $6 and store two gigabytes. To access them, of course, the data must be copied back onto a magnetic disk of some sort. There is only one vendor of the systems, it is not clear whether the format will survive, and it is not very durable.[3] Thus recopying regularly will be necessary. The drive costs about $5,000 (with interfaces, software. etc: if you can do your own mounting and driver coding, the hardware is about $3,000). It takes about two hours to read through a full cartridge.

4. Digital audio tape (DAT). Several vendors have announced DAT as a computer storage device. The cartridges hold about one gigabyte, are even smaller than the 8mm video cartridges (DAT uses 4mm tape), and the drives cost about $3,600. Again, the format is experimental and it is not clear which vendors' devices will survive. It also is not clear what the lifetime of the cartridges is, but it is unlikely to be permanent and will probably be shorter than 8mm videotape, because the tape is kept under higher tension. Access is faster than on 8mm video cartridge, another consequence of the higher tension of the cartridge. Jukeboxes for DAT tape have been announced. At present DAT cartridges cost $20, but this is certain to come down quickly as the format becomes common for consumer audio entertainment.

5. Conventional 9-track, 1/2-inch magnetic tape. The physical mechanisms needed to handle such tape are fairly expensive; a sample high performance drive is priced at $16.000. A reel of tape costs $20 and will hold .15 gigabyte, so the cost is about $120 per gigabyte. Tapes must have air-conditioned storage and must be copied every few years. but at least the format is well established and will survive. The durability is better than 8mm video or DAT.

6. CD-ROM. The CD was designed as a volume production medium but today a single disk can be made for about $1000. It stores a little over 0.5 gigabyte, and there is now agreement on the format of CD-ROM (the so-called 'High Sierra' standard). CD-ROM is long-lived, the reader costs about $500, and the format is in fairly wide use for PC data base access.

7. Magneto-optical erasable disk. These disks combine magnetic and optical technology to achieve long life,

demountable cartridges, and random access. The capacities are now limited to about 0.6 gigabyte per cartridge (using both sides). Drives cost $5000 and the cartridges are $250 each, but likely to become cheaper. Capacities are increasing steadily, and jukeboxes are available. It is not clear which companies or formats will survive.

8. Imperial Chemical Industries (United Kingdom) has announced "digital paper," a high-density WORM medium using mylar film that can be provided in various shapes and forms. Extremely high density is promised (double that of CD-ROM) but the entire technology is still experimental, more so than any of the alternatives above. No costs are known.

Here are the cost numbers more directly, with assumptions of: (a) 3-year life (2-year for magneto-optical), based on expected obsolescence of equipment; and (b) $10 charge to recopy, required once per year per reel for the non-durable media. Note that these prices are per gigabyte and should be divided by ten or so to represent the cost per book.

3

Strategy of Digital Preservation

Today, many libraries and archives are in the process of 'going digital'. The advantages of digital technology are well known and its adoption by libraries and archives seems inevitable, inexorable and well-motivated. Yet the fact remains that several key issues concerning the long term preservation of digital technologies remain unsolved. Two key problems are the fragility of digital media and, perhaps even more intractable, is the rate at which computer hardware and software become obsolete.

Moreover, as of today no one knows how to ensure the long-term preservation of multimedia documents nor how to ensure the integrity of documents that may have many links to other documents that may be anywhere in the world. Given the problems just outlined, the dominant approach to digital preservation has been that of migration. Migration is the process of transferring data from a platform that is in danger of becoming obsolete to a current platform. This process has both dangers and costs.

The notable danger is that of data loss, or in some cases the loss of original functionality or the 'look and feel' of the original platform. For these reasons, some have seen emulation as an alternative and superior strategy. The essential idea behind emulation is to be able to access or run original data/software on a new/current platform by running software on the new/current platform that emulates the original platform. If emulation is to be adopted, the first question is what is to be emulated? Three options are:

— Emulate applications

— Emulate operating sytems

— Emulate hardware platforms

It is here that emulation has its strongest attraction. One of the issues for digital preservation is what needs to be preserved in addition to the pure intellectual content of a digital object. In some cases the 'look and feel' of a digital object may be important, as may its interactivity. The fear is that migration to new platforms may lose these aspects, and that emulation may be the only strategy for preserving them. This problem is exacerbated, of course, by the increasing use of more complex digital objects (multimedia and hypermedia).

Some analysis needs to be undertaken to provide a framework for examining the issue of when these aspects of digital objects are important, with a view to providing data for a cost-benefit analysis for the justification of the likely additional costs of preserving these complex aspects of digital objects.

Intellectual Property Rights (IPR) issues may well be involved in emulating either operating systems or applications. It seems almost certain that the costs of emulation will mean that emulation will not be an option for every user. This will be one part of a case for wanting trusted organisations that can undertake the work and make this available for others to use. Of course the nature and cost of these organisations are major issues but not issues that only effect emulation.

As a general comment, if Rothenberg's scepticism with respect to approaches other than emulation is justified, and on the other hand, his optimism with respect to emulation is not justified, then the whole digital project is in serious trouble. As a simple method of preserving a digital document, why not print it out and save it as hard copy? Rothenberg rightly points out that this is not a complete solution since some multimedia documents cannot be properly printed out at all and any interactivity a document possesses will be lost. It is worth noting, however, that if one's sole concern is with the intellectual content of a document and the document is of a fairly simple nature this at least provides some form of security.

It is also worth noting that preservation strategies have often accepted loss of some of the characteristics of the originals. Rothenberg's attitude seems to be that if we can't have everything, we can't have anything. Rothenberg discusses claims made on behalf of relational databases that this provided a kind of lingua franca; since the same mathematical model underlies them all, any can be translated into any other. This, as he points out, is limited by the fact that some relational databases use proprietary features.

There are number of strategies for preserving digital documents. Charles Dollar suggested that customers should demand that vendors provide cost-effective migration paths to advancing hardware and software systems. Many vendors do provide a limited form of this capability in that an advanced version of their hardware or software system will provide the ability to migrate a customer's operations from the superseded system to the advanced. However, this type of conversion is generally limited to the previous generation of the hardware or software system and therefore, it is a short-term fix that must be repeated with each successive system upgrade.

Additionally, the translation of a digital document into successive shortterm standards over its life cycle may result in the loss of the document's original content. Without the original document and the original software to accurately interpret the document, then the format and content of the document may be compromised and the original meaning lost.

Dollar and Rothenberg also suggested promoting a "trend toward non-proprietary standardized open systems environments, which are designed to overcome compatibility between computer systems and applications and are reflected in international standards". While these open system standards would make digital documents accessible through any software system that conform to the standards, there is still the problem that even the open system standards will change as information systems technologies continue to advance.

Thus, over time, as hardware and software systems continue to evolve, it will still be necessary to either migrate digital documents to an updated standardized format or to provide some other method to maintain continual access to these documents.

Rothenberg suggested a means of maintaining long-term access to the information contained within digital documents by extending the life of the original computer hardware and software systems on which the digital documents were created. These life-cycle extensions involve the operation and maintenance of antiquated hardware systems and the archiving of the software needed to access digital documents in their native formats.

While maintaining a depository of antiquated hardware might be achievable in principle, it is also plagued with problems. The main drawbacks being the cost of operating multiple information systems and the difficulty in acquiring antiquated hardware system components. These problems make it unrealistic to expect that any organization could effectively and efficiently maintain multiple, aging information technologies in order to maintain access to superseded digital documents.

To overcome the problems associated with maintaining aging hardware, Rothenberg suggested the creation and use of system emulators that can imitate the behavior of antiquated hardware systems. This method would allow the operation of superseded software on advanced systems as a way to view digital documents in their native formats.

However, in order to emulate an antiquated information system this method requires exhaustive specifications on the original system's hardware. Therefore, this method may require extensive participation by hardware manufacturers. Many manufacturers may be reluctant to supply all of the specifications to software developers because some of the technology may still be in use in advanced systems they have developed.

None of the strategies discussed above is entirely satisfactory by itself. Therefore, as information systems and their operating environments continue to evolve it may be necessary to use some combination of one or more of these strategies in order to maintain access to digital documents in superseded formats. The strategies chosen will need to evolve from organizational requirements and conform to the limits of its financial, physical, and human resources.

Because a long-term strategic plan may call for a conglomerate of the methods mentioned here, it is conceivable that no existing organization can afford the financial, physical, and human resources necessary to carry out such a tremendous task. Therefore, it may be necessary to establish organizations or processing centers that specialize in maintaining long-term access to digital documents. Let us one of this kind.

Digital Rosetta Stone Model

At some point during the fourth century, all knowledge of ancient Egyptian scripts was lost, leaving no method available to decipher the language of hieroglyphics which had been richly preserved on ancient Egyptian monuments, stone tablets, and sheets of papyrus. Fortunately, while on an expedition to Egypt in 1799, Napoleon's army discovered an artifact which has become known as the Rosetta Stone. This stone contained the inscription of a decree issued in 196 BC by Ptolemy V Epiphanes. The decree was repeated three times in two languages, Greek and Egyptian, with the Egyptian version appearing twice, once in hieroglyphics and once in demotic, a cursive form of the hieroglyphic script. Fortunately, there is an abundance of information on ancient Greek dialects and therefore, the stone's Greek version of the decree contained the key to decipher the meaning of the ancient Egyptian texts. Today, because of the Rosetta Stone, we can interpret many ancient texts and inscriptions of Egyptian hieroglyphic and demotic scripts found on sheets of papyrus and monuments throughout Egypt.

The Digital Rosetta Stone (DRS) is so named because it offers a way for those in the future to be able to gain access to the information stored in the digital documents that have stored, and will continue to store, in increasing numbers. The DRS will contain multiple levels of knowledge about specifications and processes by which information is stored on various types of storage media. It will also contain archives of knowledge about how to meaningfully interpret that information so that the original meaning can be recovered.

If the behavior of an information system could be sufficiently described, then future generations could re-create that behavior and reproduce digital documents without the need for the original systems. However, currently, information science cannot sufficiently describe this type of behavior in a way that will allow this strategy to succeed.

One way to describe and preserve the behavior of information systems for our posterity is to create a DRS that can be used to reconstruct digital documents. The processes and metadata maintained by the DRS will catalogue the many different aspects of digital technologies. After all, "in the digital world, preservation must be concerned with entire technology systems, not one or another component, such as a film or a storage disk".

In digital equipment each component is dependent upon other components of the digital systems in order to perform a specific task. The process of viewing a file created by a word processor can demonstrate a simplified example of this interdependence. The file must be interpreted by the application program which is dependent upon the operating system which is further dependent upon the system's hardware. Each layer of digital technology involved in this process contributes some form of information necessary to view the digital document.

Components of DRS

Unfortunately, creating a DRS is not as simple as the creation of the original Rosetta Stone that held the key to Egyptian hieroglyphics. Instead, a DRS is composed of three major processes that are necessary to preserve and access our digital history—knowledge preservation, data recovery, and document reconstruction. The knowledge preservation process supports the data recovery and document reconstruction processes.

Knowledge preservation: Knowledge preservation is the process of gathering and preserving the vast amounts of knowledge needed to recover digital data from a superseded media and to reconstruct digital documents from their original formats. In a DRS, the preservation of knowledge of media storage techniques and file formats will be maintained in a metaknowledge archive.

Metaknowledge is the knowledge or awareness of facts, heuristics, and rules, and the context in which they are used and manipulated. The creation of standardized data dictionaries will be the tools used to store the metaknowledge necessary to aid document recovery personnel. The data dictionaries will contain the names and descriptions of the data items and processes necessary to recover a digital document.

The metaknowledge archive (MKA) is the foundation upon which the DRS is dependent and it must extensively preserve the knowledge in two key areas—media storage techniques and file formats. The knowledge of media storage techniques is a collection of the way data are defined and stored on specific media. While it is expected that some data will be migrated to new storage devices for archival purposes, it is likely that some data will not be migrated. Therefore, it is necessary to maintain a record of the methods in which bit patterns are used to represent data on storage devices.

The knowledge of the location and meaning of these bit patterns will be necessary to recover data if equipment to access a storage medium is not available or no longer exists. This is not to say that all specifications for storage devices must be accurately preserved so engineers can manufacture them in the future. Instead, it requires only that the techniques in which the bit patterns are stored and accessed on the media needs to be preserved.

Just as the knowledge of the techniques used to store data on a digital media must be preserved, so must the information on file formats be collected on data files created using different software applications. The knowledge of file formats is a collection of the techniques used by specific software applications to define formatting operations within digital documents.

Software applications that create digital documents use data located in specific positions and predefined character sequences to define the digital document's appearance. Interpretation software is necessary to view a digital document whether it is simply stored in an ASCII text format or in a complex database format. Software products, commercial-off-the-shelf (COTS) and Non-COTS, store digital data using a variety of techniques. Therefore, every data file is dependent upon some form of software to properly interpret and display the data file's contents.

Character sequences embedded within a digital document inform the interpretation software how the document's data is to be interpreted. For example, in order to bold a section of text using the Hypertext Markup Language (HTML), all characters following the character sequence "<B>" are bolded until the character sequence "</B>" is encountered.

Any software capable of interpreting an HTML document must recognize these character sequences and all other format character sequences that are characteristic of HTML documents. Likewise, any software capable of interpreting a digital document must recognize the formatting character sequences unique to the application that was used to create that digital document. File formats knowledge will also be stored in a metaknowledge archive.

Data Recovery: Data recovery is the process of extracting digital data from an obsolete medium and migrating it to a medium that is accessible to current information systems. The recovery will, of course, depend on the cost effectiveness of recovering the data. That is, if the need for the knowledge in the digital document(s) is greater than the cost of recovery, then the cost of the recovery method(s) may be justified.

Document Reconstruction: Document reconstruction is the process of interpreting digital documents from their original data files by using file format information gathered during the knowledge preservation process. Interpreting digital documents by describing how the original software interpreted the documents is a strategy that was suggested by. The file format information describes the formatting information used by specific software applications.

In other words it is a template that can be used to describe the way data is formatted and displayed by word processing, graphics, and other applications that create digital documents. This does not mean that the algorithms used to produce the documents are preserved so programmers can replicate them in the future. Instead, it means that the bit or character sequences and other formatting information are preserved as a template for document interpreters to use to reconstruct and view documents in their original forms.

When the reconstruction process is complete the document should appear in its original form. As in the data recovery process, the methods used during document reconstruction are dependent upon the cost effectiveness of reconstructing the document.

Knowledge Preservation

The metaknowledge archive is the foundation upon which the DRS is built. It contains templates, which can be used to extract, and display data in the form prescribed by the information systems used to create digital documents. To insure the success of the DRS the metaknowledge archive must develop a standardized format to preserve media storage techniques so engineers can extract data from the many different types of media. Likewise, it must also develop a standardized format to preserve digital document formatting information for the different types of digital documents that may need to be recovered.

As long as there is a template that can be used to interpret a document, then a document can be displayed in its original form. After the creation of a digital document, its interpretation is dependent upon the hardware and software systems that were used to create it. However, most modern computer systems have the ability to process and display the multitude of objects that appear in digital documents. Therefore, on any given hardware system routines can be designed to interpret and present the contents of digital documents that were created on another system.

Media metadata

Media metadata is probably the easiest type of data to gather for the DRS. This is because the standards for most storage media are rigidly defined before a media is brought to market. For example, ISO9660 is the standard that specifies how data are stored on a CD-ROM. This standard defines the volume structures, file structures, and all other attributes associated with a CD-ROM. This type of data must be gathered for each type of media to be included in the metaknowledge archive. When trying to recover data, recovery personnel must know where to look in order to find it. Media storage geometry defines where on a medium data are stored.

In order for data recovery personnel to find the data they must know the geometric shape of the data's path and the locations of those paths. For example, on a CD-ROM data are stored on a spiraling track with adjacent tracks 1.6 micrometers apart for a track density of 16,000 tracks per inch. Furthermore, the tracks are divided into sectors containing 2048 bytes of data and each sector has an address that is used during the file allocation. This type of geometric storage information must be collected for each type of medium.

After the medium's storage geometry has been identified, data recovery personnel must know the method used to store the data. The data storage method refers to how data are physically recorded on a medium and this information must be known so a device can be engineered to read the digital patterns. In the past, data have been stored on media using a variety of methods. Early storage media stored data as a series of holes punched into lengths of paper tape or punched cards. Hard and floppy disks store data as a series of magnetic patterns stored on a layer of magnetic particles.

More recent optical technologies, such as the CD-ROM, store data as a series of lands and pits (0.12 micrometers deep and 0.6 micrometers in diameter) burned into a plastic platter. There are many other storage methods that have been used, that are in use, and that will be used in the future. Knowing these storage methods tells data recovery personnel what to look for to identify the digital data stored on the media.

After data recovery personnel have identified where the data are stored, and the data storage method, they must determine how the data are encoded. Encoding techniques define how the data's bit patterns are stored on the media. The encoding information will be used to decode the data and restore the data bit stream to its original form. Encoding schemes may be fairly simple with one setting identifying a 0 bit and another setting defining a 1 bit. Or encoding schemes may implement coding algorithms to encrypt and compress recurring bit patterns. Two popular encoding schemes used today are multiple frequency modulation (MFM) and run length limited (RLL).

Multiple frequency modulation is a method of encoding analog signals into magnetic pulses or bits. Run length limited is another method of encoding data into magnetic pulses but its encoding scheme allows 50 percent more data to be stored on a disk than MFM. During the next step it is necessary to determine the file allocation method used on a media. File allocation is how storage space is assigned to files so that storage space is effectively utilized and files can be accessed.

Once data recovery personnel can locate, read, and decode the information on a media, they must know the file allocation method in order to properly reassemble the files. Descriptions on items such as volume and file structures are identified in media standards, such as ISO9660 for the CD-ROM.

The operating system also controls a media's file allocation method and therefore, it is necessary to access operating system specifications to gather data on file allocation methods. There are several file allocation methods in use and each operating system and media combination uses a specific allocation method. Examples of some popular allocation schemes are the contiguous, linked, and indexed allocation methods. The contiguous allocation method requires each file to occupy a set of contiguous addresses on a disk.

With linked allocation each file is a linked list of sectors and the sectors may be scattered anywhere on the disk, and with the indexed allocation method each file has its own index block which is an array of disk block addresses. The allocation method may also provide other valuable information such as distinguishing between the locations of data bytes and error detection/correction bytes.

Collecting and maintaining metadata on these four, entities, data storage geometry, storage methods, encoding schemes, and file allocation methods will provide the keys to recover data once an access system is no longer available to access that media type. As hardware and software systems become obsolete this metadata is used to develop hardware and software systems to recover data and migrate it to currently accessible storage media

File format metadata

The first step in gathering file format information is to identify all of the applications used to create the digital documents which may need to be reconstructed in the future. This includes both commercial-off-the-shelf (COTS) and non-COTS applications. Gathering and cataloging metadata to reconstruct digital documents created with COTS and non-COTS applications is going to be a time intensive and difficult task.

However, it is necessary because many organizations use these applications to create and store digital documents. The second step is to identify and catalog the objects that are supported by these applications. An object in a digital document can be text, graphics, audio, video, and any number of other structures that have been included by the document's creator. It is necessary for an interpreter to have the ability to identify the objects embedded in a digital document before the interpretation process begins. If an object is not properly identified then the document is uninterpretable.

Once the objects are identified, interpretation routines are created to present these objects in their original form on the current information system. Since objects are utilized over and over again by different applications, it is only necessary to create a routine to interpret and display that object once. A routine can be used to display an object regardless of the application used to create the digital document. For instance, most digital documents support the use of text objects.

Since text is used in multiple applications, it is only necessary to create a routine to handle a text object once. That routine can then be used to interpret and display text on the current system regardless of the software and hardware systems that were used to create the original document. The final step is to identify and catalog the formatting structures implemented within each application. These formatting structures describe how objects are identified, formatted, and arranged within a digital document.

Additionally, this information describes how to determine such things as page size, margins, line spacing, tabs, fonts, footnotes, and a multitude of other page layout information. This information must be maintained in a standardized form so that an interpreter can easily access it and switch between digital documents that were created by different applications. The formatting process may be made more difficult because there is no standardized way in which applications store formatting information.

Applications disperse formatting information (1) throughout the document, (2) in designated locations within the document, or (3) in combinations of 1 and 2. Additionally, some applications store document files in an ASCII format while others opt for a binary format. Defining a standardized method to describe these currently non-standardized procedures is one of the goals of the DRS metaknowledge archive.

Data Recovery

Once it is no longer economically feasible to maintain antiquated hardware systems, it is necessary to implement an alternate method to maintain the ability to recover data from superseded media. If data are stored on an obsolete medium that is not accessible by current systems then the data must be migrated to a currently accessible media before document reconstruction can begin. That is, the data must be recovered.

Data recovery involves the use of the storage technique information gathered during the knowledge preservation process to recover data from an obsolete media. This information is used to modify or construct the equipment needed to migrate digital data from an obsolete medium to one that is currently accessible.

An example, of this usage can be depicted by data stored on punched cards. Punched cards pass through a punched card reader at the rate of approximately 1,000 cards per minute. As the cards pass between a light source and a row of photo-electric cells the location of the holes are detected and the pattern is transformed into electric signals which are sent to the computer and translated into machine.

Because of advances in storage technologies, punched cards are seldom used as a storage medium today because they are slow, bulky, and cumbersome compared to modern storage media. Because of this, few organizations maintain punched card today. So, if stacks of punched cards were to be found and there were no punched card readers available to read the data, how could the data be read? First, the punched card storage technique information that was gathered during the knowledge preservation process is retrieved.

Once the information is analyzed and engineers understand the way information is stored on a punched card, they may find that it is a simple task to reprogram a modern scanning device, such as those used in supermarkets or on assembly lines, to read the patterns of holes on a punched card.

Therefore, a device can be modified to read, translate, and migrate the data on punched cards to a modern storage device without the need for an original punched card reader. There is no need to engineer a device to write punch cards because there is no desire to change the data. The need is only to read the data and migrate it to a currently accessible storage medium.

While this is a relatively simple example of how the storage technique information can be used, it demonstrates how easily yesterday's digital technologies can be more easily reproduced using today's digital technologies. Likewise, this same method could be used to manufacture readers for paper tapes, CD-ROMs, and other storage devices.

If someone finds a CD-ROM disk in the year 2222, perhaps he or she will be able to take it to a DRS processing center to recover the data. Instead of building a CD-ROM drive, the processing center may simply use a high-tech scanner to scan the disk and identify the patterns of lands and pits burned into the disk's surface.

Using the data gathered about CD-ROM storage techniques during the knowledge preservation process, an information system analyzes the location and patterns of lands and pits, identifies the file allocation system, processes the data, and then writes the files to a twenty-third century storage device.

Document Reconstruction

If digital documents are stored in superseded formats then they must go through an interpretation process in order to restore them to their original forms. That is, the documents must be reconstructed. Document interpreters, which accomplish reconstruction, are either (1) trained technicians or (2) software applications that use fileformatting information to reconstruct digital documents. The DRS relies upon the file format descriptions gathered during the knowledge preservation stage to describe how the original software interpreted files. These file format descriptions identify the information, such as character sequences, that identify data objects and specify formatting operations within a digital document. In addition to identifying text-based objects and operations, character sequences are used to identify other objects imbedded within digital documents.

Computer Museums

The idea that computer museums be established, where old machines would run original software to access obsolete documents is highly problematic for several reasons that Rothenberg cites. These include:

- It is unlikely that old machines could be kept running indefinitely at any reasonable cost.
- Old digital documents will rarely survive on their original digital media. The obsolete document would therefore have to be read by an obsolete machine from a new medium for which that machine has no physical drive, no interface, and no device software. The museum approach would therefore require

building unique new device interfaces between every new medium and every obsolete computer in the museum as new storage media evolve, as well as coding driver software for these devices, which would demand maintaining programming skills for each obsolete machine.

— Computer chips have a limited life-time. Rothenberg does see two possible minor roles for computer museums in digital preservation: testing emulators and helping data recovery.

Rothenberg is extremely scathing about migration. He provides a whole list of reasons why he believes migration to be inadequate as a digital preservation strategy. Rothenberg states that migration is:

— Labour intensive

— Time-consuming

— Expensive

— Error-prone

— Risky (causing lost or corrupted information)

— Non-scalable and that migration can require new solutions for each new format.

Migration has been the only serious candidate thus far for preservation of large scale archives. (Emulation has been used in some marginal cases, but currently no major archive will adopt emulation as its primary digital preservation strategy). Not all of the points apply with equal force all of the time, with migration many of these claims will vary on a case-by-case basis.

The ideal approach should offer alternatives for levels of safety and quality, volume of storage, ease of access, and other attributes at varying costs, and it should allow these alternatives to be changed for a given document, type of document, or corpus at any time in the future. It should provide single-step access to all documents, without requiring multiple layers of encapsulation to be stripped away to access older documents, while allowing the contents of a digital document to be extracted for conversion into the current vernacular, without losing the original form of the document.

It should offer up-front acceptance testing at accession time, to demonstrate that a given document will be accessible in the future. The major parts of Rothenberg's approach to emulation are:

1. developing generalizable techniques for specifying emulators that will run on unknown future computers and that capture all of those attributes required to recreate the behavior of current and future digital documents;
2. developing techniques for saving—in human-readable form—the metadata needed to find, access, and recreate digital documents so that emulation techniques can be used for preservation; and
3. developing techniques for encapsulating documents, their attendant metadata, software, and emulator specifications in ways that ensure their cohesion and prevent their corruption.

The information that has to be encapsulated comprises the document and its software environment. Central to the encapsulations is the digital document itself, consisting of one or more files representing the original bit stream of the document as it was stored and accessed by its original software. In addition, the encapsulation contains the original software for the document, itself stored as one or more files representing the original executable bit stream of the application program that created or displayed the document.

Rothenberg argues that—normally at least—what should be emulated is the hardware platform on which an application runs rather than emulating an application or emulating an operating system. This raises quite a large number of issues. With respect to multimedia systems, for example, the number of possible configurations is very large—consider the rapid rate at which the speed of CD ROMs changed. The preservation of the precise quality of a given multimedia production would be a formidable challenge.

Role of Infrastructure

The roles of infrastructure in the digital process give rise to differing perspectives and interests. Undoubtedly, some of these interests will be in conflict, but many will simply be different. It is against this background that collaborative structures need to be built. Where possible, these collaborative structures may lead to conflict resolution, but it would be optimistic, to say the least, to suppose that such resolution will always be possible. Nevertheless, there surely is scope for a vast amount of collaborative effort that may lead to solutions not possible for a single group or community to achieve on its own.

Increasingly, individuals are making greater investments in their use of digital objects. Consider their use of Personal Digital Assistants (PDAs), for example. PDAs, like other technologies, can become obsolete virtually overnight - even when they appear to be well established. Although important from an individual's point of view, it also raises two points with respect wider community interests. Cliff Lynch makes the point that with respect to physical objects, individuals, rather than institutions, have often been the ones who preserved the objects that have later become recognized as significant.

Therefore, we should be cautious with respect to solutions to digital preservation problems that would take the form of allowing special treatment for institutions (e.g., certified archives) but not for individuals. Many actions an institution must undertake in order to preserve digital objects are such that the actions will need to be taken by the institution itself—or at least by a third party undertaking the actions on the institution's behalf. However, there are other actions not of this nature - actions that a few people could undertake on behalf of the many. For these actions, it would make sense for institutions to collaborate in supporting centralized research centers—if only for cost reasons. These actions could include:

— Developing and maintaining emulators

— Developing metadata tools

— Providing data recovery services.

Of course, establishing such centers, especially and preferably on an international basis, would clearly be a large undertaking; nevertheless, it is clearly desirable to do it. The legal environment in which digital preservation occurs most obviously raises two difficult subjects: Intellectual Property Rights (IPR) and electronic deposit.

In a reasonable world, there ought to be a balance between the interests of copyright holders on the one hand, and information consumers on the other. In the world of books, a reasonable balance has been achieved. Authors are entitled to royalties and are protected by copyright law. This balance depends on contingent practical factors, such as the fact that photocopying an entire book is not an attractive option both in terms of the effort required and in terms of cost. Readers' interests are protected by policies of fair use and first sale.

First Sale, in particular, makes public lending libraries possible. In US, as reported by the 'Committee on Intellectual Property Rights and the Emerging Information Infrastructure' 'going digital' threatens this balance. From the content provider's point of view, threats arise from the ease with which digital objects can be copied without loss of quality, and because the objects can be easily distributed across networks. Conversely, the information consumer may be threatened by the imposition of draconian conditions of use and by new business models that would lead to the demise of 'first sale'.

The Digital Dilemma, which is that achieving a reasonable balance between the interests of users and those of content providers is not solely a legal issue; rather, it is getting a balance between the legal framework, the extant technology and the business model. With technology in its current state of flux, it is impossible for all these issues to be definitively resolved at the current time.

The hoped-for intellectual property law and public policy evolutionary process mentioned above should include developing systems for electronic deposit similar to those used for books. The intent here is to extend into the digital world the traditional balancing act of IP - providing enough control over the work to offer an incentive for creation, yet ensuring that in the long term all work becomes a part of the public intellectual record to the benefit of society as a whole.

Modern versions of these operating systems are advertised as being more reliable—as though reliability was not thought to be an essential requirement in the first place. At the same time, users have been virtually compelled to constantly upgrade both hardware and software, regardless of the users' real needs, since after a relatively short time, failure to upgrade will result in having an unsupported system.

Faced with these threats, there is the consoling thought that if vendors attempt to push things too far, they will meet with consumer resistance. For example, if makers of e-book readers attempt to impose draconian conditions of use, they will kill the goose they hope is laying the golden egg. However, it is currently unclear how much consolation this provides, since these same vendors may be able to push things far enough to create problems for digital preservation before deterring potential consumers.

The development and adoption of standards would contribute toward making that optimistic scenario become a reality. Perhaps part of the scepticism about standardization derives from the assumption by some that when one talks about standards, one must be talking about an ISO (International Standards Organisation) or similar standardization process. ISO standardization is notoriously slow—chances are that by the time a standard is delivered, it is out of date—or at least that is the perception.

Some ISO standards do prove their worth. The ISO model is not the only model for standardization—the Internet Engineering Task Force (IETF) works on a quite different model. Network protocols (i.e., standards) are the sine qua non of the Internet. The Internet works, and it would be hard to claim that the Internet does not change and evolve quickly.

Preserving Access to Digital Information (PADI)

The PADI (Preserving Access to Digital Information) initiative aims to provide mechanisms that will help to ensure that information in digital form is managed with appropriate consideration for preservation and future access. Now that digital preservation has emerged, if not into maturity, at least into a kind of toddlerhood of trial and discovery, it has become platitudinous to assert that unless consideration is given to preservation, much of our heritage in digital form will be lost.

In its unique role of selecting, describing and 'bringing together' digital preservation resources, PADI appeared to be well-positioned to provide a basis for such an undertaking. Cooperation has characterized the development of the PADI subject gateway. This has been seen as one of the initiative's strengths-according to one user, "It is extremely valuable in sharing knowledge around the world in a rapidly changing field. It helps prevent individual programs from being isolated and falling behind on new developments."

PADI receives advice and guidance from an Advisory Group, comprising experts in digital preservation from a number of countries. The safekeeping project-to build a library of digital preservation resources that will be accessible in the long term-extends this model of collaboration, relying on the application of many safekeeping strategies to form a distributed network of safekept material. It is founded on the understandings made between PADI and a range of resource owners with the latter indicating their intention to preserve access to their own networked resources.

A significant element of this project is the selection of resources for the PADI subject gateway that provides an initial step in the selection of resources for safekeeping. However, one of the most challenging and resource intensive parts of the safekeeping project has been making decisions about which material, of all that is contributed to the PADI database, will be of long-term interest or value.

Material selected for safekeeping may therefore be less current than other material on PADI and may not reflect current practice in digital preservation. PADI links to many types of resources. Digital preservation topics included on PADI range from emulation and legal deposit to topics such as intellectual property rights management, persistent identification and preservation metadata. Only those resources that very closely relate to digital preservation have been selected for safekeeping, with those providing contextual information only being excluded.

4

Information Retrieval and Record Keeping

The rapidity of technological change and the instability of the media have meant that traditional approaches to archives and records management, where they have been tried, have not been satisfactory for the long term preservation of electronic records. Technological change impacts on electronic environments as hardware and software undergo evolutionary change at an exponential rate.

At the hardware level changes to both machinery and capability as well as to storage media are in some cases an almost annual event. On the software side development is even more rapid to the point where companies 'market' software which doesn't even exist yet; i.e. vaporware. Examples of these changes include:

— upgrades to newer versions of operating systems or application programs;

— upgrades of hardware platforms and changes in storage device density and compression algorithms;

— the development of compound multimedia documents; and

— migration issues arising from the first three.

In the process of upgrading systems it is usually the practice for records and data which are 'current' to be migrated to the new platform to meet current business needs. The non-current records / data will often not be migrated. The longer the non-current records / data await conversion the more difficult the process becomes as the time increases after the system upgrade. In certain cases the records / data may actually be written off because it has no immediate value or as a cost cutting measure. This can cause problems down the line if the process is not conducted systematically and valuable records / data are lost or becomes inaccessible.

If the functionality of the system changes then the new or 'improved' system is different from its previous manifestation. Even if the function which is being managed is the same, improvements or alterations to any given system can affect user views via changes to the data, applications and access privileges. This process has implications for the production of evidence. In the last ten years of computing the power has literally gone to the people. With a computer on 'every desk' now and the development of inter and intra agency networks large amounts of computer power and much control now rests with individuals. The negative side this shift in power has occurred without an accompanying management or regulatory structure. A very similar result, in fact, to that which has occurred with the decentralisation of traditional paper document registry systems.

Individuals now have a great deal of control of the documentation process, whether it be in paper or electronic environments, without procedures and structures in place to enable them to exercise an informed choice. Many organisations have only recently awoken to the fact that their greatest asset (after people and dollars), information, is not adequately or systematically managed.

As a consequence resources which could be more effectively utilised in the pursuit of organisational priorities are often wasted because of poor access to and control over this information. There are a number of risks associated with this changing electronic environment, whether it be unregulated end users or poor systems design. They are:

— uncontrolled accumulation of records, documents and data;

— inadvertent destruction of records, documents and data;

— unauthorised tampering with records and documents;

— lack of or absence of systems documentation and associated metadata; and

— poor uncoordinated recordkeeping and duplication caused by the maintenance of parallel paper and electronic systems

If these characteristics are present in your system they can cause:

— system paralysis or at the very least hindrance in accessing information;

— additional costs associated with the purchase of additional storage;

— increased risk of wholesale, unsystematic and possibly illegal destruction;

— loss of valuable business and archival records;

— increased risk of security breaches;

— unauthorised alteration or deletion of records (loss of evidence);

— public embarrassment;

— unnecessary delays in or breakdowns in the business process; and

— lack of public accountability.

Because electronic records are software and hardware dependent and these change with time, the notion of the life-cycle management of electronic records is difficult to sustain. The life-cycle approach, based on the 'movement' of self-contained paper based records from creation through administrative use to ultimate destruction or retention, is unsatisfactory in a changing technological environment. In the traditional life-cycle approach, decisions are made about the value of records as archives at the end of their active life.

Only archives are then transferred to the archival repository. Following this approach these decisions could only be made about those electronic records that survived to the end of the active life. Given electronic records' dependency on software and hardware and their susceptibility to inadvertent loss through technological obsolescence this would be a huge risk. As a consequence attention must be given to records and archival issues from the outset for electronic records.

The ideal time is for this occur is as part of the systems development process at the point systems are being established or upgraded ie even before the records are created. Another consequence of the continuum approach is the breaking of the connection between the status of records and their physical custody. This has important implications for the control of and access to electronic records as physical location becomes somewhat redundant, both for the organisations which create and manage electronic records for business purposes and for archival institutions who are required to ensure the preservation of those electronic records which have archival value.

For example some organisations within the Commonwealth sphere have already outsourced the provision of their IT (information technology) services to other Government agencies or to private companies. We live in a virtual world. In the electronic environment, because records are not self evident and need appropriate software, hardware and associated metadata to be understood we have concluded that it is imperative to specify not only what values records have but which records are to be captured.

As a consequence, to enable the records to be captured, we need to provide more specific details about what data might be needed to make the record linked to good descriptions of the functions to which they relate. This can be done as part of the business process modelling phase. This process is part of the system development life-cycle. IT managers are clearly key to this process as it is they who will be responsible for:

(a) the capture and maintenance of electronic records; and

(b) the development or up-grade of systems

Records managers and archivists and others associated with the process of records creation and recordkeeping, therefore have to be involved in the systems development process in order to provide sufficient information about what records need to be kept and for how long. Appraisal, of electronic records, should be undertaken at the logical level i.e. the high-level diagrammatic representation of the system where it is relatively easy to see what functions the system manages, what business processes are involved and where records of transactions need to be kept. Appraisal done at this level is independent of how the records are physically stored.

The next step is then to build a link between the logical level of a system and the physical level (the level of databases, files, data etc). This approach, i.e. functional / logical level appraisal, is advocated, as it produces a simple, integrated and non-redundant definition of the records that is independent of frequent system and software changes. This detail is then enshrined in the business rules for the new system. Regardless of the way in which records are kept, be it electronic or otherwise, they can be appraised using standard appraisal methodology and employing standard appraisal criteria.

It is the record-keeping systems of agencies which must be appraised; looking at information flows, the interrelationships between elements of the record-keeping system, what (or even if) records are created in the documentation of activities and functions, and crucially what information needs to be provided about the records in disposal authorities to ensure that there is sufficient detail for IT practitioners to do their job.

The archival value of records needs to be determined at creation and preservation strategies employed from that point to avoid loss through planned obsolescence or separation from business context or unsystematic destruction. It is fairly clear, in the new technological environment, that the distinct roles of archivist, records manager and IT personnel are becoming less distinct and have begun to intersect at the edges.

For the archivist and records manager the key concept to communicate is that of records as evidence of business transactions. The Archives Act 1983 defines a record as:

> a document (including any written or printed material) or object (including a sound recording, coded storage device, magnetic tape or disc, microform, photograph, film, map, plan or model or a painting or other pictorial or graphic work) that is, or has been, kept by reason of any information or matter that it contains or can be obtained from it or by reason of its connection with any event, person, circumstance or thing.

This definition constructed in the early 1980s views records as physical objects such as paper files, tapes, disks etc. This type of definition presents major problems when we are dealing with electronic records. Firstly, records are neither purely documents nor objects. Secondly, in the electronic age of digital copying, records are independent of the medium (an object) on which they originally sat or currently sit. Thirdly, in electronic systems individual records and their components parts are not physically located in a logical sequence or (often) in the same physical space. Lastly, the definition does not provide any evidentiary test.

Because of these problems the Archives has decided, after some research and deliberation, that we needed an updated definition of a 'record' which has a generic set of characteristics and that is independent of format:

— A record is that which is created and kept as evidence of agency or individual functions, activities and transactions.

— To be considered evidence a record must possess content, structure and context and be part of a recordkeeping system.

By contrast in the IT environment a 'record' is defined as:

(1) an aggregate that consists of data objects, possibly with different attributes, that usually have identifiers attached to them or more succinctly

(2) a set of data treated as a unit or a set of one or more data items grouped for processing.

More recently the distinction between current and non-current records and archives has undergone a re-examination because of the need to appraise electronic records at the creation stage. This re-examination has now changed the way we look at archives in a distributed custody environment. Archiving is not a term in formal use in the archives / records management field although it is used colloquially.

In any event, to do the archiving or to archive refers to the practice of preparing consignments of records and transferring them to archival custody. Turning to the term 'document' we can see some measure of commonality in usage. The IT usage has 'document' defined in a number of ways:

(1) a named, structural unit of text that can be stored, retrieved, and exchanged among systems and users as a separate unit

(2) information and the medium on which it is recorded that generally have permanence and can be read by humans or machines.

The archives and records management definition is:

(1) a combination of a medium and the information recorded on or in it, which may be used as evidence or for consultation

(2) a single archival, record of manuscript item

Management of Electronic Records

In a virtual electronic world the need for archives to be held physically inside the walls of an archival institution becomes somewhat redundant. Accessibility becomes the issue not location. The best prospects for preserving access to archival electronic records will be to retain those records within a technological environment:

— which can maintain accessibility to the records in question;

— maintaining authenticity, in conformity with the changes and developments in technology as they occur over the time.

In most cases, this environment will not be found in the custody of the Archives, but in the custody of the Federal government agencies which have generated the records originally or have actively managed them in the course of their operations. Traditionally, archives have preserved the essential characteristics of records, (their content, structure, context and authenticity), by preserving the media on which they are recorded, in the original order in which the records were used and accumulated.

In the case of electronic records, this approach will not achieve the objective of preserving access to the records over the lengths of time required for archives. This is because the technology necessary to retrieve the records in an intelligible form from their physical carrier changes at a faster rate than the carrier themselves deteriorate. For example, in computerised systems, records come into being through transactions which occur within or between systems and the interaction of both hardware and software.

Such records will not necessarily continue to be retrievable over extended time merely because their component parts are stored on any particular medium. Access to or retrieval of electronic records created in specific environments will usually require a capacity to replicate those measures at a later time to ensure authentic versions of records are available, even though the technical retrieval process may be different. It would be very expensive for the Federal Government to duplicate within the Archives every possible configuration of software and hardware which might at any time have been in use within the Government sector.

To maintain generations of obsolete software and hardware as well as the technical expertise and environments would be extremely difficult to justify logically, practically and economically. Such an approach would result in wasteful expenditure of resources by the Australian Federal Government, without any assurance that the records concerned would continue to be accessible or retrievable when required in the future. It would also not be practical to convert the entire body of Federal Government records of enduring value to one standard medium or software and lodge that with the Archives.

Standards for software and hardware are helpful in promoting compatibility and continued accessibility, but they themselves change over time in response to industry and commercial needs, so they provide no certainty in themselves of continuity over the lengths of time required for archives. Such an approach would also involve the unnecessary conversion of records at the same time as agency computer systems continued to have the capacity to regenerate them in their original business context.

This would involve an increase in the overall cost to the Federal Government without any enhanced preservation of accessibility to the records. Normally, conversion to a standard format will not be the most cost-effective alternative for the Federal Government. This approach will only be used as a strategy by the Archives where all other alternatives have failed. Electronic records are generated in the computer systems which agencies use to facilitate their normal operations.

For this reason, maintaining the accessibility of electronic records of enduring value over time should not normally require significant analytical, design, programming, or hardware resources over and above those which are normally required for the maintenance of the computer systems generally. As applications are reviewed and re-developed, the carrying-forward of the records and their translation into the updated softwares and hardware technologies can be incorporated into the established system development processes. This requirement to ensure continued accessibility of electronic records of enduring value simply makes explicit in the electronic environment a way of meeting statutory requirements with which agencies must in any case comply.

In Australia the Archives only requires agencies to maintain accessibility to records in this way when they are of such enduring value to the Federal Government as a whole that the cost of such an approach is justified. Each review of the structure and operation of a functional computer application will not only be an opportunity to identify the record-keeping requirements for the revised system but also to review the retention requirements for electronic records which may need to be carried forward from the previous system to the new generation of technology.

At this time specific measures could then be taken within the systems to bring about the creation of records with the essential characteristics outlined in the definition of a records and with retention periods assigned. In such a review, a central criterion for determining whether such records continue to be carried forward will be that such an approach continues to be the least-cost alternative for the Federal Government as a whole in providing the required level of access to these records.

Normally the retention of accessibility to existing records will cost less than the potential cost of reconstituting such records in the future, even if such a reconstitution is in fact feasible. But the Archives recognises that there will come a time when the outcome of such a review is that the continued cost to the Federal Government incurred by keeping records actively accessible within an agency is not justified. In such a case, it is even less likely that the cost of keeping them accessible within the Archives would be less than it would be in the agency.

Alternative disposal arrangements may need to be examined, including the option of preserving the records in less accessible forms such as computer-output-microform. Ultimately the formal disposal arrangements set out in Records Disposal Authorities (schedules) may have to be revised in a new authority where the records in question could no longer be kept accessible at all.

Functional Requirements for Recordkeeping

The Archives has established a Systems Integration project to review the operation of the existing functional applications running on the organisation's mainframe system. Our recommended strategy for building in recordkeeping requirements at the systems development or up-grade stage is being tested as part of this project. The establishment of recordkeeping requirements are being determined using the following steps:

— preliminary investigation

— analysis of business activity

— identification of recordkeeping requirements

— assessment of existing systems

— identification of strategies for recordkeeping

— design of recordkeeping system(s)

— implementation of recordkeeping systems(s)

— post-implementation review.

Preliminary investigation

Through the examination of documentary sources and the conduct of interviews the role and purpose of the organisation, the organisational structure, the organisation's legal, regulatory, business and political environment and any critical factors affecting or associated with recordkeeping are examined.

Analysis of business activity

Following a similar process to the first step identify and

document each business function, activity, transaction. Establish a hierarchy of business functions, activities and transactions and identify and document the flow of business processes and the transactions which comprise them.

Identification of recordkeeping requirements

Identify the requirements for evidence affecting each business function, activity and transaction which must be satisfied through recordkeeping. These requirements for evidence can be derived from an analysis of the regulatory environment to which your organisation belongs and from an assessment of risk or failure. Determine how each requirement for evidence may be satisfied through recordkeeping and creation of records and then document the recordkeeping requirements.

Assessment of existing systems

Identify and analyse existing recordkeeping and other information systems and measure their performance against recordkeeping requirements.

Identify strategies for recordkeeping

Identify strategies for satisfying recordkeeping requirements which may include adopting policies, procedures and practices, designing new systems, implementing systems in a way which supports the satisfaction of recordkeeping requirements, or developing standards. They may be applied separately or in combination to each recordkeeping requirement. Strategies should be chosen on the basis of the degree of risk involved in the failure to satisfy a recordkeeping requirement within the business function, systems environment and the corporate culture in which the strategy must succeed.

Design of recordkeeping system(s)

Design a recordkeeping system which captures and maintains access to those records which have been identified in the earlier processes. Ensure that the system supports, and does not hinder, business processes. Assess and, if necessary, redesign business processes to incorporate recordkeeping requirements. The metadata and contextual information required for the maintenance and accessibility of the records to be created and captured in the recordkeeping system should be identified. There is no point in creating records to begin with if they cannot be efficiently retrieved and used. Records should have links to business functions activities and be accessible in transactional order.

Implementation of recordkeeping system(s)

Identify and use a suitable mix of implementation strategies. Integrate the operation of recordkeeping systems with business processes and related systems.

Post-implementation review

Monitor the performance of the recordkeeping system and carry out random checks of the quality of records and control information. Assess the performance of the system and initiate and monitor corrective action.

It is worth noting at this point that while this methodology was originally designed for electronic records management it has been more recently concluded that the methodology is equally applicable to records and recordkeeping systems in any environment. Where you enshrine these recordkeeping requirements into the new or pre-existing electronic systems you should ensure that the persons responsible for their development or up-grade take these requirements into account.

Modern Information Retrieval

The term 'archive' has come to be used to refer to a wide variety of storage and preservation functions and systems. Traditional archives are understood as facilities or organizations which preserve records, originally generated by or for a government organization, institution, or corporation, for access by public or private communities. The archive accomplishes this task by taking ownership of the records, ensuring that they are understandable to the accessing community, and managing them so as to preserve their information content and authenticity.

Historically, these records have been in such forms as books, papers, maps, photographs, and film, which can be read directly by humans, or read with the aid of simple optical magnification and scanning aids. The major focus for preserving this information has been to ensure that they are on media with long-term stability and that access to this media is carefully controlled.

The explosive growth of information in digital forms has posed a severe challenge not only for traditional archives and their information providers, but also for many other organizations in the government, commercial and non-profit sectors. These organizations are finding, or will find, that they need to take on the information preservation functions typically associated with traditional archives because digital information is easily lost or corrupted.

The pace of technology evolution is causing some hardware and software systems to become obsolete in a matter of a few years, andt these changes can put severe pressure on the ability of the related data structures or formats to continue effective representation of the full information desired. Because much of the supporting information necessary to preserve this information is more easily available or only available at the time when the original information is produced, these organizations need to be active participants in the long-term preservation effort, and they need to follow the principles espoused in ISO's Open Archival Information System (OAIS) reference model to ensure that the information can be preserved for the Long Term. Participation in these efforts will minimize the lifecycle costs and enable effective long-term preservation of the information.

The explosion of computer processing power and digital media has resulted in many systems where the Producer role and the archive role are the responsibility of the same entity. These systems, which are sometimes known as Active Archives, should subscribe to the goals of Long Term Preservation. The design process must realize that some of the Long Term Preservation activities may conflict with the goals of rapid production and dissemination of products to Consumers. The designers and architects of such systems should document the solutions that have been reached.

A major purpose of this reference model is to facilitate a much wider understanding of what is required to preserve and access information for the Long Term. To avoid confusion with simple 'bit storage' functions, the reference model defines an Open Archival Information System (OAIS) which performs a long-term information preservation and access function. It includes archives that have to keep up with steady input streams of information as well as those that experience primarily aperiodic inputs.

It includes archives that provide a wide variety of sophisticated access services as well as those that support only the simplest types of requests. The OAIS model recognizes the already highly distributed nature of digital information holdings and the need for local implementations of effective policies and procedures supporting information preservation. This allows, in principle, a wide variety of organizational arrangements, including various roles for traditional archives, in achieving this preservation. It is expected that organizations attempting to preserve information will find that using OAIS terms and concepts will assist them in achieving their information preservation goals.

A person, or system, can be said to have a Knowledge Base, which allows them to understand received information. For example, a person who has a Knowledge Base that includes an understanding of English will be able to read, and understand, an English text. Information is defined as any type of knowledge that can be exchanged, and this information is always expressed by some type of data. For example, the information in a hardcopy book is typically expressed by the observable characters which, when they are combined with a knowledge of the language used, are converted to more meaningful information. If the recipient does not already include

English in its Knowledge Base, then the English text (the data) needs to be accompanied by English dictionary and grammar information (i.e., Representation Information) in a form that is understandable using the recipient's Knowledge Base.

Similarly, the information stored within a CD-ROM file is expressed by the bits it contains which, when they are combined with the Representation Information for those bits, are converted to more meaningful information as long as the Representation Information is understandable using the recipient's Knowledge Base. For digital information, this means the OAIS must clearly identify the bits and the Representation Information that applies to those bits. This required transparency to the bit level is a distinguishing feature of digital information preservation, and it runs counter to object-oriented concepts which try to hide these implementation issues.

This presents a significant challenge to the preservation of digital information. As a further complication, the recursive nature of Representation Information, which typically is composed of its own data and other Representation Information, typically leads to a network of Representation Information objects. Since a key purpose of an OAIS is to preserve information for a Designated Community, the OAIS must understand the Knowledge Base of its Designated Community to understand the minimum Representation Information that must be maintained.

The OAIS should then make a decision between maintaining the minimum Representation Information needed for its Designated Community, or maintaining a larger amount of Representation Information that may allow understanding by a larger Consumer community with a less specialized Knowledge Base. Over time, evolution of the Designated Community's Knowledge Base may require updates to the Representation Information to ensure continued understanding.

As a practical matter, software is used to access the Information Object, and it will incorporate some understanding of the network of Representation Information objects involved. However, this software should not be used as rationale for avoiding identifying and gathering readily understandable Representation Information that defines the Information Object, because it is harder to preserve working software than to preserve information in digital or hardcopy forms.

The OAIS reference model emphasizes the preservation of information content. As digital technology evolves, multimedia technology and the dependency on complex interplay between the data and presentation technologies will lead some organizations to require that the look and feel of the original presentation of the information be preserved. This type of preservation requirement may necessitate that the software programs and interfaces used to access the data be preserved. This problem may be further complicated by the proprietary nature of some of the software.

Various techniques for preserving the look and feel of information access are currently the subject of research and prototyping. Though the OAIS reference model does not focus on these emerging techniques, it should provide architectural basis for the prototyping and comparison of these techniques.

Content Information

The Content Information is that information which is the

original target of preservation. It consists of the Content Data Object (Physical Object or Digital Object, i.e., bits) and its associated Representation Information needed to make the Content Data Object understandable to the Designated Community. For example, the CDO may be an image that is provided as the bit content of one CD-ROM file together with other files, on the same CD- ROM, that contain Representation Information.

Only after the Content Information has been clearly defined can an assessment of the Preservation Description Information be made. The Preservation Description Information applies to the Content Information and is needed to preserve the Content Information, to ensure it is clearly identified, and to understand the environment in which the Content Information was created. The Preservation Description Information is divided into four types of preserving information called Provenance, Context, Reference, and Fixity. Briefly, they are the following:

— Provenance describes the source of the Content Information, who has had custody of it since its origination, and its history (including processing history).

— Context describes how the Content Information relates to other information outside the Information Package.

— Reference provides one or more identifiers, or systems of identifiers, by which the Content Information may be uniquely identified. Examples include an ISBN number for a book, or a set of attributes that distinguish one instance of Content Information from another.

— Fixity provides a wrapper, or protective shield, that protects the Content Information from undocumented alteration. For example, it may involve a check sum over the Content Information of a digital Information Package.

The Packaging Information is that information which, either actually or logically, binds, identifies and relates the Content Information and PDI. For example, if the Content Information and PDI are identified as being the content of specific files on a CD-ROM, then the Packaging Information would include the ISO 9660 volume/file structure on the CD-ROM, as well as the names and directory information of the files on CD-ROM disk. The Descriptive Information is that information which is used to discover which package has the Content Information of interest. Depending on the setting, this may be no more than a descriptive title of the Information Package that appears in some message, or it may be a full set of attributes that are searchable in a catalog service.

It is necessary to distinguish between an Information Package that is preserved by an OAIS and the Information Packages that are submitted to, and disseminated from, an OAIS. These variant packages are needed to reflect the reality that some submissions to an OAIS will have insufficient Representation Information or PDI to meet final OAIS preservation requirements. In addition, these may be organized very differently from the way the OAIS organizes the information it is preserving.

Finally, the OAIS may provide information to Consumers that does not include all the Representation Information or all the PDI with the associated Content Information being disseminated. These variants are referred to as the Submission Information Package (SIP), the Archival Information Package (AIP), and the Dissemination Information Package (DIP).

The Submission Information Package (SIP) is that package that is sent to an OAIS by a Producer. Its form and detailed content are typically negotiated between the Producer and the OAIS. Most SIPs will have some Content Information and some PDI, but it may require several SIPs to provide a complete set of Content Information and associated PDI to form an AIP. A single SIP may contain information that is to be included in several AIPs. The Packaging Information will always be present in some form.

Within the OAIS one or more SIPs are transformed into one or more Archival Information Packages (AIP) for preservation. The AIP has a complete set of PDI for the associated Content Information. The Packaging Information of the AIP will conform to OAIS internal standards, and it may vary as it is managed by the OAIS. In response to a request, the OAIS provides all or a part of an AIP to a Consumer in the form of a Dissemination Information Package (DIP). The DIP may also include collections of AIPs, and it may or may not have complete PDI.

The Packaging Information will necessarily be present in some form so that the Consumer can clearly distinguish the information that was requested. Depending on the dissemination media and Consumer requirements, the Packaging Information may take various forms. Management provides the OAIS with its charter and scope. The charter may be developed by the archive, but it is important that Management formally endorse archive activities. The scope determines the breadth of both the Producer and Consumer groups served by the archive.

Some examples of typical interactions between the OAIS and Management include:

— Management is often the primary source of funding for an OAIS and may provide guidelines for resource utilization (personnel, equipment, facilities). Œ Management will generally conduct some regular review process to evaluate OAIS performance and progress toward long-term goals.

— Management determines, or at least endorses, pricing policies, as applicable, for OAIS services.

— Management participates in conflict resolution involving Producers, Consumers and OAIS internal administration.

Effective Management should also provide support for the OAIS by establishing procedures that assure OAIS utilization within its sphere of influence. For example, management policies should require that all funded activities within its sphere of influence submit data products to the archive and also adhere to archive standards and procedures.

Some Submission Agreements will reflect a mandatory requirement to provide information to the OAIS, while others will reflect a voluntary offering of information. Even in the case where no formal Submission Agreement exists, such as a World Wide Web (WWW) site, a virtual Submission Agreement may exist specifying the file formats and the general subject matter the site will accept.

A Data Submission Session may consist of a set of Content Information corresponding to a set of observations, which are carried by a set of files on a CD-ROM. The Preservation Description Information is split between two other files. All of these files need Representation Information which must be provided in some way. The CD-ROM and its directory/file structure are the Packaging Information, which provides encapsulation and identification of the Content Information and PDI in the Data Submission Session.

The Submission Agreement indicates how the Representation Information for each file is to be provided, how the CD-ROM is to be recognized, how the Packaging Information will be used to identify and encapsulate the SIP Content Information and PDI, and how frequently Data Submission Sessions (e.g., one per month for two years) will occur. It also gives other needed information such as access restrictions to the data. Each SIP in a Data Submission Session is expected to meet minimum OAIS requirements for completeness.

However, in some cases multiple SIPs may need to be received before an acceptable AIP can be formed and fully ingested within the OAIS. In other cases, a single SIP may contain data to be included in many AIPs. A Submission Agreement also includes, or references, the procedures and protocols by which an OAIS will either verify the arrival and completeness of a Data Submission Session with the Producer or question the Producer on the contents of the Data Submission Session.

There are many types of interactions between the Consumer and the OAIS. These interactions include questions to a help desk, requests for literature, catalog searches, orders and order status requests. The ordering process is of special interest to the OAIS Reference Model, since it deals with the flow of archive holdings between the OAIS and the Consumer. The Consumer establishes an Order Agreement with the OAIS for information. This information may currently exist in the archive or be expected to be ingested in the future.

The OAIS must:

— Negotiate for and accept appropriate information from information Producers.

— Obtain sufficient control of the information provided to the level needed to ensure Long-Term Preservation.

— Determine, either by itself or in conjunction with other parties, which communities should become the Designated Community and, therefore, should be able to understand the information provided.

— Ensure that the information to be preserved is Independently Understandable to the Designated Community. In other words, the community should be able to understand the information without needing the assistance of the experts who produced the information.

— Follow documented policies and procedures which ensure that the information is preserved against all reasonable contingencies, and which enable the information to be disseminated as authenticated copies of the original, or as traceable to the original.

— Make the preserved information available to the Designated Community.

An organization operating an OAIS will have established some criteria that aids in determining the types of information that it is willing to, or it is required to, accept. These criteria may include, among others, subject matter, information source, degree of uniqueness or originality, and the nature of the techniques used to represent the information (e.g., physical media, digital media, format).

The information may, in general, be submitted using a wide variety of common and not-so-common forms, such as books, documents, maps, data sets, and moon rocks using a variety of communication paths including networks, mail, and special delivery. The OAIS negotiates with the Producer to ensure it acquires appropriate Content Information and associated PDI for its mission and the Designated Community. Considerable iteration may be required to agree on the right information to be submitted, and to get it into forms acceptable to the OAIS.

It is important for the OAIS to recognize the separation that can exist between physical ownership or possession of Content Information and ownership of intellectual property rights in this information. If it has created the information and is the legal owner of the Content Information, the OAIS already has the independence to do what is required to preserve the information and make it available. When acquiring the Content Information from any other producer or entity, the OAIS must ensure that there is a legally valid transfer agreement that either transfers intellectual property rights to the OAIS, or clearly specifies the rights granted to the OAIS and any limitations imposed by the rightsholder(s).

The OAIS must ensure that its subsequent actions to preserve the information and make it available conform with these rights and limitations. When the OAIS does not acquire the intellectual property rights, the agreement should specify what involvement the rightsholder(s) will have in preservation, management or release of the information. In most cases, it will be preferable for the OAIS to negotiate an agreement that specifies the rightsholder(s) requirements and authorizes the OAIS to act in accordance with those requirements without active involvement of the rightsholder(s) in individual cases.

The OAIS must assume sufficient control over the Content Information and Preservation Description Information so that it is able to preserve it for the Long Term. The problems of assuming sufficient control of the Content Information and Preservation Description Information, when they are largely digital, are addressed in three related categories, as follows:

— copyright implications; intellectual property and other legal restrictions on use;

— authority to modify Representation Information;

— agreements with external organizations.

Copyright implications, intellectual property and other legal restrictions on use: An archive will honor all applicable legal restrictions. These issues occur when the OAIS acts as a custodian. An OAIS should understand the copyright concepts and applicable laws prior to accepting copyright materials into the OAIS. It can establish guidelines for ingestion of information and rules for dissemination and duplication of the information when necessary.

Authority to modify Representation Information: Although the Fixity information within the Preservation Description Information of an AIP ensures that the Content Information-related bits have not been altered, there will come a time when Content Information bits are not in a form that is convenient for the Consumers from the Designated Community. The Content Information bits may be fully documented in available hardcopy forms, so technically the information has not been lost, but practically the information has become inaccessible. The OAIS needs the authority to migrate the Content Information to new representation forms. If it is acting as a custodian, it may need to seek additional permission to make such changes. If the information is copyrighted, the OAIS should already have negotiated permission to make the changes needed to meet preservation objectives. It may employ subject matter experts, from outside the OAIS, to help ensure that information is not lost. Ideally, when this situation arises, both the original AIPs and new AIPs will be retained.

Agreements with external organizations: An OAIS may establish a variety of agreements with other organizations to assist in its preservation objectives. For example, it may establish an agreement with another OAIS so that it does not have to preserve all the common Representation Information objects related to its Content Information objects. Agreements with other organizations should be monitored to be sure they are being followed and remain useful.

Preservation Policies and Procedures

It is essential for an OAIS to have documented policies and procedures for preserving its AIPs, and it should follow those procedures. The appropriate policies and procedures will depend, at minimum, on the nature of the AIPs and any, backup relationships the archive may have with other archives. For example, migrations that alter any Content Information or PDI will need to be carefully monitored and the appropriate PDI fully updated. This attention to detail, while also ensuring against processing errors, requires that strong policies and procedures be in place and that they be executed.

The Producer and Consumer communities should be provided with submission and dissemination standards, policies, and procedures to support the preservation objectives of the OAIS. The Designated Community should be monitored to be sure the Content Information is still understandable to them. The Designated Community may lose its familiarity with some terminology, and the definition of the community may be broadened to include other members with different backgrounds.

By definition, an OAIS makes its AIPs visible and available to its Designated Communities. Multiple views of its holdings, supported by various search aids that may cut across collections of AIPs, may be provided. Some AIPs may only exist as the output of algorithms operating on other AIPs. They appear as DIPs that, upon dissemination, should include documentation on how they were derived from other AIPs. The expectations of OAIS Consumers regarding access services will vary widely among archives and over time as technology evolves.

Pressures for more effective access must be balanced with the requirements for preservation under the available resource constraints. Some AIPs may have restricted access and therefore may only be disseminated to Consumers who meet access restrictions. The OAIS should have published policies on access and restrictions so that the rights of all parties are protected. In general, DIPs may be distributed by all varieties of communication paths, including networks and physical media.

Archival Storage functions include receiving AIPs from Ingest and adding them to permanent storage, managing the storage hierarchy, refreshing the media on which archive holdings are stored, performing routine and special error checking, providing disaster recovery capabilities, and providing AIPs to Access to fulfill orders.

Data Management entity provides the services and functions for populating, maintaining, and accessing both

Descriptive Information which identifies and documents archive holdings and administrative data used to manage the archive. Data Management functions include administering the archive database functions (maintaining schema and view definitions, and referential integrity), performing database updates (loading new descriptive information or archive administrative data), performing queries on the data management data to generate result sets, and producing reports from these result sets.

Preservation Planning also designs IP templates and provides design assistance and review to specialize these templates into SIPs and AIPs for specific submissions. . Preservation Planning also develops detailed Migration plans, software prototypes and test plans to enable implementation of Administration migration goals.

Modern, distributed computing applications assume a number of supporting services such as inter-process communication, name services, temporary storage allocation, exception handling, security, backup and directory services. Much excellent work has already been done in the area of open system environment reference models.

Operating system services provide the core services needed to operate and administer the application platform, and provide an interface between application software and the platform. These services include the following:

— Kernel operations provide low-level services necessary to create and manage processes, execute programs, define and communicate signals, define and process system clock operations, manage files and directories, and control input-output processing to and from the external environment.

— Commands and utilities include mechanisms for operations at the operator level, such as comparing, printing, and displaying file contents; editing files; pattern searching; evaluating expressions; logging messages; moving files between directories; sorting data; executing command scripts; and accessing environment information.

— Real-time extension includes the application and operating system interfaces needed to support those application domains requiring deterministic execution, processing, and responsiveness. The extension defines the applications interface to basic system services for input/output, file system access, and process management.

— System management includes capabilities to define and manage user resource allocation and access (i.e., what resources are managed and the classes of access defined), configuration and performance management of devices, file systems, administrative processes (job accounting), queues, machine/platform profiles, authorization of resource usage, and system backup.

— Operating system security services specify the control of access to system data, functions, hardware, and software resources by users and user processes. Network services provide the capabilities and mechanisms to support distributed applications requiring data access and applications interoperability in heterogeneous, networked environments.

There are many types of information involved in the long-term preservation of information in an OAIS. Each of these types can be viewed as a complete Information Object in that it contains a data object and adequate Representation Information to understand the data. Information Objects that are used in the OAIS. The objects are categorized by their content and function in the operation of an OAIS into Content Information objects, Preservation Description Information objects, Packaging Information objects, and Descriptive Information objects.

The Archival Storage functional entity takes the AIPs produced by the Ingest process and merges it into the permanent archive holdings. The Data Management functional entity takes the Package Descriptions produced by Ingest and augments the existing Collection Descriptions to include their contents. The logical model of the ingested data should already be mapped into the logical model of the archives holdings.

Thus the major transformation that occurs in this step is the mapping of the acquisition session from the ingest physical data model. This will tend to be on staging storage, to the permanent storage of the OAIS, which could range from Database Management Systems (DBMS) to Hierarchical File Management Systems (HFMS), or any mixture of the above.

The internal view of the OAIS is the permanent representation of the archived data, so all encoding and mappings must be well documented and understood. The process of transferring the ingest objects is frequently by a software process such as an HFMS driver or a DBMS. In this case, it is the responsibility of the OAIS to maintain an active copy of the software or careful documentation of the internal formats so the data can be transferred to other systems in the future without loss of information.

The OAIS may have to spend significant time and effort developing Associated Descriptions and Finding

Aids such as catalogs that will aid the Consumer in locating AIPs or AICs of interest. A Consumer will establish a Search Session with the Access entity. Once the Consumer identifies the OAIS holdings to acquire, the Consumer uses an OAIS supplied Ordering Aid to develop an order request to acquire the data.

The Consumer produces a logical view of the desired AIPs and associated Package Descriptions to be included in the Dissemination Information Package and specifies the physical details of the Data Dissemination Session such as media type and object format. This process may involve no visible interaction between the Consumer and the OAIS if adequate defaults exist. This order can also specify any transformations the Consumer wishes applied to the AIPs in creating the DIP.

The fast-changing nature of the computer industry and the ephemeral nature of electronic data storage media are at odds with the key purpose of an OAIS: to preserve information over a long period of time. No matter how well an OAIS maintains its current holdings, it will eventually need to migrate much of its holdings to different media and/or to a different hardware or software environment to keep them accessible. Today's digital data storage media can typically be kept at most a few decades before the probability of irreversible loss of data becomes too high to ignore.

Further, the rapid pace of technology evolution makes many systems much less cost-effective after only a few years. Digital Migration is defined to be the transfer of digital information, while intending to preserve it, within the OAIS. It is distinguished from transfers in general by three attributes:

— a focus on the preservation of the full information content;

— a perspective that the new archival implementation of the information is a replacement for the old; and

— full control and responsibility over all aspects of the transfer resides with the OAIS.

Three major motivators are seen to drive Digital Migrations of AIPs within an OAIS. These are:

— *Improved Cost-Effectiveness*: The rapid pace of hardware (e.g., disk/tape drives) and software evolution provides greatly increasing storage capacities and transfer bandwidths at reducing costs. It also drives the obsolescence of some media types well before they have time to decay. In addition, improved AIP packaging designs may be less dependent on underlying media and supporting systems, and therefore simplified migration efforts may be recognized. To remain cost-effective, an OAIS must take advantage of these technologies. Depending on the particular technologies involved, the AIP information may have to be moved to new media types not previously supported and it may have to revise its AIP implementations to take advantage of the new technologies.

— *New Consumer-Service Requirements*: The Consumers of an OAIS also experience the benefits of new technologies and consequently raise their expectations of the types and levels of service they expect from an OAIS. These increased services may require new forms of DIPs to service particular Designated Communities, which in turn may drive an OAIS to hold new forms of AIPs to reduce output conversions. Additionally, AIPs typically go through popularity swings and the OAIS may need to provide different levels of access performance to meet Consumer demands over time. This is likely to be satisfied by moving some AIPs to different media that provide increased or decreased levels of access performance. Finally, the Designated Community for a given AIP may be broadened, resulting in the need to revise AIP forms so as to be understandable and usable by this broader community. All of these can result in the migration of AIPs within an OAIS.

— *Media Decay*: Digital media, over time, become increasingly unreliable as secure preservers of bits. Even those that are used with some level of error correction eventually need to be replaced. The net result of media decay is that AIP information must be moved to newer media.

Digital Migrations are time consuming, costly, and expose the OAIS to greatly increased probabilities of information loss. Therefore, an OAIS has a strong incentive to consider Digital Migration issues and approaches. The OAIS Consumer interface in Access provides one or more Content Information IDs, with associated name spaces, to assist in identifying a particular Content Information object of interest. One or more of these Content Information IDs will be included in the PDI Reference Information associated with that Content Information object. The Descriptive Information in Data Management will map each of these IDs to the same AIP ID.

The Access Function uses this information to obtain the AIP ID and gives it to Archival Storage to retrieve the associated AIP. Within Archival Storage, the AIP ID is mapped to the location of AIP Packaging Information by the Archival Storage mapping infrastructure. The AIP Packaging Information, in turn, logically delimits and identifies the Content Information and the PDI, and binds them into a single entity for preservation.

For example, if the Content Information and PDI are determined to be the content of several files, the pointers to documents describing the representations of those files, and the documents themselves, then the Packaging Information would logically be defined as the implementation of the file system holding the file content bits, the data structure holding the pointers, the information which is used to distinguish the Content Information from the PDI, and an encapsulating data structure which identifies the files and other data structures as the components of the AIP Package.

The associated Archival Storage mapping infrastructure might then be implemented as a database which relates the AIP ID to the location of the encapsulating data structure. The transfer of any part of the Content Information, PDI, or Packaging Information to the same or new media, with the intent that it replaces that part of the previous AIP, is considered to be a Digital Migration of the AIP. Note that a change to the Archival Storage mapping information only, which is outside of the AIP concept, is not considered to be a migration of the associated AIP, although such changes need to be carefully controlled to ensure that access to the AIP is maintained.

Digital Migration

There are four primary digital migration types. The primary types, ordered by increasing risk of information loss, are:

— *Refreshment*: A Digital Migration where a media instance, holding one or more AIPs or parts of AIPs, is replaced by a media instance of the same type by copying the bits on the medium used to hold AIPs and to manage and access the medium. As a result, the existing Archival Storage mapping infrastructure, without alteration, is able to continue to locate and access the AIP.

— *Replication*: A Digital Migration where there is no change to the Packaging Information, the Content Information and the PDI. The bits used to convey these information objects are preserved in the transfer to the same or new media-type instance. Note that Refreshment is also a Replication, but Replication may require changes to the Archival Storage mapping infrastructure.

— *Repackaging*: A Digital Migration where there is some change in the bits of the Packaging Information.

— *Transformation*: A Digital Migration where there is some change in the Content Information or PDI bits while attempting to preserve the full information content. There is the smallest risk of information loss under Refreshment because none of the bits that are used to hold AIP information or to support finding and accessing AIPs are altered. There is also little risk of information loss under Replication because none of the bits representing AIP information have changed.

However if a new media type is involved there will be some changes needed in the Archival Storage mapping infrastructure. The risk is that something may go wrong in the process and some unintended changes to bits may take place. Repackaging recognizes that some bit changes will take place, but these are mostly confined to information used to delimit the Content Information and the PDI, and so generally do not alter the information carried by the Content Information or the PDI. There is the usual risk that something will go wrong, and there are also cases where some interaction between Packaging Information and the Content Information or PDI cannot be avoided. This poses additional risk of information loss.

Finally, Transformation poses the most risk because changes to the Content Information or PDI are made. To understand more clearly what may be involved in these migration types it is necessary to look at possible implementation approaches. It will be seen that some migrations are a mixture of Repackaging and Transformation. It is also important to recall that, for any given AIP the OAIS must first clearly identify what constitutes the Content Information, and only then can the PDI be identified.

A migration involves Replication when there are no bit changes to the Packaging Information, the Content Information, and the PDI. Ensuring that none of these bits has changed may be a significant effort, depending on the implementation.

A migration involves Repackaging when there is some change to the Packaging Information during the transfer. The Packaging Information plays the critical role of delimiting and relating, at a minimum, the Content Information and PDI. If the Content Information and PDI are themselves composed of multiple components, the Packaging Information may be asked to delimit and relate these as well. These are implementation decisions that the OAIS needs to explicitly recognize.

Digital Migrations that require some changes to the Content Information or PDI are referred to as Transformations. These changes will be to some of the bits in the Content Data Object of the Content Information or PDI with corresponding changes in the associated Representation Information. In all cases the intent is to provide maximum information preservation. The resulting AIP is intended to be a full replacement for the AIP that is undergoing Transformation. The new AIP qualifies as a new Version of the previous AIP.

The Representation Information plays a key role in Transformations, and the impacts of the changes on the Representation Information may be used to categorize the Transformations. A Representation Information object can be modeled as consisting of a base set of entities, a set of resulting entities, and mapping rules that define the resulting entities and their relationships in terms of the base entities.

A Reversible Transformation occurs when the new representation defines a set (or a subset) of resulting entities that are equivalent to the resulting entities defined by the original representation. This means that there is a one-to-one mapping back to the original representation and its set of base entities.

All the Content Information bits for an AIP are contained within the body of three files on a CD-ROM. The Packaging Information includes the bits used to implement the file and directory structure that provides access to these three files. The contents of the three files are transferred to a new CD-ROM and in the process they are compressed using a lossless compression algorithm. This transfer is a Transformation because the compression process has altered the Content Information, and it is a

Reversible Transformation because there is a decompression algorithm that will return the original file content bits.

The relevant Representation Information components of the original Content Information needs to be updated to include the decompression algorithm, and the PDI information also needs to be updated, in forming this new AIP Version. The following scenario identifies a Non-Reversible Transformation that can occur when Content Information is migrated to a new format that can express a more varied data model than the original format.

All the Content Information bits for an AIP are contained within the body of three files on a CD-ROM. The Packaging Information includes the bits used to implement the file and directory structure that provides access to these three files. The contents of the three files are transferred to a new CD-ROM and in the process the third file is altered because there are no longer readily available tools to make effective use of the third file's content in its current form.

The new format, which is in common use, employs a different data model from that of the original format and there are many ways in which the information may be mapped into the new format. This mapping must be carefully done to ensure there is no significant information loss to the Designated Community. This The Content Information for an AIP is defined to be the body of three files on a CD-ROM. The first file contains an internal name that links the third file and specifies a relationship between them. The Packaging Information includes the directory and file structure that identifies the three files. During a migration to a new media type, these three files are put into a new directory and given new names. This constitutes a Repackaging migration because there is a new implementation of the directory and file structure, which is providing the packaging function.

Unless a Digital Migration involves Transformation, it is not considered to create a new AIP Version and it is not required that its PDI be updated. In other words, the AIP version is considered to be independent of Refreshment, Replication, and Repackaging that does not affect the Content Information or PDI. This does not mean that the OAIS does not track such migrations; rather it is not required to update the PDI as part of such tracking. If this process is carried out entirely within Archival Storage, the AIP ID remains the same and there is no implied impact to Associated Descriptions or Access Aids.

An OAIS may also find it convenient to provide an AIP that is derived from an existing AIP. It may do this by extracting some information, or by aggregating information from multiple AIPs, to better serve Consumers. This type of resulting AIP may be referred to as a Derived AIP. It does not replace any of the AIPs that it was derived from and it is not a result of a Digital Migration. This also results in a new AIP ID and a new Associated Descriptions. This may also require updates to, or new, Access Aids depending on how they have been implemented.

An OAIS may wish to preserve a Consumer access services in the face of changing technology. Conceptually, the OAIS provides an environment that allows the Consumer to view the AIUs Content Information through the application's transformation and presentation capabilities. For example, there may be a desire to use a particular application that extracts data from an ISO 9660 CD-ROM and presents it as a multi-spectral image. This application runs under a particular operating system, requires a set of control information, requires use of a CD-ROM reading device, and presents the information to driver software for a particular display device.

In some cases this application may be so pervasive that all members of the Designated Community have access to the environment and the OAIS merely designates the Content Data Object to be the bit string used by the application. Alternatively, an OAIS may supply such an environment, including the Access Software application, when the environment is less readily available. However, as the OAIS and/or the Designated Community moves to new computing environments, at some point the application will cease to function or will function incorrectly.

The OAIS response to preserving an Access Software application would likely depend, in large part, on whether or not it had or could obtain the source code for the Access Software. The major factors in the use of these techniques would be the cost/benefit ratio to the OAIS and the associated Designated Community. If source code or commercial bridges are not available and there is an absolute requirement for the OAIS to preserve the Access look and feel, the OAIS would have to experiment with iiemulationls technology that is currently being researched in the Digital Library domain.

The OAIS response to preserving an Access Software application execution service would likely depend, in part, on whether or not it had the source code for the application. If the OAIS had the source code and adequate documentation on the application, the expected approach would be to port the application to the new environment and attempt to test it adequately to ensure it was functioning correctly.

If the Access Software was a proprietary package, which was widely used and available commercially, it is likely that there will be commercially provided bridge (i.e., conversion) software which Transforms the current Content Data Objects to other forms used by the new Access Software having a similar look and feel. If no commercial alternative is seen, the OAIS may contract with the owner of the original Access Software to develop and provide source code for a simplified tool that can read but not modify instances of data written using the format.

This approach might not be viable due to cost or legal issues. In any of these cases, the OAIS will need to establish mechanisms to verify that no preserved information has been lost. In addition the OAIS must investigate the issues of ensuring that the new Access Software is available to the Designated Community. There may be a mandatory requirement from the Designated Community to maintain the look and feel of proprietary Access software due to the large number of AIUs that are dependent on that Access Software. In this case, if the OAIS is unable to obtain the source code, it may find it necessary to investigate use of an emulation approach.

The OAIS could consider emulating the application. If the application provides a well- known set of operations and a well-defined API for access, the API could be adequately documented and tested to attempt an emulation of the application. However, if the Consumer interface is primarily one of display or other devices, which affect human senses (e.g., sound), this reverse engineering becomes nearly impossible.

Another approach is emulation of the underlying hardware. One advantage of hardware emulation is the claim that once a hardware platform is emulated successfully all operating systems and applications that ran on the original platform can be run without modification on the new platform. However, this does not take into account dependencies on input/output devices.

Once emulation has been adopted, the resulting system is particularly vulnerable to previously unknown software errors that may seriously jeopardize continued information access. Given these constraints, the technical and economic hurdles to hardware emulation appear substantial. There have been investigations of alternative emulation approaches, such as the development of a virtual machine architecture or emulation at the operating system level. These approaches solve some of the issues of hardware emulation, but introduce new concerns.

None of the emulation techniques is mature enough for significant comment. In addition, the current emulation research efforts involve a centralized architecture with control over all peripherals. The level of complexity of the interfaces and interactions with a ubiquitous distributed computing environment (i.e., WWW and JAVA) with heterogeneous clients may introduce requirements that go beyond the scope of current emulation efforts.

Archive Interoperability

Users of multiple OAIS archives may have reasons to wish for some uniformity or cooperation among them. For example, Consumers of several archives may wish to have:

— common finding aids to aid in locating information across several archives;

— a common Package Description schema for access;

— a common DIP schema for dissemination; or

— a single global access site.

Interaction between OAIS Archives

OAIS associations can be categorized technically by both external and internal factors. External factors include characteristics of the Producer and Consumer communities. There are four categories of archive association. The first three categories have successively higher degrees of interaction:

— *Independent*: Archives motivated by local concerns with no management or technical interaction among them

— *Cooperating*: Archives with potential common producers, common submission standards, and common dissemination standards, but no common finding aids.

— *Federated*: Archives with both a Local Community (i.e., the original Designated Community served by the archive) and a Global community (i.e., an extended Designated Community) which has interests in the holdings of several OAIS archives and has influenced those archives to provide access to their holdings via one or more common finding aids. The Access needs of the Local community usually have priority over those of the Global community. Global dissemination and Ingest are optional features.

— *Shared resources*: Archives that have entered into agreements with other archives to share resources, perhaps to reduce cost. This requires various standards internal to the archive (such as ingest-storage and access-storage interface standards), but does not alter the user community's view of the archive.

Independent Archives

An independent archive is assumed to serve only a single Designated Community. The archive and the Designated Community must agree on the design of SIPs, DIPs, and Finding Aids. An independent archive may choose to design these structures based on formal or de- facto standards, which would allow cooperation with other archives that implement the same standards. However, the design decisions to use these standards are not based on the possibility of inter-operation with other archives, but rather on local requirements and cost savings.

The classification of an archive as independent is not based on its size or distributed functionality. An independent archive may occupy one site, or may be physically distributed over many sites. It may use many standards for a given internal element. However, if there is no interaction with other archives, the archive is independent.

Cooperating Archives

Cooperating archives are based on standards agreements among two or more archives. The simplest form of cooperation between archives is when one archive acts as a Consumer of material from another archive. In this case the consuming archive must support the DIP format of the producing archive as a SIP format. Cooperating archives have related communities of interest, so they order and ingest data from other cooperating archives and possibly have common data Producers.

5

Metadata: The Foundations of Digital Record Keeping

Records and archives form a significant sub-set of the information resources increasingly being created and made available in the Web environment. Records are a by-product of doing business and they have an important role to play in doing it electronically. A simple way of defining a record is as a document that has taken part in a business process, and thereafter provides evidence of the transaction of that business.

Records document business activity of all kinds, and are critical to corporate, democratic and historical accountability. They constitute a vital part of organisational and collective identity and memory, and provide important sources of value-added information. As records provide evidence of social and organisational activity, they need to be managed in ways which take account of their evidential nature as well as those characteristics they share with other information resources.

In networked environments, records, like other information resources, need to be adequately identified, described and authenticated. They need to be readily accessible via common user interfaces to authorised users, and retrievable for as long as they are required, then to be disposed of in a systematic way. Terms and conditions of access, including freedom of information law, privacy protection and confidentiality requirements, need to be managed and monitored.

But records, as accountability traces and evidence of business activity, have additional metadata requirements. Authoritative well-structured metadata which specifies their content, structure, context and essential management needs must be embedded in, wrapped around or otherwise persistently linked to them from the moment they are created if they are to continue to function as evidence.

Growth of Internet

The explosive growth of interest in the Internet in recent years has created a digital extension of the academic research library for certain kinds of materials. Valuable collections of texts, images and sounds from many scholarly communities—collections that may even be the subject of state-of-the-art discussions in these communities—now exist only in electronic form and may be accessible from the Internet.

A number of well-designed locator services, such as Lycos, are now available that automatically index many of the resources available on the Web and maintain up-to-date databases of locations. But indexes are most useful in small collections within a given domain. As the scope of their coverage expands, indexes succumb to problems of large retrieval sets and problems of cross disciplinary semantic drift. Richer records, created by content experts, are necessary to improve search and retrieval.

Formal standards such as the TEI Header and MARC cataloging will provide the necessary richness, but such records are time consuming to create and maintain, and hence may be created for only the most important resources. An alternative solution that promises to mediate these extremes involves the creation of a record that is more informative than an index entry but is less complete than a formal cataloging record.

If only a small amount of human effort were required to create such records, more objects could be described, especially if the author of the resource could be encouraged to create the description. And if the description followed an established standard, only the creation of the record would require human intervention; automated tools could discover these descriptions and collect them.

In US, the Online Computer Library Center (OCLC) and the National Center for Supercomputing Applications (NCSA) convened the invitational Metadata Workshop on March 1-3, 1995, in Dublin, Ohio to address this issue. Fifty-two librarians, archivists, humanities scholars and geographers, as well as standards makers in the Internet, Z39.50 and Standard Generalized Markup Language (SGML) communities, met to identify the scope of the problem, to achieve consensus on a list of metadata elements that would yield simple descriptions of data in a wide range of subject areas, and to lay the groundwork for achieving further progress in the definition of metadata elements that describe electronic information.

Goals of the workshop included fostering a common understanding of the problems and potential solutions among the stakeholders and promoting a consensus on a core set of metadata elements to describe networked resources. Since the Internet contains more information than professional abstractors, indexers and catalogers can manage using existing methods and systems, it was agreed that a reasonable alternative way to obtain usable metadata for electronic resources is to give authors and information providers a means to describe the resources themselves.

The major task of the Metadata Workshop was to identify and define a simple set of elements for describing networked electronic resources. To make this task manageable, it was limited in two ways. First, only those elements necessary for the discovery of the resource were considered. It was believed that resource discovery is the most pressing need that metadata can satisfy, and one that would have to be satisfied regardless of the subject matter or internal complexity of the object. Secondly, the discussion was further restricted to the metadata elements required for the discovery of what were called document-like objects, or DLOs by the workshop participants.

It was believed that DLOs are still the most common type of resource sought in the Internet and that whatever solution could be proposed for DLOs could be extended to other kinds of resources. More importantly, the likelihood of making progress on this challenging problem would be increased if attention could initially be restricted to something familiar. DLOs were not rigorously defined, but were understood by example. For example, an electronic version of a newspaper article or a dictionary is a DLO, while an unannotated collection of slides is not. Of course, the crux of the problem is that in a networked environment, DLOs can be arbitrarily complex because they can consist of text with callouts to images, audio or video clips, or to other hypertext documents.

The Metadata Workshop participants made no attempt to limit the complexity of DLOs, except to say that the intellectual content of a DLO is primarily text, and that the metadata required for describing DLOs will bear a strong resemblance to the metadata that describes traditional printed texts. The goal was to define a core set of metadata elements that would allow authors and information providers to describe their work and to facilitate interoperability among resource discovery tools. But because the core elements do not yield a complete description of objects in a networked environment, careful consideration was also given to mechanisms for extending the element set.

The primary deliverable from the workshop was a set of thirteen metadata elements, named the Dublin Core Metadata Element Set (or Dublin Core, for short). The Dublin Core was proposed as the minimum number of metadata elements required to facilitate the discovery of document-like objects in a networked environment such as the Internet. The syntax was deliberately left unspecified as an implementation detail. The semantics of these elements was intended to be clear enough to be understood by a wide range of users.

The discussions at the Metadata Workshop revealed several principles that should guide the further development of the element set. Adherence to these principles increases the likelihood that the core element set will be kept as small as possible, that the meanings of the elements will be understood by most users, and that the element set will be flexible enough for the description of resources in a wide range of subject areas. These principles are intrinsicality, extensibility, syntax independence, optionality, repeatability, and modifiability.

Intrinsicality

The Dublin Core concentrates on describing intrinsic properties of the object. Intrinsic data refer to the properties of the work that could be discovered by having the work in hand, such as its intellectual content and physical form. This is distinguished from extrinsic data, which describe the context in which the work is used. For example, the "Subject" element is intrinsic data, while transaction information such as cost and access considerations are extrinsic data. The focus on intrinsic data in no way demeans the importance of other varieties of data, but simply reflects the need to keep the scope of deliberations narrowly focussed.

Extensibility

In addition to its use in dealing with extrinsic data, extension mechanisms will allow the inclusion of intrinsic data for objects that cannot be adequately described by a small set of elements. Extensibility is important because users may wish to add extra descriptive material for site-specific purposes or specialized fields. In addition, the specification of the Dublin Core itself will change over time, and the extension mechanism will allow revisions while maintaining some backward compatibility with the originally defined element set.

Syntax Independence

Syntactic bindings are avoided because it is too early to propose formal definitions and because the Dublin Core is intended to be eventually used in a range of disciplines and application programs.

Optionality

All the elements are optional. The Dublin Core may eventually be applied to objects for which some elements have no meaning. It also seems counterproductive to mandate complex descriptions if the creators of the content are expected to provide the descriptive material. A simple description is better than no description at all.

Repeatability

All elements in the Dublin Core are repeatable. For example, multiple author elements would be used when a resource has multiple authors.

Modifiability

Each element in the Dublin Core has a definition that is intended to be self-explanatory. However, it is also necessary that the definitions of the elements satisfy the needs of different communities. This goal is accomplished by allowing each element to be modified by an optional qualifier. If no qualifier is present, the element has its common-sense meaning; otherwise, the definition of the element is modified by the value of the qualifier.

Qualifiers will be typically derived from well-known conventions in the library community or from the field of knowledge appropriate to the resource. Qualifiers are important because they give the Dublin Core a mechanism for bridging the gap between casual and sophisticated users. For example, the data in the Subject element consists of any word or phrase that describes the object's content. However, a professional cataloger may wish to supply the name of the authoritative source from which the subject terms are taken.

The NEDLIB project

NEDLIB was initiated by CoBRA+, a permanent Standing Committee of the Conference of European National Libraries (CENL). The project was launched on January 1, 1998, with funding from the European Commission's Telematics Application Programme, and will run till the end of 2000. Eight national libraries in Europe, one national archive, two ICT organisations and three major publishers are participating in the project. The Koninklijke Bibliotheek, National Library of the Netherlands, leads the project.

NEDLIB, which stands for Networked European Deposit Library, aims to develop a common architectural framework and basic tools for building deposit systems for electronic publications (DSEP). The project addresses major technical issues confronting national deposit libraries that are in the process of extending their deposit, whether by legal or voluntary means, to digital works. One important piece of work being carried out by the project is the functional specification and overall design of a DSEP.

The main objective is to identify functional requirements that are common to all deposit libraries in order to arrive at a "generic" high-level design of a DSEP that can serve as a basis for local implementations by individual deposit libraries. A common workflow for handling deposited electronic publications was defined and helped to identify common functional requirements. A major step forward in the conceptual design of a DSEP was made in December 1998, when the project consortium agreed to adopt the Open Archival Information System (OAIS) model as a Reference Model.

The fact that the model was being used by other, similar, projects such as CEDARS in the UK and PANDORA in Australia, prompted the decision. Now work is being carried out to detail a DSEP process model and data model, based on the OAIS framework, applicable to all deposit libraries, and detailed enough to enable consistent implementation design and development work. The second main objective of the project is to address the issue of long-term digital preservation. Work in this area should provide better insight into the pro's and con's of different long-term preservation strategies as applied to digital deposit collections.

The characteristics of electronic publications and other categories of digital deposit material and their associated preservation and authenticity requirements need to be defined. The NEDLIB partners recognise that many aspects, including cost-effectiveness, legal restrictions, agreements with publishers, and user access requirements, ultimately need to be taken into account when policy choices for preservation strategies are set. For NEDLIB, however, the focus lies on the technical issues of preservation. Besides work on abstract modelling and experimental preservation strategies, NEDLIB is very much geared towards producing pragmatic, ready-to-use results.

Recommended standards and conventions for technical solutions are documented in order to provide deposit libraries with practical guidelines when implementing a DSEP. Practical experiences, technical infrastructures and organisational approaches taken by individual NEDLIB partners are gathered and compiled in such a way that these experiences can be of use to other libraries. The third and last main objective of the project is to build a demonstrator system, with tools and software already in use by project partners or developed by NEDLIB, covering all functional aspects of a DSEP.

Software and tools are being developed, tested and integrated in functional building blocks of the demonstrator. Existing library systems, such as the online public access catalogue (OPAC) and the library acquisition and cataloguing systems, which are external to, but need to interact with a DSEP, will interface to the demonstrator.

The OAIS document, drafted by the Consultative Committee for Space Data Systems (CCSDS) of NASA, is a technical recommendation prepared for formal review as a draft ISO standard. It establishes a common framework for functional and information modelling concepts applicable to any archive. It is specifically applicable to organisations that have a responsibility to provide long-term access to digital information. As such, the OAIS model is relevant to deposit libraries.

The prospect that such a model can provide a solid basis for standardisation within digital archives and promote greater vendor awareness and support of archival requirements, was decisive for the NEDLIB partners. They decided to map deposit library requirements to OAIS and to detail the OAIS model into a DSEP model for deposit libraries. In this way, NEDLIB hopes to contribute to the OAIS standardisation work and, ultimately, to promote DSEP implementations conforming to the OAIS standard.

In the same way as the OAIS model presents a high-level view of the interaction between the OAIS and the environment surrounding it, it is necessary to position a DSEP in the digital library environment. Which functionality is within scope of a DSEP, and which belongs to the Digital Library System (DLS) as a whole? Most of the functionality relating to the selection and description of digital works, the creation of finding aids (such as bibliographies, catalogues, subject-guides and indexes), and the provision of user access, is part of the broader digital library configuration. Consequently, OAIS functional entities, such as Data Management and Access, which overlap general functional requirements of a digital library, need to be delimited in some detail, for DSEP purposes.

The library acquisition system and the associated procedures are responsible for selecting and acquiring the deposit copy of a publication. The procedures may vary with each library, each publisher and each publication type (CD-ROM, Web pages, etc.). To be able to ingest publications into a DSEP, an interface is needed to ensure the publication is (re-)packaged according to the specifications of a SIP (Submission Information Package). This interface may need to generate, if necessary, accompanying instructional data, in order for the Ingest module of the DSEP to be able to process the publication properly.

This "pre-processing" interface is needed because deposit libraries cannot dictate submission formats to publishers: in principle, they have to accept all formats published on the market. Most development work at deposit libraries presently concentrates on this interface. It requires much tailoring, as some publishers provide table of contents and others don't, some provide full-text versions for indexing and others don't—it often leads to re-negotiating the deposit procedure with publishers and upgrading the quality of deposit submissions. For publishers, this interaction helps them to redesign their publishing process according to higher quality standards.

In some cases a SIP may contain only metadata. This may be primary metadata, coming straight from the publisher or from identification agencies, or it may be a full bibliographic description coming from the library cataloguing system. This interface can request and accept a DIP (Dissemination Information Package) from the Access module of a DSEP. The DIP consists of the requested publication in one of the available formats with accompanying software and/or metadata needed to install and display it, to assess its authenticity or to reconstruct the original copy.

The interface takes care of all processes needed to unpack a DIP and to make it fit for use by the library visitor. Through this interface, deposited material can be made available, taking account of all kinds of access variables of the digital library environment, such as user authorisation, user access rights, publisher license access conditions and other access controls. Presently, for example, deposit license agreements with publishers only permit installation of publications onsite, on a library workstation, and access by registered library users.

This "post-processing" interface is needed because deposit libraries cannot anticipate all access modes and future variables. This interface also transfers, upon request, metadata from the DSEP through to other systems that need to process the data, either within the digital library system or external to it, such as systems from bibliographic utilities. Usually this concerns metadata uploads from DSEP to other systems. In some cases, it may also involve passing a whole publication through to a content indexing system, in order to generate, for example, a full-text index of the publication.

The DSEP itself consists of six processing modules: the five OAIS modules, plus an additional module for preservation. The need for this additional module is clarified below.

Ingest

Ingest only accepts publications packaged as a SIP. Ingest unpacks and verifies the publication, collects, generates and re-distributes data to other processes. Routines include integrity check of the medium, of the file formats and of the logical document structure. The process identifies the informational contents, the primary metadata, special access controls to be placed on the contents, abstracts, full-text indexes and other additional data accompanying the publication, technical data for installation and de-installation. The different data are copied to and processed in different environments (for cataloguing, for access control, and for finding aids). In the process, the publication is installed and de-installed and its authenticity is established and recorded. Finally, Ingest prepares the publication for transfer to storage, as an AIP (Archival Information Package).

Archival Storage

Archival storage only accepts AIPs. This module consists of all procedures necessary for the secure storage of the electronic publication in the digital store, including storage management procedures, quality assurance, disaster recovery, etc. It also includes regular medium migration, in order to preserve the bit stream of a publication from decaying carriers.

Data-Management

Data-Management mainly stores and retrieves metadata. We distinguish between two types of metadata:

— metadata and technical data associated with the publication, such as bibliographic descriptions, access control information, (de-)installation data, authenticity and integrity control information, preservation data, etc.

— metadata associated with the administration of the DSEP, such as status report information, statistical data, etc.

The metadata associated with the publication may also be duplicated in other (external) systems. The cataloguing process, which creates a title-description of the electronic publication and also involves subject indexing, takes place in the cataloguing environment of the digital library system. It may re-use primary metadata provided by the publisher and return descriptive metadata to the DSEP system, through the Delivery and Capture interface.

Access

In the DSEP model the Access module is much more limited than in the OAIS model, because many related processes belong intrinsically to the digital library environment and not specifically to a DSEP, such as creating finding aids, registering library users, applying access controls, etc. The DSEP access module takes care of retrieving an AIP and making it available in such a way that it is fit for use. This may entail extracting parts of the electronic publication, or adding a full-text index to it, or converting (parts) of the publication into appropriate formats for viewing, printing or downloading. It may involve providing a viewing configuration. It may even involve providing emulation software for displaying the publication. The resulting DIP (Dissemination Information Package) is then fed into the library access system.

Administration

The administration module is central to a DSEP. It regulates all the operations of the system and takes care of monitoring, quality control and auditing. It requests status reports from all processing modules and controls, regularly, if DSEP standards and policies set out by the deposit library management are applied throughout the system.

Preservation

The OAIS model does not explicitly include a preservation module. Medium migration (refreshing or copying a publication) is a preservation procedure that takes place in Archival Storage. It should be associated with storage because the stored bits need to be preserved. But archival storage does not have (and does not need to have) any knowledge of the content of a publication.

As formats become obsolete and the viewers needed to interpret and render these formats also become obsolete, it will be necessary to take measures to preserve the content of a publication and all related aspects such as data, layout, structure and functionality. To this end, several strategies may be followed, such as migration and emulation. In the OAIS model, digital migrations that require changes to the content are referred to as transformations. In all cases, transformation leads to a "new version" of the original publication. However, it is not clear where transformation processes take place in OAIS.

We have added a dedicated Preservation module to address this need. The module is configured according to the deposit library preservation policies. Both transformation and emulation approaches are worked out in some detail in the DSEP model. The resulting output is either a new version of a formerly deposited publication, in which case it is ingested anew in the system, or it is a set of specifications for building emulators that can render a whole generation of publications on a future (unknown) platform. In both cases, new preservation metadata will be generated and fed into Data-Management.

The data model for a DSEP is based on the OAIS information model. The deposit copy of an electronic publication is exchanged and managed within a DSEP as an OAIS information package (SIP, AIP and DIP). Such a package contains the following:

— The original bit stream of the digital publication

— Metadata

This may be primary metadata as provided by the publisher (title information, system requirements information, etc.) in the case of a SIP, or functional metadata necessary for specific functional entities (storage, preservation, access, etc.) in the case of an AIP or DIP.

However, it should be noted that the OAIS information objects are logical objects. In actual DSEP-implementations, the metadata, the software and the data bit stream need not be stored physically together in one AIP. In fact, it is proposed that, within a DSEP, all metadata is stored in Data-Management and not together with the data bit stream in Archival Storage. This is done because metadata updates will be more or less frequent, whilst the data bit stream of the publication content will not change over time. It is therefore not deemed sensible to store both types of data together in one physical container. All logical data entities that belong together and pertain to the same publication need to be linked together via interoperable identifier systems (identifier of the publication, of the information package, of the metadata records, etc.).

The OAIS concepts of "Representation information" and "Preservation description information" allow for the correct interpretation of the data bit stream over an indefinite period of time. In DSEP, the "Preservation description information" includes all recorded metadata giving information about the authenticity of a deposit copy and the preservation measures taken by the DSEP. Depending on the preservation strategy followed, both types of information need to change over time.

Management of change and versioning of AIPs are central to the migration strategy: when the original data bit stream is converted, the data formats, the rendering software, the system requirements and associated (de-)installation data, and the amount of information/functionality loss change and need to be recorded. Assessing the digital original and authenticity control are central to the emulation strategy: choices need to be made as to what needs to be preserved of the original publication, what needs to be recreated (emulated) and what is an acceptable loss of authenticity.

The parts that need to be emulated need to be specified in detail (metadata) in a high-level language and the user needs to be educated to "use" the digital original—as future generations will not know how to interact with obsolete IT-based end user environments.

SPIRT—Recordkeeping Metadata Research Project

The genesis of the SPIRT Recordkeeping Metadata Research Project lies in the increasing opportunities for information accessibility and transmission of knowledge in distributed networked environments, and the seemingly unlimited scope for the transaction of business of all kinds via the Web. The late 1997 announcement by the Commonwealth government of the delivery of all appropriate services electronically via the Internet by 2001, and the establishment of electronic commerce as a normal means for Commonwealth payments by the year 2000 signaled the emergence in the public sector of radically different ways of structuring service provision and business processes, areas already being explored in the private sector.

To support business activities in cyberspace, reliable and robust mechanisms are required to enable the continuing accessibility of essential evidence of business activities and ensure that the accountability protections provided by the electronic record persist over time. The recordkeeping community, recognising that new approaches to managing records were needed, identified as a priority the development of a framework for standardising recordkeeping metadata and defining a high level set of metadata elements to support the persistence in networked environments of reliable, authentic, meaningful and accessible records.

The SPIRT project, "Recordkeeping Metadata Standards for Managing and Accessing Information Resources in Networked Environments Over Time for Government, Social and Cultural Purposes" [HREF6], involves Monash University, the University of New South Wales, and a consortium of industry partners ñ the National Archives of Australia, the New South Wales State Records Authority, the Queensland State Archives, the Australian Council of Archives and the Records Management Association of Australia. The broader social context of the project relates to enabling society, government, commerce and individuals to continually access the information they need to conduct their business, protect their rights and entitlements, and securely trace the trail of responsibility and action.

Maintaining authentic, reliable and useable evidence of transactions has significant social and cultural implications as records are a bastion of democratic and cultural accountability. They enable democratic rights of review and examination, and the transmission of our cultural heritage. Such rights have been increasingly protected in legislative mandate. Without the appropriate frameworks for the creation and management of electronic records in the networked environment equivalent to those well established in the paper world, society will be unable to exercise these rights and the cultural record of endeavour will be lost.

The immediate challenge to the records and archives profession is to develop recordkeeping metadata management regimes that will meet organisational, social and cultural needs relating to:

— the creation and management of records in electronic environments, especially distributed networks

— making records and archives accessible with an array of other genres of recorded information through common user interfaces

— enabling records to continue to function over time and space ñ for a nanosecond or millennia:

— as evidence for governance, accountability, memory and identity purposes

— as sources of value-added information ñ information that can be accessed, exploited and reused for reasons unrelated to the business or social activity they document.

A significant factor in the shaping of the SPIRT Recordkeeping Metadata Research Project was recognition that managing records effectively in distributed networks involves ensuring that recordkeeping metadata regimes are compatible with the metadata development framework initiatives in the broader information community, in particular the DC and AGLS initiatives. Much of the metadata work undertaken so far in electronic networked environments is based on a passive notion of document-like information objects, seeing them as existing only to provide and disseminate information.

The records and archives metadata community in Australia takes a different perspective in relation to records, regarding them as "active participants in business processes and technologies" rather than "passive objects to be described retrospectively". Envisaging records as information objects that act as the transactors of business informs the SPIRT Recordkeeping Metadata Research Project and links the dynamic world of business activity to the passive world of information resource in cyberspace.

The SPIRT project's work on standardising recordkeeping metadata and defining metadata elements is based on an analysis of the business, organisational and social contexts of recordkeeping, national and international standards which specify recordkeeping requirements, and existing generic resource discovery and recordkeeping sector specific metadata schemes.

The elements defined in the Recordkeeping Metadata Scheme [HREF13] identify and describe significant features of the business contexts in which records are created, managed and used. They identify and describe the people or agents involved, and the records themselves. They also link business contexts to the people or agents doing the business and the records that document it, and they reference the mandates, laws, policies and business rules that authorise and control business activity. They enable description and management of recordkeeping actions, e.g. the processes which fix the content of records, enable their forms to be re-presented and rendered over time, manage their physical preservation, classify and index them.

They enable the stringing together of related records, the administration of terms and conditions of access, use and disposal, and the tracking and documenting of the recordkeeping actions themselves, as well as the history of the use of the records. The Recordkeeping Metadata Scheme elements are presented as three sub-sets:

Business Metadata

— identifies and describes business dealings, broadly defined as social and organisational activity of all kinds; and

— establishes relationships between the business being done, the people or agents involved and the records created and used

Business metadata can be used to identify and describe business transactions and activities, as well as the business functions and broader societal purposes that they serve.

Agent Metadata

— identifies and describes people or agents that create, control, manage and use records; and

— establishes relationships between an agent and other agents, the business being done and the records that document it

Agents may be corporate bodies or persons. They may operate at any level in a hierarchy. Examples include an operational position, an organisational unit or work group, an organisation, an institution, a person or a family.

Record Metadata

— identifies and describes records;

— establishes relationships between a record and other records, agents and the business context; and

— describes and manages recordkeeping processes.

Records may be at any level of disaggregation or aggregation, e.g. a component of a record, a file, a records system, a corporate archive, a collective archives.

Recordkeeping Metadata Scheme (RKMS) is made up of a set of highly structured metadata elements, sub-elements and qualifiers, and provides for the specification of the schemes used to determine the values of the metadata elements. A significant feature of this high level set of metadata is that it is scaleable, i.e. when it is implemented it can apply to records at any level of aggregation, to business dealings ranging from an individual transaction to the societal purpose it ultimately serves, and to agents acting at any level in organisational and social hierarchies.

6

Digital Collection Management System

For several decades, information technology has been an important tool for meeting the library's objectives. However, growth in use of the Internet as a publication medium and as a mechanism for service delivery has presented significant new challenges and opportunities not yet being adequately addressed by the library's current systems and services. These include the increasing amount of material published only in digital form, material referred to as being "born digital", and the emergence of digitisation as a cost-effective means of enhancing access to traditional library materials.

In recent years the library has given increased attention to collecting digital information resources, as part of its statutory obligation to collect, preserve and make available library material. This includes both "born digital" Internet-accessible material captured for archiving and preservation and creation of "digital surrogates" of physical objects in the library's collection through scanning or digitisation.

In Australia, library has now initiated a project to obtain an integrated technical infrastructure for digital services. The Library defines digital services to mean services exploiting digital technologies to provide access to traditional documentary resources and to ensure the long-term preservation of, and access to, documents available only in digital form. The Library is calling this new project the Digital Services Project. The Digital Collection Management System Project will build on existing Library facilities in the following areas:

a) It will provide the Library with systems supporting integrated collection management in a digital environment.

b) It will enable the Library to build and provide access through the National Bibliographic Database and the NLA Catalogue to a distributed national collection of Australian electronic publications in cooperation with Australian creators, publishers, libraries and collecting bodies.

The Library envisages that the capabilities required to achieve these outcomes may not all currently be available or may be unusual in the marketplace. The Library will be seeking the best overall "fit" to the requirement.

Strategies for Digital Collection Management

These environmental changes meet its service objectives more effectively, the Library has developed a set of strategies specifically directed to the management of its digital collections. These are outlined below under the following headings:

a) Electronic publications.

b) Digitisation of collection items.

c) Audio recordings.

d) The NLA Catalogue.

e) Administrative support.

Electronic publications

In Australia, the National Library Act requires the Library to "maintain and develop a national collection of library material, including a comprehensive collection of library material relating to Australia and the Australian people". This mandate requires the Library also to collect electronic publications. Electronic publications are considered to include physical format digital publications such as CD-ROMs and computer disks as well as online publications stored using digital technology, such as e-journals and materials held on web sites. The Library will collect, organise and preserve Australian electronic publications within a framework of cooperation that recognises that other collecting institutions have responsibility for collecting and preserving certain segments of Australia's documentary heritage.

In the second half of 1996, the Library set up the PANDORA project. PANDORA stands for Preserving and Accessing Networked Documentary Resources of Australia. During 1997 the Library began work to develop a proof-of-concept archive to provide long term preservation and access to significant Australian online publications. The archive is now operational. The Library is also developing a national model for the long-term preservation of Australian online publications and has begun to talk to the Australian State libraries about a collaborative approach to achieve broader coverage of the national output. The Library has also undertaken significant policy development and some research in relation to the preservation of and access to physical format digital publications in its collection.

The collection contains physically unstable media as well as an increasingly diverse set of software dependencies that complicate longer-term access. The Library has set up mechanisms to identify what comes into the collection, and interim procedures to record relevant information to support on-going management of the titles. The Library's strategy for dealing with the problems of unstable media has been to copy titles from magnetic floppy disks to CD-R (CD-Recordable) with appropriate descriptive concordances. This does not address the software dependency problems, for which the Library has initiated a modest research program looking at software archiving, migration, and emulation.

Digitisation of collection items

For physical format material in the collection, the Library will use digital technologies where it is cost effective and legal to do so, to enhance both preservation and access. Microfilm and photographic transparencies are still used as the Library's main strategy for preserving the content of physical collection items in case of loss of the original. This is because the shelf life of digital file formats and storage media is still uncertain. However, the Library is actively exploring digital reformatting as a future preservation option when the technology permits this.

Since 1995, the Library has been operating a service, Images1, that provides access to digital copies of items in the Library's Pictorial Collection. The Images1 database contains records with linked thumbnail and medium resolution images for approximately 20 000 collection items, with new items being added at a rate of over 5 000 a year. It can be searched directly through its own Web interface or accessed via a hypertext link in the NLA Catalogue record. External users may order a reproduction-quality copy of the image through a manual process. There are no online ordering facilities yet, pending national infrastructure support for digital signatures and cost-effective solutions for online payment facilities.

The Library routinely produces finding aids or guides to the papers and manuscripts of individuals, families and organisations deposited with the Library. Over 300 of these are now accessible in electronic form on the Library's Web server and also through links from the NLA Catalogue record. Similar finding aids are produced for the Library's oral history recordings. The Library is currently investigating the feasibility of migrating its existing electronic finding aids from HTML to the Encoded Archival Description (EAD) format. This is an SGML/XML Document Type Definition (DTD) developed especially for describing archival and manuscript collections.

The Library provides a digitisation-on-demand service whereby the Library's Document Supply Service scans print articles for delivery to customers over the Internet. Currently, the scanned file is discarded after the document is delivered. Subject to resolution of copyright issues, the Library is considering the benefits of storing these files for re-use. The Australian Public Affairs Information Service (APAIS) and the Australian Medical Index (AMI) are routinely scanned, with the intention of making the scanned copies available to external users via the Web, pending resolution of copyright issues.

Audio recordings

The Library has an extensive collection of audio recordings consisting of around 32,000 hours of unique material. Some of the recordings are commercial publications but the Library itself has created or commissioned many of the items, which include interviews with eminent Australians, social history interviews, songs, dance music, recitations and stories. The Library has begun to use digital technology "in the field", but most of the existing material is recorded in analogue form. A project is under way to copy these audio tapes to digital masters for preservation reasons, with the analogue copies being kept as backup copies until the Library is sure that risks with digital reformatting have been resolved.

About 3,000 hours of audio have been converted and are now stored on 3,500 CDs. Conversion is expected to proceed at a rate of about 2,500 hours per year. The current Integrated Library Management System provides a good level of support for managing the printed collections but does not yet deliver full support for the Library's collections of manuscripts, rare books, maps, oral history, printed music and pictorial materials.

These collections have special curatorial requirements for recording the provenance and condition of items, their preservation history, intellectual property rights and conditions of access that are currently met through a range of separate manual and automated systems. Another limitation of the current system is that the catalogue supports only a single level of bibliographic description. This has meant that external users have needed to come to the Library to discover the existence of material described in the catalogue at collection level only (for example, a set of photographs or the papers of an eminent Australian).

The Web interface to the Library's catalogue has partially addressed this problem, by enabling hypertext links to be inserted in the catalogue record to more detailed finding aids and listings. The Web interface is also the means by which external users gain access to the online electronic publications in the PANDORA archive and to digital copies of collection items. The Library will maintain and develop its public access catalogue as a comprehensive listing of materials in its collection - both print and electronic - with hypertext links from the catalogue description to:

a) A digital copy, transcript or summary where one has been created to enhance access.

b) The digital object itself, for items in the collection published in electronic form.

c) More detailed information about items catalogued at collection-level only.

The Library will provide access to more detailed information about the content of its manuscript collections through electronic finding aids in the Encoded Archival Description (EAD) format. For its pictorial collections, the Library will ensure that the system replacing the current Images1 management system provides support for up to five levels of description for collections and sub-collections and that this information can be accessed from the catalogue through hypertext links.

The current Integrated Library Management System supports the definition of separate logical views of the catalogue. These have been set up for journals and newspapers, manuscripts, maps, oral histories and folklore, pictorial material and printed music. The Library will continue to provide separate logical views for the special collections and plans to merge its Images1 service with the pictorial subset when the technology allows it. The Library will also develop separate digital services, guides, online exhibitions and other multimedia publications tailored to promote specific aspects of the collection. As a general principle, the Library will make digital content developed for these products accessible through the catalogue and vice versa.

Administrative Support

The Library's collection managers require comprehensive and integrated administrative support for the efficient and cost-effective management of the Library's digital objects. This includes the ability to monitor and control access to systems used to collect, store, deliver and manage these objects and the ability to produce reports for management of usage of digital objects. The Library may use its infrastructure to hold digital objects for an archiving partner and needs the ability for collection managers from such agencies to have remote access to and control of their objects in the Digital Collection Management System.

The Library operates on the principle that there should be no charge for access to its collections, taking into account the framework for protecting the intellectual property rights of creators and publishers provided by the Commonwealth Copyright Act and the costs of reproduction and delivery. In accordance with this principle, where it is cost effective to do so, the Library will provide onsite users with free access to commercial electronic publications and network services. The Library will strive to ensure protection of the intellectual property rights of the creators and publishers of content to which it mediates access, in line with fair use for research purposes.

Digital objects can have complex rights involving multiple parties and in some cases royalty payments associated with their provision and access. Temporal or locational restrictions on access to digital objects are also often required by the copyright holder. The Library may in future also require use of electronic commerce features such as online ordering of and/or billing for access to digital objects.

At the end of the Project the PANDORA proof-of-concept archive must have been migrated to a permanent archive based on robust commercially available software modified to meet the Library's needs. This will enable the Library to begin in earnest to build the distributed national collection of Australian electronic publications in cooperation with Australian creators, publishers, libraries and collecting bodies.

The collection will operate within a distributed framework for the discovery, appraisal and selection of digital material, its description and organisation, its archiving and preservation and its access as an integrated part of the distributed national collection. The technical framework will consist of distributed digital object servers separately maintained by the cooperating collecting bodies, with unified access at whole item level provided by the National Bibliographic Database.

A broad policy framework underpinned by Commonwealth and State legislation, published collection development policies and established guidelines will be the primary means of sharing responsibility for archiving Australian electronic publications. The Library's own archive to be delivered by this Project must be supported by systems or services configured to:

a) Capture objects selected for archiving.

b) Take in new versions of objects in the archive.

c) Keep both old and new versions to reflect changes to the original copy over time.

d) Preserve both data and information or software required to interpret what the data means (for example, specifications or copies of enabling software such as browsers, plug-ins, conversion or decryption utilities, Java applets, style sheets).

e) Support on-going access as technologies evolve.

The Library's digital archive of Australian electronic publications and Images1 digital collection will be two components of a comprehensive collection of library material relating to Australia and the Australian people that is maintained and developed by the Library. At the end of the Project, the Library's collection managers should be significantly better positioned to develop and maintain this collection through a single, coherent user interface, regardless of material type. Collection development, description and maintenance processes that are well handled by the current Integrated Library Management System will continue to be supported to the current level of service.

In addition, support should be provided as a logical extension to the Integrated Library Management System for a range of business processes currently managed through separate manual and automated systems. This should enable the Library to begin a program of migration of these systems to the new facility during 2001 and streamline procedures and workflows for managing:

a) Physical format digital publications collected by the Library.

b) Digital copies of items in the Library's collection.

c) The Library's digital audio recordings.

d) Other physical format materials in the Library's collection that require special curatorial control (desirable).

The acquisition of original materials should be supported by appropriate mechanisms for tracking the selection and negotiation process. There should be facilities for managing information about the provenance, condition, preservation history, intellectual property rights ownership and conditions of access of any item in the collection for which this information needs recording.

Processes should be available to support the detailed description of the content of collection items as part of a hierarchical data model that supports multiple levels of description. Collection managers should be able to navigate between related processes and data with the minimum of effort and to input or update data once only when it is needed in the collection management life cycle.

The Library has modelled its requirements for the Digital Collection Management System on the need for four logical system Configurations. These are the Collecting System, Digital Object Storage and Delivery System, Object Management System, and Rights Management and Access Control System.

Digital objects are captured for the Digital Collection Management System by the Collecting System. The Collecting System handles both the digital objects themselves and metadata describing the digital objects which are passed to the Digital Objects Storage and Delivery System and the Object Management System respectively. The Digital Object Storage and Delivery System provides for storage and delivery of the Library's digital objects.

The Object Management System provides for the integrated management of the Library's digital objects through recording of information (metadata) about the objects. The Rights Management and Access Control System manages external user access to the Digital Collection Management System and access to the Library's digital collections where conditions apply.

Where possible, the Library will base its Digital Collection Management System on products and services available or currently becoming available in the marketplace. The aim of this strategy is to minimise future systems development and operations costs, based on a development path which is sufficiently flexible to take advantage of market place developments. This strategy will be implemented by:

a) Adopting a modular 'mix and match' architecture that provides a clear separation between servers, underlying databases, communication infrastructures and user interfaces.

b) Utilising and supporting standards with broad marketplace and industry support to integrate individual products and services.

c) Avoiding Project software development as far as possible by working within and influencing the development priorities of vendors.

d) Maximising interoperability with other systems and databases through standard protocols.

e) Eliminating the Library's involvement in the distribution of client software by using the World Wide Web as the common access method for all users.

Configurations

There are four "Configurations" of systems and services:

— Collecting System.

— Digital Object Storage and Delivery System.

— Object Management System.

— Rights Management and Access Control System.

The Library intends to contract for a System that includes hardware, systems and applications software and on-going supply, maintenance and support services. The Library is included in Group 11 of the Commonwealth's "Whole of Government" information technology infrastructure and telecommunications services outsourcing program, known as the "IT Infrastructure Initiative", whose implementation is being administered by the Office of Asset Sales and IT Outsourcing (OASITO).

The Library therefore wishes to contract for a System in a manner that will facilitate appropriate novation or transfer to any service provider appointed as a result of the IT Infrastructure Initiative. The Library wishes to contract for the acquisition of a System (which may include lease of hardware) in a manner which:

a) ensures that the System is installed, tested and integrated to meet the NLA's requirements.

b) allows for on-going, up to 5 years, supply, maintenance and support including for the applications and applications software in the System.

c) allows for novation or transfer without penalty to the Library of part or all of the Contract to any service provider appointed as a result of the IT Infrastructure Initiative, after acceptance of the System by the Library.

The Collecting System will interface with the Object Management System and the Digital Object Storage and Delivery System to provide for collection of objects for the Library's digital collections. The Collecting System will be configured to build and maintain the Library's archive of online electronic publications and its collection of pictorial digital surrogates.

The Collecting System will replace the existing PANTRACK system currently used to gather electronic publications for the PANDORA digital archive. After implementation, the Library should also be able to configure the Collecting System to build and maintain its other collections of digital surrogates and its collection of digital audio recordings. The process of creating and disseminating digital objects is not seen as falling within the scope of the Collecting System.

The Digital Object Storage and Delivery System

The Digital Object Storage and Delivery System will play

a central role in the delivery of the Library's digital services. It will store the digital objects required to support these services. It will interface with the Object Management System and the Rights Management and Access Control System to deliver these objects to external users as an integral part of the resource discovery workflow. It will support the long-term preservation of these objects for access by future generations of Australians.

The Digital Object Storage and Delivery System will be configured to support storage of and access to the Library's archive of online electronic publications and its collection of pictorial digital surrogates. After implementation, the Library should be able to configure the Digital Object Storage and Delivery System to support storage of and access to its other collections of digital surrogates and its collection of digital audio recordings.

The following functions are sought for the Digital Object Storage and Delivery System:

a) Store the Library's collections of digital objects in ways that support on-going access as technologies evolve, including the preservation of "look and feel" to the extent this is technically feasible and cost-effective.

b) Deliver access to these objects via publicly available client software as an integral part of the resource discovery process.

c) Support an environment for the Library to undertake development of customised or tailored digital services providing access to material stored in the Digital Object Storage and Delivery System.

Storage functions

All storage functions are to be performed efficiently, with minimum collection manager intervention. The following capabilities are sought for the storage function across all categories of digital object:

a) Store digital objects as arbitrary binary objects.

b) Preserve the relationship between objects implied by directory structures captured by the Collecting System and/or made explicit through metadata in the Object Management System.

c) Maintain a master copy of the digital object in the original collected format or an appropriate archival format.

d) Maintain additional copies of the digital object in as many variant formats as is deemed necessary by the Library to meet current access requirements.

e) Support the long-term preservation of master copies separate from copies created to support current access requirements, using an appropriate management model.

f) From time to time, on instruction, convert all files of a given type in the archive (excluding master copies) to another file type as standards change and technologies evolve.

g) Interface with the Object Management System to maintain a complete migration history of each digital object.

h) Minimise the impact of migration processes on the delivery function by ensuring appropriate instructions and/or processes are invoked for the new file type.

i) Delete digital objects (on instruction) meeting specified criteria identified through the Object Management System.

j) Archive digital objects (on instruction) meeting specified criteria identified through the Object Management System to a physical carrier for offline storage, mirroring at another site or transfer to another digital object storage and delivery System.

k) Enable the deletion or archiving of sets of related digital objects (for example, all content under the title level for a given publication, all surrogates for a given collection item) through a single process.

Delivery Function

The following capabilities are sought for the delivery function across all categories of digital object:

a) Support access to stored objects via the HyperText Transfer Protocol (HTTP).

b) Interface with the Rights Management and Access Control System to allow or deny access (with an appropriate error message) depending on:

   i. Access conditions specific to an object or set of related objects.

   ii. User class.

   iii. User location (for example, a supervised reading room in the Library)

   iv. Object status (for example, temporarily withdrawn, no longer in the collection).

c) Where access is conditional on user class, interface with the Rights Management and Access Control System to verify that the user belongs to the specified user class before providing access.

d) Provide external users with contextual information, navigation pathways and service delivery options appropriate to the category of object being accessed, generating this information dynamically from data stored in the Object Management System.

e) Deliver files in formats that can be accessed online using a standard browser or public domain software.

f) Convert files dynamically at the point of delivery as instructed for specified formats (for example, to encrypt a file for delivery, or to generate a variant format such as a thumbnail image from a stored copy or an HTML version of an XML/SGML file).

g) Maintain a software repository and provide options for users to download software from this repository for objects with special software requirements.

h) Interface with appropriate digital signature and/or public key services to enable external users to ensure the authenticity of documents, when the infrastructure is in place to support this.

i) Interface with the Rights Management and Access Control System to perform one or more of the following functions to support the management of conditions applying to use of stored digital objects:

   i. Notify potential external users of an object of any conditions applying to use of that object.

   ii. Enable the external user to order a copy of an object not directly accessible online, through a variety of offline delivery options (for example, e-mail, CD, floppy disk).

iii. Enable the external user to submit a request to the Library for access to an object for which the permission of the rights holder is required.

iv. Enable the external user to access an object once only, or a limited number of times, on presentation of a password or key obtained from the Library once the permission of the rights holder has been gained.

v. Enable online payment of copyright, reproduction and/ or delivery fees using a credit card number by interfacing with appropriate third party network payment systems.

vi. Collect information to support the generation of billing reports by the Rights Management and Access Control System at a later stage.

vii. Log usage where a copyright fee applies to support the generation of usage reports by the Rights Management and Access Control System at a later stage.

Development Function

The following capabilities are sought for the development function across all categories of digital object:

a) Enable the Library's Web developers to develop and maintain a range of templates for the user interface component of the delivery function, with contextual information, navigation pathways and service delivery options appropriate to the category of object being accessed, including contextual messaging.

b) Provide support for production, development and archive versions of these templates, with appropriate mechanisms for change management and version control.

The Digital Object Storage and Delivery System will be used to support the storage and delivery of online electronic publications for which the Library has taken custodial responsibility as part of the distributed national collection of Australian electronic publications. The following specific capabilities are sought for the digital archive:

a) When the request for access is for a whole-item, provide external users with the following information:

   i. A brief description of the publication.

   ii. Information about special software requirements to access the publication.

   iii. Information about any differences between the copy at the publisher's site and the archived copy (or a link to this information).

   iv. A summary list of holdings, updated automatically as new holdings are added, with the option of linking to one of the holdings or to the publisher's site.

   v. A general warning that copyright may apply, with a link to the publisher's copyright statement, if one exists.

   vi. Information about the frequency with which updates are collected and a warning that more recent information may be found at the publisher's site.

vii. Links to other information the Library may wish to provide to external users about the archive.

viii. Information about which agency archived the item, in cases where the Library is storing publications archived on behalf of another agency.

b) For publications with large numbers of holdings, list holdings by year, with the option of navigating to a more detailed listing for each year.

c) When the request for access is for a component part of a publication that has been discovered through the service indexing the content of the distributed national collection of Australian electronic publications, provide a title page for the requested item with an option to view the title page for the whole publication.

d) Restrict access to onsite or registered remote users until a specified duration of time has elapsed since the publication was archived, where required.

e) Restrict access to a specified number of users where required.

f) Support a range of other access restrictions on an exception basis.

g) Satisfy the publisher's security mechanisms where it is not possible to remove these from the archived copy.

h) For publications the user is not allowed to access, provide information explaining why the publication is unavailable and referring the user to the publisher's site.

i) Ensure users are aware that they are accessing archived content, not the publisher's version.

j) Warn users attempting to activate an external link within the archived object that the cited item is not contained in the archive and provide the option of exploiting the link directly.

k) Warn users attempting to interact with a remote database that the input form is not active.

l) With the exception of the requirements in to, provide the user with as accurate a version of the original copy as possible, with minimum technical intervention.

Digital Surrogates and Audio Recordings

The Digital Object Storage and Delivery System will be configured to support storage of and access to pictorial digital surrogates. After implementation the Library should be able to configure the Digital Object Storage and Delivery System to support storage of and access to digital surrogates of other collection items and digital audio recordings in the Library's collection. This category of material also includes digital surrogates of digital audio recordings and pictorial material created originally in digital form.

Object Management System

The Object Management System will provide for the maintenance of information supporting the collection, storage and delivery of access to the Library's digital collections and could provide this for other items in the Library's collections requiring special curatorial control.

The Object Management System will be configured to support the Library's collection of online electronic publications, replacing the existing PANDORA Archive Management System (PAMS), and digital surrogates of pictorial collection items, replacing the existing Images 1 management system (Pictorial Manager). After implementation the Library should also be able to configure the Object Management System to support its other collections of digital surrogates and digital audio recordings.

The following functions are sought for the Object Management System:

a) Register documentary resources.

b) Record the content of documentary resources.

c) Maintain digital objects.

d) Maintain information about the selection and negotiation process for documentary resources identified as candidates for the Library's collection.

e) Maintain information supporting the collection of digital documentary resources and digital surrogates.

f) Maintain information about the condition, physical and/or technical characteristics and preservation history of documentary resources and their digital surrogates.

g) Enable users to search the information created and maintained by the above functions using a range of search criteria.

h) Provide a range of support functions, including the capability to output data in standard formats, archive or delete data and generate reports and audit trails.

Capabilities sought for the Object Management System require support for a range of data elements above and beyond those defined for automated library systems in ISO 8459. In the absence of established standards in this area, the Library has prepared a high level logical data model for the Digital Collection Management System.

The following capabilities are sought for the content recording function:

a) Record the content of collection items by enabling collection managers to:

   i. List the content within the record for the whole item.

   ii. Create a new record for each component part, linked to the parent record.

   iii. Import data in a standard format from another source, preserving links between parent and child records.

   iv. Allow update of records by imported data through matching on key fields such as control number and date of last update.

   v. Link the record for the whole item to a digital finding aid or guide that has been created and collected through a separate process.

b) Enable collection managers to specify certain data elements to be protected from replacement during data import.

c) Enable collection managers to update information about the content of registered items at any time.

d) For items issued serially (for example, APAIS and AMI titles), enable a record to be kept of the content for each issue.

e) For items registered at collection level only (for example a collection of photographs), enable content to be recorded for at least five levels of sub-collection.

f) Enable children in a parent-child relationship to inherit attributes of the parent, so that changes made to the parent record are reflected in all child records, except for protected fields or fields specifically overridden in a given child record.

g) Interface with the DB Textworks System to import metadata for items indexed for APAIS and AMI.

h) Interface with the Collecting System to import metadata describing the content of online electronic publications.

i) For items registered at collection level only, enable import of metadata conforming to the Encoded Archival Description (EAD) SGML/XML Document Type Definition (DTD).

The following capabilities are sought for the digital object collecting function:

a) Provide support for at least the range of collecting data elements defined in the logical data model.

b) For any item registered in the Object Management System, enable the recording of data supporting, limiting or tailoring the collection of associated digital objects.

c) Where the collection instructions apply to a whole item with component parts, enter the information once only, at registration level, indicating that the instructions will apply to all component parts.

d) Have the option of creating separate collection instructions for one or more component parts that would override the registration-level instructions.

e) Enable collection managers to create and maintain lists of collection items that are to be digitised as a batch, with appropriate mechanisms for uniquely identifying each batch and each item within each batch.

f) Interface with the Collecting System to maintain a record of the status of batches and of individual items within batches that may have failed quality control checks for a given reason.

g) Interface with the Collecting System to collect information about collected object

The following capability is sought for the preservation function:

a) Provide support for at least the range of preservation data elements defined in the logical data model which are found in the file, process and delivery method entities.

b) Allow collection managers to record information about the condition of physical format collection items and processes that have been undertaken to support its preservation.

c) Enable information about the technical characteristics of electronic collection items and digital surrogates to be maintained:

   i. Online by collection managers.

   ii. Through data supplied by digital object creators in a standard format either as a separate file, in digital object file headers or as embedded metadata.

d) Interface with the Collecting System to capture technical information about collected objects, including file type and version, source location, date and time of capture, index points (for audio recordings) and a checksum where appropriate.

e) Enable this information to be updated on a field-by-field basis.

f) For each file type and version maintain information about software dependencies that can be used by the Digital Object Storage and Delivery System to support current access.

g) Interface with the Digital Object Storage and Delivery System to identify digital objects meeting criteria for migration to another format, deletion or archiving.

h) Interface with the Digital Object Storage and Delivery System to maintain a complete record of the migration history and status of each digital object.

Rights Management and Access Control System

If it is implemented, the Rights Management and Access Control System will provide support for the management of access to the Library's digital collections where conditions apply. This could include the commercial aspects of rights management and access control to digital objects. If it is implemented, the Rights Management and Access Control System will be configured to manage access to:

a) Online electronic publications the Library has archived.

b) Reproduction quality digital surrogates of pictorial items.

c) Digital surrogates or photographic copies of other collection items.

d) Physical format collection items where access conditions have been imposed by the rights holder.

The Rights Management and Access Control System should be capable of interfacing with a future third party system acquired by the Library that provides integrated administrative support to deal with access to and use of any product or service delivered by the Library, for example, the Library's digital services or online ordering from the Library's bookshop.

The following functions are sought for the Rights Management and Access Control System:

a) Record information about who holds the rights to a collection item and any conditions imposed on access to the item.

b) Register and authenticate external users.

c) Collect and maintain information about requests for access to specific collection items where permission of the rights holder needs to be sought offline.

d) Collect and maintain usage information.

Rights recording function

The following capabilities are sought for the rights recording function:

a) Provide support for at least the range of rights management data elements defined in the logical data model.

b) Maintain information about who holds the intellectual property rights for a collection item.

c) Support the recording of different rights holders for different categories of rights (for example, moral rights, copyright).

d) For collection items with multiple variant copies and/ or component parts, enter the information once only at title level, indicating that the rights holder hold the intellectual property rights to all copies and/or component parts.

e) Have the option of recording different rights holders for one or more copies and/or component parts that would override the title-level information.

f) Maintain access profiles for collection items where access conditions apply.

g) Support access conditions based on elapsed time and automatically change the access status to unrestricted when the specified time period has elapsed.

h) Allow access to be dependent on user category.

i) Allow access to be dependent on payment of a copyright fee.

j) Where access depends on payment of a copyright fee, maintain information about who is to receive payment, if it is different from the rights holder.

k) Where the access conditions apply to an item with multiple variant copies and/or component parts, enter the information once only, at title level, indicating that the profile will apply to all copies and/or component parts.

l) Have the option of creating a separate access profile for one or more copies and/ or component parts that would override the title-level profile.

m) Enable access to an item to be temporarily denied (for example, in cases where there may be a legal issue under dispute).

n) Enable rights management information at registered item and/or content level to be loaded from an external source through an offline process.

o) Support a mechanism that would flag in the NLA Catalogue that access conditions apply to a given item and the nature of the condition (for example, written permission of owner required; access restricted to onsite users).

User registration and authentication function

The following capabilities are sought for the user registration and authentication function:

a) Use information about external users of the Library's digital collections maintained in an independent directory system including:

   i. Name, address and other contact information.

   ii. Mailing and billing addresses.

   iii. Electronic addresses.

   iv. Organisational affiliation (if an individual user).

   v. Contact (if an organisational user).

   vi. Customer number from the Library's Financial Management Information System.

vii. Customer order number(s).

viii. Confidential information such as a password or public key for access to the Library's digital collections or the user's credit card number.

b) Interface with the Digital Object Storage and Delivery System to authenticate external users as appropriate.

c) Authenticate external users for a given time frame or a given number of accesses only.

Permission function

The following capabilities are sought for the permission function:

a) Collect requests to the Library for access to an object for which the permission of the rights holder is required from the Digital Object Storage and Delivery System.

b) Register the external user on a temporary basis.

c) Once the permission of the rights holder has been acquired (through a separate offline process), generate a password or key granting the external user access to the object on a once-only basis or for a limited number of times.

d) Interface with the Digital Object Storage and Delivery System to authenticate the external user until the object has been accessed the specified number of times.

Usage function

The following capabilities are sought for the Usage function:

a) Maintain usage logs.

b) Generate usage reports in a prescribed format for transfer to a third party copyright broker such as CAL.

c) Generate billing reports in a prescribed format for transfer to the Library's Financial Management Information System.

Security Management

Protection of the authenticity of the Library's digital objects and the intellectual property rights of creators and publishers are critical to the Project. The Library requires the System to provide security functionality equivalent to the ITSEC F-C2 standard. The Library also requires appropriate levels of security to be applied to any chargeable services and to any business process involving update of data. The Library is committed to the use of international standards and actively participates in the development and monitoring of standards relating to library and information services.

Long-term Access to Digital Documents

Any library has the need to retain and, on occasion, refer to various stored documents. Until recently, documents were generally paper or microfilm based. However, modern data storage methods have evolved to include digital storage as well. Due to the rapid evolution of storage technologies, future digital systems may not be able to read and/or interpret the digital recordings made by older systems, even if those recordings are still in good condition.

Within many organizations today, digital documents that are official records must be categorized and managed in accordance with approved records schedules. This means that these records must be retained and accessible throughout their life cycle in accordance with the same laws and standards that govern paper records. In the case of government documents for instance, the law dictates that an official Government record must be classified into one of 26 retention periods set forth by the Archivist of the United States. These retention periods range from 30 days to Permanent storage and include time periods of 30 years, 50 years, and 75 years.

Digital documents that require long retention periods face accessibility problems due to the technology obsolescence of hardware and software. As time goes on, we can expect the problems to become worse, as more and more documents are stored in digital format.

As digital technology continues to evolve at a rapid pace, superseded technologies are quickly discarded and new technologies are embraced in the hopes of gaining improved efficiency, effectiveness, or a competitive advantage. It is crucial that, in the haste to adopt newer and generally better technologies, we don't lose the ability to access historical digital documents.

As information systems are upgraded the ability to view digital documents in superseded formats becomes a problem due to the technological obsolescence of the hardware and software systems needed to access them. This is because most digital documents contain information that is only meaningful to the software and hardware systems that were used to create, edit, and access them. Therefore, because of these non-standard digital document formats, organizations that archive digital documents must develop a method that will allow them to maintain continual access to digital documents in their native formats.

7

Intellectual Property and Access Technology

Intellectual Property Conservancies

Conservancies, which hold real property in trust for public purposes or administer easements restricting future uses of private property, are a successful means of securing public benefits within the system of private property ownership. They have been widely encouraged by governments, through tax regulations. The property owners may deed rights or donate easements limiting future development or exploitation to a non-profit organization, while continuing to live on their land or in their historic property. With the increased attention that businesses and individuals are paying to the value of knowledge assets, it should be no surprise the conservancy metaphor is now being extended to intellectual property (IP).

Intellectual Property Conservancies (IPCs) are a new idea, being conceived as a means to provide public benefits by making digital content donated, or licensed to them, freely available and by ensuring its long-term preservation. The Knowledge Conservancy is a non-profit IPC incorporated in August 2000; here, the author, who was involved in its planning, explores the issues any such organization will face. IPCs are digital libraries and therefore have all the problems associated with digital libraries.

In addition, IPCs face a large number of challenges that most digital libraries do not confront. These include:

- Obtaining content donations (persuading IP owners of the benefits of giving, possibly without any tax advantage)
- Obtaining financial contributions (persuading philanthropists and the general public of the value of free public access)
- Obtaining usable digital assets
- Creating metadata to support discovery, rights management and preservation
- Providing access to potential readers worldwide
- Providing long-term, or even 'perpetual', access

Obtaining content

Content owners may, or may not, be ideologically committed to free-to-read. Those who are persuaded in principle that free-to-read is a good idea probably need only to be given a way to do it. The challenge with these owners will be to make the opportunity known and make contribution methods convenient to use. An IPC will also need to attract those who would not be inclined to give away access rights without persuasive arguments of the benefits to them.

Several strategies can be employed to convince them. Tax benefits are central to land conservancies and historic trusts, but it is not clear whether meaningful tax benefits will, in fact, be available for Intellectual Property Conservancies. If the original creator of the intellectual property donates it, current tax laws restrict them to writing off the value of the raw materials that were consumed in its creation.

If the donor is an owner (such as a publisher, music label or employer) who has paid to acquire an intellectual property right, outright donation of the intellectual property should be eligible for a tax credit. Concepts such as easements', however, though well established in tax law for real property, are novel ideas in intellectual property law and will, at the very least, need to be tested with tax authorities. They may well need to be legislated. Providing public access to free-to-read content is a way to promote value-added content.

In the physical bookstore, we often browse a book, or listen to a few tracks of a CD, before making a purchase. Free-to-read online content may serve this same purpose. One challenge to an IPC will be to develop a model for free-to-read functionality that is accepted by publishers as not unduly competitive with their value-added products, and by online readers as useful in its own right. The IPC concept will be viable if at least some publishers are willing to provide a level of free-to-read access as a means of promoting their value-added products.

The IPC will need to protect the publishers' interests in order to obtain an early donation of limited rights and, as the threat to a publishers' commercial interests subsides, the promise to make more valuable access available over time. Individual IP owners will readily appreciate the benefits of making a gift of rights to an organization that ensures their work a sort of immortality. But an IPC can also attract publishers with the benefits of perpetual access. Publishers who provide free-to-read content on their web sites (and this is increasingly going to be necessary for competitive reasons) are faced with a new liability—either they have to keep their digital content online and free (which costs them money if it doesn't continue to sell) or they need to take it down (which could cause a degree of public anger).

It makes sense to give the limited rights-to-read (and the obligations to maintain it permanently) to an IPC early in the life of the intellectual property, thereby avoiding the liability and reaping the reward of public service. Since the mission of the IPC is to make content to which it has rights easily available online, and its promise to the owners of that IP is to make the free-to-read content easy to find, an IPC needs to invest in rich descriptive metadata to make its content readily discoverable on the web.

If, by donating content to an IPC, IP owners cannot only make the availability of their intellectual property better known, but also acquire metadata about their own properties in standard formats, they would have substantial incentives to donate content to an IPC.

Obtaining financial contributions

IPCs, like other non-profits seeking donations from the general public, will need to provide concrete benefits to supporters in order to maintain a sufficient stream of financial contributions. A "membership" organization gives public supporters a sense of belonging and of receiving concrete, perhaps even personal, benefits. A newsletter and the web site that communicate news of the success of the IPC and review recent additions to the properties it holds, would be attractive to many such general members.

An IPC may also need to solicit cash donations from intellectual property owners to help pay the costs of digitizing, transforming, or cataloging gifts of intellectual property that are not suitable for digital delivery or preservation in their current form. Individual IP donors, in particular, may need to help bear these costs since metadata creation for their donations will be a one-off cost and the transaction costs are likely to be higher. But even donors of large quantities of IP may need to be asked to contribute financially for an IPC to absorb a sizable gift in a reasonable time.

Obtaining usable digital assets

The most critical issue in the success of an IPC is probably the technical characteristics of the Intellectual Properties it acquires. If selective, the IPC could obtain content in a way that enables it to deliver the content in the future without substantial additional investment and to offer a range of value added views without requiring costly intervention. Without careful selection, an IPC could be saddled with overwhelming costs to initially capture the data in usable formats, transform what it receives, or to manage the digital data over time.

Its presumed digital assets would instead become liabilities that could far exceed its likely resources. One of the most costly factors in acquiring content is negotiating the terms and conditions for its donation and subsequent use. But depending on what those terms and conditions are, the cost of administering access could also be very high. Contractual terms that define a limited number of concrete levels of rights (for example, rights to provide free public access one page at a time and print the page being viewed) must be easily translated into levels of functionality.

With such fixed levels of rights, a donor could agree on a sequence of further future rights releases (for example, granting the right to print a chapter at a time, or search any word in context, or view an hierarchical table of contents).6 It is critical that the donation of different levels of functionality, and the progressive release of further permissions over time, not result in additional operational costs for an IPC. Metadata captured up front must interact with the format captured up front to dictate levels of functionality.

Some formats of donated content will require substantial investment to make them usable online, or to be kept online in perpetuity. Hence, an IPC needs to consider the risks involved in selection, based on decisions about what formats to acquire. Text and image can be delivered with layered public-access-level functionality using existing web-based distribution servers. In planning The Knowledge Conservancy, we decided that while issues about how best to digitize sound and motion images could be resolved, it would be more difficult at the present time to define appropriate levels of 'low-fidelity' delivery acceptable to copyright holders, because their business models are currently in such substantial flux.

Also, the public is presently quite confused about the copyright status of online sound, and adding another entity offering free sound at this time seems likely to increase the public confusion. Acquisition of patents, though these are just another form of intellectual property, raises quite different and complex issues for an IPC. An IPC must have defined rights adequate to make content available to users under some terms, but it need not own the IP to do so. If a donation with some access or development limits is accepted by the IPC, the donor is brought into a relationship with the Conservancy that might also be translated later into donations of further public rights.

Conditional agreements and agreements to release content for free public viewing at a future date, are common in archives. In such a case, the property owner would provide the IPC with a copy, but the specific rights granted to the IPC would only come into effect at a designated time or under specific conditions. One of the benefits of an IPC is that it promises to keep IP always available, while the current system of publishing makes much IP difficult to obtain.

There are a variety of technical aspects to this claim, one of which is to ensure that some server with the content must always be available. First, the IPC needs to be able to determine whether the copy at the primary location is available, and if not, shift to a secondary location. The Universal Library at CMU developed a system that keeps track of the on-line books in its catalog and will display locally cached copies of the books if the link to the original work on a remote site disappears.9

Metadata issues

Metadata management will be critical to an IPC's success. Like any Digital Library it needs to invest in discovery (content description) metadata. An IPC must additionally invest substantially in rights management metadata and technical (migration specification) metadata. While the IPC can rely on natural partners in the library community to help provide descriptive metadata for simple resource discovery, it also needs to be able to incorporate metadata conforming to standards in the publishing community.

An IPC will need to determine the requirements for rights metadata linked to delivery functionality, as discussed above. Finally, an IPC needs to manage a digital artifact over time. As such, it needs to determine what metadata will need to be acquired and kept for long-term preservation. The OAIS reference model seems a probable framework for preservation of archival originals. Recent proposals by the Open Archives Initiative may be adequate for distribution of metadata between an IPC and its mirror sites and between IP owners and the IPC.

Providing access to potential readers worldwide

Where the content resides is more than simply an operational consideration for an IPC. IP owners prefer that the digital data be located on their own servers; the terms of the gift would ensure that, should the IP owner fail to keep it available, the IPC can shift access to its own servers. The benefits to the IPC suggest that an architecture enabling this kind of distributed access will be necessary.

Perpetual access

The fundamental objectives of an IPC are to offer free access to its catalog of intellectual property in perpetuity. For this, the IPC does not need to be the archival repository of the authentic, verifiable, record copy. Like a digital library, which holds a copy of a work and makes the accurate and full content available to users, the IPC doesn't claim to preserve contextual or structural authenticity.13 Both an IPC and a digital library focus on preservation of content as required for preservation of public access and the right-to-read.

Therefore an IPC need not preserve the initial delivery format, nor any particular subsequent delivery format. Instead, the IPC can return to its escrowed copy to generate a delivery copy in a new format, or move from one delivery format to the next, depending on cost and technology availability. Of course, an IPC still must make strategic decisions about when and how to convert data from one delivery and or long-term storage format to another, to keep the content accessible over time. Media migration needs to be conducted on an on-going basis as new, more efficient, storage media are developed.

Resolving Internal Contradictions

There are considerable social, legal and organizational tensions in the organization of an IPC. During the past several months of planning for The Knowledge Conservancy, as we have been getting into those infamous details wherein the devils reside, we have uncovered many contradictions between the likely requirements for successful IPCs and the ideologies of those most committed in the abstract to their formation.

— Knowledge is universal but tax laws and some IP laws are national. How an IPC organizes to collaborate with parallel organizations worldwide will be important to its long-term success.

— IPCs could add value to works, especially social value,15 but the IPC, as a non-profit, must be careful about how it earns income.

— An IPC's credibility would be severely impugned if the 'catalog' of available free-to-read material ends up skewed by propaganda from whatever quarter or self-published works. Indeed, like any library, digital or physical, the collection of an IPC will be assessed as a whole. Loss of legitimacy could be fatal since legitimacy is crucial to any new social concept.

— An IPC should initially avoid the temptation to accept content that is not in digital form. A loss of focus on online accessibility could result in an IPC being buried under huge volumes of potential rights for materials that it cannot afford to convert.

— Obtaining rights involves negotiations and contracts. Under the most ideal conditions with the most ready donor, it takes time and energy to reach such agreements. For this reason, an IPC needs to target owners of large and/or highly visible and prestigious quantities of I.P., and particularly those who will continue to generate large quantities of IP in the future. Individual owners should be provided with standard terms and opportunities to submit content online.

— Clarity of purpose and mission focus will be crucial. Confusion in the public mind could be a major barrier to success.

Digital and Media Conversion Processes

The digital computer technology revolution continues to open up concepts, many of which are only just beginning to be understood or accepted. These concepts are critically important to librarianship in general and preservation in particular. In a world historically dominated by paper, the same medium is used for document capture (creation, recording), storage, access, distribution and use, and there has been no compelling need to consider these as separate entities.

There has also been no compelling need to distinguish between the format of a document and the medium in which it is embodied, since there is only one dominant choice of medium. Indeed, the terms have traditionally been used somewhat interchangeably and indiscriminately. The introduction of non-paper forms such as phonograph recordings and films has modified this straightforward view somewhat, but traditional cataloging makes every effort to foster the constraint that there is a one-to-one correspondence between the format and the medium, with the objective of identifying the combined format-medium with some physical shelf location.

Further efforts to foster this constraint increasingly break down when digital technologies enter the picture. Digital technologies open a world that paradoxically is simultaneously more complex and, in some ways, simpler. It is more complex because now the same document or document format may intrinsically be represented in different media for different purposes, forcefully motivating the need to distinguish carefully between the format and the medium.

Furthermore, different media may be used interchangeably for different stages of document handling, that is, for capture, storage, access, distribution, and use. To complicate the situation even more, the documents may be encoded in a myriad of ways at each of these stages. And yet, separation of the format and the medium—and treating each stage of document handling separately--may open up a more logical structure free from traditional constraints. In this sense, digital technologies may simplify certain aspects of librarianship.

Digital technologies present many new challenges, however, that must be considered. For example, although these varying formats may be decoded and translated back and forth among each other, many fear that the means of decoding may become lost as a result of technological obsolescence, conceivably making digitally stored documents inaccessible. There are also many who question the longevity of the physical media used in digital technologies. Others suggest that the appropriate way to address both of these problems—as well as to take advantage of the declining costs of computer storage and of increasing storage densities—may well be to copy stored documents periodically onto new media.

Indeed the main advantage of the world of digital technologies, namely that they represent a kind of "esperanto" of mutually comprehensible and interchangeable formats, may, if not properly managed, also represent their biggest weakness, because of the rapidity of change and obsolescence, and because of the wide range of choices available at any given time. Their very attractiveness could lure the unwary or the uninformed into dangerous territory. Periodic recopying onto new media represents a whole new approach for libraries to the operation and financing of "inventory management".

The implications could be quite extensive. Librarians tend to think in terms of periods of centuries rather than having (or wanting) to recopy every few years. Such considerations may either hinder the adoption of digital technologies for preservation or other purposes or eventually cause some rethinking of the underlying economics of librarianship. The incentive for such potential reevaluation, however, is not limited to the preservation of older materials, nor is the influence of technology the only driving factor.

The underlying stimulus is a gradual transition over the centuries—perhaps spurred by the exponential growth of recorded knowledge and information—from documents with associated physical or conceptually useful lifetimes, times between new editions, or, more generically, times between "instances", that can be measured in decades or centuries; to documents with associated times between instances measured in much shorter units of time—even, in the case of "active documents", measured in minutes or seconds.

These are concepts that are familiar to the world of digital electronic processing and quite normal outside of universities, but that have been avoided in worlds—such as research libraries—that depend to a greater or lesser extent upon irregular gifts or grants of varying or unpredictable size, donations directed to the purchase and immediate storage of documents, but not to their maintenance. Indeed, one of the most serious questions facing librarians in the future may be how to effect a match between the changing economic demands of "continuous processes" and the traditional nature of many funding sources.

Yet the potential of digital technologies and of the flexibility they offer is boundless. Over the coming decades, these technologies may open up vistas of ever-increasing storage densities to where entire libraries can be electronically stored in the space of a single room; of blinding access and distribution speeds allowing whole documents to be moved almost instantly across the nation's data networks, leading to the concept of the "distributed library;" of ease of replication at very modest cost; of "print-on-demand" where paper copies of documents are only printed "just in time" and not inventoried in advance of need; of accessibility at a distance away from where the "digital document" or preservation copy was created or is stored; and of intelligent automated document analysis.

Indeed, the means of creation and production of documents have already been revolutionized by these technologies. These technologies also open up horizons for totally new document formats, such as active documents whose contents may combine different media such as text, sound, video or voice; or whose contents may change dynamically with time, what Harvey Wheeler called "the fungible book." The preservation of these new "active" formats is not of direct interest to the subject of preservation of more traditional formats, but is of indirect interest because digitally preserved traditional documents can be incorporated into such active documents.

Furthermore, contemporary active documents will become a subject of future preservation interest. Some view the introduction of digital technologies into the world of libraries as likely to cause a revolution as far-reaching as that caused by the printing-press: a massive paradigm shift. Others view the introduction with concern (one cannot help but recall that the monks at first also viewed the introduction of the printing press with equal concern), an intimidating perturbation that disturbs an equilibrium and modalities of scholarship that have served well for many decades or even for centuries.

Either way, digital technologies cannot be ignored. They are already with us. The question is not whether they will have a presence, but the pace and degree to which that presence will grow and influence. The next twenty years are likely to be times of extraordinary change. Our libraries—indeed our universities, colleges, and our scholarly communities—may well be remade by the consequences of this technological revolution.

And yet—in spite of technology's impact and of the revolutionary consequences of that impact—it must be recognized that technology itself is not the ultimate driving force. It is the inexorable pressure caused by the exponential growth of recorded knowledge, and the ever-increasing complexity, costs, and other problems associated with the storage and distribution of, and access to, such information.

Technology can provide some solutions: it is not an end in itself. Furthermore—for many reasons too numerous to detail here—the "digital library" is not about to replace the "paper library." Both will need to coexist in a shifting environment, at least for the foreseeable future. This in itself will present librarians with many economic, organizational, social, technical, and other challenges. Between the eager apostles of technology and those who approach change with extreme caution lies the mass of professionals who are trying to understand and grapple with the potential of this shifting environment, many of them implementing prototype activities designed to elucidate greater insight, many working to close the gap between promise and reality.

The Glossary is not intended to be so comprehensive as to satisfy the technologist only concerned with technologies, or the librarian exclusively concerned with librarianship and preservation. It is intended to satisfy the intersection of their concerns. On the other hand, issues of preservation and access raise concepts that have implications for librarianship as a whole, so that, in that sense, this Glossary has consequences that are not limited to the preservation arena alone.

The Glossary is not intended to solve all issues associated with the definition of technological and other terms associated with preservation and access. It is a conceptual document. Not all terms are defined with equal precision; indeed, the degree of precision is largely directed by the extent to which it is necessary to distinguish among these terms. The Glossary is intended to be adequate to support further research and development on the subject. Indeed, one measure of success of the Glossary will be the extent to which it stimulates additional work in the field, including refinements of the Glossary itself.

The Glossary departs from many well-established norms. Furthermore, excluded in any detail are terms primarily associated with conservation, such as paper deacidification, where every effort is made to preserve the documents in their original physical form, or hand conservation. The focus, as stated, is on preservation through media conversion, where the objective is to preserve the intellectual content of the original document on some other medium, and also if desired to produce at some later stage a close physical facsimile of the original, at least to the extent allowed by the technology.

The focus is also for the most part on paper documents requiring preservation. These represent the principal area of national and international attention: paper documents have the longest history and exist in the greatest numbers. They are also in urgent need of preservation because of the "embrittlement" caused by the high acid content of paper manufactured since the mid-nineteenth century and by improper storage environments. In the years to come, the focus may well shift to other media.

There is already, for example, considerable attention paid to film preservation, and video recordings are already deteriorating at an alarming rate. Different technologies are more or less suitable to preserve different classes of documents or for achieving different access or other objectives. One of the main applications intended for this Glossary is for the classification of ranges of activity that can be used to describe different investigations into preservation and access methodologies.

The Glossary is divided into three main sections: the Original Document, the Selection Process, and the Preserved Copy.

Original Document

Different preservation or media conversion technologies are appropriate to different kinds of original material. This section, therefore, is devoted to a classification of terms used in describing the original document to be preserved, particularly those terms that need to be referenced in the context of media conversion. The term document is used generically throughout this Glossary to include all forms of books, manuscripts, records and other classes of material containing information or other matter of intellectual content, regardless of the actual medium or format employed.

The Glossary takes free license with terms that have taken on a traditional meaning in the context of cataloging and other library activities, and in fact frequently departs from traditional norms used in this area. As stated in the Introduction, the reason for this is that such traditional definitions often confuse the format and content of the document with the medium used to record it, terms that have traditionally been used somewhat interchangeably and indiscriminately. This made sense when paper was the primary medium used for document capture, storage, distribution, and use. With newer technologies, however, and particularly with those used for media conversion, different media can be used for each of these stages, and, in fact, different media can be used for different instances of each stage.

Document Medium

Document Medium refers to the material upon which the original document was recorded.

Paper

Paper is a medium traditionally used for printed books and other documents that are the most frequent target of preservation efforts. Paper is defined to be sheets usually made of vegetable fibers laid down on a fine screen from a water suspension. Marks are imprinted on the paper using any of a number of techniques including handwriting or drawing using a variety of media such as pencil, pen and ink, or pastel; various forms of printing using inks (numerous technologies are used to accomplish this); photographic printing, where paper coated with light-sensitive emulsion is exposed to various intensities of light); xerographic printing, where an electrically charged photoconductive insulating surface is selectively exposed to light and the latent image is developed with a resinous powder; thermographic printing, where the paper is exposed to a directed heat source that selectively modifies parts of the surface that may have been pre-treated with a heat-sensitive powder; and chemical transfer printing, where the surface of the paper is chemically coated and selectively modified by pressure or other means.

Microform

Microform refers to a document medium for producing or reproducing printed matter. It records microimages, that is, images too small to be read without some form of magnification. In a general sense, microforms may be on film or paper, but for purposes of this Glossary the definition is restricted to film. Reading a microform requires the assistance of a microform reader. Microform comes in different styles including microfilm (a film roll that contains microimages arranged sequentially) and microfiche (sheets of film in which many microimages are arranged in a grid pattern). Both usually contain a header that can be read without magnification).

Microforms are an economic and compact form of document representation for archival storage, but are inconvenient to read when compared with a printed book. Microform technology is used as a preservation medium, as a means of saving space, or as a means of duplicating scarce or unique documents, that is, microreproductions of other original documents. However, microform is sometimes used for original documents, for example, those created on a computer and directly printed out onto a computer-output-on-microfiche (COM) device; and for microreproductions of material assembled for the purposes of releasing an original edition in microform.

Video

Video is normally an analog electronic technology for recording still or moving images, usually combined with sound. Following standards defined for television playback and broadcasting, the images are normally recorded on magnetic tape, when it is known as videotape, but also on other physical media such as optical disk (videodisk). Playback is usually achieved through a television set or video projector, although it is now possible and becoming common to play video recordings back through a computer or multimedia workstation.

Film

Film is a recording medium consisting of thin sheets or strips of transparent or translucent material, such as polyester or acetate, coated with a light-sensitive emulsion. Recording occurs by exposing the film to the light emitted or reflected by the entity being recorded. Film is also the medium used for microfilm recording. A photograph is produced using essentially the same technology, except that normally the light- sensitive emulsion is adhered to paper or some other opaque medium.

Audio

Audio documents are recordings made on a variety of (usually) magnetic media of sounds only. The evolution of such audio recordings has traversed a large number of different formats and physical media, including phonograph disks of varying size and tape cassettes, both of which are analog recording technologies; and, more recently, compact disks and digital acoustic tapes (DATs), which are digitally encoded.

Digital Electronic

Digital Electronic Technologies are technologies used to capture, store, transform, distribute or present information in quantized electronic form (normally as a sequence of O's and l's known as bits). Digital, in which information is quantized discretely, is to be contrasted with Analog, in which information is not quantized but maintained in a continuous format. A video recording, is an example of an electronic technology that is analog.

For a variety of reasons, digital technologies are gradually replacing analog technologies. Reasons of importance to this Glossary are the convertibility of digital technologies among each other and into and from other technologies (such as paper and voice), so that digital technologies become a kind of lingua franca of communication and storage; and the ease of transmission of information by digital technologies across networks to facilitate communication at a distance.

Original documents that are of concern for library preservation purposes are not normally encoded in a digital electronic medium. Since this may become a subject of future concern, the category is included for completeness.

Multi-Media

Multi-Media is a term used to denote documents created using a number of different media simultaneously, usually those with an electronic technological basis: for example, a digital electronic recording that also combines video and audio, and that may, as part of the document, intrinsically produce paper outputs.

Document Format

Document Format refers to the class of document with respect to its style, arrangement, or layout. Although this Glossary emphasizes the distinction between format and medium, some formats are more closely associated with a given medium. Thus, formats such as documentary, short, feature, and newsreel are most closely associated with the medium of film. Consistent with the main thrust of this Glossary, we emphasize those formats that are mostly associated with the medium of paper, even though several of these formats may also be embodied in other media.

The term "format" itself may be too all-encompassing. There may be a need to further distinguish between the "type" of a document, such as "book," and the arrangement or layout of the book--such as formatted text on pages, or simply linear text that is not formatted into pages (as in the "talking book" where pages are not distinguished). However, this Glossary does not make this distinction, partly because of its focus on the paper milieu, where such a distinction may not be necessary, and partly because in the emerging world of digital tèchnologies it may be premature to attempt such a distinction.

Manuscript

For purposes of this Glossary, an original, unpublished document directly created by its author(s), usually on paper or parchment, and often in the author's own hand.

Book

A monograph publication containing more than 49 pages, usually on paper.

Pamphlet

A complete monograph of at least 5 but not more than 49 pages, usually on paper.

Newspaper

A serial publication issued at stated, frequent intervals containing news, opinions, advertisements, and other topical material, usually on paper.

Printed Sheet

A single sheet of printed paper such as a poster, broadside, folded leaflet, or memorandum, usually on paper.

Cartographic Materials

Representations of a selection of abstract features of the universe, most often in relation to the surface of the earth, often on paper but also on other substrates.

Music

In this context, printed representation of musical notation for instrumental, chamber, orchestral, and vocal scores, usually on paper.

Data File

The term Data File is used generically to denote a document consisting of a collection of data, normally organized in some logical fashion so as to facilitate access. Such data may consist of factual information, statistics, numbers, textual, or composite records to be used as a basis for reasoning, discussion, or calculation. An entity within a data file is known as a record. A collection of data files is sometimes known as a databank, particularly when the data files are electronically encoded.

Although data files may be encoded in any media (for example, a paper card index file is an example of a data file), the term has most often come to be used in connection with data files that are electronically encoded and stored in digital electronic form.

Table

A data file arranged into two-dimensional form, normally consisting of rows and columns together with headings or labels to depict the contents of the rows and columns. Tables may themselves contain other tables as elements resulting in a "latticed" arrangement of data. A spreadsheet is a special form of table originally used for accounting purposes and containing financial data, but which now includes a wide variety of complex reports arranged in tabular form, often with the aid of computer workstations.

Document Properties

Document Properties refers to a classification of various components of documents as to their different tonal or color content and as to the types of objects they contain. Emphasis is placed on those properties most closely associated with documents produced on paper.

Tone

Tone refers to the color quality or color content of the document or parts of the document regardless of form or material content.

Monotone

Monotone documents (or parts of documents) are printed or otherwise produced using one color hue only, most often black or near-black.

Two-Tone

Those parts of a monotone document that are represented in only two contrasting tones (regardless of the hue of the color, although the term is most often associated with black hues), with no intermediate shades. Thus, for purposes of this Glossary, a book printed with red ink on yellow paper would be considered two-tone. When one of the shades is black or near- black, and the other white or near-white, the document is described as being produced in black-and-white.

Greyscale

Those parts of a monotone document that are presented using a range of tones (regardless of the hue of the underlying color). The range of tones may either be continuous (such as in a photograph), where all possible values may essentially be taken on, or discrete, where only a finite set of values may be taken on.

Document Condition

Condition refers to the physical state of the document compared with its state when originally published. The following presents only those characteristics of the physical state of a document that are pertinent to the main thrust of this Glossary, that is, to the paper milieu.

Archival

A document that can be expected to be kept permanently as closely as possible to its original form. An archival document medium is one that can be "expected" to retain permanently its original characteristics. A document published in such a medium is of archival quality and can be expected to resist deterioration.

Permanent paper is manufactured to resist chemical action so as to retard the effects of aging as determined by precise technical specifications. Durability refers to certain lasting qualities with respect to folding and tear resistance.

Non-Archival

A document that is not intended or cannot be expected to

be kept permanently, and that may therefore be created or published on a medium that cannot be expected to retain its original characteristics and resist deterioration.

Copyright

Copyright refers to a means of legal protection provided to the author(s) of original published and unpublished works that have been "fixed in a tangible form of expression," in order to afford such authors the exclusive right of exploitation, in particular the right to control the reproduction, distribution, performance, or display of the work, or to control the preparation of derivative works. Often, exploitation of the work by others requires the consent of the author(s) and the payment of a royalty to the author(s), usually in the form of a fixed sum of money for each copy made, shown, or distributed.

For works copyrighted in the United States after January 1, 1978, protection afforded to the author(s) or the author(s)' estate is usually for the author(s)' lifetime plus 50 years. For works created prior to that date, the copyright period was 28 years from the date of publication, plus an additional period of 47 years for works whose copyright was renewed during the last year of the first term.

Works published in the United States may be afforded protection in countries that were members of the Universal Copyright Convention or of the Berne Convention for the Protection of Literary and Artistic Works. Conversely, works published in such member countries are protected within the United States. Most works that are the subject of preservation interest were published before 1978.

The copyrights on the majority of those works were not renewed for the optional second term. Thus, the copyrights have expired on most of the works of current preservation interest that were subject to United States copyright protection. However, since this is not true of all such works, the normal practice is to check copyright ownership to verify clearance.

The Selection Process

The Selection Process refers to the means whereby original documen.s are selected for preservation purposes. The choice of selection strategy may be intrinsically affected by the choice of preservation or media conversion technology used, since the latter may well affect costs and other parameters associated with the former. Thus, the total costs of preservation will be a complex combination of the effects of selection strategy and choice of technology.

Thus, for example, with the use of microform, it is highly desirable to obtain a complete copy of the document to be preserved prior to recording. This may require replacing missing or damaged pages from the prime copy being microfilmed, and the expense of obtaining these pages from copies held in other libraries. Microfilming also places a premium on recording only once. With the use of digital technologies, on the other hand, such replacement pages could be scanned at a later date and electronically "edited" into the main electronic document: with digital technologies, it may in fact be cheaper to scan more than one copy to facilitate such "editing" rather than to expend excessive manual labor on assembling the most perfect paper copy possible prior to microfilming.

"Preservation", however, may also be applied to the conversion onto other media of materials that, while in quite good condition, are scarce or unique, thus allowing patrons to handle facsimiles instead of the precious originals.

By Title

Selection is made from among individual works, perhaps by professional bibliographers who, possibly working in consultation with others, make a determination of the value of the selected work to a given collection, discipline, or field of study.

By Category

Selection is made by choosing essentially all documents from a within a given category, such as within a given time period, or of a given format (for example, all newspapers), subject classification, special collection, or, say, American imprint. The essence of this approach is that all documents within the category be readily and conveniently definable and accessible, without having to resort to time-consuming selection processes. Colloquially, this approach is sometimes erroneously termed the vacuum cleaner approach", an appellation that is overly pejorative insofar as some prior review is almost always made to reject materials within a category that for various reasons are not suitable or desirable for preservation. In particular, a check is made to ensure that the material has not already been preserved.

By Bibliography

Selection is made by choosing essentially all documents specified in a published bibliography.

By Use

Selection is made by choosing essentially all documents in poor condition that are actually used by patrons as judged by some criterion such as, for example, frequency of circulation.

By Condition

Selection is made by preserving the documents in the worst physical condition.

The Preserved Copy

This section addresses technologies employed in the preservation process. The first section broadly classifies different kinds of preservation processes. The remaining sections focus on the different technological stages associated with preservation processes dependent upon media conversion technologies. These are: capture technologies, storage technologies, access technologies, distribution technologies, and presentation technologies.

In the world of paper, these are usually all one and the same, even though the same paper book, say, may play different roles at different times. When it is on the library bookshelf, it is a storage medium; when it is being messengered through interlibrary loan, it is the distribution medium; and when it is being read by the patron, it is the presentation medium. In the world of convertible technologies, the separation becomes more than convenient sophistry—it becomes essential, since different media may well be used at any stage of the process.

Indeed, in the preservation milieu, this conceptual separation also offers considerable flexibility. It offers the flexibility of separating the act of preservation itself from the ultimate means of storage and delivery. Thus, for example, microfilming may be used as a preservation process, but the microfilm contents may be printed later onto paper for user presentation purposes. Thus, preservation technologies that offer the greatest flexibility are to be preferred to those that offer less flexibility, although lack of funds and patron preference often dictates the use of the latter.

Many different technologies have been proposed to address the problems of preservation. These can be divided into three broad categories: those directed at preserving both the content and physical embodiment of the original, those directed at preserving the content and copying the physical embodiment, and those directed at preserving the content only, without concern for the physical embodiment.

Conservation and paper deacidification fall into the first category. The remaining technologies described below fall into the other categories. In the second category every effort is made to copy the physical embodiment or format of the original as faithfully as possible, normally onto another medium. The term media conversion technologies is thus used for this class. Media Conversion includes photocopying, microform recording, and the use of electronic digitization techniques.

Conservation Treatment

The treatment of a document to preserve it in its original form, in recognition that the original medium, format, and content are all important for research and other purposes. Pure conservation approaches are normally hand-tailored to the individual document and, as such, may be relatively expensive. Use is normally, therefore, limited to those situations where such expensive treatment is justified by the research requirements.

Paper Deacidification and Strengthening

The treatment by chemicals to stabilize a document and/or to strengthen it. The alkalization treatment also usually entails depositing an alkaline reserve to buffer against further acidification. Deacidification or strengthening can be applied to individual documents or, with some treatment processes, to a large number of documents at once (mass or bulk deacidification). The latter is a relatively cheap approach, and pilot plants have been or are being established in a number of countries to support different processes.

There is, however, no standard approach at this time even though there appear to be a number of promising alternatives. There are also a number of unanswered questions at this time regarding the longevity of chemical stabilization processes, toxicity, the feasibility of scaling processes to full production requirements, the potential continuing "offgassing" implications to patrons resulting from the storage of thousands of treated volumes in confined library spaces, and other issues.

Deacidification is essentially a stabilization process that arrests deterioration. It does not turn brittle books back to their original state, although coating or impregnation can strengthen the paper to extend its useful life. Its greatest utility may lie in arresting embrittlement in books that are not too far gone, or for prophylactic protection of new or old books that have not yet started to turn brittle. Deacidification may also "buy time" in anticipation of later preservation by other processes.

Photocopying

Photocopying refers to the process of preserving the document by making a full-size (usually bound similarly to the original) facsimile copy on archival paper by creating a photographic copy of the images of the pages contained in the document, possibly using a photocopier. As used here, photocopying refers to an in-line process where the original is scanned and one or more photocopies made all in one pass, with no form of retained intermediate storage being automatically generated so that more copies can be made in the future.

In actual practice, however, when photocopying is used for preservation it is customary to make a second photocopy that is retained in unbound form, so that further copies can readily be made in the future from this master copy. A distinction is made between straight photocopying, which does not necessarily involve the use of archival paper, and preservation photocopying, which does require the use of archival paper. The advantages of making such a facsimile are that normally a single paper facsimile is produced that is quite faithful to the original, there is no machine interface required other than the photocopier itself, the medium and format of the original are retained, and the cost is usually less than other processes, particularly if the original is a monochrome document.

Microform Recording

Microform Recording refers to the process of preserving the document by filming the original document onto a microform film negative, that is, storing microimages of the pages or segments of the document on film. Positive film copies, which can be produced inexpensively, are made from this original film negative or master. Such a positive copy is both a storage and distribution technology, and is normally viewed using a microform reader, or paper positive prints may be made from the positive microform using printing devices designed for the purpose.

Access to microfilm using such a reader is serial, whereas access to microfiche is random ike a book. The advantages of microform are that the process is economically competitive with other processes; that film has a long useful life; and that microform copies—made from a second negative copied from the original negative—may be made cheaply and distributed among other institutions, so that access is not limited to a single facsimile. Microform preservation is a well-tried, tested, and accepted method of preservation.

The disadvantages are that there is usually a loss of information in the recording process, particularly in recording continuous tone imagery, since the film used is usually of high contrast; and that readers dislike using microform readers compared with, say, reading books.

Microform-preserved documents can subsequently be converted to other media besides paper. They can be scanned and converted to digitally-encoded documents to take advantage of the benefits of digital encoding for storage, distribution, and access.

Electronic Digitization

Electronic Digitization refers to the capture of the document in electronic form through a process of scanning and digitization. The scanned image is stored electronically, usually on magnetic or optical storage media. The electronically stored image may be further transformed for reasons such as compression or information interpretation; and subsequently selected through the use of access technologies, distributed through the use of distribution technologies, or viewed through the use of presentation technologies.

When originally scanned, or as a result of subsequent transformations, the document may in whole or in part be stored in image, unformatted text, formatted text, or compound form. The distinction is important insofar as it affects inter alia the extent to which information such as text in the scanned document may be interpreted and used for purposes of information access.

In the context of preservation, image representations are likely to dominate, since the cost of transforming image into text representations with sufficient accuracy may be prohibitively high, at least in the immediate future. Thus full-text searching, for example, is not likely to be a feature of digitally-preserved documents. This is unlike the situation that exists with documents where the text already exists in digital electronic form, such as if the publisher had preserved the original tapes used in typesetting.

If and when OCR techniques are able to convert image format to text format with sufficient accuracy and performance, then the archives of digitally-preserved material in image format can be converted to text format using ICR techniques, provided the original material was scanned with sufficiently high resolution. Furthermore, promising research has been done recently on the searching of documents for retrieval purposes using the "corrupted" text derived from the OCR or ICR scanning of image documents at existing levels of OCR/ICR accuracy and performance.

The advantage of electronic digitization is that it potentially combines the advantages of photocopying and microform recording while eliminating some of the disadvantages. Paper facsimiles can be produced at will by printing-on-demand on paper, thus eliminating the need for awkward microform readers. Alternatively, the stored images can be reconstructed and viewed at computer workstations. Furthermore, the stored digital images can be distributed essentially at will across data networks for sharing among institutions.

Photocopier

A Photocopier is a device for making photographic copies of graphic images. A common form of the photocopier involves the use of the xerographic process, where light reflected from the original document is focused onto an electrically charged insulated photoconductor, and the latent image is developed using a resinous powder. For the purposes of this Glossary, the term photocopier is restricted to devices that use analog technologies, such as the use of light lens technology.

Digital technologies are incorporated separately. With photocopiers so defined, the image is normally scanned and printed essentially in a single operation, and an intermediate scanned latent image is not normally stored for re-use at a later stage—although the two stage processes of photography, which indeed may be used for photocopying, do permit the use of the photographic negative as an intermediate storage device.

Microform Recorder

A Microform Recorder is a camera or other photographic device for photographing the original document and printing it onto one of several forms of microform. The microform film in essence becomes both a storage medium and a presentation medium. Other film copies and paper copies may also be made from the microform negatives for presentation.

Digital Image Scanner

A Digital Image Scanner is a device for scanning the images contained on pages of a document and transforming the scanned image into digital electronic signals corresponding to the physical state at each part of the search area, that is, into image documents. Digital Image Scanners may scan in one or more different modes, depending upon their capability and depending upon whether they are scanning monotone or color, or whether they are scanning line art, greyscale, halftone, or continuous tone objects. Performance, in terms of speed, accuracy, and resolution depend upon the degree to which these attributes can be accommodated. The speed of digital image scanners range from one or two pages per minute to around fifty per minute.

A FAX machine is a special form of digital image scanner. Other special forms of digital image scanners exist for scanning from media other than paper, such as digital image scanners that scan directly from microfilm. Such images scanned from microfilm, however, can be no better than the original microfilm image itself. Digital image scanners may come equipped with different physical devices for accommodating the original documents. These may include flatbed platens equipped with manual feeds, semi-automatic feeds (one page at a time is fed into an automatic hopper), or fully-automatic feeds.

Manual feeds offer the greatest safety from potential jamming, a point of importance in the scanning of unique documents. Flatbed scanners generally require either books to be disbound and one page at a time placed on the platen, or require books to be laid open face-down on the platen, which may cause some distortion. They may also come equipped with edge-scanners, which scan right up to the binding of the book, avoiding this distortion; or with cradle scanners, where the book is opened in a cradle (such devices are also used in some microform recording devices) and two angled scanning heads are lowered into the open, cradled book. In all cases, quality control of scanning is an issue with respect to fidelity of the scanned image and registration of the scanned image with respect to a defined standard.

Optical Character Recognition Scanner

An Optical Character Recognition (OCR) Scanner is a digital image scanner that in addition interprets the textual portion of the images and converts it to digital codes representing formatted or unformatted text. The less sophisticated such devices can only "recognize" one or a few fonts of a fixed size, and can only interpret such information as unformatted text. The more sophisticated devices can represent multiple fonts of different sizes, and can interpret limited information as formatted text.

OCR devices are most often used where scanning errors and unformatted text are acceptable limitations, such as, for example, where the input material can be subsequently proofread and corrected, or where redundant information is scanned and the redundant information used to correct any inconsistencies arising from scanning errors. In the context of document preservation, most uses of OCR devices are limited to where text information only suffices, and the form of the original document is not an important aspect of preservation.

Internal Character Recognition

Internal Character Recognition is the term sometimes used when the same interpretation technology that is used in OCR devices is applied to an already stored digital image at a later date. This separates the functions of scanning the images digitally, and of interpreting the images. Interpreting the scanned and stored images at a later date also allows for using different recognition technologies in the tradeoffs between accuracy, speed, and function. In the context of preservation and media conversion, it also allows for the immediate focus to be placed on scanning and storage, deferring the option of character recognition and its applications to a later date—at such time, massive-volume character recognition and information interpretation is likely to be more economically feasible at higher levels of accuracy than with present technology.

Intelligent Character Recognition

Intelligent Character Recognition is the term sometimes given to Optical or Internal Character Recognition where the scanned and recognized information is further interpreted to take advantage of contextual information, that is, words, phrases, and so forth, rather than simply treating the text as a string of independent characters. Intelligent Character Recognition, for example, may be used by sophisticated computer programs to construct concordances automatically, or to create highly-sophisticated indexes. At this stage, intelligent character recognition is a field of research, rather than production, interest .

Page Recognition

Page Recognition is the term given to the automatic interpretation of features contained within the printed page such as titles, subheads, columns, paragraphs, figures, figure captions, footnotes, and so forth. Additional capabilities of sophisticated page recognition algorithms include the ability to determine fonts and font sizes. In essence, Page Recognition "reverse engineers" the image into marked-up copy.

Rekeying of Text

As an alternative or complement to OCR, textual information can be encoded by directly keying alphanumeric text into computer files manually. This has some advantage in accuracy over OCR, but is slower.

Storage Technology

Storage Technology refers to the technology used to store the images or information obtained through the use of some form of Capture Technology. This includes the medium used for storage, the compression methodology used to minimize the amount of storage medium employed, the format used to program the image or information onto the medium, the encoding methods used to represent any interpretation of the stored information, and the useful life of the storage medium.

A family of storage devices where information or data are represented by a series of quantized changes to the surface of the storage medium, where such quanta are recorded or modified using electronic means. There are two main classes in this category: magnetic devices where, in recording, the magnetic state of a coated surface is altered by the electronic digital signal, and, in reading, the surface is sensed using reading heads conceptually similar to those used in common tape recorders; and optical devices where the optical properties of a coated surface are altered.

Such devices are further classified according to whether they are read/write devices, read only memory (ROM) devices (that is, prerecorded information can be read from the device, but the information cannot be modified), or write-once-read-many (WORM) devices (that is, information may be written once by the consumer onto the device, but thereafter it can only be read). Most optical devices are either read only or WORM devices, but a class of devices that combine both magnetic and optical technologies (magneto-optical devices) are indeed read/write devices.

Typically, magnetic devices are of higher performance in terms of access time to a given segment of recorded information and transfer time of such accessed information to the host device. Optical devices, however, are generally more economic in terms of storage capacity. Magnetic technologies have a longer history than optical technologies, and more is known about their useful life, for example. Both technologies seem to be following similar cost/performance curves with performance parameters doubling in capability approximately every two to three years, and cost per bit halving about every two to three years.

Magnetic Disk

A rotating circular plate having a magnetized surface on which information may be stored as a pattern of polarized spots on concentric or spiral recording tracks. These plates or platters are usually stacked in disk drives, several to a drive. These platters may either be removable or not, although in high performance disk drives, the platters are usually not removable. They are, however, read/write devices. Some removable magnetic disks of lower capacity are known as floppy disks, since originally the recording medium was made of a flexible plastic.

Magnetic Tape

A plastic, paper, or metal tape that is coated or impregnated with magnetizable iron oxide particles on which information is stored as a pattern of polarized spots. These are read using magnetic tape drives. Access times with magnetic tapes are slower than those associated with correspondingly priced disks, since they are serial access devices, but the tapes are almost always removable so that the information can be stored off-line, thus making tapes useful for archival storage.

Optical Disk

A rotating circular plate on which information is stored as submicrometer-sized holes and is recorded and read by laser beams focused on the disk. This includes the class of CD-ROM devices, which embodies the same 5 1/4" diameter format used for CD recordings. CD-ROM's are usually read by inserting the CD-ROM disk into a CD-ROM player. Other typical formats involve 12" or 14" diameter formats, but there is a dearth of standards. The latter are usually read by inserting them into optical jukebox devices, which perform the role suggested by their name. Even when mounted, access times for optical disks are typically relatively slow, because of the lag time needed to "spin up" the disk. However, the cost per stored bit is extremely low. Error rates may also be higher than for magnetic technologies. As such, optical disks are most useful where there is an abundance of redundant information contained in the stored data, such as would be the case with the storage of scanned document pages.

Magneto-Optical Disk

Disks that combine the use of magnetic and optical technologies. To record data, elements of the crystal structure of the substrate are aligned by using a laser to heat the element in the presence of an applied magnetic field.

Storage Format

As used in information storage and retrieval, Format or Storage Format refers to the actual representation of the stored data on the storage medium, that is, the specific way in which it is encoded or programmed onto the medium. Classifying such methodologies is beyond the scope of this document. Indeed, for the most part—and particularly as applied to digital electronic storage technologies—there are few general standards that are accepted by all or most manufacturers. The implication is that access to the information stored on the medium depends upon specific software or computer programs supplied by the manufacturer, software that may become obsolete with the passage of time. One result may be that stored information may need to be reformatted or transferred to newer storage media periodically in order for the information to remain accessible with current software and technology.

Encoding Method

Encoding Method refers to the extent to which the information content of the document has been interpreted and encoded, rather than merely recorded. Such interpretation may be beneficial for a number of reasons including as a means of achieving reversible compression; for the construction of document indices to facilitate searching and access; or for efficient distribution of the information across data networks.

No Encoding

No interpretation of the information contained in the original document has occurred. If the document were originally scanned using a digital image scanner, then the document in this instance is generally stored in some image format, compressed or not. If portions of the document were originally scanned using optical character recognition, then those portions will be stored as either formatted or unformatted text.

Textual Encoding

The text contained in the original document has been interpreted so that each character has a separate representation. Such interpretation may have occurred at the time of scanning if an optical character recognition device is used, or later using internal character recognition programs applied to documents in image format. Such textual interpretation may result in either unformatted or formatted text, depending upon the degree of sophistication of the device or program. Recognition accuracy may also be limited.

Markup Language Encoding

A computer markup language is a means for describing,

for an electronically stored document, the complete positioning, format, and style of text and image segment representations within the document. When combined with textual representation, it is a means for achieving fully formatted text. When combined with relevant image information about document graphics material, it may be a means of archiving fully reversible compression of the document. An example of a markup language is SGML (Standard Generalized Markup Language) that has been adopted by the United States Government and by many publishers as a pseudo-standard.

Page Description Language Encoding

A computer language in which segments of text and images are economically described with respect to form, orientation, size, density, and other characteristics for purposes of economic transmission across networks and between host devices and output devices such as printers. Page Description Languages are another form of compression, as well as a form of encoding.

Digital electronic storage media have a varying useful life projected to range from a few years to over 100 years. The latter has not been formally tested by experience, but is projected based on laboratory stress tests. Such media, however, become obsolete for other reasons long before their physical properties render them useless. It becomes economically and functionally infeasible to maintain the information stored on the original medium of capture, since it becomes far cheaper to transfer the information periodically to higher density and cheaper newer technologies.

The implications of periodic recopying for libraries are quite far- reaching. Libraries are not used to having to maintain their inventory by periodic recopying, even though such practices are quite common in data centers. Indeed, the recent impetus of preservation may have caused some librarians to rethink their position in this regard, although librarians still tend to think in terms of periods of centuries rather than having (or wanting) to recopy every few years. Such considerations may either hinder the adoption of digital technologies or eventually cause some rethinking of the underlying economics of librarianship.

Access Methodology or Technology

Access Methodology or Technology refers to the means of selecting information from among all the information that is stored.

Indexed Access

A Document Index is a systematically ordered file of objects that refer to a collection of documents or to specific parts of those documents, organized in such a way as to facilitate searching the document collection for purposes of selection of single documents or groups of documents contained in the collection. Such document indices may be stored on different media depending upon how they are to be used.

Via Catalog

Access via a file of bibliographic records, created according to specific and uniform principles of construction and under the control of an authority file, which describes the documents contained in a collection. The file is usually organized in a systematic manner to facilitate access and document selection. Catalogs historically have been implemented in card files, but increasingly such card files are retroactively and prospectively giving way to computerized data files which may be accessed and searched by patrons with the use of computer workstations and data networks. Such computer-based catalogs are increasing in sophistication to support complex queries, including Boolean queries, which support logical searching.

Print-on-Demand

Print-on-Demand refers to the capability to print documents right at the time they are required by patrons and consumers, rather than following traditional norms of printing documents in advance of need and coping with the need to distribute and inventory printed documents in anticipation of demand. This approach to distribution mirrors the "just-in-time" approach to inventory control. Print-on-Demand techniques are normally used in conjunction with digitally stored documents and data networks. The approach offers the promise of closing the gap between the world of digital technologies and those who maintain the superiority or simply prefer the characteristics of paper documents. Documents may be printed right in the patron's office or at a shared local facility from where it is delivered to or picked up by the patron.

Data Networks

A Data Network, is a communications network that transports data between and among computers and computer workstations. Such networks may depend upon different physical media to transport the encoded digital signals (twisted pair copper wire, coaxial cable, fiber optic cable, satellite, and so forth); different protocols to encode the signals; and different ways in which the encoded signals are interpreted for use in applications. They also include bridges, routers, and gateways for connecting different media and for translating one protocol into another. Data networks vary considerably in speed and capacity, depending upon the physical media, the protocols used, and the particular architecture of the network. Network speeds and other performance characteristics appear to be more than doubling every two to three years.

Local Area Network

Local Area Network (LAN) is a data network used to connect nodes that are geographically close, usually within the same building. In a wider view of a local area network, multiple local area networks are interconnected in a geographically compact area, usually by attaching the LANs to a higher-speed local backbone.

Wide Area Network

A Wide Area Network (WAN) is a data network connecting large numbers of nodes and LANs that are geographically remote, such as within a broad metropolitan area, or between widely-separated metropolitan areas. This would also include regional networks, such as NYSERNet, which interconnects research and educational institutions in New York State.

A WAN, or a federation of interconnected WANs, that span the nation, such as the NSFNet, BITNet, CSNet, CREN, and, more generally, the Internet and the anticipated NREN (National Research and Educational Network). These national networks often use a high-speed spanning national backbone to interconnect regional WANs. Protocols are established to facilitate routing of information across the national networks to users at connected nodes. The national networks often have international connections and outreach.

Voice Networks

Voice Networks are local, national, or international networks used to carry voice or telephone traffic. They may be either analog or digital. Because of different technical requirements, the transmission of data and voice usually is conducted using different transmission protocols, although it is increasingly common to share the same wiring plant. In general, there is increasing integration between the voice and data milieus.

Usability of Digital Resources

In recent years, libraries have been fortunate to have increasing access to new and innovative digital resources. A number of factors contribute to this trend:

— advances in networking technology and the growth of the JANET network mean that UK libraries can deliver more information more quickly directly to their end-users;

- — an influx of funding following on from the Follett Report has provided libraries with an opportunity to experiment with and integrate new technologies into the services they provide;
- — the emergence of consortium purchasing and the prevalence of nationally negotiated dataset deals which grant better and cheaper access to a wide variety of commercially produced digital products.
- — Libraries in the UK over the past few years have certainly benefited from new funding, technology and business approaches. Relatively speaking it has happened very fast and consequently our reliance on these resources is growing exponentially

Digital Preservation is a complex and exciting area. Libraries now rely increasingly on digital resources, many of which do not have a print equivalent. Examples include new electronic journals, web-based information gateways or electronic courseware. Since the introduction of digital material, the technologies through which a great deal of digital resources are delivered have continued to evolve, mutate and develop.

Libraries in the UK have pursued relatively conservative collections management policies, and continue to retain print journals where there are new electronic versions. However, electronic journals (even those in parallel) are beginning to include technology-dependent content such as animation, sound or video which is simply not available/possible in the print version. Although the Research Libraries Group (RLG) is currently funding a study to support this assumption, it is unlikely that many libraries in the UK have policies which address the long-term access to and preservation of electronic materials.

Despite this potential gap, libraries continue to invest in digital resources that may not have a print equivalent and funding continues to be poured into digitisation projects without a clear understanding of the future of the digital files. In research libraries, preservation of material has always been a priority. Indeed research libraries (and in particular the UK copyright deposit libraries) are largely responsible for preserving access to our most valued UK scholarly resources.

Although much of current digital libraries activity may have happened anyway in the fullness of time, there has been a surge of new funding (both in the UK and abroad) for the creation and application of new technology in libraries. Most notably in the UK, the eLib Programme has overseen the establishment of over 70 different projects and studies in the UK in digital libraries. As a result of this, eLib has recognised that some investment into the problems of long-term access to digital resources was probably wise.

Digital preservation is a process by which digital data is preserved in digital form in order to ensure the usability, durability and intellectual integrity of the information contained therein. Although a list of working definitions is still evolving, the project has agreed a more specific definition for digital preservation which is "storage, maintenance and access to digital objects/materials over the long term. this may involve one or more digital preservation strategies including technology preservation, technology emulation or digital information migration." According to Hendley, at a basic level, digital preservation involves the following tasks:

— Preserving the digital medium that holds the digital information by storing it in the correct environment and following agreed storage and handling procedures

— Copying the digital information onto newer, fresher media before the old media deteriorates past the point where the digital information can be read or becomes so obsolete that we can no longer find a storage device to read it on referred to as refreshing.

— Preserving the integrity of the digital information during the copying process. Cedars is most concerned with digital preservation beyond this basic level to ensure that the information can be retrieved and processed in a meaningful way in the future and is therefore useable.

The relative novelty of digital preservation as an issue for libraries, and the fact that expertise in this area resides in other sectors (e.g. electronic records management) means that defining what we mean by specific terms is sometimes contentious. Where librarians, archivists, records managers and computing technologists assemble, the term "archive" can (and does) mean very different things.

Digital preservation includes many materials for which there is no print equivalent - these materials have been referred to as "born digital". Indeed it is the latter which present the most complex problems of preservation because they are often inextricably linked to the technical environment in which they are produced. Digitised images may need routine "refreshing", but will generally not require disentangling from a technical environment which is often necessary with a 'born digital' object.

Preservation of the technical environment by conserving copies of the software and specific hardware is referred to as "technology preservation". For some digital objects this may be the best solution - at least in the short-term - because it ensure the material is accessible by preserving the access tools as well as the object itself. However, longer term this is more problematic. For example, issues of space and maintenance for hardware as well as costs may make this an impractical solution for the long term.

There are other options however which focus on preserving the environment for a digital object. It is possible in the case of something like Encarta to preserve data about how the technical environment was created in the first place in order to re-create a new technical environment which mimics the original. If we preserve enough information about Windows 3.1 then instead of preserving it, we can simply re-engineer it again when we need it. This option is called "emulation" and is probably the most complex option for preserving digital resources. This relies on a robust system for preserving the metadata which describes the technical environment.

In an emulation situation, like the case described above, nothing is done to the original object (it is left simply as a bitstream) and it is the environment which is re-created. The costs of emulation are as yet unknown and it is expected that the costs of re-creating complex technical environments could be astronomical. However, unlike the technical preservation model, the costs fall further along in the resource's lifecyle. Instead of spending money now and for the foreseeable future, by preserving both software and hardware, emulation loads the costs at the far end. If a resource is needed in future, only then are resources required to emulate the necessary technological environment.

Emulation is more like the "just in time" option where technology preservation means we will have the necessary soft/hardware "just in case". (However, this option also requires a leap of faith in terms of the power of future technologies and in the abilities of future software engineers).

As part of the UK Electronic Libraries Programme (eLib), the Cedars project has been funded to explore issues and practical exemplars for the long-term preservation of digital materials. The Consortium of University Research Libraries (CURL) in the UK represents the major national, academic, and research libraries in England, Wales, Scotland, and Northern Ireland. So, it is well placed to lead in this relatively new and increasingly urgent area.

Cedars stands for "CURL Exemplars in Digital Archives," and the project focuses on strategic, methodological, and practical issues for libraries in preserving digital materials into the future. The 3-year project, which is in its second year, is led by the universities of Oxford, Cambridge and Leeds. The UK Office of Library Networking is also a partner in the project with a focus particularly on metadata issues for long-term preservation.

One of the first challenges in establishing the project was the implementation of an agreed model or standard for archiving materials. If the demonstrator projects are to illustrate a scaleable distributed digital archive, technical development and implementation across all three sites must converge. Cedars is also focusing on a number of other areas related to digital preservation, including technical approaches to preservation, intellectual property rights, and the copyright implications for preserving digital materials.

The UK currently has a system for the legal deposit of most non-digital material published in the UK. Deposit is limited to six specific libraries: the British Library, the National Libraries of Scotland and Wales, Cambridge University, Oxford University, and Trinity College Dublin. Similar to the system for print materials, future legislation for digital resources will almost certainly be based on a distributed system composed of several repositories.

The adoption of standard approaches to management of a digital archive is critical - even more so than for archiving non-digital resources. For instance, in a digital archive system, there may be only one copy deposited with a single repository within the distributed archive that relies on interoperability and sharing of resources among archives. Convergent development and implementation across the repositories or archives is therefore paramount.

The Open Archival Information System (OAIS)

ISO has been collaborating with the Consultative Committee for Space Data Systems on the development of a standard framework for implementing a digital archive. The OAIS reference model includes the complete range of functions within any archive (whether digital or not): acquisition (referred to hereafter as "ingest"), data storage, data management, administration, and access (referred to as "dissemination").

The OAIS model provides a useful framework including concepts and vocabulary that facilitates clear and meaningful discussions and implementation of archival repositories. Although developed initially for archiving geographical information systems and satellite data, OAIS is intended to be applicable to any archive. Cedars has been testing the applicability of the OAIS model within the context of a distributed digital archive of library materials.

Before describing the Cedars Architecture, which implements the OAIS model, it is worth noting that Cedars is also addressing issues external to the OAIS model. The OAIS model does not focus on the environment external to the archive, which includes key stakeholders such as producers, consumers, and management. In a Cedars context, these external factors must also be considered. Metadata that describes the software and systems necessary to make the data useable is referred to as "representation information," while the metadata that describes an object's preservation status is referred to as "preservation description information." Making a clear distinction between these two types of metadata within the OAIS model is not always easy.

Within Cedars, there are ongoing discussions about what metadata constitutes representation information, and what is included in the preservation metadata. Indeed, this may vary depending on the nature of the object to be preserved. Perhaps the distinction is more clear for GIS data, which constitute the basis for the OAIS model. However, for complex multi-media materials found in library collections, the distinction can be blurry. Cedars plans to use its practical exemplars based on specific digital library resources to better understand this distinction.

Archival Information Packages (AIPs)

AIPs encapsulate preserved digital objects, and are physically stored in the archive. For ease of media independence, an AIP is handled as a byte stream, however, the metadata elements can be stored by reference rather than being placed within the AIP (i.e., each digital object is stored as a byte stream along with pointers to metadata that allows their rendering and describes their preservation process). In the case of representation information metadata, which provides a rendering scheme for the digital object, a whole network of references may be used to link each AIP with the relevant resources.

For example, a PDF file would require storage of the byte stream itself as well as a "rendering scheme" that would include the version of PDF, and information about the required software and hardware. By keeping the rendering tools separate from the digital object itself, the archive can update the representation network without trawling through every AIP and incorporating the change.

Submission Information Packages (SIPs)

The OAIS model suggests that to usefully preserve a digital object, that object should be fully understood. That is, without meaningful retrieval or rendering, there is no preservation. As a digital object is submitted to an archive, sufficient information needs to be included in SIPs during the ingest phase. Cedars proposes that "the level of abstraction" of the digital object should be identified to enhance the understanding of the digital object. This is a particularly useful approach for complex, multi-layered objects.

For this CD-ROM, the underlying digital object could be seen either as an SGML document, or as a PC-based piece of software that runs using the Dynatext-viewer included on the same CD-ROM. Alternatively, taking the abstraction further, the underlying layer can be seen as a set of pages of text that can be navigated in a well-defined manner. Identifying the level of abstraction also allows the formulation of recommendations about the "best" or "most suitable" choices for an object's preservation and management within the OAIS.

Dissemination Information Packages (DIPs)

The OAIS model includes an access component, which relies on a system of metadata that Cedars may include as part of the PDI (preservation description information) for resource discovery or searching and retrieval of material from the archive. DIPs contain the resultant digital object responding to a user's request based on the search and retrieval metadata. It only carries the elements of metadata that are relevant to retrieving and rendering the digital object on the requested platform. The implementation decisions made about the AIP and SIP heavily influenced how DIPs are utilized.

Archive Administration and Data Management

Having looked at the three information packages, the remaining function of the OAIS model concerns data management and the overall administration of the archive. It is critical to ensure that digital object integrity is adequately maintained, involving activities ranging from controlling the objects within the archive (security) to running a validation and media refreshment program. An archive might also wish to manage system configuration (audits, performance, and usage monitoring).

Authenticity of Digtal Resources

Traditionally, when scholars encountered original sources (artifacts, documents or works of art) many physical clues assisted in establishing their authenticity. If sources are studied in the surrogate (in photographs, microfilm or other reprographic form), all the questions concerning the authenticity of the original are overlaid with additional questions about the methods of representation.

When the source is itself is distant from the original, such as a transcription of selections from a census or a collation of statistics, the methods employed and choices made in its creation are assessed by scholars along with the intepreted results; these methods impinge upon its subsequent utility for other kinds of analysis and interpretation. Concerns about authenticity in sources, then, are not new. With the ubiquity of digital representations and the proliferation of source information on the Internet, these issues are further complicated. It is not unusual to find resources purporting to represent the same thing at many different sites.

But we are without widely understood and employed methods of assessing and establishing authenticity of digital sources. It is crucial for the ongoing development of knowledge in many fields that it be possible to determine the relative authenticity of a number of different representations, through an analysis of the methods that have been chosen to transform the original into a digital form, or through an assessment of the methods used to capture original digital data. It is also essential that it be possible to establish the integrity of a particular digital copy.

The community of users and creators of scholarly digital documentation is not without proposed solutions to this problem. Many companies offer technologies, and a variety of institutions have established or proposed social mechanisms of control which make promises to satisfy some part of the requirements for digital authenticity. The appropriateness of these solutions cannot be assessed until we are clearer about its needs in this area. Further articulation of requirements is a necessary precursor to systematic assessment of the degree to which different types of technical and social offerings satisfy scholarly needs. This note calls for both such further definition of requirements and the associated assessment of mechanisms being offered in order to hasten the development of trusted and widely adopted solutions.

Many cultural agencies are making substantial investments in transforming heritage information into digital form. For the scholars who study these works, the ability to distinguish an "authoritative" digital representation, from that made by someone who might have paid less attention to the requirements or impact of digital transformation, is important. Knowledge of digital representation and modeling methods and access to appropriate capture technologies are not necessarily resident with those who have access to the original documents themselves.

While a collecting institution may always have an apparent advantage in having access to "the real thing", a scholar may have far greater understanding of the content and context of a particular artifact, and/or greater sophistication about the implications of specific approaches to re-presentation. Faithfulness in representation, a self-conscious awareness of the issues in digital conversion, and assurances of the authenticity of available resources will greatly influence the decision of a scholar to use a particular digital document or dataset.

Forgeries and fakes have long been a concern of students of culture and the humanities, but fakery has not been a major issue for most researchers in the past, both because of the technical barriers to making plausible forgeries, and because of the difficulty with which such fakes entered an authoritative information stream. This changes with the broadening of the number of sources for information, the ease with which digital information can be altered, and the likelihood of the existence of many digital "copies" of the same work with slight differences.

The underlying technology makes purposeful fakery easier and more tempting. In addition, lack of understanding of the distorting effects of specific methods of digitization makes the creation and distribution of copies that were designed to be faithful, but are, in fact, misleading in some manner, very common. New digital works are also challenging our concept of authentic representations, particularly in realms such as photography, where digital manipulation has extended the practice of retouching photographic prints beyond cosmetic to the misleading.

Some of the most promising characteristics of digital objects are those which reveal the greatest authenticity problems. For example, objects tied to methods are programmed to behave in particular ways. Performance of works has generated an important literature on the nature of authenticity.

Automatic "performance" of a work based on its symbolic representation is enabled by digital presentation and can have some benefits—but its limitations must be understood. For example, a speech by a nineteenth century political figure can be "read" by a computer or a quartet can be "played" by computer simulated instruments, but both will be misleading in many respects. Even more complex re-enactments or re-creations can enable visualization of realities that are otherwise hard for people to understand, but it is important that those who are experiencing such manifestations understand the rules by which they were created.

It is interesting to note that the last time a significant shift took place in the technologies of copying, with the invention of printing, a similar concern about authenticity gave birth to the entire discipline of Diplomatics. Diplomatists are again active in the search for methods of establishing digital authenticity. Quite possibly, societal responses ultimately create mechanisms that are sufficient for most general assurances of authenticity as a basis for the widespread adoption of such new technologies—if so, we are currently crafting such mechanisms for the 21st century.

Three quite distinct technical and social strategies for asserting authenticity can be identified in proposed solutions: public, secret, and functionally dependent.

Public methods for asserting the authenticity of sources include:

— the creation of copyright deposit "collections of record",

— certified deposits of original sources combined with record certification services,

— registration of unique document identifiers,

— publishing "key" data about documents which, when hashed, or otherwise calculated in a publicly available way, should match that of the document in hand, and

— defining metadata structures to carry document authentication declarations or proofs.

Secret methods involve hiding data in the object to reveal its source. Techniques include:

— digital watermarking

— stegonography and

— digital signatures.

Functionally dependent methods employ specific technologies that are bound together with the information source. Methods employing technical dependencies include:

— object encapsulation

— crypotolopes (TM)

— encryption and

— embedded active agents.

Each of these technologies addresses problems beyond simple resource authentication. Questions of authenticity and assessment arise throughout the process of scholarly research, whenever a potential scholarly user finds, retrieves, or subsequently uses, a digital resource. Because we believe that ultimately expressions of the requirements for authenticity will need to reflect both specific disciplines and their working methods, the various stages in the research process: information discovery, retrieval, and use.

Information discovery

Information discovery, the identification and location of relevant resources, most often takes place through a query process. A user searches a database or index for a particular resource or type of resources. Such a query most often results in a list of citations. Unique identifiers offer one solution to the problem of disambiguation. If each version or edition of a resource has a distinct identifier, the researcher is then able to request a particular source.

This source could be known to meet certain authenticity criteria. Or it could be that a specific source is sought because it was the basis for a previous analysis. In either of these cases, the unambiguous identification of a particular digital information source is key. For example, unique identification by a Digital Object Identifier or Serial Item and Contribution Identifier, registration with a copyright agency, or assignment of a Permanent URL (purl).

But unique identifiers only address one aspect of authenticity in discovery. Often, however, the researcher is faced with the difficulty of choosing between different sources, as a query identifies numerous versions of the same source. In making a decision to act upon the results of information discovery, the user wants further assurances of authenticity.

Information retrieval

Once a resource is discovered, and judged to be of interest, the researcher makes a choice to retrieve it, consciously moving a copy of a digital source to a local workstation for future use. Here the authenticity of a copy of a known resource might be assured by digital verification methods such as (public) hashing algorithms, (hidden) watermarks, or (functionally dependent) unlocking encryption. Such comparisons of a specific copy to a known version of integrity can assess and/or assert the integrity of the copy.

The retrieval process itself is software enabled. If we trust the specific retrieval system to check the received copy against what was transmitted, this post-facto comparison may seem unnecessary. But methods we have constructed for convenience, to use data constructed in one environment with tools resident in our own environment, involve transformations between representations. End-users are unlikely to be aware of the types of approximations made in these "automatic" and behind-the-scenes translations, and will encounter "the original" in their own software environment complete with any such changes that have been introduced.

Information Use: Collation, Analysis, and Representation

At the stage of analysis and use of resources retrieved, the scholar confronts questions of authenticity that are both similar to and distinct from the traditional assessments of primary or secondary source material. The analog world gives us some models for comparative analysis. Reprints, changes of scale, and loss of color in black and white photography may either emphasize or obscure particular characteristics in the original source.

Scholars have historically relied on metadata provided by repositories to determine the meaning of otherwise ambiguous documents, to more or less success. Representations may also implicitly impart a particular "point of view", either consciously or sub-consciously.

Since digital resources are often representations of information previously created in analog format, the verisimilitude of these representations are matters of considerable scholarly dispute.

Different representations amplify different aspects of the "real thing"; for example, mark-up of a text may or may not identify particular linguistic elements; images taken with different wave lengths of light will show different features of an object; and images digitized with different degrees of attention to color will show different degrees of accuracy/fidelity.

The issues of authenticity in digital transformations are, properly, about how well certain representations serve a desired purpose. When we are using a representation (and all digital resources are representations), many of the issues which figure prominently in the field of translation become critical. Issues of authenticity have always been critical in some areas of scholarship in which a resource is going to be used in a new way.

Authenticity is, therefore, of concern for both information providers and information users throughout the entire research process. Researchers are concerned about identifying and assessing the integrity of a particular source of interest. Agencies may wish to identify copies of digital transformations they have made. This may be to assert their original care in the creation of a representation, or if they no longer physically control copies, to be able to identify them in the future, possibly replace them subsequently methods of representation change, or to ensure their continued integrity through association with an authoritative source.

The creators of authentic digital representations may also feel that their investment in high quality authoritative knowledge representation requires compensation, requiring the ability to track copies of authoritative originals as part of licensing and protection mechanisms. Many technical methods are being developed or offered that purport to address the issues of authenticity and integrity of information resources.

In future, the roles are shifting, and publishers are increasingly expected to preserve their own content. Librarians, still leery about how adequately publishers will perform the role, are nonetheless relinquishing some of the responsibility. They have no choice when they do not own the information, as is the case for many electronic products. Even when the access versus ownership issue is resolved, the sheer volume of information to be preserved and the cost of archiving will lead to shared responsibilities.

E-print and Long-term Services

E-prints are seen as a catalyst for the freeing of the scholarly and scientific literature from the cost barriers imposed by journal publishers. Supporters of the self-archiving concept (as it is sometimes known) argue that the easiest, fastest and cheapest way for authors to make their papers available is to store electronic copies of these (both pre-prints and reprints) on e-print servers. In US, the successes of the arXiv e-print server based at Los Alamos National Laboratory (LANL) and other e-print services are cited as exemplars of how authors' distribution of e-prints can start a revolution in scholarly and scientific communication.

The LANL-based service initially gave access to e-prints in the domain of high-energy physics, but has since expanded to cover other areas of physics, mathematics and computer science. Stevan Harnad has recently noted that the Los Alamos physics service holds over 150,000 papers, is mirrored on over 14 sites world-wide and gets about 160,000 user hits each weekday at its US site alone. The arXiv e-print server and services like CogPrints (the Cognitive Sciences Eprint Archive) and WoPeC (Working Papers in Economics), are examples of a centralised discipline-based service.

Harnad initially suggested an alternative approach based on authors self-archiving their papers on their home pages or on institutional servers. The core of Harnad's original 'subversive proposal' was the establishment by authors of publicly accessible 'archives' of their own papers. It is a simple subversive proposal that we would make to all scholars and scientists right now: if from this day forward, everyone were to make available on the Net, in publicly accessible archives on the World Wide Web, the texts of all their current papers then the transition to the PostGutenberg era would happen virtually overnight.

The main problem with this model was that papers distributed across many Web pages or FTP archives could not be collectively searched or retrieved. So, back in 1994, Paul Ginsparg argued that creating a distributed 'database' was technically possible, but not at that time logistically feasible. The standards under development by the OAI, however, now mean that the distributed model can now be made to work. Harnad has argued that widespread implementation of the OAI standards would enable e-prints stored on both distributed institution-based servers and centralised services like arXiv.org to be harvested into a single virtual archive.

authoring packages. This quality of hypertext lends itself to this application. The first method of access to the information uses the *classification information*. This is the information that that is held in the Document Management System (DMS) and is almost exactly equivalent to the information that is held in a library catalogue. It contains the position(s) within the document hierarchy that the file will be located, and it contains all the attributes, such as title, author, date of creation, physical media type and keywords.

This information is very high quality, as it provides specific information about documents, and Microcosm provides tools for traversing the subject hierarchy, and for querying the documents by attributes such as keywords. The second method of access is *hypermedia link following*. It is generally supposed that hypermedia links are manually authored in order to indicate some relationship between the two items at each end of the link. Such links are of very high value, but creating them requires considerable manual effort.

However, the Multimedia Research Group at Southampton always considered that the reduction of this effort, and the automation of link creation, was an important research issue. One of the earliest results of this research was the introduction of *generic links*, which are links with a fixed end point, but which may start at any point where the source object is located. Typically this means any place where a particular text string is located. The third method of data access is text based information retrieval.

The interface to this functionality requires the user to make a selection of text from some document, or else to type in some text, and then choose "compute links" from the menu. One of the strengths of the traditional libraries is that many large collections of books and materials in other media are catalogued with great care and attention to bibliographic detail and accuracy using standard cataloguing rules such as Anglo-American Cataloguing Rules (AACR2).

As Howard Rheingold points out 'Librarians and other specialists have a toolkit and syntax for dealing with well-known problems that people encounter in trying to make sense of large bodies of information. However even key libraries such as the Library of Congress are constantly having to review their strategies and approaches to alternative methods of cataloguing such as copy cataloguing and minimal cataloguing in order to dramatically bring down their backlogs. On-line journal abstracting databases also traditionally provide very thorough bibliographic detail created by professional graduate level staff. The combination of a variety of materials from different sources may provide a variety of classification schemes and types of subject headings. These can be added to the bundle's hierarchies.

Although at the document level the classification may not easily convey a sufficient level of separation, nevertheless it can be used in the way a library user traditionally browses a library shelf. On the World Wide Web we see subject catalogues such as the WWW Virtual Library being developed to give a useful alternative way to access a huge amount of information. At the same time Internet Yellow Pages directories, while they become obsolete fairly quickly, still sell because they provide an overview of accessible items which is not yet so easily scanned from today's computer screen. The options for locating information are varied and different ones will suit different users at different times and also the same users at different levels of understanding.

The level of a item - who it is intended for- has less frequently been emphasised in the past. It may perhaps be highlighted by a pointer such as a treatment code or a readership category, but this may become more important in the future with the enormous volumes generated by both paper and electronic publication. The catalogue entries produced by the information specialist may give a degree of rigour to the information retrieval process. However, a multimedia bundle will frequently contain documents produced by and often further modified by the authors, particularly in the academic environment, which do not have the advantage of such in-depth indexing.

One way to compensate for this might simply be to provide or point to a glossary or dictionary which helps the searchers choose their terms. The linking mechanisms of Microcosm do, in any case, give considerable help in retrieving relevant items. Free text terms used by the author are often more up to date in style and therefore more akin to the searcher's own vocabulary. The art is in balancing the effort required versus the result, particularly as terminology can change dramatically as one moves forwards or backwards in time.

The Web is complicated by the fact that only part of it is publicly accessible and by unresolved issues over rights. It is not clear, for example, that a Web site may be "harvested" for purposes of preservation without the knowledge and permission of the various rights holders. Several people in both the technical and the arts communities urged attention to "ephemera" as well as to "published" works. A number of respondents in film, television, and sound noted that again, the distinction between publication and ephemera is blurred.

Within the Web itself are emerging distinctions between the "surface" Web and the "deep" Web. E-books and e-journals download content from the Web to their respective formats and include hyperlinks to the Web for ancillary augmentation. The advent of interactive television also invites new forms of multimedia that combine resources built for the Web with those created for broadcasting in digital form. Moreover, an item that appears seamless to the user is frequently a composite document.

Formats as well understood as electronic scholarly journals are built as multimedia objects in which the constituent elements may include text, images, animation, or advertisements, each of which may be encoded in a different format. Finally, several people from the arts communities emphasized the importance of collecting the version of the object that the creator (e.g., the director of a film) considered final in the format that he or she considered final.

There are complexities to notions of "authorship"; many of these are not new to digital but are magnified by the circumstances under which digital products may be distributed and used. These complexities are related to the complicated intellectual property considerations that surround digital information. Even in a format as carefully studied as is that of electronic scholarly journals, creation and deposit can involve numerous stakeholders, and the number of interested parties multiplies in sound, television, and film, in which individuals and entities have traditionally had rights in the processes of creation and distribution. Frank Romano points out that the e-books world is witnessing changes in traditional roles and functions; for example, writers can self-publish and thus become distributors, while software companies can behave like publishers.

The issues, which include technical obsolescence and standards, metadata, information security, and the overall architecture of the system, are by no means discrete. Several writers pointed out that the issue is not only making sure that bits survive but also ensuring the preservation of a technical environment that will permit future retrieval of the information, the work as envisioned by the author or creator, and the experience of the user. The longevity of the storage medium was a consistent concern, as was signal degradation and software obsolescence.

One technical expert urged that degradation be compared with the process by which a photograph ages. The image fades; the medium on which the image is printed also disintegrates. There are methods for error detection; however, at some point, there is concern that the integrity of the digital object is compromised. One solution is migration from one medium to another. Particularly for e-books, where so much of the design is predicated on screen size, re-creating the experience for future users implies access to the device that was intended to display the content.

The rapid obsolescence of some formats, as well as the plethora of standards, was widely considered to be a barrier both to creation and to preservation. Those who had opinions on open versus proprietary standards favored the former because they were believed to facilitate management of the archive and its content. This applies to a broad range of issues, from operating systems to markup language, compression, and fonts. Before September 11, 2001, few people consulted had strong opinions on information security, but those who did thought that it was important as a guarantor of trust.

One example that was offered was the information typically provided on copyright registration concerning the authors, who might use a pseudonym or who might wish to keep their own addresses, or the addresses of their agents, from general use. There are overlaps between this kind of information and the information included in metadata. At least one person cautioned against excessive restriction, arguing that too many restrictions inhibit accountability. Those who addressed technical issues tended to favor distributed rather than centralized systems, because the former would accommodate a high degree of "local" variation within shared protocols.

There were also calls for interoperability, which would make it possible for information to be shared across platforms and among vendors. Metadata, or "data about data," are simultaneously a standard, a management and access tool, and a feature of the system architecture. Moreover, as pointed out by Lyman in his study of archiving the Web, the metadata discussions reveal the different visions of archiving as embodied by the library and computer science communities. He writes, "The librarian tends to look at the content of the Web page as the object to be described and preserved. The computer scientist tends to look at the Web as a technology for linking information, thus looks at the Web as a system of relationships."

One of the functions of metadata, as the various schemes have evolved since 1995, is outlining the terms and conditions of use-that is, access. Few failed to identify intellectual property rights (IPR) management and fair use as key issues. The complexity of this set of issues varies across media. Some arose from unfamiliarity with the distinction that is common among traditional preservation circles in which use of rare objects, for example, can be calibrated and surrogates used in their stead. While there was near unanimity on the importance of managing intellectual property responsibly, no voices called for some version of complete lockout.

Indeed, one representative from a major company with interests in several areas thought that the most important issues were both protection of intellectual property rights and ease of use (with appropriate accommodation for potential users with special needs). There was widespread acknowledgment of the need to find a balance between the economic needs of the creators and distributors and the legitimate uses of the works, but there was a range of opinion as to what that meant. Some suggested ways to handle management of intellectual property "behind the scenes" through technological means, which could be coupled with pricing that discouraged inappropriate use.

Several people felt that existing laws were sufficient: what is required, they maintained, is appropriate enforcement. Others believed that there was a need to clarify the law. Given that the Web is an international phenomenon, attention to international law is particularly important. Several people pointed out that copyright as a mechanism, which had arisen in the context of print, had already begun to fray under the stress of its application to media other than text, and that it was becoming increasingly unwieldy.

Bibliography

Arms, William Y., *Digital Libraries*, Cambridge, MA: The MIT Press, 2000.

Blandford, Ann, and George Buchanan, "Usability of Digital Libraries: A Source of Creative Tensions with Technical Developments." *TCDL Bulletin*, Summer 2003.

Borgman, Christine L., "Digital Libraries and the Continuum of Scholarly Communication." *Journal of Documentation* 56: 412-430, July 2000

Borgman, Christine L.,"Multi-Media, Multi-Cultural, and Multi-Lingual Digital Libraries: Or How Do We Exchange Data in 400 Languages?" D-Lib Magazine, June 1997

Bishop, Ann Peterson, "Measuring Access, Use, and Success in Digital Libraries." *The Journal of Electronic Publishing* 4, no. 2, 1998.

Chowdhury, G.G., and Sudatta Chowdhury, "Digital Library Research: Major Issues and Trends." *Journal of Documentation* 55 : 409-488, September 1999

Cole, Timothy W., "Creating a Framework of Guidance for Building Good Digital Collections", First Monday 7 May 2002

Graham, Peter S., "Requirements for the Digital Research Library", *College & Research Libraries* 56 : 331-339, July 1995.

Greenstein, Daniel, "Digital Libraries and Their Challenges" *Library Trends* 49 : 290-303, Fall 2000

Harter, Stephen P., "Scholarly Communication and the Digital Library: Problems and Issues." *Journal of Digital Information*, 1, no. 1 1997

Kilker, Julian, and Geri Gay, "The Social Construction of a Digital Library: A Case Study Examining Implications for Evaluation." *Information Technology and Libraries* 17: 60-70, June 1998.

Klemperer, Katharina, and Stephen Chapman, "Digital Libraries: A Selected Resource Guide." Information Technology and Libraries 16, : 126-131, September 1997.

Lesk, Michael, "Going Digital." Scientific American 276 : 58-60, March 1997.

Lesk, Michael, "The Organization of Digital Libraries." *Science & Technology Libraries* 17, nos. 3/4 : 9-25, 1999

McKay, Sally, "Digitization in an Archival Environment." *Electronic Journal of Academic and Special Librarianship* 4, no.1, 2003

Marchionini, Gary, and Hermann Maurer., "The Roles of Digital Libraries in Teaching and Learning." Communications of the ACM 38 : 67-75, April 1995

Pope, Nolan F., "Digital Libraries: Future Potentials and Challenges." Library Hi Tech 16, nos. 3-4 : 147-155, 1998.

Smith, Terence R., "A Brief Update on the Alexandria Digital Library Project: Constructing a Digital Library for Geographically-Referenced Materials." *D-Lib Magazine*, March 1996.

Schatz, Bruce R. "Information Retrieval in Digital Libraries: Bringing Search to the Net." *Science*, 327-334, 17 January 1997

Schwartz, Candy, "Digital Libraries: An Overview." *The Journal of Academic Librarianship* 26 (November 2000): 385-393.

Shiri, Ali, "Digital Library Research: Current Developments and Trends." *Library Review* 52, no. 5 : 198-202, 2003

Waters, Donald, "Developing Digital Libraries: Four Principles for Higher Education." EDUCAUSE Review 36 : 58-59, September/October 2001

Index

Additional application services 13
Art Museum Image Consortium (AMICO) 23

Business to consumer (B2C) 284

Collaborative Digital Reference Service (CDRS) 276
Collection management 177
Computer-Aided Design (CAD) 105
Cooperative Online Resource Catalog (CORC) 276
Council on Library and Information Resources (CLIR) 45

Digital Convergence 40
Digital Libraries Initiative (DLI) 166
Digital Object Identifiers (DOIs) 183
Digital Repository Service (DRS) 186
Digital representations 162
Digital responsibilities 179
Digital Revolution 32
Document Type Definition (DTD) 153

E-journals 168
Electronic Business XML (EbXML) 15
Electronic library 2
Encoded Archival Description (EAD) 26, 153
Environmental controls 21
Extensible Markup Language (XML) 14, 53

Fault-isolated dynamic system 12

Geographic Information Systems (GIS) 105
Global Legal Information Network (GLIN) 120

Information retrieval 173
Information Technology (IT) 6
Information-seeking activities 273
Intellectual Property Conservancies (IPCs) 59

Machine-Readable Cataloging (MARC) 1
Metadata 18
Metadata Encoding and Transmission Standard (METS) 19
Microfilming initiatives 21
National Information Standards Organization (NISO) 30
National Institute of Standards

and Technology (NIST) 30
National Science Foundation (NSF) 8

Open Archival Information System (OAIS) 112

Personal information retrieval systems 1
Plagiarism 4
Policy base mechanism 13
Portable Document Format (PDF) 124
Preservation Description Information (PDI) 114
Preservation strategy 50
Preserving Access to Digital Information (PADI) 24

Reliability, Availability, and Serviceability (RAS) 11
Research Libraries Group (RLG) 23, 42
Rich Text Format (RTF) 159
Rules for Archival Description (RAD) 153

Simple Object Access Protocol (SOAP) 14
Standard General Markup Language (SGML) 14, 53
Submission Information Package (SIP) 187
Sun Microsystems 5

Tax-supported research institutions 4
Technological obsolescence 100
Text Encoding Initiative (TEI) 53
Traditional research library 3

Uniform Resource Locator (URL) 110

Virtual Learning Environment (VLE) 10

Web Services Description Language (WSDL) 15
Web-accessible resources 272
Web-enabled device 7
World Wide Web 274

DIGITAL LIBRARIES

DIGITAL LIBRARIES

(In 3 Volumes)

DIGITAL LIBRARY AND ARCHIVES

(Volume-2)

Editor

Dr. Vijya Lakshmi

ISHA BOOKS

DELHI-110 033

Digital Libraries

Rs. 2500 (Set)
Rs. 835 (each volume)

ISBN: 81-8205-109-6 (Set)
ISBN: 81-8205-111-8 (Vol.2)

Reprinted in 2011 in India by
Isha Publications
B-63, Ist Floor
New Gupta Colony
Near DDA Market
Delhi-110009

Printed at: G. Print Process, Delhi

Contents

Preface vii

1 **Digital Archives** 1
Records Management Programme; Role of Audiovisuals; Organisation of Archives; Rights and Responsibilities of Archives; Archival Life Cycle; Open Archive Initiatives.

2 **Digital Library Development** 78
Content Management in Web Environment; New Measures for Digital Collection; Impact of Library on Teaching and Learning; Institutional Repositories in the Digital Age; Importance of Institutional Repositories; A Global Resource Programme; Role of Bibliographer; Role of Library in Education; Online Service Providers.

3 **Preservation of Digital Heritage** 118
The UNESCO Draft Charter on the Preservation of the Digital Heritage; Digital heritage and Digital Continuity; Types of Digital Heritage; Understanding Digital Preservation; Strategies for Preserving Digital Materials; Data management; Responsibility in Digital Preservation; Managing Digital Preservation Programmes; Tools for

Preservation Programmes; Perspectives of Management; Metadata Management; Preservation of Metadata; Data protection in Digital Preservation; Role of documentation.

4 **Roles and Responsibilities of Archiving** **200**
Collaborative Digital Reference Service (CDRS).

5 **Digital Library Classification** **214**
Study of Digital Archiving by Research Libraries Group (RLG); High Performance Digital Library Classification System; Knowledge Networking; Digital South Asia Library (DSAL).

6 **Digital Library Collections and Access** **263**
Electronic Publishing; Role of Online Catalogs; Scholarly Communication Issues; Preserving Digital Content; Research Library Collections; Elements of Institutional Repository; Promoting Open Access; Open Archives initiative (OAi); Open Archives Metadata Set (OAMS); Open Archives; Dienst Subset; Dienst System.

Bibliography 307

Index 309

Preface

The primary goal of a library is to collect, preserve and give access to recorded knowledge, in all documentary forms, for the benefit of all engaged in research and learning, or with other information needs. Library traditionally have formed a preservation safety net for materials that will be transmitted to subsequent generations of information seekers and scholars. For paper-based documents, provision of adequate storage conditions was the best means to help ensure that materials would remain readable far into the future.

The digital age creates new delivery and access alternatives for libraries, as well as new preservation challenges. In turn the expectations of library users are changing. As people discover information resources online at their computer workstations, they also want access to the contents of libraries in that same online environment.

Digital libraries and archives play a critical role in organizing, preserving, and providing access to the various information resources of society. In the relatively stable world of printed, hand-written, and mechanically reproduced information, repositories managed to preserve a rich array of scholarly communications, documentary evidence, and useful information for specialized scholars and for the general public.

However, libraries and archives, face technical, legal, and organizational challenges in responding to the new demands of digital preservation. Digital materials are especially vulnerable to loss and destruction because they are stored on fragile magnetic and optical media that deteriorate rapidly and that can fail suddenly from exposure to heat, humidity, airborne contaminants, or faulty reading and writing devices. Even if the media are preserved intact, digital materials become unreadable if the playback devices necessary to retrieve information from the media become obsolete or if the software that translates digital information from machine-to human-readable form is no longer available.

The present publication provides a comprehensive analysis of set-up, processes and significance of digital libraries and archives. It also narrates the serious challenges confronted by them. The content of the book will be highly valuable to librarians, information scientists, teachers and students of library science and anyone dealing with digital library collections.

Editor

1

Digital Archives

Archives have been involved in great changes with the use of modern information technology to automate archives management, especially through the application of computers for the arrangement and description of records. The result is faster and more accurate arrangement and description, as well as more efficient information retrieval. The use of computers in Asian archives is not widely developed, but the employment of word-processing or database systems to produce finding aids or to undertake other aspects of the management of archival material is now to be found in Australia, China, Indonesia, Japan, Macao, Malaysia, the Republic of Korea, Singapore and Viet Nam.

An Asian computer network for exchanging archival information does not yet exist. Archives in Asia play an important role as an indispensable instrument for the history of both the whole continent and the individual nations. Consequently they must offer well-organized and structured services in order to give easier access to citizens and researchers. Until recently most archives in

Asia were very isolated and unprivileged institutions. They have been gradually developed and provided with increased resources, as a result of the growing awareness of the important role they play in society. Yet the present situation is far from ideal.

The scarcity of economic resources and the lack of proper archival policies are the main problems. The situation of archives in Asia, assume that all countries have archives at the national level, together with archival legislation which defines and establishes general policies and standards for the preservation of the national archival heritage. Many archives use microfilming technology to preserve records and a few have now started to implement and develop computerised systems to help with the arrangement and description of archival materials. Almost all the archives issue archival publications and are members of international associations.

However, there are less positive aspects: lack of specialised human resources and almost non-existent professional archival education and training. In the absence of qualified personnel the archives are experiencing difficulties in tackling the problems of records and archives management. Another major problem is the uncertain financial background -often archives institutions have very limited budgets which do not guarantee them adequate resources for the implementation of a proper archives policy. The statutes of most countries in the Arab region have appeared in various publications.

The number of countries without any real legislation on archives none the less remains high. However, apart from Morocco, they are small countries where the state apparatus is relatively new, and whose institutions until recently amounted to local governments. Furthermore, many of these countries are still monarchies. Morocco is a special case: archives are kept for the King's private administrative offices but little is done in the sphere of public administration. The shortage or absence of legislation on archives is a function of the lack of importance some decision-makers attribute to it. The public conception of archives and their purpose is another factor here.

Almost everywhere archives are esteemed only for their heritage value; the role documents play in managing the country's affairs and assisting the decision-making process is forgotten. As record-keeping practices are not changing, there is no incentive to draft new legislation. Standardisation is everywhere less developed in the archive sector than in other information sciences. In the Arab States, standardisation is at best confined to applying known standards, particularly as regards conditions of conservation and building construction. Archival institutions are relatively recent in Arab countries.

Many countries took over the archive system established by the colonial power; others set up archive services much later. Some countries, such as Oman and Jordan, still have no real administration for archives. The attachment of an archival institution to a supervisory body can have an enormous influence on the development of the archive sector. Archival institutions under the supervision of a body well placed in the political hierarchy have more facilities at their disposal for the accomplishment of their task, provided that decision-makers are willing. Many Arab archival institutions are not only attached to ministries of culture with little political authority, but are often dependent on other cultural sectors such as archaeology.

The subordination of archive services to other structures often results in the marginalisation of the field. As far as the administrative organisation of archives is concerned, a distinction can be drawn between institutions regarded as departments coming under a ministry and those established as autonomous bodies with a legal status and financial autonomy.

Organization of Arab archives at regional and local levels is embryonic. Except for Algeria and the Sudan, which have set up regional archive services, such organization is non-existent in Arab countries. The same is true of municipal archives, which exist in only a few large Arab towns. Purpose-built premises for archives are important tools for any national policy in this field. This type of building is still rare in Arab countries. The comprehensive view of archives which sees documents as records from the moment they come into being is not widespread in Arab countries.

Records Management Programme

The aim of the records management programme is obviously to improve the efficiency of government agencies. For some public establishments and businesses the tools have already been prepared and applied. As regards government departments, the plan has just begun and should be completed by the year 2000. Records management in the private sector in Arab states is no better than in the public. The strategic sectors of the economy are still controlled by the state, so the private sector consists essentially of small and medium-sized companies, many of which have become aware of the importance of records management as an aid to the decision-making process and a factor in more rational management.

Records management is not a common practice in the administration of Arab countries; it is not inherent to Arab civilization. Although the Arab world had a highly developed administrative and documentary tradition in the Middle Ages, the region went through a long period of decadence marked by political instability that lasted until the colonial period.

The collection and organization of records determines the development of historical studies. It should be noted in this respect that records concerning the twentieth century are relatively little developed in Arab countries, and the same is true of historical studies of the modern period. Historical study often remains the prerogative of specialised researchers. Some research on genealogy or local matters is carried out by individuals, especially the elderly, but not much in comparison with that in developed countries.

Few catalogues of inventories or archive documents, or books based on archive documents for a general audience or for educational purposes, are published. In contrast, the publication of annotated manuscripts, particularly religious and even scientific manuscripts, is flourishing. Multimedia techniques are making slow progress in the Arab States. Their use calls for financial resources and a propitious administrative and human environment. Information retrieval applications are being developed in some countries and a few CD-ROMs relating to heritage have been produced including the CD-ROM on the fragments of the Sanaa Koran produced within the framework of UNESCO's Memory of the World Programme, and the CD-ROM on archaeological sites produced by the Regional Information Technology and Software Engineering Centre (RITSEC) in Egypt.

The spread of multimedia in the archives sector, however, encounters the question of the medium's durability; conservation of original documents, because of their probative value, is indispensable. Multimedia at the moment, therefore, is more useful for distribution than for conservation. The archival situation in Africa is as varied as the multiplicity of nations that make up the huge continent. In as much as the more than fifty countries that comprise Africa vary in size from a geographical coverage of less than 1,000 square kilometres to 2.5 million square kilometres, populations of less than 100,000 to over 96 million, Gross Domestic Products (GDP) ranging from US$279 million to over US$110 billion and per capita incomes of US$60 to US$6,000, so too does the archival situation vary enormously.

At one end of the spectrum are nations that have only the most rudimentary of archival infrastructures and where even the most basic of archival services are absent; at the other end are countries which have established advanced archival services and whose facilities and infrastructures compare favourably with other nations in the developed world. While some countries in North Africa have archival institutions that date back several centuries, most sub-Saharan countries established national archives only after the Second World War. Benin, Burkina Faso, Namibia, Senegal, South Africa and Zimbabwe are among the few exceptions in sub-Saharan Africa that established national archives before 1950.

Most countries have promulgated national archives or public archives acts which provide the legal framework under which national archives institutions operate and which control and preserve the archival heritage. The very few that as yet have no archives legislation, such as Uganda and Ethiopia, have draft legislation which is in the process of being formalized.

The legislative instruments in general give the national archives the authority to deal with the records and archives of public entities such as central government, local government and parastatals. The degree of authority and control differs from country to country, ranging from giving advice to the right to inspect records and issue instructions for their proper management and handling. In most of the legislation, the destruction of public records is forbidden without the consent of the national archives.

In a number of countries the national archives also administer the legal deposit or printed publications acts which require the deposit of copies of all publications produced in the country. This in effect creates within the national archives the national reference library. The ministerial placement of national archives is varied, but the vast majority of the national archives are in the ministries of home affairs, education/ sports/art and culture, and the president's office. In a few countries advisory boards or committees have been created to assist the national archives. The standards applied in the acquisition, processing, preservation, conservation and usage of records and archives in general are those that have been developed by the International Council on Archives (ICA). In West Africa, standards from the Association Française de Normalisation (AFNOR) and the

International Standard Organisation (ISO) have been adopted.

There are also standards which have been developed by other organisations such as the International Records Management Council (IRMC), the Association of Records Managers and Administrators (ARMA) based in the United States, the Records Management Society of Great Britain, and other specialist organizations. Standards also tend to be influenced by the practices of the former colonial powers, because most of the national archival institutions are based on the records of the former metropolitan entities and are reflective of the latter's administrative structures and systems.

The type of training received by the records managers and archivists, and the institutions giving the training, also have a bearing on the standards used. Almost all countries in Africa have national archives or public records offices. The national archival institutions play the key role in the organisation, management and preservation of records and archives at the national level. Their mandate tends to be allembracing because of the absence of similar facilities at the local government and parastatal levels and in the private sector, as is the case in other regions of the world such as Europe and North America.

In a few countries there are municipal and local government archives, but these are the exception. In quite a number of countries the national archives have established regional offices but the functionality of these in the majority of cases is rather weak. Privatesector archives exist in some countries but these tend to be limited to large multinational corporations. In a number of countries private commercial records centres have been established. Architecture plays an essential role in the preservation and conservation of the archival heritage. The national archives in most countries occupy either purpose-built or converted buildings.

But many archival institutions are housed in buildings which are inadequate. In some cases, such as Cape Verde, Ethiopia, Guinea, Lesotho and Uganda, the archives are temporarily housed in such places as the university library, the basement of a former colonial secretariat building or the national library. Few countries, however, have adequate space for the storage of the archives and most, even those in purposebuilt repositories, are facing severe space shortages in buildings that were filled long ago.

Many of the institutions are unable to receive new accessions because there is no storage space. There are also problems concerning airconditioning. Although most of the purpose built repositories originally included air-conditioning systems, these systems in several cases have broken down or become non-functional for one reason or another. This has created serious difficulties, as often such buildings do not allow for adequate natural ventilation and the archival holdings are therefore at risk. The size of holdings of conventional archives varies enormously from country to country.

These archives can be varied and diverse: diaries and collections of eminent and scholarly individuals, archives of churches, educational institutions and sporting organizations, and business archives recording official transactions such as policies, procedures and meetings. Archival collections are also held by various other institutions and individuals: religious organizations, universities, libraries and some large corporations can contain sizeable archival holdings. In 1987, for example, the National Archives of Mali and Guinea were to be handicapped by insufficient human resources.

The high staff turnover is attributed to a number of factors including low salaries, low grading, lack of attractive career structures and the lure of the private sector. Government registry staff constitute the bulk of the records management staff in all countries. The registry staff, however, are not well trained and of low calibre. The morale of registry staff is quite low in most countries and they operate without recognition and some of the basic necessities. Most national archives in Africa have reprographic and conservation units or laboratories.

These reprographic facilities consist mainly of microfilming equipment but there is also other document-reproduction equipment such as photocopiers and duplicators. Microfilming is used primarily for acquiring copies of documents whose originals cannot be obtained, for preservation purposes when documents are in a fragile condition or are constituted of materials which deteriorate rapidly, such as newspapers, and for the production of multiple copies of documents, as in the case of the records of the former Federation of Rhodesia and Nyasaland, which were microfilmed to provide copies to each of the three successor countries: Malawi, Zambia and Zimbabwe.

Document conservation unit have been created to repair and rehabilitate archival materials from depositors that are received in a deteriorated condition. The main method of repair and restoration utilised is lamination, although a limited amount of encapsulation is done in some countries. Most of the countries with conservation units have lamination machines and only in a few countries is the hand method used.

Countries such as Ethiopia and the United Republic of Tanzania do not have conservation units. The need for conservation in a continent with such a harsh climatic environment is self-evident. Unfortunately, in the government ministries and departments of a number of countries in Africa, the condition in which records are being maintained is a cause for great concern. There are numerous detailing situations in which records were exposed to excessive heat, humidity, mould, light, air pollution, insects and rodents.

Records have often been dumped in storerooms and sheds where the roofs leaked, the windows were broken and doors were only partially effective. This grave situation has given rise in the last ten years to international rescue missions which have been used to salvage the situation and avoid total disaster. Such missions have been launched in the Gambia, Uganda and the United Republic of Tanzania. For those countries that do have reprographic and conservation facilities, there are often insurmountable difficulties in maintaining equipment and acquiring adequate and appropriate supplies of chemicals and other materials.

With a few exceptions such as Botswana, Kenya, Namibia, South Africa and Zimbabwe, the national archival institutions only concern themselves with semi-current and non-current records due for transfer to the national archives. And yet by that time, irreparable damage will have been caused to the records. Many countries have established records centres for semi-current records, but in a good number of the cases the records centres have been completely full for many years, making it difficult for new accessions to be received. As a result the records remain in the ministries and departments. The crisis that faces many countries in terms of records management was aptly captured in one consultant's described file index systems that were rudimentary or nonexistent. In several registries records were strewn all over the floors and under shelves; file covers were often torn and crumpled, frequently with large numbers of pages missing; heaps of dirty, tattered and misfiled records could be found in corners and on tops of cupboards; there was a lack of discipline among staff who seemed to be driven more by tradition than by need; and office equipment was in short supply, the few filing cabinets available being rusty and damaged.

This is by no means the scenario in all African countries, and indeed many have well-organized registries, but all the same such situations are a cause for concern. Only in a few countries do national archives carry out regular visits to ministries and departments. While standing instructions for the disposal of time-expired records exist in many countries, these are often outdated and cover only a small proportion of the records produced by the ministries and departments. There are cases where time-expired records are not disposed of because of lack of capacity in the national archives.

In most countries public records become archives and accessible to the public after thirty years. Some countries of huge backlogs in the appraisal of records and the processing of archives, thereby delaying the availability of the archives to the public. There are often finding aids to the collections, and in some cases guides have been published. Unfortunately, in many countries these have not been updated for many years and some predate the attainment of national independence. Many of the archival institutions have search room facilities for researchers and the public. Some of these rooms have facilities for viewing stored cine films and microfilms, but in certain cases these collections are inaccessible because microfilm readers and projection equipment have broken down or become unserviceable. Both static and mobile exhibitions are occasionally mounted by some institutions while a few have educational programmes.

Very few in the private sector have received records management training other than the cursory treatment that it receives in secretarial and office management training courses. The standards of records management in the majority of businesses is therefore very low and no real attempt has been made to mobilize resources and effect improvement. The notable exceptions are the large multinational corporations, which often have elaborate records management procedures developed at their head offices. They also often have established in-house records centres and archives facilities. The availability of unemployed archivists has contributed to the development of archives in banks and large firms in countries like Senegal.

In a few countries, such as Zimbabwe and South Africa, commercial records centres have also been established. In some countries consulting firms are providing services in records and information management. Although increasing numbers of private firms are manufacturing and distributing records management materials, supplies and equipment, a large technology gap remains in comparison with the developed world. South Africa is probably the main exception in this regard. The privatization of public enterprises has also endangered the welfare of large quantities of records. Even when the national archives could cater for the archival collections of former public enterprises such as parastatals, very few of these enterprises made use of this facility or had any relations with the national archives.

When privatizing, little attention has been paid to the fate of the records which in the first instance were public records and archives but now belong to a private entity. The national archives have in any case, by and large, lacked the capacity to intervene in order to ensure that the records are adequately catered for. ICA is by far the most prominent professional archival association in Africa. It has established a network of regional branches: the West African Regional Branch of the International Council on Archives (WARBICA); the Central African Regional Branch of the International Council on Archives (CENARBICA); and the East and Southern African Regional Branch of the International Council on Archives (ESARBICA). Many national archives are also affiliated to such international organizations as the International Association of Sound Archives (IASA) and the International Federation of Library Associations and Institutions (IFLA).

There are other international professional associations in Africa. Archivists from countries in the Commonwealth, for instance, have generally affiliated with the Association of Commonwealth Archivists and Records Managers (ACARM). Some countries such as Benin, Ghana, Mali and Senegal have established national associations of records managers and archivists, but many others find that the number of archivists and records managers is too small for the establishment of viable associations. Africa lacks adequate training facilities for professional and technical staff. Attempts made in the early 1970s to establish regional training schools were only partially successful.

While the school at Dakar, Senegal, for French-speaking Africa seems to have fared better with its two degrees (technical and professional), the school for English-speaking Africa in Ghana has now become no more than a national centre. A number of countries have as a result established their own educational facilities at the national level. Countries such as Botswana and Kenya have graduate schools in archives and information science. Training facilities have been established also at the paraprofessional level, but technical training facilities in conservation and reprography are virtually unavailable.

In the absence of such facilities, it is not surprising that most archives staff have to be educated or trained overseas. For English-speaking Africa, this has mostly been done by University College London (United Kingdom) which runs a Master's programme. France has provided much of the training for French-speaking Africa, and Germany and Portugal have provided training for their former colonies. India has also done a lot of training, especially in conservation. A number of countries, such as South Africa, run their own national programmes within the national archives or through longdistance training, as in the case of the South African Higher Diploma in Archives Studies run by Technikon SA. Other countries with their own training programmes include Senegal and Mauritius. Continuing training in Africa is provided at the national, regional and international levels through workshops and seminars that are organized from time to time

The curriculum being developed within Africa is beginning to put more and more emphasis on the management of current and semi-current records and on automation. While traditional archives principles and practices are still being taught, some elements which are less relevant to the African continent, such as palaeography and sigillography, are now being dropped.

The historical bias and orientation is also becoming less pronounced in accordance with a changing professional perception of the role of archivists and the demands of information technology that are requiring a different breed of archivist. Archives are recognized as the primary instrument through which a nation's historical heritage is preserved. African nations by and large recognize the importance of archives in the preservation of the nation's history, and African scholars make extensive use of archival sources.

A large part of the written archival sources, however, relate to the period after colonization of the continent, and this has forced African nations to mount programmes for the collection and preservation of oral historical sources which narrate and chronicle the lives of the indigenous people. Many countries have developed active programmes for oral history and oral tradition. Some are based at universities and special institutions while others are run by national archives. The latter has resulted in soul-searching by some African archivists, who feel that national archives should not dissipate scarce resources by indulging in activities for which they are neither well equipped nor trained. Archives in Africa have long been viewed as a cultural heritage. There are many instances where there has been conflict with museums who do not view favourably the retention by national archives of museum artefacts.

Archivists hold the view that these constitute an integral component of archives collections bestowed on them. There is an increasing perception, though, that while archives cannot be divorced from the national cultural heritage, nevertheless national archives must pay more attention to information management operations, especially the management of current and non-current records.

This view is strongly supported and promulgated by the United Kingdom based International Records Management Trust (IRMT), which has conducted several rescue missions in Africa and has concentrated on overhauling registry systems in those countries. IRMT currently in several countries including the Gambia, Ghana, Uganda and the United Republic of Tanzania.

The increasing emphasis on records management has also refocused archival activities on the administrative structures of government. Whereas in the past archivists viewed administrative history in relation to those records and archives received and registered, they are now being encouraged to be proactive and to be involved in the current operations of the record-generating agencies. France, Germany, Portugal and the United Kingdom were the major colonial powers in Africa.

On the attainment of independence and nationhood by the African countries, some records were transferred to the metropolitan countries while other natural accumulations of administrative records remained in situ. The new nations laid claim to some of the transferred records, and a limited amount of repatriation was done. By and large, however, the former colonial powers remained steadfast in their claims on the records and instead encouraged the copying of these records to give the new nations access.

In many countries government requirements for automated data processing are fulfilled by central computing departments which usually have mainframe computers. Little has been done by national archives in Africa to deal with electronic media and the electronic records being generated by various agencies. In a few cases, such as Namibia, South Africa and Zimbabwe, special facilities have been put in place, but still the services provided are limited and do not embrace control back to the point of electronic record creation in the agencies.

South Africa began automation in 1974 and today has a database of almost 6 million records. The information technology revolution has provided both an opportunity and a challenge for archives. On the one hand, the availability of such mass storage devices as optical disks creates an opportunity for archives, and computerization can enhance the national archives' capacity to process, manipulate and make information accessible. On the other hand, this opportunity has not been grasped, and this failure of archival institutions has been accompanied by a failure generally to cope with the challenges that the multimedia society poses as record-creating agencies adopt new technologies. Most African archivists feel that it is inevitable that the disciplines of archives, records management and library science, hitherto seen as separate and distinct, will merge.

African archivists nevertheless caution against failure to recognize the unique nature of archives or to discard the time-immemorial principles of 'provenance' and 'sanctity of the record group'. The major problems facing archives in Africa are as much archives-specific as they are reflections of the general malaise afflicting the continent. Many parts of the continent have been ravaged by wars, droughts and other man-made as well as natural disasters which have inflicted untold misery and suffering.

Infrastructures and technical facilities established in the 1960s and early 1970s have disintegrated in some countries. Government ministries and departments operate without functional registry systems, with untrained and sometimes uncaring staff and without manuals to give guidance. The overall archival situation is one of severe crisis requiring urgent remedial measures.

This must not detract, however, from the achievements of those African nations that have established viable and vibrant archival systems, and which in some respects have pioneered significant breakthroughs in archives development and are at par with similar institutions worldwide.

This sharp contrast gives hope to African archives; the need is for international support to those nations and institutions which already have achieved excellence and international help to foster development in those less fortunate and facing catastrophe. The capacity for classification—for seeing patterns in practices—is an essential characteristic of archivists. Characterizing the state of archives in the countries of Europe, together with Canada and the United States, requires identifying the faultlines that divide the region as well as the considerable bonds that bind it together.

Archives have three universal purposes: to select the records of institutions, the papers of individuals and families and the artificial collections of documentary materials that have enduring value; to preserve them; and to make them available for use. Individual nations and archival institutions accomplish these purposes through programmes which vary in emphasis and administration. Identifying the varieties of archival practice in Europe and North America requires assembling and analysing a sizeable quantity of data. All European archives owe a debt to the Greco-Roman archival tradition. There are, however, several obvious groupings of archives, either by virtue of the legislative structure of the nation or by tradition.

All archives, however, whether in governments, businesses or private organizations, must soon manage electronic records. At the European Summit on Archives in 1996, delegates agreed that the three principal issues for European archivists are the management of electronic records, training for personnel and preservation of the European archival heritage.

Consequently, the critical issue for most European archives is providing guidance to the records creators, in particular in the area of electronic records, not in finding ever larger storage facilities for semi-current records. The electronic records issue binds Europe together. Although the development of the computerized office generally occurred earlier in Western Europe, the computerization of Central and Eastern Europe has occurred at lightning speed, as external donors put computers in parliaments and courts and as businesses snapped them up for commercial ventures. This means that the intensity of the computer question, particularly for the very latest systems, is at least as pervasive in Eastern Europe as in the West.

Archival education increasingly is challenged to provide the new skills needed to manage archives in the current information age. Two shifts are occurring simultaneously: first, records are created and maintained electronically in the entities that are the sources of archival holdings, requiring archives to move aggressively to protect the archival information in the complex environment of modern management systems; second, archives are themselves introducing and adapting automation to facilitate work in the archives. Recent graduates from academic archival programmes emphasizing digital, processrelated information are entering European archival institutions and challenging with their enthusiasm the staff already employed there.

Effective in-service training programmes are urgently needed throughout the European archival world in order to ensure that serious divisions of competency do not occur within the professional community. The third major concern identified at the archival summit in spring 1996 was preservation. Facilities are a central concern of archivists everywhere. The nature of archives is that the holdings are continuously expanding, and space utilization is a constant preoccupation.

European archives also 66% of central repositories with temperature and humidity controls, and 49% with microform storage accommodation to international standards. By contrast, state archives in the United States, 92% with purpose-built repositories and 92% with climate controls. All this suggests that European archives have major problems of adaptive re-use of older buildings, and consequently must struggle to maintain adequate preservation conditions for the materials stored within them. The average European national archives had 93,000 square metres of holdings in 1993.

In any event, the apparent lack of reformatting capacities in most European archives suggests that original records are made available to users, even those records that are extremely popular, setting up a future need for expensive conservation treatments. Preserving electronic records requires both physical facilities and the management of the physical and logical structures of the item. The technical facilities available in archives to handle electronic records are not as yet widespread. The techniques for preserving electronic records have evolved with the changes in the information industry; the preservation of flat files is well understood, the preservation of relational databases is fast becoming a standard practice and the preservation of electronic mail is rapidly emerging as a basic technique.

The fast advances in imaging technology are currently causing very serious problems for European archives, both because their popularity means that more and more images are created, and because the hardware and software dependency of imaging systems is extremely high and the rate of innovation extremely fast, leaving orphaned systems littering the way. Add to this the developments in the television industry, linking sound, image and text, and the problems mount. At present the only means of preservation is duplication to a current system, assuming that the system on which the image was generated is still operating (or can be made to operate). And yet it is essential that archives grapple with these issues, for in the long term this is the way records will be created, maintained, and used. The purpose of an archives is both preservation and use. One of the most significant developments for archives around the world has been the adoption of international standards for archival description, based on traditional archival practices but adapted for using computers to describe the holdings.

This is particularly important, because European archivists estimated in 1993 that only about 50% of their holdings were adequately described but 83% were using computers to describe holdings. There is considerable variation between Eastern and Central Europe on the one hand, and the rest of Europe on the other; in the former 55% of the institutions use computers for description while in the latter the figure is 91%.

As computers are rapidly introduced, adopting a standard format that can be shared electronically through the Internet will revolutionize archival use. No longer will users be tied to opening hours or transcontinental mail deliveries for service; neither will they have to consider wide variations in national descriptive practice. The day is approaching when the information about holdings can be searched in compatible versions worldwide.

The use of archives is increasing everywhere in Europe, but with particular ferocity in Central and Eastern Europe. As holdings long unavailable are now released for use, scholars and genealogists (to name only two user groups) are streaming into research rooms. The 1993 figures, based as they are on 1992 data, capture only the beginning of this wave.

Archives from Estonia to the Republic of Moldova faced new archival legislation; in addition, legislatures proposed other laws that had a vital impact on archival practices. In 1993, 63% of archives in Europe were operating under legislation passed or revised in the preceding ten years. While avoidance of obsolescence is all to the good, this means that the archivists must learn to interpret these laws, develop a body of practice that accords with them, and consider what further revisions are necessary.

Archivists unite in mourning the actual destruction of documents, but the problems of restitution and division have separated as much as they have united archivists. The break-up of the Ottoman and Habsburg Empires, and the fragmentation of the Soviet Union and the Yugoslavia of Tito, to name only a few examples in this century, caused documents of signal importance to one people to be lodged in the archives of another.

The European Summit on Archives, held in March 1996 in Munich, reaffirmed the desire for this continued, co-operative archival enterprise in Europe. The Council of Europe, UNESCO and the European Commission are major partners for the European Board. At the same meeting, UNESCO gave support to archives through the Memory of the World Programme and the Records and Archives Management Programme (RAMP), and an emphasis on access to archives as a basis for democratic societies.

The development of the Internet and the World Wide Web is bringing unprecedented changes to the archival enterprise. In describing and making available holdings, archivists have long developed finding aids, printed them and distributed them in person or by mail. Records have most often been used in research rooms; sometimes records are used through photocopies ordered after consultation with an archivist; sometimes records are used on microform ordered by an archivist and accompanied by some form of description. The general pattern, however, has been of direct communication, one-to-one, between archivist and user, with the archivist able to answer questions, clarify the structure of the holdings and in general mediate the research use.

The World Wide Web and the Internet have changed that. The new pattern is unmediated communication in multiples. Archivists place descriptions on a Web site, and users from all over the world have simultaneous access without intervention of the archivist. Copies of documents placed on the Web site may be used in the order the archivist envisions, or may be used in random sequences over the course of the research. These four great engines of change are reflected in the work of the European archival profession at large.

Ethical and legal issues are now more visible than at any time since the start of the Cold War, resulting in the development of an international Code of Ethics for Archivists, the above-mentioned statement of principles on replevin, the development of a model for archival legislation and a statement on the management of records of former repressive regimes. Bilateral efforts, particularly within the framework of a multilateral body such as ICA or the Council of Europe, have a renewed vigour. But perhaps the most striking feature is the growing importance of professional associations. In North America, professional archival associations have a long, strong history. In both Canada and the United States the majority of archives are outside the administrative control of the national archives, and therefore the professional associations have played a critical role in fostering uniquely important bonds among individual archivists employed in widely divergent institutional settings. Many of these archivists are employed within a library, particularly a university library, and library practice has often influenced the archival tradition in the United States.

Standards for archival education, codes of ethics, statements of best practices, publication of the major journals and newsletters, and a host of other initiatives have come from these societies of professionals organized in their own self-interest, rather than from the central archival institution. In Western Europe, the tradition of professional associations is also strong. The German archival association, the Netherlands association (now well over 100 years old) and the Society of Archivists in the United Kingdom, among others, are influential in shaping archival practice in their countries.

In Central and Eastern Europe the pattern is different. A few strong national associations, such as in Poland, do exist, but in most countries the association is weak and in some countries does not yet exist. What are emerging are regional groups, led by national archivists. European archivists are beginning to have new means of professional development at hand. Co-operative networks, not all dependent upon the intervention of national archives and national governments, are developing. A healthy, vital profession, with no fundamental barriers to professional conversations or to shared competencies, has emerged over the last decade. The archival profession as we know it is largely an invention of the twentieth century. It is now ready for the challenges of the twenty-first. The task of assessing the current situation affecting archives in Latin America and making valid generalizations about it is certainly not an easy one.

Although it is true that many shortcomings in the region's archives still exist and that in some countries there has been scant improvement, in others a sustained process of change has been taking place since the 1980s that allows us to claim a qualitative leap forward in the history of archives. All kinds of limitations have traditionally affected Latin American archives: administrative neglect, a lack of definition of their legal and administrative status, organizational weaknesses, inadequate and insufficient buildings and facilities, budget constraints, obsolete technical working methods, non-professionalized staff, and poor theoretical and methodological development of record-keeping. Most national archives in Latin America were created back in the nineteenth century once the process of achieving independence from the colonizing nations had been completed in the region.

The archives were set up with the twofold aim of collecting and preserving the documentary heritage corresponding to the colonial period and, at the same time, of receiving new records as they were created by the bodies and institutions in the new states. For a variety of different reasons, however, this latter function tended to be overlooked. Thus, by the second half of the twentieth century, many of the national archives had long since ceased to receive transfers from government departments. The overall image they presented was one of inward-looking institutions that devoted all their energy to research and were poorly represented within the wider administrative organization to which they belonged.

Moreover, their internal organization was oldfashioned, making them inoperative. This shortcoming was never corrected despite the attempts that were made to that effect by the different countries. Likewise, the second-rank position they held within the administrative structure made them, as a general rule, subordinate to other higher bodies, and that considerably reduced their capacity for action. However, recent years have seen an intensive overhaul take place in many national archives. This aims, on the one hand, at restoring their link with the government's archives in order to return the flow of documents to normal and, on the other, at reinforcing their institutional position within the national archive structure. In several countries this process has been further consolidated by the recent enactment of legislative provisions that place national archives at the head of the respective national archive systems and significantly extend their previous tasks.

The responsibilities conferred on the national archives by their new status include: drawing up, coordinating and overseeing national archive policy; organizing and managing the national archive system; setting technical standards and guidelines with a view to modernizing public records management; training the human resources required for the smooth running of the archives; guaranteeing and improving access to the information in the archives; and so on. In parallel with this process, and with a view to making it feasible for the national archives to perform these wide-ranging functions, in some countries they have been granted a higher-ranking position in the administrative hierarchy as well as the autonomy needed to develop and finance their own working programmes.

Take, for instance, the 24th International Conference of the Round Table on Archives (CITRA), the first of its kind to be held in Latin America, the various seminars on archival description that have been held, the International Seminar on Construction of Archive Buildings, the Preventive Conservation Course, the Seminar on Restoration, the Seminar on Appraisal or the International Seminar on Archive Policy in Central America. Another patent example of the dynamism of these archives can be found in their activity within ALA, whose working programme is the most far-reaching of all the regional branches of the International Council on Archives (ICA).

Nevertheless, it must also be acknowledged that in a handful of countries the limited support lent by the public authorities to their national archives makes it impossible for these structures to overcome their backward and poverty-stricken situation and become modern institutions. The oldest records held in Latin American archives date back to the time of the Spanish and Portuguese conquest and colonization in the sixteenth century, and many are of extraordinary value.

Most of the holdings in Latin American archives are conventional archives. Cartographic material is also common and some repositories—not just the national ones—boast rich collections of maps and plans. Many of the national archives also hold documents on new media, particularly collections of photographs. At present, however, the existence of records held on computerized media is practically nil. The conservation of the vast documentary heritage held in their archives throws up enormous challenges to countries and its survival is sometimes under serious threat. The administrative archives of bodies attached to the central or federal administration rarely have any professional-level staff, since the people who are responsible for them are administrative public officials who have not been required to undergo any specific training.

Most archives have no other source of income than the budget allocated to them by the state. The possibility of obtaining additional outside resources through the sale of publications, reproductions, etc., is practically non-existent as the budget they are given is not enough to develop this type of activity. Other national archives, whose position within the administrative organizational hierarchy leaves them under the responsibility of a higher body do not have this financial autonomy.

Role of Audiovisuals

The audiovisual heritage is an important element within the cultural heritage and has achieved prominence in the twentieth century, the first to have been recorded on audiovisual formats. Audiovisuals are not new but have become of increasing importance as art, entertainment and information carriers. In some cases the transmission of sound and visual data has greater value and impact than the printed document - where, for example, there is a literacy or language barrier. Audiovisuals may also be the only suitable records for the oral or sonic transmission of culture and the arts, news and other current items. The spread and development of modern technologies mean an increase in the role of audiovisual data carriers for communication, information and culture.

Today's radio and television rely heavily on archive material and it is estimated that more than 60% of radio and television programmes use archival or stock material for programming. The definitions are still being formulated, but audiovisual materials are to be understood as visual recordings and sound recordings irrespective of their physical base or recording process. The carrier usually requires a playback device. This definition is meant to cover the maximum number of forms and formats.

Audiovisual materials should not be confused with multimedia; the former provide source material for the latter, and multimedia as such are not archival material. Two features of audiovisual materials add an extra dimension to the principles of collection and preservation: a proliferation both of formats and of systems of production and playback. These cause incompatibility problems between formats and systems. Archives have to maintain original playback devices and employ technical staff who know how to use and maintain the machinery. Audiovisual archives are storehouses for a large proportion of the social and cultural heritage of the twentieth century.

An audiovisual archive is defined as an organization or department of an organization which is focused on collecting, managing, preserving and providing access to a collection of audiovisual media and the audiovisual heritage, applying archival principles. Such archives contain huge treasures of unique material. Archives of audiovisual materials are relatively new, but they have proliferated in the past few decades. Television was originally recorded on film, but video has been the principal material since the later 1960s.

Although audiovisual materials have appeared so recently, time is not on their side and the longer we delay in gathering, conserving and preserving the materials, the less we shall be able to retain. It is vital that steps are taken now to collect and manage audiovisual materials properly before their fragile nature takes a further toll. Already much has been lost owing to ignorance, lack of awareness of the dangers and careless handling. Audiovisual archives vary in type, purpose and function, and until recently most of them were singlematerial archives: moving image, sound and still-image archives, the latter frequently housed in more conventional archives of print materials.

As the technologies converge so do the archives, to unite effort and conserve resources. Some archives take responsibility for all recorded materials, others take smaller bites and combine one or two of the materials. The larger archives cannot always combine materials in one department; the physical techniques required to deal with each material from the point of view of storage, handling and restoration need different expertise and materials are therefore separated by this parameter alone. Other functions of collection management can be applied to all the materials: documentation and information retrieval, and selection.

Storage vaults may have to accommodate more than one material and the resulting environmental considerations will be different from those more stringently applied to individual materials. Alternatively, an archive may decide that it must apply the optimum storage and environmental values which apply to each material: single-material archives are more fortunate in these cases. Academic archives also house audiovisual materials, many in universities for research, and latterly educational materials for distance learning. These may be small and specialized, or have substantial collections and preservation programmes. Specialized or thematic archives concentrate on a particular format, subject-matter or locality, or relate to specific cultural groups. Many of these archives have developed within larger organizations.

Film companies, broadcasting companies and record companies maintain archives primarily for use and exploitation by the parent company. Many of these preserve and restore their materials for re-use, but the archives' main obligation is to the parent organization rather than to preserving the cultural heritage. This may be left to a national archive, which obtains a selection of the production company's material by deposit. Other institutions with archival responsibility include museums, cinematheques, videotheques and national libraries.

Most of these are more concerned with maintaining stock for exhibition purposes, and originals may be deposited for long-term preservation in a national archive. There are also collections of last resort which attempt to conserve copies of material in usable condition, but seldom retain archival originals or masters. Audiovisual materials result from a huge level of investment.

Archives in organizations such as broadcast associations or film production companies have commercial backing and motivation, and meet costs from their revenue. Once that commercial motive is fulfilled, however, it is generally acknowledged that, as with other records of the national cultural creativity, the cost of maintaining the collection reverts to government and granting bodies. Many valuable collections have disappeared for ever as a result of production company closures or changes in franchise when materials are not taken over by already overstretched archives. The basic tasks of an audiovisual archive are collection, preservation, documentation and access provision.

Methods of collection and acquisition vary, and include the legal or voluntary deposit of collections or individual items, the deposit of in-house productions, donations, special agreements for copying nationally produced materials, and purchase. Other archives collect their own materials in the form of oral or video history programmes, with the purpose of recording cultures, languages and music before they disappear. Closely allied to acquisition are evaluation, selection and appraisal.

The audiovisual archive acquires materials according to a particular remit, balancing new acquisitions against existing stock and the purpose and function of the archive. Storage space and resources being what they are, archives have to select material for preservation on the basis of relevance, uniqueness and quality. Wherever possible an archive should be dealing with original materials, but originals are hard to come by. There is strictly only one original film, video or master sound recording. Such originals seldom survive and there are various forms of tampering with the products - cut/ uncut versions, director's/producer's cut, censored and unexpurgated versions. Owners of original material may be reluctant to deposit their master material in an archive until they have no further use for it, by which time the technical quality has deteriorated. Three elements in audiovisual documents have to be considered in the selection process: the artefact or carrier, the information content and the aesthetic content, particularly with film and sound recordings. The artefact or carrier will designate the form of the audiovisual and influence selection for technical reasons. Audiovisual archives, therefore, do not have a huge selection of material, but most of it has unique value, and such archives retain more material than many other archives.

Some audiovisual collections will include several interpretations of the same work—for example, music recordings—or several records of the same event carried in different documents: a film, video or sound version. Guidelines for archival selection exist, but they are usually those of organizations with their own parameters. Selection of material is dependent upon the function of the archive, the quality of the material and the uniqueness or rarity of the content.

Audiovisual archives should concentrate on recordings of national origin. To avoid duplication of effort, material should be offered back to the country of original production or to archives with a more relevant collection remit. The main function of any archive is to preserve the heritage and the artefacts which make up that heritage.

Organisation of Archives

In a well-designed archival network, institutions can share the burden of archiving journals, and libraries and researchers needing to use archival materials can locate and retrieve appropriate copies from a participant in the network. However an archival system is set up, though, it must be clear who takes responsibility for the material being archived and how this responsibility is enforced.

Self-archiving

Some authors and organizations may attempt to archive their own material. A publisher may declare that it will archive its own back issues indefinitely, for instance. Many authors have also provided preprints of their papers and journal articles on their Web sites for years. This informal practice is now encouraged by manifestos like the Budapest Open Access Initiative."Self-archiving" can also be done by authors' institutions. For instance, MIT's Dspace repository promises stable long-term storage for the scholarly work of its faculty.

Self-archiving, however, will not suffice to preserve scholarly journals, let alone scholarly communication as a whole. It essentially relies on the self-interest of the original creators and publishers to keep the archive viable, but Web sites often disappear when an individual changes institutions or careers. Copies of papers on individual sites are often preprints, so they may lack important revisions and supplementary information that appeared in the journal version.

Publisher-run archives may disappear without warning if they are no longer cost-effective to the publisher, or if the journal or the publisher fails or is acquired by another company. Contents of archives may be changed, corrupted, or withdrawn, either by accident or intentionally. As holders of copyrights to the content they archive, publishers and authors have exclusive rights to disseminate this content unless they grant rights to archives run by disinterested third parties. With exclusive rights comes near-exclusive responsibility for their material.

Without very strong certification and backup strategies, self-archiving with this level of exclusivity is not likely to be widely trusted to preserve scholarly information for the time spans researchers and libraries have come to expect. This does not mean that self-archiving is useless, however. Self-archiving can be a backup to trusted archives run by other parties.

Integrated Responsibility

Whether run by content creators and publishers or by third parties, archives have traditionally taken full responsibility for the content they archive. They are responsible for quality control, continued preservation, and providing appropriate access. If they themselves cannot maintain the content in perpetuity, they are responsible for finding someone else who can. While they may delegate some of their functions, such as ingestion or migration, to outside service providers, they are ultimately responsible to their clients for making sure these functions are carried out correctly and that the content is preserved for future access.

This "integrated" responsibility for preserving and providing access to content may earn the trust of users, since the buck stops, as it were, with a definite party. Publishers, too, may be more willing to grant rights to a specific agent who takes responsibility for their work. Of course, the archive must live up to this responsibility, with its attendant certification and sustainability requirements.

Distributed responsibility

The LOCKSS (Lots of Copies Keep Stuff Safe) project at Stanford suggests a more distributed form of responsibility, similar to the distributed responsibility for print journals discussed earlier. With LOCKSS, no one institution takes responsibility for a journal. Instead, many institutions maintain sites that cache copies of journal content published on Web sites. Content can be accessed from the cache if it is no longer available on the original publisher's Web site. Cache contents are automatically checked against each other on a regular basis, and corrupted or lost copies of items replaced with other copies.

The cache correction protocol is slow and relies on records of past holdings. These features make it highly unlikely, given enough participants, that a copy of an object will be completely lost, be corrupted, or become unavailable to any site that originally cached the content. Because the protocol also checks what content a site has previously demonstrated that it owned, the protocol does not "leak" content to sites that were not authorized to see it.

LOCKSS is designed to run on low-cost machines with as little maintenance as possible, making it attractive for libraries to set up LOCKSS caches. If enough libraries continue to cache the same content, that content (at least in its original format) can be preserved reliably even if no single institution takes final responsibility for it. The system can be queried to see how many sites are caching content. Institutions that see a need for greater reliability, can arrange to put additional copies on caches run at their own site or other sites.

In its original form, LOCKSS makes a number of simplifying assumptions about what is being cached, that may not be applicable to all journal archives. For instance, LOCKSS obtains publishers' content by automatically polling their Web sites for HTML and image files, but while those sites may include presentation forms of journals they typically do not include source forms. However, the basic LOCKSS model can be generalized to cover a broader range of journal archiving strategies, especially if caching sites can individually decide what to cache and how.

Useful generalizations of the model include:

— *Introducing an explicit representation of trusted sources for journal content.* The basic LOCKSS model assumes the publisher's Web site is the trusted source for journal content. However, other trusted sources might be needed to provide content not available on the Web site such as source forms for journal content, metadata, and updates and migrated versions of journal content.

— *Caching Archival Information Packages (AIPs).* If AIPs and not just Web pages and images are cached, then a distributed archive can reliably cache both source and presentation forms of content, as well as appropriate metadata and migrated forms. These AIPs would need to come from a trusted source.

— *Identifiers for AIPs and other journal content.* A distributed archiving system requires a consistent way of identifying content so that different servers can check consistency between different copies of the same material. As originally designed, LOCKSS simply uses URLs as identifiers, but this only works for material pulled directly from the Web at static URLs. A distributed archiving system could use AIP identifiers to identify content, but would have to settle on a suitable global scheme for assigning such identifiers. Other globally addressable entities, such as directories, will need globally unique identifiers as well.

— *Metadata*. A distributed archiving system should agree on a common core set of metadata to maintain for journal content, including descriptive and technical metadata, to support searching and browsing and maintenance of particular journal content.

— *Directory services*. Once the metadata above is in place it should be possible for archive users to be able to see what content is in the system, even if they cannot actually view all the content. They should also be able to search and browse it in customary ways, such as looking up an article by its citation, or browsing tables of contents for a particular journal volume. Directory information needs to be updateable as more journal content is added.

— *Versioning*. LOCKSS' cache consistency protocol works well for objects that do not change once they are imported into the system, but a general-purpose distributed archiving system includes several types of changing objects. AIPs for particular journal articles may change as new manifestations of the articles are added (such as through migration) or if publishers issue a corrected version of an article after its original publication. Directories change as new articles, issues, and journals are added to the system. A versioning discipline would allow LOCKSS-like consistency checks for updates and new manifestations of these objects. A new version could be identified as an update of an existing version of an object in the system, and distributed archive sites could decide whether or not to accept the version.

The sites could use acceptance criteria of their choosing, such as the trustworthiness of the source and the nature of the differences between the new version and the older version. Some types of updates may be expected to be monotonic: new data gets added, but old data does not get taken away. Sites could also decide whether or not to retain older versions. Most legitimate updates to journals would not occur more frequently than issues of journals are published, a pace which is compatible with the deliberately slow coherency protocol that LOCKSS uses.

— *Controlled expansion of access.* LOCKSS' access control model is also monotonic: if a site has had a copy of some content in the past, it can be given a copy again, if its old copy has been lost or corrupted. Trusted sources could also grant new copies to sites that previously did not have copies of particular content, when this is permitted, without any further changes in the access control model. It would also be useful to be able to designate that certain content could be given to a wider set of sites. The simplest approach would be to include an "open access" flag that could be given to journal content or metadata that can be distributed freely. Trusted sources could set this flag, either on original distribution, or when previously arranged "triggers" applied that opened access to content.

In making these extensions, one must avoid introducing so much overhead into the system that the primary advantages of LOCKSS — reliable distributed archiving with minimal cost and maintenance — are lost. Each of the enhancements mentioned above should not be overly burdensome in itself, but designers of a distributed archiving system should make sure the enhancements are kept as simple as possible.

Service providers

Service providers perform specific functions on behalf of the archival system. In an "integrated responsibility" model, service providers are essentially subcontractors for the main archive. In the "distributed responsibility" model, service providers are trusted sources, as defined above. Service providers help scale up an archival system by spreading out responsibility for archival tasks. They can be useful when an archival function requires specialized expertise or resources. For instance, if a company provides low-cost, highly replicated reliable data storage, an archive might out-source backups to that company rather than maintain backups itself. Or, if content is submitted or stored in a variety of protocols and formats, ingestion and migration of this content might be usefully parceled out to service providers, each specializing in a particular format or data provider, instead of trying to have one organization handle everything.

Service providers often do not need to make the same sort of long-term commitments as archives themselves do, unless their service includes long term information storage. However, they still need to be visible in the design and operations of an archiving system. Archive users may want to make sure they are certified for carrying out their service correctly. Publisher agreements may need to allow them to access copyrighted material, and publishers may want to be assured that they do not distribute or alter this material without authorization. The business model for the archive or archival system also needs to include some sort of compensation for the services of the providers.

Registries. Several organizations, including JSTOR, Highwire, PubMedCentral, and various publishers and national libraries, are currently archiving journal material. As the population of archives and archived materials grows, it will be increasingly important for archive maintainers and users to be able to keep track of who is doing what and with what content. A registry of journal archiving activity would make this possible. It would allow users to find content they needed, and allow archive maintainers to find service providers, look up technical information on archiving formats and practices, and track redundant archiving of journal content.

Several architectures are possible for such a registry. A centralized knowledge base could be set up to accept information about archival activities. The Jointly Administered Knowledge Environment (Jake) is already set up to record journal information in this manner, though it does not currently record archiving information for journals. Peer-to-peer systems can also act as decentralized "registries." The Typed Object Model, for instance, propagates information about data formats and their conversions between peer "type brokers."

The Open Archives Initiative (OAI) suggests a particularly promising architecture for a registry. Using OAI, repositories can expose metadata about their contents which can then be harvested incrementally by any interested service. The OAI protocol is lightweight and easy to implement and add on to existing systems.

One or more archival information sites could harvest information from appropriately certified archives, and allow archive users and maintainers to search and browse the aggregated metadata. Setting up such a system would require some agreements on "core" metadata that the archives would export, but it would be in the interest of most archives to agree on such metadata. The aggregated information site would not need to be particularly expensive to maintain. It would be automatically updated from the certified archives, and the software to browse and search its records would only need to handle the common "core" metadata format.

A journal archive registry should include at least the following information:

— Information on journals being archived including

— their names and identifiers

— the archives or archival systems preserving them, the scope of the issues and articles preserved by these archives, and the formats being archived

— who is authorized to access the content

— Information on the archives and service providers themselves

— For "integrated responsibility" archives, information on their certification including how they are certified, when they were last certified, and relevant reports from the certifiers

— For "distributed responsibility" archival systems, information on how to find out the archival status of journal content, including how to locate and check the reliability and redundancy of the storage of particular journal content.

Rights and Responsibilities of Archives

An electronic journal archive has responsibilities to scholars and their institutions and to publishers. The archive is responsible for ensuring scholars can access journal content for as long as it is of scholarly value in a form that allows it to be used effectively for research, teaching, and learning. The archive is responsible for respecting the copyrights of authors and publishers in its stewardship of electronic journal content. It is also responsible for helping maintain a healthy climate of scholarship and scholarly communication. It should neither hinder publishers or libraries with overly burdensome procedural and economic constraints, nor hinder scholars themselves with overly restrictive policies for access or deposit. Archives need to be granted sufficient rights to carry out these responsibilities.

Selection Responsibilities

The archive is responsible for identifying journals it wishes to archive and making these selections known to a publisher for the publisher's approval. The selection does not have to be enumerated. For instance, archives that plan to include all electronic journals of particular publishers, could agree that any newly added journal will be included in the selection unless either the publisher or the archive notifies the other that the new journal should be excluded. In such cases, the publisher should also inform the archive about newly added electronic journals or of journals that it no longer publishes.

Of course, this notification, and other provisions of information given in this section, can be made simply by publishing the information in an agreed-upon location, such as a Web page or a mailing list. The archive and publisher also need to agree on what content in the journals is being selected. Normally, the archive should collect at least all issues published from the time the agreement is made. Back issues, where feasible, are also desirable to include.

The archive and the publisher also have to agree on a set of formats that will be collected, and protocols for collecting content and metadata. Either the archive or the publisher should be able to request, with sufficient advance notice, that archiving for a journal be cut off: that is, no further issues will be deposited into the archive. The archive is responsible for notifying its clients, including appropriate registries, of its selections.

Ingestion Responsibilities

The publisher is responsible for providing content and metadata for the journal issues being archived. Content should include the journal content as provided to subscribers in presentation forms such as PDF and HTML. Even if an archive does not store presentation forms, it is helpful for an archive to be able to compare any source forms it receives against what the publisher actually supplied to subscribers in the electronic journal. This provision may simply consist of allowing the archive access to the online journal for testing.

When the archive is preserving source forms of content, the publisher is responsible for providing them and for ensuring they are correctly formatted; the publisher is also responsible for ensuring the source forms correspond appropriately to the published presentation forms. The publisher should likewise be responsible for providing metadata for the journal content in sufficient detail to allow standard scholarly citations to be built for all articles and other citable contributions. This includes title, authors, issue information, page numbers or other section delimiters where applicable, and other standard identifiers for the content such as ISSNs and DOIs. Abstracts and keywords would also be useful, when available.

The archive is responsible for collecting content and metadata in a timely fashion, checking it for consistency and proper formatting, and either ingesting it into its repository or informing the publisher of any errors or problems with the data. If the archive reports errors the publisher should remedy them, and the archive should then reingest content. Generally, the archive should try to ingest an issue while it is still the current issue. If the archive is harvesting data from the Web or another published source, it should be able to assume the data is in its final form unless the publisher has notified it otherwise. For example, if the publisher posts "draft" or pre-publication material which it then modifies before an issue's "official" publication, the publisher is responsible for telling the archive when and when not to harvest this information.

The archive is responsible for collecting appendices to articles such as datasets, audiovisual clips, program code, and other multimedia when this is within the archive's stated selection criteria. The publisher may need to assist the archive in collecting these appendices. If the appendices have unusual size or format, they might not be required to be migrated as is regular content. "Appendices" external to the journal itself — a Web site referred to by a URL in a journal article, for example — need not be collected.

If content is to be collected by harvesting from the publisher's site, the publisher is responsible for allowing access by the archive's harvesters, while the archive is responsible for ensuring the harvesters do not unduly load the archive's servers.

Rights and responsibilities for storage and maintenance. The archive is responsible for ensuring the long-term persistence and stability of the archived content. It is also responsible for making sure the content does not become unusable due to technological obsolescence. Therefore, the publisher should give the archive the right to store copies of the journal content and metadata, make and store backup copies, and create derivative works based on the original data for the purpose of maintaining their suitability for research and scholarship. Such derivative works could include migrations to new formats, indexing for searching and browsing, and transformations required for emulation. Ideally, the right to create derivative works would also allow enhancements to the content, at least when the enhancements are for services that researchers come to expect in online journals. Such enhancements, for instance, could include converting static images to wavelet-based forms that allow panning and zooming, or inserting hyperlinks to make it possible for readers to go to referenced articles.

Users expect that reliable, persistent electronic archives will not lose content. Therefore, the rights above and other intellectual property rights given to the archive should be irrevocable by the publisher, provided that the archive fulfills its responsibilities. Publishers can retain copyright; they just need to assign appropriate rights for the archive to do its job.

Rights and responsibilities for access and distribution. The archive is responsible to its clients for providing authorized users with its content and metadata, and it is responsible to publishers for providing content only to authorized users. Content provided to authorized users should include:

— Copies of the journal content as originally published (byte-for-byte copy, in original formats) for journals archived in presentation form.

— Images of the journal pages in formats commonly readable at the time of access for journals archived in presentation form. This may require migration if common data formats change.

— The text of the journal content in formats commonly readable at the time of access. This may also require migration.

— Where feasible and cost-effective, other journal content, such as data sets and audiovisual materials, in formats commonly readable at the time of access.

Metadata should include at least citation information for the journals and their articles. The archive should also provide reasonable facilities for locating an article or journal with a known citation.

It seems relatively uncontroversial to allow general access at least to citation-level descriptive metadata. This allows users to know what is in an archive. Richer descriptions, such as abstracts, may be more controversial, but if they encourage a user to seek out the full content and become more interested in the journal as a whole, providing such detailed metadata can benefit both archive and publisher.

Likewise, allowing access to content by the publisher and by the archive maintainers seems uncontroversial. Widening access further, though, proved more problematic. Even providing access to subscribers to the journal for content that was also available on the publisher's Web site raised concerns that the archive would compete with the publisher's own offerings.

The concerns here seemed to be not just possible loss of marketing opportunities on the publisher's own Web site, but also possible degradation of image. The look, the services, and the authority that the publisher took pains to establish on their Web site could be lost on the archive site, thus weakening the "brand" or reputation of the publisher. This seemed to be less of a concern if the archive just offered material that was no longer available on the publisher's own Web site. Concerns about image may also be alleviated if appropriate links are made between the archive site and the publisher's site.

Even more controversial is allowing access to archived journal content to those who are not subscribers to the journal. JSTOR and Highwire, two established projects that archive journal content, allow such access after a certain time has passed from publication. The point at which access is opened is referred to as the "moving wall." There are several advantages to this sort of access:

— It satisfies, at least in part, the desire of many scholars that scholarly information should be generally accessible to all for little or no cost, whenever feasible.

— It provides an electronic counterpart to the long-standing custom of researchers obtaining older journal articles by interlibrary loan if their institution did not subscribe to the journal or retain their volumes.

— It avoids the overhead of the archive having to keep track of exactly what users should be allowed to access each item in the archive.

— It allows a wide audience of readers and third-party automated programs to examine the archived content and verify that it is being accurately preserved or report problems if it is not, thus enhancing trust in the archive. This may be especially important when material needs to be migrated to a new format, a process that may risk losing information or usability in unexpected ways.

— It may make it easier for mirror sites and other service providers to access the content.

— It provides an ongoing service of document delivery to the scholarly community, instead of just being an unseen "insurance" policy as an inaccessible or "dark" archive would be. This strengthens support for the archive in that community.

These are all benefits for the archive and its users, but they are not direct benefits to publishers. Of greatest concern was the possibility that libraries would cancel subscriptions to their journals or not sign up for them in the first place if they could have access to the archive without a journal subscription. Martin Richardson of Oxford University Press, for instance, reported that institutional subscriptions to eleven journals made available via Highwire had declined by three percent per year in the three years since they had been placed online, even though they had been increasing prior to that time.

Faced with such declines in subscriptions, publishers might have to raise prices for the subscribers that are left, or cut the budgets to produce the journals. As an alternative to general free access Richardson recommended free access to readers in developing countries and low article pricing for infrequent users of journals.

Richardson's report does not prove that opening access caused the drop in subscriptions or that a more distant moving wall, such as the three to five years that is common for JSTOR journals, would not solve the problem. Both Oxford and Cambridge have been willing to experiment with allowing some of their journal content to be accessible to nonsubscribers through JSTOR and Highwire as well as PubMedCentral.

Some may argue that copyright law already specifies a moving wall when works enter the public domain and are available to anyone. However, this moving wall has been extended repeatedly in the United States and is now up to ninety-five years after publication for older publications and works for hire, and to seventy years after the death of the last surviving author for other works. The distance and uncertainty of copyright expiration in these circumstances makes an archive that requires public domain verification before providing access to electronic journal content equivalent to a "dark" archive for most practical purposes.

Other "trigger" events besides a fixed moving wall are also worth considering. For example, opening up access when migration is required would ease user concerns that migration might not be successful. It might also benefit publishers if they found migration too expensive or troublesome to carry out themselves. It is also reasonable for archives to be able to provide general access to content that is no longer being offered online by the publisher or the publisher's agents.

The archiving agreement should not abridge the traditional rights recognized by copyright law. These rights include fair use, first-sale rights, and unrestricted use of public domain material. All of these rights play important roles in scholarship, so archives whose purpose is to support scholarship should avoid restricting them. Some publishers digitizing older material may want to make an exception to this rule for new digitizations of public domain content from early in a journal's run. An archive should weigh this proposed exception carefully.

In some cases, a short-term embargo on unrestricted use of this material may be necessary if the only likely digitizer of the content is worried about the investment going to waste, but there is little justification for extending this embargo beyond the same moving wall term that is given to copyrighted content. On the whole, the copyrighted content of most electronic journal archives will usually be much more valuable than recently-digitized public domain content. Users are also much more likely to trust and support a comprehensive and authorized archive of a journal's run than an unauthorized provider of part of the journal's run.

Rights and responsibilities for certification and evaluation. The archive is responsible for specifying a process for certification of its content and procedures, and for reporting the results of this certification to its clients, including its publisher partners. The RLG-OCLC Trusted Repositories paper notes two basic approaches to certification: an approach based on auditing and an approach based on standards and usage.

For a "dark" archive, or an archival system that uses software that is not available for public inspection, certification will generally need to involve auditing, to satisfy the concerns of constituents who cannot examine the content or the software themselves. In a more open system, such as LOCKSS, each site can examine its own contents and the software it is using. In such cases, separate auditing is less important though it may be desirable for the designers of the system to have the code reviewed and certified by an outside party.

Publishers may want to know how the content they publish is being used in an archive as well as the cost of the archiving processes. It is reasonable for an archive to share aggregated usage information with publishers as long as the form of the information sharing protects the privacy of individual readers. If publishers are subsidizing the archiving they also have a right to be informed of the costs involved. Archives and publishers should agree in advance on the data an archive will collect, what an archive can be expected to provide, and for how long an archive should retain usage data.

Responsibilities for sustainability. The archive is responsible for ensuring it has appropriate technology, procedures, and funding for it to continue archiving activities for as long as needed. Responsibility for funding, however, is related to the other rights and responsibilities of an archive.

Funding for an archive can come from various sources including:

— The organization running the archive (self-funding)

— External sponsors (e.g., private foundations, government grants, marketers)

— The publishers of the journals in the archive

— Users of the archive materials (e.g., individual researchers and libraries)

Self-funding is viable for most academic libraries if the archival system is sufficiently lightweight and inexpensive to run and provides commensurate benefits. We can run a LOCKSS server on a commodity PC, for example, and in its current form it requires very little maintenance. Even a more ambitious system, such as the distributed archiving system described earlier, could easily pay for itself if its cost were similar to the original LOCKSS system and it made it easier for us to move older journals to inexpensive remote storage.

Full-service "integrated responsibility" archives are much more heavyweight. According to discussions with its maintainers, PubMedCentral, run by the National Center for Biotechn0logy Information (NCBI) of the National Institutes of Health (NIH), requires seven full-time employees to run on an ongoing basis. The project archives fewer than thirty externally published journals, plus a few dozen very low volume journals published by NCBI, and makes extensive use of automation. PubMedCentral staff represent only a small fraction of the staff of the NCBI, itself a small division of NIH. Organizations like this, which have national mandates as collectors and providers of research information, should find it a relatively small stretch to maintain an archive of online scholarly journals in-house and to justify it in their budgets.

Many publishers can fund an archive if the archive provides them sufficient benefit. The costs of funding will ultimately be passed on to someone else. For subscription-based journals, the price of subscriptions may account for the cost of funding the archive. Journals that charge authors for publication might build charges for preservation of the article into the author's fee. Journals published by scholarly societies may have those societies fund their preservation.

Costs for preserving journal material are ongoing but publishers may be unwilling or unable to pay for archiving the material indefinitely. One solution to this problem is to structure publisher funding as an endowment. When a publisher deposits a journal volume or issue in an archive, it would also include a one-time payment to endow the future archive needs of the deposited content. Income from this endowment would fund ongoing archiving, backup, mirroring, maintenance, and migration of that journal content in perpetuity. If the archive decided to transfer responsibility for the content to another institution or back to the publisher, the content's endowment would be transferred as well. If a publisher stopped supporting an archive, the endowments associated with previously deposited content could still fund the preservation of that content.

For the publisher and journal subscribers, the endowment would provide a guaranteed source of funds to ensure the ongoing availability of journal content. Funding would not be dependent on an archive's ongoing revenue stream. By guaranteeing long-term availability of journal content, an endowment-funded archive could ultimately save money both for the publisher and subscribers to the journal. Subscribers who can rely on preserved electronic copies may be willing to forgo print versions or keep them in less expensive storage, thereby lowering their costs. Hence, they may be willing to contribute to an endowment fund via their subscription fees. If the archive is sufficiently trustworthy and accessible, it may even be possible to discontinue print production which would lower costs and subscription fees for the publisher.

For the endowment model to work, however, costs have to be well-understood and kept under control. If the costs can be kept down to a small percentage of subscription revenue, the endowment model may be financially viable. For instance, a journal that costs $350 per volume, with 300 annual subscribers, brings in about $100,000 of subscription revenue. If endowment income were five percent per year, then each one percent surcharge for archiving would pay $50 per year of archiving costs for that volume. So if the true costs to the archive were $150 per year per volume, three percent of subscription revenues would need to go towards archiving.

Unfortunately, this may be an optimistic estimate of archiving costs, which are still uncertain and likely to change as archives develop and as technology changes. Long-term costs may be difficult to measure in the early stages of an archiving project, especially since it may be unclear what costs are startup costs and what costs are ongoing or recurrent, given the fluid nature of technology and archiving standards. Automation of as many tasks as possible may help, as long as the cost of computers continues to decrease while the cost of labor increases. The endowment model also works best when an archive's fixed costs of operation are low compared to costs that vary with the size of the archive, favoring larger archives. For similar reasons, high endowment requirements may also favor larger publishers which might be an undesirable side-effect for libraries already worried about over-consolidation of scholarly journal publishing in for-profit conglomerates. If scholarly archives are ultimately designed to meet the needs of scholars and scholarly institutions, a funding model that relies on publishers may produce a less useful archive than one that is funded more directly by scholars and their libraries.

Funding by users appears to be a viable alternative to endowments by publishers. JSTOR has found success through funding from libraries and other journal users. Libraries pay a one-time capital development fee and an annual subscription fee to access JSTOR content. Publishers are not charged for deposits into the archive. JSTOR has proven highly popular with libraries and their patrons.

JSTOR's convenient access is the carrot that encourages libraries to pay for subscriptions that cover both access services and archiving. JSTOR's success with libraries, scholars, and publishers makes a powerful case for this type of funding model. Of course, it is possible for journal archives to have multiple funding sources, but complicated funding models may produce more problems than they solve.

An archive faced with high ingestion costs could depend on users to fund its general operations and development, as JSTOR does, but charge publishers for ingesting their content unless their content came in a prepackaged, easily-validated form prescribed by the archive. In effect, the archive would offer to sell publishers a packaging service for their content. The publisher could pay for the archive to package their content, or pay some other service provider to do it, or do it on its own and avoid having to pay. In any case, the archive's own costs for ingestion would be reduced and publishers would have an incentive to provide their content in accordance with archival standards. Both of these developments would make the archive more reliable and sustainable.

Funding and control of access rights represent a tradeoff. Publishers can provide funds or they can provide access rights to users after a suitable delay. They are reluctant to provide both. Libraries and scholars, on the other hand, may be disinclined to fund an archive that does not give them access except in some far-distant or unforeseeable circumstances. Thus, archives funded primarily by publishers may tend to be "dark," whereas archives funded primarily by libraries and archives should be more open to access by their funders.

Responsibilities and rights for transfer and delegation. Archives must be ready for unforeseen changes in the scholarly or online community that may render the archive unsustainable or make it far preferable to archive content elsewhere. Therefore, agreements with the publisher should allow the transfer, if necessary, of the archival material and its associated rights to another party that agrees to assume the archive's responsibilities. The publisher, if it is still in existence, may want to stipulate some additional qualities of the new party, for instance, that it not be a commercial competitor.

Similarly, the agreement should allow third parties to act as service providers for delegated archival functions as long as the third parties do not distribute archival material or use it for any purpose other than to carry out legitimate archival functions on the archive's behalf. For example, integrated archives may need to have a third-party off-site mirror of the archive's contents in case of a disaster at the main archival site.

Archival Life Cycle

The OAIS model breaks down the archiving process into distinct functional modules which manage archival information packages throughout their life cycles. The key modules defined by OAIS and some of their functions are:

— *Ingest*. This includes the archive's acquisition of journal content and metadata, validation of the content, and packaging for archival storage as Archive Information Packages (AIPs).

— *Archival storage*. This includes maintaining AIP data and ensuring the continued survival and integrity of binary representations of archival data.

— *Data management*. This includes, among other things, maintaining metadata on archived content, managing storage, and handling queries on stored data.

— *Administration*. Among other things, this includes migration.

— *Preservation planning*. This includes planning and implementing further development of the archival system, including migration planning.

— *Access*. This includes delivery of content both to end users and to other archives under appropriate access controls.

— *Ingestion*. Ingestion of presentation content and metadata from Web sites helps to construct a modular prototype harvester that could collect metadata and links to content from different publisher Web sites, then deposit the metadata and links into a common data structure that could be browsed and accessed uniformly.

Size of the content varied greatly among journals. For example, PDFs for American Law and Economics Review, a semi-annual journal, took up little more than 2 MB of storage space per year, whereas PDFs for Brain, a monthly medical journal, took up closer to 100 MB of storage space per year.

Articles in PDF form were generally easy to harvest, usually as one PDF file per article, although in some instances the PDFs were page-oriented instead and included content from multiple or adjacent items in the same file.

Correctly harvesting HTML presentation forms was considerably more problematic. Many of the HTML-formatted articles were clearly generated from source files and included numerous automatically generated links, some of which led to content that was important to the article, such as high-resolution versions of illustrations, while others led to related material that was not part of the article itself. Many of these HTML articles were produced by the same organization, Highwire Press.

Ingesting material into an archive, whether manually or automatically, is far from foolproof. When publishers manually send a journal issue to an archive they may accidentally leave out articles, send misformatted files, or even send the wrong files altogether.

Occasionally, articles published on Web sites included mistakes. An early spot-check of one mathematics journal article revealed a PDF file in which the last pages could not be read as the file was initially posted. Human checks may turn up some of these errors but can be expensive to perform.

Migration. Left alone, archived content and metadata are not likely to stay usable forever. Preserving the integrity of the original digital forms of archived electronic journals is not difficult with proper planning and the right to make copies as needed for archiving. The strategies of generating checksums, making backups and offsite mirrors, regularly refreshing media, and conducting regularly scheduled consistency checks and disaster drills are well-known in digital preservation and data security circles. However, more uncertainty exists about whether the digital forms can continue to be understood and used effectively as technologies and expectations change.

Data structures and formats based on simple, openly-specified, and widely-used standards are the easiest to preserve, and journal archives should encourage their use. The definition of XML, for instance, is straightforward and widely publicized. Even if XML is eventually replaced by some other standard for structured data, it would not be difficult to migrate XML files to the new standard or to maintain programs that continue to parse XML in its original form.

To understand and use archival files formatted in XML or SGML, though, it is not sufficient to be able to parse the markup; it is also necessary to know what the markup represents. In addition, we need to preserve the DTDs or schemas used, as well as the documentation for defining DTDs, schemas, or whatever syntactic convention next comes along to describe markup formats. And, above the level of DTDs or schemas, we need to document and preserve the semantics of the schemas: the meaning of the markup elements and how their composition turns a set of angle-bracketed words and sentences into a journal that speaks from mind to mind.

The semantics may be expressed in English-language descriptions, stylesheets, a program that renders markup as a visual display like that of a Web browser, or all of these. Particularly since some of the syntax and semantics may be specific to the world of electronic journal publishing and archiving, the archival system will need to include a preservation mechanism for both the syntax and semantics of its data.

Preserving format information is not a new idea. The Multipurpose Internet Mail Extensions (MIME) registry maintained by the Internet Assigned Numbers Authority (IANA) preserves descriptions of data formats commonly used on the Internet, as well as standard methods for encoding, packaging, and transmitting them. The Typed Object Model (TOM), adds semantic capabilities to a distributed format registry mechanism, supporting automated services like migration, format identification, and interpretation of data formats by remote servers.

An ideal registry for journal archiving data structures would allow the combination of the prose descriptions and canonical authority of IANA's MIME registry, the computational power of TOM, and the expertise of digital librarians, archivists, and publishers.

Preserving presentation forms presents some special problems: they are often complicated, defined by vendors, and dependent on external information in unexpected ways. Fortunately, the presentation forms of most electronic journals are designed to be viewable by ordinary Web browsers without esoteric plugins. The capabilities of Web browsers are well-documented, for the most part, so it should be possible to deal with the formats they handle.

Open Archive Initiatives

The Open Archives Metadata Harvesting Protocol, an important new infrastructure component for supporting distributed networked information services. The Metadata Harvesting Protocol-a mechanism that enables data providers to expose their metadata-is seeing very rapid deployment, and enables a fascinating array of new services and system architectures for a diverse set of communities.

There has been considerable confusion about the Open Archives Metadata Harvesting Protocol, mostly beginning with and stemming from its name. The protocol no longer has much to do with archiving or archives, other than in terms of its heritage. The Open Archives Metadata Harvesting Protocol grew out of an effort to solve some of the problems that were emerging as e-print servers became more widely deployed; it originated in the community concerned with advancing the development of e-print archives.

However, as work on the protocol advanced it became clear that it provided a very general-purpose mechanism that could address a surprisingly wide range of urgent needs and, in order to be useful in the widest variety of contexts, this mechanism had to be defined so that it was agnostic to assumptions about types of content, economic models, intellectual property constraints, or systems of information flow.

For better or worse, by that time the protocol was widely known as the Open Archives Protocol, and the program to develop it was widely known as the Open Archives Initiative, so the decision was made to maintain the popularly known terminology. The protocol is now often referred to as the Open Archives Metadata Harvesting Protocol in an attempt to reintroduce a bit more clarity.

This Metadata Harvesting Protocol (MHP), is simply an interface that a networked server (not necessarily an e-print server) can employ to make metadata describing objects housed at that server available to external applications that wish to collect this metadata. A server does not need to be part of an e-print program to use the protocol; indeed, it does not need to house journal papers at all. The server does not need to offer free access to the digital objects that it stores.

The Metadata Harvesting Protocol can be implemented by servers housing commercial products available by subscription (like scientific journals) or available for transactional purchase, by libraries or museums offering access to digitized images, or by scientific data archives, to list only a few potential applications. Many of the people who have been involved in the work on the MHP are also strong proponents of the broader program to open free public access to the scholarly journal literature, but they are usually careful to differentiate between the two; the MHP can certainly advance the deployment of e-print archives, but it is not limited to supporting that program. It is a much more general and more neutral technical-enabling mechanism.

The term "Open Archives Initiative" is ambiguous; it refers both to a specific, organized, funded effort to advance the Metadata Harvesting Protocol, and to a separate, diffuse movement to promote the deployment and use of e-print archives involving a lot of the same people.

The Open Archives Metadata Harvesting Initiative had its roots in work done by Herbert Van de Sompel (then of the University of Ghent) working in collaboration with groups that included researchers and librarians at Los Alamos National Labs in the United States. In late 1999, a meeting was convened in Santa Fe, New Mexico to address a series of problems that he had been exploring in the e-print server world.

Fundamentally, the problem was that as disciplinary e-print servers proliferated, often with overlapping disciplinary coverage and geographical affinity, there was a need to develop services that permitted searching across papers housed at multiple repositories. Repositories also needed capabilities to automatically identify and copy papers that had been deposited in other repositories.

Further complicating matters, institutional e-print archives (such as the DSpace project being carried out at MIT in collaboration with Hewlett-Packard3) were beginning to emerge that would house the intellectual output of specific campus communities; it was undesirable to require scholars to deposit their work in multiple repositories, and hence it would be necessary for disciplinary archives to be able to identify and replicate material from these institutional archives and for federated search services to be able to search across both institutional and disciplinary archives.

The Metadata Harvesting Protocol uses a very simple HTTP-based request-response transaction framework for communication between a harvester and a repository. A harvester can ask for metadata to be returned with optional restrictions based on when the metadata has been added or modified (in other words, it can obtain new or changed metadata since its last harvest interaction with a repository); it can also restrict metadata by server-defined "partitions" (think of these as gross subject-oriented subcollections housed on a server).

The server returns a series of sets of metadata elements (in XML) plus identifiers (i.e., URLs) for the objects that the metadata describes. Supporting this core harvesting transaction are a few ancillary transactions: for example, to permit a harvester to obtain a list of the names of partitions that a server has defined and which can thus be used as restriction criteria in harvesting requests.

Multiple metadata schemes are supported in the Open Archives Metadata Harvesting Protocol-this is really the key architectural change from the Santa Fe Convention. The protocol requires that all servers offer unqualified Dublin Core metadata (encoded in XML) as a lowest common denominator; however, each server is also free to offer metadata in one or more other schemes, and a harvester can request that metadata be provided in a scheme other than Dublin Core as part of the harvest request.

There is also another auxiliary transaction that permits a harvester to obtain a list of the names of the metadata schemes that a given repository supports. The underlying idea here is that we will see communities of practice evolve that define metadata schemes that are richer and more precise than unqualified Dublin Core; for example, the e-print archives community is already working on one that encodes various important data elements for e-prints, such as author affiliations, bibliographic information if the paper has been published in a journal, and even the paper's cited references in a structured form.

These community-specific schemes could be handled as qualified Dublin Core, or as de novo schemes; the only requirement is that they be transportable in XML. This is a very powerful method of enabling communities with common metadata to work together while still ensuring some minimal level of interoperability for very broad federated search or other services based on unqualified Dublin Core.

It seems very likely that the MHP will drive development of community-specific metadata schemes. It will also be helpful in clarifying our understanding of the value of unqualified Dublin Core for lowest common denominator cross-domain resource discovery.

Authentication and access management are not covered. A given repository can use a range of access-management mechanisms that are external to the protocol to decide which harvesters it will provide with metadata if it wishes to impose access control. Independent of access control decisions about providing metadata, the server only includes a pointer-such as a URL or URN-to each object described by metadata that it makes available for harvest; access controls on this base object may or may not exist.

In addition, any authentication that the harvester wants to conduct on the repository is handled by external mechanisms. The protocol does not address the very real issue of how harvesters will identify repositories that they wish to harvest, nor does it provide information to help determine when harvesting should occur, or how frequently.

There will clearly be a need for some kind of registry of names for well-known community-specific metadata schemes. The MHP does not address this, though it clearly must be part of the broader infrastructure associated with the protocol. The most obvious applications that are enabled by the Metadata Harvesting Protocol are those that helped to motivate the work at the initial Santa Fe meeting: repository synchronization and federated search.

For repository synchronization, one compares metadata from two or more repositories and decides what objects should be copied from one repository to another. The hard part here is in the application: deciding what repositories to examine, and determining the criteria for identifying what to copy. There is also a problem with the propagation of metadata from one repository to another; it's not clear how to determine the most comprehensive metadata set describing an object so that all of the relevant metadata can be copied over.

Similarly, federated search using MHP is not hard in principle; one collects metadata from a number of sites, normalizes it, clusters it in some fashion to deal with duplicates as appropriate, and offers search services against the resulting database. In practice, all of the details are complex: what sites to harvest, how often to harvest them, how to normalize metadata (especially if one wants to do better than the lowest common denominator-unqualified Dublin Core-offered by each site), how to handle duplicate objects-these are all key design issues that need to be addressed.

MHP provides a very powerful framework for building union-catalog-type databases (in the broad sense; not just union bibliographic catalogs, but all sorts of union descriptive databases) for collections of resources by automating and standardizing the collection of contributions from the participating sites, which has traditionally been an operational headache in building and managing union catalogs.

But there are many complex specifics that need to be coded into any actual implementation. A set of applications closely related to federated search deal with the potential enhancement of web search engines in at least two distinct dimensions. One is providing a more efficient way for web search engines to crawl static HTML pages, and also to obtain metadata associated with these pages (there are other methods of getting the metadata, such as in-line META tags, but the MHP provides a much more flexible way of doing this).

The second is being able to integrate various parts of what is sometimes called the "deep web" or the "invisible web" with the indexing of static web pages, including repositories of digital objects and databases that do not exist as retrievable and indexable static web pages, and also proprietary content, where the content owner may be willing to make metadata about the content available to facilitate finding it, but may be unwilling to permit arbitrary web-indexing programs to have direct access to the content in order to index it.

The Metadata Harvesting Protocol allows a server to enumerate the objects it houses and to provide metadata associated with these objects, no matter what the nature of these objects and the access constraints that might apply to them. Any application dealing with metadata created and stored on distributed sites faces issues about whether it can trust the metadata it is relying upon.

This means, for example, that it is unlikely that the public web search engines will use an OAI interface to harvest arbitrary sites anytime soon; however, federated searching or customized indexing of sites that are selected in some fashion-by being part of an organizational intranet, or through some type of editorial policy that selects quality sites as part of a subject portal, for example-will likely make wide use of the protocol.

These are the most obvious applications (and the ones that will probably be available soonest), in that they directly extend or enhance existing practices. Interesting and novel applications are likely to emerge as well. For example, one can easily imagine the rise of intermediary services (reminiscent of the brokerage services in the original Harvest system) that collect raw metadata from sets of sites, consolidate and enhance it, and then redistribute it as a single feed or as custom-selected subsets to still other sites for reuse.

Creative applications designers are at the very early stages of exploring the services that the MHP can enable, and we can expect some fascinating and unexpected developments in the next few years. While the Open Archives Metadata Harvesting Protocol solves one very important set of problems, it also focuses attention on a number of other issues that will have to be addressed as applications proliferate.

Some of them will require progress in standards and/or other networked information infrastructure components; others are simply not well understood at this point and will require considerable research and experimentation to allow the development of a body of design knowledge and community practice. Many sites make metadata about their holdings publicly available today in the sense that they offer publicly accessible search services operating against that metadata, which can then result in the display of individual records.

This is the case with most library catalogs; for example, they offer searching to anyone who wants to search the database, and some systems will even provide formatted displays of individual, full MARC records that are retrieved by such searches as an option. There is a great difference between this practice and simply making the entire catalog's contents, or major subsets, available for bulk downloading and re-incorporation into other databases and services.

In a world of MHP-enabled network resources, metadata becomes migratory and recombinant. Owners and operators of large databases and repositories will need to think through how comfortable they are in making their metadata generally available on this basis, and what limits, if any, they want to place on permissible reuse. In addition, this may focus new attention on metadata ownership; while nobody may much care about who reuses the odd individual bibliographic database record, copying an entire bibliographic database may be viewed quite differently.

There is no real way to encode acceptable-use policies or restrictions on metadata harvesting within the MHP; while it would not be difficult to make reference to textual statements about such policies, encoding them in a machine-understandable way is a difficult problem that calls for collaboration between computer scientists, lawyers, and standards developers, among others.

Many applications will use manually-curated lists of sites to harvest, and, indeed, the editorial processes and selectivity that go into the development and maintenance of these lists will be part of the value of the application itself. As these services multiply, operators of new repositories will face the problem of bringing their site to the attention of the appropriate service operators so that their metadata can be harvested.

If we look at the operation of the public web search engines, which seek to be comprehensive, we find much more complex methods of identifying sites to crawl (the details of which vary from search engine to search engine, and are viewed as representing proprietary advantage to these search engines).

They start with a base of websites that they have identified, or that site operators have submitted to the indexing services, but then they also dynamically discover new sites to index by analyzing links on sites that they visit. They also use a variety of techniques (both manual and automated) to determine how often to revisit sites looking for new material to index. Some applications performing metadata harvesting will want to do a similar dynamic discovery of sites that are available to be harvested. This could be done in a number of ways.

Certainly, for systems that harvest static HTML pages, it would be possible to program their crawlers to also attempt to do an OAI query against each site to see if it offered metadata for harvesting. It would be possible to establish a central registry of sites that offered metadata via the OAI secretariat; setting up a database that allowed sites to register themselves and interested parties to search the registry to identify harvestable sites is technically straightforward and not terribly resource intensive.

A prototype of this exists today on the Open Archives website; this is simply a list of MHP-compliant sites that have submitted their addresses to the OAI secretariat. The secretariat does some essentially mechanical validation of the sites by running a program periodically that issues OAI queries; it checks that the site is still there and provides syntactically well-formed responses to these queries. This mechanical validation is very valuable in these early days of experimental implementations.

But it is important to recognize the very limited value of such a registry. It does not address how one might classify sites (for example, by the nature of their content or their subject coverage) in order for applications to decide which sites should be harvested. Developing computer-based methods of doing this, at any level of generality, is a complex proposition.

Many applications will likely be structured around the principle of offering in-depth access to high-quality information resources, which means that they will have to be concerned with the assessments of the quality of the metadata offered by the sites they choose to harvest. It's difficult to see how this can be handled at this point other than by evaluation and/or trust decisions by the individual applications.

Scaling these decisions past manual editorial management of lists of sites to harvest takes us quickly to research areas such as reputation management systems, further complicated by the fact that both the harvesting services and their end users may want to be able to make choices about trust and reputation in their use of metadata.

In developing MHP interfaces to databases or repositories, a key design decision has to do with the granularity of the objects for which the site exposes metadata. For the original e-print-archive applications this was straightforward; the objects of interest were individual article e-prints and thus they made available metadata for each article e-print.

But as metadata harvesting is deployed in a wider range of contexts, the answers are less clear. For many repositories we have little or no metadata at the individual object level, and instead have various forms of collection-level description (such as the Electronic Archival Description, or EAD, files); in other cases we may have both collection- and item-level records, each of which has value in its own right, but it is not clear how to link the two and it also isn't always clear that it is useful to make huge numbers of item-level records available.

OAI-enabled service would use the MHP to pull metadata for all of the individual records in a database, and would then perform computations that allow it to provide some kind of summary metadata record for the entire database as output; these summary records could then be returned to the database owner or operator or could be made available to other resource discovery services.

The Metadata Harvesting Protocol is a means of making machine-processable metadata widely available for use. It will create tremendous pressure for standards programs that are now developing schemes to codify and represent such metadata, especially the Dublin Core Metadata Initiative.

MHP specifies unqualified Dublin Core as the lowest-common-denominator mandatory metadata scheme for interoperability purposes. This will likely lead to the first truly large-scale test of the real utility and practicality of unqualified Dublin Core for resource discovery. It is certainly clear that almost any metadata scheme can be "downgraded" into unqualified Dublin Core (in a non-reversible fashion), but the actual usefulness of such a coarse metadata scheme has been the subject of considerable debate and speculation.

The Dublin Core Initiative is also codifying the notion of qualified Dublin Core-a series of extensions to the base Dublin Core elements that can provide much greater precision but that can be "interpreted down" to unqualified Dublin Core in a consistent fashion by applications that are not knowledgeable about specific extensions. At a broader level, the idea of community-based metadata schemes is central to the vision of the Metadata Harvesting Protocol. There has been a great deal of work in this area over the past few years, in part driven by the promise of XML and the growing interest in the interchange of computer-processable information using the Internet.

Fundamentally, the development of these standards is a social process within a community, though it calls upon a poorly-codified body of knowledge in data structuring, descriptive practices, classification, and other areas. It is still very slow, and very expensive, to develop these community standards, and it is hard to predict which ones will be successful in terms of broad adoption or in terms of effectively meeting community needs over reasonably long periods of time.

The Research Libraries Group (RLG) manages one of the largest union library catalogs in the world. It received support to explore how this major scholarly resource could be completely redesigned to take advantage of Internet portal technologies.

In its proposed project, RLG catalog records would be made accessible via the Open Archives protocol to a standard Internet search engine, such as Google, and search results would be expected to link the user not only to a set of catalog entries, but also to a set of service options that might, for example, direct users how to purchase the book, find the nearest library that owns the title, find related works by the author or on the subject, or link to an online version if one exists.

2

Digital Library Development

There are many thousands of digital library projects currently underway, in all sectors of the library community. These projects have taken widely varying approaches, dependent on the needs of the different libraries, the sector in which they are based, and, in part, the definition of digital library that has been applied.

This has led to a variety of digital libraries being developed, with no common model being available. The many existing digital library studies can give a useful pointer to the general development of digital libraries. However, the majority of published digital library research has occurred in the academic and public library sectors.

Watson and Streatfield were concerned that there has been a major focus on digital library developments in recent years, yet there has been relatively little attention paid to special libraries, especially those outside the "commercial" arena. Missingham concurred with this view, noting that the use of new technology in special libraries has been quite different to that of academic and public libraries. Government libraries usually fill a quite different role within their agency than their academic and public library counterparts.

The basic concept underlying the digital library is not new. In 1945, Dr Vannevar Bush of the U.S. Office of Scientific Research and Development discussed a device called a "memex". He envisioned this device being used by individuals as "a sort of mechanised private file and library". It would be able to store large amounts of books, pictures, periodicals, newspapers, correspondence, and so on, with material being indexed for easy retrieval. According to Saffady, the Bush vision is "one of the most influential and frequently cited precursors" of the modern digital library concept. He continued to note that although the digital library seems a revolutionary development, the concepts and technologies involved are more accurately described as evolutionary.

Although not a recent concept, in terms of actual development, digital libraries are still relatively new. Because of this, there is as yet no universally agreed terminology in place. In the literature, the digital library may also be called the library without walls, virtual library, electronic library, e-library, desktop library, online library, future library, library of the future, logical library, networked library, hybrid library, gateway library, extended library or information superhighway.

Of these many terms, digital library, virtual library, hybrid library and electronic (or e-) library are most common. Just as there is no universally agreed upon terminology for digital libraries, neither is there a common definition for this concept. In the 1990s, terms such as digital library, virtual library and electronic library became widely used, but considerable uncertainty remains about what they actually mean.

The term digital library has been defined both broadly and narrowly. In the narrower form, a digital library is construed as a mainly, if not wholly, digital entity , although this fully digital scenario is dependent on the necessary materials being available in an appropriate format. In the broader construction, the digital library is defined as a hybrid of traditional library services and new electronic sources and methods.

One of the more comprehensive definitions by Gapen, who defined digital libraries as:

...the concept of remote access to the contents and services of libraries and other information resources, combining an on-site collection of current and heavily used materials in both print and electronic form, with an electronic network which provides access to, and delivery from, external worldwide library and commercial information and knowledge sources. In essence, the user is provided the effect of a library which is a synergy created by bringing together technologically the resources of many, many libraries and information services.

The broader definition of digital libraries offered by Gapen was adopted. No distinction was made in defining the various terms used to describe the digital library concept, and for the sake of clarity, the term digital library has been used throughout..

Regardless of the wide variety of terms used to describe the digital library concept, it is clear from the literature that there are certain common elements, regardless of the terminology applied. There must be, in some sense, a collection, to which clients must be linked in an efficient and satisfying manner. There is also a set of services, either human or electronic, which link clients to the collections.

The technologies involved in providing digital library services should support document creation, retrieval, transfer, dissemination, manipulation and management. Finally, there must be an institution in which the digital library collections and services are embedded. A major study, conducted by the Association of Research Libraries (ARL) in 1992, identified series of different activities considered essential to the formation of digital libraries. These included:

— Use of, or development of electronic document delivery services;

— Policies, services, or reallocations that emphasise access [to information] over ownership;

— Participation in cooperative development or purchase of electronic files;

— Participation in the development of a campus-wide information system;

— A written plan that states its goal as access to information from a single workstation;

— Enhancement of the online public access catalogue (OPAC) to include the holdings of other libraries besides those held locally;

— Providing a gateway from the OPAC to other databases or networks, such as the Internet;

— End-user access to online files from on or off campus;

— Connection with the Internet;

— Training faculty and students:

— in the use of Internet sources; and,

— in end-user searching;

— Subscribing to electronic journals;

— Digitisation of text for electronic storage, retrieval and/or dissemination.

These elements, then, may be considered the basic building blocks of the digital library, although the nature and extent of the application of each component will depend upon the circumstances and needs of the library and/or organisation to which the digital library is attached.

There are number of activities that together make up digital libraries, so too does it show that the development of digital libraries is heavily dependent on a number of inter-related enabling (or hindering) factors. These include such issues as copyright, client attitudes, changes to funding and financial structures, the need for new organisational structures, technological issues, staff training, and so on.

A study of Commonwealth library digital library developments was conducted in 1998-1999, with one of its objects to determine if the model developed from the general literature on digital libraries was appropriate to digital library development in the Commonwealth library sector. Libraries included in the study were libraries within those agencies, statutory and non-statutory authorities administered by the Commonwealth Government. Where an agency had more than one library, only those libraries that had policy and budgetary control over their individual library or network was included.

The National Library of Australia was excluded from this study as, although it is a Commonwealth library, it is also a national library, and as such, has different foci, programs and priorities than special libraries delivering information services to public sector organisations. An examination of the digital library activities undertaken in Commonwealth libraries showed that some activities were undertaken by far more libraries than were others.

This suggests that the various issues that impact on the digital library environment have relatively equal importance, with none assuming much greater significance than another.

Content Management in Web Environment

The idea of "content management" is multifaceted. One's choice of a perspective on the idea carries with it distinctive terminology, particular alliances with facets of a complex information technology infrastructure, specific limits on what content is and is not, and implied commitments to organizational and administrative priorities. Each of the three perspectives outlined below attempts to deal with various aspects of the content management issue, ranging from digital content (as objects or assets), to the people who add value to the content, to the tools one uses to add support or manage the process of adding value.

For many people in the IT community, content management simply means WEB content. The key concept in Web content management is the creation of value through a reduction in "time to web." In practice, this concept translates into more dynamic web delivery systems built on the back of a relational database tied to a template-driven workflow process that allows fewer people to create and deliver more web content.

A database-driven approach to web content management opens up new possibilities within an organization to share content across units and to share in the costs of creating and maintaining digital content. Some writers on content management have chosen to focus almost exclusively on protecting the asset value of digital objects, without regard to the purposes to which the objects may be put. From an asset management perspective, the organization of digital objects in well structured and well-documented databases is the most critical activity.

The digital preservation community in libraries has tended to emphasize asset management as a key value. The present movement to specify preservation metadata requirements within the construct of the Open Archival Information System reference model is the most dramatic example of efforts define content management in terms of the archival repository.

Knowledge management has traditionally suffered from the hubris of modernism: the belief that we can discover ultimate truths and organize the world according to rational principles using clever code. The idea was that we should capture and organize bits of "knowledge" in central databases. The people involved were relevant only as donors to the common ontology or as empty vessels into which knowledge could be poured.

Therefore, postmodern KM can't be about management at all, because management implies external control of some definable resource. Its goal is simpler yet deeper: leveraging people. Postmodern KM operates within and on the basis of existing behavior patterns, mining conversation streams and relationships automatically to incorporate structure and context into the information human users already manipulate. It fosters human intelligence and interaction rather than trying to replace them.

This vision of content management suggests that librarians must reconcile the tensions between the structured and the dynamic, between "control zones" and empowerment, and between the Web that we access and the digital content that we provide. These tensions are not new or particularly interesting, except in so far as they help to extend the concept of "content" to encompass a much wider range of management responsibilities for digital content than we have heretofore chosen to consider appropriate.

Increasingly, libraries are being asked or expected to step up to the challenge of acquiring, organizing, and protecting digital content that they have neither created themselves (digitization) or licensed from publishers. Examples of new generations of digital content that are just beginning to flow into and through libraries include digital products produced and distributed or otherwise published by faculty, the output of research collaboratives, graduate student theses, the electronic records or the university's administrative offices, courseware content, and streaming audio and video resources generated from courses, conferences, and other campus activities.

In the Web environment, the business community has adopted the term "knowledge management" to refer to processes that use technology to leverage human expertise and know-how to create new value for the organization. In the higher education context, knowledge management constructs are most closely tied to scholarly communication processes. A critical issue for libraries is tension between possibly competing commitments to the process of scholarship as a discipline-based enterprise and the product of the process as an institutional imperative.

Another critical aspect of considering "content management" to be an important but limited component of the scholarly communication process is the relationship of librarians and libraries to content creators, whether those creators are faculty/authors or publishers/ owners. Today's library is "all digital" in the sense that all services and content (digital and non-digital) are mediated via web gateways. Users begin and end their scholarly work with digital information, even if there is a considerable amount of paper in between.

Without some form of digital accessibility, library resources in any format are invisible and therefore unusable. Physical browsing for all but a vocal few has become a chimera. Libraries are already in the new business of digital product development by nature of their creation of digital resources, regardless of whether creation encompasses only digitization or extends to the development of specialized aggregations of digital resources.

Libraries and archives cannot possibly assume full responsibility for preserving digital information, but rather must participate in a marketplace that itself has not come to terms with the idea of lost value. Librarians are critical players in the conception of the IT marketplace but have neither exclusive claim on content management concepts or a particularly strong share of the marketplace that is driving the development of content management tools.

Content management in the "all digital" environment within higher education can only function effectively at the corporate (i.e., university) level, even when the digital content itself is created and managed to support disciplinary or interdisciplinary scholarship.

New Measures for Digital Collection

Within the past four years, "new measures" has entered the lexicon of library performance and assessment literature. In the 1990s, escalating economic pressures and demands for accountability from governing boards, university administrators, and government agencies strongly encouraged ARL member libraries and many other libraries to find new ways to illustrate the contribution their collections and services provided to their constituencies.

Traditional, input measures (i.e., size of collections, budget, and staff) were not meeting institutional accountability needs. Although efforts were in place to measure some forms of output--e.g., activities such as circulation, interlibrary borrowing, and group presentations--these, too, did not always provide a good or complete indication of library performance and the cost effectiveness of their services.

Impact of Library on Teaching and Learning

For many institutions, the accreditation process has provided the strongest impetus for a shifting campus emphasis on institutional outcomes. The retreat participants recognized that some of the more difficult measures to develop would identify how a library contributes to the teaching and learning process.

Recent literature on higher education assessment illustrates evidence that general education outcomes and, in some cases, outcomes for some professional programs are being developed and used. Common themes and learning objectives have arisen that can be applied by institutions beginning to develop their own outcomes assessment efforts. Accrediting agencies are a key source in encouraging these developments.

Libraries are now in an environment that asks for outcomes (what is the benefit of your service) or impact (what difference do you make). Institutions are identifying their outcomes, defining criteria for success, and determining methods to look for evidence of success. Responding to user demand, libraries have steadily been shifting the focus of their collection development to the acquisition and licensing of electronic content, much of it via consortia.

In the last decade, the average percentage of acquisition dollars that ARL member libraries directed to electronic resources rose from 3% to 20%. Increasingly libraries are called upon to demonstrate the educational impact and outcomes achieved because of the increased availability of electronic resources. In the new measures environment, we are faced with the challenge of identifying (a) new "species" of metrics and (b) new methods for measuring the effectiveness of these new species.

In US, the National Science Digital Library (NSDL) Educational Impact and Evaluation (EI&E) Standing Committee is developing a strategy for evaluating the educational impact of digital libraries. As in all new measures work, the lack of common definitions or understood vocabulary is a challenge. NSDL is a National Science Foundation (NSF) program with over 100 projects. It is a network of digital libraries and services that are targeting different audiences.

A large component of this network is the core integration effort that attempts to create shared technologies, protocols, a central repository, and a core portal. The mission of NSDL is (a) to encourage and sustain continual improvements in the quality of science, technology, engineering and mathematics (STEM) education for all students, and serve as a resource for lifelong learning and (b) a collective effort to build a national digital library of high quality STEM educational materials for students and teachers at all levels, in both formal and informal settings.

Evaluation of NSDL has been primarily formative in nature with different projects and participants bringing forward their own assessment activities. In addition, there is continuous NSF program evaluation and encouragement to broaden participation of other NSF programs that support the development of assessment capacity.

Institutional Repositories in the Digital Age

The development of institutional repositories emerged as a new strategy that allows universities to apply serious, systematic leverage to accelerate changes taking place in scholarship and scholarly communication, both moving beyond their historic relatively passive role of supporting established publishers in modernizing scholarly publishing through the licensing of digital content, and also scaling up beyond ad-hoc alliances, partnerships, and support arrangements with a few select faculty pioneers exploring more transformative new uses of the digital medium.

Many technology trends and development efforts came together to make this strategy possible. Online storage costs have dropped significantly; repositories are now affordable. Standards like the open archives metadata harvesting protocol are now in place; some progress has also been made on the standards for the underlying metadata itself. The thinking about digital preservation over the past five years has advanced to the point where the needs are widely recognized and well defined, the technical approaches at least superficially mapped out, and the need for action is now clear.

The development of free, publicly accessible journal article collections in disciplines such as high-energy physics has demonstrated ways in which the network can change scholarly communication by altering dissemination and access patterns; separately, the development of a series of extraordinary digital works had at least suggested the potential of creative authorship specifically for the digital medium to transform the presentation and transmission of scholarship.

A university-based institutional repository is a set of services that a university offers to the members of its community for the management and dissemination of digital materials created by the institution and its community members. It is most essentially an organizational commitment to the stewardship of these digital materials, including long-term preservation where appropriate, as well as organization and access or distribution.

While operational responsibility for these services may reasonably be situated in different organizational units at different universities, an effective institutional repository of necessity represents a collaboration among librarians, information technologists, archives and records mangers, faculty, and university administrators and policymakers. At any given point in time, an institutional repository will be supported by a set of information technologies, but a key part of the services that comprise an institutional repository is the management of technological changes, and the migration of digital content from one set of technologies to the next as part of the organizational commitment to providing repository services.

An institutional repository is not simply a fixed set of software and hardware. While early implementers of institutional repositories have chosen different paths to begin populating their repositories and to build campus community acceptance, support, and participation, that a mature and fully realized institutional repository will contain the intellectual works of faculty and students—both research and teaching materials—and also documentation of the activities of the institution itself in the form of records of events and performance and of the ongoing intellectual life of the institution. It will also house experimental and observational data captured by members of the institution that support their scholarly activities.

At the most basic and fundamental level, an institutional repository is a recognition that the intellectual life and scholarship of our universities will increasingly be represented, documented, and shared in digital form, and that a primary responsibility of our universities is to exercise stewardship over these riches: both to make them available and to preserve them.

An institutional repository is the means by which our universities will address this responsibility both to the members of their communities and to the public. It is a new channel for structuring the university's contribution to the broader world, and as such invites policy and cultural reassessment of this relationship.

Importance of Institutional Repositories

Scholarship and scholarly communication are changing. These changes start with risky and bold acts of individual creativity. They will extend slowly to cultural changes at the disciplinary levei and ultimately to new interdisciplinary standards that are expressed in the decisions of institutional tenure and promotion practices. Institutions of higher education have overlooked an opportunity to support our most innovative and creative faculty for at least a decade now, to the detriment of both the faculty members and the institutions themselves.

These faculty have been exploring ways in which works of authorship in the new digital medium can enhance teaching and learning and the communication of scholarship; such innovations are essential to keeping scholarship vital and effective, and they must not only be supported but nurtured. Indeed nurturing these innovations reaches to the core mission of our universities, and to the core values of our universities.

A much broader and generally more conservative group of faculty have exploited the Net as a vehicle for sharing their ideas worldwide, whether these ideas are expressed in relatively familiar forms such as digital versions of traditional journal articles or (less commonly) in entirely new forms that begin to map out the future evolution of, for example, the scholarly monograph in the digital medium. This embrace of new dissemination opportunities is also important for what it says about the roles of scholars and universities in society and in a global environment.

Over the past few years, this has ceased to be a reasonable activity for most amateurs; software complexity, security risks, backup requirements, and other problems have generally relegated effective operation of Web sites to professionals who can exploit economies of scale, and who can begin each day with a review of recently issued security patches.

Institutional repositories can address both the near-term questions about continuity of access by providing an environment in which such new works of scholarship can be managed and disseminated—including such basic things as professionally managed systems and systematic backup procedures—and also the longer-term questions about preservation by creating an institutional commitment to such preservation.

The revolution in scholarly communications is not limited to the development of new genres of scholarly works that are enabled by the digital medium; even traditional forms such as journal articles now frequently include supplementary datasets and analysis tools. Scholarship has become data intensive; it is supported and documented by data and tools that complement interpretive works of authorship.

Most scientific journals are now accepting what they characterize as "supplementary" materials as part of the publication of traditional journal articles, but it is much less clear what commitments these journals are making to actually integrating these supplementary materials into the permanent record of scholarship in the same way that they maintain the journal articles themselves as a part of that record.

Journals will move too slowly and too unevenly to manage these resources, and disciplinary data repositories cannot be comprehensive. Institutional repositories can maintain data in addition to authored scholarly works. In this sense, the institutional repository is a complement and a supplement, rather than a substitute, for traditional scholarly publication venues. Institutional repositories also have roles beyond disseminating and managing the works of individual scholars that are part of the dialog of scholarly communications.

Institutional repositories are a place where they can put much of the material that research libraries identify as worth collecting. Finally, at least a few institutions themselves are changing their culture and are making commitments to globally disseminate extensive teaching and learning materials through the Net or, at a less systematic but still important level, to digitally capture and preserve the many of the events of campus life--symposia, performances, lectures.

Institutional repositories offer a framework for organized stewardship and accessibility of these materials. To summarize, institutional repositories can facilitate greatly enhanced access to traditional scholarly content by empowering faculty to effectively use the new dissemination capabilities offered by the network. This is also occurring on a disciplinary basis through the development of e-print and preprint servers, at least in some disciplines.

In cases where the disciplinary practice is ready, institutional repositories can feed disciplinary repositories directly. In cases where the disciplinary culture is more conservative, where scholarly societies or key journals choose to hold back change, institutional repositories can help individual faculty take the lead in initiating shifts in disciplinary practice. Institutional repositories can encourage the exploration and adoption of new forms of scholarly communication that exploit the digital medium in fundamental ways.

Institutional repositories can support new practices of scholarship that emphasize data as an integral part of the record and discourse of scholarship. They can structure and make effective otherwise diffuse efforts to capture and disseminate learning and teaching materials, symposia and performances, and related documentation of the intellectual life of universities. Institutional repositories will succeed precisely because they are responsive to the needs of campus communities, and advance the interests of campus communities and of scholarship broadly.

To the extent that they try to enforce behavioral or cultural changes--and particularly controversial ones--within the campus community they will and should fail. The theme is accepting responsibility, not exerting new levels of control. This is not to say that policies mandating the deposit of materials that are broadly recognized as part of the institutional record are inappropriate. But institutions should move very conservatively down this path.

Institutional repositories may legitimately serve as infrastructure to advance some of these interests—for example, groups might construct a peer-review process that certifies selected works that are accessible in various institutional repositories and even develop overlay systems that span a complex of institutional repositories and create a "virtual" journal. Such an effort would have to be extra-institutional and cross-institutional to have much scholarly credibility, for the same reason that university presses aren't simply publishing outlets for the faculty at their parent institutions, and the editorial boards of institutionally hosted journals are drawn from beyond the host institution.

Its extra-institutional nature should help to clarify that it shouldn't be confused with the development of individual institutional repositories. But this is not, to my mind, the primary point of institutional repositories. Indeed, it dramatically underestimates the importance of institutional repositories to characterize them as instruments for restructuring the current economics of scholarly publishing rather than as vehicles to advance, support, and legitimize a much broader spectrum of new scholarly communications.

But recognize that the institutional repository isn't a journal, or a collection of journals, and should not be managed like one. That's not the point or the purpose of an institutional repository. Institutional repositories are not a challenge or alternative to disciplinary repositories; rather, they complement them, just as they can complement existing venues of scholarly publication. The Open Archive Initiative Metadata Harvesting Protocol gives the tools for an institutional repository to act as an entry point for redistributing works to systems of disciplinary repositories. It is desirable to make this as simple as possible, and to insulate faculty from having to deal with the details of a constantly evolving multiplicity of disciplinary services. Better to present the faculty with a simple and stable submission interface to the institutional repository.

In this sense institutional repositories can be an infrastructure upon which disciplinary services and repositories can build. In the near future, many campus communities may expect and demand that such services be made available rapidly; creating institutional repositories may also become fashionable in some administrative circles. It's vital that institutions recognize institutional repositories as a serious and long-lasting commitment to the campus community (and to the scholarly world, and the public at large) that should not be made lightly.

In establishing institutional repositories, institutions are both accepting risks and making promises; they are creating new expectations. In a budget crunch, the institutional repository may be one of the last things that can be cut, given the way that digital preservation demands steady and consistent attention and hence funding. Faculty who choose to rely on institutional repositories to disseminate and preserve their work are placing a great deal of trust in their institution and in the integrity, wisdom, and competence of the people who manage it.

An institutional repository can fail over time for many reasons: policy (for example, the institution chooses to stop funding it), management failure or incompetence, or technical problems. Any of these failures can result in the disruption of access, or worse, total and permanent loss of material stored in the institutional repository. As we think about institutional repositories today, there is much less redundancy than we have had in our systems of print publication and libraries, so any single institutional failure can cause more damage.

Institutional repositories make promises about stewardship and preservation. These promises are necessarily qualified. Institutions will make choices based on a balance of campus community demand and local assessments about technical feasibility, which will result in lists of file formats that they will commit to preserve in accessible forms (presumably through format migration); in other cases, they may preserve the bits that make up a file, but will offer no guarantees that these bits can be interpreted in the future without the development of specialized programs to read them.

These choices can then be collected into broader community consensus within the higher education and research community as a form of bottom-up standards development that benefits from active work in curation and ongoing faculty involvement. The ability to make persistent reference to materials in institutional repositories will clearly be critical as these materials will form an important part of the scholarly dialogue and record. This will have to include provisions to deal with issues like versioning.

Higher education and the library community have not been sufficiently active in this area, largely ceding the field to commercial interests and traditional publisher agendas. The deployment of institutional repositories will drive pragmatic solutions in this area. The management of rights for digital materials will be essential. The whole point of institutional repositories is to facilitate access, reuse, and stewardship (which may itself involve reformatting) of content, and we need methods of recording and documenting the rights and permissions associated with works that facilitate these goals of the research and education community.

Part of this is a technical problem involving metadata structures; the other part is building consensus around a relatively small number of sets of terms and conditions that can cover the majority of the materials in practice. University institutional repositories have some very interesting and unexplored extensions to what we might think of as community or public repositories; this may in fact be another case of a concept developed within higher education moving more broadly into our society. Public libraries might join forces with local government, local historical societies, local museums and archives, and members of their local communities to establish community repositories. Public broadcasting might also have a role here.

It is clear that the institutional repository is a very powerful idea that can serve as an engine of change for our institutions of higher education, and more broadly for the scholarly enterprises that they support. If properly developed, it advances a surprising number of goals, and addresses an impressive range of needs. Some of the results seem clear, though there are also likely to be any number of unexpected consequences.

A Global Resource Programme

A globally oriented program is by definition ambitious, especially when it is focused on information and its dissemination. Despite an increasing reliance on electronic information, print book and journal publishing worldwide continues to expand dramatically. Accordingly, the strategies adopted to tackle the goals of the Global Resources Program are multiple and varied:

— providing seed money for an initial set of six diverse regional projects (on Africa, Germany, Japan, Latin America, South Asia, Southeast Asia);

— gathering information into a clearinghouse on ARL libraries' linkages with institutions abroad;

— building bridges to scholars who use international materials, and to the scholarly associations to which they belong, in order to develop a better understanding of the research resources they need and how libraries can facilitate access to them; and

— helping to create new models for recruiting and training future area specialists who have strong subject knowledge, initiative, and the right skill set.

The systematic identification of collection strengths of North American libraries will be another important step toward the Program's full implementation, and the launching of other area- and subject-specific projects as they are designed is an ongoing objective. The overarching strategy for the Program is to scale up from the projects by selecting, from among the models they are testing, the elements that will contribute to a comprehensive, cooperative, distributed program of access to international resources, regardless of their format or location.

The eventual goal is to move beyond a set of discrete, area-specific projects to an interconnected, globally oriented program in which "lead institutions" provide users throughout North America with both physical collections and access points to diverse resources published in or relating to a given world area. Another long-term goal of the Program–essential for making the vision into reality–is to develop a system of financial incentives that will benefit a broad range of institutions, as well as sustain the Program well into the future.

The six regional projects currently underway offer an impressive array of approaches to addressing some of the most urgent information needs of scholars researching individual world regions. These approaches range from the creation of a web-based union list of sub-Saharan African newspapers to an international document delivery service between North American and German research libraries, from a Latin American table-of-contents database with direct, user-initiated article requesting capability to the digitization, in India, of South Asian reference works and periodicals, and the creation of an image database of Thai journal literature.

The full impact of the Program, however, extends beyond this set of projects. For example, awareness of the factors that negatively affect the ability of libraries to provide the materials that users need, that litany of pressures with which librarians are all too familiar, has been heightened among faculty and within scholarly associations.

Librarians with responsibility for one region of the world are finding common ground with those whose principal focus is another. The Overseas Offices of the Library of Congress are key participants in many of the projects and are uniquely prepared to address directly the key issue of access through the expansion of the services they provide in Cairo, Islamabad, Nairobi, New Delhi, Jakarta, and Rio de Janeiro.

The Center for Research Libraries has launched the International Coalition on Newspapers (ICON), an ambitious and much-needed effort to identify, preserve, and make accessible as wide a range of foreign newspapers as possible. Collaboration with institutions outside North America, both formal and informal, has been stimulated by the identification of reciprocal relationships for collection development, interlibrary lending and borrowing, and document delivery.

In short, the AAU/ARL Global Resources Program has been a catalyst in stimulating interest and action to strengthen international library resources. This new Department of Education program has stimulated the development of projects that bring together librarians and faculty in creative joint undertakings whose goal is exactly consistent with that of the Global Resources Program: to expand access to international resources through the use of new technologies.

The initial focus of the Global Resources Program was on cooperative collection development. This is arguably the necessary first step toward a distributed network of interdependent collections, and yet the Program has since shifted focus within some of the regional projects to concentrate on document delivery. At first glance, this would seem to be a major change; however, they are part and parcel of the same theme.

For years, at meetings of collection development librarians and other conferences, inadequate document delivery and interlibrary loan capability has been pinpointed as a major obstacle to successful cooperative collection development, whether it be on a relatively small, regional scale, or at the national or North American level. Certainly, to gain faculty acceptance of a distributed collection it is critical to guarantee rapid access to needed materials that are not held locally.

And since engaging faculty as supporters of the premises of the Global Resources Program and illustrating for them the potential of structured interdependence are among the Program's original goals, a focus on rapid delivery of the resources they need seems logical. It is important to demonstrate to faculty that the Program and other cooperative collection-building structures will expand access, not decrease it. They are gaining, not losing.

An acute awareness of the importance of building collections cooperatively still characterizes the Program, although several current efforts focus on disseminating information about what is held where rather than on orchestrating firm cooperative agreements. In order to distribute responsibility for collecting, it is important to know who has what, a need that has promoted the development of projects to establish union lists of journals and newspapers, or periodical indexes, for example.

Nevertheless, the Program will only achieve its goals and realize its full potential when participants take the difficult steps of redefining collecting policies to focus on local strengths and reallocating resources accordingly, while simultaneously moving toward a more inter-reliant network of research libraries. An emphasis on cataloging and preservation is inherent in all of the activities of the Global Resources Program.

The American Council of Learned Societies (ACLS) featured a special session on the AAU/ARL Global Resources Program. Executive directors of area studies scholarly associations and delegates to each organization, along with other interested participants, responded to a presentation about the Program and expressed their views on its future development. The environment, human rights, migration, popular culture, ethnic studies–these are examples of areas of scholarship with a significant international dimension, in which research requires access to a multiplicity of resources that may be ephemeral, difficult to locate, poorly preserved, and undercollected in North America.

A Global Resources project that takes a topical rather than a regional approach would encourage links among library collections that are not based on the traditional area studies model, that span national boundaries, and yet still address the core challenges of the Reed-Scott book and the studies that preceded it.

There are many nonaffiliated projects underway that bear a relationship to the Global Resources Program. Similarly, any distributed collection development structure will take advantage of existing consortia and work in progress. Links among libraries and scholars, and the active involvement of faculty in helping to imagine and anticipate future needs, will be critical to the Program's continued success. Just as important will be a practical vision of a new interdependence among libraries.

Although it has focused on projects that expand access to international research materials, in many cases vernacular resources, the lessons of the Global Resources Program are not limited to the acquisition and distribution of foreign materials. The Program is also raising issues with broader, more general implications. In this way, the Program contains a microcosm of the newest challenges and concerns for research libraries, issues that are not peculiar to area studies.

These include, of course, the creation of cooperative structures for collection development and document delivery services that are rapid, efficient, and international. The Program is built on the need to discover ways to stretch budgets so that libraries collectively can offer access to more than they currently do individually. The Program has stimulated new thinking about service to users, especially those who are remote but rely on specialized collections held in our libraries, and has shifted focus to a user-based model of distributed collection development and away from an emphasis on amassing collections locally.

Participation in large-scale collaborative endeavors requires a significant commitment of staff time and energy, and this in turn requires a re-thinking of the collection development librarian's job description. The success of the Global Resources regional projects would have been impossible without the ideas, initiative, and action of a number of area studies librarians. Such energy and creativity will continue to be prerequisites for achieving the goals of multi-institutional collaboration, whether international or not.

To achieve the goals of the Global Resources Program, and any program based on cooperative collection development, we must view "collections" as a wide array of resources, some held locally but many found elsewhere–even outside North America–and not necessarily in libraries, or in print form. We do not need to own the physical object to consider it part of our "collection."

Technology makes it feasible to consider remote collections to be local resources as long as it is reasonably straightforward for users to gain access to these materials. It is apparent that university administrators, faculty, library administrators, and collection development librarians need a new vision for their local library collection, and new ways of measuring its strength as part of a shared North American collection.

The Global Resources Program forces a redefinition of "collections" if we are to meet the needs of current users of our libraries and anticipate those of future generations. Bringing about the change in perspective that is necessary for distributed collecting to succeed will require progress in several interconnected areas:

— an understanding on the part of faculty that it is in their long-term interest for their university's library to have an interdependent relationship with other institutions, so that someone, somewhere, is collecting the materials that they, and their colleagues within North America, need;

— the autonomy for collection development librarians to craft cooperative policies that share responsibility for collecting and commit their institutions to a particular set of areas, the will and authority to cancel journals that are widely held elsewhere in favor of more specialized acquisitions in their areas of collecting responsibility, and the political sensitivity to explain these decisions to library users in compelling and convincing terms;

— an acknowledgment of the critical role of document delivery and interlibrary loan in making distributed collections feasible, and a commitment to invest in the redesign of systems of access;

— the necessary determination and support for rapid cataloging of international materials, which will not only make these resources more accessible to users but will also provide bibliographers with important information on holdings that may influence their acquisitions decisions; and

— a firm commitment on the part of library and university administrators to a new vision of interdependent collections, acknowledgment of the benefits of the strategy, and adequate, long-term financial support to continue building and preserving the collections for which their institution has accepted responsibility.

The Latin Americanist Research Resources Project is experimenting with distributed collecting responsibilities through its "Distributed Resources" component, in which each participating institution commits to redirecting a minimum of either $3,000 or 7% of its monographic budget for Latin American materials towards an area of locally established collection strength. By implication, they will rely on other Project libraries for materials they will no longer be acquiring.

Participating bibliographers have confirmed that, through reallocation, they have been able to acquire items that enrich their local collections in areas of emphasis while also providing access to these materials for users anywhere. In the division of responsibilities among the participating libraries, based on local strengths and local choice, nearly all countries are represented. Thus, the Project is demonstrating broad coverage and balance.

This element of the Latin American project is a significant step towards strengthening North American collections of Latin American publications. The Project has succeeded in large part because it is allowing individual institutions to emphasize local strengths (thereby eliminating the tension between local program needs and national-level commitments) and because it is focusing on materials that do not generally receive high use.

Role of Bibliographer

An expansion and redefinition of the role of the collection development librarian, or bibliographer, has been underway for some time as the job has required more contact with the public and advanced technological skills. In the Global Resources arena, bibliographers have the opportunity to serve as intellectual leaders in crafting new models for access and new structures for cooperative collection building.

Rather than being marginalized, bibliographers have become even more central to the success of complex international projects. They play a visible role in fund raising, including drafting proposals and administering grants. Designing area- and subject-specific projects to address the goals of the Global Resources Program also brings bibliographers together with faculty to think strategically about the variety of future scholarly resource needs.

Working with a much broader definition of "collections" than ever before, bibliographers are collaborating with colleagues at other libraries and in other countries to ensure that research libraries are together providing access to the widest range of resources possible. The creation and maintenance of web pages with detailed collection descriptions and links to many other carefully selected and vetted resources is increasingly part of the bibliographer's job.

As the Global Resources Program moves toward the identification of a network of lead institutions, bibliographers' knowledge and experience will become even more important. The Global Resources Program has opened positive new lines of communication within individual libraries as well. The implementation of the regional projects, particularly those with significant document delivery components, encourages a closer relationship between collection development librarians and interlibrary loan staff.

ILL librarians are in an excellent position to help identify where there may be gaps in local collections coverage. They are also key players in determining the nature and usefulness of new document delivery mechanisms that are at the core of enhanced access. Additional intra-institutional collaboration will flourish as cross-regional projects are developed, and subject and area studies bibliographers begin to work together to implement and publicize the projects and to evaluate their effectiveness.

Role of Library in Education

Today, the library and education community faces a series of fast-paced copyright and other intellectual property issues. The issues addressed in The Digital Millennium Copyright Act (DMCA), PL 105-304, that are of utmost importance for libraries and the education community are: access to and fair use of copyrighted works issued in encrypted form; the liability of online service providers for infringing behavior by a user of the service; the proper uses of copyrighted works in distance education programs; and the use of digital technology to preserve library and archival materials. In the case of all but the last of these issues, major questions remain about application of the new statutory provisions in educational settings.

Many electronic works are distributed in encrypted form and the DMCA established stiff penalties for anyone accessing a copyrighted work protected by "technological protective measures" (TPMs) without the consent of the copyright owner. The law also bans equipment or services whose primary purpose is for use in defeating technology that limits access to a copyrighted work.

Taking effect in two years, the new anti-circumvention and access rules will encourage publishers to distribute digital works online; by CD, CD-ROM, or DVD; or in other formats in either encrypted or protected form by providing greater assurance to copyright owners that those who abuse access barriers will be subject to severe penalties.

Legislators and content owners both hope that the severity of the penalties will discourage widespread piracy. The new law does provide for certain exemptions to the anti-circumvention penalties. However, the one exemption included for nonprofit libraries, archives, and educational institutions is solely for the purpose of determining whether to acquire the work or not. A central question not answered in the new law is how a library, archive, or school may obtain the means to circumvent, since the selling of such equipment is prohibited in the law. It also remains unanswered in law whether any fair use can be made of a work protected by TPMs, absent a future rulemaking.

The TPM and anti-circumvention provisions of the DMCA will most likely ensure that more works come with licenses and with an obligation to pay for each use or access. This change could hit libraries particularly hard because it challenges the way in which libraries function as archives of our published history. Libraries must be prepared to review contracts for the acquisition of digital works more closely than ever before and bargain for full access rights. Libraries must be alert to limitations on access and use of works that are licensed. In short, they must be prepared:

- to bargain for the right to a hard copy;
- to realize that digital access means limited access, unless you own a copy of the work;
- to pay for the cost of access; and
- to understand that equipment that decrypts works may be illegal to acquire or use.

The library and education community needs to organize itself and understand how it is using digital works today, how it is likely to use them in the near term, and what the economic and social impacts of the new regime will be. As with many agency rulemaking proceedings, active participation in the initial case will be very important, because procedures will be established for managing the record and early precedents will carry forward for years to come.

All issues raised by the legislation will be novel for the Librarian in the first rulemaking case. The central focus of these proceedings will be to determine (1) the "adverse affects" of the rules upon library and educational users, the significance of licensing alternatives ("pay per use"), and, ultimately, (3) the particular classes of works that should be exempted from the scheme.

Since the burdens of obtaining relief fall on the proponents, library and educational institutions will have to make a persuasive record that justifies appropriate relief. It will be a challenge, but one that will help shape the future role of libraries in the digital age.

Online Service Providers

Creation of a new limitation on liability for online service providers (OSPs) was perhaps the most complex task of the DMCA legislators. The new rules establish certain procedures and conditions that grant OSPs, including libraries and educational institutions, an exclusion from monetary liability for copyright infringement by a user of the service.

Balancing a myriad of interests and fashioning legislation for technology that is arcane and evolving are no simple tasks. Thus, the OSP limitation of liability represents a very important contribution of the DMCA to copyright law. Also, the process used to develop this statutory limitation-congressional committee supervised negotiations-may also serve as a model for preparing legislation on other issues that require discreet balancing of concerns of contentious but politically powerful interests.

For libraries, the initial issue is whether to assert status as a "service provider" and register with the Copyright Office. This is not an easy question to resolve. Certainly, the definition of "service provider" is broad enough to encompass many of the libraries' online activities. However, the legislation's complex rules will require very careful compliance practices, including the use of sophisticated software and systems and the development of notification and termination policies.

Although monitoring of sites is not required, once a service provider receives notice of an infringement, actions such as "notice and take down" or "counter notice and put back" must also be taken. In weighing the benefits of coming within the statutory limitation terms, libraries should appreciate the reduction of potential damages for innocent, but contributory, infringements.

For libraries that are part of larger, educational institutions, exposure to money damages from cyberspace violations by patrons, students, and faculty-as well as third parties-must be deemed a real threat. It should be understood that online copyright infringements are a "hot button" issue for publishers. It should also be anticipated that a test case or two would be brought in the near future.

Further, it must be underscored that even though monetary damages may be avoided, all service providers are subject to all other copyright legal remedies, including injunctive relief. It is not known whether content owners will use the website list of service providers maintained by the Copyright Office as the "go-to group" that receives all the infringement notifications.

Since each OSP is an online ramp to the cyber-violations, whether more than a limited group will receive infringement notices is not yet known. If many owners adopt an approach that blankets the potential universe of OSPs, then those identified OSPs could be flooded with requests for take down. Such a situation could render operations at small- to medium-sized libraries into an immediate state of chaos. Then, too, how much technological support in terms of advanced software and personnel is required to satisfy the legal strictures is unknown.

Although DMCA did not include explicit expanded protection for educational activities involving the Internet, the creation of a congressionally-mandated study of the subject by the Copyright Office is important and deserves immediate and active attention by the library community. From its inception, copyright law has balanced owners' rights with users' rights.

Despite copyright owners proclaiming the need for fair return on their creative works and the importance of securing economic rewards in a global economy, principles like fair use and exemptions for classroom teaching and library preservation survive. Distance education is the latest major battleground in the effort to balance educational interests in a federal law that increasingly emphasizes the commerce of copyright.

Extending the face-to-face and transmission exemptions to Internet education will not happen without aggressive and active participation by the library and educational communities. In the initial hearings held in January 1999 by the Copyright Office, owners have already asserted there is no need to change the law. They argue licensing and other permissive approaches to incorporating works into course content will suffice.

Moreover, they claim to be the primary producers of course texts and thus any exemption hurts their markets and damages them competitively. Unless educators are energized by the opportunity to create a new and important expansion of principles embodied in the current classroom and closed circuit transmission limitations, no change will occur. The central points to be made include the following:

— Obtaining clearances for spontaneous use of copyrighted works in online courses is virtually impossible.

— Identifying copyright owners of certain works, like photographs, is so daunting as to make it a task not worth pursuing.

— Licensing is not an acceptable alternative because, when offered, the price is often far too high to justify the use.

— Unless the copyright law is modified, the playing field for parties negotiating licenses is out of balance. Libraries and educators will find they have less leverage to negotiate fair terms for digital use within their communities.

— The transaction costs associated with clearances and licensing requirements threatens to perpetuate or exacerbate the traditional disparities between "have" and "have-not" communities that distance education and the Internet could otherwise help to mitigate.

But if the library and educational communities are unified in their desire to update copyright law exemptions so that online education is treated on a par with classroom learning, then there is a chance that reform can be accomplished in the near future. With congressional and presidential elections coming in the next year, education will be a very important electoral issue and distance education should be a central topic in all races.

The DMCA provides the most significant updating of library and archival preservation rules since procedures to cope with photocopy machines were established in 1976. The changes permit preservation and storage of a copyrighted work in a digitized format and describe a mechanism for handling preservation of works originating in outmoded formats.

The updating of Section 108 to enable libraries to work in digital preservation was surprisingly hard fought. Even with the endorsement of the authors of the White Paper3, it required extensive negotiations in the House and Senate. The content community is very nervous about allowing digital copies of works to exist anywhere without explicit authorization. In the end, this update is a modest, yet important, change for libraries that will make their task of maintaining collections easier in a technologically advanced environment.

Moving in tandem to the DMCA legislation was another copyright reform bill-term extension. For the past three years, there was a drumbeat by certain copyright proprietors, especially those owning movies and musical works, for extension of the copyright term. Although the legislation had strong support, it was held hostage to a debate over the demand of certain groups-notably restaurants, bars, and religious broadcasters-to be entitled to relief from the high charges for use of music on their premises and in their broadcasts.

For the library community, concern about extension of the copyright term was expressed early in the debate. It was posited that the overwhelming majority of works are neither commercially exploited nor readily accessible in the marketplace after several decades, much less 75 years. Yet, for researchers and scholars, access to such works from the library's collection are important and no limitation should be made on such noncommercial uses.

Moreover, with regard to already-existing works, no "extra incentive" is needed to spur creativity.

In an effort to resolve the concerns expressed by library interests, an understanding was reached regarding the ability of nonprofit libraries, archives, and educational institutions to exploit older works during what constitutes the extended copyright term. Suggesting that libraries should be able to exploit works that have lain fallow for decades should not strike one as an explosive proposal.

The Copyright Office, through the vehicle of regulations, will help determine the reach of the new exception that permits libraries to continue to freely use old works in the last 20 years of the extended term, just like public domain works. This is a vital concern for the library and education community, because maintenance of the public domain assures the role of libraries as archivists of history, not licensees of commerce.

Participation in the regulatory process that will define the terms and establish rules is a relatively efficient way to get one's key points across. Just as was noted with regard to the anti-circumvention rulemaking and the distance education study, active participation in these administrative proceedings assures that the library and education community's voice will be heard at the opportune time and its views not ignored.

3

Preservation of Digital Heritage

The technologies we use to create and enjoy the digital heritage have many advantages that explain their extraordinarily rapid take up in many parts of the world. But there are very serious challenges in keeping our emerging, but already burgeoning, digital heritage usable and available. The media we use to carry and store it are unstable, and the technology needed for access is quickly superseded by newer technologies, wave after wave.

As technologies lose support, access to the digital heritage that they fostered is also lost. These challenges are not only technical in nature; they have organisational and societal dimensions as we struggle with the responsibility of keeping access lines open over extended periods of time, often with insufficient resources and uncertain strategies.

The interest of UNESCO in this situation comes as no surprise. UNESCO exists in part to encourage and enable the preservation and enjoyment of the cultural, scientific and information heritage of the world's peoples.

The growth of digital heritage and its vulnerability could hardly go unnoticed.

The UNESCO Draft Charter on the Preservation of the Digital Heritage

Introduction

The UNESCO Draft Charter on the Preservation of the Digital Heritage presents a compelling case for digital preservation. It is included in the Guidelines to provide a clear link between the two documents, and to present those advocacy and public policy issues that are outside the scope of technical and practical guidelines.

Preamble

The General Conference,

Considering that the disappearance of heritage in whatever form constitutes an impoverishment of the heritage of all nations,

Recalling that the Constitution of UNESCO provides that the Organization will maintain, increase and diffuse knowledge, by assuring the conservation and protection of the world's inheritance of books, works of art and monuments of history and science, that its "Information for All" Programme provides a platform for discussions and action on information policies and the safeguarding of recorded knowledge, and that its "Memory of the World" Programme aims to ensure the preservation and universal accessibility of the world's documentary heritage,

Recognizing that such resources of information and creative expression are increasingly produced, distributed, accessed and maintained in digital form, creating a new legacy - the digital heritage,

Aware that permanent access to this heritage will offer broadened opportunities for creation, communication and sharing of knowledge among all peoples, as well as protection of rights and entitlements and support of accountability,

Understanding that this digital heritage is at risk of being lost and that its preservation for the benefit of present and future generations is an urgent issue of worldwide concern,

Bearing in mind the UNESCO Universal Declaration on Cultural Diversity,

Proclaims the following principles and adopts the present Charter.

The Digital Heritage as a Common Heritage

Article 1 - Digital heritage

Resources of human knowledge or expression, whether cultural, educational, scientific and administrative, or embracing technical, legal, medical and other kinds of information, are increasingly created digitally, or converted into digital form from existing analogue resources. Where resources are "born digital", there is no other format but the digital original.

Digital materials include texts, databases, still and moving images, audio, graphics, software, and web pages, among a wide and growing range of formats. They are frequently ephemeral, and require purposeful production, maintenance and management to be retained. Many of these resources have lasting value and significance, and therefore constitute a heritage that should be protected and preserved for current and future generations. This heritage may exist in any language, in any part of the world, and in any area of human knowledge or expression.

Article 2 - Access to the digital heritage

The purpose of preserving the digital heritage is to ensure that it remains permanently accessible. Accordingly, access to digital heritage materials, especially those in the public domain, should be equitable and free of unreasonable restrictions. At the same time, the security of sensitive and personal information should be protected from any form of intrusion. It is for each Member State to cooperate with relevant organizations and institutions in encouraging a legal and practical environment which would maximise accessibility of the digital heritage.

A fair balance between the legitimate rights of creators and other rights holders and those of the public to access digital heritage materials should be reaffirmed and promoted.

Guarding Against Loss of Heritage

Article 3 - The threat of loss

The world's digital heritage is at risk of being lost to

posterity. Contributing factors include the rapid obsolescence of the hardware and software which brings it to life, uncertainties about resources, responsibility and methods for maintenance and preservation, and the lack of supportive legislation.

Attitudinal change has fallen behind technological change. Digital evolution has been too rapid and costly for governments and institutions to develop timely and informed preservation strategies. The threat to the economic, social, intellectual and cultural potential of the heritage - the building blocks of the future - has not been fully grasped.

Article 4 - Need for Action

Unless the prevailing threats are addressed, the loss of the digital heritage will be rapid and inevitable. Awareness-raising and advocacy is urgent, alerting policy makers and sensitizing the general public to both the potential of the digital media and the practicalities of preservation. Member States will benefit by encouraging legal, economic and technical measures to safeguard the heritage.

Article 5 - Continuity of digital information

The digital heritage is part of the wider continuum of digital information. To preserve digital heritage, measures will need to be taken throughout the information's life cycle. Preservation of digital heritage begins with the design of reliable systems which will produce authentic and stable digital objects.

Measures Required

Article 6 - Developing strategies and policies

Strategies and policies to preserve the digital heritage can be developed, taking into account the level of urgency, local circumstances, available means and future projections. The cooperation of creators, holders of copyright and related rights, and relevant institutions in setting common standards and compatibilities, and resource sharing, will facilitate this.

Article 7 - Defining what should be kept

As with all documentary heritage, selection principles may vary between countries, although the main criteria for deciding what digital materials to keep would be their significance and lasting cultural, scientific, evidential or other value. Selection decisions and any subsequent reviews need to be carried out in an accountable manner, and be based on defined principles, policies, procedures and standards.

Article 8 - Protecting the digital heritage

Member States need appropriate frameworks to secure the protection of their digital heritage. Market forces alone will not achieve this. As a key element of national preservation policy, archive legislation and legal or voluntary deposit in libraries, archives, museums and other public repositories should embrace the digital heritage. Copyright and related rights legislation should allow preservation processes to be undertaken legally by such institutions.

The right to permanent access to legally deposited digital heritage materials, within reasonable restrictions, should be guaranteed without causing prejudice to their normal exploitation.

Legal and practical frameworks for authenticity are crucial to prevent manipulation or intentional alteration of digital heritage. Both require that the content, functionality of files and documentation be maintained to the extent necessary to secure an authentic record.

Article 9 - Promoting cultural diversity

The digital heritage is inherently unlimited by time, geography, culture or format. It is culture-specific, but potentially accessible to every person in the world. Minorities may speak to majorities, the individual to a global audience.

The digital heritage of all regions, countries and communities should be preserved and made accessible, creating over time a balanced and equitable representation of all peoples, nations, cultures and languages.

Responsibilities

Article 10 - Roles and responsibilities

It is for each Member State to designate one or more agencies to take coordinating responsibility for the preservation of digital heritage, and to provide the necessary staff and resources. The sharing of tasks and responsibilities may be based on existing roles and expertise.

Measures should be taken to:

(a) urge hardware and software developers, creators, publishers, producers, and distributors of digital materials as well as other private sector partners to cooperate with national libraries, archives, museums and other public heritage organizations in preserving the digital heritage;

(b) develop training and research, and share experience and knowledge among the institutions and professional associations concerned;

(c) encourage universities and other research organizations to ensure preservation of research data.

Article 11 - Partnerships and cooperation

Preservation of the digital heritage requires sustained efforts on the part of governments, creators, publishers, relevant industries and heritage institutions. In the face of the current digital divide, it is necessary to reinforce international cooperation and solidarity to enable all countries to ensure creation, dissemination, preservation and continued accessibility of their digital heritage.

Industries, publishers and mass communication media are urged to promote and share knowledge and technical expertise.

The stimulation of education and training Programmes, resource-sharing arrangements, and dissemination of research results and best practices will democratize access to digital preservation techniques.

Article 12 - The role of UNESCO

UNESCO, by virtue of its mandate and functions, has the responsibility to:

(a) take the principles set forth in this Charter into account in the functioning of its Programmes and promote their implementation within the United Nations system and by intergovernmental and international non-governmental organizations concerned with the preservation of the digital heritage;

(b) serve as a reference point and a forum where Member States, intergovernmental and international non-governmental organizations, civil society and the private sector may join together in elaborating objectives, policies and projects in favour of the preservation of the digital heritage;

(c) foster cooperation, awareness-raising and capacity-building, and establish standard ethical, legal and technical guidelines, as a companion sourcebook to this Charter;

(d) determine, on the basis of the experience gained over the next six years in implementing the present Charter and the Guidelines, the need for further standard-setting instruments for the promotion and preservation of the digital heritage.

Digital preservation is used to describe the processes involved in maintaining information and other kinds of heritage that exist in a digital form. In these Guidelines, it does not refer to the use of digital imaging or capture techniques to make copies of non-digital items, even if that is done for preservation purposes. Of course, digital copying, may well produce digital heritage materials needing to be preserved.

Digital materials is generally used here as a preferred term covering items of digital heritage at a general level. In some places, digital object or digital resource have also been used. The terms have been used interchangeably and generically: they do not imply a particular kind of item unless that is clearly stated. Preservation programme is used to refer to any set of coherent arrangements aimed at preserving digital materials.

More commonly used terms such as digital archive and digital repository have been avoided because of their potential ambiguities: archive has different meanings for the records management community and the ICT community, whereas both archive and repository may imply a single storage site - not an appropriate implication where very distributed arrangements may be in place.

Of course, the term programme also comes with some baggage. It should be understood to cover all the aspects of preservation responsibility, including policy and strategy as well as implementation. Presentation, re-presentation are used to describe the processes of providing access to digital materials. The second term has been consistently (and idiosyncratically) hyphenised to emphasise the understanding that digital preservation seeks to re-present what was previously presented.

Not all digital materials need to be kept, only those that are judged to have ongoing value: these form the digital heritage. For those materials that warrant keeping, continuity of survival and accessibility is critical. The chances of recovering lost access to large amounts of data are very slim. Continuity requires sustained, direct action (called digital preservation) rather than passive 'benign neglect.'

Digital materials cannot be said to be preserved if access is lost. The purpose of preservation is to maintain the ability to present the essential elements of authentic digital materials. Digital preservation must address threats to all layers of the digital object: physical, logical, conceptual and essential.

Digital preservation will only happen if organisations and individuals accept responsibility for it. The starting point for action is a decision about responsibility. Everyone does not have to do everything; everything does not have to be done all at once. Comprehensive and reliable preservation programmes are highly desirable, but they may not be achievable in all circumstances of need. Where necessary, it is usually better for non-comprehensive and non-reliable action to be taken than for no action at all. Small steps are usually better than no steps.

Currently, preservation efforts have to work against the prevailing trend of digital technology and how it is developed and used. Digital materials are very often created without long-term preservation intentions in mind. Working with producers to influence the standards and practices they use, and to increase their awareness of preservation needs, are important investments.

Preservation programmes must clarify their legal right to collect, copy, name, modify, preserve and provide access to the digital materials for which they take responsibility. Digital heritage materials must be moved to a safe place where they can be controlled, protected and managed for preservation.

Digital heritage materials must be uniquely identified, and described using appropriate metadata for resource discovery, management and preservation. 18. Taking the right action later depends on adequate documentation. It is easier to document the characteristics of digital resources close to their source than it is to build that documentation later. Preservation programmes should use standardised metadata schemas as they become available, for interoperability between programmes.

The links between digital objects and their metadata must be securely maintained, and the metadata must be preserved. Authenticity is a critical issue where digital objects are used as evidence. It may also be important for other kinds of digital heritage. Data that underlies digital objects must be safely stored and managed if there is to be any chance of re-presenting authentic objects to users.

Digital preservation programmes are subjected to increased authenticity concerns because they so frequently have to use processes that involve change. Authenticity is best protected by measures that ensure the integrity of data is not compromised, and by documentation that maintains the clear identity of the material. Data protection is built on the principles of system security and redundancy.

For preservation programmes, redundancy must include securely stored backups designed around the long-term maintenance of data rather than a cycle of overwriting old data with new. The goal of maintaining accessibility is to find cost-effective ways of guaranteeing access whenever it is needed, both in the short-term and the long-term. Standards are an important foundation for digital preservation, but many programmes must find ways to preserve access to poorly standardised materials, in an environment of changing standards.

Preservation action should not be delayed until a single 'digital preservation standard' appears. Digital data is always dependent on some combination of software and hardware tools for access, but the degree of dependency on specific tools determines the range of preservation options. It is reasonable for programmes to choose multiple strategies for preserving access, especially to diverse collections.

They should consider the potential benefits of maintaining the original data streams of materials as well as any modified versions, as an insurance against the failure of still uncertain strategies. Strategies for preserving accessibility do not stand alone: they are supported by other responsibilities, and many strategies can be combined to good effect. Preservation programmes are often required to judge acceptable and unacceptable levels of loss, in terms of items, elements, and user needs.

Preservation programmes require good management that consists largely of generic management skills combined with enough knowledge of digital preservation issues to make good decisions at the right time. Digital preservation incorporates the assessment and management of risks programmes are usually faced with more material and more issues than they can cope with, so they must set priorities.

The costs of preservation programmes are hard to estimate because they encompass so much uncertainty, including evolving techniques, changing technologies and very long timeframes. Costs may well be lower per unit of information than for non-digital materials, but the amount of information to be managed in digital form is very large so total costs are also likely to remain high, including set-up costs and significant recurrent costs.

Preservation programmes may start as pilot projects but they eventually need to establish sustainable business models. While suitable service providers may be found to carry out some functions, ultimately responsible for achieving preservation objectives rests with preservation programmes, and with those who oversee and resource them. Working collaboratively is often a cost effective way to build preservation programmes with wide coverage, mutual support and the required expertise.

Digital heritage and Digital Continuity

Digital heritage is made up of computer-based materials of enduring value that should be kept for future generations. Digital heritage emanates from different communities, industries, sectors and regions. Not all digital materials are of enduring value, but those that are require active preservation approaches if continuity of digital heritage is to be maintained.

Heritage is explained in UNESCO documents as "our legacy from the past, what we live with today, and what we pass on to future generations." A heritage is something that is, or should be, passed from generation to generation because it is valued. The idea of cultural heritage is a familiar one: those sites, objects and intangible things that have cultural, historical, aesthetic, archaeological, scientific, ethnological or anthropological value to groups and individuals.

According to the Draft Charter for the Preservation of Digital Heritage:

> Resources of human knowledge or expression, whether cultural, educational, scientific and administrative, or embracing technical, legal, medical and other kinds of information, are increasingly created digitally, or converted into digital form from existing analogue resources.

Where resources are "born digital", there is no other format but the digital original. Digital materials include texts, databases, still and moving images, audio, graphics, software, and web pages, among a wide and growing range of formats. They are frequently ephemeral, and require purposeful production, maintenance and management to be retained. Many of these resources have lasting value and significance, and therefore constitute a heritage that should be protected and preserved for current and future generations.

This heritage may exist in any language, in any part of the world, and in any area of human knowledge or expression. Using computers and related tools, humans are creating and sharing digital resources - information, creative expression, ideas, and knowledge encoded for computer processing - that they value and want to share with others over time as well as across space. This is evidence of a digital heritage. It is a heritage made of many parts, sharing many common characteristics, and subject to many common threats.

For example, UNESCO defines a world heritage made up of globally outstanding sites of cultural and natural value that should be preserved; many national and state legislatures also define their own national, regional or state heritage. However, heritage value may also be based on what is important at a group or community level. Heritage materials can exist well beyond the limits suggested by national legislation or international conventions. Anything that is considered important enough to be passed to the future can be considered to have heritage value of some kind.

This digital heritage is likely to become more important and more widespread over time. Increasingly, individuals, organisations and communities are using digital technologies to document and express what they value and what they want to pass on to future generations. New forms of expression and communication have emerged that did not exist previously. The Internet is one vast example of this phenomenon.

It is also likely that the development of tools to support greater multi-lingual and multi-script use of the Internet will lead to further rapid growth in digital heritage in parts of the world that are currently disadvantaged by the predominant use of English on the Internet. Making sure this burgeoning digital heritage remains available is thus a global issue relevant to all countries and communities.

Types of Digital Heritage

Over time, new types of digital heritage can be expected to emerge: we have already seen the enabling power of the technology in forms as diverse as word processing, email, websites, relational databases, computer models and simulations, digital audio and video, space imagery and computer games. Electronic publications, being information that is made available for wide readership.

Publications are distributed in various ways including online via the World Wide Web, or on portable carriers such as CDs, DVDs, floppy disks and various electronic book devices.

Some publications manage to combine both online and portable carrier access to different parts of the publication. As well as their means of distribution, digital publications may be classified by genres, some familiar from traditional publishing formats like monographs and serials, and others less easily defined like websites and e-zines. Some publications are released as complete items, but others evolve over time, their creators taking advantage of the interactive potential of the Internet.

Print publishing continues to grow, but increasingly publications are appearing in digital versions, increasingly in digital-only versions. Both commercial and non-commercial publishers produce digital publications, as do millions of other people who would not see themselves as publishers at all. 'Semi-published' materials such as pre-print papers and theses held in e-print and other archives available for restricted use within specific communities such as universities and scholarly societies

Organisational and personal records of activity, transactions, correspondence, etc. A very large part of the world's business and government records now exist in electronic record keeping systems. Email, messages to discussion lists and bulletin boards, web diaries, 'blogs' and 'cams' - dynamic, informal interactions enabled by digital technology - may also include important digital records amongst a tidal wave of data.

Datasets collected to record and analyse scientific, geospatial, spatial, sociological, demographic, educational, health, environmental and other phenomena · Learning objects used in technology-assisted education · Software tools such as databases, models, simulations, and software applications · Unique unpublished materials that may include research reports, oral history and folklore recordings.

Electronic 'manuscripts' such as drafts of works and personal correspondence. Entertainment products from the film, music, broadcasting and games industries, both commercial and non-commercial. Digitally generated artworks and documentary photographs. Digital copies of images, sound, text and three-dimensional objects from non-digital originals.

Many of these materials exist only in a digital form (even if carried on a physical carrier of some kind). With no equivalent non-digital version, their content is especially vulnerable to the influences that threaten digital materials. There are also rapidly growing collections of digital copies. Having originally been generated from non-digital sources, these might appear to be less vulnerable, but many of them are the only surviving version of originals that have since been damaged, lost or dispersed.

Continuity of the digital heritage is profoundly important. Increasingly this is a heritage that documents the actions of governments, the results of scientific research, the debate of ideas, the aspirations and imagination of communities, the histories of the current and coming world. If these are not to be lost or distorted, continuity is required: continuity of production, continuity of survival, and continuity of access. This must be achieved in the face of many threats:

— The carriers used to store these digital materials are usually unstable and deteriorate within a few years or decades at most

— Use of digital materials depends on means of access that work in particular ways

The Internet is an interesting scenario in which many of these threats are played out. In assessing the risks associated with the Internet, it is necessary to distinguish between two overlapping but different concerns. One concern is to look at the Internet as a whole. There is no central agency that can decide what happens to material made available through the Internet. Typically, users connect with a kaleidoscope of information for which no single creator, publisher, or any other agency is responsible.

A different viewpoint is to look at individual resources published through the Internet. These may also be quite unstable, but their instability reflects the decisions and actions of their owners in deleting, changing, moving, or renaming them. The loss of materials in this environment is attributable to how they are managed at a local level, exposed to many of the same threats that other kinds of digital materials experience.

While it is largely beyond the power of Internet users to control whether information remains available, it is very much within the power of those owning and managing digital objects and sites. If they are committed to maintaining access, it is generally within their power to do so. However, the Internet does present some special risks. For example:

— There is a strong novelty factor, so some publishers choose to change things frequently - sometimes the way information looks, sometimes also the content

— Many Internet resources are a virtual composite drawn from a number of sources, which may not be stored together anywhere.

Understanding Digital Preservation

Digital preservation consists of the processes aimed at ensuring the continued accessibility of digital materials. To do this involves finding ways to re-present what was originally presented to users by a combination of software and hardware tools acting on data. To achieve this requires digital objects to be understood and managed at four levels: as physical phenomena; as logical encodings; as conceptual objects that have meaning to humans; and as sets of essential elements that must be preserved in order to offer future users the essence of the object.

Digital preservation can be seen as all those processes aimed at ensuring the continuity of digital heritage materials for as long as they are needed. The most significant threats to digital continuity concern loss of the means of access. Digital materials cannot be said to be preserved if the means of access have been lost and access becomes impossible. The purpose of preserving digital materials is to maintain accessibility: the ability to access their essential, authentic message or purpose.

There is an underlying similarity in the way digital objects are accessed in the present, and how they will be accessed in any future use. In both cases, access can be seen as a performance. Digital objects are made accessible by applying software and hardware tools to data in order to create a presentation or performance that has meaning to a user. It may be the presentation of a word processing document, or a piece of recorded audio, or a Web page, or results from a database query, or any other kind of digital object depending on the way the data is encoded and on the actions the tools are programmed to perform.

Digital preservation must work in the same way, somehow re-presenting what are judged to be the essential elements of the original performance when required at some later time. Conceptualised in this way, digital preservation can be seen as straightforward. Indeed, copying data from carrier to carrier, and providing the right tools to recreate the intended performance will preserve continuity of access to most digital objects.

However, this simple model encompasses great complexities: it may be hard to define the performance that must be re-presented; it is usually difficult to work out what tools are needed once the original ones have been lost; the tools themselves typically rely on other tools that also may have been superseded; and it may be difficult to find tools that will create the required performance in a reliable, cost-effective and timely way, especially in the context of many thousands, millions or more of digital objects.

Despite such underlying complexities, the performance model helps in recognising what digital preservation programmes must aim for: the best means of re-presenting what users needs to access. Preservation programmes must deal with digital objects in four guises:

— As physical objects, consisting of 'inscriptions' (usually binary states of 'on-ness' or 'off-ness') on carrier media such as computer disks or tapes.

— As logical objects consisting of computer readable code, whose existence at any particular time depends on the physical inscriptions but is not tied to any particular carrier

— As conceptual objects that have meaning to humans, unlike the logical or physical objects that encode them at any particular time.

— As bundles of essential elements that embody the message, purpose, or features for which the material was chosen for preservation.

This multi-layered nature of digital objects has profound implications for digital preservation. Preservation means different things for each layer. Preservation programmes for non-digital heritage have traditionally worried about preserving the physical object as the embodiment of the object's meaning. However, individual physical manifestations of a digital object are almost inevitably lost, one after another, because the media used for physical storage are typically unstable and liable to short-term deterioration.

Preservation requires a succession of data transfers from one physical carrier to another. Despite this shift in focus from the physical object to a conceptual object inherent in digital preservation, it must never be forgotten that digital objects cannot survive without some kind of appropriate physical form.

The logical encoding normally has a much longer life than any particular physical inscription, but it is by no means sacrosanct. As the layers of technology used for access - hardware such as computer processors, disk drives and peripheral equipment, and many layers of software such as operating systems, specific applications, and presentation tools - become obsolete, it may be necessary to change the logical encoding so that it can present the same conceptual object using different technology.

The conceptual object is the ultimate focus of preservation concern; as noted above, it is at this level that digital objects convey meaning to human users. However, for most digital objects there is a further layer that must be considered. Many objects consist of several elements, some of which are more important than others in carrying the object's essential message. Preservation programmes have to decide which sub-set of elements should be preserved for re-presentation to users.

Strategies for Preserving Digital Materials

Digital preservation involves choosing and implementing an evolving range of strategies to achieve the kind of accessibility discussed above, addressing the preservation needs of the different layers of digital objects. The strategies include:

— Working with producers (creators and distributors) to apply standards that will prolong the effective life of the available means of access and reduce the range of unknown problems that must be managed

— Recognising that it is not practical to try to preserve everything, selecting what material should be preserved

— Placing the material in a safe place

— Controlling material, using structured metadata and other documentation to facilitate access and to support all preservation process

— Protecting the integrity and identity of data

— Choosing appropriate means of providing access in the face of technological change

— Managing preservation programmes to achieve their goals in cost-effective, timely, holistic, proactive and accountable ways.

Preservation programmes have certain responsibilities and functions that have been defined, at least at a conceptual level. Comprehensive programmes must take control of appropriate digital materials and ensure they remain understandable and usable as authentic copies.

This generally involves taking the materials, properly prepared, along with associated documentation or metadata, into an archival digital storage system of some kind, where they can be managed to deal with the threats of data loss an technological change. The characteristics or attributes of programmes that can be relied upon to deliver ongoing digital preservation have also been described, in terms of responsibility, viability, sustainability, technical suitability, security, and accountability.

Digital information objects are generally not understandable or re-presentable by themselves: users need help to use them. Preservation depends on maintaining digital objects and any information and tools that would be needed in order to access and understand them. Together, these can be considered to form an information package that must be managed either as a single object or as a virtual package.

Preservation programmes must identify a safe place where digital materials can be stored and managed. Because the concept of the preservation programme allows for distributed arrangements and shared responsibilities, it is quite conceivable that while some programmes will create their own repositories, others may decide to look for a suitable 'safe place' operated and managed by someone else.

The processes of receiving, preparing and transferring digital materials into the archival system are usually referred to as ingest. Preparing material for entry into the archival information system is critical to the way the whole system is managed. It involves a number of important steps that may determine how easy or difficult it is to maintain the archived information packages in the system. These steps include:

— Applying collection policies and selection criteria to assess whether material is in scope so that it can be sought, or accepted if submitted

— Clarifying or negotiating rights issues with rights owners

— Checking the quality of the submitted information package, including its completeness, the functionality of its component parts, its authenticity, and whether it contains unwanted material such as viruses

— Labelling the material with unique identifiers

— Assessing the elements that must be maintained, and assigning preservation objectives

— Setting retention and review periods for the material, if appropriate

— Checking and if necessary upgrading the documentation that describes the material, including the technical and preservation metadata

— Assessing the file format(s) and deciding if they need to be changed to comply with the Programme's policy on what formats it will manage

— If necessary, changing the file formats to comply with the policy

— Adjusting the documentation to reflect any changes.

Once the digital object and its metadata have been prepared and associated with each other to form an information package, they are saved to the archival storage system. A preservation programme must provide archival storage that maintains, protects and verifies the integrity of the stored information packages, both the digital object and the metadata, whether stored as a single data stream or as separate but linked data streams.

To achieve this, the storage function must include practices that protect the data stream from unintended change, damage or loss: this will usually require regular copying of the data stream to fresh media, and when necessary copying to new media types. Storage practices must also include checking that the data stream has not been corrupted; system security; backup regimes that place copies at remote sites; and disaster recovery plans that address contingencies such as complete loss of the system's operating infrastructure.

Obviously, this requires technical capabilities to provide a suitably secure and reliable storage service. Such a capability can be achieved with modest equipment so long as the equipment and the whole system are well managed. The more material there is, and the more diverse and complex it is, the more sophisticated the storage system needs to be.

For most digital materials, preserving accessibility requires more than the data protection offered in the Archival Storage function. Only material being kept for very short periods could be stored without further attention to the means of providing access. The purpose of the Preservation Planning function is to monitor threats to accessibility, and to specify action to pre-empt or respond to them. The relevant threats mostly relate to changes in the technology that underlies access, so this function looks for such changes and takes action to maintain accessibility despite these changes.

Data management

Managing information packages in the archive generates its own data about what material is stored, what can be accessed, and about the management of the archive. This data must be managed to support use of the archive, and to support its effective administration. This function provides a user interface to the archive, allowing users to discover what is held, to request material and if appropriate to receive copies.

For many archives, access will be subject to restrictions for some or all potential users. The Access function may well require mechanisms to control access. The preservation programme must find ways to advocate good practices among producers, aimed at facilitating preservation of the material for which the programme will be responsible.

There is also a need to understand who the likely users of the material will be, so that preservation and access arrangements can be tailored to their needs and expectations. The overall operation of the programme must be managed. In part this responsibility involves the development of policy frameworks and standards covering all areas of operations; in part it involves the ongoing supply of appropriate resources and infrastructure including suitable technical systems; and in part management processes such as monitoring and reporting on the programme's operations.

Reference Model for Open Archival Information Systems (OAIS), released in 2002 as a draft international standard by the International Standards Organisation. The OAIS Reference Model is the most successful attempt to define both a conceptual model for managing digital materials of enduring value, and a vocabulary with which to discuss it. Anyone contemplating a responsibility for managing digital materials should seek to understand the concepts articulated in the Reference Model itself.

The Reference Model is a high level conceptual framework that can be used as a reference point for those designing, using and evaluating real implementations. It is important to realise that it is not an implementation specification: it does not provide a set of instructions on how to preserve digital information. Its value lies in explaining what is required at a highly conceptual level, regardless of the means chosen to achieve it.

The reliability and trustworthiness of digital preservation programmes are very important issues to many stakeholders. Producers, users, investors and the broad community have a strong interest in ensuring that digital heritage materials are managed by arrangements that can be trusted. Those potentially responsible for the programmes also have an interest in assessing what they can offer and the risks of accepting responsibility.

Preservation programmes offering long-term reliability are expected to have the following characteristics:

— *Responsibility*: a fundamental commitment to preservation of the digital materials in question · Organisational viability, including the prospect of an ongoing mandate; a legal status as an organisation that would support an ongoing preservation role; and a demonstrated ability to put together the resources, infrastructure and work teams that could manage the complexity of digital preservation

— *Financial sustainability*: a likely prospect of the organisation being able to continue to provide the required resources well into the future, with a sustainable business model to support its digital preservation mandate

— *Technological and procedural suitability*: the use of appropriate systems and procedures to do what is required to manage and preserve digital resources

— *System security of a very high order:* Procedural accountability, with clear allocation of responsibilities and mechanisms for reporting and assessing performance.

Arrangements that are able to demonstrate these attributes should be trustworthy. Development of trust may be a matter of demonstrating these characteristics over time. In the long term, certification programmes will probably be needed but at the time of writing no certification programmes for digital preservation arrangements have appeared. It remains very much the responsibility of those proposing digital preservation programmes to show why their arrangements should be trusted, and very much the responsibility of other stakeholders to determine that any arrangements on offer can provide an acceptable level of reliability.

Responsibility in Digital Preservation

Responsibility is a crucial issue in the preservation of digital heritage. The starting point for action is a decision about responsibility. Because the cost implications for an organisation can be significant, and because the requirements may be complex and uncertain, it is no small thing to accept a responsible role. The purpose of such arrangements is to provide a good prospect of preservation continuing beyond their own involvement, should that become necessary.

Fail-safe arrangements extend along a continuum, from a commitment to find someone else to take over responsibility before discarding digital materials, through to legally mandated arrangements for one agency to take over the management of data held by another agency if it fails to meet its preservation responsibilities. Responsibility for initiating and maintaining succession plans obviously lies with whomever is managing the material, but there may be other players who should accept some responsibility.

In facing the daunting challenges of preservation responsibility, it may help to consider some pragmatic principles:

— *Someone has to take responsibility*: if no one does, the chances of any particular materials surviving are very small

— *Everyone does not have to do everything*: responsibility can be shared. As these guidelines indicate, there are more than enough responsibilities for one preservation Programme. Many tasks, such as deciding what should be preserved, are best managed in partnership with others. If there is no one suitable to share responsibilities, preservation programmes should make realistic judgments about the responsibilities they can carry alone

— *Everything does not have to be done at once*: developing all the components of a large-scale, comprehensive preservation programme takes time. It is good to approach the task with a sense of urgency, but it may also be necessary to look for ways of buying time. This might require prioritising the issues that need to be addressed, or the material that needs attention. It may involve looking for easily managed materials ('low hanging fruit'). Some problems must be addressed without delay; some can be addressed in stages; and some can wait

— *Responsibility does not have to be forever*: there is definitely a place for time-limited contributions to an overall preservation programme, so long as the time limits are explicitly understood

— *Limited responsibility should not mean causing harm*: preservation programmes may need to take steps before all problems are solved and all techniques settled, but they must also try to minimise the harm of making later preservation efforts more difficult

— *Someone must take a leading role*: even when responsibility is shared, progress usually depends on at least one partner accepting the responsibility to lead.

Some people believe that new institutions will be needed to take on the task of preserving digital heritage. Presumably these agencies would offer specialist expertise and facilities dedicated to digital materials, and possibly dedicated to preservation rather than a wider range of functions which existing collecting institutions perform, like arranging and interpreting materials and promoting their use.

Many data archives fit into such a field already, as they exist solely to manage and preserve digital materials. They often have the paradoxical advantages of being able to focus on a limited range of materials and management tasks, while being able to offer services to a wider range of data-producing communities.

Just as it is too early to judge the long-term role of libraries, archives and museums, it is too early to attempt a definitive list of others who may play an important role. Universities and other institutes of research and learning have a natural interest in ensuring ongoing access to certain kinds of digital materials, and may have both the long-term viability and the technical infrastructure to play a preservation role · Publishers and creators of digital content have a range of interests in ongoing management and accessibility.

In many cases this extends beyond immediate commercial considerations to a longer-term investment in the exchange of ideas and the intellectual and cultural capital that ongoing accessibility encourages. Some publishers and creators may be willing and able to provide the infrastructure needed to maintain digital heritage materials in which they have an interest.

When preservation programmes have decided what kind of responsibility they will take, it is very important that they declare their intentions. This makes it easier for others to work with them, reduces the likelihood of effort being unnecessarily duplicated, and provides a clearer picture of what material is likely to survive and what is not.

Managing Digital Preservation Programmes

Preservation programmes require good management, often drawing on generic management skills such as tailoring programmes to the priorities and circumstances of the case, and making the right decisions at the right time. Digital preservation programmes present some particular management issues associated with their developing nature, the range of stakeholders, and the long-term impacts of current decisions.

Like all programmes, preservation programmes need to be managed in a coherent way. Digital preservation management should not be seen as a mysterious art: it draws on good general management skills, allied with enough subject knowledge and understanding of technical issues to see realistic possibilities and to make good decisions. The discussion that follows focuses on those issues specifically relevant to digital preservation.

Good management often comes down to knowing what decisions have to be made and making them at the right time. The important decisions do not have to be made all at once, but eventually they will be required on issues including:

— Whether to get involved in preserving digital materials at all

— The mission of the programme

Preservation programmes must seek to understand and respond to threats that would jeopardise ongoing accessibility and other aspects of the programme's mission. A risk management approach provides an appropriate basis for deciding what risks warrant attention, and for planning action that will lower the level of risk. There are many suitable risk management models available. Risk analysis, even undertaken informally, helps in a number of ways:

Recognising:

— The most pressing threats (such as web publications disappearing; media failure of magnetic carriers; impending replacement of equipment or software; a change in government agency arrangements that will threaten record keeping systems)

— Threats that may not require immediate action (such as the eventual obsolescence of a standardised, ubiquitous file format such as TIFF, the impact of which should be manageable when a replacement standard appears) - Threats over which the programme may have no influence (such as the business imperatives of producers)

— Threats that are so pressing but so intractable that the programme may decide to withdraw from responsibility (such as a refusal by rights owners to allow any form of access or preservation copying at any future time).

Deciding:

— Where to allocate resources

— What steps to take as a priority
— When action may be needed
— What supporting action is needed to address priority risks.
— Planning ahead
— Justifying decisions.

Risk assessment is especially helpful if it is extended beyond the immediately apparent risks to include:

— The risks associated with the action that is proposed to deal with the threat. For example, the programme may not have the required skills, resources, permissions, etc. This in turn might lead to action that is a prerequisite for dealing with the priority threat
— The causes of the original threat. For example, web publishers may not be aware of steps they could take; producers may be using standards incorrectly; or producers may be at risk of business failure. This analysis might lead to action that addresses the causes, such as education campaigns, the development of standards in conjunction with producers, or development of indicators of impending business failure including signs that web sits are not being maintained or personal knowledge that projects are coming to a close.

A broad range of stakeholders have an interest in digital heritage materials and how they are managed. They may include those creating or distributing the materials, those who need to use them now or in the future, and those who cite the materials, assuming that they will remain available. Some stakeholders may be hidden but play a very influential role behind the scenes, such as hardware and software manufacturers, providers of funds, and bodies authorised to control access to certain materials.

Some stakeholders may be of direct interest to the preservation programme itself, such as potential collaborative partners, standards bodies, and researchers developing new digital preservation methods. Preservation programmes must recognise those who have an interest in their objectives or who could exert an influence on them. Risk assessment is likely to indicate which stakeholders will be most important, as well as suggesting the kind of relationship the programme needs to develop with them.

Because the windows of opportunity for preservation are much narrower than for non-digital heritage, preservation programmes may have to be much more active in pursuing relationships with producers of heritage materials. They may also have to look for ways of influencing the 'hidden' stakeholders whose decisions may have a critical impact. Reliable preservation programmes must be sustained over long periods, so they require business models that guarantee adequate resources will continue to be available.

Unfortunately, such guarantees are rare in the real world. Most programmes have to survive with less certainty. Especially in the initial stages, sustainability presents a dilemma: programmes must eventually have it, but they often cannot tell what resources will be needed to fulfil their responsibilities, nor what resources may become available once a successful programme has been established.

Programme managers have the challenge of finding long-term business models, but they may also have to find short-term funding arrangements, and recognise the appropriate time to switch from one to the other. (In fact, some managers may find they can only build a long-term programme on the back of a series of short-term funding arrangements.) Some of the business models commonly considered for preservation programmes include:

— General community funding, often through taxes or the allocation of grants from special sources such as lottery funds

— Funding by a specific community with an interest in the programme, such as a local community project, or an industry peak body levying members

— Central funding by a parent organisation as a normal cost of business, such as a university library or a business archive

— Payments by users of the material

— Payments by producers who deposit material with the programme.

— Sponsorship or philanthropic assistance

— Cross subsidisation by other activities within an organisation

Standards and practices in digital preservation are evolving rapidly (though perhaps not as rapidly as they are needed), and programme managers must find ways to keep their knowledge up to date. There are a number of international initiatives dedicated to just such a purpose, including the journals, websites and subject gateways included in the Reading List. Despite some overlap, these initiatives complement each other; they offer excellent ways of keeping abreast of developments.

There also appears to be an opportunity to explore solidarity relationships between programmes with different levels of experience and expertise. Most existing programmes are willing to share information and ideas but often find themselves overwhelmed with requests. Formal information sharing arrangements may ease that burden while offering real benefits to those developing new programmes.

Digital preservation programmes often start as experiments and projects with a speculative mission and an uncertain future. They can be easily dismissed as important but bothersome add-ons to already overstretched organisations. It often takes some time for a definite set of workflows to emerge and for the programme to take shape.

Availability of resources is always a critical constraint. It is important to tailor the ambitions of the programme to a reasonably realistic idea of what can be achieved: it may not be possible to do everything! It is difficult to estimate the long-term costs of digital preservation. While unsatisfactory from a planning point of view, it may be necessary to estimate expected costs over a short- to medium-term period, such as five years, and to use the knowledge gained in that timeframe to inform more accurate estimates of long-term costs.

However, there is always likely to be a problem in estimating the costs of long-term actions that are still unclear, such as migration costs. Some costs do become much easier to predict following a few years' experience in collecting material, preparing it for storage, and protecting it. Some cost assumptions can be reasonably made:

— Development costs are likely to be high, depending on how ambitious the programme is from the start. Systems design is a necessary investment in the long run but it can be a significant set up cost

— There are obvious recurrent costs associated with staff, accommodation, energy supplies, network use, telecommunications costs, storage media such as disks and tapes, and consumables. Although often funded as capital expenditure, equipment and software should be seen as recurrent costs because they will have to be replaced on a regular basis

— The staff costs of working with producers can be high because of the need to address new issues with each change in technology. The costs of negotiating rights may vary depending on the complexity of rights ownership and on whether or not rights need to be purchased

— The costs of identifying and selecting materials for preservation are likely to be low per unit, but there may be many units. A nonselective approach may reduce costs, although adding to long-term preservation costs overall, as more material must be stored, processed, preserved and organised for access. Human judgments about selection are expensive where labour costs are high; automating decisions may reduce costs if the high set-up costs can be spread over a large amount of material, and if it is feasible to automate what are often complex human judgments

— The costs of collecting or transferring materials are likely to be low per unit but large programmes may generate significant transfer costs overall. This may incorporate high transmission costs where automated gathering searches and downloads large amounts of data. The cost of quality control checking is likely to be high unless it can be automated

— Converting material to a restricted range of standard formats may be inexpensive if the conversion is easy, but expensive if individual handcrafting or correction is needed. However, there may be considerable long-term cost benefits in being able to deal with a restricted range of formats

— The costs of describing material and adding metadata are likely to be high because of the amount of information to be recorded, and the difficulty of finding it in some cases. Costs could be greatly reduced by producers using more standardised structures and creating good metadata and documentation themselves. For heavily standardised formats such as those widely used for archival versions of images and audio, costs will be reduced by automated gathering of metadata from files and during production processes

— Costs associated with storage are theoretically low and decreasing, but in total they reflect the amount of data to be stored, which may be large. Estimates of storage and processing costs should take account of backups and multiple versions of material. The cost of regularly copying data to new media is generally discounted by regular increases in storage densities

— The costs of providing means of access - such as analysing data structures, writing new code for migration, writing or finding emulators, quality checking, and so on -may be high or low, depending on how difficult the process turns out to be. For example, if a conversion software tool can be developed that works automatically for millions of similar files, the unit costs may be extremely low, although the total cost of computer time could still be significant. On the other hand, strategies that must be managed item by item will be very expensive

— Computer costs to store and serve large numbers of access copies, or to generate them on request, should not be ignored. These would generally not be counted as preservation costs, but preservation programmes may still have to bear them as part of their business function.

Where the material is very similar and well organised, and where the preservation tasks are straightforward, it may be possible to automate most processes and reduce staffing requirements to a minimum. On the other hand, where repeated human intervention is needed, the programme will need staff who are adequately equipped to provide it. It is very hard to automate processes that require subjective judgments, although not impossible.

Even highly automated programmes, however, will eventually need staff to deal with changes in the operating environment and with the need to replace systems.

Programme managers need to have:

— Good problem solving skills, and an ability to deal with complex problems for which there may be no current long-term answers

— A pro-active approach that considers short-term, medium-term and long-term issues

— Adequate awareness of the relevant technical, preservation, corporate, legal and political aspects

— An ability to think critically, but also to receive new ideas and to adapt to change

— Collaborative abilities and in interest in sharing information and looking for ways to work with others.

Preservation programmes require sophisticated systems and tools, although small programmes dealing with largely un-automated processes and with carriers that can be stored on shelves may be able to get by using quite modest computer equipment that is already available. Where services have been contracted from an outside supplier, the programme itself may not need to provide much of the technological infrastructure.

The systems and tools likely to be required include those for:

— Storing and managing the collection material

— Storing and managing metadata

— Managing the transfer of material to the collection, possibly including gathering

— Managing information about rights and managing access in accord with rights

— Storing and managing accessibility tools such as original software, plug-ins, conversion and emulation programmes

— Searching by users

— Making appropriate copies available for users

— Managing many of the processes described in these guidelines, especially those that generate management information, copy material from one place or format to another, or require automated process checking.

Procurement of appropriate systems is a significant task, requiring special attention to specifications and the evaluation of options. Some existing programmes are willing to share information on the specifications they have used and their experience in procuring suitable systems.

Tools for Preservation Programmes

Standards lie behind almost everything that computers do, so they form a crucial foundation to the creation and use of digital materials. However, they have not yet been great enablers of preservation. They can be expected to make several important contributions if they are well chosen and well used. Those contributions can be seen in:

— The creation of digital materials that should be relatively straightforward to preserve. Some file formats (themselves standardised) have proven to be so widely useful that they have been adopted by creator communities as a best practice, raising the prospect that they will continue to be used for a long time. Examples include the Tagged Interchange File Format (TIFF) for images, and the Structured General Markup Language (SGML) family of formats including HTML and XML, for structured documents

— Where such widely adopted formats are based on open source, non-proprietary specifications (as is the case with TIFF and SGML), it should be relatively easy to find or develop tools when they are needed to provide ongoing access across changes in technologies

— Agreed approaches to a number of preservation processes, including the recording of metadata, migration processes, data protection and item identification. Standards are still evolving in these areas

— Defining the responsibilities and functions of certain kinds of preservation programmes. The outstanding example of this to date is the Reference Model for an Open Archival Information System (OAIS), accepted by the International Standards Organisation in 2002.

Standards should not be seen as a preservation panacea. Even where they exist, they are subject to change, versioning and non-standard use by producers. Many format standards are in fact proprietary specifications that may not be publicly available, so it may be impossible to know whether tools for future access will be available. While increased standardisation of processes can only help preservation programmes, it is important not to wait for a single 'digital preservation standard' to emerge before taking sensible preservation action.

There are many different models that have been used as organisational structures to manage digital preservation. Some possibilities include:

— Setting up a single separate digital preservation unit to look after all aspects

— A series of specialist units looking after different aspects

— A matrix of people working in different areas, responsible to an overall programme manager

— Mainstreaming of the work through existing work areas so that it becomes part of the normal work integrated with other operations

— Embedding the programme in a particular existing work area such as IT, preservation, collection development, or collection management sections.

These different models tend to produce different emphases, reflecting various levels of comfort with IT tools, collecting objectives, preservation thinking, etc. Any model can be made to work effectively, so long as it draws on the perspectives and skills that are needed and has strong management support.

Preservation programmes should be guided by a policy framework that says what the programme is trying to do and how it will try to achieve it. In a field of such complexity and evolving understandings, a policy document needs to provide clear, long-term direction as well as regularly reviewed guidance. In implementing policy and developing action plans, it is almost always necessary to decide what issues, actions and materials should be given priority for attention, and to understand what work is critical before other work can be attempted.

There may be alternative paths for achieving the preservation commitments of the programme. Organisations should consider whether they will get a better result from doing the work in-house, or by contracting with someone else to do it, or by a combination of approaches. Many processes such as storage and documentation may be amenable to contracting, which may offer access to specialised expertise and facilities that would not be available otherwise.

In many cases, programmes may not be able to afford the initial investments involved in setting up and maintaining infrastructure, so paying for someone else to provide services may be attractive. Contracting may present some potential risks, including:

— Creating a distance between programme objectives and service provision

— The possibility of being locked into the service provider's services because the cost of seeking alternatives is greater than the cost of continuing

— Less control over what happens on a day-to-day basis

— Higher costs (they may also be lower) than in-house arrangements over the long term ·

— Fewer learning opportunities that might suggest better ways of doing things.

The success of contracting may depend on the programme manager's ability to define what is needed; finding a reliable supplier who can offer the services required at a suitable price; being able to negotiate a suitable contract with adequate safeguards; and skills in managing the contract. In working with service providers, preservation managers must ensure they:

— Understand their business and what they need to achieve

— Communicate their needs

— Rigorously assess the capabilities, motivations, and understandings of potential suppliers

— Prepare and negotiate an appropriate contract

— Ensure communication channels are open so that any problems that be reported early

— Monitor performance closely and evaluate arrangements regularly. Ensure there are responsible exit strategies and succession plans in place for when arrangements come to an end.

There are good technological, economic and political reasons for preservation programmes to cooperate. Decisions about collaboration should be based on assessment of the benefits expected and the costs involved. There are a number of possibilities regarding where to look for partners, what the focus of the relationship should be, and structural frameworks that would be suitable. Successful cooperation is usually the result of careful attention to these choices, and to putting in the effort required to manage the collaboration in practice.

Perspectives of Management

Digital heritage and collaboration go together very well. The technology of digital materials supports collaboration: such materials are easy to duplicate, and many are designed for networked access, so remote management is not difficult. It is also expensive - often too expensive - to set up the whole infrastructure of digital preservation for every preservation programme, so there is a strong incentive to look for ways of sharing facilities.

There may even be a political imperative to work cooperatively: the community may reasonably expect that programmes will collaborate to ensure as much digital heritage as possible can be preserved, as coherently as possible.

Organisational priorities can be sidetracked by problems in the collaborative relationship itself, taking attention away from the real mission of preserving digital materials. In the face of such potential costs and difficulties, it is important to identify the benefits that any collaboration is meant to deliver. Benefits driving a cooperative effort could include:

— Access to a wider range of expertise

— Shared development costs

— Access to tools and systems that might otherwise be unavailable

— Shared learning opportunities

— Increased coverage of preserved materials

— Better planning to reduce wasted effort

— Encouragement for other influential stakeholders to take preservation seriously

— Shared influence on agreements with producers

— Shared influence on research and development of standards and practices

— Attraction of resources and other support for well-coordinated programmes at a regional, national or sectoral level.

The benefits of collaboration usually do not happen by accident, but result from careful attention to choices. Programmes need to consider their potential partners, ways of working together, structural models, and the steps involved in making the proposed collaboration work. Potential partners are likely to be others working in the same sector. Examples could include a consortium of university libraries, or networks of data archives, or government agencies agreeing to use the same application software, or a group of recording studios sharing storage facilities for masters.

It may be possible to join an existing collaboration, or to form new partnerships. However, there may also be benefits to be gained from looking beyond sectoral boundaries, especially as digital technologies and users expectations are increasingly blurring the edges between sectors. For example, a number of libraries, archives, research institutes, data archives and producers in a regional area may consider joining forces to develop a local programme that meets all their needs.

There may also be opportunities for formal cooperative arrangements between preservation programmes and interested stakeholders including groups of producers, industry peak bodies, user groups, IT industry groups, or government bodies interested in fostering good practice. There are many ways that preservation programmes can work together, depending on the benefits they want to achieve and what each partner has to offer. They include:

— *Shared standards*: agreements to do things in the same ways, either with a view to interoperability between programmes, or simply based on a shared understanding of what practices will best support preservation objectives

— *Information sharing*: agreements to share information either at a general level or on specific issues, such as procurement specifications or research results

— *Speaking with a common voice*: agreements to develop and present a common message in advocacy campaigns, or in publicity aimed at raising the profile of digital heritage preservation

— *Division of labour*: agreements to work together at an operational level, taking preservation steps in a coordinated way, with responsibilities either carried out in parallel or divided between programmes

— *Shared resources*: agreements to share resources such as systems, staff or funds to work on a common programme.

Technical and Practical Perspectives

It is usually necessary to decide what digital materials are worth keeping, as has been the case with non-digital materials. Many of the same approaches - selection based on criteria embodied in collection development policies, and good knowledge of the materials and their context - are fundamental for digital heritage selection. Preservation programmes also need to define the elements or characteristics of the materials they select that give them value, so that those elements can be maintained.

Deciding what should be preserved, by whom, and for how long, have been fundamental decisions in managing all kinds of tangible heritage. Such decisions are necessary because there are usually more things - more information, more records, more publications, more data than we have the means to keep. Every choice to preserve is at the expense of something else.

The selection of digital heritage is conceptually the same as selection of non-digital materials. Any existing programme with well-established procedures for assessing and selecting material for preservation will already have policies, skills and tools that can help in selecting digital materials, even though they may need some adjustment. However, digital materials do present some new challenges that programme managers must take into account in making the best selection decisions they can.

— There is often a large amount of material to be assessed

— The means of producing and disseminating digital materials are widely available, so their quality is often inconsistent

— At the same time, there may be pressure to preserve the entire traffic carried by new communication channels such as the World Wide Web, regardless of quality

— Timing of selection is usually critical, as digital materials quickly de-select themselves by becoming unusable. It may not be possible to wait for evidence of enduring value to emerge before making selection decisions

— Some digital objects may be hard to pin down. New genres may not fit into existing classifications; some digital resources consist of linked or overlapping parts; many also exist in parallel versions.

— Even when external boundaries have been defined, it may be hard to tell which elements need to be maintained if the digital object is to fulfil its essential purpose

— It may even be difficult to tell where digital materials come from, making it hard to decide who is responsible for their preservation and with whom to negotiate the rights required by preservation programmes.

There are dangers in assuming that current value assessments are a completely reliable guide to future values. For example, remote sensing data collected in previous decades has become unexpectedly important for assessing environmental change. This experience suggests it is probably better to err on the side of collecting more material rather than less, if the preservation programme can manage it.

Where digital materials can only be understood by reference to a set of rules such as a record keeping system, database or data generation system, or other contextual information, selection processes must identify the documentation that will also need to be preserved. Producers of digital materials may have a significant role to play in selecting what should be preserved. They are often well placed to understand why digital objects were brought into being, their essential 'message', and the relationships between objects and their context. If that information is not captured from the producer it may be too difficult to reconstruct it later.

Both comprehensive and selective approaches are supported by strong arguments. Advocates of a comprehensive approach argue that any information may turn out to have long-term value, and that the costs of detailed selection are greater than the costs of collecting and storing everything. Advocates of a more selective approach argue that it allows them to create collections of high value resources, with some assurance of technical quality and an opportunity to negotiate access rights with producers.

There may well be a place for both approaches, as they are likely to produce quite different collections of digital heritage that are valued for different purposes. To minimise the risk of important materials being missed, and to avoid unnecessary duplication of effort, it may be necessary to seek agreements with other potential collecting and preservation agencies about respective roles and responsibilities.

Selection policies may have to decide whether to select whole items and whole collections, or samples only. It is generally preferable to preserve whole items to retain their integrity, but it may be necessary to restrict collecting to representative samples as a way of at least evidencing the existence of some kinds of materials. Selection policy may also have to consider whether the re-use of material constitutes a new item that should also be preserved.

Rights issues may influence selection decisions. Preservation programmes often select materials that are still subject to rights, but generally would not select material if rights were so restrictive that arrangements for giving access at some future stage cannot be negotiated. If the material can never be made available for use, or if necessary preservation steps cannot be taken, there is little point in selecting it as heritage material.

Managing selection also requires the development of criteria for appraisal. Where the amount of material is so large that it is not feasible to assess items individually, it may be necessary to establish classes of material that can be assessed on the basis of representative samples. Preservation programmes often act as agents for other stakeholders: they take preservation action on behalf of someone who wants material kept for a reason.

The 'someone else' may be as broad and many-faceted as 'the nation' or 'the general community', who may mandate a programme to collect and preserve a very broad range of materials; or it may be as narrow as the members of an organisation or researchers working in a particular discipline who want their own research output preserved for later use.

The needs of the 'community' - however defined - for whom the material is being kept will drive many decisions, from what material is selected, to the kind and level of documentation that is recorded, to the level of concern with authenticity, to the strategies that are used. For example, some programmes must offer users the option of interrogating old data to produce new results, whereas others have a brief to present material in a read-only form to that it cannot be changed or manipulated.

Some programmes may even have to ensure users can run old simulations, play old computer games, or view digital art in ways that reproduce the original experience rather than a speeded up experience that later technologies may provide. Defining the essential elements or characteristics (also referred to as significant properties by some programmes) is not conceptually difficult, as the examples above illustrate. In some circumstances - such as clearly defined and constrained user expectations, and easily characterised materials that are all similar - defining and encoding the essential elements should be straightforward.

For instance, a programme may decide that users of a large collection of electronic mail messages only need to see elements that can be characterised as 'content information', such as the name and address of the sender, subject, date and time, recipients, and the message, in a standardised structure with only the most simple of formatting. A government archive with this approach could expect to apply this essential elements template to very large numbers of email records.

On the other hand, some materials are much more difficult to characterise, and expectations about how they will be re-presented for use, especially to an open-ended community of potential users, may be so hard to define in advance that it becomes almost impossible. Approaches to this issue are developing as more people encounter the problems of describing, storing and planning to re-present digital objects in growing collections over long periods of time.

Preservation programmes with few resources must still make decisions about the materials for which they accept responsibility. Because the costs of preservation are related to the amount of material to be managed, such programmes may need to be highly selective, limiting their ambitions to a small amount of highly valued material. Preservation costs are also related to the range of problems and formats that need to be managed, so it may also make sense to severely limit the kinds of materials selected to a very few formats.

Collecting agreements with other programmes may shift some of the burden of selecting materials. While these would normally be negotiated with other preservation programmes, there may be potential for agreements with producers that would lead them to make decisions about what should be collected and preserved. The preservation programme would still need to take some responsibility for quality control, as well as articulating the criteria by which material should be chosen.

Digital heritage is often created without consideration of ongoing use and accessibility. However, there are definitely standards and practices that producers can use that either help or hinder preservation. Programme managers need to look for ways of exerting a positive influence from as early in the digital heritage life cycle as possible. This often requires a willingness to work with producers.

Digital materials are created by producers who are not necessarily concerned with long-term availability: creation of 'digital heritage' may not be part of their intention. Even those hoping to make something of enduring value may not have the knowledge or the means to do so, or be constrained by other impediments in their working environment. Without some kind of intervention, it is unlikely that digital heritage materials will automatically be made in ways that will minimise costs and remove barriers to preservation. Many practices in fact make preservation much harder.

Preservation efforts that wait until problems start to appear are likely to be more costly, more difficult, and less effective than efforts that start early. Organisations that have both heritage-creating and heritage-preserving functions have learnt from experience that care invested from the start in the use of standards, documentation, good file management and other practices, pays dividends later in lower preservation and maintenance costs, as well as more easily accessed, re-used and managed collections.

While all preservation programmes do not have the same opportunities to influence production practices, all programmes should seek to influence the way materials are created, and managed, from as early in their life cycle as possible. It is important to recognise that creators of digital materials work in different environments and are likely to be quite diverse in many ways: how they approach their work, their size of operations, the organisational and technical support at their disposal, and their interest in long-term access issues.

For example, scientists collecting data are likely to have an overriding interest in how accurately and securely their data is protected; how well any proposed formats and standards fit with their working needs; the convenience of transfer arrangements; and maintenance of moral rights and access controls over their data. On the other hand, commercial publishers of CD-ROM packages are likely to be more interested in controls on unauthorised copying; the costs and risks associated with providing 'unprotected' versions to a preservation programme; the potential re-use of their content; and their licence obligations to software owners whose products they have used.

There are many ways in which those responsible for preserving digital heritage may approach working with those who create and disseminate it. Preservation programmes should proactively promote awareness of their own role. It may be advantageous to identify particular groups of producers and work with them, addressing specific issues, rather than trying to resolve everyone's concerns at a generic level. At a broader industry level, it may be helpful to develop a code of practice that sets out agreed understandings about roles and responsibilities, and defines the scope and terms of ongoing cooperation.

Many sectors have active industry groups that provide forums for discussing issues. As well as offering opportunities for dialogue with industry leaders, such forums may help in establishing new norms of thinking that incorporate a longer term perspective. It is important for preservation programmes to offer positive encouragement and feedback for the steps producers are willing to take, and to provide a level of accountability for the way preservation programmes deal with their materials.

In many situations, working with producers means a real input by the preservation programme, not just the producer. Possible areas of input may include:

— Providing written guidelines and specifications

— Providing training for staff

— Help in designing systems and workflows

— Exchange of information and working tips

— Succession arrangements for material in a producer-managed preservation programme.

Specifications and best practice guidance Guidance on good practice is likely to include advice on the following:

— *Organisational issues that will make it easier to manage digital materials:* Project planning, emphasising system design prior to the creation of any records or publications

— *Choice of carrier*: Producers should be encouraged to use 'industrial strength' products that will survive long enough for the data to be transferred to other carriers, either by the producer or on transfer to the preservation programme

— *Choice of appropriate file formats and data standards*: Unless there are very good reasons to do otherwise, creators should be encouraged to use very widely adopted, well-standardised file formats that fit their purposes. Generally speaking, data in simpler formats using open source, non-proprietary software are easier to preserve (although some proprietary applications achieve such widespread use that they may be accepted as an industry standard, especially if their specifications are openly published).

Online materials published for public access should be readable by commonly used browsers. Structuring documents in a standard, easily recognised and durable format such as XML (Extensible Markup Language) should be considered for material of enduring value

— *Validation of formats*: It is not enough simply to choose a standard format and then to use it in non-standard ways: formats should be implemented in compliance with their standard and if necessary validated to remove any idiosyncrasies likely to complicate preservation.

— *File names should be consistent and unambiguous*: Online files should be managed for persistent access through the use of a persistent identifier and resolver service, or re-direct messages if files are moved. A number of PI schemes are in use internationally in different sectors, although none are in universal use. The DOI (Digital Object Identifier) scheme used by commercial publishers to manage rights has the widest acceptance.

Creators should create good quality metadata for the resources they create, using a widely accepted schema such as MARC, the Dublin Core metadata elements or one of its many sector-based enhancements. The metadata will help users find and use their resources. Metadata should also be recorded that describes the technical nature of the digital objects, what is required to access them, and any changes in these details over their life cycle: this information will be needed in managing them. The metadata can be either embedded in the resources or stored in a linked metadata file

— *File management*: Preservation master files should be stored and managed separately from dissemination copies. Database management procedures should ensure that data is not overwritten before it is captured

— *System security*: Files and systems should be fully protected from damage or loss by adopting best practice security measures and by appropriate backup arrangements even for short-term storage

— *Authenticity*: All files should be identified and their provenance and history documented to provide continuous evidence of authenticity

— *Training*: Staff, contractors and others coming into contact with the digital materials should be guided by appropriate procedures and manuals, and be adequately trained, motivated and equipped to use them

— If access or copying barriers are considered necessary to protect intellectual property, they may well make preservation impossible. Arrangements will be needed to allow preservation processes such as copying to take place.

Initial steps in maintaining access may include keeping all the software required for access, as well as any specialised hardware. This will not be an effective long-term strategy but may well be necessary in the short term. There may be a need to evaluate digital materials, decide how long they should be kept and by whom, in accordance with an approved policy such as an archival disposal authority.

Digital preservation programmes with few resources may find they are unable to spare any resources to work with producers. However, it may be possible to make a worthwhile investment in reducing future costs by taking limited, targeted actions aimed at influencing the material they have to manage.

Metadata Management

Controlling what happens to digital materials is a key preservation step. In most cases this requires the safe transfer of data and documentation to the care of a preservation programme, where they are given unique identification, and described using various kinds of metadata. Metadata enables digital materials to be found and, crucially from a preservation point of view, to be managed and re-presented accurately.

Although preservation metadata standards are still developing, programmes must describe the technical characteristics, provenance and preservation objectives of the digital materials in their care. In most cases this requires the transfer of data into the care of a responsible preservation agency. The transfer process itself is not without risks as it provides opportunities for data to be lost, changed, misidentified, or divorced from the context that gives it meaning.

Because the producers of digital materials generally have some rights in the materials they produce, transfer raises a number of legal and moral rights issues. Once digital materials have been transferred, they must be controlled and organised in effective and efficient ways. This generally includes requirements that materials can be easily located, accessed, used, managed and preserved, in accord with permissions.

Transfer and control are long-established practices in managing non-digital heritage. When applied to digital materials, these processes must be modified. An appropriate legal basis for transfer is required. It must address concerns over the ease with which materials can be re-used, as well as the need to copy data for its preservation. Transfer must affected without loss of data, often using quite different methods from those used for transfer of non-digital materials. The transfer of accompanying documentation is particularly critical for digital data that may not be understandable without it.

Most transfer strategies are variations of two basic concepts: producers pushing digital materials to the preservation programme, or the preservation programme pulling materials from the producer. Programme managers must decide which approach will be most suitable for the materials being transferred and for the workflows of the parties involved.

Many programmes impose controls at the point of transfer on the formats of the material they receive. The purpose of this is to simplify preservation by reducing the variations that have to be managed in storing the material and in keeping it accessible. Not all programmes are able to restrict the formats they accept, but they should seek to verify that formats have been used in a standard way.

Digital files must be given suitable file identifiers so they can be retrieved. Each file within a storage system must be identified with a unique file name so that it cannot be confused with any other file. It is also most important for preservation programmes to ensure that the materials they keep can be reliably found, whatever their location. The Universal Resource Locator (URL) used to identify Web-based resources, for example, does not allow users to find material once it has been moved. Thus, items can be effectively lost even though it may still exist and be well protected.

Overcoming this problem requires some form of persistent identification, built around an identifier and a means of resolving or linking to the file in its current location. There are a number of schemes proposed or in place including the Digital Object Identifier (DOI) used by publishers, and various schemes being investigated by libraries and archives, but none has yet found universal acceptance.

Preservation programmes use metadata - structured information about data resources - to describe the digital materials in their care. Preservation programmes generate large amounts of information about way material is created, transferred and used; about rights and who is authorised to do what; and other management processes. Preservation metadata describes the means of providing access, along with those elements of resource management metadata required to manage preservation processes. It is critical for any preservation programme; its careful design and management is especially important for large collections that must be processed with as much automation as possible.

Metadata is itself an information resource that must be managed and preserved, along with the material that it describes. Individually developed metadata schemes can be successful in describing collections of digital materials, but there are increasingly good reasons to use a standardised approach in line with other widely adopted schemes:

— To reduce the considerable costs of developing individual schemes

— To take advantage of available software tools that automatically recognise and record standard metadata elements from digital materials, greatly reducing the cost of metadata capture

— To allow preservation programmes to share information, making their collections visible and searchable to a much wider audience

— To allow collection materials to be moved from one repository to another without the need for wholesale rewriting of metadata

— To encourage the standardisation of preservation processes that are described and controlled by the metadata.

The reproducibility of digital materials means that transfer no longer requires removal of the material from one site in order to move it to another. Perfectly authentic copies can be transferred for preservation while 'live' copies remain with the creator · The timing of transfer may be critical. Even though material may have been selected for preservation, selection of itself does nothing to slow down processes like media deterioration or obsolescence of technology.

There is no standard way of effecting the physical transfer of digital materials. Data can be transferred on a wide range of physical carriers such as various forms of diskettes, CDs, tapes, cartridges, and disk drives; or through communication networks using means such as email attachments, file transfer protocol (FTP), and downloading from Web sites. The choice of transfer media depends on the needs of the parties involved.

Whatever means are chosen, the data must remain secure. Some transfer environments may present particular risks for specific media; for example, physical carriers may be easily lost or stolen, while communication networks may be unreliable and it may be safer to hand deliver a physical carrier. The transfer medium must allow the data to be loaded and retrieved. When both sender and receiver use the same technologies, transfer should be relatively straightforward. When technologies are mismatched, one or both parties will need to bear the cost of using different technologies.

Preservation programmes may have facilities to handle a wide range of media, or their.facilities may be more restricted. Physical carriers require specific hardware which preservation agencies may not be able to provide. In such cases they will need to decide whether it is reasonable to require transfers via specific media that they can process, or to invest in facilities to handle a wider range of media.

On the other hand, preservation programmes relying on deposit may find that transfers depend on production factors beyond their control, including changes in personnel, changes in priority, or declining levels of interest, all leading to inconsistent transfers. Pull approaches place more control in the hands of the preservation programme regarding timing and content of transfers. Some producers consider this an infringement of their rights and either block the software used to copy their files or demand rights agreements, so the control offered by pull approaches is not absolute.

Digital objects can have a number of identifiers variously used for local control, for system-wide identification, and for global access, (just as a book on a library shelf can be identified by its title, a classification number, a shelf location, an accession number, a record number in the catalogue database, an International Series Book Number, and so on). Persistent identification of some kind is needed so that items can be found even if they are moved in a storage system. Any links embedded within objects will only continue to work if linked to persistent identifiers.

It has already been noted that metadata must be not only recorded, but also looked after. There are a number of elements to this:

— *Structuring*: Organising metadata into a standardised document structure such as an XML template should make it easier to preserve

— *Linking*: The links between metadata records and the digital objects they describe must be maintained. There is much debate about the best place to store metadata to achieve this. While some metadata must be attached so that software tools can automatically process the material, there is disagreement on whether full metadata records should be stored separately, attached to, or even become part of, the objects they describe.

Separate storage allows metadata to be accessed and updated without needing to extract the linked digital objects from storage - a great advantage. On the other hand, many programme managers worry about the potential for the essential link between object and record to be disrupted over long periods of time. Managers should assess the risks they operate with and decide which approach is more suitable

— *Quality control*: Ensuring the trustworthiness of metadata records is a high priority. Quality control measures are needed whenever metadata records are created or changed

— *Protection*: The integrity of metadata records must be ensured, requiring the same preservation attention as the objects they describe.

Once the digital material has been transferred and any necessary control and description work undertaken, it must be prepared for entry into a storage system, ensuring the various part of the information package (including the content and any metadata) are linked, and a data stream created that can be safely stored on the storage media in use and can found by the appropriate file searching programmes. The package is then saved to storage.

Preservation of Metadata

Preservation metadata is structured information about a digital object, which:

— Identifies the material for which a preservation programme has responsibility

— Communicates what is needed to maintain and protect data

— Communicates what is needed to re-present the intended object (or its defined essential elements) to a user when needed, regardless of changes in storage and access technologies

— Records the history and the effects of what happens to the object

— Documents the identity and integrity of the object as a basis for authenticity

— Allows a user and the preservation programme to understand the context of the object in storage and in use.

Arrangements for recording preservation metadata must accommodate the fact that the same basic content (or conceptual object) may exist in many manifestations during its life. Some of these manifestations will co-exist as digital objects, while others may follow each other in a series of separate or overlapping generations.

Some preservation programmes reflect this by creating a record for a single version identified as a Preservation Master, documenting variants and changes as part of the history of that object. Other programmes create a record for each manifestation requiring preservation action, ensuring the relationships between manifestations are explicit in their metadata records. The information required for preservation metadata is often divided into two classes:

— Content information, consisting mainly of details about the technical nature of the object which tells the system how to re-present the data as specific data types and formats. As access technologies change, this re-presentation metadata also needs to be updated

— Preservation description information, consisting of other information needed for long-term management and use of the object, including identifiers and bibliographic details, information on ownership and rights, provenance, history, context including relationships to other objects, and validation information, Obviously, some of this metadata may refer to other information objects such as software tools and format specifications that must also be managed.

The interdependent nature of digital materials means that programmes often have to manage networks of linked objects and their metadata. There are still no accepted standards for preservation metadata schemas for universal use, so programmes may have to choose between accepting (and possibly adapting) one of a number of models being used by others, or designing their own schema (either as a complete solution or as a minimal interim one until a standard emerges).

Legal Rights for Management

There are a range of right and expectations held by stakeholders, which preservation programmes must be aware of and, if necessary, include in their management planning. Many of these rights have legal implications, including intellectual property rights and privacy rights. Because preservation programmes must copy digital materials to preserve them, and because most programmes aim to provide some level of access, active rights management approaches are needed.

Digital heritage materials are subject to a range of rights and expectations, some of which have legal force. Many, such as copyright, result from the intellectual property invested in the material. However, there may be other rights and expectations that also need to be taken into account. The range of rights and expectations that preservation programmes may encounter and have to manage typically includes:

— Intellectual property rights of producers including copyright, which may exist in various layers associated with different aspects of the material; the right to set conditions of access and use; and the creator's moral right to be recognised

— Legislated rights of certain institutions to collect, preserve and provide access to some materials. The rights and expectations of privacy, confidentiality and authorisation of use associated with some subjects of materials such as organisational records, oral history recordings, personal data and private communications.

Preservation involves many processes where rights issues are relevant. In order to achieve continuity of digital heritage, preservation programmes must:

— Obtain and hold material, usually involving making copies

— Make further copies for preservation purposes

— If necessary, bypass devices used by producers to limit access and prevent copying

— Decide what materials and what aspects of materials should be preserved

— Add metadata

— Modify file structures and file names if necessary

— Use whatever means are available at the time to preserve accessibility

— Provide managed access for authorised users.

Preservation programmes must be aware of the legal frameworks in which they operate, including their legal rights, constraints and obligations. This may require reference to specific legal advice from a competent source. Even with good intentions to preserve important heritage materials, preservation programmes are responsible for seeking ways to achieve their mission without infringing the legitimate rights of others.

Preservation programmes must decide on the extent to which they should engage in advocacy on rights issues, presenting arguments for legislation that would make it easier for a wide range of digital materials to be preserved. At a minimum, preservation programmes should ensure that interested parties are aware of the rights required for effective preservation action.

There may be a number of frameworks which allow preservation programmes to assume the right to collect and preserve specific digital materials. The most common include:

— Legal deposit or records management legislation

— Organisational rules governing corporate information

— Contractual requirements to deposit data

— Conditions of grants, awards, employment, or membership of organisations

— Rights inherited by one organisation from another

— Negotiated or purchased licence agreements

— Rights implied by voluntary submission of material to a preservation programme

— Some preservation agencies capture and store materials such as publicly available, free access Web sites without seeking prior approval. Some do this on the assertion of 'fair use' for material in the public domain; others rely on an 'opt out' option whereby rights owners are generally invited to express an objection.

It is the responsibility of the preservation programme to determine, on the basis of competent legal advice, whether any of these or other approaches is applicable, and what is required as an adequate legal defence.

Each situation requires its own set of arrangements, but preservation programmes should consider the need to take some common steps including:

— Determining the legal situation regarding rights specified by legislation, existing organisational rules, or licence agreements

— Identifying the rights that will be needed to carry out a preservation responsibility

— Identifying relevant rights owners, and other stakeholders with an influential interest in what rights are negotiated

— Preparing a clear explanation of what is needed and how it will be managed

— Approaching rights owners and negotiating a rights regime that is mutually acceptable

— Recording rights management responsibilities in metadata that is clearly and securely associated with the relevant materials.

— Ensuring the responsibilities are understood by staff

— Having secure systems, procedures and tools in place to control access and copying, and to monitor compliance

— If necessary, isolating preservation actions from other kinds of access and use

— Ensuring users understand their legal rights and obligations

— Regularly evaluating systems and procedures to ensure they do what they are supposed to do

— Monitoring any triggers for a change in rights, such as the passing of a specified period of time.

The level of access that preservation programmes should seek will depend on their mission: it may be appropriate for some digital heritage materials to be subject to very limited access for privacy, security, or other reasons, whereas it seems reasonable to expect that published materials would be available for ongoing access through a well-managed preservation programme. Some possibilities that may be attractive in negotiating access conditions include:

— Geographical restrictions, such as limiting access to onsite users

— Restrictions on the ability to copy, such as use of a stand alone computer without access to external networks or disk drives

— Restrictions on the number of users who can access the material at any one time

— Time thresholds allowing unrestricted access after a reasonable period for commercial exploitation

— Mutually agreeable triggers for a transfer of access rights, such as when the material is no longer available from a publisher's site

— Restricting access to authorised users who are required to meet specified conditions.

When rights have been negotiated, they must be managed as a core business responsibility of the preservation programme. Preservation programmes can expect to deal with large amounts of material, so the use of standard licence agreements covering classes of material will avoid the need to negotiate and manage rights item by item. System tools to manage rights are available and can be expected to continue to evolve. Such tools record access conditions applying to individual items, record and filter requests for use, and report on usage.

In choosing rights management tools, it is important to decide what tools are appropriate to support a balanced approach to rights management. It should be made easy for users to contact rights owners to negotiate their own permissions, such as the right to copy, where it is the user's responsibility to do so. Making authorised access as easy as possible may act as a disincentive to unauthorised access and use. Encouraging creators to use open source software should help reduce complications and costs involved in negotiating rights with proprietary software developers.

Rights issues have the potential to add greatly to the costs of preservation programmes, so all programmes have an interest in finding efficiencies and in avoiding exposure to litigation. programmes with few resources may particularly need to look for standard agreements that reduce the costs of negotiating rights approvals. They may also have to accept that rights management is a limiting factor on the size of their operations.

Data protection in Digital Preservation

Data protection is a fundamental of all preservation

programmes. For many programmes, authenticity is also critically important. Authenticity relates to the ongoing integrity of data, and its clear and sustained identification. Data protection strategies include allocation of responsibility, technical infrastructure, maintenance, data transfer, proper storage of data carriers, backup, system security and disaster planning. Authenticity also relies on clear documentation of the origins and history of digital materials.

Data must be stored. While it is appropriate to focus preservation attention on how best to re-present digital objects as originally intended, it must never be forgotten that the digital object has an underlying form as data. It is as data that it must be stored, managed and protected if any digital object is to be available for presentation to a user.

Heritage materials are often valued, at least in part, for their authenticity - the degree to which one can trust that they are indeed what they are thought to be. For archival records, scientific data, and many other kinds of digital materials, trust in their ongoing authenticity is critical, for without it they are of virtually no value. Authenticity derives from being able to trust both the identity of an object - that it is what it says it is, and has not been confused with some other object - and the integrity of the object - that it has not been changed in ways that change its meaning.

Maintenance of both identity and integrity implies sustained and documented links between an object as originally created and as currently presented. Evaluating, maintaining and providing evidence of continued authenticity are key responsibilities for most preservation programmes.

The nature of digital materials, and how they must be managed for preservation and access, both present challenges:

— Digital materials can be changed easily, with or without fraudulent intent, and even without any intent at all

— Changes that happen may not be obvious

— Preservation processes almost always involve making changes - transferring data from one system to another, from one carrier to another, adding or updating metadata, creating new copies that need new file names, changing the means of presentation as technologies change, and so on.

Where digital materials have value as records that offer evidence of some kind, authenticity is extremely important. Not all digital materials are made or selected to provide evidence: for example, they may reflect creative expression, the debate of ideas, or the desire to entertain and be entertained.

Even for these materials authenticity may be an issue, as the integrity of their creators' work or ideas should be protected. Ultimately, preservation programmes must decide how much to invest in ensuring that the authenticity of material in their care can be trusted, bearing in mind that object identity and data integrity are fundamental responsibilities.

Data protection must play a key role in any preservation programme, for two reasons: i) So that there is a digital object for a user to access. This is a fundamental requirement: if data is lost or seriously corrupted it may be impossible to re-present the intended digital object at all, and the preservation process must be judged to have failed ii) So that the integrity of the data can be maintained without tampering or corruption in order for users to trust the authenticity of the represented object.

Role of documentation

Documentation also plays a key role, for two reasons:

- — By explaining the links between objects and by clearly distinguishing between them, it provides evidence of identity
- — By showing what changes, if any, have taken place, with whose authority, and to what effect, it provides an audit trail to attest to authenticity.

Of all the responsibilities of preservation programmes, storage and data protection may be the ones for which it is easiest to find suitable third party service providers. The considerable investments required for equipment and expertise may make this an attractive alternative to managing data in-house. However, the critical nature of data protection means that the preservation programme must still accept responsibility for ensuring that any contracted services deliver the necessary levels of care and control.

Data must be stored and managed with appropriate systems and on an appropriate carrier. There are digital asset management systems or digital object storage systems available that meet the requirements of digital preservation programmes. Once requirements have been determined, they should be thoroughly discussed with potential suppliers. Different systems and carriers are suited to different needs and those chosen for preservation programmes must be fit for their purpose.

The overall system must have adequate capabilities including:

Sufficient storage capacity. Storage capacity can be build up over time, but the system must be able to manage the amount of data expected to be stored within its life cycle -As a fundamental capability, the system must be able to duplicate data as required without loss, and transfer data to new or 'refreshed' carriers without loss -Demonstrated reliability and technical support to deal with problems promptly -The ability to map file names into a file-naming scheme suitable for its storage architecture. Storage systems are based around named objects.

Different systems use different architectures to organise objects. This may impose constraints on how objects are named within storage; for example, disk systems may impose a hierarchical directory structure on existing file names, different from those that would be used on a tape system. The system must allow, or preferably carry out, a mapping of system-imposed file names and existing identifiers

Error checking. A level of automated error checking is normal in most computer storage. Because heritage materials must be kept for long periods, often with very low human usage, the system must be able to detect changes or loss of data and take appropriate action.

Technical infrastructure must also include means of storing metadata and of reliably linking metadata to stored digital objects. Large operations often find they need to set up digital object management systems that are linked to, but separate from, their digital mass storage system, in order to cope with the range of processes involved, and to allow metadata and work interfaces to be changed without having to change the mass storage.

While the cost of replacing data carriers must be considered, replacement media typically offer increased storage capacity. Unfortunately, any savings are usually offset by growth in the amount of data to be stored. The market for data storage and management systems extends well beyond preservation programmes, so there are good COTS (Commercial Off The Shelf) products available.

Using COTS technology is possibly the most easily managed, iow risk and cost effective approach as technical support and upgrades are provided by vendors in a competitive marketplace. Standards are sufficiently widely used in the storage market to allow mixing and matching products from various vendors so that a number of upgrade and replacement paths are available when needed.

Storage systems rely on safe and complete replication of data, rather than enduring carriers, for data protection. Data must be copied from carrier to carrier to avoid the impact of carrier deterioration. As new kinds of carriers prove their usefulness in storage systems, data is transferred from older kinds of carriers. This must happen before any hardware or software required to retrieve the data are discarded. Planning for data transfers is a management challenge, whatever the system used.

For example, a small, low use archive storing data on shelved CDs, must keep track of the age and condition of the CDs as well as signs that CD technology will have to be replaced. More sophisticated mass storage systems generally automate decisions about regular transfer of data between carriers, but managers still need to decide when carriers should be replaced with new media, and when underlying technology has been superseded. Appropriate storage and handling conditions for carriers.

Digital data carriers must be stored in conditions that do not accelerate their rate of deterioration. The main risks for data carriers are excessive temperature and humidity which endanger the carrier; dust or other particulates which may obscure access to the data; and in the case of optically encoded material, light, which may damage the optically inscribed data. Modern data tapes are of such a high coercivity, that accidental erasure by a magnetic field does not constitute a major risk.

Magnetic data tapes may be integrated into a digital storage system. Typically this would be housed in a clean computer room with controlled temperature and relatively humidity set at 18°C, and 40% RH, a continuous influx of clean, dust-free air, with daily cleaning to prevent contamination. The conditions would fluctuate no more than 2°C and 10% RH in any given 24 hour period. Magnetic data tapes stored for optimum carrier life should be stored under more stringent conditions, at a temperature between 18°C and 10°C, with a daily tolerance of no more than 1°C, and between 30 and 40% RH with a tolerance of no more than 3%RH.

Optical carriers, such as CD-Recordable, should be stored under similar conditions, in a darkened environment due to their sensitivity to light. There are suggestions that very low temperatures (approaching or lower than 0°C), may be detrimental to the life expectancy of certain carriers, however, this has not been proven.

While storing multiple copies of the same data does offer some protection against failure, preservation programmes must also consider the risks of a disaster which damages all copies stored at the same site. Storing copies at different sites is a basic requirement; to avoid the impact of region-wide disasters such as floods, earthquakes, wildfires, and war, programmes should consider the need to store additional backup copies of important data outside their own region.

Preservation programmes may also need to adjust normal backup schedules so that preservation data, which must be kept, is refreshed (i.e. rewritten) not overwritten with new data.

Data protection is such a critical responsibility that even programmes with few resources must give it a high priority. The simplified risk analysis above may suggest areas of lower risk for some programmes. It also suggests that some risks may be reduced at the cost of reducing the level or speed of access. This may be perfectly acceptable for some collections.

Changes in software and hardware add up to a loss in the means of access to digital heritage materials. This is expected to be the core challenge for most preservation programmes. Using understandings of the relationship between digital objects and their means of access, and taking account of what has to be presented to a user in providing access, programme managers must decide on strategies that will guarantee accessibility whenever it is needed.

Strategies, which are likely to vary over time and according to needs, are still evolving. The strategies discussed are grouped into those based on investment of resources from early in the life cycle of digital materials, those with short-term and with medium- to long-term effectiveness, and some alternative 'non-digital' and 'non-preservation' strategies.

4

Roles and Responsibilities of Archiving

The well-ordered world of the university library is giving way to a new era of promise and uncertainty, of technology, of new forms of engagement and redefined roles in learning. The assumptions and rationales that have been relied on in the past are inadequate as a guide to future developments. To be successful in this new environment those responsible for academic libraries need to understand:

— the changing expectations faced by universities,

— how universities are responding to these new expectations,

— how this affects the library's mission,

— how libraries can develop a strategy to be a central part of the university's response, and

— how the Association of Research Libraries can assist its members to take on new roles.

This concept of learning requires a shift in focus from the teacher's knowledge to the student's understandings and capabilities. This shift in focus leads to a new perspective on the development of quality in the academic enterprise. More than anything, it requires the faculty to bring the strength of the research paradigm into the learning process. The high quality of research in American universities is, in part, the result of the central role of assessment in the research process.

With an understanding of student learning objectives, the scholarship of teaching and learning identifies critical issues, uses research methods, and applies results to understand and improve learning outcomes. For over a decade, institutional and professional accreditation bodies have been shifting their attention from input measures (faculty, courses, books) to outcomes measures (what students learn). Universities and colleges are required to develop and implement a student outcomes assessment program. Assessment requires academic organizations (departments, colleges, universities) to:

— make expectations and standards for quality explicit and public

— systematically gather evidence on how well performance matches those expectations and standards

— analyze and interpret the evidence

— use the resulting information to document, explain and improve performance.

The focus on learning involves looking at the academic program not from the perspective of its subject matter content but from the perspective of the competencies to be developed by students. These competencies include knowledge, skills and abilities, and attitudes and values that are important to a graduate's future success. It is easy to treat these new expectations as one more example of a demand for accountability in higher education.

A closer examination leads me to conclude that they represent a recognition of the changing needs of graduates to be successful in an increasingly complex knowledge economy. Faculty have always assessed the performance of individual students within their individual courses. The focus of outcomes assessment is on the collective success of the program in developing the competencies of the students in the program.

The faculty is being asked to accept responsibility for a broader set of outcomes. To a significant extent this represents a new challenge because while faculty are knowledge experts, they are not necessarily learning experts. Students will also be required to approach the learning experience differently. They are being asked to become more actively involved in the learning process. While they have mastered the passive accumulation of knowledge, they are less comfortable with the responsibility to demonstrate their ability to use knowledge in unstructured situations.

They must become proficient as members of teams, in communicating their solutions, and effectively taking advantage of access to information and the use of technology. Finally, they must begin to develop and demonstrate maturity in how they approach their work. The focus on learning outcomes leads to a consideration of the learning process and the learning community.

From the University's perspective, they are achieved as a result of a total experience over a four (or more) year period. Each element of the educational program contributes, directly or indirectly, to their achievement. Looking at the learning process allows us to recognize the various activities that contribute to learning. On the far left of the figure we see how foundational courses (math, composition, etc), general education courses and special prerequisite service.courses prepare the student for the major.

The requirements for the major are designed to produce the learning outcomes necessary for the graduate to be successful. Across the bottom of the figure we see how the program offerings of the library, student life and technical services can contribute to the learning outcomes of the graduate.

Looking at the learning community allows us to consider how faculty, students and other learning professionals can contribute to learning outcomes. The faculty responsible for the major is in the best position to develop the complete set of learning outcomes, since those outcomes will depend on the specific objectives for the degree program.

The American Association for Higher Education's Principles of Good Practice for Assessing Student Learning recognize that "student learning is a campus-wide responsibility, and assessment is a way of enacting that responsibility. Faculty play an especially important role, but assessment questions can't be fully addressed without participation by student affairs educators, librarians, administrators, and students. ...assessment is not a task for a small group of experts but a collaborative activity; its aim is wider, better informed attention to student learning by all parties with a stake in its improvement."

The University is made up of various communities, each of which has a direct and/or indirect view of student learning outcomes. For example, faculty with responsibility for designing and delivering a general education program must define outcomes that assure students across the University will have a common foundation and also contribute to the learning outcomes that are important in many degree programs. An academic department has a direct interest in the learning outcomes for students in their majors.

A department with an important course that serves a critical role in preparing students in another department's degree program has an indirect interest in the learning outcomes for students in that major. For example, physics is an important service course for students in an engineering program. The Physics faculty can not be effective unless they are working with the Engineering faculty to produce a clear set of learning outcomes for their service courses that will help achieve the outcomes desired for the engineering students.

Within the new environment, we need to measure the ways in which the library is contributing to the learning that the University values. Like the general education program, the library has a direct and an indirect interest in the learning outcomes for all the students at the University. Like the Physics Department, the Library should be able to contribute to the achievement of learning outcomes for various academic programs across the University.

Developing a set of learning outcomes will allow libraries to determine the extent to which their interests are aligned with the expectations of other academic communities in the University. They will find that faculty responsible for the general education program as well as those responsible for many of the academic degree programs also are interested in critical thinking, the effective use of information and technology, the search process and collaborative reasoning.

The library can build on a shared view of what are important student learning outcomes. All the individual communities are being asked to prepare students in ways that go.beyond their expertise in their fields. It is this shared need to go beyond our traditional focus on what students need to know that creates an opportunity for the library. Consider for a moment the way in which a department faculty might look at the learning outcomes for their degree program and how they are achieved through the course requirements. Having agreed on what outcomes they believe are important to their graduate's future success, they can ask the faculty responsible for each course to identify the extent to which each outcome is a focus of the course.

Collectively, across the curriculum, they can determine which outcomes are covered to a major, moderate or minor extent. At this point, while they haven't yet assessed how well their students have developed on each learning outcome, they can evaluate whether enough attention is being paid to individual outcomes. The library must take the initiative in determining what the library has to offer that will help the department achieve greater success in achieving their learning outcomes.

As an example, the University of Arizona Library is offering instruction sessions based on the ACRL Information Literacy Competencies, using the Kuhlthau "Information Search Process" model. The instruction will be integrated into a general education natural sciences course offered by the Astronomy department. The library team has developed learning modules that focus on entry-level information literacy competencies.customized for use in Astronomy related studies.

They will be a required part of the course but offered at a variety of times outside the normal class period. The aim is for students to become confident and skillful information users. To pursue this strategy also requires that the library create new roles for its learning practitioners. To some extent and in some libraries this process of change has begun.

Libraries have developed organizational strategies to serve the various academic communities. But the focus to date is primarily on making information more and more accessible rather that addressing specifically the learning outcomes important to student success. The library needs to ask what kind of expertise is required to be actively engaged in the learning process and an effective partner in achieving learning outcomes. It then will be in a position to adapt roles and responsibilities of its professionals to take full advantage of the opportunity.

Collaborative Digital Reference Service (CDRS)

In United Kingdom the Collaborative Digital Reference Service (CDRS) provides professional reference service to researchers anytime, anywhere, through an international, online network of libraries and related institutions. Launched by the Library of Congress in June 2000, CDRS now includes more than 200 member libraries—academic, public, special, and national—worldwide and that number is growing weekly.

The collaboration has been very beneficial in that each library brings its professional experience, knowledge of user behavior and needs, and subject expertise to bear on the project. CDRS uses technology to provide the best answers in the best context, by taking advantage not only of the millions of Internet resources but also of the many more millions of resources that are not online and that are held by libraries around the world.

CDRS supports libraries by providing them additional choices for the services they offer their patrons. Libraries can more ably assist their patrons by sending questions that are best answered by the expert staff and collections of CDRS member institutions from around the world. An advisory board, comprised of representatives from CDRS member institutions, meets to discuss policy and future directions of the program. Business meetings with member representatives are also regularly held to get feedback, report on and solve workflow problems, discuss training and performance measures, and build esprit de corps.

The CDRS homepage posts general information and news links, information for members, and project milestones. An electronic mailing list allows members to communicate frequently with one another, get technical questions addressed, and comment on the efficacy of the network.

At no other time in history has the emergence of technology affected so significantly the core mission of a library. These technological advances have created new service opportunities for libraries and library patrons. For information to have relevance, it must be up-to-date and receive the hands-on touch of the skilled reference librarian to provide context and added value.

Through the CDRS network, LC and its partner libraries can serve researchers everywhere and, in so doing, bring control, context, greater choice, and timeliness to the world of information. CDRS includes two component parts: submission of a question and answer, and archiving the answer for future use. The workflow looks like this: An end user requests information through a CDRS member institution. The member institution sends the query to the online Request Manager (RM) software for processing and assigning.

The RM searches a database of CDRS member institution profiles looking for the institution best suited to answer the question. Once a match on an institution has been made, the query is sent to that institution for answering. After the query has been answered, it is routed back to the original CDRS requesting library via the RM to allow for closing out the case and completing other administrative tasks. The library profile is the core of the routing and assignment activity, and each institution can "code" itself as broadly or as narrowly as it chooses.

Library profiles contain basic information about the library, including hours of service (and time zones), collection strengths, staff strengths, education levels served, languages covered, geographic location of users served, whether there are special services provided and what they are--as many as 28 data fields. This information is captured in a table, where it is used by the online RM to sort, assign, and track incoming questions and to deliver answers to the end user.

Further, the profile tool is flexible enough to allow for regular updating to reflect staffing changes or special circumstances that would affect the automatic routing by the RM. For example, if the astronomy specialist is on sabbatical for several months and no back-up is available, the library might choose to remove that subject strength from its profile until the staff member returns.

Answers are edited and stored in a separately searchable knowledge base of information. The knowledge base, to be populated with the diverse and authentic information provided by CDRS librarians, will ultimately serve as a front end to CDRS, designed to "catch" and answer incoming questions if there is a ready match. If there is no match on the knowledge base, the question will be routed through the RM and assigned to a library.

There are no restrictions on the types of libraries that can participate. Size of a library or collection is not a factor in determining whether a library can become a member. The aforementioned Service Level Agreement defines the nature of the member library's relationship to the CDRS and that agreement is codified in the library profiles.

Many types of agreements are possible and are limited or expanded depending upon the strengths (e.g., subject) or limitations (e.g., staffing or hours of service) of the individual library. For example, a library may agree to ask and answer questions; only ask questions; ask or answer questions only during specified periods; serve as an editor for the knowledge base; or serve as the on-call library if the automatic Request Manager function is inoperable.

In addition, many libraries have local collections that are unique to them. These local, specialized collections make a potent contribution to CDRS overall, filling special niches that larger research institutions may not be able to fill. In addition to defining roles and responsibilities among the partner libraries, the SLAs will ultimately be used to determine what it will cost a library to be a member of CDRS.

We have encouraged maximum flexibility in developing the many component parts of CDRS. For a library to want to participate, CDRS has to be perceived to have value. Just as there are no "one size fits all" libraries, so too are there no "one size fits all" arrangements with CDRS. Libraries are structured and organized differently, they have different local audiences, and they have different policies and procedures for ensuring quality control.

To be useful to a library, CDRS must fill an unmet need and offer something that the library does not already have, e.g., adequate staff, a subject strength, or a special collection unique to a participating library that the whole collaboration then has access to. When the participating library defines the terms of that value, that library will have greater incentive to make the arrangement work, for itself and for CDRS.

Currently, libraries participating in CDRS connect with other libraries on behalf of patrons so that the libraries can conduct the reference interview before sending the question, define the parameters of the service, determine what works and what does not work, and create a service that is scalable and maximally responsive to user needs.

From the beginning, however, we have envisioned that CDRS will become a service that is available directly to patrons, recognizing that many individuals never go to their local library but still need information. In January

2001, the Online Computer Library Center (OCLC) and the Library of Congress, on behalf of CDRS member libraries, signed a cooperative agreement to guide CDRS through its next phase of development. OCLC will provide technical and development support to CDRS by building and maintaining a database of participating institution profiles that will route questions and answers through CDRS; building and maintaining a question-and-answer database system that will enable CDRS participants to catalog answers and store them in a searchable and browsable database; and providing administrative support for CDRS, including marketing the service, registering new members, and providing training and user support.

Together, the Library of Congress and OCLC will develop a viable model for a self-sustaining digital reference service and promote CDRS in the library community. The major factors that influence the level of investment an institution can make are software and hardware costs (including laptops for telecommuting librarians), staffing/hours issues, and training. Some libraries are offering experimental services that are open only a couple of hours a day and use inexpensive software, while others are committed to 24/7 service, delivered via sophisticated call center software from the corporate sector.

As when planning any new public service, it is helpful to conduct a needs assessment to look at the type of Internet connectivity that your users have and when they are using library resources. When choosing software, there are a large number of chat software programs and services on the market to choose from. Libraries also have the option of installing the software on their own computer networks or having it hosted by a commercial vendor or by a free service such as Yahoo! Chat. Each approach has its associated challenges, including response time, maintenance issues, and control over the user interface.

While expensive call center software may be out of reach for a smaller library's budget, many libraries are banding together in consortia to purchase software and to collaboratively staff virtual reference desks. The Biblioteksvagten consortium of academic and public libraries in Denmark, using Live Person, is one example. Many libraries are purchasing hosted service from companies named LSSI or 24/7 Reference that offer use of NetAgent or eGain software at a reduced price, and even librarians to staff your service, if staffing is an issue. In addition to the chat space, some of these features are:

— Users do not need special software to connect, only a Java-enabled web browser, such as Netscape Communicator, Opera, or Internet Explorer.

— A powerful client to help librarians answer questions quickly.

— The ability to show users web pages on their screen (push page).

— The ability to escort a user through a web search.

— Private messaging between librarians (independent of the chat space).

There are many challenges in setting up a chat reference service, not the least of which is selecting and installing usable software and marketing the new service to your users. The real challenges are overcoming staff resistance to a new and unfamiliar service, teaching effective online communication, and training librarians to field questions outside their areas.

All of these challenges can be addressed by training and experience with working on the service. It is important to give staff ample time to practice their skills before going online, and to provide them with a safety net for their first few shifts. It is also important to realize that not every question that begins in a chat session is best answered via chat. Sometimes it is more effective to e-mail the answer, to ask the user to come to the library, or to refer the question. Chat reference is a convenient and very effective way to extend reference services to users outside the library, and requires the same kind of teamwork that keeps the traditional in-library reference desk operating smoothly.

5

Digital Library Classification

Libraries and archives play a critical role in organizing, preserving, and providing access to the cultural and historical resources of society. In the relatively stable world of printed, hand-written, and mechanically reproduced information, repositories managed to preserve a rich array of scholarly communications, documentary evidence, and useful information for specialized scholars and for the general public.

The introduction of digital technologies into the processes of production, distribution, and storage of information challenges the capacity of libraries, archives, museums, and other cultural institutions to carry out their responsibilities for preservation. This problem has been the focus of numerous reports designed to raise awareness of digital preservation issues and to propose general strategies for addressing them.

The general outline of digital preservation challenges is well established. Digital materials are especially vulnerable to loss and destruction because they are stored on fragile magnetic and optical media that deteriorate rapidly and that can fail suddenly from exposure to heat, humidity, airborne contaminants, or faulty reading and writing devices. Even if the media are preserved intact, digital materials become unreadable if the playback devices necessary to retrieve information from the media become obsolete or if the software that translates digital information from machine- to human-readable form is no longer available.

Libraries, archives, and other repositories that traditionally have assumed responsibility for preserving information face technical, legal, and organizational challenges in responding to the new demands of digital preservation. Repositories need access to technical resources — both information systems that support digital preservation and the technical expertise to use these technologies effectively.

Institutions also face legal obstacles in fulfilling their mandates to preserve valuable information when copyright or licensing agreements prohibit duplication or local storage of digital information. Institutions can take action on their own, but there is a strong consensus that coordinated strategies and shared resources are essential to achieving broader solutions to digital preservation and enhancing the success of local efforts.

Study of Digital Archiving by Research Libraries Group (RLG)

In early 1998, the Research Libraries Group (RLG) funded a study of digital archiving needs and requirements in RLG member institutions. RLG is an international consortium of close to 160 members, including universities and colleges, national libraries, archives, historical societies, museums, independent research collections, and public libraries.

The purpose of the study was twofold: (1) to gather baseline data on the nature and extent of digital preservation problems in member institutions and the status of their digital preservation programs, and (2) to identify needs and requirements of member institutions in meeting their responsibilities for preserving digital information.

Methodology

The methodology used for the research was a combination of a survey distributed to all RLG member institutions and follow-up interviews with one or more administrators at 15 institutions. This combination of data collection methods was used to gather and analyze data on the nature and types of digital collections in member institutions, the policies and programs in place for digital preservation, digital preservation needs and requirements, and future plans for developing digital preservation programs. The interviews with administrators provided additional qualitative insights into the problems they face and their perceptions of various strategies for digital preservation.

Libraries, archives, museums, and other repositories acquire digital materials through several different channels, which include purchasing digital information from publishers or distributors, legal deposit or transfer, donations, and licensing access to online databases. Many institutions also are creating digital information through programs or projects that convert print, photographic, and manuscript material to digital form. Libraries and archives do not necessarily assume responsibility for long-term preservation of all these materials. Some print-to-digital conversion projects exist primarily to improve access to materials, and some institutions consider the originals or a microfilm copy to be the preferable version for long-term preservation.

Online databases that are updated regularly may only be useful in their current version. Licensing agreements and copyright restrictions governing online digital resources and hand-held digital products might prohibit institutions from maintaining copies of digital works for preservation purposes.

For the purposes of the project, the survey focused on digital materials for which an RLG member institution assumes long-term preservation responsibility. The materials within the scope of the study include: (1) information created originally in digital form and acquired by a repository through purchase, transfer, or legal deposit; and (2) digital materials that are created when repositories convert print, photographic, and manuscript materials to digital form, provided that the institutions considered it their responsibility to preserve the information.

The term "digital preservation" refers to both preservation of materials that are created originally in digital form and never exist in print or analog form (also called "born-digital" and "electronic records") and the use of imaging and recording technologies to create digital surrogates of analog materials for access and preservation purposes. While this broad use of the term digital preservation can cause confusion, data on both aspects of digital preservation were analyzed.

Digital materials, regardless of whether they are created initially in digital form or converted to digital form, are threatened by technology obsolescence and physical deterioration.

The survey was designed to gain an understanding of member institutions' current holdings of digital materials and to gather data on present and near future needs related to preservation of digital materials. The survey questions were grouped into the categories of:

— digital materials policy,

— digital holdings,

— storage methods and formats,

— digital knowledge/training, and

— future needs for services and training.

A survey was distributed in late April 1998 to the designated member representative in all 158 RLG member institutions. E-mail was the primary distribution method, but copies were distributed in print form via fax or express mail to institutions without e-mail access.

A test survey consisting of the scope, definitions of terminology, and 25 questions had been distributed by RLG in March 1998. Based on feedback from eight individuals, the survey was revised and simplified to its final form of 18 questions, a statement about the scope of the survey, and definition of six key terms used in the survey. The survey was designed for ease of completion on a computer screen and reply via e-mail, with provision for returning the survey via fax or postal service. Although a May 6 deadline was specified, all surveys received by the end of August 1998 were included in the data analysis.

A total of 54 completed surveys were received between April and August 1998 for a response rate of 34%.

Interviews were conducted to gain additional insights that would supplement the quantitative data from the surveys. The interview script consisted of six open-ended questions designed to encourage spontaneous and reflective responses. Three questions focused on the current situation within the institution regarding:

— the impact of digital preservation demands on the interviewees and their institutions,

— experience(s) with outsourcing services, and

— availability and effectiveness of technical support within the institution.

One question asked administrators for feedback on the major issues that their institution will be facing with digital materials during the next four years; another focused on their insights regarding consortial arrangements for preservation of digital materials. The final question was a wish-list scenario, situating respondents "outside the box" to voice concerns about a particular problem regarding preservation of digital materials that they would like to see "magically solved."

RLG provided a list of 25 member representatives who were targeted for interviews. An e-mail message was sent to all, requesting their participation in individual thirty-minute interviews. Representatives of 16 institutions responded, and it was possible to schedule interviews with 14 of these. A test interview was also done, and as it was determined that no changes to the script were necessary, this was included in the final compilation for a total of 15 interviews. All interviews were conducted over the telephone, with the interviewer typing responses immediately into Microsoft Word. Fourteen interviews were completed between April 21 and May 7; the final interview was completed on June 15. Three interviews were conducted as conferences with two or three representatives from different departments in one institution.

Interview length was determined by the interviewee, and ranged from approximately 15 minutes to one-and-a-half hours, with the average being about 25-30 minutes. At the end of each interview the interviewee was asked to return the institution's survey so that complete data would be represented in the analysis. The non-respondents in this interviewed group were the only institutions to which follow-up appeals were made to return surveys. Of the 15 institutions that provided interviews, 12 institutions are represented in the survey data.

The survey data was compiled in a database in Microsoft Access. This database was then exported into a Microsoft Excel spreadsheet, and all statistical comparisons were made using formulas in a series of spreadsheets.

Owing to their qualitative nature and unstructured format, the interviews were more challenging to record. While complete interview responses were available in their entirety, for ease in comparison the major components of each response were distilled into abbreviated phrases (maximum 75 characters), coded by institutional identifier and question number, and arranged in an Excel spreadsheet. This produced a brief document that could be quickly scanned, with the responses arranged in columns by question number, and in rows by institution. Based on analysis, 10 major themes were then identified, and a second spreadsheet was created in which the coded, abbreviated phrases were matched with the themes they represented. This again produced a document in which responses could be easily scanned by theme, as well as by institution identifier and question number.

The data gathered and analyzed in the research permits drawing several conclusions about the current state of digital preservation in RLG member institutions and about their perceptions of needs and requirements for digital preservation. There are three aspects of the research that may limit broad generalizations from the results.

The sample was drawn from RLG member institutions to provide RLG with analysis of conditions and needs of its member institutions. It has the advantage of gathering data from a variety of institutions with digital preservation responsibilities, including research libraries, archives and historical societies, special research collections, and museums. However, there may be systematic differences between RLG member institutions and similar institutions that are not RLG members; and consequently, findings from the survey may not apply to all libraries, archives, museums, and special collections with digital preservation responsibilities.

Although 34% is a reasonably good response rate for a survey of this sort, there are two potential problems with the number of respondents and the nature of the response rate. The total of 54 responses allows detecting patterns and drawing certain conclusions across the entire data set. However, when one breaks the data into smaller categories by type of institution, location, whether or not the institutions have holdings or policies, etc., the small number of cases in some categories makes it difficult to draw statistically significant conclusions. Given this limitation, many of the findings are descriptive of the entire population, and trends within categories are suggested where the data supports such conclusions.

The potential bias in response is toward institutions with some digital materials in their holdings for which they assume preservation responsibility. Although there is no way of comparing the characteristics of non-respondents with institutions that responded, it is possible that institutions which consider digital preservation an important problem because they have digital materials in their holdings were more motivated to respond to the survey.

This cautionary note is reinforced by anecdotal information gathered from respondents while they were completing the surveys and through informal feedback received after the surveys were completed. Several institutions reported difficulty completing the survey because there was no single individual or source of information for answering all of the questions on the survey instrument. Compiling all of this information and answering the questionnaire thoroughly required a significant amount of time on the part of member institutions, suggesting that a high level of motivation was necessary for member institutions to respond.

Digital preservation is a multi-faceted problem that is viewed differently by different institutions and different professionals. The broad umbrella of digital preservation includes preserving both materials created and acquired in digital form and digital files generated when institutions convert analog materials to digital form. The survey instrument took special measures to explain the scope of the survey and to define the technical terminology used. While acknowledging that there are different interpretations of the terminology used, it requested the respondents to refer to and use the definitions provided. Nevertheless, one cannot be certain that all respondents shared exactly the same concepts and terminology in all of their responses.

Findings

Digital Preservation Responsibilities

Digital preservation is not an isolated problem affecting only large libraries and archives. Two-thirds (36) of the institutions in the survey have some digital materials in their holdings for which the institution assumes preservation responsibility. In fact, the 30 research libraries, which tend to be larger than the 24 archives, museums, and special collections, are not quite as likely to hold digital materials as the other types of institutions. About two-thirds of the research libraries assume responsibility for preserving digital materials, whereas 71% of the other types of repositories hold digital materials. A higher percentage of institutions outside the US have digital preservation responsibilities — 83% as compared to 62% of the institutions in the US.

Most repositories with digital holdings both acquire material in digital form and create digital files through conversion. Two-thirds of the institutions with digital holdings both acquire and create digital materials. One-quarter of the institutions are responsible for preserving only information that they create through conversion. Two institutions acquire information in digital form, but do not create digital files through conversion.

In the survey overall, almost half of the member institutions acquire digital materials and nearly two-thirds are involved in conversion activities. Through both acquisition and conversion activities, RLG member institutions are taking on responsibility for preserving unique digital materials that appear not be duplicated elsewhere. Twenty-eight institutions reported that irreplaceable information would be lost if the digital materials in their holdings are not adequately preserved for future use.

The digital holdings that member institutions are responsible for preserving vary in size, age, and the types of formats used for storage. Taken together, RLG member institutions that responded to the survey hold a minimum of 275,000 digital files and a total of at least 4.1 terabytes of information. These estimates are stated as minimum values because complete information on the quantity of digital materials was not available. Many institutions do not know how much digital material they hold and those that do use different measures to keep track of the quantity of digital materials in their holdings.

The survey asked institutions to report the number of digital files, the number of volumes (reels of tape, CDs, etc.), and the total storage volume (in MB, GB, etc.). Only 26 of the 36 institutions with digital materials were able to estimate the quantity of material using any one of these measures. Holdings range in quantity from less than 200 files at one institution to 96,600 files in another repository. Three repositories account for almost 75% of the total number of files and 90% of the total volume of 4.1 terabytes. In the 19 institutions that estimated the quantity of their holdings in megabytes or gigabytes, storage volumes range from a low of 500 megabytes in one institution to a high of 2 terabytes.

Many file formats and storage media are present in the digital holdings of these institutions. Among the 36 institutions with digital holdings, the most common formats are image files (97.2%), text files with mark-up (75.0%), and ASCII files (66.7%). More than one-third of the institutions had digital information in at least one of the following formats: word processing files (55.6%), audio (50.0 %), video (38.9%), and spreadsheets (38.9%), while fewer than a third of the institutions maintain digital information in geographic information systems, vector graphics, databases and other miscellaneous formats.

When institutions create digital information through conversion, they also create archival master files in a wide variety of formats for preservation. The most common formats for archival master files of converted images are TIFF (80.6%); text files with mark-up (55.6%); JPEG (38.9%); and PDF, GIF, and ASCII (30.6% each).

The survey shows that at least 24 different storage formats are present across the 54 responding institutions. Many institutions are maintaining digital information in several different formats. 24 of the 36 institutions with digital holdings maintain digital information in at least six different formats, and 13 of these institutions have 10 or more different formats.

Most of the institutions with digital holdings maintain relatively recent material, with some notable exceptions. The oldest digital materials reported were written to their current storage medium in the late 1970s, but the vast majority were generated in the last one to three years. Of 33 institutions reporting on the age of their oldest digital materials, 15 have materials created since 1995; only seven have materials created prior to 1990. Institutions with recent acquisitions and those that started conversion projects only in the last few years are just beginning to confront problems of long-term management of digital information.

In spite of the relatively young age of digital collections in most institutions, 15 institutions reported that they lack the operational and/or technical capacity to mount, read, and access some digital materials in their holdings. The most common storage media for which institutions lack access capability are floppy disks (five institutions) and open reel nine-track tape (three institutions); there are also scattered problems with CD-ROMs, magneto-optical disks, DDS DAT tape, 3480 cartridges, and various audio and video formats.

The research on digital preservation responsibilities and the nature and extent of digital holdings provides concrete evidence about digital preservation problems facing libraries, archives, museums, and other repositories. Digital preservation is a widespread problem in RLG member institutions.

Typically, institutions with digital preservation responsibilities both acquire materials in digital form and create digital files through conversion. While a few institutions have large collections of digital materials, most are modest in size but growing rapidly. Most member institutions began acquiring or creating digital materials during the last one to five years. Nevertheless,

15 of the 36 institutions with digital holdings cannot access some of their materials because they lack the operational or technical capacity to mount, read, or access files stored on some of the storage media in their holdings. Three-fourths of the institutions with digital holdings report that irreplaceable information will be lost if the digital materials in their holdings are not adequately preserved for future use.

Digital Preservation Policies and Practices

Digital preservation policies and practices are not well developed in member institutions. Two-thirds of the institutions do not have written policies for digital preservation. One common reason that institutions appear not to develop digital preservation policies is that they have not yet assumed responsibility for preserving materials in digital form. However, taking responsibility for digital preservation does not necessarily mean that institutions use policies to govern their digital preservation activities. Only half of the institutions with digital materials in their holdings have written digital preservation policies.

Fourteen institutions with policies considered their policy adequate, two institutions said it met the institution's needs poorly, one said well, and one was not sure. Most of the policies govern the acquisition of materials in digital form, but less than half of the policies govern storage of digital information, conversion of materials from print to digital form, refreshing, and migration. Only five institutions have policies that cover acquisition, storage, migration, and refreshing. Of the 34 institutions that are generating information in digital form through conversion, only seven have policies governing conversion.

This data and additional information gathered through interviews allows speculation about the lack of written policies. Most institutions that have not yet acquired materials in digital form or created digital materials through conversion have not yet experienced the need for written policies.

The interviews suggest that among those institutions with digital preservation responsibilities, the lack of good models for digital preservation and confusion about the most appropriate methods and approaches are major obstacles to developing effective policies and practices. Several administrators who were interviewed believe that policy development is important, but they do not yet see stable standards or effective models that can be used as the basis for institutional policy. Some expressed concern over competing strategies and the wide variety of approaches being advocated or followed by different institutions. At the same time, there is little information available on the costs or the effectiveness of different strategies. For some institutions, the perceived lack of a consensus in the community serves as a disincentive to policy development.

Effective digital preservation requires life-cycle management of digital information from the point of creation through storage, migration, and providing access on a continuing basis. Only 13 institutions reported that they have established methods in place for digital preservation.

Some of the institutions in the survey have adopted practices that limit the formats of digital information that they must manage. Two institutions limit the acceptable formats to flat files while others accept several different formats such as PDF, TIFF, SGML, and word processing formats. Only seven of the 34 institutions that create materials through conversion have adopted a standard format or formats for preservation master files, and there are a wide variety of formats present across the institutions.

The institutions in the survey use a wide range of methods for storing the digital information in their holdings. It appears that a majority of institutions store some materials on the media in which they are received and transfer some materials to another digital medium, most commonly magnetic tape or cassette (68%), a hard drive (64%), or CD-ROM (52%). One-quarter of these institutions transfer some files to open reel magnetic tape. The use of rewritable magneto-optical disk and WORM optical disks is uncommon. One institution reported using a robotic tape storage system,5 while another prints its digital information on paper for preservation. Four institutions contract with a third party for storage. While there are several different storage methods in use, most institutions are avoiding proprietary and highly vulnerable media, such as magneto-optical and WORM disks.

Most institutions do not have established methods for digital preservation beyond transferring some material to new storage media. Eighteen institutions "refresh" digital materials, which the survey defined as copying digital materials in their original digital format from old to new media. A wide variety of practices are used for refreshing digital information. Nine institutions have refreshing cycles that range from as often as daily or weekly as part of the routine operations of a hierarchical storage management system to as infrequently as once every 10 years. The most common refreshing cycle is in the range of once every three to six years. One institution cleans and rewinds magnetic media on a yearly rotation and copies those files that exhibit access problems or physical deterioration. Two institutions reported that they refreshed digital materials only as a by-product of a larger system upgrade, while two others reported that the problem of refreshing had not arisen yet because of the newness of digital activities. One institution reported that refreshing services were provided by centralized information technology services and that the details of their practices were not available.

Seventeen institutions also reported that they migrate digital materials. The survey defined migration as the periodic transfer of digital materials from one hardware/software configuration to another, or from one generation of computer technology to a subsequent generation. Migration practices also vary among institutions and they do not appear to be well integrated into regular digital preservation processes. Rather, migration has mostly occurred on an ad hoc or project basis.

Most institutions that described their migration methods indicated that they performed migration as necessary to ensure continuing access or as a by-product of a larger system upgrade. One institution reported that they had migrated digital images from a Xerox proprietary format (XDOD) to TIFF 5.0/6.0 and another institution was launching a similar project. When migration takes place, it appears to occur in response to impending technological obsolescence or in conjunction with larger system upgrades.

The policies and practices for digital preservation are underdeveloped in member institutions, especially given the increasing prevalence of digital materials in their holdings. Those institutions with the largest digital collections also appear to have the most developed policies and practices, and those without holdings have not yet experienced the need to address digital preservation issues.

Most institutions have not adopted policies that limit the variety of digital formats and storage media and few have adopted standards for the master files of materials that they generate through conversion. As a consequence, there are a significant number of institutions that maintain digital materials in many different formats. Many of these files are relatively new and the institutions have not yet confronted problems of technology obsolescence or systems upgrades. When migration is necessary or when the systems are upgraded, these institutions may face a complex and expensive task of converting files from many different formats, including proprietary formats. While more than half of the institutions with digital holdings refresh and/or migrate digital materials, these activities are not well integrated into digital preservation programs and tend to occur on an ad hoc basis or in conjunction with system upgrades.

Digital Preservation Staffing and Expertise

Lack of staff expertise is a common problem both in institutions with digital preservation responsibilities and in institutions that have not yet assumed responsibility for digital materials. Only eight institutions ranked the highest level of digital preservation knowledge on their staff as expert, while 21 ranked the highest level of in-house knowledge at the intermediate level. The largest group of institutions reported that the level of staff expertise was at the novice level, and two reported that they had no expertise available.

There is a relationship between having responsibility for preserving digital materials and levels of expertise. All institutions with experts available and 80% of the institutions with intermediate-level expertise have digital materials holdings in their holdings. This is true of only half of the institutions with novice-level expertise available and neither of those with no expertise. It is not clear from the data, however, whether taking responsibility for preservation encourages institutions to develop the requisite expertise, or whether institutions are reluctant to assume responsibility for digital preservation until at least a modicum of expertise is available in their institutions.

The telephone interviews gathered data about additional sources of support and about the experience of institutions that had used third-party services for some aspect of digital preservation. Some institutions get technical support from centralized institutional computing services such as the campuswide computing services in universities.

Interviewees were asked about the role of institutional computing services in meeting digital preservation needs. About two-thirds reported that they used institutional computing services, most often for backup, telecommunications, setting up systems, and as a source of expertise. Several of the interviewees mentioned that although they have access to centralized computing services, these services do not meet the needs of the repository. One interviewee pointed out that the computing services organization is responsible for meeting the institution's business needs and not the special requirements of digital preservation. Another mentioned the "intermediate view" of computing services, but a lack of awareness of long-term preservation.

Several respondents reported that, as organizations, the centralized computing services are also small or understaffed and lack technical expertise, while two people mentioned a "lack of imagination" and a conservative orientation among centralized computing staff. It appears that centralized computing services are potential sources of support for some digital preservation programs, and several people reported that they had initiated or established relationships with these organizations. Nevertheless, centralized computing organizations usually cannot meet all of the digital preservation needs of repositories.

Twenty institutions also use external sources such as consultants or contracts with third-party vendors to gain access to expertise in digital preservation or to outsource certain digital preservation functions. Interestingly, those institutions with the highest levels of staff expertise are most likely to acquire expertise from outside sources three-fourths of the institutions with in-house digital experts do so, as well as almost half of those with intermediate-level in-house expertise and one-fifth of those with novice-level in-house staff. Neither of the institutions with no in-house expertise available use outside sources for digital expertise.

Interviews also yielded some insights into the experiences of member institutions that had outsourced preservation activities or contracted with third parties. A few institutions had outsourced digital conversion and preservation microfilming, but no institutions have experience with outsourcing digital preservation activities. Several interviewees expressed an interest in outsourcing conversion and one mentioned services related to access.

The interview research suggests some of the concerns about outsourcing. A few interviewees mentioned the need for quality services and for agreements between the institution and the vendor about acceptable quality. Others mentioned that the third-party services have to be flexible, affordable, and beneficial to the institution. Several respondents also discussed the potential for a consortium of institutions to share leads and experiences with vendors and to develop quality services without redundancy.

The lack of expertise in digital preservation appears to be a significant obstacle to developing digital preservation programs. The programs with the highest levels of staff expertise also tend to have significant holdings of digital materials. Those institutions with expert staff also are more likely to take advantage of outside experts by hiring consultants with expertise to supplement that available on their staffs.

Although the research did not collect quantitative data specifically on the expertise available from centralized institutional computing services, the information gathered through interviews suggests that centralized computing services provide needed expertise and services only in exceptional cases. Some institutions have developed or are starting to form effective relationships with centralized computing services, but computing services often lack the staff, specific knowledge of digital preservation requirements, and vision to meet the digital preservation needs of many institutions. Finally, institutions have limited experience using third-party service providers for digital preservation. This may be due primarily to the lack of service providers in this area, but concerns over quality control and cost are also deterrents to outsourcing digital preservation services.

Needs and Requirements

The survey and interviews captured information about administrators' perceptions of digital preservation problems, their anticipated changes in digital preservation responsibilities in the next three years, and their sense of the most important issues facing their institutions. The research also gathered data on plans for increasing the institutions' capacity for digital preservation and respondents' perspectives on various types of services that consortia and/or third-party providers might develop to assist member institutions to implement sound digital preservation programs.

Problems and Threats to Digital Preservation

Respondents were asked to rank the significance of four issues as threats to digital preservation: technology obsolescence, insufficient resources, insufficient planning, and physical condition of materials. Member institutions ranked technological obsolescence as the greatest threat to loss of digital materials, followed closely by insufficient resources and an insufficient policy or plan for digital preservation. Only one institution ranked physical condition of the materials as the most serious threat. The lack of resources for digital preservation is ranked as the greatest threat by institutions that have policies in place for digital preservation and by the institutions that have digital materials in their holdings. Although the size of the sample is too small to reach statistically significant conclusions, this suggests that as institutions assume responsibility for preserving digital materials and as they develop policies, they then confront the resource requirements in concrete terms.

The interviews with managers of digital collections provide additional insights into how this problem is perceived and which strategies institutions are using to address it. When asked about the impact of digital preservation on their institutions, the interviewees mentioned changes in the way information management and preservation are organized and carried out, additional resource requirements, changing relationships with other professionals and specialists, and the need to hire new staff with digital preservation expertise.

Several digital collection managers mentioned the lack of standards, planning, infrastructure, and models for digital preservation as significant problems for their institutions. Several administrators in archival repositories expressed concern about the changing nature of institutional memory, where paper records are disappearing but the repositories are not prepared to handle electronic records.

Another common theme is the strain that digital preservation places on resources, including staff, equipment, and funds. Several administrators mentioned the need to hire staff with technical expertise and a few had plans in place to do so. Cooperative efforts with experts in technology or with other individuals responsible for digital preservation were also mentioned as strategies to share expertise and learn from others. Several administrators mentioned the increasingly complex relationships between libraries or archives and information technology and service providers.

As responsibility for digital preservation becomes spread across several different divisions there is a need for more coordination. Two interviewees also raised lack of awareness and support from top administrators as a problem for dealing with digital preservation in a concrete manner. Some interviewees felt that administrators paid lip service to digital preservation issues but were not willing to support serious institutional efforts to address the problem. Finally, a few interviewees mentioned the positive impact of digital initiatives on their institutions, especially in the way that conversion of materials to digital form offers new means to deliver information to users and to preserve the originals.

The respondents had mixed reactions about the impact of digital preservation on them personally and professionally. They were fairly evenly divided between those who found digital preservation interesting and stimulating and who had made large personal investments to keep up with the issues, and those who were concerned about the challenges, the absence of clear guidance, and the need for greater expertise. Many of the interviewees said that digital preservation was forcing them to re-examine traditional practices, change the way they administer their departments, develop more interdepartmental relationships, and learn new skills.

Anticipated Changes in Responsibility

Member institutions appear to take digital preservation seriously. Almost all of the institutions in the survey anticipate an increase during the next three years in the quantity of digital materials that they are responsible for preserving. Fifty-two institutions expect an increase in digital materials from conversion projects, while 47 institutions expect digital preservation responsibilities to grow as a result of new acquisitions or accessions of electronic records.

In the interviews with administrators, several mentioned new acquisitions or the increasing size of the collections as a major issue that they would have to confront in the next four years. An archivist in a state archives anticipates that with a change in administration, records in electronic form will begin to arrive in the archives for the first time. The institution needs to develop information systems immediately that can support cataloging, access, and preservation of this material. In a different state archives, the archivist considered the need for more staff and funding to deal with the growing number of digital records as a major issue facing the institution. In this case, developing a fairly technical system to describe, preserve, and provide access to digital materials is considered a priority so that it is possible to make access more self-service. The director of a university library that may be designated as a national repository for digital materials considers the problem very serious because the library will have to be able to take responsibility for digital preservation if required to do so through legislation.

When asked about the major digital preservation issues facing institutions in the next four years, the digital collection managers who were interviewed mentioned a wide variety of issues along several common themes. A few respondents stressed the importance of raising the level of awareness about digital preservation problems, especially among top administrators.

Some collection managers expressed concerns that institutions would sidestep the issue of long-term preservation by viewing digital technologies as a way to provide access to materials, but that at some point this approach would fail, leaving institutions with a preservation crisis. This presents a challenge of convincing administration to see digital preservation as a priority and to take some immediate steps to avoid even greater problems in a few years.

Several interviewees discussed human resource implications, including the need for more staff to carry out labor-intensive digital work, the demand for staff with new and different skills, the challenges of "upskilling" and retraining, and the need to redefine job descriptions and skill requirements.

A third theme relates to the absence of standards, clear models and best practices, especially in the areas of migration and frequent updating of hardware and software. Several digital collections managers stressed the importance of working together as a community to drive the development of needed products, services, and international standards so that vendors will begin to create products that meet digital preservation needs. The interviewees also mentioned the need to address preservation in the context of materials that institutions license, but do not own; better coordination among the various parties involved in digital preservation; and the development of tools for appraisal and risk assessment.

Proposed Actions

Most member institutions are planning to take concrete measures to build up their capacity for digital preservation. Almost all of the institutions (51 of 54) anticipate developing new policies for preserving digital materials in the next three years. This includes all of the institutions that currently have written policies as well as 33 of 36 that do not currently have a policy.

Institutions also anticipate using a variety of methods to increase the level of available staff expertise with digital preservation. Thirty-one institutions hope to hire people with digital preservation knowledge or expertise.Institutions plan to use multiple sources for training and staff development, ranging from training provided by professional organizations (42 institutions) to hiring consultants (20 institutions.)

Institutions also expressed an interest in using a variety of digital archiving services if they were made available at a reasonable cost. The broad interest in model policies, standards and best practices, training, and specific storage, maintenance and conversion services suggest useful roles for institutions, consortia such as RLG, and commercial service providers.

In the interviews the researchers also asked about attitudes toward the possibility of institutions pooling resources into a consortium or network for digital preservation, and how each interviewee would see his or her institution fitting into such a network. In general, the interviewees supported cooperative efforts, but they differed in their views of how such cooperative efforts should be organized and exactly which activities could be done best through a consortium. The strongest support was expressed for having a consortium that could provide leadership and coordination in best practices and standards, serve as a source of technical information and expertise, provide training, and bargain collectively with publishers and vendors for more affordable services. The response was mixed to the idea of having a consortium assume responsibility for storage, preservation, and access to digital materials. While a few interviewees said they would be relieved if a trusted organization were available for storage and management of digital materials, many interviewees expressed concerns about losing control over their material.

Interviewees favored the idea of pooling resources to eliminate redundant efforts and reduce preservation costs, but they expressed several concerns. One manager pointed out that outsourcing and pooling of resources is popular politically, but it is difficult to achieve. This represents a major change from the way institutions have worked traditionally. Some of the keys to developing successful cooperative efforts appear to be a clear definition of the role and responsibilities of any consortium-based service and a proven ability to provide a quality service at a lower cost than the institutions can achieve on their own.

The research also compiled a "wish list" of issues that digital collection managers would like to see solved. When asked to choose "one concern or problem to be immediately and magically solved," most interviewees had trouble limiting their response to a single issue. Interviewees provided a lengthy wish list of issues to solve, but some issues appear repeatedly among the top concerns. One request is for a clear, coherent set of guidelines and standards to follow.

Some respondents were frustrated by the multitude of competing strategies and the varied and confusing voices addressing digital preservation. Several respondents considered technology obsolescence the most important issue to resolve, but they proposed different priorities for resolving this problem. One interviewee wanted to avoid migration by using standards as a way to ensure continuing access to materials. Another stressed the need for cost models and process models to deal with migration and obsolescence issues. Two interviewees mentioned fast, reliable and stable storage media.

There was also considerable interest in dealing with the economics of and funding for digital preservation. First, there is an interest in better data on the costs of digital preservation and the need for cost and funding models which in turn might be used to increase institutional understanding and commitments to digital preservation. This is often coupled with a desire for more resources and for more reasonably priced services.

Finally, several respondents mentioned legal and organizational issues, including the changing nature of ownership of information, the role of publishers and their responsibility for preserving digital products, and the issues of access, licensing, and copyright. Several interviewees also stressed the need for a long-term vision oriented toward the future to avoid rapid obsolescence of guidelines, resources, and technology.

Member institutions expect their digital preservation responsibilities to increase during the next three to five years. During this time period, all but one institution in the survey anticipate some involvement with digital materials through acquisition, the creation of digital materials, or both. Institutions that already have responsibility for digital preservation expect that their digital holdings will grow during this time period. Many institutions that only recently started digital initiatives will confront the need to convert materials from older formats to current formats for the first time.

The institutions that responded to the survey are planning a number of actions to prepare for increased digital preservation responsibilities. Many institutions plan to hire additional staff with expertise in digital preservation, provide training to current staff, and hire consultants to help with the development of digital preservation programs.

Member institutions are seeking leadership in the development of standards and best practices, guidance on model policies and practices, and various types of training from consortia such as RLG. The respondents also expressed an interest in a variety of services from third-party vendors, especially conversion services, migration services, hardware and software to meet archival needs, and archiving or preservation storage services. Acceptance of third-party services is contingent on reliability and a reasonable cost.

High Performance Digital Library Classification System

In this era of the Internet and distributed, multimedia computing, new and emerging classes of information systems applications have swept into the lives of office workers and everyday people. New applications ranging from digital libraries, multimedia systems, geographic information systems, and collaborative computing to electronic commerce, virtual reality, and electronic video arts and games have created tremendous opportunities for information and computer science researchers and practitioners.

As applications become more overwhelming, pressing, and diverse, several well-known information retrieval (IR) problems have become even more urgent. Information overload resulting from easy creation and transmittal of information via Internet and WWW, has become prominent in people's lives (e.g., even stockbrokers and elementary school students, heavily exposed to various WWW search engines, are versed in such IR terminology as recall and precision).

Significant variations of database formats and structures, the richness of information media (text, audio, and video), and an abundance of multilingual information content also have created severe interoperability problems. The conventional approaches to addressing information overload and interoperability problems are manual in nature, requiring human experts as information intermediaries to create knowledge structures and/or classification systems.

Such manually-created classification systems, which represent subject vocabularies and their relationships, are often used to index and/or organize collections or to suggest search terms during retrieval processes. But as information content and collections become even larger and more dynamic, thus rendering manual knowledge creation to become more difficult, if not infeasible, we believe a complementary system-aided, algorithmic, bottom-up approach to creating large-scale digital library classification systems is needed.

Knowledge Networking

In US, the Information Infrastructure Technology and Applications (IITA) Working Group, the highest level of the country's National Information Infrastructure (NII) technical committee, held an invited workshop in May 1995 to define a research agenda for digital libraries. The shared vision that emerged is an entire Net of distributed repositories, where objects of any type can be searched within and across different indexed collections.

In the short term, technologies must be developed to search across these repositories transparently, handling any variations in protocols and formats (i.e., addressing structural interoperability). In the long term, technologies must be developed to handle the variations in content and meanings (knowledge) transparently as well.

In a new NSF Knowledge Networking (KN) initiative, a group of domain scientists and information systems researchers were invited to a Workshop on Distributed Heterogeneous Knowledge Networks at Boulder, Colorado, in May, 1997. They considered that scalable techniques to improve semantic bandwidth and knowledge bandwidth are among the priority research areas, as described in the KN report: The Knowledge Networking (KN) initiative focuses on the integration of knowledge from different sources and domains across space and time.

KN research aims to move beyond connectivity to achieve new levels of interactivity, increasing the semantic bandwidth, knowledge bandwidth, activity bandwidth, and cultural bandwidth among people, organizations, and communities. "Knowledge networking" or, using a more general term, "knowledge management" (KM), has attracted significant attention from academic researchers and even executives in Fortune 500 companies.

KM is formal in that knowledge is classified and categorized according to a pre-specified - but evolving - ontology into structured and semi-structured data and knowledge bases. Many commercial software systems are considered enabling technologies for KM, including Internet/Intranet search engines, groupware, electronic document management systems, full-text retrieval systems, database management systems, and electronic mail.

Major consulting firms, on the other hand, are promoting KM practices such as organizational development, strategic planning, performances metrics, and methodology. Despite of obvious differences in technologists and consultants views of what KM should be, their calls for advanced classification and categorization technologies to help analyze, organize, and present mission-critical information and knowledge are the same - turning information overload into knowledge assets.

In "Practical Digital Libraries", Lesk describes knowledge representation methods by which people have tried to organize and arrange knowledge, with the idea of making searching simple.

Library classification systems and thesauri often capture nouns or noun phrases and represent only limited relationships (e.g., broader terms, narrower term, etc.). The representations are often coarse, but precise, and they do support their practical goal of supporting indexing and searching, but significant human efforts are needed to create and maintain such large-scale classification systems.

Artificial intelligence representations such as semantic networks, expert systems, or ontologies represent another approach to capturing knowledge, e.g., Lenat's CYC common sense knowledge base. Their representations are often richer and more fine-grained and the goal of capturing human intelligence is ambitious and difficult. Due to the granularity required of such representations, knowledge creation is slow and painstaking. Only experimental prototypes in small, limited domains have been created. Their usefulness in large-scale digital library applications remains suspect.

The traditional approach to creating classification systems and knowledge sources in library science and classical AI is often considered top-down since knowledge representations and formats are pre-defined by human experts or trained librarians and the process of generating knowledge is structured and well-defined. A complementary bottom-up approach to knowledge creation has been suggested by researchers in machine learning, statistical analysis, and neural networks.

Based on actual databases or collections, researchers develop programs which systematically segment and index documents in various databases (text, image, and video) and identify patterns within such databases. Analyzing databases which contain structured and numeric data (e.g., credit card usage, a frequent flyer program) is often referred to as data mining or knowledge discovery.

Generating knowledge algorithmically from multimedia databases (especially text, e.g., customer complaint email, machinery repair reports, brainstorming outputs) is considered the core of knowledge management. Two stages of such a bottom-up knowledge management approach are often required:

— Object Recognition,

— Segmentation, and

— Indexing:

The most fundamental techniques in IR involve identifying key features in objects. For example, automatic indexing and natural language processing (e.g., noun phrase extraction or object type tagging) are frequently used to extract meaningful keywords or phrases from texts automatically. Texture, color, or shape-based indexing and segmentation techniques are often used to identify images.

For audio and video applications, voice recognition, speech recognition, and scene segmentation techniques can be used to identify meaningful descriptors in audio or video streams. Many of these techniques have been developed previously in the six large-scale DLI-1 projects. Several classes of techniques have been used for semantic analysis of texts or multimedia objects.

Symbolic machine learning, graph-based clustering and classification, statistics-based multivariate analyses (e.g., latent semantic indexing, multi-dimensional scaling, regressions), artificial neural network-based computing (e.g., backpropagation networks, Kohonen self-organizing maps), and evolution-based programming (e.g., genetic algorithms) are among the popular techniques.

Most of these are computationally intensive and are particularly suitable for creating classification systems or knowledge structures from unstructured textual collections. Large-scale image (and video) based knowledge extraction is still at an early stage of development due to the difficulty of designing image-invariant content-based segmentation and indexing algorithms.

Digital South Asia Library (DSAL)

The Center for Research Libraries (CRL) proposes a three-year collaborative project to improve electronic access to vital resources for understanding South Asia. Through this project scholars, public policy officials, business leaders, and other citizens will benefit from an improved electronic information infrastructure and expeditious delivery of digital research materials directly to them from the South Asian subcontinent and England.

The Digital South Asia Library (DSAL) project will produce:

1) On-line information about contemporary and historical South Asia - including full-text documents, statistical data, electronic images, cartographic representations, and pedagogical resources for language instruction;

2) Delivery on demand of page images from South Asia, scanned from both paper and microform sources;

3) Internet-based indexes to highly select journals in the regional languages of South Asia;

4) Use of Unicode electronic character encoding for non-roman language data disseminated under the project;

5) An international cooperative venture whose contributing members will include leading

universities in the U.S., Britain, and South Asia as well as libraries with a focus on South Asian studies; and

6) A detailed plan of operation for phase three of the Digital South Asia Library.

The Internet will be used to its full potential in facilitating full-text delivery of documents created under this project. A distinctive feature of the approach successfully tested under the current pilot phase of the Digital South Asia Library involves direct delivery from India of scanned page images to scholars in the U.S.

The wide-ranging collaborative base established for DSAL includes indexing for highly select periodicals, cataloging of vital official publications from South Asia, and access to electronic databases of bibliographic information via the Internet. The Digital South Asia Library program is committed to full implementation of the internationally recognized Unicode encoding standard as the means of displaying DSAL texts in the regional scripts of South Asia over the World Wide Web.

While this means of text encoding is beginning to be included in standard software packages, it is currently used only rarely for South Asian texts.

Collaboration in the use of technology is a hallmark of this proposed program. Evidence of this approach is presented throughout the proposal. The collaborative nature of the enterprise is reflected in the wide array of institutions joined together to enhance language instruction, expand resources for scholarship on South Asia, and improve the position of international studies.

Participants in the Digital South Asia Library include leading U.S. universities, the Center for Research

Libraries, the South Asia Microform Project, the Committee on South Asian Libraries and Documentation, the Association for Asian Studies, the Library of Congress, the Asia Society, the British Library, the University of Oxford, the University of Cambridge, MOZHI in India, the Sundarayya Vignana Kendram in India, Madan Puraskar Pustakalaya in Nepal, and other institutions in South Asia.

South Asian studies encompasses the subcontinent which lies south of the Himalayan range and comprises India, Pakistan, Bangladesh, Nepal, Sri Lanka, Bhutan, and the Maldive Islands. This area has been the site of major civilizations since at least 2,500 B.C. Both in geographical area and chronological expanse, the intellectual domain is enormous. The size of the subject is matched by the American contribution to the study of this region.

Since 1960 scholars from North America have done more to enhance knowledge of South Asia than their colleagues from any region, save the subcontinent itself. This assessment is based on the number and quality of books and articles written, Ph.D.s awarded, courses taught, and language instruction offered. The growth of knowledge about the region has been supported by forty-one years of funding from the U.S. Department of Education for foreign language and area training.

This sustained support has produced an intelligent and demanding body of scholars and policy makers with demonstrable capacity to use the languages of South Asia and comprehend the nuances of South Asian civilizations. They expect and deserve more extensive and flexible access to electronic resources in order to train succeeding generations of researchers and leaders as well as to further their own inquiries.4 This project will address that need.

South Asian studies in the United States has historical roots in nineteenth-century philological and religious studies, both focused on classical India. In the aftermath of World War II, however, there was a marked change. The war highlighted America's profound ignorance about the civilizations of South Asia and systematic efforts were made to develop programs of study, first at a few universities, but at many more by the 1960s.

These new South Asia programs had distinctive intellectual characteristics and disciplinary orientations that were shaped by founding faculty. Yet, in general, there was a strong emphasis on the social sciences and regional rather than the classical languages. The social sciences have remained vital and continue to attract the interest of new students and of scholars without backgrounds in South Asian studies.

Some researchers have been engaged by the writings of South Asian scholars addressing traditional issues such as colonialism from varied perspectives. Others have been interested in more novel approaches to knowledge such as those surrounding popular culture (or public culture), cinema, and gender studies. During this period of economic liberalization and increased foreign investment, economics and political science continue to attract the attention of many.

The humanities are also vital areas of research related to South Asia. As an example, scholars of regional literatures are writing new histories of the enormous and varied literary traditions in the subcontinent that challenge presuppositions of literary and language boundaries, chronological divisions, nationalism, and canon that undergirded earlier publications.

While most researchers come from a discipline - both as a departmental home and also as a methodological disposition - there is increasing interest in interdisciplinary studies and trans-regional research on South Asia. In addition to their wide geographical scope, these inquiries often have a global impact. The need for this project on South Asia is acutely felt in research libraries.

More specifically, books and periodicals in South Asia's regional languages are often targeted for sharp reductions. In response to decreased acquisition budgets, consortia of U.S. research libraries are beginning to share collecting responsibilities in order to ensure that the aggregate national collection remains strong. This cooperation entails a greater reliance on inter-library loan. For less commonly consulted publications inter-library loan remains an acceptable alternative to widespread duplication in acquisition.

However, for many core resources widespread demand requires alternative solutions that can provide a number of readers with important works in a timely fashion. The direct delivery of selected documents to readers via the Internet as proposed in this project is such an alternative. Beyond the primary audiences of scholars and policy makers, other important bodies of readers will be well served by the electronic resources prepared and disseminated under the Digital South Asia Library. These include:

— businesses;

— outreach coordinators at National Resource Centers, Centers for International Business Education, and

Undergraduate International Studies and Foreign Language programs;

— school teachers;

— governmental and non-governmental organizations (NGOs);

— cultural institutions, especially museums and libraries; and

— media.

Through this project, the needs of a wide array of U.S. citizens for ready access to new and unique resources will be met. They will be able to turn to the project's site on the World Wide Web for free and dependable access to information of the highest accuracy and integrity. This project achieves significance through effectively addressing needs registered by national foundations and associations of scholars and librarians.

Association for Research Libraries (ARL) and the Association of American Universities (AAU) inaugurated the Global Resources Program (GRP). Its principal goals are to improve access to international research resources and help libraries contain costs through the creation of cooperative structures, the use of new technologies, and the expansion of international document delivery. This approach ensures more focused collection development at individual institutions resulting in access to a broader array of these often difficult-to-acquire resources.

The GRP coordinates its efforts with those of other libraries and organizations that share common interests with AAU and ARL. Current GRP regional projects include: the Cooperative African Newspapers Project; the German Resources Project; the Japan Journal Access

Project; the Latin Americanist Research Resources Project; and the Digital South Asia Library.

The Digital South Asia Library pilot project is the only one funded by the Association of Research Libraries for South Asia. During the pilot project DSAL has developed an Internet-based infrastructure for intercontinental electronic document delivery to and from selected South Asian libraries. DSAL's large target audience will be well served by the digital resources provided. The Association for Asian Studies lists more than 760 of its members as having South Asian countries as a major focus of academic interest.

In addition, many members of other scholarly associations have a primary interest in South Asia-the American Academy of Religion, the American Political Science Association, the American Anthropological Association, and the American Oriental Society, to name a few. Looking to the larger body of citizens, the 1990 U.S. census shows that slightly more than one million Americans trace their heritage to the cultures of South Asia.

DSAL resources will serve "heritage learners" among this population. Finally, those outside the U.S. will be well served by the resources freely available over the Internet. It is important to recall that the South Asian subcontinent encompasses more than 22% of the world's population and that access to the Internet is expanding rapidly in that region.

Scholars in virtually all disciplines of the social sciences and humanities will be able to consult the DSAL Web site for an array of documents, statistics, images, and bibliographic data supporting their research, teaching, and planning efforts. Economists and political scientists will use the periodical indexes to locate current articles, both in English and in the regional languages, in the on-line Bibliography of Asian Studies (BAS).

Beyond the art historical and museological uses of photographs scanned from the British Library's collection, anthropologist and historians will consult the finding aids for photographs made accessible under this project to locate images from the Anthropological Survey of India or street scenes of urban India. Professors of art will be able to project pictures of South Asian buildings in class from the DSAL Web site when discussing the architectural heritage of the subcontinent.

Businesses and government policy makers will rely on current data from the statistical abstracts of South Asian countries presented with accompanying programs for statistical analysis of the data. Criminologists with interests in jail populations, rates of crime, and size of police forces will be able to query the same abstracts to derive data from as early as 1840.

Language teachers will be able to direct their students to the pedagogical resources for instruction in less commonly taught languages, knowing that the best available materials created under Department of Education grants will have been converted for easy access. The same teaching resources will enable distance language learning by students not able to meet face-to-face with one of the few U.S. instructors for certain least commonly taught languages.

Carefully selected on-line dictionaries will complement the grammars and readers if our complementary proposal to support their conversion is awarded. These language resources will be valued by "heritage learners" as well as others. News reporters and others in the media will find it easy to consult background articles from full-text documents such as the Economic and Political Weekly and India Briefing.

Systems staff of ARTFL will implement the project's computational and Web delivery components in the U.S. ARTFL, an acronym for American and French Research on the Treasury of the French Language, is a University of Chicago program for humanities computing and one of the first large-scale digital libraries developed on the Internet.

ARTFL's involvement will ensure high quality results. Further, it is highly significant that work done under this program will draw upon the body of software previously created by ARTFL thus reducing project expenses. At the same time project funds will support development of new computer algorithms and modes of dissemination over the World Wide Web that will further augment the software library ARTFL maintains.

The electronic resources created by ARTFL are shared widely throughout academic computing and will therefore serve the needs of a larger audience than this specific project. Overseas implementation of the project is significant for its method as well as its objectives. The DSAL project builds upon and expands existing cooperative relationships, particularly in the United Kingdom and South Asia.

More than a decade of close collaboration between the Center for Research Libraries' South Asia Microform Project, the University of Chicago, and the British Library's Oriental and India Office Collections have led to the preservation on microfilm of nearly 10,000 publications at the British Library. This project will extend that relationship into the realms of digitization and delivery of electronic files - files containing textual, pictorial, cartographic, and bibliographic data - to readers.

While much of this work will be undertaken overseas, multi-directional flow of information is central to the DSAL model. In other words, benefits accrue in South Asia, the U.S., and elsewhere in the world. In addition to the electronic resources on the Web, one is already beginning to see the results in India of DSAL workshops held to train librarians and archivists in preservation and bibliographic access, topics inadequately addressed in university training programs for professionals.

Another element in DSAL's overseas implementation is taking concrete form as this proposal is submitted. Effective dissemination of the resulting digital resources and information about the project will enhance the project's significance. The free DSAL Web site will allow readers around the world easy access to the texts, images, and bibliographic data created under this project.

The Co-Directors will notify scholarly organizations, libraries, and the general public of progress during the course of this project by means of news notes and articles in relevant scholarly publications, academic news publications such as the Chronicle of Higher Education, postings to the listservers for South Asian scholars, and press releases to national news media. We will send information about this project to the all members of the Association for Asian Studies' Committee on South Asian Libraries and Documentation, a group including representatives of all significant North American research libraries with collections on South Asia.

The two original sister institutions in India will continue to grow under this project, expanding to provide a larger array of digital resources while also helping to train those at new DSAL sites in the subcontinent. One of DSAL's fundamental objective is building a "new library movement" in South Asia, a new library movement more responsive to local needs and also more capable of joining in international collaborations.

A commitment to international standards is central to the project's design. For a more detailed statement of those standards, please see Appendix 5 with extracts from relevant Web sites. Where display of text in non-roman characters is required, DSAL will use Unicode. Further, DSAL staff will report to the Unicode Consortium on how the character sets for South Asian languages could be usefully expanded through the inclusion of conjunct characters for a more felicitous display of texts.

All electronic resources delivered over the Internet will contain Dublin Core metadata. Where bibliographic files are created the project will follow the USMARC standard for bibliographic records. The Encoded Archival Description (EAD) will be the standard where finding aids are created. The statutory standard for equitable access under Section 427 of the Department of Education's General Education Provisions Act is met through free dissemination of the project's resources via the Internet and through wide publicity of the availability of the project's Web site.

Further, the Center for Research Libraries is an equal opportunity employer and provides equitable access to, and participation in, its programs for students, teachers, and others with special needs. The constituent elements within this proposal include a wide variety of formats and types of documents. However, those elements can be classified into three broad categories. These categories are: full-text documents [a through d], graphics [e through f], and bibliographic information [g].

All of these categories grow out of the DSAL pilot project which was intended to develop an Internet-based infrastructure for intercontinental electronic document delivery to and from selected South Asia libraries. Collaboration with South Asia National Resource Centers in the United States will include:

1) conversion to Web resources of existing grammars and readers created under earlier Department of Education support;

2) creation of electronic paleographic guides for the scripts of South Asia; and

3) preparation of proposals to convert standard dictionaries of South Asia for the modern literary languages to files available via the Web and via file transfer protocol.

The University of Chicago and the British Library will provide other in-kind contributions for cataloging and integration of cataloging records into international bibliographic utilities. The South Asia Microform Project (SAMP), based at the Center for Research Libraries, will create preservation microfilm of at least 300 volumes, with the microfilming work done at the Roja Muthiah Research Library in Madras. This will build on an earlier and highly successful SAMP program to microfilm the Indian land settlement reports held by the British Library. SAMP will be engaged for preservation while DSAL is the vehicle for digital dissemination of selected titles.

Collaboration with governments in South Asian countries will include: 1) conversion of key historical data from the Statistical Abstract Relating to British India and its successor publications for presentation as a database available on the Internet along with software resources for interrogating the file; and 2) negotiations with South Asian governments for release of current statistical data in electronic form to be mounted in the countries and mirrored on the DSAL Web site.

The British Library's collection of maps on South Asia is one of the finest in the world. The British Library will create these digital images in London using equipment already owned. Additionally, project staff in India will experiment with conversion of selected maps to vector or GIS format. A joint initiative with the Association for Asian Studies, the producer of the Bibliography of Asian Studies (BAS), will result in incorporation of text in Asian languages into the BAS database. Further, DSAL staff will assist BAS staff in implementing Unicode for delivery of index information in the future and collaborate in developing statistical measures of Web usage. The BAS has received major support from the National Endowment for the Humanities for retrospective conversion of the early printed volumes to create the current on-line Bibliography. Its collaboration with DSAL will extend the temporal range and depth of indexing.

The support requested for this project is modest relative to its benefits. This is in large measure due to contributions by the Center for Research Libraries, University of Chicago, Columbia University, and other members of the Digital South Asia Library. There will be no charge for bibliographers' time or for material infrastructure. In the U.S., the project will use computer facilities and other resources already in place at CRL, Chicago, and Columbia. Conducting digitization work in collaboration with institutions in South Asia is prudent and productive.

6

Digital Library Collections and Access

Within this changing environment, research libraries understand more keenly than ever the new ways in which clients are seeking and using information. Libraries see an expanding base of users and, in many instances, changing service demands. There is ample evidence that when libraries make quality content available through the Web, its use increases and it reaches more people within the institution.

In addition, the user base for any individual library has expanded to include users beyond the institution. This has been achieved through more efficient resource-sharing arrangements (often statewide) as well as by targeting new user groups for digitized content and e-services.

In many cases, openly accessible digitized collections on the Web are also being used heavily by people from beyond the educational world. Despite press accounts to the contrary, research libraries report that use of the library's physical facility remains heavy, especially for collaborative learning and research activities and for access to computers and information technologies.

As a result, many libraries have moved to provide 24/5 access to the library buildings. At the same time, there is growing evidence in the data collected from ARL member libraries that the service demands of users may be changing. Many libraries see declining use of some traditional services, such as use of some print materials, circulation transactions, and reference transactions.

However, the data confirm that the demands for interlibrary borrowing and for user education are steadily increasing. These trends signal a shift in the behavior of information users that is being closely monitored. Research on the information-seeking behavior of people is growing almost as fast as the Web itself.

The Pew Internet & American Life Project5 creates and funds original, academic-quality research that explores the impact of the Internet on children, families, communities, the workplace, schools, health care, and civic/political life. The project aims to be an authoritative source for timely information on the Internet's growth and societal impact, through research that is scrupulously impartial.

An overwhelming number of college students reported that the Internet, rather than the library, is the primary site of their information searches. "Many students are likely to use information found on search engines and various Web sites as research materials....A great challenge for today's colleges is how to teach students search techniques that will get them to the information they want and how to evaluate it....While few universities require college students to take courses on information seeking, many include a session on it during freshman orientation meetings.

To better understand how usage patterns are changing, the Digital Library Federation (DLF) and Council on Library and Information Resources (CLIR) commissioned Outsell, Inc., to conduct a large-scale study of over 3,000 undergraduates, graduate students, and faculty members from a wide range of academic institutions.

The results revealed that the highest percentage of resources used were print materials, which students ranked higher than library and non-library electronic sources in four out of five factors. The Internet-based sources scored high only on the factor of convenience, while print materials scored high on the factors that make a difference in the quality of research and learning: generating the information for which the student is looking, the usefulness of the material, its reliability, and the availability of assistance.

There are differences across disciplines in terms of how information is used and to what extent new technologies are being embraced; libraries are recognizing these differences as they offer new services. There are also differences in the pace of change in different institutions; institutional cultures that allow, for example, some flexibility in personnel policies and practices as well as in budgetary reallocations, are more accommodating of experimentation and change.

In this rapidly changing environment, libraries must continue monitoring trends, assessing their performance by seeking feedback from current users, and anticipating the needs of future users. To meet and anticipate these needs of the academic and research communities, libraries are collaborating as never before, forming partnerships both within and outside their own institutions, often sharing control in order to effect critical change.

While circumstances will vary from library to library, the results of the task force survey demonstrate many ways that libraries are responding to user expectations. Libraries are expanding the amount and variety of high-quality information resources that are directly available to academic and research users via the Web. They are also expanding the definition of collections to include "born-digital" content that is neither owned nor licensed by the library.

The varied efforts toward this goal may be characterized as · follows: changing collection development policies to emphasize the acquisition of electronic resources, engaging in digitizing and electronic publishing projects, and assuming responsibility for managing and servicing born-digital content that resides outside the domain of the library.

Even in the electronic and networked environment, the economic model continues to feature the library as the central agency on campus that buys and/or manages information resources on behalf of the institution. Libraries have shifted the focus of their collection development policies to the acquisition of more electronic content, much of it via consortia.

While aggregate data documenting the quantity of e-resources currently being made available by libraries has proven elusive, there is data on the spending trends. Over the last decade the average percentage of a research library's materials budget that is spent on electronic resources has grown from 4% to 16%. One hundred six ARL university libraries report spending more than $132 million on electronic resources in 2000-01.

The vast majority of that was spent on electronic serials and subscription services, expenditures which have increased sharply, from just $11 million in 1994-95 to more than $117 million today. To support this increased spending on electronic content, libraries have reallocated resources from the purchase of print. The extent of such reallocations will vary depending on institutional user expectations and financial circumstances.

Many libraries have adopted a policy of adding the e-version of journals when available and are showcasing titles of e-journals available to users via the Web by making this a staff priority and by applying software management tools for titles included in aggregated electronic databases. The processes for selecting, budgeting, and acquiring electronic materials are continually changing and greatly differ from those for the selection and management of print.

The print process is orderly: discrete amounts of money are allocated by discipline, the marketplace is fairly predictable, and materials are selected and ordered using established procedures. By contrast, the processes for selection and management of electronic resources are chaotic. The migration from print to electronic varies in speed and extent by discipline; electronic products are interdisciplinary and expensive, giving rise to selection by committee; projections for future funding are guesswork; and archiving and content control are problematic.

Legal and negotiation skills are now mandatory. To complicate matters, decisions are often made through a consortium. The process for acquiring electronic resources turns the traditional acquisitions and user service model topsy-turvy. In building electronic collections, libraries must also constantly respond to changing publisher behavior.

The most profound influence on a library's collection management and access strategies has been the extraordinary price increases for scholarly journals, combined with publishers' use of licensing to define the terms under which a library may make the content available and to whom. It is reasonable to speculate that these phenomena, driven by some of the larger publishers but now employed widely, make up one of the forces that prompted libraries to blend the previously distinct operations of collection management and access.

Some libraries have fully embraced initiatives stimulated or endorsed by SPARC (the Scholarly Publishing and Academic Resources Coalition) and other affordable publishing venues and are using acquisitions funds as investments in the future of scholarly communication. These libraries focus acquisitions on publications from scholarly societies and less expensive publishers, nonprofit and for-profit, that provide high-quality titles at affordable prices.

These less expensive titles tend to be the most highly ranked by faculty but labor intensive to obtain, since each publisher has only a few titles and often lacks sales and technical staff. These libraries try to consistently view collection expenditures as investments, and to seek out publishers likely to contribute to a sustainable future for scholarly information. Libraries are also supporting open access projects that experiment with alternatives to the current subscription-based funding model or the current journals-based publishing model for scholarly communication.

These approaches are seen as those of a good citizen, especially in an institution whose needs for funding include many urgent priorities in addition to library needs. These libraries are investing in initiatives that may help solve the long-term problem of high prices for journals.

Electronic Publishing

Most libraries are also pursuing a proactive strategy to increase user access to quality information resources on the Web by digitizing materials and collaborating with others to publish digital collections on the Web. For example, libraries are:

— Creating new electronic collections by digitally reformatting existing collections in the library and institution, including the collections of senior faculty and retired faculty

— Collaborating with other libraries, academic departments, scholarly and historical societies, museums, and others to build virtual collections from originals that are geographically dispersed

— Giving greater emphasis to developing and showcasing special collections of manuscripts and rare books, foreign-language resources, images, music, maps and geospatial data, numeric data sets, and making them accessible to discovery via the Web and in other learning environments

— Supporting faculty's e-publishing efforts by consulting and by offering technological infrastructure to develop the next generation "journal" and to create Web-based research tools and resources for teaching

— Partnering with university presses and other publishers to develop new publishing models

— Partnering with faculty departments and/or societies to mount discipline-based and/or institutional e-print servers

Libraries have expanded the traditional view and definition of collections so that the concept no longer equates with those materials that the library "owns". The boundaries have expanded far beyond the print collections on site or the electronic files mounted locally to include electronic materials licensed or managed by the library and materials available through consortia.

Increasingly libraries are taking responsibility for born-digital collections (such as geospatial or numeric data sets, faculty or class Web sites) and developing tools for their management and use. In a growing number of cases, a library's collection also includes resources that reside outside the domain of the library but for which the library takes some responsibility for managing and servicing.

An example of the latter is the movement by libraries to support the development of institution-wide knowledge management systems, where an institution's intellectual capital is centralized, preserved, and made accessible. In a university, this might include collections of digital material created by faculty, research staff, and students, e.g., research collaboratives, graduate student theses, electronic records of the university's administrative offices, courseware content, and streaming audio and video resources generated from courses, conferences, and other campus activities.

The content of print collections continues to play a critical role in libraries but that role is changing, as is the way that libraries are managing print collections. Less frequently used print resources are being relocated to storage with paging/retrieval services; more convenient resource sharing makes book collections accessible to wider audiences. Instead of describing collections as "those things owned", a better definition may be "information resources for which the library invests financial resources—directly or indirectly—to manage, service, or preserve on behalf of library users, regardless of the location of content."

"Collections" now include resources owned by the library and those accessed in remote locations; the norm is now an interdependent mix of ownership and access, with the location of the material increasingly irrelevant to users. Libraries are increasingly providing users with services and tools that enhance access to electronic resources and support an integrated approach to discovering and receiving this content--along with library services--in classrooms, on the "desktop", and on PDAs.

In many cases, libraries deliver unrestricted content and services to users far beyond those affiliated with the institution. Libraries are pursuing this in many ways, including offering new services, adapting the role of the online catalog, experimenting with the Open Archives Initiative (OAI) metadata harvesting protocol, and writing or adapting software tools.

Role of Online Catalogs

It is clear that the role of the online catalog has changed. That catalog has become one of many databases available to users; libraries are linking to and from the catalog to integrate all of these resources. In recognition of this broader role for the library catalog, some libraries are considering modifying cataloging to favor timely access to a wider variety of formats.

One proposal called for reallocating funds that are devoted to describing books and journals to materials that are proportionately underrepresented in today's catalogs, such as films, music, photographs, and digital objects. Libraries are also reconsidering their current efforts to collect and catalog free Web resources, concluding that these labor-intensive activities can be avoided by perfecting nascent machine harvesting and cataloging techniques.

A small number of libraries and library organizations are participating in experiments funded by The Mellon Foundation to test the application of harvesting and search engine technologies. Using the recently developed OAI metadata harvesting protocol, these libraries are delivering information from the "hidden Web" not normally found by Internet search engines and from databases with retrieval formats that present special processing or presentation problems.

For example, several libraries are working with vendors to adapt existing portal software into multifunctional products with features and services desired by users in research communities. Other examples of library involvement in development of software applications are ILL management systems, instructional tutorials, management of content and services for digital libraries, and institutional repositories.

Although where information resides matters less to the user, the library as place—the physical entity—

remains more important than ever and performs a host of functions vital to learning and research. Much research library space is busier than ever before. Library facilities are being reconfigured to provide space for collaborative learning and research. There are classrooms and media labs where faculty and librarians may interact in providing student learning experiences, group study spaces, and community spaces where students can meet to discuss ideas.

The transformation of library space has also become an opportunity to attract new academic collaborations such as writing studios and academic skills tutoring. Library space is now seen as learning space on an equal footing with classrooms and laboratories. Libraries are being renovated to expand e-access and foster community by providing electronic classrooms, wireless data networks, offering laptops, and expanding library hours.

Libraries are establishing spaces called "information commons" where library reference services are offered jointly with information technology support. At the same time, libraries are responding to decreasing use of in-person reference service by combining service points and shifting resources to online reference service and online tutorials. To make the best use of prime real estate, libraries are adopting new approaches to managing large print collections by using storage centers with delivery services for less frequently used materials and engaging in cooperative approaches to long-term preservation copy retention.

The branch or departmental library remains valuable but its role too is changing. While access to information and library services is far less geographically based, branch and departmental libraries still play a role in development of community and serve as sites for collaboration. Yet, in the Internet world there are opportunities to rethink the role of multiple libraries and their configuration within an institution.

One library reported establishing a program to replicate the opportunities for personalized services and contacts that characterize branch library service without the cost of creating additional branches. Some of the same opportunities for reorganization may present themselves when libraries work in collaboration with other libraries outside their institutional boundaries.

Libraries are active participants in building awareness among researchers, faculty, and students of uses of high-quality content and information technology in teaching and research. Curriculum review and changing expectations for teaching faculty present opportunities for libraries to contribute expertise and resources.

Libraries provide classrooms; training and consulting in finding and evaluating information; and assistance with creating electronic theses and dissertations, displaying and visualizing data, publishing journals on the Web, and using geographic information systems (GIS) and remote sensing. Recognizing that disciplines are adopting new technology at different rates, librarians are:

— Working with faculty to integrate information literacy skills and digital content into the course curricula

— Expanding the number of people reached by offering basic information literacy and fluency training through online tutorials

— Assisting researchers in acquiring, accessing, displaying, and visualizing spatial and numeric data by providing training in use of software and partnering with faculty to provide classroom instruction in its use

— Developing systems and instructional tools for pedagogical use of digital resources, including images

— Managing campus instructional technology initiatives

— Making Organizational Changes within the Library to Innovate and Improve Services

Libraries are embracing change—being willing to change what libraries do and how it is done—and, as a result, are reorganizing their operations and re-deploying staff to respond to the new environment. Examples of recent organizational change in ARL libraries include:

— Many libraries report having instituted an integrated approach to collection management, bringing together the activities of building, maintaining, and providing access to library resources in all formats, both in-house and remote, both acquired and locally created.

— Many libraries also report taking interdisciplinary approaches, training library staff to perform across traditional roles and to build bridges between the culture of the library and that of the faculty and information technology. An example is the creation of information commons jointly staffed by the library and information technology, often developing services in collaboration with faculty.

— Others report organizational redesigns to achieve a system-wide view of services to coordinate communications with all library users and to deploy staff more flexibly.

— Libraries are experimenting rigorously with organizational transformation reflecting strategies for team-based decision making, learning organizations, and quality management.

Scholarly Communication Issues

Libraries are assuming leadership within their institutions to advocate for enduring institution-wide knowledge management policies and programs that contribute to a robust system of scholarly communication. Some libraries are accomplishing this goal by:

— Sponsoring scholarly communication seminars to broaden faculty and graduate student awareness of trends that threaten the long-term sustainability of the current system of scholarly communication

— Advocating for institution-wide intellectual property policies that balance the rights of copyright owners and those of users and libraries in educational settings, including the development of principles that guide the licensing of electronic resources for the institution

— Promoting individual behavior and building institutional support that contributes to the long-term health and viability of scholarly communication channels, including developing infrastructure for such alternative publishing practices as publishing open access journals or creating institutional repositories

All research libraries are innovating and adapting to the changing needs of their patrons, as well as to the changing requirements of their institutions. There is no clear evidence to suggest definitive trends in change based on the size of the library collection.

There are specific types of innovation, however, that seem to be related to library or institution size. There is anecdotal evidence that library size has been influential in the development of digital library programs; libraries with more mature digital library programs tend to be libraries with larger collections and more staff members. On the other hand, smaller institutional settings may encourage innovative collaborative activities, either because of the financial necessity to join forces to make something happen or because of the potential in smaller communities for more interaction across campus units.

There is also anecdotal evidence that the institutional climate for change and the active support of groups and key individuals within the institution play a central role in the library's orientation and opportunities to innovate; to the extent that the size of the institution impacts this climate, size may be a contributing—if not driving—factor. Research libraries' ability and desire to collaborate with other research libraries, with non-university libraries, or with other organizations and industries will determine the success of many library programs.

Motivations for collaborations vary greatly and include leadership, political support, the lure of available funding, and the desire to transform the library, to move it into the digital age. An increasingly important collaboration is consortial buying of print and electronic content and services. Consortial buying and licensing for access to electronic resources have become central in every research library's arsenal of strategies for acquiring information more economically than could be accomplished by acting alone.

Many libraries find user-initiated consortial borrowing combined with rapid delivery a successful avenue for making their users' access to books as easy as access to electronic resources. There is evidence that fast delivery of books within a consortium has increased book use, especially by undergraduates. Consortia also offer accompanying services that greatly expedite the discovery and delivery of non-book content for users affiliated with libraries participating in the consortium; some consortia are centrally managing image data banks, electronic theses and dissertations, and other digital materials.

Consortial structures vary and reflect the political framework of the state or region in which they operate and the institutions they represent. In some cases, a state legislature appropriates funds centrally to support consortial activities on behalf of libraries; in others, individual libraries pay to a common fund. External funding facilitates the process of individual institutions' making the adjustments and compromises that consortia require and tends to support consortial relationships among libraries of varying sizes and characteristics.

Consortia funded solely by the participating libraries tend to be formed of libraries of similar size and characteristics. Consortia are on the front line of controversies between libraries and publishers about pricing, the terms of use defined by licenses, and publisher practices that make it difficult for a library to cost-effectively tailor its purchases from the publishers' lists or to reduce the total amount of money spent with that publisher.

The tendency of consortia to acquire or license electronic resources from the larger, commercial publishers raises concerns that content from scholarly societies or other smaller publishers will be overlooked. Research library staff are actively working with their partners in consortia to assess the benefits and challenges of consortial licensing and to influence publisher behavior in favor of scholarly communication needs.

A closely related factor to collaboration is the degree to which the organizations involved in a joint effort are willing to share control, at both the intra- and the inter-institutional levels. This sharing of control has implications for many activities such as archiving; consortial buying; expanding online resources; collaborative efforts with faculty, information technology groups, instructional technology centers; and cooperative publishing projects.

Libraries are promoting team operations to advance collaborative projects and to encourage a convergence of different organizational cultures where control is truly shared (for example, between the library culture and faculty culture and computing center culture). Many research libraries are willing to establish new partnerships and share control in order to innovate.

Research libraries' ability to recognize their strengths and their willingness to leverage those strengths influences the success of library integration into the research institution. Libraries have a special kind of space on campus, space that is seen as politically neutral and representative of the intellectual commons--public-good space. This nature of space gives libraries leverage to attract and nurture collaboration with other parts of the institution.

Libraries also have human talent they may deploy for the institution. Research library staffs have a wide range of expertise that can support new approaches to meeting user and institutional needs. Many libraries are leveraging their space and human resources to the advantage of the institution, for example, in creating an information commons, establishing an institutional repository, or providing campus management of copyright clearances.

A major factor in innovation is the degree to which research libraries and their institutions are willing and able to embrace change. The willingness of the library leadership (at all levels) to change its vision of what a library is and does, and to transform library operations to reflect that vision, obviously influences innovation. However, the culture of the institution itself also influences how the library engages and supports change.

Many research libraries find themselves in the impossible position of being expected by some disciplines to implement systemic change while continuing to be responsive to the needs of other disciplines that have slower rates of adoption of new technology.19 During this period of transition, this is a major factor influencing how libraries implement change and how that change is received within the institution.

The degree to which people in the institution exhibit "interdisciplinarity" or demonstrate effectiveness in working with the various cultures of the institution—library, faculty, and information technology cultures—is another important factor in innovation. Success in collaboration depends on some degree of convergence of these cultures.

Convergence or integration of cultures is being approached in several different ways. Examples include convergence of cultures in shared space; convergence of technical and bibliographic expertise; and convergence of human capital to consolidate efforts, encourage cooperation, and provide institution-wide access to the latest equipment, software, and support as well as a wide and deep collection of high-quality content.

Experience reported in the task force survey suggests there is a need to support greater cultural integration. Some libraries pursue this goal by establishing cross-cultural task forces, developing cross-training and mentoring programs for effective performance across and outside traditional roles, adopting position classification schemes that reflect the changes required of staff, providing opportunities for staff to cross boundaries, and by giving people time to work through the process of cultural convergence.

Preserving Digital Content

Converting existing collections and new acquisitions from paper to electronic-only is currently inhibited by the nascent state of strategies for preserving digital content. Internationally, publishers are working with national libraries (or their proxies) for them to assume the role of the publishers' archives for digitized texts; the reliability and terms of use of these archives are still being determined.

When library, publisher, and technology communities reach consensus on how best to manage the preservation of digital resources, the transformation of library collections to largely electronic will accelerate. In this rapidly changing environment, there are many opportunities for entrepreneurial activities, which often require the financial risk of investing resources in new activities even as budget pressures tighten.

Entrepreneurship may also create new activities that bypass or challenge the standards, rules, and policies that are part of library operations. Success depends on the library's ability to reach informed judgments, usually with less than complete information, on the strategic importance of an opportunity and whether it warrants the financial and other risks that accompany change.

Research Library Collections

Responding to user expectations for easy searching and convenient access to an expanding array of information sources, libraries are spending increasing amounts of their materials budgets on electronic resources. While up to now many libraries have actually also maintained the print, where dual versions exist, recent budget and space constraints have led many to make a choice of the format they collect.

The nascent state of strategies for preserving digital content makes some libraries reluctant to relinquish print editions. However, seeing that these preservation issues are now being addressed, and given the significant advantages of the electronic editions, many libraries have decided to collect electronic-only. Libraries are also offering printing services to meet users' expressed need for print.

As professional print-on-demand technologies become more cost effective, this option may offer, for users who require it, a way to generate high-quality bound printed editions from electronic information resources. At the same time, libraries have not abandoned print. They continue to acquire print in disciplines that are not moving as quickly into the digital world as others and in formats, such as monographs, that are still published primarily in printed form.

Thus, integrating print and electronic resources and making print resources almost as easy to access as electronic content are challenges facing libraries in this hybrid environment. Portal software is being designed to enable users to search library catalogs simultaneously with both open and licensed databases to find content regardless of format, thereby building a bridge between the library's print and digital collections.

Timely, self-service resource sharing and other user-initiated services such as book renewals and book- and article-delivery are also making access to print resources much easier. In the future more information will be created, stored, delivered, and preserved digitally, but print—because of its physicality, flexibility, perceived reliability, ease of reading and sharing—will be used for reading and editing for some time to come. Even as print retains importance, the library's physical space has increasing value for other activities, especially collaborative learning and research.

Thus, to free up prime real estate, libraries are moving lesser-used print collections to storage centers (with rapid delivery service) and are exploring cooperative approaches to long-term preservation copy retention. For now, research libraries' print collections continue to play a critical role for users even as that role and how users gain access to the material are changing.

Given the rapidly changing environment, however, libraries are carefully monitoring the information-seeking and reading habits of their users to see how their use of print and digital resources changes or does not change over time. Institutional repositories—digital collections capturing and preserving the intellectual output of a single or multi-university community—provide a compelling response to two strategic issues facing academic institutions. Such repositories:

— Provide a critical component in reforming the system of scholarly communication--a component that expands access to research, reasserts control over scholarship by the academy, increases competition and reduces the monopoly power of journals, and brings economic relief and heightened relevance to the institutions and libraries that support them; and

— Have the potential to serve as tangible indicators of a university's quality and to demonstrate the scientific, societal, and economic relevance of its research activities, thus increasing the institution's visibility, status, and public value.

Institutional repositories represent the logical convergence of faculty-driven self-archiving initiatives, library dissatisfaction with the monopolistic effects of the traditional and still-pervasive journal publishing system, and the availability of digital networks and publishing technologies. This convergence manifests itself in several ways:

— *Attitudinally*: Institutional repositories build on a growing grassroots faculty practice of posting research online, most often on personal web sites, but also on departmental sites or in disciplinary repositories.

— *Economically*: While the variety of institutional contexts and potential implementations make it difficult to project institutional repository development and operational costs with any precision, the evidence so far suggests that the resources required would represent but a fraction of the journal costs that libraries now incur and over which they have little control.

— *Technically*: Digital publishing technologies, ever-expanding global networking, and enabling interoperability protocols and metadata standards are coalescing to provide practical technical solutions that can be implemented now.

The rationale for universities and colleges implementing institutional repositories rests on two interrelated propositions: one that supports a broad, pan-institutional effort and another that offers direct and immediate benefits to each institution that implements a repository.

While institutional repositories centralize, preserve, and make accessible an institution's intellectual capital, at the same time they will form part of a global system of distributed, interoperable repositories that provides the foundation for a new disaggregated model of scholarly publishing. This model unbundles the principal functions of scholarly communication, thus presenting the potential to realize market efficiencies previously hidden by the vertically integrated publishing model that now characterizes academic journal publishing.

Altering the structure of the scholarly publishing model will be neither simple nor immediate. The stakes are high for all the well-entrenched participants in the system--faculty, librarians, and publishers--and the inertia of the traditional publishing paradigm is immense. In the near-term, large journal publishers have both the power and the incentive to maintain the status quo: the prestigious journals they control appear integral to the very structure of academic professional advancement.

However, digital publishing and networking technologies, harnessed by an increasingly dissatisfied library market—as well as by authors themselves--are now driving fundamental changes to this publishing model at an accelerating pace. And new communications paradigms, especially when constructed by the scholars themselves, can eliminate seemingly insurmountable publisher advantages in relatively short order. Institutional repositories, by capturing, preserving, and disseminating a university's collective intellectual capital, serve as meaningful indicators of an institution's academic quality.

Under the current system of scholarly communication, much of the intellectual output and value of an institution's intellectual property is diffused through thousands of scholarly journals. While faculty publication in these journals reflects positively on the host university, an institutional repository concentrates the intellectual product created by a university's researchers, making it easier to demonstrate its scientific, social and financial value. Thus, institutional repositories complement existing metrics for gauging institutional productivity and prestige.

The current system of scholarly communication limits, rather than expands, the readership and availability of most scholarly research (while also obscuring its institutional origins). Rounds of journal price increases and subsequent subscription cancellations act to reduce the audience further. The role of alternative scholarly publishing models, such as institutional repositories, in breaking the monopolies of publishers and increasing the awareness of university intellectual output grows increasingly clear. Further, institutional repositories can serve this function whether they are implemented on individual campuses or in collaborative consortial projects.

Elements of Institutional Repository

Stated broadly, a digital institutional repository can be any collection of digital material hosted, owned or controlled, or disseminated by a college or university irrespective of purpose or provenance. A particular type of institutional repository—a digital archive of the intellectual product created by the faculty, research staff, and students of an institution and accessible to end users both within and outside of the institution, with few if any barriers to access.

In other words, the content of an institutional repository is:

— Institutionally defined;

— Scholarly;

— Cumulative and perpetual; and

— Open and interoperable.

Institutional repositories can assume many forms and serve a variety of purposes. Indeed, the technical and administrative infrastructures developed by academic institutions for existing digital library initiatives might often be modified or repurposed to serve the requirements of an institutional repository. The institutional repository might form a component of a more comprehensive institutional initiative, one encompassing virtually all of an institution's digital assets.

In contrast to discipline-specific repositories and subject-oriented or thematic digital libraries, institutional repositories capture the original research and other intellectual property generated by an institution's constituent population active in many fields. Defined in this way, institutional repositories represent an historical and tangible embodiment of the intellectual life and output of an institution. And, to the extent that institutional affiliation itself serves as the primary qualitative filter, this repository becomes a significant indicator of the institution's academic quality.

Depending on the university, an institutional repository may complement or compete with the role served by the university archives. University archives often serve two purposes: 1) to manage administrative records to satisfy legally mandated retention requirements, and 2) to preserve materials pertaining to the institution's history and to the activities and achievements of its officers, faculty, staff, students, and alumni. Compared to institutional repositories, which aim to preserve the entire intellectual output of the institution, university archivists exercise broad discretion in determining which papers and other digital objects to collect and store.

Developing institutional repositories does not require that each institution act entirely on its own. For many colleges and universities, existing state or regional institutional or library consortia will provide a logical infrastructure for implementing institutional repositories via collective development. Such cooperation could deliver economies of scale and help institutions avoid the needless replication of technical systems. Indeed, consortia might well prove the fastest path to proliferating institutional repositories and attaining a critical mass of open access content.

Depending on the goals established by each institution, an institutional repository could contain any work product generated by the institution's students, faculty, non-faculty researchers, and staff. This material might include student electronic portfolios, classroom teaching materials, the institution's annual reports, video recordings, computer programs, data sets, photographs, and art works—virtually any digital material that the institution wishes to preserve.

This content may include pre-prints and other works-in-progress, peer-reviewed articles, monographs, enduring teaching materials, data sets and other ancillary research material, conference papers, electronic theses and dissertations, and gray literature. To control and manage the accession of this content requires appropriate policies and mechanisms, including content management and document version control systems. The repository policy framework and technical infrastructure must provide institutional managers the flexibility to control who can contribute, approve, access, and update the digital content coming from a variety of institutional communities and interest groups (including academic departments, libraries, research centers and labs, and individual authors).

Several of the institutional repository infrastructure systems currently being developed have the technical capacity to embargo or sequester access to submissions until the content has been approved by a designated reviewer. The nature and extent of this review will reflect the policies and needs of each individual institution, possibly of each participating institutional community.

Essential to the institutional repository's role both within the university and within the larger structure of scholarly communication is that the content collected is both cumulative and maintained in perpetuity. This has two implications. First, whatever the content submission criteria for a repository, items once submitted cannot be withdrawn--except in presumably rare cases involving allegations of libel, plagiarism, copyright infringement, or "bad science." This removal would be the functional equivalent of revoking the registration initially granted to the contribution on accession into the repository. This does not necessarily mean that all content will be universally accessible in perpetuity.

Institutions must develop criteria and policies--and implement rights management systems--for allowing access to a repository's content, both inside the institution and from outside, that balance the goal of the broadest available access with the reality of encouraging faculty participation. The cumulative nature of institutional repositories also implies that the repository's infrastructure is scaleable. While initial processing and storage requirements might prove modest, institutional repository systems must be able to accommodate thousands of submissions per year, and eventually must be able to preserve millions of digital objects and many terabytes of data.

Second, institutional repositories aim to preserve and make accessible digital content on a long-term basis. Digital preservation and long-term access are inextricably linked: each being largely meaningless without the other. Providing long-term access to digital objects in the repository requires considerable planning and resource commitments. The institution needs to balance the desire to accept the farrago of file formats popular with various disciplines, in order to simplify content submission and encourage faculty participation, with the complications that migrating some of those formats or media might present as new standards evolve.

While it is possible for an institution to dictate digital formatting standards for students—in the submission of electronic theses and dissertations, for example—prescribing such formats for faculty, for both attitudinal and practical reasons, proves far more problematic. The goals motivating an institution to create and maintain a digital repository—whether pan-institutional, as a component in the changing structure of scholarly communication, or institution-centric--require that users beyond the institution's community gain access to the content.

For the repository to provide access to the broader research community, users outside the university must be able to find and retrieve information from the repository. Therefore, institutional repository systems must be able to support interoperability in order to provide access via multiple search engines and other discovery tools. An institution does not necessarily need to implement searching and indexing functionality to satisfy this demand: it could simply maintain and expose metadata, allowing other services to harvest and search the content.

This simplicity lowers the barrier to repository operation for many institutions, as it only requires a file system to hold the content and the ability to create and share metadata with external systems. Given the disparate publishing practices amongst academic disciplines, an institution's content accession and access policies need to accommodate legitimate researcher concerns about access to pre-publication material deposited in the repository.

Institutional repositories typically do not permit content to be removed once submitted. However, a variety of legitimate circumstances might require an institution to limit access to particular content to a specific set of users. These circumstances might include copyright restrictions, policies established by a particular research community, embargoes that an institution's Sponsored Programs Office might require to keep the institution in compliance with the terms of sponsor contracts, and even monetary access fees for certain data.

Promoting Open Access

The advent of the Internet, the World Wide Web, and digital technologies has revolutionized scholarly communication. Creative applications of these technologies are leading to innovations in the conduct of research as well as in the conveyance of ideas to readers. And the growing availability and application of these technologies has dramatically altered how readers may discover, gain access to, and use information.

As positive and liberating as these developments are for many researchers, authors, and readers, they have also accelerated the commodification of information and drives by some content industries to make their channels of information distribution more secure. As a result, changes are taking place in copyright, license/contract, and related laws that govern the management and use of intellectual property.

For the most part, the changes result in more limited access and more restrictive uses for copyrighted material.

It is no surprise then that, as the laws change to secure content for publishers, there is a negative impact on those in the educational and research communities where the creation, dissemination, and use of intellectual property is expected and, in fact, forms the very core of learning and research.

Historically, the library and academic communities looked to copyright law as the policy framework for balancing competing interests of creators, publishers, and users of copyrighted works. To achieve its constitutional purpose to promote the progress of science and the useful arts, copyright law provides a copyright owner with a private monopoly to reproduce, distribute, perform, display, and revise a work, while simultaneously providing exceptions for the special circumstances of education and libraries.

This balance has been significantly eroded as copyright and other laws have been revised to apply in the digital and networked environment. Changes in the laws have come from many directions but are largely driven by players who are part of a large and diverse commercial marketplace seeking changes in the legal framework in order to maximize their profits from e-commerce in publishing and entertainment.

The rules promoted by these players to govern a sizeable, general marketplace of users do not lend themselves well to the educational and research communities because, with a few notable exceptions, they do not provide for the special qualities and needs of education and scholarship. Even in licensing, where libraries have made some progress in negotiating broad uses for their communities, efforts to legitimize mass-market licenses could eliminate fair use and erode the willingness of providers to negotiate at all.

In the U.S. and Canada as well as other parts of the world, the library community has been actively engaged in policy debates as laws have been revised, consistently advocating the need to retain a balance among the interests of creators, owners, and users. Our involvement has been significant but these efforts have not been able to stop the economic and political forces of the marketplace that now so clearly dominate society.

It is critical that library community advocacy activities be sustained so there is no further erosion of the balance of interests among creators, copyright owners, and users. At the same time, it is essential for the community to step back, assess the current reality, and consider additional strategies for achieving our commitment to "promote equitable access to and effective use of recorded knowledge in support of teaching, research, scholarship, and community service."

The current environment clearly favors commercial interests and thus mitigates against effective use of intellectual property for purposes of education and research. After many years of the library community's struggle to retain the balance in copyright law, scientists and scholars have cast a new light on the debate. Researchers have come to depend on new technologies for rapid peer-to-peer communications and sophisticated searching and manipulation of data. They have begun to insist that publishers support articles with large datasets, image files, and simulations. And, as the original authors, they are demanding open, easy access to the literature as soon after publication as possible.

Some publishers have been resistant to open access, fearing loss of revenues and loss of control over their content. To date, librarians have exhibited mixed responses to open-access initiatives. Some librarians, like their scientific and scholarly colleagues, see open access as an opportunity to exploit technology more fully in support of research and teaching; others express concern, particularly with the Public Library of Science, that some libraries will cancel journal subscriptions thereby motivating publishers to raise subscription prices and increasing the overall cost of access. Now is the time for librarians to fully embrace the goal of open access, and join with scholars, scientists, and their institutions in working toward this goal.

Open Archives initiative (OAi)

The goal of the OAi is to contribute in a concrete manner to the transformation of scholarly communication. The proposed vehicle for this transformation is the definition of technical and supporting organizational aspects of an open scholarly publication framework on which both free and commercial layers can be established. The origins of the Open Archives initiative lie in the growing number of electronic preprint (eprint) archives. While several of these began as informal vehicles for the dissemination of preliminary results and non-peer reviewed "gray literature", a number of them have evolved into an essential medium for sharing research results among the colleagues in a field.

These archives demonstrate a shift in the traditional scholarly communication model, which has relied on formally published scholarly journals. There is a growing consensus that the scholarly journal system is facing significant challenges:

— The explosive growth of the Internet has given scholars almost universal access to a communication medium that facilitates immediate sharing of results.

— The rapidity of advances in most scholarly fields has made the slow turn-around of the traditional publishing model an impediment to collegial sharing.

— The full transfer of rights from author to publisher often acts as an impediment to the scholarly author whose main concern is the widest dissemination of results.

— The current implementation of peer-review-an essential feature of scholarly communication-is too rigid and sometimes acts to suppress new ideas, favor articles from prestigious institutions, and cause undue publication delays.

— The imbalance between skyrocketing subscription prices and shrinking or, at best, stable library budgets is creating an economic crisis for research libraries.

The e-print archives exemplify a more equitable and efficient model for disseminating research results. An important challenge is to increase the impact of the e-print archives by layering on top of them services-such as peer review-deemed essential to scholarly communication. This is the focus of the Open Archives initiative.

The aim of the archive initiatives described above is to try to create a more effective scholarly communication mechanism that addresses problems that exist in the established system. The approaches that are taken by individual archives differ in a number of ways. Some initiatives build on a centralized model, others on a distributed departmental, or by extension, institutional model. Some deal with gray literature only, others incorporate metadata of peer-reviewed papers or try to establish some form of peer-review outside of the established system. Some deal with metadata only, others with both metadata and full content. Yet all share the attribute of offering scholars a vehicle to conveniently and immediately disseminate research results to peers. The reason for launching the Open Archives initiative is the belief that interoperability among archives is key to increasing their impact and establishing them as viable alternatives to the existing scholarly communication model.

The Open Archives initiative has been set up to create a forum to discuss and solve matters of interoperability between author self-archiving solutions (also commonly referred to as e-print systems), as a way to promote their global acceptance. Interoperability is a broad term, touching many diverse aspects of archive initiatives, including their metadata formats, their underlying architecture, their openness to the creation of third-party digital library services, their integration with the established mechanism of scholarly communication, their usability in a cross-disciplinary context, their ability to contribute to a collective metrics system for usage and citation, etc.

Interoperability among archives offers substantial benefits to the scholars that use them. An important attribute of the traditional research library as an information provider is its role as a common entry point for a variety of information resources, not necessarily divided along disciplinary or institutional boundaries. The move from physical to digital sources should not be accompanied by the breakup of this entry point into a collection of fragmented archives.

An increasing number of scholars move fluidly in their research across domain boundaries; the technology for delivering digital information should facilitate rather than hinder such fluidity. Mechanisms for interoperability offer the potential for discovery tools and virtual collections that extend across the contents of multiple archives. Interoperability is also beneficial to the archive and service provider. Rather than having to provide an entire suite of services for its users, individual archives can instead establish a welldefined interface on which external providers can build enhanced services.

A variety of such services can be envisioned, including those that facilitate discovery, linking, and reviewing. An intriguing and essential set of services would be those that provide metrics to assist in the evaluation of the impact of certain scholarship and aid in tenure review and promotion decisions. Although interoperability has been a watchword for a variety of efforts in digital libraries and networked information, the actual meaning of it and the implementation thereof has often proven elusive.

In UK, the Santa Fe Convention presents a technical and organizational framework designed to facilitate the discovery of content stored in distributed e-print archives. It makes easy-toimplement technical recommendations for archives that-when implemented-will allow data from e-print archives to become widely available via its inclusion in a variety of end-user services such as search engines, recommendation services and systems for interlinking documents.

In addition, the convention introduces an organizational framework for making information available about archives that adhere to the technical recommendations of the convention-the data providers-and about trusted parties that build end-user services for data originating from such archives-the service providers. As such it provides a communication mechanism between providers of data and providers of services and creates a community of open archives.

The Santa Fe Convention builds on on a number of definitions and concepts that are essential for its understanding. The Convention considers the following to be crucial components of an e-print archive:

— A submission mechanism;

— A long-term storage system;

— A management policy with regard to submission of documents and their preservation;

— An open machine interface, that enables third parties to collect data from the archive.

The last item is crucial for enabling third parties to create services that support the discovery, presentation and analysis of data in the archive. Most e-print archives will also provide native end-user services. However, facilitating the broad dissemination of archive data through third party services is a crucial feature of an e-print archive. Therefore, the open interface is a key part of the Santa Fe Convention.

The convention uses the notion of a record in an archive. Some archives may store metadata that describes full content without storing the full content itself. In this case, the metadata is a record. Other archives may also store full content. However, the convention assumes that if full content is stored, there will always be associated metadata stored in the archive as well as a mechanism to tie metadata and content together. In this case the combination of metadata and full content is a record.

Open Archives Metadata Set (OAMS)

The Open Archives Metadata Set (OAMS) is a collection of nine metadata elements intended to facilitate coarse granularity resource discovery among the records in distributed and dissimilar archives. The semantics of this set have purposely been kept simple in the interest of easy creation and widest applicability. There is no provision for qualification or extension of the nine elements. The expectation is that individual archives will maintain metadata with more expressive semantics and the Open Archives Dienst Subset provides the mechanism for retrieval of this richer metadata.

Open Archives Dienst Subset

The Open Archives Dienst Subset is a set of protocol requests that are delivered via HTTP. This protocol is a subset of the full Dienst protocol. The protocol requests in the subset provide the following functionality:

— List the full identifiers for records stored in an archive. An optional argument permits the client to specify that the list should only include records added after a specific date. Another optional argument allows the client to specify that the records should be accompanied by the metadata associated with the identifier.

— Return the metadata for a specific record in a requested format.

— Return the list of metadata formats supported by an archive.

— Return the list of metadata formats available for a specific record.

— Return the structure of the partitions by which an archive is organized.

Santa Fe Convention also introduces an organizational framework to facilitate its implementation and to establish a communication mechanism between data providers and service providers. An understanding of this framework can be obtained from an exploration of the core document of the Santa Fe Convention that gives a step by step approach for making an e-print archive or a service comply with the Santa Fe Convention.

Metadata

The requirement to have a shared, basic metadata set to facilitate interoperability across communities was reconfirmed. Also the notion of parallel metadata sets that serve specific needs of communities and archives was reconfirmed.

The shared metadata set developed during the original Santa Fe meeting-the OAMS-was deemed inappropriate for cross-community use due to some e-print specific aspects. Instead, the Dublin Core Element Set was selected as the common metadata set. This selection leverages years of work in the Dublin Core Metadata Initiative in developing cross-community consensus.

Initial steps were taken to encourage the development of community-specific harvestable metadata sets. Representatives of the e-print community at the meeting decided to propose a metadata set targeted at the e-print community under the name EPMS by the beginning of 2001. Representatives of the research library community proposed a similar effort and calls for proposals from other communities (e.g., the museum community, Open Language Archives) will be issued.

To distinguish between metadata specific to harvesting functionality and other metadata (both shared and community specific), a carrier syntax in XML was developed. This syntax transports packages of specific sets (e.g., Dublin Core, EPMS) within a contextual wrapper that contains metadata specific to the harvesting interactions between data and service providers.

The concept of unique identifiers within an OAI namespace has been maintained. Its implementation has been revised for compliance with general URI principles and to allow for the building of resolution mechanisms and services across OAI-compliant archives.

OAI Harvesting Protocol

At the heart of the technical agreements of the OAI is the metadata harvesting protocol, which provides a simple interface to transfer metadata from a data provider to a service provider. The original specifications for this interface in the Santa Fe Convention were a subset of the more expressive Dienst protocol (called the Open Archives Dienst Subset). This protocol contains the following service requests:

— *Identify* - returns a self-description of the archive, containing information submitted at time of registration and other administrative information;

— *ListMetadataFormats* - returns a list of identifiers of metadata formats that are offered by the archive in general or for a particular record;

— *ListSets* - returns a structured list of sets (formally called partitions) within which records may be located;

— *ListRecords* - returns a list of record identifiers, and optionally metadata, within a specified range of dates and/or a specified Set. Flow control is achieved by the use of server-generated continuation tokens;

— *GetRecord* - returns the metadata associated with an identifier.

These service requests and their parameters are encoded into standard HTTP URIs. Responses to the requests are XML documents. This allows for simple implementation using CGI scripts or similar technology for data providers while service providers can exploit the proliferation of XML parsers to ease the harvesting of data.

Dienst System

The word "Dienst" refers to a number of things:

— A conceptual architecture for distributed digital libraries.

— A protocol for service communication in that architecture.

– A software system that implements that protocol.

Conceptually, Dienst is a system for configuring a set of individual services running on distributed servers to cooperate in providing the services of a digital library. The open architecture of the Dienst system - exposure of the functionality through an defined protocol - makes it possible to combine Dienst services in flexible ways and augment the existing services with other mediator services, which build on the functionality of the existing services.

The Dienst system originated with the Computer Science Technical Reports Project, a DARPA-funded collaboration to establish a digital library of computer science technical reports. Broadly speaking, there are three ways that Dienst is used:

1. Organizations that wish to join an existing digital library built using Dienst.
2. Organizations that wish to create a new distributed digital library with Dienst.
3. Organizations that wish to undertake research in digital libraries using an existing Dienst digital library or by experimenting with the software.

The modular nature of the software encourages researchers who wish explore mechanisms for enhancing existing services or using the interfaces to existing services to built other services. Notice: While the software has been built and tested according to conventional software engineering standards, we stress that it is research software. Organizations wishing to use it for mission critical applications should consider a thorough review of the architecture, protocol, and software for robustness and security.

The distributed Dienst software is configured to handle textual resources (documents) in a variety of formats. However, the Dienst architecture includes a sophisticated document model that accommodates a wide variety of digital resources. Using the Dienst software for these other resources will require some programming. The Dienst protocol and software is copyrighted but is available for free and can be used and redistributed for non-commercial uses. The Dienst protocol and software is used in a variety of existing digital libraries and projects.

In short, the Open Archives Initiative is providing a framework for the extensive interoperability of archives of scholarly research literature (and potentially other digital materials too). For this initiative to become a widespread reality, the participation of large numbers of individuals and institutions is required. In order to be able to participate, what institutions need is working, interoperable, configurable software that is freely available and easy to set up. It is this need that the EPrints software was developed to fulfill.

EPrints is a feature-rich open archive software system that is as simple to install as any normal application. It runs right "out of the box" with a comprehensive default setup that should serve most people's needs. However, it has also been designed to make it extensively and flexibly re-configurable for customized needs; almost any aspect of the archive's operation can be adapted to suit a particular requirement. This means that the archive can be used by institutions, individuals, journals or any other organization wishing to interoperate with Open Archive services.

This adaptability is achieved by using a modular design methodology. The system is divided into two main components: The core archive component, which provides the functionality required for all open archives, and the site-specific component, providing details about exactly what is stored in the archive, how it is presented and how it may be searched. The system is supplied with a richly featured site-specific component that requires minimal changing (handled by an installation script) to set up a fully working, interoperable open archive.

Bibliography

Arms, William Y., "Digital Libraries", Cambridge, MA: The MIT Press, 2000.

Bishop, Ann Peterson, "Document Structure and Digital Libraries: How Researchers Mobilize Information in Journal Articles." Information Processing and Management 35: 255-279, May 1999.

____________, "Measuring Access, Use, and Success in Digital Libraries." The Journal of Electronic Publishing 4, no. 2, 1998.

Blandford, Ann, and George Buchanan, "Usability of Digital Libraries: A Source of Creative Tensions with Technical Developments." TCDL Bulletin, 2003.

Borgman, Christine L., "Digital Libraries and the Continuum of Scholarly Communication." Journal of Documentation 56: 412-430, July 2000.

____________, "Multi-Media, Multi-Cultural, and Multi-Lingual Digital Libraries: Or How Do We Exchange Data in 400 Languages?" D-Lib Magazine, June 1997.

Buttenfield, Barbara, "Usability Evaluation of Digital Libraries", Science & Technology Libraries 17, nos. 3/4: 39-59, 1999.

Ferrer, Robert, "University of Illinois the Federation of Digital Libraries: Interoperability Among Heterogeneous Information Systems", Science & Technology Libraries 17, nos. 3/4: 81-119, 1999.

Greenstein, Daniel, "Digital Libraries and Their Challenges", Library Trends 49: 290-303, 2000

Hill, Linda L., Greg Janee, Ron Dolin, James Frew, and Mary Larsgaard, "Collection Metadata Solutions for Digital Library Applications." Journal of the American Society for Information Science 50, no. 13: 1169-1181, 1999.

Klemperer, Katharina, and Stephen Chapman, "Digital Libraries: A Selected Resource Guide." Information Technology and Libraries 16: 126-13, September 1997.

Lynch, Clifford, "Today and Tomorrow: What the Digital Library Really Means for Collections and Services", In Virtually Yours: Models for Managing Electronic Resources and Services, ed. Peggy Johnson and Bonnie MacEwan, 85-97. Chicago: American Library Association, 1999.

McKay, Sally, "Digitization in an Archival Environment." Electronic Journal of Academic and Special Librarianship 4, no.1, 2003

Pope, Nolan F., "Digital Libraries: Future Potentials and Challenges." Library Hi Tech 16, nos. 3-4: 147-155, 1998.

Schatz, Bruce R., "Information Retrieval in Digital Libraries: Bringing Search to the Net." Science, 327-334, 17 January 1997.

Smith, Terence R., "A Brief Update on the Alexandria Digital Library Project: Constructing a Digital Library for Geographically-Referenced Materials", D-Lib Magazine, March 1996.

Waters, Donald, "Developing Digital Libraries: Four Principles for Higher Education." EDUCAUSE Review 36: 58-59, September/October 2001.

Witten, Ian H., and David Bainbridge, "How to Build a Digital Library", San Francisco: Morgan Kaufmann Publishers, 2003.

Index

Administrative organisation 4
Administrative organizational hierarchy 30
Archival information 1
Archival Information Packages (AIPs) 39
Archives management 2
Association of American Universities (AAU) 254
Audiovisual materials 31
Automate archives management 1

Bibliography of Asian Studies (BAS) 256

Center for Research Libraries (CRL) 249
Commercial Off The Shelf (COTS) 196

Database systems 1
Digital copies 135
Digital heritage 147
Digital Library Federation (DLF) 265
Digital Object Identifier (DOI) 180
Digital preservation 137
    policies 227
    programmes 138
Digital technologies 166

Educational programmes 13

Fail-safe arrangements 147

Geographic Information Systems (GIS) 274
Global Resources Program (GRP) 254
Gross Domestic Products (GDP) 6

Indispensable instrument 1
Information retrieval (IR) 244
Information retrieval applications 5
Information technology revolution 18
In-service training programmes 21
International Association of Sound Archives (IASA) 14
International Conference of the Round Table on Archives (CITRA) 29
International Council on Archives (ICA) 7
International Records Management Council (IRMC) 8

International Records Management Trust (IRMT) 17
International Standard Organisation (ISO) 8
Internet Assigned Numbers Authority (IANA) 63

Knowledge management (KM) 245
Knowledge Networking (KN) 245

Legislative instruments 7
Lots of Copies Keep Stuff Safe (LOCKSS) 37

Metadata Harvesting Protocol (MHP) 65
Metadata Management 178
Microfilming technology 2
Modern management systems 21
Multimedia society 18
Multimedia techniques 5
Multinational corporations 13
Multipurpose Internet Mail Extensions (MIME) 63

National Information Infrastructure (NII) 245
Non-Governmental Organizations (NGOs) 254

Open Archives Initiative (OAI) 43 271
Open Archives Metadata Set (OAMS) 300

Plagiarism 290
Professional archival associations 25
Public records management 28

Record-keeping practices 3
Records and Archives Management Programme (RAMP) 24
Regional Information Technology and Software Engin 6
Reprographic facilities 10
Research Libraries Group (RLG) 76

Single-material archives 32
South Asia Microform Project (SAMP) 260
Standardisation 3
Structured General Markup Language (SGML) 160

Tagged Interchange File Format (TIFF) 160
Technology-assisted education 135
Typed Object Model (TOM) 63

Universal Resource Locator (URL) 180

West African Regional Branch of the International 14
World Wide Web 25

DIGITAL LIBRARIES

DIGITAL LIBRARIES

(In 3 Volumes)

ISSUES OF DIGITAL LIBRARY ENVIRONMENT

(Volume-3)

Editor

Dr. Vijya Lakshmi

Dr. S.C. Jindal

ISHA BOOKS

DELHI-110 033

Digital Libraries

Rs. 2500 (Set)
Rs. 835 (each volume)

ISBN: 81-8205-109-6 (Set)
ISBN: 81-8205-112-6 (Vol.3)

Reprinted in 2011 in India by
Isha Publications
B-63, Ist Floor
New Gupta Colony
Near DDA Market
Delhi-110009

Printed at: G. Print Process, Delhi

Contents

Preface vii

1 **Origin of Digital Library** 1
Open Digital Library; Digital Revolution; Digital Convergence; Challenges; Digital Conservancies.

2 **Digital Resources** 67
Role of Hybrid Library; Digital Environment; Interoperability.

3 **Digital Preservation** 100
Long-term Preservation.

4 **Intellectual Access to Digital Information** 131
Challenges to Traditional Cataloguing Practices.

5 **Archival Collections** 151
E-journal Archiving; Management of Library Collection; Information Retrieval; Issues.

6 **Control Measures of Digital Libraries** 190
Web Content Management; Cataloguing Electronic Publications; Importance of Digital Library Evaluation.

7 **Metadata and Digital Libraries** 215
Metadata Models and Schemas; Genres of

Digital Content; OAI-Protocol for Metadata Harvesting (OAI-PMH) ; Metadata Harvesting; Open Archives Initiative (OAI).

8 **Surfing Digital Information** **266**
Networked Information.

9. **Information Automation** **285**
Knowledge Management Context.

Bibliography 305

Index 307

Preface

The term digital libraries refers to a new way of carrying out the functions of libraries encompassing new types of electronic information resources, new approaches to acquisition, especially more access to other libraries collection and sharing it. It also undertake new methods of storage and preservation, new approaches to classification and cataloguing, especially of electronic data, intensive use of electronic system and networks, and dramatic shifts in intellectual, organisational and electronic practices. It may have several provisions to access documents, which are of high value, mostly from outside the organisation.

In a digital library environment, publication need not owned to be readily accessible. Many sources of information can be made available to the user community that could not be available if the library were to acquire or purchase and store the same. An electronic collection can be more flexible and dynamic, leaving wider variety and choice of selecting only that part of the document that is relevant and the whole source need not be acquired. Location of all items in the machine readable form is quicker than that of the conventional printed shelf collection.

All the libraries in developed nations have totally shifted to electronic environment and those of them in the developing countries are in the process of marching towards the new electronic environment to find their place and fit into the changing information society with all its limitations.

In digital environment, only digital information is disseminated and most of the information is obtained by remote accesses. Much of this information is less permanent in nature. The data or information may be of different types. To organise the data or information, we require cataloguing practice and it calls for an appropriate data model for organising data with standard point. Specialised technologies are needed for compressing as well as for organising information. These are the major challenges in digital library environment.

The opportunities and challenges in the digital library environment are described elaborately in the present volume. Besides librarians and information scientists, students and teachers of library science will find this work informative and useful.

Editor

1

Origin of Digital Library

The term "digital library" is simply the most recent in a long series of names for a concept that was written about long before the development of the first computer. The idea of a "computerized library" that would supplement, add functionality, and even replace traditional libraries was invented first by H.G. Wells and other authors, who caught the imagination of millions with speculative writings about "world brains" and similar fanciful devices.

There is general agreement that much of the early actual application of computers to information retrieval was stimulated by the prominent scientist Vannevar Bush, who wrote about the "memex," a mechanical device based on microfilm technology that anticipated the ideas of both hypertext and personal information retrieval systems. The first real-world applications of computers to libraries began in the early 1950s with IBM and punched card applications to library technical services operations, and with the development of the MARC (machine-readable cataloging) standard for digitizing and communicating library catalog information.

In 1965, J. C. R. Licklider coined the phrase "library of the future" to refer to his vision of a fully computer-based library, and ten years later, F.W. Lancaster wrote of the soon-to-come "paperless library." About the same time Ted Nelson invented and named hypertext and hyperspace. He also analyzed some of the problems to be identified later in this paper in some detail, but never built an operational system. Many other terms have been coined to refer to the concept of a digitized library, including "electronic library," "virtual library," "library without walls," "bionic library," and others.

The relatively recent use of the term "digital library" can be traced to the Digital Libraries Initiative funded by the National Science Foundation, the Advanced Research Projects Agency, and the National Aeronautics and Space Administration in the United States. In 1994 these agencies granted 24.4 million dollars to six U.S. universities for digital library research, impelled by the sudden explosive growth of the Internet and the development of graphical Web browsers. The term was quickly adopted by computer scientists, librarians, and others. Thus, while the term "digital library" is relatively new, work in bringing digitized information resources to libraries has a history spanning several decades.

The most inclusive view takes a digital library to be, as its starting point, essentially what the Internet is today. But from this extreme perspective it can be seen that the metaphor of the traditional library fails in several respects. A digital library contains digital representations of the objects found in it. Most understandings of "digital library" probably also assume that it will be accessible via the Internet, though not necessarily to everyone. But the idea of digitization is perhaps the only characteristic of a digital library on which there is universal agreement.

A digital library may be organized and represented in the form of object surrogates created by human specialists or it may be entirely unorganized, with no "added value" whatever, using free text searching of the objects themselves — rather than object surrogates — to gain access to the objects in the library. The digital coherence of the objects, the near elimination of distance or physical location as an important consideration, and the existing computer and communications infrastructure will give rise to a myriad new possibilities for enriching and redefining what we think of as a library. But there may be a tradeoff. We may be asked to give up some important properties to gain new ones.

The traditional research library has a physical location, embodied in its physical building. Most of the objects in the library are information resources of some kind. The works are also selected. Criteria for the selection process are defined, and these criteria typically include measures of quality. The objects (information sources) in it are organized — classified, catalogued, and indexed by human beings, in what are called value-added processes. Authority control is a key feature, in which names of authors, variants of works (editions), and subject headings or descriptors are all controlled.

The concept of authorship and ownership are extremely important in a traditional research library, in which various forms of an author's name are brought together in a name authority file. Surrogates of the objects in the library — called index records, or in digital library terminology, metadata — are created for purposes of representing the value added by catalogers and indexers. Data are recorded in dozens of specific fields and subfields of these records, and are "finely searchable." That is, highly specific searches can be conducted on particular combinations of fields or subfields of the index records. Retrieved records are linked to the objects themselves, which can then be obtained and used. The treatment of authorship and ownership in the traditional research library reflects the importance of these ideas in traditional scholarly communication, in which scholars and scientists cite in reference lists the authors and works from whom they have borrowed ideas, words, or facts, thus paying intellectual debts and acknowledging original authorship.

Ownership of intellectual property is central to publishing and scholarship. Plagiarism — stealing the words of others without attribution — is considered unethical in scholarly writing and science. Formal legal rights of ownership are also defined by national and international copyright law. The objects in a traditional research library have certain properties as well. First, they are fixed — they do not normally change, or if they do, various editions are identified and considered to be different from one another. Objects are also permanent — they do not normally disappear from a collection. A variety of services to users are offered by librarians who work in the traditional library.

These include assistance with searching for information resources, reference and research services, readers advisory services, and others. A traditional research library typically offers only limited access to materials and services; access to certain services may be restricted to certain classes of potential users. Use of basic services in many traditional research libraries is free for defined user populations. Some of these libraries are large, tax-supported research institutions.

There are many definitions, ranging from the electronic catalog that describes physical items in a "brick and mortar" library to advanced multimedia environments housing all-digital collections. H. Thomas Hickerson, Cornell University's Associate University Librarian for Information Technologies & Special Collections, believes it is time to erase the line between physical and digital libraries. "A major portion of library activities are technology-supported and have been for years. The Internet has had an incredible impact, but libraries have a history of managing large systems and using technology to deliver bibliographic information," Hickerson says.

Sun Microsystems defines a digital library as the electronic extension of functions users typically perform and the resources they access in a traditional library. These information resources can be translated into digital form, stored in multimedia repositories, and made available through Web-based services. The emergence of the digital library mirrors the growth of e-learning (or distance learning) as the virtual alternative to traditional school attendance.

As the student population increasingly turns to off-campus alternatives for lifelong learning, the library must evolve to fit this new educational paradigm or become obsolete as students search for other ways to conveniently locate information resources anywhere, any time.

Digital libraries began to appear on the campus in the early 1990s as research and development projects centered within computer science departments, sometimes funded by government grants. Campus librarians were often uninvolved in these early projects, which focused on digitization technology, metadata schemes, data management techniques, and digital preservation. Dan

Greenstein, former director of the Digital Library Federation and now head of the California Digital Library, characterizes this experimental period as the "second-generation digital library," exploring new opportunities and developing new competencies.

With this new knowledge in hand, Greenstein suggests that the third-generation digital library abandoned this experimentation and the "build it and they will come" philosophy that characterized early digital collections, focusing instead on fully integrating digital material into the library's collections through a modular systems architecture. "This modular approach is fundamentally liberating since it permits libraries to think creatively about how to build upon services supplied by others." As these projects matured and led the way toward more practical digital library implementations, the library began to take a more central role.

Digital library use shifted to a large and diverse campus audience, and information technology (IT) groups began to partner with the library to develop campus-wide standards for the deployment and operation of digital libraries as an integral part of the education enterprise. This development paralleled the development of heightened student requirements for access to library resources. With the advent of the Internet, individuals' expectations for access to information have increased dramatically.

It is no longer considered practical or acceptable to travel to a specific location during certain hours to locate needed information. Library patrons are not satisfied to locate an item of interest that is housed at yet another physical location, request the item, and then wait days or weeks for the item to arrive at the building where it was requested. Patrons increasingly expect instant access to all the information resources they require, from any location, at any time, and from any device. This is the objective that the digital library is fulfilling. With digital libraries, an individual can:

— Gain access to the holdings of libraries worldwide through automated catalogs.

— Locate both physical and digitized versions of scholarly articles and books.

— Optimize searches, simultaneously search the Internet, commercial databases, and library collections.

— Save search results and conduct additional processing to narrow or qualify results.

— From search results, click through to access the digitized content or locate additional items of interest.

All of these capabilities are available from the desktop or other Web-enabled device such as a personal digital assistant or cellular telephone. Additionally, the user can customize his or her information request so that search results reflect individual needs and preferences. Sun considers personalization the next killer application, creating a more valuable and richer user experience in the digital library environment.

These components might not all be part of a discrete digital library system, but could be provided by other related or multi-purpose systems or environments. Accordingly, integration is a consistent issue cited by digital library developers. To interoperate with the existing library infrastructure, the digital library must be designed to work with existing library catalogs and incorporate industry standards, formats, and protocols.

The term "digital library" is often used to describe any multimedia management system holding digitized information, but this does not mean it will deliver true library application functionality. Thus, these digital library components must also be tailored to capture, encode, and deliver information according to the standard practices adopted by the library industry. Because of the rapid pace of technological change, some standards are concrete and others are emerging.

Throughout the world, libraries, museums and archives are digitizing the important documents and images of our culture, both to preserve them for future generations and to make them more accessible to our own. As digital imaging technology has advanced, so have opportunities for preservation of irreplaceable artifacts. Today, students, researchers, information professionals, and the general public can directly access many of the world's rarest artifacts-from high-quality images of each page of the Gutenberg Bible to a digital likeness of the Mona Lisa-right at the desktop or other Web-enabled device, at any time and from any location. Audio recordings of historic speeches or exotic birdcalls, video clippings from televised news programs, geospacial data, and more are being delivered directly to the desks of students and researchers.

Through the 1990s, digital library projects were largely experimental activities. Digital library techniques came about through research sponsored by the U.S. National Science Foundation (NSF) and the U.K. Joint Information Systems Committee (JISC). In 1999 these projects began expanding internationally when NSF linked its digital library research program with similar activities being undertaken by JISC, resulting in the JISC-NSF International Digital Library Initiative. The objectives of this three-year program were to:

— Assemble collections of information that were not otherwise accessible or usable because of technical barriers, distance, size, system fragmentation, or other limits.

— Create new technology and the understanding to make it possible for a distributed set of users to find, deliver, and exploit such information.

Evaluate the impact of this new technology and its international benefits. through research sponsored by the U.S. National Science Foundation (NSF) and the U.K. Joint Information Systems Committee (JISC). In 1999 these projects began expanding internationally when NSF linked its digital library research program with similar activities being undertaken by JISC, resulting in the JISC-NSF International Digital Library Initiative. The objectives of this three-year program were to:

— Assemble collections of information that were not otherwise accessible or usable because of technical barriers, distance, size, system fragmentation, or other limits.

— Create new technology and the understanding to make it possible for a distributed set of users to find, deliver, and exploit such information.

— Evaluate the impact of this new technology and its international benefits.

The development of digital libraries must be considered in the overall context of initiatives to unify the IT structures of the campus and to transform the learning process through innovative technology. Economic, social, and cultural pressures are forcing schools and universities to reinvent themselves. As in the business process re-engineering activities of the last decade that transformed corporate enterprises, education organizations are now viewing themselves in a new light.

New types of students and changing student expectations are driving the integration of core campus functions and deployment of student services on the Web. Fragmented, monolithic approaches are falling away as educators realize the need to link learning and administrative resources in a more effective way to become a "knowledge enterprise," the 21st century version of the traditional campus. During the past decade steep declines in the cost of commodity components, combined with the availability of high bandwidth networks, have made sophisticated IT applications for education affordable.

A mix of sophisticated digital and Internet-based services and rapidly expanding global digital content have made possible a "virtual learning environment" (VLE) that delivers the capability to enhance the classroom experience or conduct learning apart from a physical campus. The digital library is a core component of this VLE. "These developments are extending the role of the library, and changing the relationships between the library and other parts of the academic enterprise," according to Clifford Lynch, Director of the Coalition for Networked Resources and a noted authority on digital libraries.

The NSF in the United States has joined with the JISC in the United Kingdom to sponsor a major research program called "Digital Libraries and the Classroom: Testbeds for Transforming Teaching and Learning." This program will promote the use of large-scale, distributed digital content and advanced networking technologies for learning. Running from 2002 to 2007, the sponsored projects are expected to demonstrate how integrating recent technical developments with digital content improves the learning experience of students and provides new models for classroom instruction.

Open Digital Library

By its nature, digital collection development requires extensive use of technological resources. In the early days of digital library development, when collections were typically small and experimental, a wide variety of hardware and software was utilized. Today, the leading digital library developers are putting substantial collections online. Some of these collections include millions of digital objects; collections are being planned that will require storage measured in petabytes-the equivalent of more than 50,000 desktop computers with 20-gigabyte hard drives. As digital libraries scale in size and functionality, it is critical for the underlying technology platform to deliver the performance and reliability required.

Many digital libraries are considered "mission critical" to the overall institution. In addition, patrons expect high service levels, which means that downtime and poor response time are not tolerable. Moreover, because cost is a foremost concern, scalability and efficiency with a low total cost of ownership are also key requirements. This type of digital library implementation requires a scalable enterprise-level technology solution with built-in reliability, availability, and serviceability (RAS) features. Storage capacity also must be scalable to adapt to rapid growth in demand, and must be adapted to the mix of media types that may be stored in a digital library, such as:

— Text, which is relatively compact.

— Graphics, which can be data-intensive.

— Audio, which is highly dynamic.

— Video, which is highly dynamic and data intensive.

Storage capacity should be expandable in economical increments and should not require redesign or re-engineering of the system design as requirements grow. An open systems architecture provides both a robust platform and the best selection of digital media management solutions and development tools. The inherent reliability and scalability of open platforms have made them the most popular choice of IT professionals for Internet computing. This computing model features an architecture that is oriented totally around Internet protocols and stresses the role of Web sites for a vast and diverse array of services that follow a utility model.

The use of new Internet and portal computing models, the explosion of off-campus, lifelong learners, and the growing need to better manage heterogeneous, round-theclock IT environments has fueled the move to Sun technologies. Sun Microsystems continues to lead the way in RAS, resource management, real-world performance capabilities, and cost of ownership, setting a standard that other technology platform offerings cannot match.

Sun midrange and high-end servers also offer high-availability features such as full hardware redundancy, fault-isolated dynamic system domains, concurrent maintenance, and clustering support. Exceptional performance is achieved through fast processors, outstanding system interconnect performance, fast I/O, and linear scalability. Sun also offers one of the industry's most economical storage environments, providing modular storage capacity that can be added incrementally.

Sun's flexible storage products enable the user to purchase precisely the increments needed. Spindle limits, capacity, and bandwidth can be increased with a simple upgrade. Sun's enterprise storage products are designed to have no single point of failure. Increasingly, IT specialists are implementing campus portals. In a portal environment, the client connects to a portal server via a browser or other device. The portal server presents an authentication screen to the user. With the connection running https, all username and password information is encrypted in transport. If the user name and password is accepted and verified within the directory services, the portal server can then read all dynamic attributes for the customer from the directory services and start to build the primary screen.

This screen will include all services and applications that the customer has permissions to access -including library services. Meanwhile, the portal server establishes connections to all the back-end application servers while waiting for the customer to choose where to go next. All of this functionality can create a management nightmare, which is why it is important to support a scalable management and policy base mechanism.

Software is evolving from local desktop and client-server software applications to Web applications. Today, it is very common for organizations to move their local applications to the Web, and in some cases to subscribe to additional application services over the Web from external service providers. The next phase of this evolution is the development of true Web services.

A Web application offers a service that requires the intervention of a user, while a Web service facilitates direct program-to-program interaction without user intervention. Web services are functional components that can combine with other services dynamically to create a more useful or powerful application. The digital library of the future will deliver "smart media services"; that is, Web services that can match "media content" to user "context" in a way that provides a customized, personalized experience. Media content is digital content that includes elements of interactivity.

Several key technologies must interact to allow Web services to work in this way. Extensible Markup Language (XML) and Standard General Markup Language (SGML) are important standards influencing our ability to create broadly interoperable Webbased applications. SGML is an international standard for text markup systems and is very large and complex, describing thousands of different document types in many fields of human activity. XML is a standard for describing other languages, written in SGML.

XML allows the design of customized markup languages for limitless types of documents, providing a very flexible and simple way to write Web-based applications. This differs from HTML, which is a single, predefined markup language and can be considered one application of XML. The primary standards powering Web services today are XML-based. These include:

— Simple Object Access Protocol (SOAP).

— Universal Description, Discovery and Integration (UDDI).

— Web Services Description Language (WSDL).
— Electronic Business XML (ebXML).

These standards are emerging as the basis for the new Web services model. While not all are fully defined standards, they are maturing quickly with broad industry support. An educational institution's digital library environment will likely encompass both local collections and externally provided resources from such sources as subscription services and other libraries. There is often a desire to structure this blend of internal and external resources as a unified collection from the user's point of view, with a single gateway and a comprehensive set of support services.

Some resources are "born digital"while others originate in physical form and require transformation into digital form, a process that can be difficult and costly. Most of today's digital library environments are the result of custom development, but as packaged library solutions are now available, the next group of digital library adopters must reach a "make versus buy" decision. Much of the utility and long-term ease of maintenance of digital collections is dependent upon the types and quality of metadata that is stored with the digital objects, but agreed-upon standards for metadata are only beginning to emerge.

The first organizations to build large-scale digital libraries encountered many challenges in organizing, funding,managing, and ensuring the long-term maintenance of the digital library environment. These challenges and share experiences of the early adopters. Some of these experiences may help others avoid pitfalls and take advantage of evolving best practices. The funding issue is probably the single largest barrier to digital library development; this is why most existing collections are essentially pilot projects or R&D activities.

The challenge of mounting a large-scale digitization effort, encoding appropriate metadata to ensure ease of discovery and use, and making a commitment to longterm preservation can be daunting to libraries already struggling to pay for existing activities. Some institutions like Harvard University have been able to generate start-up funding with the philosophy of "build it and they will come."

Custom development has been the predominant means of constructing digital libraries simply because off-the-shelf solutions have only become available relatively recently. Leading digital library implementers who have gone this route consistently cite the lack of commercially available solutions that met their requirements as the reason for developing custom systems.

There are both benefits and drawbacks to doing custom development. On the plus side, there is a high degree of assurance that the completed system will closely fit the specific user requirements, since there are (theoretically, at least) no competing communities with different needs or opinions about the best way of accomplishing a certain task. The up-front cost of development can be spread over a long period of use, with no further license fees or charges to be paid as time goes on.

Future development is completely controllable and predictable, and there is no doubt about continued availability of the system. On the other hand, the cost of developing and maintaining a complex multimedia management environment is very high. Says a veteran digital library implementer, commenting on one particularly well-funded project: "Even a million dollars doesn't go very far in developing this kind of a system." Another experienced digital library developer says, "If you're going to do it by yourself, bring your checkbook." There is also the threat that evolving standards would result in one-off systems that lack interoperability with other digital environments.

The school of thought advocating the development of commercial digital library solutions revolves around the value of a large number of buyers supporting the research and development required to bring a robust "turn-key" solution to market. The nature of the marketplace will dictate that the system for sale will meet a majority of the buyers' needs at a more reasonable price than developing unique systems. The continuing force of the market will exert pressure for improvement and evolution of the product to continue to meet users' requirements, protecting the buyers' long-term interests.

Many libraries simply do not have access to the types of technologists required to develop and maintain these systems, nor do they have any interest in staffing to maintain a complex digital library system. The key to locating, using, and preserving digital content is metadata, or structured data about digital objects and collections. Many digitization efforts have been unsuccessful due to inadequate metadata. There are three different types of metadata, all essential to ensure the usability and preservation of the collection over time.

Descriptive metadata

This metadata provides information that a) allows discovery of collections or objects through the use of search tools, and b) provides sufficient context for understanding what has been found. When collections become large or when searching multiple collections (such as over the

Internet) the discovery of objects of interest becomes a "needle in a haystack" exercise.Without agreed-upon metadata standards and the discipline of capturing and storing appropriate descriptive metadata, all but the smallest digital collections would be useless.

Metadata for individual objects varies by the type of object, but would include such things as its title, what it is, who created it, contributors, language, when it was created, where it is located, the subject, etc. At the collection level, users should be able to determine the scope, ownership, any access restrictions, and other important characteristics that would assist in understanding the collection. Probably the best-known descriptive metadata standard for libraries is MARC (MAchine-Readable Catalog) used for cataloging books and other publications.

MARC has served the traditional library well, but was not designed for describing images, sound files, and other new media types. An important emerging descriptive metadata standard for images and other multimedia objects is Dublin Core, a group of 15 items of information designed to be simple to understand and use. Dublin Core was designed to provide a very widely accepted mechanism to allow discovery, but with the option for different communities of users to adapt and customize it by adding more fields of particular importance to the community. In this way, the same base standard can be used for a wide variety of purposes and business models.

Structural metadata

The second type of metadata is structural metadata. This describes the associations within or among related individual information objects. A book, which consists of pages and chapters, is one of the most straightforward examples of structural metadata. The structural metadata would explain how individual page images make up individual chapters, and how chapters make up the book. There could also be individually imaged figures, and structural metadata could also relate these to chapters or to a list of all figures in the book. Structural metadata aids the user in navigating among individual objects that comprise a compound object.

Administrative metadata

Administrative metadata facilitates access,management, and preservation of the digital resource. It can describe the viewer or player necessary to access the object, automatically opening that viewer or player when a user selects that resource. It can describe attributes such as image resolution, file size, or audio sampling rate. It can provide a record of how and when an object was created as well as archival and rights management information.

An important emerging standard for interoperability of digital collections is the Metadata Encoding and Transmission Standard (METS), which provides a uniform framework for managing and transmitting digital objects. The Making of America II project (MOA2) developed an encoding format for descriptive, administrative, and structural metadata for textual and image-based works. Supported by the Digital Library Federation and the Library of Congress, METS builds upon the work of MOA2.

It provides a format for encoding metadata necessary for both management of digital library objects within a repository and exchange of such objects between repositories (or between repositories and their users). Leading academic and research libraries are citing METS as an important standard for digital library interoperability, and seem to be rallying behind this standard.

As libraries increasingly focus on building gateways that direct patrons both to the library's own content and to networked digital resources owned or controlled by other entities, rights management becomes a major concern. "In constructing a digital library service environment, the library becomes responsible for configuring access to a world of information of which it owns or manages only a part," says the California Digital Library's Dan Greenstein. "Accordingly, the digital library is known less for the extent and nature of the collections it owns than for the networked information space it defines through a range of online services."

In this type of cooperative resourcesharing environment, mechanisms for identifying information users and their access privileges are essential. With increased use of the Internet to buy, sell, or license the use of documents, images, video, and other copyrighted content in digital form, comes the need to protect that content from unauthorized use once it is outside the control of the publisher or distributor.

Digital content is very easy to copy and disseminate with little or no loss of quality. Accordingly, the ability to positively identify library patrons and their associated access privileges is required to assure that materials are being accessed and used by the appropriate parties. From a more practical perspective, it is also useful to integrate these identification and authorization mechanisms with other campus requirements, providing an environment where individuals can use a common facility for a "single signon" identification process shared with other campus computing applications.

Ideally, a common authentication/authorization process would be capable of positively identifying any computer user, linking that user to groups of other users with similar access requirements, and passing the user's identity and access profile to all campus computing applications that require such intelligence. A student enrolled in a particular class should be able to seamlessly access reserve materials in digital form (held in the digital library system) as well as online course materials available through the curriculum management system, the student's enrollment in the course being verifiable through the course registration system.

Libraries place high value on preserving the irreplaceable contents of their collections, making the historical and cultural artifacts of our civilization available for future generations. Stanford University's Michael Keller comments, "Libraries are communications devices from preceding generations to succeeding generations. Preservation of scholarly publications are tremendously important." Fire prevention systems, environmental controls, and microfilming initiatives guard against catastrophic loss of irreplaceable items. Even the move from acid to alkaline paper in publishing has worked for long-term retention of printed items.

In 1991, the American Library Association published a preservation policy outlining the responsibilities of the library profession for preserving access to information of all forms. In 2001, that policy was updated to reflect changes brought about by the Internet. The preamble of the revised policy states: "Librarians must be committed to preserving their collections through appropriate and non-damaging storage, remedial treatment of damaged and fragile items, preservation of materials in their original format when possible, replacement or reformatting of deteriorated materials, appropriate security measures, and life-cycle management of digital publications to assure their usefulness for future generations."

With digitized resources, it would seem that preservation would be much easier to achieve, especially since an unlimited number of copies can be created of the individual object. There are, however, a number of issues that complicate the maintenance of digital objects over long periods of time:

— *Deterioration of media*: Stone tablets have a considerable advantage over today's digital media for long-term storage. The problem of deterioration limits the useful life of today's digital media to between 5 and 50 years, while librarians debate how to retain the artifacts of our civilization for thousands of years to come.

— *Evolution in type and format of media*: In addition to the concerns of physical deterioration of media, we must be aware of the challenges posed by changes in media type and format. In the relatively recent history of personal computer use, we have seen an evolution from 5-1/4" floppy disks to higher density 3-1/2" diskettes to high-density zip disks, all requiring different physical disk drives and reader software. Optical storage technology is next, and there will undoubtedly be continual change in storage technologies.

— *Changes in applications and operating systems*: New software constantly appears on the horizon, rendering older versions obsolete. The hardware required by applications and operating systems software also changes over time. Any information stored in a given software/hardware environment will eventually be rendered obsolete through technological obsolescence, most likely before deterioration of the actual storage media occurs. Today, locating a system capable of reading 20-year-old Visicalc spreadsheet files or Multimate word processing files is a difficult proposition; in 50 years' time it will likely be impossible.

— *Preservation of processing results*: Some digital resources exist only fleetingly as a program runs and cannot be preserved as static objects. Preservation of such resources requires maintenance of the program and the surrounding operating environment in operable form. Of course, not all digital resources have the same preservation requirements. "We are more concerned about persistence and authenticity of the collection of images than the long-term preservation of the surrogate," explains David Bearman, director of the Art Museum Image Consortium (AMICO). "Museums are in the business of pre-serving the real thing." The skill set of the archivist, establishing criteria for selection of content to be preserved, will become even more essential as the amount of digital content expands.

Today, most digital libraries follow a schedule of copying archived digital resources to address the issue of media deterioration. As organizational standards for formats and applications evolve,many libraries also convert the objects over time to maintain readability. Specific preservation policies and best practices, however, are not well developed. The Research Libraries Group (RLG) is an international member alliance, including universities and colleges, national libraries, archives, historical societies, museums and independent research collections, and public libraries dedicated to "improving access to information that supports research and learning."

The National Library of Australia sponsors an initiative called "Preserving Access to Digital Information" (PADI) with the goal of providing mechanisms that help ensure that digital information is managed with appropriate consideration for preservation and future access. PADI recommends these strategies for long-term preservation of digital collections:

1. The migration of digital information from one hardware/software configuration to another or from one generation of computer technology to a later one offers one method of dealing with technological obsolescence.

2. Adherence to standards will assist in preserving access to digital information.

3. Technology emulation potentially offers substantial benefits in preserving the functionality and integrity of digital objects.

4. Encapsulation, a technique of grouping together a digital object and anything else necessary to provide access to that object, has been proposed by a number of researchers as a useful strategy in conjunction with other digital preservation methods.

5. It is universally agreed that documentation is an important tool to assist in preserving digital material. In addition to the metadata necessary for resource discovery, other sorts of metadata, including preservation metadata, describing the software

hardware and management requirements of the digital material, will provide essential information for preservation.

Deployment of portal technology has occurred side-by-side with digital collection development and access. As libraries create, license, or negotiate access to more and more digital content, the need for an easy-to-use interface becomes increasingly important. Library portals typically include an online catalog of materials as well as gateways to collections of digital resources accessible to the user.

Broadcast search tools allow library users to search all of these sources simultaneously with a single query. Portals may include electronic reference services ("ask a librarian"), personalization features ("my bookshelf," custom intelligent searches), and other research tools. Enriched content, such as author biographies and book reviews, tables of contents, and jacket images can be provided to supplement the online catalog. Some libraries have built interactive features into their portals, allowing development of virtual communities.

The resulting nonprofit organization, the Art Museum Image Consortium (AMICO) now includes more than 35 major museums in the United States, Canada, and the UK. As the museums grew their digital collections and usage increased, they found that the task of dealing with requests by students and faculty took increasing amounts of time. AMICO provides a more efficient means of dealing with the work of rights management and access by clearing a licensed set of rights and delivering access to the consolidated collections through a variety of distribution mechanisms.

More than three million AMICO Library subscribers access not only the images, but also find detailed provenance information, curatorial text, multiple views, and other related multimedia for many of the works. AMICO maintains the half-terabyte master repository in a custom-developed relational database that is growing by 20,000 works per year. Current challenges include expanding the multilingual capabilities of the user interface to encourage more internationalization of membership and use, as well as encouraging the inclusion of more multimedia items in the collection. Clearing digital rights for works sought for inclusion in the AMICO Library also remains a continuing challenge.

The University of California at Berkeley has been in the forefront of digital library innovation for many years. Projects begun at Berkeley included the creation of specifications for encoding electronic finding aids that are used to access special collections and archives. These specifications later evolved into the XML-based Encoded Archival Description (EAD). Current work involves development of a modular object management environment, called GenDL (for "Generic Digital Library"). GenDL includes three components that can be thought of as three separate systems:

— The Web-based content management system, where creation and maintenance of the digital content is controlled. Descriptive, administrative, and structural metadata is created and linked to digitized or born-digital content. The resulting digital library objects are then encoded to the METS standard.

— The preservation repository (a joint project with the California Digital Library), where the digital content is managed to ensure its integrity and longevity.

— The access system, which is used to discover, display, and navigate objects that may have complex internal organizations (i.e., structural metadata).

Having undertaken one of the world's most aggressive digitization programs, Cornell library has been a developer of best practices and a leader in the field of digital libraries. As a Sun Center of Excellence for Digital Libraries, Cornell has served as a co-developer with Endeavor Information Systems for the product "ENCompass," a specially tailored multimedia management system intended for library implementations. Although Cornell has gained international recognition for its computer science advances in digital library technology, this university also recognizes the value of off-the-shelf products.

Cornell has attained recognition for the substantial digital collections it has developed. One of the best known is the "Making of America" collection, a multi-institutional digitization initiative making available primary sources of 19th century American culture and history, including popular magazines like Harper's, Atlantic Monthly, and Scientific American. To date, more than 900,000 pages, which are full-text searchable and freely accessible over the Internet, are in the collection.More than 40 other digital collections have been established, ranging from audio recordings of rare birdcalls to digital facsimiles of essential works in the literature of witchcraft and demonology, drawn from Cornell University's Rare Book Collection.

There are several strategic digital library priorities. One is to establish a central repository for all information resources deemed worthy of long-term maintenance. The repository's aim is to support the total lifecycle of those materials. Harvard University has a very large and decentralized library system including more than 100 libraries and 35 major research collections. There is no hierarchy tying these libraries into a single organizational group.

Harvard's digital library activities are designed to provide a common technology infrastructure, consulting assistance, and guidance on policy issues to all of the Harvard libraries. Unlike many universities, Harvard has established major funding to support the development of a comprehensive infrastructure for digital libraries. The $12 million, 5-year program is called the "Library Digital Initiative," deliberately emphasizing the library orientation of the program. The goal of centrally funding this initiative to serve the decentralized network of libraries is to create incentive for participation in a common, standardized solution featuring a robust production IT environment and common practices for digitizing, reformatting, metadata creation, digital licensing, preservation, and migration of objects, etc.

The central Oracle repository supports all types of multimedia objects and a set of catalogs. A portal sits over the catalogs, allowing cross-catalog searching. Although born digital information is at the heart of the program, a program of internal grants has also been established to foster additions to the collection. It is expected that there will be a lot of activity devoted to the interface with learning systems in the future. There will also be increased emphasis on scholarly communication and the libraries' role in capturing the university's intellectual output.

The problems associated with storing back issues of printed journals and locating articles of interest in those back issues led to the creation of JSTOR, an electronic archive of scholarly journals. JSTOR began as a pilot project sponsored by the Andrew W. Mellon Foundation in 1990. Ten journals in economics and history were selected initially, and all back issues were digitized. High-resolution images of each page were captured and linked to a text file generated with optical character recognition software. Table of contents indices were developed as well, to provide search and retrieval of journal content of interest. When five test libraries showed enthusiasm about the space savings and ease of access, JSTOR was born.

In 1995 JSTOR was established as an independent non-profit organization with the goals of providing a trustworthy archive of important scholarly journals, reducing the cost of accessing these materials, and assuring their long-term preservation. JSTOR now provides 1,100 user institutions worldwide access to 169 journals. Originally written in Perl, the Web interface has been ported to Java. Java's object-oriented approach makes it easier for JSTOR's geographically distributed developers to quickly write small pieces of reusable code. More than five million requests per month are satisfied through three sites at Princeton, the University of Michigan, and the University of Manchester.

The entire JSTOR archive requires 2.2 terabytes of storage for more than eight million pages of journal content. Usage has been growing at a rate of 50% per year, with rapid growth among international users. There is also increasing emphasis on allowing access to the JSTOR archive by secondary schools and public libraries. The University of Maryland has opportunistically grown its unique digital collections, beginning with the Performing Arts Library and the Broadcasting Archives. Both were highly motivated to make their holdings more accessible and usable.

A 1996 implementation of a commercial multimedia management platform had mixed results, due to the difficulty of integrating the product into the existing environment and the lack of specific library functionality. The University of Maryland has since taken a different approach, becoming an Ex Libris "Premier Partner" for the Ex Libris "DigiTool" product. This involves full implementation of the Ex Libris digital asset management product, as well as ongoing participation in product design, development, and testing. The implementation will emphasize streaming audio and video, as well as images. The university's goal is an environment that handles all types of digital objects.

Advanced object management technologies are envisioned to assist users in accessing the Performing Arts Library audio collections. An example of an enhanced digital service is the capability of displaying sheet music images simultaneous with the music being played. "It's good to have a vendor who works with library problems as a mainline business. Other commercial products don't necessarily map to the library business," says University Dean of Libraries Dr. Charles Lowry. Lowry also cites the ability to integrate the digital library software into the Web-based user interface as a benefit, so users can access the physical collection catalog in the same way as the digital collections. It is also important to the University of Maryland that the digital library software supports. National Information Standards Organization (NISO) and National Institute of Standards and Technology (NIST) standards and protocols

Stanford University is well known for its pioneering work in digital library development and electronic publishing. Stanford has participated in both phases of the NSF Digital Library Initiative, provided online publishing services to nearly 100 scholarly societies, developed extensive digital collections, and is currently implementing an advanced digital repository. Stanford has entrusted the responsibilities of University Librarian, Publisher of the

University Press, Publisher of the HighWire Press, and Director of Academic Computing to a single individual at Stanford.

This assignment has fostered functional synergy that has integrated many information management activities across these disciplines and facilitated coordination between related activities such as digital repository and learning management system development. After putting up many digital collections on custom-developed systems, the Stanford Libraries have selected the "TEAMS" multimedia management software from Artesia Technologies as the base for its new digital repository. It is also utilizing Luna Imaging's "Insight" software for managing high-resolution images, and it will utilize the METS standard for managing multimedia objects.

"METS is tremendous, an XMLimplemented generalized metadata environment that lets you describe and interrelate any digital entity.We'll be able to store objects one time in one repository, encode them using different descriptive metadata, and make them available to all different types of applications on campus," explains Stanford Libraries' Chief Information Architect Jerry Persons. The repository will handle authentication using Kerberos certificates and will include rights management and charging mechanisms.

In future, the pace of change in digital library technology and its applications has accelerated in recent years as the focus has begun to shift from R&D to full-scale deployment. Several key trends are emerging and will continue to gain momentum:

— The shift from text and image-based systems to audio and video will continue.

— As network bandwidth becomes more economical and streaming technologies improve, increasing numbers of institutions will have access to the practicality of full multimedia solutions.

— Broadly accepted best practices will emerge for digitization, rights management, preservation, metadata encoding, and other key digital library processes. The library discipline is highly collaborative and has a history of sharing successful approaches. Debate about these issues will recede as proven techniques mature and spread.

— Standards will move from the discussion and trial stage to widespread adoption.

It is clear that digital library technology is becoming an essential enabler of library services. In fact, one recent posting to a digital library e-mail list commented that the term "digital library" is starting to sound as anachronistic as "horseless carriage."

Digital Revolution

The past brought recognizable information formats such as books, journals, film, and other fixed media. Many electronic information resources, however, are brand-new creations that resemble traditional media less and less. They include the millions of Web pages and databases produced all over the world by individuals, companies, institutions, and government agencies. These creations represent a variety of information types, including descriptive materials, corporate reports, datasets, educational offerings, theses and dissertations, and many more.

But, along with these recognizable publication types are many new kinds of publications beyond anything anyone has ever imagined, in terms of size, scale, complexity, and function. These resources spring out of the energy and creativity of society's best minds in a ferment of excitement, and it is reasonable to expect that their variety and novelty will only increase. For example, Corbis offers a huge collection of digital images derived from traditional photo archives, and the Survivors of the Shoah Visual History Foundation collects thousands of videotaped memoirs from Holocaust survivors and integrates them with related materials.

Microsoft's Terraserver project, a collaboration with the U.S. Geological Survey, is a collection of satellite photos of many parts of the United States and selected parts of the rest of the world. The project, which is freely available and offers high-quality information, is an experiment in managing a very large database for public access. It is impossible to describe any of these projects in traditional terms that would allow comparing their collections to items now collected by libraries, nor is it easy to imagine how a given library would collect such items, although they are fully analogous to, and might well substitute for, library holdings. Even resources that seem to be more traditional, such as the research projects fostered by the Institute for Advanced Technology in the Humanities (IATH) at the University of Virginia, challenge traditional expectations by virtue of their constant state of flux.

The institute's Web site contains no single stable artifact to "collect"—it is very much a work in progress. Arts and Letters Daily (A&LD) is a Web site that goes one step further. In appearance, it is a daily "newspaper" whose content is cultural. But all that the editors provide is a front page with short descriptions and links to content found on hundreds of other freely available sites, many of them well-known resources in their own right. The repackaging accomplished by linking articles intelligently to a single site makes A&LD a hugely popular and highly useful site.

Long-established standard newspapers are avoiding links to material from other sources (for legal reasons, possibly); many of the newer newspapers and magazines, however, are filled with links to other sites. Preserving the news nowadays requires collecting not just the specific news source, but also the content of links to other Web spaces. The nation is investing significant sums to advance research in scientific areas, investments that will bear fruit in many directions now little surmised. Both the Los Alamos National Laboratory's e-print archive and the Human Genome Database are collective works that bring together new global communities based on special interests and have extraordinary power to advance and build scientific research.

It is entirely reasonable to imagine that, particularly in scientific and technological fields, such initiatives offer only an inkling of what is to come. As the committee was deliberating, initiatives such as PubMed Central (sponsored by the National Institutes of Health) and the Department of Energy initiative PubSCIENCE were set to be scaled up in the very near future. Other resources are the electronic equivalents of printed information.

The electronic mode makes it possible to deliver the information wherever the reader may be (for instance, to his or her computer in the home or workplace or, by wireless technology, to any place), to present information that cannot be captured in print (such as video attachments, tables that can be manipulated, and so on), and to facilitate use of the information through quality interfaces and search capabilities. Some of the speed with which this transformation is happening in the world publishing industry can be captured by briefly considering two well-established publishing formats—journals and books.

Online Electronic Journals

There is no truly reliable or single source of information on the growth of electronic journals. A study of the World Wide Web archives of the e-journal and magazine electronic announcement list NewJour reveals that in 1989, fewer than 10 e-journals were available. They were created in basic ASCII (.txt) form and had to be distributed in small chunks, lest they crash the mailboxes of subscribers. Today, many large publishers around the world, both for-profit and not-for-profit, maintain Web sites that make available their full collections of print journals (with only limited back-file runs, so far) to subscribers.

Given this penetration of new technologies into scholarly, scientific, and popular journal and magazine publication, a list such as NewJour will one day soon no longer be needed. In this decade (or even half-decade), most print magazines and journals will have a Web version, if they do not already have one. Furthermore, although for the moment it is convenient to think of print and Web versions as providing the same or identical information, the two styles are already beginning to pull apart and will only diverge further.

Not only will the same name ultimately denote collections of content that are in fact very different, but some of the e-journals also will evolve into new genres. The prevailing vision is that this wealth of journal literature will be linked through indexing services and search engines and cross-linked internally online; indeed, this vision is rapidly being realized. For as long as print versions continue to be published, tracking and collecting will be much more difficult. The most significant problem for ubiquitous electronic access is that of long-term archivability and preservation, an issue that begs to be solved if publishers and libraries are not to maintain costly parallel print and electronic systems.

So far, very few electronic journals (or any other resource) have had to survive on the Internet for even one decade. While some experts say that long-term sustainability is a trivial matter, studies suggest high costs and tremendous uncertainties. Fundamental to these uncertainties is the matter of ownership, which libraries rarely have, given that electronic information produces no fixed artifact for libraries to possess and cherish. While rapid growth characterizes scholarly and research journals, the committee found similar or even faster growth in the even broader universe of all continuing publications that includes popular magazines and newspapers as well as annual reports, directories, series, and so on.

Standard periodical indexing and abstracting services began to become available electronically in the 1970s through specialized vendors such as Dialog and BRS, whose proprietary systems required the mediation of expert searchers; by the mid-1990s, they were available through easy-to-use Web interfaces for any licensed subscriber. Thus it is no surprise that the journal articles cited by these sources would become quickly available online. However, books—such as novels and scholarly monographs, for example—have seemed far less susceptible to electronic transformation.

While some books are consulted in bits and bytes (for particular facts or small sections), many (the argument goes) need to be deliciously savored and contemplated from beginning to end, and an online screen is hostile to such prolonged congenial or intense reading. "You can't take it to bed or to the beach or onto the plane with you," is the oft-heard lament. The vision now being articulated by many players in the book publishing industry and its partners (in printing, distribution, and software) is that the full text of all published books, at least from mainstream publishers, will exist on vast electronic information servers, there to be channeled to the output of the reader's choice: traditional print formats or digital formats (by accessing a local copy on a PC or portable device or by viewing a remote copy through the Web). That is, the authoritative source file of many books may soon be an electronic version that can generate various derivative versions.

The e-book may be on the verge of acceptance and success because of the convergence of large computer servers, big network pipelines, rapid progress in developing e-book standards, and the increasing sophistication and utility of handheld book-reading devices, as well as business partnerships to take advantage of all this. Like e-journals, e-books also have a history that goes back to the 1980s.

In the mid-1990s, an entrepreneur making a car trip with his wife had a vision of "the world's largest bookstore," a virtual shop in which the discerning reader could obtain every book—or nearly every book—currently in print. Jeff Bezos, founder and CEO of Amazon.com, Time Magazine's Person of the Year for 1999, achieved his dream: situating bookselling at the core of e-commerce and radicalizing the bookstore concept, to say nothing of notions of business success. Through the Web, the Amazon.com shopper fills a virtual shopping cart with the desired books, which are delivered a day or two or three later to the reader's address of choice.

Through Amazon.com, large collections of books have come one step nearer to their readers—and no library has played a part in this dramatic convergence of reader and book. In the case of the virtual superstore, the reader controls the atmosphere, which need not be as public as a library or bookshop and may be as comfortable as reading in a lounge chair wearing fuzzy slippers and a dressing gown. Most significantly, the rise of the book superstore has implicitly changed the overall economics of access to books and information.

Where once a good public library was the best and most accessible source of materials for many, if not most, communities, bookstores of similar size may be a few doors down the block, open longer hours, and with enough copies of popular titles to satisfy almost all comers. And, most libraries and physical bookstores are dwarfed by online bookstores. These book superstores offer a remarkably wide range of library-like services—lectures, discussion groups, ready access to books, a sense of community. What they do not yet offer is information service--labor-intensive, provided by experts—but it is probably not wise to predict that they will not continue to expand their range.

For now, it is most noticeably the information navigation functions of the library--the instruction in finding, filtering, and evaluating information from a welter of available sources—and its provision of historical depth that the bookstores make the least attempt to supplant. Borders began its career with claims about the literacy and helpfulness of its staff, all of whom had to pass a test to demonstrate their book lore as a condition of employment. Despite this, the library is less than ever a primary supplier of access to new and current books. Libraries continue, however, to be strong in providing access to both older and more specialized material.

Another implication of the shift in the economy of information is that collecting and storing materials are arguably somewhat less the jobs of the library than before. The current emphasis is on services. Indeed, many public libraries have always had this bias, retaining from among older books only those of continuing interest to their readers, while clearing out shelf space for what a current generation demands.

In any case, the superstores and Amazon.com have by no means reached the end state of the publishing industry's book-to-reader vision, nor do libraries seem to have much of a role in that next vision either. The concept of books on demand has been in gestation for some time. For example, in the early 1990s, Xerox partnered with a few large publishing houses in an OD experiment. The products were acceptable, but computer servers and network pipelines were less capacious than today and so the results were slow. The need to resolve rights and permissions issues also posed a significant challenge. The concept needed time to ripen, and ripen it has.

Most individuals, organizations, and publishers agree that at the very least, the traditional book format is facing competition from formats that do some things better. In 1999, the American Historical Association announced an electronic book prize to be awarded annually for several years to half a dozen brilliant dissertations in various fields of history, dissertations that take full advantage of the converging multimedia capabilities that computers and networks can offer and books cannot. The results will enliven the books, attract readers, promote the new medium as a viable one for serious scholarship, and give young scholars a leg up.

Digital Convergence

Traditional libraries are most often conceived of as repositories of textual artifacts. High culture constructs itself around artifacts that can be managed and cataloged in particular ways. But the technological changes of the next decade will no doubt challenge that conservatism in new ways. The technical convergence of data, voice, and video technologies, coming to the desktop (or palmtop) through a single network connection, will encourage consumers to think first of data and only secondarily of media.

Libraries will then be particularly challenged to decide whether and to what extent their traditional focus on textual or mostly textual artifacts fulfills their responsibility. At the very least, libraries in the year 2000 should be actively assessing the possibility that they will be called upon in the future to be the repositories of whole classes of artifact quite unlike what they owned before, placing very different demands on their various skills.

These artifacts will be emphatically commercial in purpose and appeal but no less important than traditional artifacts for documenting American culture in decades to come and therefore inescapably part of the collecting mission of the Library of Congress as now articulated. In the past, the Library of Congress successfully accommodated the introduction of media such as sound recordings and film.

Formally published online information resources are expensive to license, often costing more than one would expect to pay for print. Start-up costs for both sellers and purchasers of information are higher than the costs of maintaining traditional print information:

- information providers are investing in new technologies and skills, and a database or subscription price attempts to recover many, if not all, of the start-up costs over time;
- institutions are developing their own technological and human capabilities, also with significant new costs; and
- libraries and publishers are maintaining parallel information systems and resources in traditional and electronic media.

These additional costs will not disappear for some time. But the primary barrier to the use of online information resources is the cost of licensing the electronic resources marketed by publishers and vendors. Most libraries are funded on a model for the acquisition of fixed-format materials. License agreements, or even specialized CD-ROM products and services, are being offered at prices that encourage many libraries to consider cooperative purchasing. Furthermore, the new model for library acquisitions must consider not only the cost of access to the information, but also the cost of maintaining the technical capability (hardware, software, personnel) required to make these resources available to readers.

Various contemporary students of the economics of information have asserted that the only financial survival option of libraries is to scale up into efficient, cooperating entities. The large consortia that build national catalogs—the large utilities such as Research Libraries Group (RLG) and OCLC—clearly have a part to play in organizing any such meta-system. Although librarians and publishers have, as yet, little quantitative data or user analysis to show how much or even how electronic information resources are used, there is no question that usage, to the extent it can be measured, is shooting up with every passing month.

Readers regularly demand more and more such resources and protest loudly if online access to any index, dictionary, encyclopedia, text, or collection is removed, even if the reasons are seemingly good ones—for example, if a library or institution believes the price is too high or the usage too small to justify continuance. This reaction is no surprise and from the reader's point of view makes perfect sense. Because we live in an age of intense national, institutional, and personal competition, information is essential, and meeting the need for knowledge is an indisputable requirement.

Traditionally, libraries have purchased physical objects for their collections and permitted these to be used as allowed by copyright law and best practices. Many electronic resources, on the other hand, are maintained by publishers, vendors, or others designated by them, and libraries or individuals can obtain rights of access through custom or mass-market licenses.

A library's readers then access the works through high-speed information networks. A library's electronic resources licenses generally permit readers a broad range of educational, research, and personal uses, and, increasingly, the book and journal suppliers promise, in the licenses, to deliver ongoing ("perpetual") access or to give the institution a residual "product" should the publisher or vendor discontinue the work, sell it to another supplier, or leave the business altogether.

Nonetheless, this new business and (non)ownership model raises many questions for libraries and for society. What future, if any, is there for the largest research libraries in an era when, increasingly, materials that readers want are available without going to the library? More importantly, when libraries or other entities do not have contractual rights to archive and preserve electronic content, can they develop adequate archival and preservation mechanisms for electronic materials? These questions speak to large and vital questions of societal well-being.

The traditional regime of copyright, enshrined in the copyright law (Title 17 of the United States Code) and its provisions for fair use (section 107) and libraries (section 108), creates for libraries (institutions that for at least the last century have been designated as holders of materials for the public good, materials that they then make freely available to the reading public) a role that now appears to be challenged if not attacked outright.

As libraries generally shift toward a service rather than a collection orientation, and as the economics and technologies of publishing (particularly for digital materials) make it harder for libraries to own their materials, the concept of freely accessible information, at least to the academic and public library user at the point of use, may well be at risk. The Library of Congress has a unique and privileged position in the acquisition of cultural materials. While all other libraries in the United States must find willing sellers and must have the financial wherewithal to become willing buyers in a freely made commercial transaction, the requirement of legal deposit with the Copyright Office gives LC a presumptive right to full ownership of a copy of each and every artifact published in the United States.

The multitude of electronic databases, the rapid growth of Web sites, the increase in the number of electronically available print journals, and the availability of numerous full-text resources such as reports, dissertations, and electronic books all represent a dramatic change in the dissemination of scholarly and cultural content. The history of this revolution is short and there is still much to learn, on all levels and in all areas. Not a great deal has been published about how the great libraries are transforming themselves to greet the electronic age, although Maurice B. Line notes that three factors have caused an almost ceaseless questioning of the roles and futures of national libraries:

1) automation, information, and communications technology;
2) the intrusion of the private sector into areas formerly sacred to libraries; and
3) the globalization of libraries. He writes:

A great deal of information exists about the emerging practices of the largest research libraries in the United States and Canada, particularly in the publications and data gathered by the Association of Research Libraries

(ARL). In particular, about 25 of these libraries are also members of an initiative named the Digital Library Federation, under the auspices of the Council on Library and Information Resources (CLIR), which leads its members in exploring various key infrastructure issues and helps them to formulate useful projects and experiments.

While the continent's large research libraries in no way begin to compare in collecting scope, mandate, or size with the Library of Congress, they have, nonetheless, begun to move aggressively in the direction of becoming hybrid libraries (i.e., libraries that embrace information in numerous formats, now including electronic formats). The transformation of library culture and practice by the adoption of information technology continues apace. An increasing emphasis on service and a decreasing emphasis on collection have already been noted. Libraries are incorporating electronic technologies and services into the everyday work of all staff by doing a number of things:

— Working for the broadest possible access for readers in the electronic environment. Not only are libraries seeking technological standards and presentation of resources in forms accessible to the broadest range of readers, but they are also lobbying to advance the public policy debate in ways that support broad access for the good of society as a whole.

— Reallocating an increasing and visible portion of collections budgets to the electronic resources needed by their readers. For example, ARL Supplementary Statistics indicate that in FY98/99, 29 ARL member libraries spent more than $1 million of their collections budgets for licensing electronic databases,41 representing anywhere from 6 to 22 percent of their library materials budgets.

— Building collections of digital resources that, while not yet rivaling traditional collections in scope and bulk, are substantial, of high value, and integrated in the traditional patterns of collection and use.

— Working to shape and support initiatives such as community education, online course support, Web page design, teaching-specialist electronic resources, and digitizing of materials for these programs—all with a view to making educational opportunities as broad, rich, and accessible as possible. Lifelong learning is the opportunity and the goal, and "distance learning" is the current buzzword for the tactics librarians seek to support.

— Finding new ways to measure the usage patterns and behaviors of readers, so as to anticipate and support their needs, bringing the right resources into play for readers. The digital environment facilitates such measurement and, accordingly, such feedback, giving a better allocation of resources than has ever been possible with print media.

— Devoting increasing effort to more sophisticated reader services associated with single and multiple electronic resources. Librarians are more often than ever teachers of how to use electronic resources, and readers spend less time pursuing simple factual information at traditional reference desks.

— Cooperating with other libraries in setting up networks that make libraries effectively a single virtual (through the locator tool of interoperable online catalogs) institution that can deliver physical materials, via advanced interlibrary loans and document delivery, to more and more readers more effectively—and more cost-effectively—than ever.

— Delivering physical materials by electronic means. As physical materials become increasingly deliverable at a distance, libraries are putting more and more electronic delivery services into operation.

— Partnering with other participants in the creation and dissemination of knowledge. Libraries can, for example, work with individual authors, organizations, publishers (commercial and noncommercial), booksellers, and software companies to create and make available functional and well-used online resources.

— Digitizing and making available to readers material already in library collections and special collections. Such materials would include, in particular, out-of-copyright material, image collections, sheet music, maps, and other traditional library treasures.

— Subscribing to online services that provide statistical data. Libraries would help readers learn to manipulate services containing anything from historical census data to financial market data.

— Creating multimedia servers for music, film, and other media. At the same time, thorny questions of access and permitted use must be addressed, and the technological capability to handle significant quantities of such material must be developed.

— Using the new generation of library management systems as a springboard not only for integrating forms of access to a wide range of materials and formats but also for reengineering the entire workflow and back-office processes of traditional librarianship. The technical services of libraries are becoming increasingly business-like, streamlined, and closely managed, with closer links than ever to vendors through electronic data interchange (EDI) and other forms of electronic interaction that work to the advantage of all parties.

— Working to understand the technical demands, possibilities, and long-term costs and responsibilities of digital media as instruments for the preservation of library information, including material from traditional print media (e.g., the contents of books printed on acid-based paper) and material created in digital form. When we fully understand the challenges of moving digitally preserved information from format to format, from one hardware and software system to a new hardware and software system, we will have made great progress in solving what many think is the biggest remaining problem in establishing truly functional and satisfactory digital libraries.

– Working through the issues that must be faced in deciding which kinds of resources are best maintained locally, library by library, and which resources are best maintained elsewhere, whether by publishers, vendors, library consortia, or third parties. Traditional librarianship achieves security and preservation by having redundant physical copies: the challenge now is to balance redundancy (and thus security) with optimal efficiency and to avoid unnecessary duplication of effort.

— Understanding evolving legal regimes such as copyright and licensing. In this arena, librarians seek not only to understand but also to shape and influence developments, thus securing agreements that offer readers high-quality, reliable, and permanent access to resources.

— Exercising responsible stewardship of library resources, which are usually purchased with public funds or from not-for-profit institutional budgets. Such stewardship requires keen understanding of the business models and economics of the new information sources in an environment in which libraries find themselves increasingly offered not ownership but access, not a once-for-all price but something closer to annual subscription or by-the-drink pricing.

— Cultivating an expertise in technology matters. The technological infrastructure of a library now faces a new degree of volatility and continuing costs as equipment and software need upgrading. The e-marketplace makes it literally impossible to choose not to play the upgrade game: in a very short time, a library's information would simply become unavailable if it persisted in using even slightly outmoded operating systems or software.

— Continuously upgrading human resources and skills. The librarians and support staff at this time of transformation must undergo no less arduous a series of "upgrades." As in other sectors of our economy, it is impossible in the library sector for staff to acquire and practice skills and then use them for a lifetime; instead, they must grow and adapt, and there are real and substantial costs for supporting the necessary training and for paying a more highly skilled staff.

— Seeking new funding sources and opportunities. Traditional funding sources—annual budgets doled out by the government or not-for-profit organizations with a tiny annual increase—no longer suffice.

Librarians are increasingly engaged in entrepreneurial efforts, whether soliciting research and development funding from granting agencies, developing partnerships with other entities in the library sector, or participating in cost-recovery projects with the commercial sector that serves and interacts with the library community.

Challenges

The challenge in utilising digital technology for enhanced access, is the need to secure that investment, and guarantee long-term access to that information. The role of digital technologies as a preservation strategy is a contentious issue, with the traditional school of library preservation clinging to microfilm as the preferred reformatting medium for long term archival storage. The challenge is to react pro-actively, to look forward to consider ways of minimising identified future risks associated with new media, and to look back into the past to understand the nature and development leading to their creation.

Digital information and electronic resources have transformed academic research fundamentally. As the price of print materials, such as scholarly journals continues to rise, the accessibility and functionality of electronic versions become more attractive, and libraries invest more heavily in new technologies. A related issue in the need to preserve digital resources is a growing reliance of libraries as service providers on digital technology, which must impact on our institutional goals. Digital technologies find their place in the preservation strategies of research libraries in the opportunities presented to one such goal - in improved public access to on-line digital surrogates. Digitisation is now a mainstream activity of the Campbell

Collections of the University of Natal, aimed at collecting, preserving and organising historical material of national and international importance in a manner that is widely accessible.

The retrieval of digital images offers a significant technological advance as a vehicle for integrated access to visual representations of historic photographs, art and ethnographic artefacts - together with traditional library resources. Preservation digitisation has focussed on reformatting rapidly deteriorating materials, with the aim of preserving the intellectual content, as separate from the medium or carrier. Because one is able to make repeated copies of digital files without the informational loss associated with analogue copies, the impact of the technology is beguiling.

Complete digital conversion comprises two process, the capture by scanning of digital data, and that of the associated metadata, wrapped as a digital object and stored using containers to hold the objects and related software modules. The integrity of the digital file is threatened by alterations to the contextual data file, and the loss of the linking mechanism between the two is the same as deleting the contextual information.

The improvements in storage media are so great as to drive market forces. Longevity of a floppy disk common until a year or two ago, can be estimated at between one and ten months. CD longevity is estimated between 10 and 100 years. Other advantages can be found in the aggregation of larger quantities of information to facilitate data management. 650Mb of data can be stored on a CD, current disk storage capacity is moving in excess of 72Gb, the equivalent of 113 CD's. Migration of information is commonly associated with archival storage. We have all known software upgrades to "orphan" or render unreadable, files created under an earlier version.

The most serious problem facing managers of digital collections, is not unstable media, but data format and software obsolescence. Transforming information from one digital format to another, migration is an essential strategy for persistent adherence to international standard formats. Infrastructure risks include the presence or lack of persistent institutional support, in terms of funding, hardware, software and staff to manage the repeated migration of digital collections. Emulation of software and hardware platforms aims to use the power of present computer technology to function as if it were the technology of a previous generation.

Rather than repeated create new versions of a digital document, recent experimentation has shown that it is possible to develop a set of specifications for the building of emulators that can render the content of digital documents on future unknown platforms. The representational information contains all the technical characteristics, including format, navigational structure such as a table of contents, application software, and the computer specifications and system requirements necessary to read that document. Secure systems technologies provide stable environment for digital archives. When preservation strategies have not been applied to systematic digital archiving and all else fails, it may become necessary to work out how to read the stored bits. Because of the manner in which magnetic media are written, it is possible, given sufficient resources, to recover much material believed lost.

Long term preservation of digital resources is feasible through the implementation of sound policies at the inception and in the development of digital libraries. The challenge lies in the need for libraries to move pro-actively in establishing digital collection development programme in an electronic environment that is conducive to preservation. The collaboration of a wide community of information professionals was responsible for developing new strategies for data management and storage for the preservation of digital information resources.

The interaction between library, archive and museum professionals, together with information technology specialists, helped to clarify the myriad technical issues. There are digital imaging projects underway at some libraries in South Africa, and a number of problems have been encountered that are difficult to overcome in isolation. The equipment is expensive, especially if it is state-of the-art, software varies in quality and local support is often lacking. Standards have not been agreed upon, and vary from one project to another.

Standard Generalized Markup Language (SGML) an international standard designed to promote text interchange, provides a definition of a document structure that can be used to encode the logical structure and content of any defined document and known by any remote system. Extensible Markup Language (XML), a simpler dialect of SGML has since been adopted, using the information community-based document type descriptions of the Text Encoding Initiative (TEI) and Encoded Archival Description (EAD), to build an infrastructure that enables interoperability between heterogeneous systems. The most comprehensive preservation strategy currently evolving is that of a collection-based persistent archive system.

A persistent archive operates in two phases, the first comprising capture of digital data wrapped as XML digital objects and ingestion to archival disk storage, using containers to hold objects along with relevant metadata and software modules for future emulation. The second is in the opposite direction, with containers brought out of storage and loaded onto new possibly new information management systems, and returned to a new, and possibly new archival storage system. The result is a product with the ability to scale its capabilities by adding resources when required.

By differentiating between the storage of the bits that comprise the digital object and the related information carried by the metadata it is possible to create an infrastructure for life cycle management for digital preservation. In fact, information products, like electronic documents and digital objects are particularly important because they represent the purest form of Electronic Commerce. Indeed Electronic Commerce, with its greatly reduced cost of production and distribution makes many new knowledge businesses practical that were previously impractical.

For example, a fully realized infrastructure for Electronic Commerce would make it practical for authors to charge pennies for paragraphs and still make a profit - because the author can reach millions world-wide over the Internet, who can pay and download the paragraph at little or no cost to the author. Electronic commerce does not completely address collaborative design and manufacturing activities, although they do share many of the same sorts of activities. The publication of compelling electronic catalogs, advertisements, and product information requires the same set of electronic publishing tools, as the author of an electronic document or digital object for a digital library.

In the ultimate "wired" society; collaborative design and manufacturing could decompose to hundreds of specialty firms that meet, negotiate and contract with each other over the network, which they would then use to purchase, sell, distribute, and assemble the various components that make up a product or service. Policies regarding customer satisfaction and return should be negotiated prior to this activity, and made part of the contract between buyer and seller. For larger, more complex, orders, distribution may involve more than two parties and entail complicated distribution coordination strategies. An ancillary distribution service involves acting as a fiduciary, and holding goods, certificates, bonds, stocks, etc., in trust. Account activity is particularly important to corporate customers and suppliers. Both buyer and seller must reconcile all electronic transactions in the accounts receivable and accounts payable, inventory information, and accounting systems.

In the information age, a large percent of the commerce will never be embodied physically. Information products are enabled by information technology and not just distributed more efficiently by it. These products can consist not just of electronic publications, catalogs, videos and the like, but can include interactive video games, software programs, electronic keys and tokens, customized design specifications, even electronic keys that can open to hotel rooms, cars, storage compartments, and airport boarding gates.

Furthermore, these information products are not just created entirely by the service provider, but can be designed or customized by the customer, adding a customer-driven activity call "design" to the purchase cycle. Indeed, information products can be continuously added to, modified, and morphed, as they pass along a chain of users. It is also likely that for these products ordering, billing, payment, and distribution would likely all happen simultaneously. Some micro-payment schemes for use over the Internet have been proposed that are significantly weaker than those being proposed for the more traditional payment schemes. The argument is that one can safely sacrifice security for processing efficiency when the transactions are low value enough.

The argument is that it is much more important to minimize the amount of computational and communications resources needed to effect payment than to ensure the integrity of the transaction—that the loss of a penny here or there will not be consequential enough to matter. But, this may not be the case when the revenue is being allocated across many parties, each getting only a small portion of the payment, and where the profit margins may be extremely thin. The user acceptability of these new forms of payment is also questionable. Advocates point to gas meters, and telephone bills, as proof of the acceptance of bills with small payments based on usage.

But, the complexity of these bills certainly pale by comparison to the sorts of bills that users might expect to see in some future "wired" world of micro-payments. Imagine sitting down to reconcile a bill comprised of thousand of penny items. Each item is small enough, but the total will probably be large enough to command attention. Also, these all these examples of usage billing are coming from businesses that have been run as a monopoly - the user has had no other alternative offered them. When given the choice, users have often opted for a more certain, fixed flat fee, even if that fee is slightly greater than their historical usage pattern. The cost of usage billing and accounting may be unacceptably high in the future economics of the "wired" society.

For example, it has been argued that a significant portion of the cost of operating the telephone and utility infrastructure today is due to the imposition of usage metering and accounting hardware and systems, and that more nimble companies offering equivalent services based on a flat fee, could operate equivalent service at much lower cost. Electronic commerce transactions currently involve all manner of devices (e.g., phone, fax, POS - point-of-sale device) and media (e.g., electronic data, image, voice, paper), and networks (cable, wire, satellite, cellular) over which they will be delivered, so the system infrastructure must accommodate all of these devices, media and communications networks, without degrading them to the lowest common denominator.

Opening up digital libraries to all these devices, at of course a greatly reduced functionality on some of the less capable devices, might still be a capability worth looking into. It would better bridge the gap between the real physical world and the future "wired" world, and it would dramatically increase the accessibility of the digital library to a much wider population faster, including the more disadvantaged citizens. The electronic commerce domain has a large quantity of legacy systems which it needs to interface to, and ultimately phase-out, as it evolves to more modern systems, applications and processes.

These legacy systems and processes will not go away overnight, and a successful electronic commerce infrastructure must allow the user to easily and transparently transfer between and switch back and forth between the new all electronic, and the older, hybrid legacy systems and processes. Digital Libraries also need to deal with similar legacy issues. A convergence of several factors has recently lifted digital libraries and electronic commerce to the promise of a new level of utility and viability. These factors include the increased availability of communications and communications bandwidth, the reduced cost and increased user-friendliness of computers and communications, the growth of the Internet and on-line services, and the drive toward global competitiveness.

There are however, a number of standardized services that are needed to fully realize their complete potential. Most of these services are common to many different applications, including electronic commerce and digital libraries. Most of the current solutions being prototyped over the Internet, all vary in their approach to security and privacy, their ability to handle micro-payments, and their applicability to various types of transactions. They also differ in their business models - for example, in their pricing strategy and in their assumptions as to who bears the risk in case of insufficient funds or disputes.

A truly interoperable common infrastructure, for applications such as electronic commerce and digital libraries, would allow parties to conduct their transactions in private, without paying any fees to intermediaries unless they provide some real added value, such as credit or search services. This infrastructure would make it easier for any and all interested persons to become service providers as well as consumers. The infrastructure must be based on a common set of services and standards that ensure interoperability. Preferably, these services and standards can be used as standard building blocks that service providers and application designers can combine, enhance, and customize.

Digital Conservancies

Digital Conservancies have been widely encouraged by governments, through tax regulations. With the increased attention that businesses and individuals are paying to the value of knowledge assets, it should be no surprise the conservancy metaphor is now being extended to intellectual property (IP). Intellectual Property Conservancies (IPCs) are a new idea, being conceived as a means to provide public benefits by making digital content donated, or licensed to them, freely available and by ensuring its long-term preservation. IPCs are digital libraries and therefore have all the problems associated with digital libraries.

An IPC will also need to attract those who would not be inclined to give away access rights without persuasive arguments of the benefits to them. Several strategies can be employed to convince them. Tax benefits are central to land conservancies and historic trusts, but it is not clear whether meaningful tax benefits will, in fact, be available for Intellectual Property Conservancies. If the original creator of the intellectual property (an author, artist or inventor) donates it, current tax laws restrict them to writing off the value of the raw materials that were consumed in its creation. If the donor is an owner who has paid to acquire an intellectual property right, outright donation of the intellectual property should be eligible for a tax credit.

Concepts such as 'easements', however, though well established in tax law for real property, are novel ideas in intellectual property law and will, at the very least, need to be tested with tax authorities. They may well need to be legislated. Providing public access to free-to-read content is a way to promote value-added content. In the physical bookstore, we often browse a book, or listen to a few tracks of a CD, before making a purchase. Free-to-read online content may serve this same purpose. One challenge to an IPC will be to develop a model for free-to-read functionality that is accepted by publishers as not unduly competitive with their value-added products, and by online readers as useful in its own right.

The IPC concept will be viable if at least some publishers are willing to provide a level of free-to-read access as a means of promoting their value-added products. The IPC will need to protect the publishers' interests in order to obtain an early donation of limited rights and, as the threat to a publishers' commercial interests subsides, the promise to make more valuable access available over time. Individual IP owners will readily appreciate the benefits of making a gift of rights to an organization that ensures their work a sort of immortality. But an IPC can also attract publishers with the benefits of perpetual access.

Publishers who provide free-to-read content on their web sites are faced with a new liability—either they have to keep their digital content online and free (which costs them money if it doesn't continue to sell) or they need to take it down. It makes sense to give the limited rights-to-read to an IPC early in the life of the intellectual property, thereby avoiding the liability and reaping the reward of public service.

Since the mission of the IPC is to make content to which it has rights easily available online, and its promise to the owners of that IP is to make the free-to-read content easy to find, an IPC needs to invest in rich descriptive metadata to make its content readily discoverable on the web. If, by donating content to an IPC, IP owners cannot only make the availability of their intellectual property better known, but also acquire metadata about their own properties in standard formats, they would have substantial incentives to donate content to an IPC. IPCs, like other non-profits seeking donations from the general public, will need to provide concrete benefits to supporters in order to maintain a sufficient stream of financial contributions. A "membership" organization gives public supporters a sense of belonging and of receiving concrete, perhaps even personal, benefits. A newsletter and the web site that communicate news of the success of the IPC and review recent additions to the properties it holds, would be attractive to many such general members.

An IPC may also need to solicit cash donations from intellectual property owners to help pay the costs of digitizing, transforming, or cataloging gifts of intellectual property that are not suitable for digital delivery or preservation in their current form. Individual IP donors, in particular, may need to help bear these costs since metadata creation for their donations will be a one-off cost and the transaction costs are likely to be higher. But even donors of large quantities of IP may need to be asked to contribute financially for an IPC to absorb a sizable gift in a reasonable time. The most critical issue in the success of an IPC is probably the technical characteristics of the Intellectual Properties it acquires.

If selective, the IPC could obtain content in a way that enables it to deliver the content in the future without substantial additional investment and to offer a range of value added views without requiring costly intervention. Without careful selection, an IPC could be saddled with overwhelming costs to initially capture the data in usable formats, transform what it receives, or to manage the digital data over time. Its presumed digital assets would instead become liabilities that could far exceed its likely resources.

One of the most costly factors in acquiring content is negotiating the terms and conditions for its donation and subsequent use. But depending on what those terms and conditions are, the cost of administering access could also be very high. Contractual terms that define a limited number of concrete levels of rights (for example, rights to provide free public access one page at a time and print the page being viewed) must be easily translated into levels of functionality. With such fixed levels of rights, a donor could agree on a sequence of further future rights releases. It is critical that the donation of different levels of functionality, and the progressive release of further permissions over time, not result in additional operational costs for an IPC. Metadata captured up front must interact with the format captured up front to dictate levels of functionality.

Some formats of donated content will require substantial investment to make them usable online, or to be kept online in perpetuity. Hence, an IPC needs to consider the risks involved in selection, based on decisions about what formats to acquire. Text and image can be delivered with layered public-access-level functionality using existing web-based distribution servers. An IPC must have defined rights adequate to make content available to users under some terms, but it need not own the IP to do so. If a donation with some access or development limits is accepted by the IPC, the donor is brought into a relationship with the Conservancy that might also be translated later into donations of further public rights.

Conditional agreements and agreements to release content for free public viewing at a future date, are common in archives. In such a case, the property owner would provide the IPC with a copy, but the specific rights granted to the IPC would only come into effect at a designated time or under specific conditions. One of the benefits of an IPC is that it promises to keep IP always available, while the current system of publishing makes much IP difficult to obtain. Metadata management will be critical to an IPC's success. Like any Digital Library it needs to invest in discovery (content description) metadata. An IPC must additionally invest substantially in rights management metadata and technical (migration specification) metadata.

While the IPC can rely on natural partners in the library community to help provide descriptive metadata for simple resource discovery (such as Dublin Core metadata), it also needs to be able to incorporate metadata conforming to standards in the publishing community. IPC needs to manage a digital artifact over time. As such, it needs to determine what metadata will need to be acquired and kept for long-term preservation. Where the content resides is more than simply an operational consideration for an IPC.

IP owners prefer that the digital data be located on their own servers; the terms of the gift would ensure that, should the IP owner fail to keep it available, the IPC can shift access to its own servers. The benefits to the IPC suggest that an architecture enabling this kind of distributed access will be necessary. The fundamental objectives of an IPC are to offer free access to its catalog of intellectual property in perpetuity. For this, the IPC does not need to be the archival repository of the authentic, verifiable, record copy. Like a digital library, which holds a copy of a work and makes the accurate and full content available to users, the IPC doesn't claim to preserve contextual or structural authenticity.

Both an IPC and a digital library focus on preservation of content as required for preservation of public access and the right-to-read. Therefore an IPC need not preserve the initial delivery format, nor any particular subsequent delivery format. Instead, the IPC can return to its escrowed copy to generate a delivery copy in a new format, or move from one delivery format to the next, depending on cost and technology availability. Of course, an IPC still must make strategic decisions about when and how to convert data from one delivery and or long-term storage format to another, to keep the content accessible over time.

An implicit mission of computing science has been to make the benefits of computing technology of use to society at large. Missions, needs and capabilities now come together so that information users can have added assistance in performing research and in assuring the continuity of scholarship, today and in the future. It will take conscious, planned efforts by both librarianship and computing to make this happen. Many libraries are now trying to provide the increasing volume of scholarly electronic information to their clienteles.

Current information needs are being provided in electronic form with varying success in public, college and research libraries around the country and the world. Research libraries have only begun to take on the provision, organization and preservation of information with the same long-term commitment they have made for print materials. It is an expensive, uncharted and difficult task. But until the long-term commitments are undertaken, many currently proposed solutions will have only temporary effects. The ability of the scholarly community to give serious weight to electronic information depends upon their trust in such information being dependably available, with authenticity and integrity maintained.

Looked-for changes in scholarly publishing to help alleviate the serials crisis, for example, are usually thought to be bound up with the prestige of electronic journals in the academic tenure process. The ability of the academy to count on long-term, secure existence of electronic scholarly work will be an important determinant of the success of academic electronic publishing. Libraries and universities have a stake in helping electronic publishing to succeed, and therefore have an interest in establishing secure digital research libraries. Users' needs will continue to be what they long have been.

Users will want information reliably locatable, so that when they go there, they can expect to find what they're looking for. Users will want information easily accessible: the cataloging must be clear and accurate, and the information must be promptly retrievable. In the electronic environment the need for access tools will be more evident, and users will expect appropriate and standard software to be readily available. Users will expect information to be available that was placed in the library's care a long time ago; and they will expect that the integrity of the information they get from the library will be assured. Implementation of a Digital Research Library will require several specific tasks, broadly familiar to a computing audience, and three kinds of new commitments. A Digital Research Library will be manifest to users as collections of information existing in various places and accessible through the use of widely available tools.

The locus of information may be called the electronic storage repository; the access tools will be described below. Over time, we will learn how collection development plays out in an access environment as well as in an ownership environment. It is sometimes loosely proposed that libraries need not acquire electronic information, for it will be available somewhere on the network. Such proposals ignore the obvious truth that some institution must still, in the end, take responsibility for the information. That has always been a definition of the library responsibility.

There will be many electronic storage repositories, responding both to requirements of redundancy and to the individual needs of institutions. In contrast to print collections, it is unlikely that there will be a high degree of content duplication across many electronic repositories, since for most purposes existence in a single place allows world-wide access.

2

Digital Resources

The Internet has grown and evolved rapidly over recent years. Growth and evolution are continuing, and are bringing great uncertainty. It is difficult to make quantitative forecasts about the Internet with any confidence. The Internet has evolved in recent years from a predominantly academic network into today's increasingly generalised and increasingly commercialised network. Its structures - standards, decision-making processes, and physical infrastructure - mostly evolved to suit the relatively small academic community rather than today's large and growing general commercial network. There are several measures of Internet size and growth, all imperfect. The two most relevant are the numbers of servers connected to the Internet and the numbers of users.

The number of servers is routinely measured by network programs which check electronic directories and which validate them by attempting to confirm the existence of servers. There is growing commercial interest in using the Internet as a medium for publishing and storing journals. The British Library currently has a presence on the Internet in the form of its Portico service. This service currently contains some 560 "pages" of information. Portico mostly holds information about the Library rather than displaying holdings. The Internet, and digital media generally, offer opportunities for the Library to distribute knowledge of its catalogue easily and efficiently.

In practice, this means that readers of all kinds could be expected to have improved access to the catalogues. This improved access would increase the demand for items from the collection, and hence for reading room space. The Library historically has made its catalogues widely available, for example on microfilm. There is considerable anecdotal evidence that improved access to catalogues results in increased demand for reading room space. Other features of digital resources will decrease demand. Specifically, readers will not occupy reading room space while awaiting delivery of requested items; and the digital medium facilitates searching, counting, extracting, cross-referencing, and other functions related to some forms of research.

The relative magnitudes of these effects will vary according to the materials involved. Access to the Library's resources within reading rooms introduces several conflicting effects. There is no quantitative basis for estimating any change in demand for reading room space, but given the conflicting trends, the most reasonable guess is that the effect will be roughly neutral. The term "BL resources" today would probably be understood to mean any items deposited at or acquired by the Library. This includes not only heritage collections but current publications such as scholarly journals.

Increasingly, current publications are being made available in digital form; so it is likely that some of the fastest-growing collections of digital works at the Library will be in the form of current serials and monographs which are deposited or acquired in digital format. As with access to digital resources inside reading rooms, only some readers will be able to use digital resources remotely; others will always require paper originals.

Role of Hybrid Library

The hybrid library tries to use the technologies available to bring things together into a library reflecting the best of both worlds. The hybrid library is on the continuum between the conventional and digital library, where electronic and paper-based information sources are used alongside each other. The challenge associated with the management of the hybrid library is to encourage end-user resource discovery and information use, in a variety of formats and from a number of local and remote sources, in a seamlessly integrated way. The hybrid library should be designed to bring a range of technologies from different sources together in the context of a working library, and also to begin to explore integrated systems and services in both the electronic and print environments.

The hybrid library should not, then, be seen as nothing more than an uneasy transitional phase between the conventional library and digital library but, rather, as a worthwhile model in its own right, which can be usefully developed and improved. This kind of library has been given other labels. The concept of the gateway library, for instance, seems to be one which describes a similar idea.

Hybrid Electronic Access and Delivery in the Library Networked Environment (HeadLine) is a 3-year programme, undertaken by the London School of Economics, the London Business School, and the University of Hertfordshire. It aims to design and implement a working model of the hybrid library in actual academic environments, providing access to a wide range of library materials, regardless of physical form, from a single web interface. The user-centered model employed by HeadLine defines authentication as a predominant issue, since the system must store information about users and their personal preferences, as well as details of resources they have rights to access by virtue of their membership of a given academic community.

In this respect, HeadLine seeks to link otherwise disparate sources of data—which may range from institutional MIS databases to browser bookmarks files—that serve to define users attributes and preferences. Authentication therefore plays a key, dual role: firstly, in securing personal data privacy, and secondly, in controlling which resources may be used. A major goal of HeadLine is the promotion of the single sign-on approach for access to networked information resources: once authenticated into a HeadLine system, the user should not be required to supply further passwords for subsequent resource access or requests.

Moreover, this facility should function consistently, independent of the user's current location. HeadLine therefore engages directly with the complexities of differing schemes of access control for resources available over an open network infrastructure. The creation of a practical, robust, yet flexible authentication model will depend on its simultaneous ability to address users as individuals and to conform to current and future developments in computer access control technology. Authentication establishes the identity of a user within a given context; its companion process—authorization—controls the levels of permitted access to resources for that user identity.

Network operating systems inherently provide this degree of administrative control; however, their locus of influence is confined to the organizations that deploy them. The open network environment of the Internet operates without any such centralised, enclosing authentication scheme; the new era of ubiquitous networked information services has rapidly exposed the limitations of authentication techniques in common use for the past three decades. Problems inevitably arise as users attempt to move between resources where different access restrictions apply.

Traditional techniques of access control employing user identifier and password combinations are becoming unsustainable due to their high administrative overhead and practical shortcomings: loss, unauthorized transfer, or theft. The password proliferation scenario familiar to librarians, information managers, IT personnel and computer users themselves is symptomatic of this problem. A number of current, widely deployed access control techniques, such as IP address filtering, rely upon a continuity of identification rather than upon an absolute identification of an individual.

HeadLine aims to formulate an authentication model that can encompass the need to store users' attributes and data privacy whilst remaining sufficiently extensible to incorporate subsequent developments in third-party authentication methodologies. Many enabling technologies already exist which can be used to achieve this deep integration. However, in some key areas there is currently an absence of tools. There is, perhaps most significantly, an absence of standards-based ways of communicating with many external services.

In an ideal world, these would be supplied by the data providers themselves in the form of an Application Programming Interface (API). Agora is developing a hybrid library management system (HLMS) to provide integrated access to heterogeneous discovery, location, request and delivery services. Agora is led by the University of East Anglia, with UKOLN, Fretwell-Downing Informatics, and CERLIM (the Centre for Research in Library and Information Management) as partners. A prototype system has been made available to provide a focus for development.

It encompasses a range of social science resources, including abstract and indexing services, library catalogues, archive databases and subject gateways. It will demonstrate two scenarios: cross-domain searching for mixed media with authentication; and search through to delivery for monographs and serials. The feedback on the Agora prototype will be sought from professional staff at the library associate sites. The Agora broker is based on the MODELS Information Architecture (MIA). This is a conceptual framework for managing distributed services. MIA suggests some principal components of such systems and provides a common vocabulary for both systems developers and information managers.

In implementing MIA, Agora will be exploring some key areas of concern for distributed service development. It is hoped to find some workable and scalable solutions which will be shared with the relevant communities via targeted dissemination activities. Most libraries today are, in fact, already hybrid libraries—they own and subscribe to a range of resources and services which are supplied in a variety of formats and media: print monographs and serials, electronic journals, abstract and indexing services on CD-ROM, music CD-ROMs, etc.

Many electronic resources are accessed on remote servers. An increasing number of end-users are also accessing these services from outside the home institution: users and services are both distributed. However, there is currently no uniform way of managing and providing integrated access to these hybrid resources. Users are forced to interact with each service individually and waste time in repeating the same steps to search different systems. At the same time, using different interfaces also increases the risk of inefficiencies—such as failure to discover relevant resources because of unfamiliarity with one service's idiosyncrasies.

In a discover/locate/request cycle, the user will also be forced to re-enter the same data when he or she moves from one stage to the next. Agora is using the Z39.50 protocol as the 'glue' to link services together and provide true integrated access via a single interface. Although Agora is principally concerned with developing an infrastructure for managing hybrid libraries, the development of understanding and the acquisition of new hybrid library management skills are equally important to producing a working demonstrator.

Consequently, the Agora hybrid library management system will be a key tool for demonstrating potential service scenarios to a range of library and information communities. The issues facing these hybrid library are those facing all library and information services. The aspects of their programmes the writers have chosen to highlight here are now—and will continue to be—at the centre of contemporary information provision.

Many archives' most significant holdings are not commercially produced recordings but are unpublished recordings of various types. Such works include radio broadcast recordings, television sound tracks, "live" musical or dramatic performances, ethnographic field recordings, and interviews. It is in these recordings in which rights issues are most complex and in need of study, and perhaps adaptation, as they relate to preservation. When a for-profit or nonprofit corporate body, such as a broadcast network/station/producer or a music producer, creates these unpublished recordings, that body often owns the rights to the recording.

As with commercially distributed published recordings, unpublished recordings are usually interpretations of music or literary underlying works that are commonly protected by copyright. In the United States, federal copyright protection was not available for sound recordings until 1972. However, state and common laws protect these recordings until the year 2067, no matter when they were created. This means that, in effect, the law grants greater protection to sound recordings than to print materials.

The radical transformations that have made digital formats the predominant form of sound recording have made available to the public more types of sound recordings, and greater numbers of hours of audio, than ever before. As a result, research library administrators responsible for collection development policies must regularly reevaluate their long-range goals as well as their day-to-day acquisitions. No longer are acquisitions limited to physical items offered by retailers and in catalogs, or bought on their behalf by contracted purchasing representatives.

Rather, librarians and archivists face a plethora of technologies, platforms, and genres. In the consumer arena, the digital audio revolution began in the early 1980s, when the compact audio disc format was introduced. Public adoption of the CD format burgeoned beyond anyone's expectations. The public, and libraries, were attracted by the lack of surface noise and hiss that was commonly heard on LP and 78-rpm records and cassette tapes and by the CDs' touted invulnerability to normal wear.

The sound on compact discs was criticized by audiophiles, collectors with high-end playback equipment, and other consumers, but most consumers never heard their arguments or the aural evidence. In fact, the 44-MHz, 16-bit sampling rate, or amount of compression, selected by the creators of the compact discs was a compromise that sacrificed sound quality at the expense of time capacity of the discs.

Initially, the content of compact discs replicated that of the LP discs they would supersede. However, record companies gained significant profits from the re-release of older catalog issues, in addition to new releases. Serious sound archives dedicated to documenting the history of music and sound recording continue to acquire LP and 78-rpm discs for their unique repertoire and their audio quality. Stored properly, these discs will last many years, but they deteriorate from repeated playback. Moreover, high-quality disc playback equipment is expensive. With compact discs came myriad recording reissues.

The complete recording careers of hundreds of notable classical, jazz, blues, and rock artists have been thoroughly documented on thousands of CD reissues.

These discs and sets have enabled libraries to build research-level, encyclopedic collections of important musicians and recording artists. These are recordings that libraries might not have obtained otherwise, either because of inaccessibility or the expense of obtaining and maintaining the original records. Two important points related to reissues must be emphasized. The first is that most comprehensive jazz, blues, and classical reissues are produced outside of the United States in countries where older recordings are no longer protected by copyright.

In most European countries, the copyright on a sound recording is 50 years from the original date of recording. Although liberal foreign copyright laws enable publication of thousands of previously out-of-print recordings, the quality of these reissues varies greatly. While the producers of comprehensive reissues make thorough searches to locate one copy of every recording an artist has made, the copy used is often generations away from the master recording and is in only mediocre condition. To compensate for the condition of the source recordings, many producers of reissues misrepresent the original recordings with signal processing: overuse of noise reduction, sound equalization, and limiting tools in order to reduce the surface noise found on the source.

Today, many archives are rethinking their acquisitions policies, preservation techniques, and delivery systems. The sheer number of new audio materials made available through the World Wide Web is astounding.

Digital Environment

Digital information environment in metacommunity needs to develop a dynamic paradigm that draws on those of its constituent communities. However, the metacommunity must also understand and account for the distinctiveness of the societal roles and missions of the different information professions as the boundaries among their practices and collections begin to blur. The archival community is one of the smallest and, arguably, the least well understood of the professional communities working in the digital information environment and in knowledge management in general.

The archival community comprises practicing archivists, manuscript curators, archival academics, and policy makers who work to define and promote the social utility of records and to identify, preserve, and provide access to documentary heritage regardless of format. Archival holdings are noncurrent organizational records of enduring value that are preserved by the archives of the creating organization. Manuscript collections, however, are also often collocated with archival holdings. Manuscript collections are unpublished materials that are created or gathered by an organization or individual but are transferred from the original custodian to an archives, a historical society, or university library. The archival perspective brings an evidence-based approach to the management of recorded knowledge.

It is fundamentally concerned with the organizational and personal processes and contexts through which records and knowledge are created as well as the ways in which records individually and collectively reflect those processes. This perspective distinguishes the archival community from other communities of information professionals that manage decontextualized information and tend to be focused more on users, systems, or institutions. Exhortations for archivists to move beyond customary custodial roles and become advocates for information that must be preserved because of its enduring legal, fiscal, administrative, research or other societal value reflect a growing awareness among archivists that along with their concern for the nature of the materials, there is a critical need to promote the materials' long-term requirements and enduring value to society.

Over the past two centuries, a range of information institutions have evolved that play distinct roles within society. These roles reflect the many ways in which information is created, used, valued, preserved, and disposed of by individuals, organizations, and communities in the conduct of business, scholarship, learning, and personal affairs. Libraries are engaged in the tangible activities of identifying, acquiring, preserving, and providing access to published information. They are also engaged in less tangible, value-laden activities such as promoting intellectual freedom and serving as focal points for various communities.

Asserting individual institutional or professional differences always carries with it the potential to confuse the user and impede interoperability. It is important, however, to recognize that variant practices have arisen for sound intellectual and pragmatic reasons as institutions have fulfilled their various societal roles and managed their collections from diverse but equally legitimate perspectives. A new paradigm needs to be created that will facilitate the right blend of commonality and distinctiveness. Archival institutions serve an important legal function in society.

Archival institutions are generally legally constituted entities responsible for identifying, managing, and preserving the integrity of an institution's official records of long-term value. These activities prove the actions of the institution and provide essential protection for the institution's legal rights and those of its constituents or the general citizenry. Archival institutions enable legally constituted access to records, access that must also constantly address a range of legal concerns that become more pressing in the digital environment.

These concerns include intellectual property, the privacy of individuals mentioned in materials, the conditions under which certain types of materials can be accessed and made available, and the protection of the integrity of digital materials from accidental or deliberate tampering. Concern for retaining the evidential value of records has placed the archival community at the vanguard of research and development in digital preservation and authentication. Archives focus on records, archivists have an awareness of the societal, institutional, and individual construction of memory and an understanding of the implications of how that memory is represented and transmitted over time.

This awareness becomes increasingly important as more of the world's collections are reformatted and represented online. It is also important for retaining evidence in time and over time, especially through digital preservation processes. Libraries have focused predominantly on the organization, dissemination, and use of existing information, archives focus on these activities too, but are also intimately engaged in the creation of information and its ultimate disposition.

Since the 1960s, the archival community has worked closely with the creators of records and record-keeping systems to develop means to identify and preserve digital records that have no paper counterpart. The problem of what to do about records that are born digital has forced archivists to reexamine and reinvent their principles and practices in light of a digital challenge that emerged before the advent of digital libraries. Archival theory, methodology, and practice together constitute archival science. Because archival science is scholarly as well as practical and uses a distinct methodology to gain knowledge, it can be considered both a discipline and a profession.

The disciplinary and professional aspects of archival science together compose the archival paradigm—a set of assumptions, principles, and practices that are common to the archival community and are a model for its activities and outlook. Although archives have existed for thousands of years, much of the archival paradigm—not unlike that of library science—coalesced between the mid-nineteenth and twentieth centuries. The archival paradigm has been extensively influenced by the so-called auxiliary and ancillary disciplines—diplomatics, history, law, textual criticism, management and organizational theory, and library science.

Perhaps most influential have been the research methods of modern scientific history and legal theories of evidence that developed during the nineteenth century largely from diplomatics. Diplomatics was developed to help establish the authenticity of medieval ecclesiastical records. It is the study of the genesis, forms, and transmission of archival documents; their relation to the facts represented in them; and their relation to their creator, in order to identify, evaluate, and communicate their true nature.

As a result of these influences, most of the archival community working with public records focused on developing principles for archival arrangement and description that emphasized the organic nature of records and the circumstances of their creation. The manuscript community and some national archives, however, adopted bibliographic practices of subject control. The bifurcation of public archives and historical manuscript descriptive practices in the United States can most easily be explained in terms of prospective use and archival setting. For archivists administering records programs within their own institutions, the primary uses of records were legal proof and administrative research, often conducted by the records creators.

For those engaged in manuscript administration, the focus was on secondary use by historical scholars, often in a research library, where there was more pressure to apply bibliographic models of description. Arguably, therefore, library science has influenced archival science less through the contribution of specific practices than through the encouragement of greater emphasis on access and user orientation. Archivists and the bibliographic community worked together to increase use and facilitate access to archival and manuscript holdings. Although MARC AMC was widely adopted by university archivists as well as many state and local historical repositories, many archivists were not comfortable with what they perceived to be the forcing of archival descriptive practices into a data structure that was still essentially bibliographic.

In 1993, encoded archival description (EAD), which took the core archival descriptive tool—the finding aid—and used it to develop a standard generalized mark-up language (SGML) document type definition. This definition could be used to disseminate archival descriptive information on the World Wide Web and could be mapped onto other kinds of descriptive metadata in digital information resources. In the United States, where archival practice developed later than in Europe, a whole new focus on the management of current records emerged between the 1930s and 1960s.

Faced with vast quantities of modern records generated by two world wars and a huge federal bureaucracy and with early adoption of new record-keeping and reproduction technologies, archivists at the National Archives realized that they could not possibly keep everything. Thus, they developed revolutionary approaches that engaged archivists at the point of record creation in identifying active records of long-term value and arranging for the orderly retiring of inactive records.

This development had two important consequences: the addition to the archival paradigm of a new set of theories relating to life cycle management of records and appraisal and the establishment of the records management profession with the founding in 1956 of the American Records Management Association. From the 1970s until the early 1990s, the archival community in the United States hotly debated the extent to which archival principles and practices were based in theory versus expediency.

Archivists needed to cope with emerging electronic record-keeping technologies, new modes of scholarly research and increasing user expectations that archivists should provide automated information access. Archivists are closely aligned with professions such as law, history, journalism, anthropology, and archaeology. Evidence in the archival sense can be defined as the passive ability of documents and objects and their associated contexts to provide insight into the processes, activities, and events that led to their creation for legal, historical, archaeological, and other purposes. The concern for evidence permeates all archival activities and demands complex approaches to the management of information; it also sets high benchmarks for information systems and services, particularly with respect to archival description and preservation.

Recently, the paramount importance of identifying and maintaining the evidential value of archival materials has been reemphasized, partly as a result of the challenges posed by electronic records but partly also to differentiate the information and preservation practices of the archival community from those of the library community. The integrity of the evidential value of materials is ensured by demonstrating an unbroken chain of custody, precisely documenting the aggregation of archival materials as received from their creator and integrated with the rest of the archives' holdings of the same provenance, and tracking all preservation activities associated with the materials. Jenkinson described this process as the physical and moral defense of the record.

The primary values of archival records are related to the legal, fiscal, and administrative purposes of the records creators; the secondary values are related to subsequent researchers. Schellenberg argued that the secondary values of public records can be ascertained most easily if they are considered in relation to "the evidence they contain of the organization and functioning of the Government body that produced them, and the information they contain on persons, corporate bodies, things [e.g., places, buildings, physical objects], problems, conditions, and the like, with which the Government dealt." His argument acknowledges both the strict legal requirements of records that must be satisfied by archival processes and the wider concept of historical and cultural evidence that is contained in the materials and can be interpreted by secondary users.

The archival concern for the description and preservation of evidence involves a rich understanding of the implicit and explicit values of materials at creation and over time. It also involves an acute awareness of how such values can be diminished or lost when the integrity of materials is compromised. Evidential value in the widest sense is reflected to some extent in any information artifact, but only a subset of all information is subject to legal or regulatory requirements concerning creation and maintenance. Publications, for example, can be analyzed for evidence of the motivations and processes associated with their creation by studying their physical and intellectual form, examining different editions of the same work, and learning about the history of the publishing house or printer that produced them.

Primary sources particularly lend themselves to such kinds of analysis and interpretation, and such materials are increasingly being incorporated into digital information resources. Maintaining the evidential value of information is important not only to creators of materials that are subject to legal or regulatory requirements but also to many researchers. In particular, reformatting, description, and preservation need to be considered. Information professionals involved in digitally reformatting their collections must understand when a user may need to work with the original information object to appreciate some intrinsic characteristic, such as the weight of the paper; when a digital copy will do; and whether a copy needs to be high or low resolution, color or black and white.

Information professionals must also decide how much of a collection needs to be digitized and what kind of metadata will enable a user to place information objects in context. Archival practice places a premium on both collective and contextual description. The key is to explain the physical aspects and intellectual structure of the collection that may not be apparent and to provide enough contextual information for the user to understand the historical circumstances and organizational processes of the object's creation.

Digital preservation techniques have moved beyond a concern for the longevity of digital media to a concern for the preservation of the information stored in those media during recurrent migration to new software and hardware. In the process, many of the intrinsic characteristics of information objects can disappear—data structures can be modified and presentation of the object on a computer screen can be altered.

Archivists have had difficulty establishing the provenance of records of multi-institutional collaborations or those contained in multifunctional databases and distributed information systems. In archival appraisal, more sophisticated conceptions of provenance, such as functional provenance and multiprovenance, have been developed for electronic records that apply business process analysis and functional decomposition. Functional provenance views the business function through which a record came into being as that record's provenance rather than the office or individual creating the record.

In archival description, developments such as EAD and the Australian series system recognize that a one-to-many relationship may exist for groups of records created by changing bureaucratic structures. Taken together, respect des fonds, provenance, and original order ensure that the intellectual integrity of aggregations of records is maintained and that individual records are always contextualized. Adhering to these principles is a less resource-intensive way of providing access to high-volume collections than are classifying by subject and cataloging of individual documents.

Considerable cataloging expertise and the availability of specialized standardized vocabularies are required for correct and consistent assignment of subject access points to heterogeneous unsynthesized and unpublished materials. Because the language used in archival materials is often archaic or technical, assigning a modern subject term that accurately reflects the concepts being expressed in the records can be difficult. On the basis of their insight about how users working with historical and organizational materials might wish to search, archivists have broadened the notion of subject access, suggesting access points such as temporal and geographic coverage and form of material.

The archival approach offers the concepts of collective arrangement and description according to the provenance of the materials; these provide benefits even when information managers or users are not interested in the evidential value of the materials. Applying these concepts makes it possible to unite related digital, nondigital, and predigital materials according to their intellectual rather than their physical characteristics. These concepts build context, which is a powerful and underused tool for facilitating understanding and ultimately creating knowledge. They prompt the user to consider the degree to which the material's source is authoritative.

The intellectual interrelationships of active and archival records are established by integrating metadata from active records into the archival authority's information system. The practices of many information communities focus on the best and most cost-effective ways to organize and retrieve discrete information objects. Archival practice assumes that materials within a fond can be most effectively organized and retrieved collectively. Although collective management and description are pragmatic ways to gain basic levels of control over large quantities of heterogeneous information, for archivists the rationale behind these practices lies in the inherent characteristics of records and other materials that are the by-product of human activities.

When materials are generated by the activity of an individual or organization, an interdependent relationship exists between the materials and their creator. A complex web of relationships also exists between the materials and the historical, legal, and procedural contexts of their development as well as among all materials created by the same activity. The organic nature of records refers to all these interrelationships, and archival practices are designed to collectively document, capture, and exploit them.

These practices recognize that the value of an individual record is derived in part from the sequence of records within which it is located. They also recognize that it can be difficult to understand an individual record without understanding its historical, legal, procedural, and documentary context. The perspective gained from working with information collectively can also be applied to the description, preservation, and use of Web resources. Resources created on the Web are not unlike archival fonds in that they include a complex of hyperlinks to pages related by provenance, topic, or some other feature.

An advantage in the Web environment is that hyperlinks are explicit rather than largely implicit, as is the case with paper records. As a result, those who manage and use these resources can more easily identify and exploit organic relationships. A Web page without its hyperlinks may be less valuable to users because of its diminished evidential content. Recent developments in information organization have exploited the structure of information content and its metadata to provide smarter access to materials, especially those that are hard to locate by subject or keyword. This is particularly evident in efforts to apply extensible mark-up language (XML) to develop structures that are more predictable for Web resources and in the application of the text encoding initiative for the SGML encoding of literary and historical texts. Structure can be both intellectual and physical; it can exist within an information object, collections of information objects, and descriptions of those information objects.

Archival practices explicitly recognize the existence of such structures and exploit those that are hierarchical. Developing and using hierarchies are intuitive ways for humans to model information; as a result, much information and many information systems have hierarchical characteristics. To ascertain authenticity, archivists use principles derived from diplomatics to analyze how the intellectual form of records reflects the functions by which they were created.

Archival description, through inventories and registers collectively referred to as finding aids, has traditionally reflected these hierarchies. In the digital environment, hierarchical and collective description lend themselves to hierarchical and object-oriented metadata structures such as SGML. The archival community is making significant contributions to research and development in the digital information environment by using integrity, metadata, knowledge management, risk management, and knowledge preservation. Each area is discussed below with reference to recent and ongoing projects in which the archival community has played a leading role in setting the agenda or integrating the archival perspective.

Interoperability

Interoperability among heterogeneous collections is a central theme of the Core Integration. The potential collections have a wide variety of data types, metadata standards, protocols, authentication schemes, and business models. They are managed by large numbers of organizations, some of which have grants from the NSF, but most of which are independent. Some are well funded, but many have limited resources. Some were established specifically for education, but most are not designed primarily for education. All have their own priorities. The Site for Science strategy for interoperability was first articulated in a memorandum that was distributed among the Core Integration demonstration projects in fall 2000. The goal of interoperability is to build coherent services for users, from components that are technically different and managed by different organizations. This requires agreements to cooperate at three levels: technical, content and organizational.

— Technical agreements cover formats, protocols, security systems, etc., so that messages can be exchanged.

— Content agreements cover the data and metadata, and include semantic agreements on the interpretation of the information.

— Organizational agreements cover the ground rules for access, preservation of collections and services, payment, authentication, etc.

Defining these agreements is hard, but the central challenge is to create incentives for independent digital libraries to adopt them. The traditional approach to interoperability is for all participants to agree to use the same standards. If each service implements a comprehensive set of standards then interoperability follows. However, experience has shown that interoperability through comprehensive standardization is hard to achieve.

Adoption of common standards provides digital libraries with valuable functionality, but at a cost. Some costs are directly financial: the purchase of equipment and software, or hiring and training staff. More often the largest costs are organizational. Rarely can a single aspect of a digital library be changed in isolation. Introducing a new standard requires inter-related changes to existing systems, altered work flow, changed relationships with suppliers, and so on. It is important to recognize that there is no best point on these curves. Every point is optimal for some purpose.

For example, libraries have developed a framework for interoperability based on the Z39.50 protocol, the Anglo American Cataloguing Rules and MARC. This combination of standards provides an excellent choice for libraries, because they value the functionality and have catalog records in this form, but the cost of adopting these standards is high unless an organization already has metadata that meets them. Hence, few other collections of information on the Internet have adopted these standards because, for most other organizations, the cost of adoption is high relative to the functionality gained.

A heterogeneous digital library, such as the NSDL, will include some collections that support powerful standards, such as Z39.50 or SGML, but must expect that most collections will use standards with lower functionality, such as HTTP or HTML, because of the lower cost of adoption. Current research and development on web information systems and digital libraries are often aimed at such changes. For instance, text-based applications clearly gain functionality if they support a range of scripts beyond English. There are three levels of digital library interoperability:

- Federation
- Harvesting
- Gathering

Federation

Federation can be considered the conventional approach to interoperability. In a federation, a group of organizations agree that their services will conform to certain specifications. The libraries that share online catalog records using Z39.50 are an example of a federation. Another federation is the ADEPT project for geospatial materials, led by the University of California at Santa Barbara, one of the partners in the Core Integration production team [Alexandria]. The principal challenge in forming a federation is the effort required by each organization to implement and keep current with all the agreements. Since the cost of participation is high, typical federations have small but dedicated memberships.

Harvesting

The difficulty of creating large federations is the motivation behind recent efforts to create looser groupings of digital libraries. The underlying concept is that the participants agree to take small efforts that enable some basic shared services, without being required to adopt a complete set of agreements. The Open Archives Initiative (OAI) is based around the concept of metadata harvesting. Each digital library makes metadata about its collections available in a simple exchange format.

This metadata can be harvested by service providers and built into services such as information discovery or reference linking. Two members of the Site for Science team act as the executive for the OAI, and Site for Science was one of the alpha test sites for the metadata harvesting protocol. Metadata harvesting was first developed by the Harvest project in the early 1990s, but the approach was not widely adopted.

The concept was revived in 1998/99 in a prototype known as the Universal Preprint Server. This prototype concluded in favor of metadata harvesting as a strategy to facilitate the creation of federated services across heterogeneous preprint systems. The OAI work, which is derived from this experiment, emphasizes the core functionality that can be achieved by digital libraries sharing metadata. It minimizes the cost by using a simple protocol based on HTTP, by providing software that is easily added to web servers, and by documentation, training and support.

While services built by metadata harvesting are usually less powerful than those provided by federations, the burden of participating is much less. As a result, many more organizations are likely to join and keep their systems current. This is confirmed by the rapid acceptance of the metadata harvesting protocol of the OAI.

Gathering

Even if the various organizations do not cooperate in any formal manner, a base level of interoperability is still possible by gathering openly accessible information using a web crawler. The premier examples of this approach are the web search engines. Because there is no cost to the collections, gathering can provide services that embrace large numbers of digital libraries, but the services are of poorer quality than can be achieved by partners who cooperate directly.

Some of the most interesting web research at present can be thought of as adding extra function to the base level, which will lead to better interoperability, even among totally non-cooperating organizations. Even though the concept of a fully semantic web is a pipe dream, it is reasonable to expect that the level of services that can be provided by gathering will improve steadily.

Metadata

In an ideal world all the collections and services that the NSDL wishes to encompass would support an agreed set of standard metadata. The real world is less simple. However, the NSDL does have influence. The prospect of obtaining NSF's funding provides useful incentive for collections. The Site for Science metadata strategy is based on two principles. The first is that metadata is too expensive for the Core Integration team to create much of it. Hence, the NSDL has to rely on existing metadata or metadata that can be generated automatically. The second is to make use of as much of the metadata available from collections as possible, knowing that it varies greatly from none to extensive. Based on these principles, Site for Science, and subsequently the entire NSDL, developed the following metadata strategy:

— Support eight standard formats

— Collect all existing metadata in these formats

— Provide crosswalks to Dublin Core

— Assemble all metadata in a central metadata repository

— Expose all metadata records in the repository for service providers to harvest

— Concentrate limited human effort on collection-level metadata

— Use automatic generation to augment item-level metadata

— Metadata formats

Early in 2001, the NSDL Standards and Metadata Workgroup, which represents all NSDL projects, identified the following list of preferred metadata element sets.

Dublin Core

Some of the collections that we would like to see in the NSDL support one of these standards, but far from all do.

The collections that have good metadata using the preferred standard are outnumbered by those that have poor or idiosyncratic metadata, or none at all. Even those collections that purport to support one of the standards often have local variations.

The strategy developed by Site for Science and now adopted by the NSDL is to accumulate metadata in the native formats provided by the collections, hopefully in the eight preferred standards. If a collection supports the protocols of the Open Archives Initiative, it must be able to supply unqualified Dublin Core (which is required by the OAI) as well as the native metadata format. Other than that, we do not ask the collections to supply any specific metadata format. Tools are available to convert from the preferred standards to Dublin Core.

Thus, three categories of metadata are available and can be stored in a metadata repository:

— *Collection-level metadata:* The repository contains a registry of the collections that are known to the NSDL. There is a metadata record for each collection. It uses qualified Dublin Core including descriptive information about the material in the collection (e.g., courseware for high school biology) and, where available, technical information about protocols, formats, etc., and access restrictions and authentication requirements. The Site for Science demonstration has collection-level metadata for about 150 collections.

— *Original item-level records:* Whenever a collection is able to supply item-level metadata that follows one of the preferred standards, the original records as supplied by the collection are stored in the metadata repository.

— *Normalized item-level records:* The preferred metadata standards differ considerably in their syntax and semantics. Many collections implement only part of a standard and others have no standardized metadata. To enable the delivery of services that require consistent information about items from such diverse collections, all item-level metadata records are normalized by metadata crosswalks to Dublin Core. We use all the Dublin Core elements and qualifiers applicable, plus the DC-Ed extensions.

By providing item-level metadata both in its original form and also as normalized metadata, the repository offers service providers a choice. Services that are able to make use of the original metadata can use it. Others can use the simpler, normalized records.

No Core Integration effort is being put into the creation of item-level metadata by hand. Every item-level record in the repository is either received from the collections or generated automatically. However, we are prepared to put human effort into creating collection-level metadata for important collections.

For collections that do not provide item-level metadata, we attempt to generate minimal records automatically. Site for Science developed tools for automatically creating Dublin Core records, both collection-level and item-level.

The metadata repository

From a computing viewpoint, the metadata repository is the key component of the Site for Science system. The repository can be thought of as a modern variant of the traditional library union catalog, a catalog that holds comprehensive catalog records from a group of libraries. Metadata from all the collections is stored in the repository and made available to providers of NSDL services. Some of these services, such as a comprehensive search service, are provided by the Core Integration team, some by other NSDL projects, and some by third parties.

For distribution to the services providers, the repository makes all the metadata available through the OAI protocol. The only restrictions are that some of the collections impose limitations on the redistribution of their native metadata. In the NSDL, the metadata repository will probably be mirrored and may be distributed over several computers, but it will be managed as a single system. The decision to have a centralized metadata repository is a consequence of the spectrum of interoperability.

In contrast, tightly knit federations often rely on distributed computing to provide services such as searching. For instance, federations of library catalogs expect every library to have its own catalog. If a user wishes to search several catalogs, the query is sent to each separately. Either the search is broadcast automatically, or the user selects the specific sites to search.

Therefore, Site for Science followed the more robust strategy of gathering metadata to a centrally managed system. It is notable that all the web search engines follow the same strategy of providing services from a central system, not by distributed processing across all the collections. The metadata repository is a generalization of this approach. Site for Science developed a prototype of the repository, with simple, well-documented interfaces that can be used by all NSDL service providers. During the current year, this repository is being reimplemented and its scope extended to include metadata for all NSDL collections. The most important of the interfaces is to make the metadata available via the OAI protocol.

To enable collections to contribute their metadata to the repository, Site for Science offered three options: metadata harvesting, FTP, and web crawling. The preferred method is to use the OAI metadata harvesting protocol. Metadata harvesting allows digital libraries to share metadata about their collections, without the need to support real-time, distributed services. This protocol is very simple, but it still requires a certain level of commitment from the participants. For important collections that have suitable metadata but are unable to make that commitment, Site for Science provided batch transfer of metadata files using FTP. This is slightly more labor-intensive, but it is well proven and sometimes is the only option.

Since the source of the information is stored in the metadata repository, the portal can display an ENC icon as part of the record. This acknowledges the source of the item. At this stage, the user has several choices. In this example, the user has clicked on a button labeled "More information" and the full metadata record has been displayed in a separate window. Where the item is available online, the user could also have clicked on a link that goes directly to the resource .The Site for Science demonstration used a very simple search service. For the production version, a search service is being developed by the Center for Intelligent Information Retrieval at the University of Massachusetts, Amherst [CIIR]. This service will extract metadata from the metadata repository, by harvesting using the OAI protocol. It will also access collections directly and, where possible, index textual materials.

This example highlights the heterogeneous nature of the NSDL and the challenges in building coherent services across collections. The search service has the challenge of finding materials when the amount of information about each varies greatly. This is a particular challenge for non-textual materials where it is not possible to combine metadata with full text indexing. The portal has the challenge of presenting the results to the user in a comprehensible manner.

3

Digital Preservation

Today, information technologies that are increasingly powerful and easy to use, especially like those that support the World Wide Web, have unleashed the production and distribution of digital information. Such information is penetrating and transforming nearly every aspect of our culture. If we are effectively to preserve for future generations the portion of this rapidly expanding corpus of information in digital form that represents our cultural record, we need to understand the costs of doing so and we need to commit ourselves technically, legally, economically and organizationally to the full dimensions of the task.

In the face of rapid technological obsolescence and to overcome the problem of media fragility, archivists have adopted the technique of "refreshing" digital information by copying it onto new media. Copying from medium to medium, however, also suffers limitations as a means of digital preservation. Refreshing digital information by copying will work as an effective preservation technique only as long as the information is encoded in a format that is independent of the particular hardware and software needed to use it and as long as there exists software to manipulate the format in current use.

Otherwise, copying depends either on the compatibility of present and past versions of software and generations of hardware or the ability of competing hardware and software product lines to interoperate. In respect of these factors- backward compatibility and interoperability-the rate of technological change exacts a serious toll on efforts to ensure the longevity of digital information.

Digital information today is produced in highly varying degrees of dependence on particular hardware and software. Moreover, it is costly and difficult for vendors to assure that their products are either "backwardly compatible" with previous versions or that they can interoperate with competing products. Jeff Rothenberg, has suggested that there may be sufficient demand for entrepreneurs to create and archive emulators of software and operating systems that would allow the contents of digital information to be carried forward and used in its original format. Refreshing digital information by copying it from medium to medium and the possibility of maintaining a complex set of emulators describe two distinct points on a continuum of approaches to preserving digital information.

However, neither refreshing nor emulation sufficiently describes the full range of options needed and available for digital preservation. Instead, a better and more general concept to describe these options is migration. Migration is the periodic transfer of digital materials from one hardware/software configuration to another, or from one generation of computer technology to a subsequent generation. The purpose of migration is to preserve the integrity of digital objects and to retain the ability for clients to retrieve, display, and otherwise use them in the face of constantly changing technology. Migration includes refreshing as a means of digital preservation but differs from it in the sense that it is not always possible to make an exact digital copy or replica of a database or other information object as hardware and software change and still maintain the compatibility of the object with the new generation of technology.

Users of intellectual property are unsure about what rights are conveyed with the use of a particular digital information object and about how much such use is worth. Government representatives seek in the public interest to manage the powerful changes that accompany digital technologies, but are unsure about what levels of influece are available to them and how to generate appropriate public policy. The state of the copyright law, which was generated and developed in an analog world but is applied in an increasingly digital universe, is itself confusing and uncertain.

And all of these concerns are exacerbated by the fact that bits know no borders. The costs and the technical, legal and organizational complexities of moving digital information forward into the future raise our greatest fear about the life of information in the digital future: namely, that owners or custodians who can no longer bear the expense and difficulty will deliberately or inadvertently, through a simple failure to act, destroy the objects without regard for future use.

Viewed developmentally, the problem of preserving digital information for the future is not only, or even primarily, a problem of fine tuning a narrow set of technical variables. It is not a clearly defined problem like preserving the embrittled books that are self-destructing from the acid in the paper on which they were printed. Rather, it is a grander problem of organizing ourselves over time and as a society to maneuver effectively in a digital landscape. It is a problem of building-almost from scratch-the various systematic supports, or deep infrastructure, that will enable us to tame anxieties and move our cultural records naturally and confidently into the future.

For digital preservation, the organizational effort-the process of building deep infrastructure-necessarily involves multiple, interrelated factors, many of which are either unknown or poorly defined. One of the biggest unknowns is the full impact on traditional information handling functions of distributed computing over electronic networks. Digital archives are distinct from digital libraries in the sense that digital libraries are repositories that collect and provide access to digital information, but may or may not provide for the long-term storage and access of that information.

Digital libraries thus may or may not be, in functional terms, digital archives and, in fact, much of the recent work on digital libraries is notably silent on the archival issues of ensuring long-term storage and access. Conversely, digital archives necessarily embrace digital library functions to the extent that they must select, obtain, store, and provide access to digital information. Many of the functional requirements for digital archives defined thus overlap those for digital libraries.

Many traditional libraries, archives and museums, as institutions, have taken and may well continue to assume digital library and archival functions. Certified digital archives will have available to them a critical fail-safe mechanism. Such a mechanism, supported by organizational will, economic means and legal right, would enable a certified archival repository to exercise an aggressive rescue function to save digital information that it judges to be culturally significant and which is endangered in its current repository.

The current repository may be a digital library, another digital archives, or some other individual, organizational, public or private source of digital information. Without the operation of a formal certification program and a fail-safe mechanism, preservation of the nation's cultural heritage in digital form will likely be overly dependent on marketplace forces, which may value information for too short a period and without applying broader, public interest criteria.

Such development is necessary for and will contribute powerfully to the overall growth of an information-based society and economy. We can afford to continue and increase economic and social investments in digital information objects and in the repositories for them on the information superhighway if, and only if, we also create the archival means for the knowledge the objects and repositories contain to endure and redound to the benefit of future generations. The digital world is still too new for us to describe fully the life cycle of the information objects that do now or will in the future reside there, but what surely unites the community of actors in their various information-based activities is their common purpose in support of the pursuit of knowledge.

The pursuit of knowledge is a process in which the emergence of new knowledge builds on and reconstructs the old. Knowledge cannot advance without consistent and reliable access to information sources, past and present. It is the archival function in the system of knowledge creation and use that serves to identify and retain important sources of information and to ensure continuing access to them. How reliable the archival process proves to be in the emerging digital environment hinges on the trustworthy operation of digital archives and on their ability to maintain the integrity of the objects they are charged to preserve. For digital objects, no less than for objects of other kinds, knowing how operationally to preserve them depends, at least in part, on being able to discriminate the essential features of what needs to be preserved.

Digital technologies increasingly serve to integrate information resources. Text, numeric data, images, voice, and video have heretofore resided in print or other analog media for storage and transmission. When they are encoded digitally, either by conversion or at the point of creation, these various kinds of resources share layers of technology-a common means of storage and transmission-that allows them to be brought together and used in both old and new ways.

Multimedia and hyperlinked objects on the World Wide Web represent some of the new kinds of information and new ways of knowing in the digital realm that bring together the traditional forms of information and transform their use. The application of computer hardware and software has also generated other new kinds of information objects, including the products of simulation, remote sensing, computer-aided design (CAD) and geographic information (GIS) systems. These objects come into being and exist as creatures of the digital environment; if nurtured well, digital technologies will certainly beget still other kinds of information objects, which we can now only anticipate. The processes of preserving digital information will vary significantly with the different kinds of objects-textual, numeric, image, video, sound, multimedia, simulation and so on-being preserved.

Whatever preservation method is applied, however, the central goal must be to preserve information integrity; that is, to define and preserve those features of an information object that distinguish it as a whole and singular work. In the digital environment, the features that determine information integrity and deserve special attention for archival purposes include the following: content, fixity, reference, provenance, and context. What digital archives are trying to preserve after all is the intellectual substance contained in information objects. The notion of content, however, is itself a complex idea that operates at several different levels of abstraction.

To preserve the integrity of objects in their charge, digital archives must decide at which level, or levels, of abstraction they are defining information content. At the lowest level of abstraction, all digital information objects consist of simple bitstreams of 0s and 1s. One can distinguish objects from one another merely by distinguishing the configuration of bits. Preserving the integrity of an information object in this sense means preserving the bit configuration that uniquely defines the object. There are various well-established techniques, such as checksums and digests, for tracking the bit-level equivalence of digital objects and ensuring that a preserved object is identical to the original. Defining content as a collection of bits, however, is often too limited and simplistic to be useful.

In the digital environment, as we have seen, ideas are typically embedded in particular formats and structures that are dependent on hardware and software technologies subject to rapid change. In addition to character set issues, digital archives must also grapple with the means of representing and preserving textual content embedded in layout and structure. Markup systems, such as implementations of TeX and the Standard Generalized Markup Language (SGML), do exist as platform-independent mechanisms for identifying and tagging for subsequent layout and retrieval detailed structural elements of documents. The use of TeX and its variants, for example, is relatively common among scholars in some scientific disciplines such as mathematics and computer science, and the federal government and scholarly publishers are increasingly employing the SGML standard in documents that they produce and distribute electronically. Beyond these relatively specialized segments, however, word processing and desktop publishing systems still dominate the market for the creation of documents with complex structure and layout, and the software for such use typically models and stores document structure and layout in proprietary terms.

Although software may provide mechanisms for converting documents to common interchange formats, use of such mechanisms often results in the loss or inadequate rendering of content such as page structures and the layout of headers, footers and section headings. The preservation of images comprises another example of the ways in which content, defined in terms of structure and format, poses integrity problems for digital archives.

Image resolution, accuracy of color representation and compression for storage all require attention, but the interaction of these structural factors tends to pit judgments about the quality of content against the need for its efficient archival storage and use. In general, one can express the tradeoffs as follows: the higher the resolution and the richer the color register, the larger the file size and more costly the storage. At the highest level of abstraction, digital archives define content in a way that transcends the limits of the hardware and software systems needed for reading and interpreting the bits of an information object and for rendering it for use in a specific format and structural representation; that is, they define content in terms of the knowledge or ideas the object contains.

The measure of integrity in the preservation process thus turns, at least in part, on informed and skillful judgments about the appropriate definition of the content of an digital information object-about the extent to which content depends on its configuration of bits, on the structure and format of its representation, and on the ideas it contains-and for what purposes. The process of identifying and preserving a digital information object as a whole and singular work goes well beyond considerations of content. It also depends, for instance, on the way that the content is fixed as a discrete object. If an object is not fixed, and the content is subject to change or withdrawal without notice, then its integrity may be compromised and its value as a cultural record would be severely diminished.

The acts of production and broadcast establish radio and television programs as discrete objects. And the act of publication marks a specific version or edition of a literary work. In each of these cases, it is virtually impossible to change or withdraw the cultural record that the release of an information object establishes. On the digital landscape, by contrast, it is still relatively easy for a creator to alter or retract previously released information. Such actions can eliminate or overlay significant content and thereby corrupt the record. To address these problems, a wide range of cryptographic techniques, such as watermarking, already exist for various kinds of digital information objects.

These could serve well to mark and identify specific, canonical versions and editions of textual, audio and visual works, and to establish trusted, protected channels of distribution for those objects. However, the standards and infrastructure and the policies and practices for applying such techniques to the creation of fixed versions of digital information objects still need considerable development. Absent such development and the fixity of information that would result, digital archives face considerable challenges in trying to preserve the integrity of digital objects.

Some kinds of digital objects present the problem of fixity of information in yet another way. An increasing number of networked information resources are better modeled, not in terms of versions or editions of works, but as continuously updated databases. The financial communities also depend on large, continuously updated databases. There is no natural way to fix these resources at the database level, no natural set of publication points for the objects as a whole. Their integrity, or singularity, as databases resides in the coherence of the database as a whole and in the continuousness of the updates.

To preserve the integrity of such information resources, the complete record of changes has to be built into the design of the database and fixed at the record level. In the absence of such a preservation-oriented design, digital archives may have no choice but to fix the database artificially in time and capture a series of snapshots of its state at periodic intervals as a way of preserving its integrity. Information objects come into being and acquire their distinctiveness in relation to various other objects in an information space.

There are several factors contribute to the unique identification of digital information objects. Two of the most important factors are the Uniform Resource Name (URN) and the Uniform Resource Locator (URL). The URL refers to the specific place where a digital object resides and is currently the dominant method of object location on the World Wide Web. The weakness of the URL however, is that it may frequently change, especially as an object migrates from one machine to the next.

By contrast, a name, the URN, is supposed to apply uniquely and permanently to a distinct object and to designate it independently of its particular location at any point in time. URNs today exist more in concept than in practice. Thus, resolving the name and location for variant digital works and thereby providing consistent reference to them means moving from a conceptual design of the relation between names and locations to an operational reality through the implementation of naming authorities, which assign URNs, and and the development of digital services that translate names into currently valid URLs.

For archival purposes, however, there are two other qualities of digital information objects that a reference system must take into account. Provenance has become one of the central organizing concepts of modern archival science. The assumption underlying the principle of provenance is that the integrity of an information object is partly embodied in tracing from where it came. To preserve the integrity of an information object, digital archives must preserve a record of its origin and chain of custody.

For some information objects, the formal process of publication creates a trusted channel of distribution and serves to establish a sophisticated record of provenance, at least from the creator through the point of release. In the digital environment, as in other domains, individuals produce and accrete much information that relates to their private lives and to their public roles and responsibilities, including their means of livelihood.

The archival challenge for establishing the provenance of such objects is to find ways to preserve an understanding of the corporate policies and processes and roles and responsibilities thus represented in the information system and its products. In some cases, the instrumentation produces data in the service of individual experiments or of clinical practice; in other cases, remote sensors gather streams of observational data about physical systems in space or on earth.

In the end, the investment that digital archives make in establishing the provenance of objects in their care serves to preserve the integrity of digital information in two distinct ways. First, a tracing of chain of custody from the point of creation helps to create the presumption that an object is authentic, that it is what it purports to be and that its content, however defined, has not been manipulated, altered or falsified. The second effect of establishing provenance through a chain of custody is to document, at least in part, the particular uses of the object by the custodians. In thus creating a record of use, the archival concern with provenance is intimately related to the notion of context as a matter of information integrity.

As network-based objects, such as video and records of confidential transactions, make their way into digital repositories, an archival account of their integrity must include an account of the features of the network context that supports their existence. Finally, the wider social environment plays a significant contextual role that contributes to the integrity of digital information objects. Networked information, for example, depends on specific policy and implementation decisions that address the bandwidth, security and other qualities of the network and related technical infrastructure.

Long-term Preservation

Different types of information involved in the long-term preservation of information in an Open Archival Information System (OAIS). Each of these types can be viewed as a complete Information Object in that it contains a data object and adequate Representation Information to understand the data. The Content Information is the set of information that is the original target of preservation by the OAIS. Deciding what is the Content Information may not be obvious and may need to be negotiated with the Producer.

The Representation Information for a digital Content Data Object (both semantic and syntactic) is needed to fully transform the bits into the Content Information. In principal, this even extends to the inclusion of definitions (e.g., dictionary and grammar) of any natural language (e.g., English) used in expressing the Content Information. Over long time periods the meaning of natural language expressions can evolve significantly in both general and in specific discipline usage. As a practical matter, the OAIS needs to have enough Representation Information associated with the bits of the Content Data Object in the Content Information that it feels confident that the members of the Designated Community can enter the Representation Network with enough knowledge to begin accurately interpreting the Representation Information.

This is a significant risk area for an OAIS, particularly for those with an expert Designated Community, because jargon and apparently widely understood terms may be short-lived. In such cases extra care needs to be exercised to ensure that the natural evolution of the Designated Community Knowledge Base does not effectively cause information loss from the Content Information. As described above for an Information Object in general, the Representation Information can also be viewed as being augmented by Access Software that supports the presentation of the Content Information to the Consumer.

Examples of this type of software include word processors supporting complex document format representations of Content Information and scientific visualization systems supporting representations of Content Information as a time series or a multidimensional array. The software uses its knowledge of the underlying Representation Information to provide these services. Often required information will be embedded in the software packages used by the Designated Community to present and analyze the Content Information.

A reason for preserving working Access Software arises from a convenience factor. Even with a complete set of Representation Information, practical access to all or part of a digital Content Data Object requires the use of Access Software. Thus a software module that provides useful access to a digital Content Data Object may be preserved in a working state as a matter of convenience.

This is not difficult to do as long as the environment, which supports the software module, is readily available. This environment consists of some underlying hardware and an operating system, various utilities that effectively augment the operating system and storage and display devices and their drivers.

A change to any of these may cause the software module to no longer function, to function incorrectly, or to be unable to present results to the application or human user. The complexity of these interactions is what traditionally makes the preservation of working software such an arduous task. In short, the use of Access Software to replace Representation Networks is attractive from the point of view of minimizing the resources needed to ingest data and provide current users with access to data. However the reliance on working software can provide major problems for Long-Term Preservation when that software ceases to function. Indefinite long-term information preservation requires a full and understandable description of the Representation Information.

Preservation Description Information (PDI)

An important function of the OAIS is deciding what parts of the Content Information are the Content Data Object and what parts are the Representation Information. In addition to Content Information, the Archival Information must include information that will allow the understanding of the Content Information over an indefinite period of time. The specific set of Information Objects, which are required for this function, is collectively called Preservation Description Information (PDI).

The PDI must include information that is necessary to adequately preserve the particular Content Information with which it is associated. It is specifically focused on describing the past and present states of the Content Information, ensuring it is uniquely identifiable, and ensuring it has not been unknowingly altered. This information is typical for all types of archives and has been classified in the context of traditional archives. However, the class definitions must be extended for digital archives. The following definitions are preserving Digital Information:

Reference Information: This information identifies, and if necessary describes, one or more mechanisms used to provide assigned identifiers for the Content Information. It also provides those identifiers that allow outside systems to refer, unambiguously, to this particular Content Information. Examples of these systems include taxonomic systems, reference systems and registration systems. In the OAIS Reference Model most if not all of this information is replicated in Package Descriptions, which enable Consumers to access Content Information of interest.

Context Information: This information documents the relationships of the Content Information to its environment. This includes why the Content Information was created and how it relates to other Content Information objects existing elsewhere.

Provenance Information: This information documents the history of the Content Information. This tells the origin or source of the Content Information, any changes that may have taken place since it was originated, and who has had custody of it since it was originated. This gives future users some assurance as to the likely reliability of the Content Information. Provenance can be viewed as a special type of context information.

Fixity Information: This information provides the Data Integrity checks or Validation/Verification keys used to ensure that the particular Content Information object has not been altered in an undocumented manner. Fixity Information includes special encoding and error detection schemes that are specific to instances of Content Objects. Fixity Information does not include the integrity preserving mechanisms provided by the OAIS underlying services, error protection supplied by the media and device drivers used by Archival Storage. The OAIS needs to explicitly decide what the exact definition of Content Information is in order to be able to ensure that it also has the PDI needed to preserve the Content Information. Once the Content Information has been determined, it is possible to assess the Preservation Description Information.

Packaging Information: The Packaging Information is that information which, either actually or logically, binds or relates the components of the package into an identifiable entity on specific media. For example, if the Content Information and PDI are identified as being the content of specific files on a CD-ROM, then the Packaging Information may include the ISO 9660 volume/file structure on the CD-ROM.

The Packaging Information does not necessarily need to be preserved by an OAIS since it does not contribute to the Content Information or the PDI. However, there are cases where the OAIS may be required to reproduce the original submission exactly. The OAIS should also avoid holding PDI or Content Information only in the naming conventions of directory or file name structures. These structures are most likely to be used as Packaging Information.

Descriptive Information: To preserving information, the OAIS must provide adequate features to allow Consumers to locate information of potential interest, analyze that information, and order desired information. This is accomplished through a specialization of the Information Object called Descriptive Information, which contain the data that serves as the input to documents or applications called Access Aids.

A library is not a last resting place for the books contained there but a place where information and ideas live and breathe in new minds. The digital age brings, here as elsewhere, opportunities and challenges. The Library can now provide access to some objects without assuming any responsibility for preserving them. The acquisition of materials and their integration into a library's collections traditionally have implied a responsibility to preserve those items for use by future generations. Its preservation responsibilities using a variety of professionally accepted practices:

— Providing adequate storage conditions (e.g., proper environmental controls and appropriate binding and shelving);

— Reformatting materials from their original fragile formats and media to more stable media (e.g., microfilming newspapers and brittle books, transferring audio recordings to more stable media, and copying content on nitrate and acetate film to more stable polyester film bases); and

— For a small percentage of rare and unique materials with intrinsic value in their original formats, restoring originals through conservation treatments.

The library also has a long history of providing leadership in the broader field of preservation. Over the last two centuries, it has conducted research and led efforts in areas such as binding and shelving books, proper environmental conditions for storage, use of microfilm for preservation, and mass deacidification of paper. The Library faces challenges in digital preservation that are widely recognized and shared by many other libraries and archives. They include the following:

— *Fragile storage media*—Digital materials are especially vulnerable to loss and destruction because they are stored on fragile magnetic and optical media that deteriorate rapidly and that can fail suddenly from exposure to heat, humidity, airborne contaminants, faulty reading and writing devices, human error, and even sabotage.

— *Technology obsolescence*—Digital materials become unreadable and inaccessible if the playback devices necessary to retrieve information from the media become obsolete or if the software that translates digital information from machine- to human-readable form is no longer available.

— *Legal questions surrounding copying and access*—Libraries, archives, and other cultural institutions have limited and uncertain rights to copy digital information for preservation or backup purposes, to reformat information so that it remains accessible by current technology, and to provide public access.

All organizations with responsibilities for preserving digital information are seeking better technical solutions, model policies, best practices, and clearer guidelines regarding legal and intellectual property issues. In US, Library Congress (LC) providing leadership or contributing actively to solving critical problems of digital archiving and long-term preservation. Until now, LC seems to have assumed a wait-and-see attitude toward its role in preserving digital information created outside the walls of the Library itself; this was probably exacerbated by the absence of a director for the Preservation Directorate.

The Library's collecting policies and mechanisms with regard to born-digital materials are closely tied to its preservation capabilities. As long as traditional collecting mechanisms guarantee a steady stream of print, other analog materials, and tangible digital objects such as CD-ROMs into the Library's collections, there is an illusion that little significant content is being lost. The absence of significant digital content in the Library's collections removes a sense of urgency about digital preservation, and the lack of organizational capacity to preserve many types of born-digital information discourages the Library from taking on responsibilities that it is not prepared to fulfill.

The methods for doing this include traditional collecting and custodianship and developing relationships with publishers, other research libraries, other national libraries, bibliographic networks and utilities, government agencies, and archives. Traditionally, the acquisition of materials through purchase, exchange, or deposit and their cataloging into the Library's permanent collection entailed a commitment to preserve those materials. In the digital environment, libraries will assume a wider variety of roles and responsibilities with regard to preservation.

One of the first steps that librareis needs to take in adapting its collecting practices to accommodate born-digital information is to delineate clearly its responsibilities for preserving digital information. As libraries identifies the areas in which it will assume the lead responsibility for digital preservation, other organizations can adjust the scope of their digital collections accordingly. Just as the

Library cannot ignore the problem of digital preservation, so also it cannot be expected to do it all. If libraries does not set clear boundaries around its digital preservation responsibilities, then many people may assume unrealistically that the Library will be the repository of last resort for everything worth keeping.

The Library of Congress must act as the owner and primary custodian for the digital collections it creates. This is a logical extension of the Library's current efforts to preserve the digital resources that it creates through the retrospective conversion of materials for the National Digital Library Program (NDLP), compilation of public-domain materials, and cataloging. The Law Library's Global Legal Information Network (GLIN) maintains an online database composed primarily of searchable legal abstracts in English of foreign laws and regulations enacted in selected countries since 1976 and over 20,000 full texts of legal instruments since 1995.

In addition, libraries has preserved its bibliographic database of some 12 million machine-readable catalog records representing the books, serials, maps, sound recordings, manuscripts, and visual materials in its collections by migrating these data successfully from older legacy systems to the new Integrated Library System. The Library can also logically be expected to serve as owner and primary custodian of materials for which it has a unique mandate and of digital resources that it has unique responsibilities for acquiring.

The Library's role in registering copyright and enforcing mandatory deposit law creates a unique opportunity for the Library to collect digital information that might otherwise vanish from the historical record. One particular concern with regard to preservation is how deposited items will be identified for integration into LC's permanent collection and which parts of LC will look after long-term preservation requirements. It is not clear when (or if) CORDS will begin retaining and preserving complete digital objects in a systematic way rather than maintaining only registration information and a digital signature of the object being registered.

In some cases, only the digital signature will be kept in CORDS, to verify potential alterations to a digital document or copyright infringements. It is also unclear whether the Copyright Office will assume responsibility for the long-term preservation of the digital content deposited in CORDS or whether some or all of this task will pass to Library Services. The Library needs to determine whether CORDS is intended to serve solely as a registration and deposit mechanism or whether it should also include a repository for digital materials with long-term value.

In the paper world, each library that decided to provide its users with a given resource both obtained and conserved its own copy of the object. This replication in the paper world served as a powerful fail-safe mechanism, helping to ensure long-term accessibility through the uncoordinated but distributed maintenance of independent copies. (The only coordination between libraries took place when materials deteriorated to the point where reformatting was required. At that point, a library would check in national databases to see whether another library had already reformatted the item.)

In the digital environment, in which much content is distributed through the centralized services of a publisher, it is not clear where the preservation responsibility lies. The Library has begun experimenting with arrangements that may help clarify its role in these instances. It is now necessary to move from these early experiments to the development of a coherent, overarching strategy for digital preservation. There are no formal arrangements that define LC's role in long-term maintenance and preservation of the portions of the NDLP that are currently in the custody of other participating institutions. Although the committee does not question the participating institutions' commitment, in principle, to preserving the digital content they have contributed, a variety of unforeseen circumstances could prevent them from doing so. This is a particular concern because of the funding model for the NDLP and the emphasis to date on digitization and the development of access mechanisms.

An important next step for the NDLP is to develop standards and agreements for long-term stewardship that define when and under what circumstances LC will serve as the fail-safe mechanism or repository of last resort. Repositories are systems for storing digital objects in a robust and managed fashion. They protect data from inappropriate access, facilitate the recording of appropriate metadata to allow the management of objects, and provide delivery facilities for both curatorial and user access.

The Library has recently acquired, through a gift, the TEAMS system developed by Thompson Publishing. TEAMS supports both object and metadata storage and maintenance and has been implemented in a variety of corporate settings. Its use by LC represents the first implementation of TEAMS in a traditional library application. The committee supports the development of a repository system as an important next step for the NDLP and agrees that this work needs to be stepped up, but it has reservations about the directions that LC is taking.

Although accepting donated hardware and software helps to mobilize private support for LC and may reduce expenditures in the short run, contributions like these can also commit LC to proprietary systems and methods that in the long run will limit the Library's ability to federate its collections with those of other repositories and interoperate easily with potential partners. One approach is for LC to coordinate its efforts to develop a repository system with those of other organizations that are using the reference model for the Open Archival Information System (OAIS). This high-level model does not specify any particular implementation of an archival information system, nor does it define standards accession, description, data management, or distribution.

The OAIS model is important for digital preservation standards and strategies because it defines the functions and requirements for a digital archive through an international standard that vendors and producers of digital information can reference. If the OAIS reference model is widely adopted (and there are indications that it will be), then it may provide the framework for a network of cooperating and federated repositories. US National Archives and Records Administration is adopting this model for some of its digital archiving requirements and is working with the San Diego Supercomputer Center on one specific implementation.

In general, for LC to develop the capacity to serve as a fail-safe mechanism, it will need to acquire a much more extensive technical infrastructure and greater expertise in a wide variety of file types and formats. While they are important experiments, neither the NDLP repository nor CORDS yet offers solutions to LC's responsibility to preserve born-digital content created outside the Library. In the case of NDLP, LC has been working with materials converted to digital form, and for these materials it has taken the lead in setting standards for formats, metadata, naming conventions, and other technical attributes.

But for born-digital materials, especially those created outside the Library, LC is unlikely to have the leverage to define or limit the formats and structures that are used. In the experimental period of the dissertation project, ProQuest is presenting dissertations in the portable document format (PDF) directly to the Copyright Office. These are being accepted as the best edition, cataloged using the cataloging specifications offered by ProQuest, verified by examiners in the Copyright Office, and stored at ProQuest. That is, registration is handled by the Copyright Office but the deposit is virtual. This arrangement presents LC with no immediate need to preserve the materials.

Because of intellectual property law and the uncertainty of some publishers regarding the deposit of copies of digital works, institutions with long-term preservation responsibilities must seek and develop new means of ensuring continuing access to the valuable documentation of history, culture, and creativity. One possible approach is contractual agreements with rights holders who maintain digital information in off-site repositories, with provisions for deposit in a library or other institution should the publisher cease to maintain the information.

Some publishers have agreed to provide perpetual access to their materials as one of the conditions of a license. The Library has initiated an experiment in reaching such an agreement with ProQuest. The committee believes that such arrangements need to be tested carefully and that other models need to be explored as well. The way in which librarians work must be totally reconceptualized for these fail-safe mechanisms to work.

Library needs to articulate carefully a policy identifying the subset of digital materials for which it will assume long-term curatorial responsibility, taking into account the following:

— The burden of preserving digital collections is daunting and must be shared with other archiving institutions.

— The archiving and preservation of digital resources normally accessed over the Internet will not take place as a by-product of normal access but must be explicitly pursued. Simply assuming that preservation will be carried out somewhere across numerous replicated research collections will not be a solution for networked resources.

Both considerations argue for libraries to define the scope of their archiving roles, in order that responsibilities be distributed across the archiving libraries of the world. The archiving and preservation responsibility is a long-term one that will serve researchers in generations to come. One advantage of digital materials is the potential to distribute preservation responsibilities among a wide variety of partners so that each institution preserves only a designated portion of the global digital record.

With careful planning, coordination, cooperative agreements, and clearly articulated boundaries around its curatorial collection, the Library could assume long-term preservation responsibility for a much smaller portion of the digital corpus than it did for the paper one. Some redundancy is necessary for backup and security purposes, but less redundancy is needed for digital collections than was required in the past because access no longer requires physical proximity to materials. Distributed curatorial responsibility will be achieved only with leadership from LC and cooperation with many partners.

A variety of roles can be envisioned for the Library in a collaborative effort among libraries, publishers, government agencies, and other stakeholders to define the parameters of distributed digital collections and delineate the roles and responsibilities of various parties for access and long-term maintenance of important digital works. One of LC's roles could involve coordination with other national libraries. Several European national libraries and the national libraries of Canada and Australia have launched programs to collect and preserve the digital portions of their national bibliographies.

If the mechanisms to acquire and preserve the digital national bibliographies of some countries succeed, LC could be relieved of responsibility for preserving most digital materials from those countries. At that point, it could concentrate its curatorial efforts on works created or published by Americans or that reflect important aspects of U.S. history, policy development, and culture. Some other countries would need help.

For the foreseeable future, many developing countries will not have the resources to preserve their digital heritage. Curatorial responsibility for these collections could be shared by LC and other libraries that have well-developed repository systems rather than assuming that LC will serve as the repository for all significant materials globally. There are many other opportunities to divide up long-term preservation responsibilities by subject area or domain. LC already cedes responsibility for materials in medicine, agriculture, and education to the national libraries set up for those subject domains. In addition, the National Archives and Records Administration preserves records of the federal government that have long-term value for documenting U.S. government, policy development, and history. A clear delineation of LC's long-term curatorial responsibilities would be critical as a means to avoid unachievable commitments to long-term preservation and enable the Library to preserve materials that it is best suited or uniquely able to collect and maintain.

Many national libraries, university research libraries, national archives, bibliographic utilities, and organizations with large holdings of digital information are actively pursuing solutions to the problems of digital preservation. Although the Library of Congress might have been expected to provide leadership in this area as it once did in others, LC has at best played only a minimal role in these initiatives. As a consequence, it has little awareness of potential solutions that are emerging from joint research and development projects and has not contributed much to this important national and international problem for the library community.

Ensuring its leadership in digital preservation will require the Library to hire or develop relevant expertise. The Library should join and, where possible, lead or facilitate national and international research and development efforts in digital preservation. There are opportunities for the Library to learn from and contribute to such efforts in preserving born-digital information and converting certain types of information to digital form as a preservation strategy.

To make it a safe haven for preservation purposes, the Library should take an active role--including working with the Congress if necessary--in efforts to rework intellectual property restraints on copying and migration.

Even if LC carefully defines its roles and responsibilities along the continuum from serving as a portal to acting as the primary custodian for digital materials, there is an urgent need for it to enhance its technical capacity and expertise in digital preservation. Such preservation will involve a wide range of activities, including the following:

— "Protecting the bits"—The making of backup copies, periodic recopying to new media, and regular checking of object coherence and validity are required to make certain that rarely accessed materials remain technically sound. Access will be enhanced to the extent that archived materials remain online rather than, say, being stored on media such as tapes, which must be mounted manually.

— Archiving appropriate copies—For many digital materials, the format most useful for current services (say, a PDF file or a GIF image) is not the most robust for long-term archiving (SGML, XML, or TIFF may serve better). A preservation program must encompass the selection and archiving of the appropriate formats for long-term use and then the derivation of current-use copies appropriate to the technological base of today's users. It must also work with users to help them undertake these tasks.

— Maintaining appropriate metadata—All preservation activities will depend on the completeness and quality of the metadata for the objects to be preserved. It will be critical for the Library to monitor developments in metadata standards and follow best practices for metadata as they develop.

— Migrating formats—Even the most careful selection of archiving formats cannot ensure that objects will be useful in the decades to come. It will be necessary to migrate objects periodically from one archival format to another. Such processes must be carefully designed and executed to ensure minimal loss of content (it is impossible to ensure that all such migrations will be loss-free). Some works, such as those that include active software (e.g., Java applets), may raise particularly difficult issues.

— Conducting research and development—Only a handful of institutions are likely to face digital preservation challenges on the scale or scope of those that LC faces in the coming years. This makes it unlikely that LC will be able to import models and solutions for all of its preservation needs. An active program of research and development in digital preservation is needed to solve immediate preservation problems--technical, legal, and economic—at LC and to provide guidance to other libraries and archives.

— Educating the relevant communities—Especially in this transitional period, when digital materials are new and preservation practices are still in flux, institutions and particular communities will need to be educated about digital preservation: What is the state of the art? What factors must be taken into account in planning for preservation? LC is well situated to participate in such efforts and possibly to take the lead.

A robust preservation program will employ curators and preservation staff with knowledge of the formats of materials in their collections and of appropriate metadata standards and practices and an understanding of the issues involved in migrating objects from one format to another. It will require well-developed production services for creating the specified metadata, sound and robust repository services, and periodic quality checking and copying of objects in the collection.

In the future, libraries will also need to make much more extensive use of digitization for preservation. Some professionals consider digital objects—whether born digital or turned digital—unacceptable as preservation masters because their longevity is uncertain. In some cases, however, digital conversion may offer the only viable means of salvaging and preserving certain materials, such as audio recordings in obsolete analog formats. The Library has used digitization to preserve severely damaged black-and-white negatives and some audio and video records on magnetic media.

The challenges of digital preservation make it easy to overlook the benefits that libraries could enjoy by rapidly enhancing its capacity to collect and preserve digital information. Digital storage media are very compact, making it possible to store enormous quantities of information in a very small amount of space. Digital information can be managed and handled more automatically. More significantly, whatever libraries collects and preserves in digital form has the potential to be made accessible to anyone, anywhere, on any day of the week or at any time of the day.

4

Intellectual Access to Digital Information

Today most libraries, invests heavily in cataloging its collections. It probably has the largest cataloging operation in the world1 and is a source of both cataloging data and standards for much of the library community. In the world of paper-based publication, its role is second to none. One enduring role of libraries during the transition from physical to digital information will be the intellectual task of cataloging—imposing order on diverse resources with the goal of making those resources easier to discover and manage.

Cataloging is arguably among the most expensive tasks in the library. Current estimates range from $50 to $110 for the creation of a single full cataloging record. What is responsible for this high cost? While some of the tasks of cataloging—for example, recording a title—are indeed mundane (in the majority of but not all cases), others are intellectually challenging and time consuming:

— *Subject analysis*—The usability of library catalogs for finding resources "about" a particular subject depends greatly on the nontrivial task of understanding the content of a resource and tagging it with a controlled subject heading.

— *Authority control*—While the subject of assigning authorship may seem superficially simple, it is confounded by the fact that people frequently use different forms of their name, and different people frequently have very similar or identical names.

There is the problem of the multiple spellings of historical figures (is it "Shakespeare" or "Shakespere" or "Shakespear" or ?), the problem of aliases ("Mark Twain" and "Samuel Clemens"), and the seemingly random use of initials, shortened names, and the like ("Samuel Langhorne Clemens," "Samuel L. Clemens," "Sam Clemens," etc.). Authority control, in the context of author names, is the task of, first, associating these name variations with a canonical name in the cataloging record to show that the variations are indeed the same person and, second, differentiating between ambiguous and overlapping names.

The development of standard cataloging practices from the end of the nineteenth century through the twentieth century made it possible to share cataloging records, leading to a significant cost savings for libraries. "Copy cataloging" exploits the fact that the overwhelming majority of resources in an average library are not unique. Rather than produce original cataloging records for the duplicated resources, libraries can use cataloging records from other libraries.

In US, the development of the machine-readable cataloging (MARC) record by the Library of Congress, in concert with the library community, in the 1960s was a landmark event in the automation of library operations. As recalled above, preautomation catalog sharing involved the physical shipment of catalog cards to fellow libraries. The introduction of computers into the library environment allowed sharing computer catalog records among libraries by exchanging magnetic tapes.

MARC consists of both an encoding scheme for labeling cataloging elements (e.g., "author" or "title") and an exchange format for packaging the encoded bibliographic data into a record for transfer purposes. The MARC record remains a critical technical foundation of existing integrated library systems and permits the transfer of records among these systems. The Library's Network Development and MARC Standards Office leads and coordinates international efforts to further develop MARC as a standard for the efficient and long-term interchange of bibliographic information.

In recent years, the office has been analyzing the relationship of MARC to standard generalized markup language (SGML) and the use of MARC for digital media. Such a catalog could have been a natural product for a national library and, perhaps, could have provided a revenue stream to underwrite the Library's cataloging operation. In fact, the Library, for reasons not entirely obvious to the committee or the individuals, failed to take advantage of this key opportunity and ceded it to the Online Computer Library Center (OCLC) and the Research Libraries Group (RLG).

While MARC provides the markup and transfer syntax for bibliographic records, the Anglo-American Cataloging Rules (AACR2) provide the rules for the actual description of a bibliographic item. The Library of

Congress plays a major role in coordinating activities in AACR2, and its Library of Congress Rule Interpretations defines common practice for the use of AACR2 in cooperative cataloging. The result, in combination with the MARC standard, is that both the meaning and encoding of cataloging records can be shared among a large number of libraries.

These activities are centered in the Library's Cataloging Policy and Support Office (CPSO), which provides "leadership in the creation and implementation of cataloging policy within the Library of Congress and in the national and international library community." In general, archival and manuscript items are handled differently from monographs and serials. Whereas the latter are cataloged at the item level, the former are described at a coarser level of granularity (for example, a manuscript box or folder). Tools for locating such items are referred to as "finding aids."

The encoded archival description (EAD) was the product of a project at the University of California at Berkeley in the early 1990s to develop a standard for machine-readable finding aids. The EAD standard utilizes SGML to mark up structured descriptions of units of archival information. The Library's Network Development and MARC Standards Office serves as the maintenance agency for the EAD standard, an excellent example of the Library stepping in to play an important role in the new metadata environment.

Challenges to Traditional Cataloguing Practices

A user of the Web who has sampled any of the numerous search engines (e.g., Google, AltaVista, Excite) might argue that digital content, networks, and full-text indexing have made human-mediated organization through cataloging obsolete. Web search engines demonstrate the great utility of such searching and the benefits of over 30 years of research in information retrieval and, to a lesser degree, natural language processing. However, there are numerous inherent limitations to the technology underlying them:

— Scalability—Most Web search engines accumulate indexes by scanning the Web and downloading full content from sites. As the volume of Web content grows, it has become increasingly difficult to keep these indexes current or complete. One study indicates that even the best search engines index only about 12 to 15 percent of Web content. Even more problematic are the limitations of the information retrieval (IR) technology used in most popular Web search engines. The nature of the Web as a corpus presents some difficult scalability challenges for IR and often leads to poor results. The sheer size of the corpus is a notable problem; a typical Web query will retrieve a very large set of potentially relevant documents. In addition, the Web corpus is usually presented as a single, unorganized collection of documents, which makes synonym clashes inevitable. Synonym clashes are well understood and can be addressed with a variety of techniques (e.g., thesauri, user feedback, local context analysis, phrase structure), but these techniques are generally not exploited by Web search engines.

— Access limitations and databases—While a great deal of useful content is freely available on the Internet, there is a growing and equally valuable portion of Internet content that is proprietary and held in protected systems. Much "valuable" content is held in databasés on special servers that require a password or other means of authorization for access. These databases also provide enhanced functions beyond what can be done with simple, static Web pages. However, they do not in general support access via crawling, the method used to build most Internet search services. Thus, while Web indexers are able to access and index a large percentage of the total content on the Web, an ever-growing percentage of the most-sought-after material is not available from Internet search facilities.

— Format—Existing Web search engines are limited to textual content. They index words in documents and process textual queries—for example, "digital imaging"—returning lists of documents ranked according to the appearance of the query words in their content. Extending this approach to images will require tools to analyze image content and respond to queries such as "find images with cars in them" or, at an even more advanced level, to queries that ask for images with features similar to those of another digitized image. The tools to retrieve images, video segments, voice, and music are being actively researched but are currently beyond the capabilities of Internet search engines.

— Context—At a more abstract level, the usefulness of indexing based solely on the text content of a resource is compromised by lack of context. The best tools to help a person locate a resource are those that are tailored to the context in which the resource occurs and to the knowledge context of the searcher. For example, content-based searches of MEDLINE (the medical index at the National Library of Medicine) might be appropriate for a professional familiar with medical terminology and with the body of medical literature indexed by MEDLINE. However, a high-school student might not be able to select documents that are appropriate to his or her background and might not be familiar with medical terms, so he or she might find content-based searching to be difficult. The lack of context is a problem for both human and automatically generated representations, but different representations can often be combined to good effect.

— Markup—HTML, the main markup language of the Web, provides only a very simplified set of tags for labeling the parts of a document. These are primarily oriented to supporting the appropriate display of the document and in general tell little about the meaning of the various sections of the document. Many search engines utilize smart markup to provide more powerful retrieval facilities, allowing users to limit which parts of a document are used to satisfy the search argument. The simplicity of HTML markup severely constrains Internet search engines' use of such facilities, which are very useful for limiting and refining search results.

The creation of structured descriptive records for resources (e.g., traditional cataloging records or, more generally, surrogates) can help to address some of these limitations. Scalability can improve if surrogates are used instead of the full content for indexing. Content providers may be more willing to distribute freely descriptive surrogates for indexing, in lieu of the full content. Surrogates can be created, and standards are being developed for describing all manner of digital objects.

Finally, surrogate records may include descriptive information that is not part of the document itself (usually the result of human analysis). For example, surrogates to facilitate searching MEDLINE by high-school students might associate more common medical subject terms with the resources, thus making searching easier for this community. On the other hand, there is broad agreement among the committee members and in the general information community that the nature of resource description needs a thorough examination in the context of digital resources.

Traditional cataloging is one kind of resource description, which, in turn, is one kind of "metadata (information that describes the structure or content of a document but is not part of the document). The nature and use of meta-data are evolving to accommodate the great variety of digital objects.

Traditional library cataloging has scaled up to serve institutions of great size—prominent among them the Library of Congress. However, over the past year the number of resources on the Web has grown to the point that they exceed the number of books in even the largest of libraries and even the number of book pages in the average library. The growth rate of these networked resources substantially exceeds the growth rate of traditional physical resources. Sheer size presents considerable challenges to the economics of traditional library cataloging, in which metadata records are characterized by great precision, detail, and professional intervention.

The high price of traditional library cataloging makes it impractical in the context of such growth, and less expensive alternatives are needed for many, if not all, of these resources. There has always been a trade-off between the cost of creating metadata and its value in facilitating access to document collections. Large print collections generally cannot be accessed without some sort of metadata, so the value of the metadata is high. The appearance of digital objects in commercially interesting collections during the 1970s changed the economic model. Then, access could be provided with relatively little investment in metadata, although higher-quality metadata could still be justified for high-value materials. Now, the steady increase in the volume of electronic materials has increased pressure to reduce the cost of metadata, although manually produced metadata are still common.

The lifespan of networked resources differs dramatically from that of physical resources. The well-known problem of "dangling URLs" bedevils any librarian who is trying to incorporate Web pages into a collection. The impermanence of networked resources is rooted in the economics of networked dissemination. The cost of distributing networked content is low compared with the cost of printing and distributing hard-copy content, so there is little benefit to the publisher of maintaining older versions of a document. With no incentive to retain older versions, the management of objects is haphazard and object permanence is problematic.

Such an environment has a strong impact on the economics and incentives for producing metadata and also points out the critical need for preservation-oriented metadata and mechanisms to manage the preservation of digital objects. The breakdown of traditional publishing roles has disrupted some of the traditional mechanisms for establishing the credibility of an information source. Since metadata is itself an information resource, the credibility issue applies to the quality of metadata created by external sources (outside the traditional library cataloging community).

The creation of bad metadata can be nonmalicious: for example, an author who lacks training or who doesn't care may assign a bad subject classification to a descriptive metadata record. It can also be malicious: so-called "index spamming," whereby content creators seed metadata fields with misleading or incorrect information to affect the ranking of their pages by search engines, is a real problem on the Web. An important challenge for networked information is developing the mechanisms and policies to verify the origin of any information, including metadata.

Libraries, deals with a considerable variety of resources, including books, serials, maps, software, movies, images, and, now, digital resources. The Library's efforts to create metadata for this spectrum of resources can be divided into two categories. First, much attention has been paid to enhancing the traditional cataloging mechanisms—AACR2 and MARC, for example—to accommodate these new genres. These efforts are motivated by the central role that the traditional cataloging formats play in the Integrated Library System and in the cooperative cataloging efforts.

Second, the Library has employed a number of other vehicles for resource description—metadata schemata tailored for individual resource characteristics. Some schemata have been coordinated with external communities; others have been developed internally. The use of other meta-data vocabularies raises the issue of how these vocabularies interact to provide integrated information spaces for users of digital libraries. After all, one of the major strengths of the standardization on AACR2 and its expression in MARC records has been the uniform search interface provided by library catalogs to large and heterogeneous collections.

The field of metadata has exploded into a major area of investigation and development over the past several years. As information becomes more of a commodity item--and, as many would argue, is the largest product of the "new economic paradigm--its management is of interest to a broad spectrum of organizations. This stands in rather strong contrast to the situation in the pre-Internet era, when the standardized management of information was more or less restricted to libraries, with the Library of Congress playing a key leadership role.

This broadening of the metadata environment will include many new players and applications and require the Library to think in new ways if it is to reassert its leadership in this area. Descriptive cataloging, exemplified by the traditional library cataloging record, is but one of many classes of metadata. Real-world applications need to make use of a much broader range of metadata than descriptive cataloging. Some other metadata types are listed below to provide a sense of this range.

— *Terms and conditions*: metadata that describe the rules for use of an object. Terms and conditions might include an access list of who may view the object, a conditions-of-use statement that might be displayed before access to the object is allowed, a schedule (tariff) of prices and fees for use of the object, or a definition of the permitted uses of an object (viewing, printing, copying, etc.).

— *Administrative data*: metadata that relate to the management of an object in a particular server or repository. Some examples of information stored in administrative data are the date of last modification, the date of creation, and the administrator's identity.

— *Content rating*: a description of attributes of an object within a multidimensional, scaled rating scheme assigned by some rating authority; an example might be the suitability of the content for various audiences, similar to the well-known movie rating system used by the Motion Picture Association of America. Note that content ratings have applications far beyond simple filtering on sex and violence levels. Content ratings are likely to play important roles in future collaborative filtering systems, for example.

— *Provenance*: data defining the source or origin of some content object, for example, of some physical artifact from which the content was scanned. The data might also include a summary of all algorithmic transformations that have been applied to the object (filtering, reductions in image density, etc.) since its creation. Arguably, provenance information might also include evidence of authenticity and integrity through the use of digital signature schemes; or, authenticity and integrity information might be considered a separate class of metadata.

— *Linkage or relationship data*: data indicating the often complex relationships between content objects and other objects. Some examples are the relationship of a set of journal articles to the containing journal, the relationship of a translation to the work in its original language, the relationship of a subsequent edition to the original work, or the relationships among the components of a multimedia work (information on synchronization between images and a soundtrack, for example).

— *Structural data*: data defining the logical components of complex or compound objects and how to access those components. A simple example is a table of contents for a textual document. More complex examples include the definition of the different source files, subroutines, data definitions in a software suite, SGML or XML tagged books, or other complex works.

The need for additional metadata types and for traditional metadata for a larger volume of materials challenges traditional means of metadata creation—manual techniques cannot be scaled up to meet demand. But automated techniques are available that can help in the production of metadata (natural language processing, automatic classification, document clustering). These techniques have yet to be integrated with more traditional manual techniques; such integration will be a huge task for the library community.

The Dublin Core Metadata Initiative (DCMI)

The Dublin Core Metadata Initiative (DCMI), begun in 1994, hoped to create a simplified metadata convention that would provide more effective resource discovery on the Web. Over the past 5 years, it has developed and refined a set of 15 elements—the Dublin Core Element Set (DCES)—for resource description to facilitate discovery. The DCMI has broad international participation from librarians, digital library specialists, the museum community, and other information specialists. Its advocates claim that the DCES has distinct advantages over traditional cataloging methods in terms of simplicity, interoperability, and extensibility.

DCMI, which is hosted by OCLC, represents a concerted effort by OCLC to extend the leadership role it has played with physical resources into the world of digital resources. The DCES plays an important role in one of OCLC's latest projects, the Cooperative Online Resource Cataloging (CORC) project, which is examining the use of new Web-based tools and techniques for cataloging electronic resources. One important aspect of CORC is that it examines the mechanics and economics of different levels of representation, whereby resources can be described simply using the DCES and, when appropriate and economically feasible, described more completely using traditional cataloging techniques (MARC).

The geospatial community's interest in metadata stems from the difficulty of managing and locating the burgeoning amount of data being produced by geographic information systems (GISs), remote sensing initiatives (e.g., satellites), and the defense and intelligence community. The U.S. Federal Geographic Data Committee has been working for several years to create a complete and complex metadata format for describing geospatial entities--Content Standards for Digital Geospatial Metadata. The Open GIS Consortium, which comprises technology companies, universities, and government agencies, manages consensus processes with the goal of achieving interoperability among diverse geo-processing systems.

The motivation for content-rating metadata grows out of the proliferation of adult material on the Internet and the desire for filtering mechanisms to keep certain individuals (e.g., children) from accessing certain content (e.g., pornography). Faced with this challenge, the World Wide Web Consortium (W3C) developed a description standard, Platform for Internet Content Selection (PICS).

The PICS standard enables content providers to label (voluntarily) the content they create and distribute and "enables multiple, independent labeling services to associate additional labels with content created and distributed by others."

The burgeoning of content available over the Internet has stimulated interest in the business community in mechanisms for managing, controlling, and receiving remuneration for providing access to digital intellectual property. So-called "rights management" is among the most active topics in digital library research and Internet business development. The proliferation of standards for metadata has motivated W3C to examine a general infrastructure for associating multiple metadata records with Web resources and packaging those records for exchange (as MARC does for AACR2 descriptions).

The result is the resource description framework (RDF), a major initiative by W3C to facilitate descriptions of Web resources. The intellectual underpinnings of RDF lie in a variety of knowledge representation efforts. The RDF is based on two key assumptions: (1) the diverse metadata needs of networked objects argue for a modular, not a monolithic, metadata solution and (2) the different meta-data modules should be created and managed by individual communities of experts (e.g., let the librarians construct the bibliographic descriptions). RDF is an area of intense development within the Web community, and the associated tools and standards promise to enhance significantly the functionality of the Web over the next several years.

Cataloging has evolved from primarily a library practice into an activity engaged in across the Internet economy. Library itself, faced with a proliferation of resource types and management needs, has undertaken and participated in a variety of metadata initiatives outside traditional cataloging. This proliferation of metadata types and standards raises a pressing need for intensive work, both technical and organizational, on issues of metadata interoperability.

The problem of interoperability is not new. Specialized metadata standards have been developed in many domains (e.g., law, medicine, chemistry) to help normalize the description of knowledge in each. Interoperability problems are exacerbated by the nature of the "Internet Commons, where multiple communities intermix and interact in nontraditional ways. By eliminating physical barriers, the Internet encourages interactions among formerly separate communities. In such interactions, one community may have good reason to use the work of another.

For example, an art museum may put a digitized map, which is the product of the geospatial community, on its Web page to provide directions for visitors. These spontaneous interactions underlie the need for common meta-data standards to support finding, evaluating, and managing content across traditional boundaries. Metadata interoperability has three dimensions:

— *Semantic interoperability*—Every metadata scheme defines its own set of data elements or categories for data. For example, the DCES defines a set of 15 categories for resource discovery. Semantic interoperability is the extent to which different metadata schemes express the same semantics in their categorization. Successful interoperation requires clarity about how the categories of metadata across schemes relate to each other: When do elements have the same meaning? When are elements derivatives, subsets, or variations of each other? When are elements completely unrelated?

— *Structural interoperability*—Each metadata record expresses a set of values for the categories described above. Humans are often quite capable of translating between unstructured values; many recognize that "Bill Gates" and "Gates, William H." are the same person. On the other hand, U.S. and British citizens are likely to interpret the date 10-1-99 differently. Computers are even worse at interpreting unstructured values and so require strict definitions of structure. Authority files, described above, have been the primary mechanism in the library community for enforcing structural interoperability.

— *Syntactic interoperability*—Creators of metadata want to store, exchange, and use metadata records from different sources. Such exchange requires common mechanisms for expressing metadata semantics and structure. These common mechanisms include hypertext markup language (HTML), the resource description framework (RDF), and extensible markup language (XML). The MARC record format, described above, has been the primary mechanism in the library community for addressing syntactic interoperability.

The last two areas of metadata interoperability, structural and syntactic, have been and are being addressed in forums such as the W3C and in the various standards agencies, such as the International Organization for Standardization (ISO), the American National Standards Institute (ANSI) and the (U.S.) National Institute of Standards and Technology (NIST).

The first area, semantic interoperability, is the subject of current research activity and the area in which the knowledge organization and classification expertise of the Library, and the library community in general, has the most to offer. Various metadata vocabularies are by nature frequently not semantically distinct but overlap and relate to each other in numerous ways. Achieving interoperability between these packages by means of one-to-one "crosswalks is useful, but this approach does not scale to the many metadata vocabularies that will inevitably develop.

A more scalable solution is to exploit the fact that many entities and relationships—for example, people, places, creations, organizations, events, certain relationships, and the like—are so frequently encountered that they do not fall clearly into the domain of any particular metadata vocabulary but apply across all of them. Mechanisms for semantic interoperability could exploit this fact by expressing the relationships between the vocabularies of individual metadata sets and the core concepts (e.g., places and events) using notions such as subtypes, supertypes, or siblings.

Although a number of these concepts in semantic interoperability are still in the early development or even the research stage, they address a critical problem that the Library needs to recognize: metadata vocabularies will proliferate, and methods for interoperability among them must be developed. The committee believes strongly that the Library needs to take an active role in such research areas if it is going to successfully deal with digital materials and information on the Internet.

Establishing and expressing the relationships among information resources is one of the most difficult aspects of cataloging. These relationships are multidimensional, bidirectional, and many-to-many. Examples of such relationships are translations, versions, editions, transcriptions, and structures (e.g., the issue of hierarchy and the relationship of articles to serials). In many ways the relationships between information resources are of primary importance in the management, discovery, and accessibility of these resources.

Yet, the basic model of the MARC record, whereby cataloging metadata is packaged into discrete records associated with individual information artifacts (that is, MARC records are resource-centric), makes it unwieldy to express the richness and complexity of these relationships. The importance of relationships among entities has been recognized for a long time in the database and knowledge representation communities. Entity-relationship modeling and E-R diagrams are tools to model information that expresses entity types (e.g., books, serials, agents, events), the permissible relationships between these entity types (e.g., authoring, creating, publishing) and the constraints on these relationships (e.g., an article must be "in" a journal).

Recent work in the international cataloging community recognizes the importance of relationships for formulating accurate descriptions of the resources commonly dealt with by libraries. The Functional Requirements for Bibliographic Records (FRBR), defined by an International Federation of Library Associations task force and contributed to by the Library of Congress, provides a provocative starting point for discussions on how bibliographic description might more accurately reflect resource relationships.

The FRBR presents a model that distinguishes among intellectual ideas ("works"), the forms in which they are realized ("manifestation," for example, a novel), and their availability as physical objects (e.g., as an individual book or an individual performance of a play). These stages in the evolution of intellectual content are connected by distinguishing relationships that affect the description or metadata for the objects.

The FRBR is just a start for rethinking the theory behind bibliographic description, but it provides an interesting foundation for the treatment of digital objects whose plasticity will require that considerably more attention be given to issues of relationships than has been required for physical artifacts. The importance of relationships in resource description of digital objects is also reflected in the metadata activities on the World Wide Web. The Web has demonstrated, even in its current primitive form, that the linkages (hyperlinks) between information objects are an integral part of their content. RDF incorporates a data model in which relationships, or "properties," play a key role in the description of digital resources.

5

Archival Collections

In 1990s, a wide variety of digital collections have emerged on the Internet. While digital collections may differ in content or structure, they all share one commonality—the need for metadata. Frequently described as "data about data," metadata is a critical component of all digital collections. Metadata facilitates the discovery and retrieval of information, it provides for resource presentation and navigation, and it contains the information needed to preserve digital data files.

While several digital collections of books have been created for the Internet, it is only recently that libraries and archives have begun to digitize archival collections for Web delivery. The Barren Lands project is a full-text online collection of archival material related to two exploratory surveys conducted by the Canadian explorer, geologist, and mining engineer, Joseph Burr Tyrrell. The collection is centred on Tyrrell's 1893 and 1894 explorations of Canada's Barren Lands region west of Hudson Bay, in the area now known as Nunavut. The first major challenge associated with the Barren Lands project centred on how to represent archival material within an online environment.

A search of the Internet for similar archival projects revealed that online archival collections were most often presented in one of two ways: as an online exhibition or as a simple database of independent archival documents. Following the "exhibition" method, institutions presented archival collections online in much the same way as they would present an exhibition of physical materials; narrative descriptions or transcriptions of items were presented with links to digital representations of those items. In these digital repositories, each archival document was treated as a separate entity and basic descriptive metadata elements such as title, author, and date were given for each item. Although the Barren Lands project team found aspects of both methods of delivery appealing, they decided that neither approach was fully compatible with their vision of the project.

While the "exhibition" approach provided an abundance of narrative contextual information, this method was deemed impracticable for the size of the digital collection. Similarly, a strict database approach was also not favoured, as it did not retain the contextual linkages between the documents. Instead, the Barren Lands project team decided to create two levels of descriptive metadata to provide the necessary contextual information for the archival materials and to allow for comprehensive searching. In most digital collections, each book, article, map, etc. is considered to be an independent digital object. The Barren Lands project was different in that the archival collection consisted of many documents that were inter-related with each other.

It was essential that these natural connections be retained within the digital environment. At the same time, it was necessary that each document remain an independent digital object for the purpose of resource discovery and retrieval. The solution to this problem was to adopt a two-tiered approach to the creation of descriptive metadata—one tier to describe the archival materials as a collective unit and another to describe each digital object. Although paper-based finding aids and item listings for some of the materials did exist for the J.B. Tyrrell and James W. Tyrrell collections, the project team was unable to use this information in the construction of the online collection.

Problems with the pre-existing descriptive metadata were three-fold: first, the metadata was not in electronic format; second, the metadata did not contain all of the necessary descriptive information; and third, the archival materials were not described consistently according to archival descriptive standards. Because of these problems, the project team decided to re-describe both collections according to the Canadian descriptive standard, the Rules for Archival Description (RAD). Once the descriptive metadata was complete, it was necessary to encode this information in a standard data structure.

In order to retain the relationships between archival materials, the project team adopted the Encoded Archival Description (EAD) data structure standard, which is jointly administered by the Society of American Archivists and the Library of Congress. EAD is a non-proprietary standard in the form of a Standard Generalized Markup Language (SGML) and Extensible Markup Language (XML) Document Type Definition (DTD). Developed specifically for archival finding aids, the EAD standard has the ability to accurately represent the multilevel nature of archives in a machine-readable format. Consequently, the EAD standard facilitates access by allowing users to "drill down" into an archival finding aid, beginning at the fonds or collection level description down to the descriptions of individual items. In the Barren Lands project, the descriptions of the J.B. Tyrrell and James W. Tyrrell fonds were encoded using the XML version of the EAD DTD. In these multi-level records, users are provided with descriptions of the entire fonds, the various series of documents that make up the fonds, and file level descriptions if they exist.

Within the description of each series or file containing digitized objects, a link is made from the title of the object to a separate item level description. While EAD does provide the capability to describe archival materials down to the item level of description, the project team decided that within the context of the project, the standard was unsuitable for that purpose. The problems associated with multiple media collections do not generally lie in the presentation of various media, but rather in their preparation for online delivery. The Barren Lands project consists of a variety of documentary forms, all of which needed to be handled in a slightly different manner. As a form of structural metadata, the file naming structure was used to distinguish between documentary forms. Directories were created for each type of document, such as letters, diaries, published text, maps, photographs, and so on.

Then, as each archival document was scanned, a unique identifier, containing a letter to identify the documentary form followed by a five-digit number, was recorded in a relational database. The project team felt strongly that no semantic information be included in the file naming system as this type of information would likely become confusing rather than helpful in the long run. This file-naming system not only ensured that we had a simple, well-organized repository for the images, it also allowed the team to quickly identify which image files required OCR and which files needed rekeying.

In the Barren Lands project, structural information such as unique identifiers, page sequence numbers, page numbers as stated on the document, special features such as tables of contents and indexes, and other relevant information was collected in a relational database at the point of scanning. Some descriptive metadata relating to individual pages of the digital object, such as titles of maps or illustrations and content dates were also recorded in the database. In addition to descriptive and structural metadata, the Barren Lands project team also captured administrative or technical metadata during the scanning process. As each image was scanned, information relating to the source type, file format, scanning date, and scanner was captured in a relational database. Adobe Portable Document Format (PDF) is a widely used standard for electronic document distribution worldwide in many institutional settings. Much of its popularity comes from its ability to faithfully encode both the text and the visual appearance of source documents, preserving their fonts, formatting, colors, and graphics.

PDF files can be viewed, navigated, and printed with a free Adobe Acrobat Reader, available on all major computing platforms. PDF has many applications and is commonly used to publish government, public, and academic documents. Many of the electronic journals and other digital resources acquired by libraries are published in PDF format. As libraries grow more dependent on electronic resources, they need to consider how they can preserve these resources for the long term. Many libraries retain back runs of print journals that are over 100 years old, and which are still consulted by researchers.

No digital technology has lasted nearly that long, and many data formats have already become obsolete and not easily readable in a much shorter time period. PDF is a platform-independent document format developed by Adobe as a follow-up to its Postscript language. Although Postscript was designed specifically for printing, PDF is meant to support on-line, secure, interactive use, as well as printing. PDF combines attributes of structured text formats and traditional image formats, so that a document can be used both in terms of its text and in terms of its "look" on-screen or on the page.

A PDF file does not always contain the full glyph specification of characters in the document, but at least includes the name of the fonts used and specifies the space all characters will occupy. PDF includes metadata on the document, specifying things such as page size, page numbering, and a structured table of contents. Add-ons, such as hyperlinks, forms, and even pieces of scripting code in Java or Postscript that control dynamic displays or the user interface, can also be included. Not all PDF documents encode the text of a document directly. It is possible to embed images of a page in PDF, so that a picture of text is encoded but not the text itself. Some scanners, for instance, can output this "uninterpreted" form of PDF.

Such uninterpreted PDF files tend to be much larger than PDF files that encode text directly as characters, and text-oriented operations such as searching and textual copying and pasting are not supported by these files. Some programs also exist that will attempt to recognize whatever text they can in a scanned PDF document, and replace the images of this text with a briefer encoding of the characters and fonts. Such programs tend to produce "hybrid" PDF files where encoded text strings in appropriate fonts are positioned inside page images, and any unrecognized characters are kept on the page in the form of images. Although such PDF files can be smaller than those that consist only of uninterpreted page images, they also often have only partial, and choppy, encoding of their underlying text, because recognition programs typically cannot recognize 100% of the text in a typical page scan.

PDF was originally designed for 8-bit character sets. Some limited support for Unicode also exists, but the format has not yet taken full advantage of Unicode's capabilities. Unlike XML, PDF was not originally designed for arbitrary structural annotations, although the last revision of PDF includes some facilities for user-defined structural markup. PDF is a less efficient format for text analysis than purely text-based formats such as XML or HTML, and readers have noted that searching for words within a PDF viewer can be noticeably slower than searching for words in an HTML viewer. The central role that appearance plays in PDF is both a strength and a weakness; it allows publishers to specify exactly how they want a document to look, but it also makes it difficult for users to reformat or repaginate the document if that would be better for them.

PDF includes facilities for encrypting content, or directing that a document not be printable. It is possible to use encryption so that a document cannot be decrypted without a password. However, once the document is decrypted, it is possible, in theory, to make an unlocked copy that can be freely copied, read, or printed. Adobe is highly invested in the success of PDF, but even if Adobe fails or abruptly changes course, a community of third-party tools for handling PDF has started to emerge. PDF is used widely by many well-funded bodies so there should be widespread support for using and migrating PDF, should Adobe fail to provide adequate support for the format. Even so, it is likely that PDF will one day be superseded by another format. It may be a successor format, or it may be a completely different format that users prefer over PDF. Hence, it is necessary to have migration strategies planned for PDF.

Currently, there is no other format that can encompass all of the features of PDF in a form that standard tools can interpret. Most page image formats are pixel-oriented, where pictures are encoded using a grid with each grid cell (known as a pixel) associated with a particular color (or with no added color). Some image formats, including PDF and Postscript, are stroke-oriented, encoded with instructions about lines to plot, regions to color, and text to place. They can also include instructions to embed pixel-oriented images at specified locations. Pixel-oriented formats have a well-understood mathematical representation, making them easy to migrate.

Stroke-oriented image formats are not so standardized. They can encode information about the structure of a picture, such as the lines that are drawn in it, that can only be approximated to a certain resolution in purely pixel-oriented formats. On the other hand, since pixel-oriented formats can typically accommodate very fine resolutions, an image converted from a stroke-oriented format to a pixel-oriented format at fine enough resolution can be visually indistinguishable from its original. PDF can also be converted into text, at least when the text (rather than pictures of the text) has been directly encoded in PDF files.

Formatting and layout information would be lost in a straight text conversion, and the text conversion of certain pages with complex layout may not always be read in "logical" reading order, without human intervention. Different PDF-generating programs may be more or less accommodating about rendering PDF text in a logical reading order. A straight text conversion would also lose structural information and other PDF extras, as well non-textual items such as pictures, diagrams, and possibly equations. However, it is possible to write conversions to HTML or XML that would include a "table of contents" header that incorporated the structure of the PDF document, and that would preserve certain types of PDF hyperlinks.

Text in non-European languages may also be difficult to migrate correctly, because of the previously-described limitations of PDF's support for Unicode, unless a standard set of well-defined fonts, with widely available specifications, is used to represent non-European characters. Although it is possible to migrate the appearance of PDF files, or the text, migrating both of them into a single document would be more difficult. The only other formats commonly used to specify both the text and the appearance of documents are word-processor formats, and those tend to be proprietary, system-dependent, and more ephemeral than PDF itself is likely to be.

Converting to these formats may also lead to subtly different appearances, depending on the implementation of the word processing program. RTF (Rich Text Format) may be the best target for word-processor-oriented conversions at this time, though it is far from a perfect choice. Even if it is infeasible to migrate both the text and the look of PDF into a single document, it may still be possible to migrate PDF documents into a presentation that allows one to switch between text-oriented and image-oriented views of the same document. In theory, it is possible to convert all of the information in a PDF file into an XML format with appropriate tags and attributes.

Libraries extend the power of the word over time and over space. The world over, it is emblematic of the largest and most complete collection of written materials. In US, Library of Congress (LC) is incomplete, incomplete in a thousand ways. It holds millions of titles but has no precise idea of how many books in the world it does not hold, although the number is certainly large. The greatness of the Library of Congress since the Second World War lies in the fact that it has developed its own collection at the same time as it has facilitated the growth and interdependency of the worldwide collection of the treasures of human creativity.

It is evidently impossible that copies of everything should ever be found in a single place—it takes an Alexandrian monarch or an Argentinian poet to imagine such things. But it is far from impossible that collections great and small will one day be so tightly interlinked by the exchange of data about their holdings that we will eventually know where and how to find a vastly larger percentage of the materials held in them. The last two generations have already seen huge progress in this regard, going back to LC's epochal agreement to disseminate cataloging information from its holdings and now leveraged to a wider world by such widely accessible catalogs as the Research Library Group's (RLG's) Eureka or the Online Computer Library Center's (OCLC's) WorldCat.

All of these real achievements pale by comparison with what can be imagined for the world of cyberspace. Far more information from far more sources can be brought together in nearly real time. The floods of new, increasingly available electronic information can be drawn together, sorted, filtered, and made usefully accessible. Such a possibility is easy to evoke but difficult to achieve. For a long time, traditional library materials have formed only a part of the collection: beyond books and journals and maps, LC has been collecting advertising materials, motion pictures, and baseball cards.

Today, at least three additional categories of information material challenge LC's traditional practices. The categories of material are as follows:

— *Born-digital*—Under this heading fall materials containing socially valuable and interesting information created in electronic form. Typically, we regard such materials as necessary either because they have no corresponding print form or, if they have one, they possess significant individuality in electronic form to merit inclusion in a serious library collection. Born-digital materials in turn fall into two categories:

— *Artifactual:* These are digital information materials that are published and distributed in ways that depend on particular physical media and artifacts--floppy disks, CD-ROMs, laser video disks, and the like.

— *Nonartifactual:* Increasingly, digital information does not appear in forms that lend themselves to physical collection by libraries. Web sites increase the number of sources where information of the highest social value may be found, but it is often functionally impossible to "acquire" a Web site—even if one copied all the public pages of a site, substantial additional bodies of material that lie behind it (e.g., databases that are accessed by commands issued from the Web pages) would not be publicly available. The quantity and quality of material available in this form can only be expected to grow in the coming years.

— *Turned digital*—By this phrase is meant materials that were originally created in a traditional artifactual form (usually print) but have been converted to digital media for reasons of preservation and/or access. There is already a history of cooperative activity surrounding preservation decisions (that is, decisions to change the media of presentation in order to preserve the content of the original), but this movement must now be accelerated, for two reasons:

  — The use of electronic media for preservation has advantages in cost and accessibility over many other media (though electronic media may introduce new preservation problems of their own).

  — Digital representations of print materials and other physical artifacts are increasingly popular when the purpose is not only preservation but also a concomitant increase in ease of access and use, particularly for rare or fragile materials.

For digital materials, both "born" and "turned," there is a nationwide and worldwide need for coordination and communication so that expensive and time-consuming projects do not duplicate other efforts. Furthermore, the results of digital preservation efforts can and should be widely shared, and for that reason turned-digital materials will quickly begin to behave just as born-digital materials do. A library such as LC will presumably first digitize treasures of its own but will then wish to have access to those of other libraries. In the world of print materials, LC's strategy was straightforward: to leverage its statutory rights of collection (through copyright deposit) to achieve physical collections of unparalleled size and quality.

In the digital realms, LC starts with many fewer advantages. The digitization of its own existing collections can give it, to be sure, tremendously rich and exciting materials for a new digital collection. But no matter how aggressively LC collects digital materials, achieving a truly universal collection will now increasingly mean recognizing that not everything can be collected, because the volume of digital information is so great. Also, many publishers and distributors of material of high value will produce material in a form that must be consulted remotely and cannot be physically added to the working collections of the Library.

When physical possession is not possible or desirable, it will be all the more important that firm and secure links between LC and other stakeholders in the information community are established. If LC possesses a physical book, it can take its own steps to ensure preservation and accessibility—or even, if appropriate, to practice relative neglect—thereby making it possible for a book to be usable generations after its creation. Where LC possesses the original source files or identical copies, preservation will be a demanding chore. Where LC does not possess the digital source files, assurance of preservation and access will require coordination of a complicated social, legal, and economic strategy.

No library in the world has the prestige or the influence of the Library of Congress, if LC will only use it. Over the last two decades, the Library has been too little visible on the national and international stage, particularly in the digital arena. Too many of the stunning achievements of LC leadership and collaboration are now receding into the hallowed past. Moreover, it has been the case that projects and/or exhibitions of great significance have not always been consistently institutionalized as ongoing services.

At the same time, it is important to be clear about the kind of role that LC can and should take. The vast size of its collections and its national importance to the United States do not elevate it—or any other player—above the rest of the library community. The Library should see itself as a particularly privileged, and therefore particularly responsible, partner in a wide range of conversations. The important role LC could play in establishing standards for a wide variety of infrastructural elements of the library of the future, just as it did in the past when it created the MARC record. But LC cannot dictate the outcomes of such a process to others. Rather, its true value would be to bring stakeholders together in a collaborative process that begins by identifying issues and needs that cut across broad swathes of the information community.

While LC and all of the other stakeholders are sobered by the realization that the outcomes of high-level summits are always debatable and never last forever, they can take heart from knowing that LC would participate in such conversations not as one of several hostile parties seeking influence but rather as the genuine representative of a common public good that can advance the interests of other participants in the process. A genuinely broad vision and a determined insistence on turning that vision into reality must be accompanied by a collegial, humble manner that seeks the broadest possible common good for both the users and the producers of information.

The Library must recognize and genuinely respect other senior partners in these undertakings. Over the last three decades, both RLG and OCLC have emerged as serious and respected players in advancing broad and reliable access to library materials. Relations among these three organizations have at times been no better than cool. RLG's and OCLC's joint representations to the committee suggested that they see the value and necessity of working with each other in productive ways and with LC.

Collaboration of this sort may not prove easy for LC, because decisions taken two decades ago led to the creation of a highly successful system whereby OCLC distributes catalog records to a wide variety of libraries, and these records include the very substantial body of cataloging created by LC. The results for users have been overwhelmingly positive, however, and the cost savings to the library community extraordinary. Great things have been achieved by LC, OCLC, and RLG, and it is time to look to the future in a trusting and collaborative spirit.

The experience of installing the new Integrated Library System in 1999 shows that even when the Library waits until a technology is well established and in use at other libraries, its size and scope make it hard to tailor the technology to the Library's needs. The Library should look for ways to influence the technologies it will use earlier in their development cycle, ensuring that both library technology research and product development address issues of scale early on. In order to succeed, it is necessary for LC and its leaders to be seen and heard widely in the library community in the United States and abroad. It is unfortunate, although understandable, that none of the three senior officers of the Library has chosen to dedicate time to becoming heavily involved with the library community.

In US, the National Science Foundation distributed funds through the 1990s for its Digital Libraries Initiative (DLI). The inclusion of LC as a partner of DLI is a promising step in the right direction, but more substantive involvement in the DLI and engagement in other, comparable initiatives need to be pursued aggressively. The Library is at a disadvantage owing to its lack of a research capability and its inability to provide significant funding for research by others, for even when it sees an opportunity it has only modest means to exert influence. Still, LC could provide small research grants to be used for cooperative efforts with others, or it could develop other means to support the needed research (e.g., sponsor visiting research fellows at LC, if such a program were in place).

The Library of Congress must seek out, generate, and empower leaders who will be visible and influential as spokespersons for the library community and the interests of a broad range of information users. Such leadership could be credible and effective at creating the connections that the future of libraries requires. By U.S. law, the Library of Congress is only Congress's library, not the nation's. The Library's role and function thus differ significantly from those of counterpart libraries in other countries. It is important, however, to understand that a number of the Library's functions are characteristic of the functions of a national library. These include but are not limited to the following:

— It serves as the national (copyright) depository library with a mission to assemble a comprehensive national collection.

— It is the authoritative national source of cataloging information.

— It de facto represents the United States in bodies and organizations where the other participants represent the national libraries of their countries.

There is today no easy replacement of paper with digital materials, and comparatively few cost-saving benefits will be reaped from automation per se: those days are largely over. We live in a time when libraries will see their missions expanded as they continue to collect and preserve analog materials while at the same time participating wholeheartedly in the digital revolution. The users of libraries—from senators to ordinary citizens to research scholars—will demand (and deserve) no less.

The Library owns precious content that many publishers and entertainment industry producers would be happy to develop. It has reservations, however, for it has had some negative experiences with such partners. These reservations are understandable, but they should transmute not into suspicion but into a strategy for partnership. Insofar as LC remains committed to the business of disseminating its collections to a broad public, and in particular to schoolchildren, it should look for neither a core congressional allocation nor charitable contributions to support that commitment. Rather, LC should seek to disseminate its collections to a wider public by means of a mutually beneficial partnership with the private sector—a partnership that goes beyond the contribution of funds or equipment by using the partnership to develop the technical and marketing expertise of the Library (i.e., to effect technology transfer).

To the extent that there are legal and practical restrictions on such partnerships, the committee strongly urges Congress to respond by facilitating the creative exploitation of a cultural treasure. In the end, of course, LC's collections belong to the nation, and that fact sets limits to the rights that LC can assign to its prospective partners and thus, inevitably, to the degree of exploitation that is possible.

Traditional processes can also be facilitated through the use of information technology to improve access for clients and to increase revenue. For example, the Photoduplication Service might sell its products through the Web. There are surely other strategic opportunities of a nontraditional kind, for example, with "portals" that would let the portals' customers link more effectively to LC, while LC would find in such (presumably nonexclusive) arrangements an effective and essentially cost-free marketing strategy.

E-journal Archiving

E-journals may publish articles as they are ready, without waiting for a whole issue's worth of articles, but this change is sequential addition. Dynamic e-journals can be defined as those that contain moving elements or make elements move. Moving elements include, for example, audio and video clips as well as animations. Because moving elements are not printable, libraries can no longer rely on printing the e-journals as a primary preservation strategy. Microfilm and microform are likewise static and cannot accommodate moving elements either. E-journals that can make elements move typically include embedded software that enables movement, or scripts and programs that render content on the fly. Because one cannot print dynamic e-journals to preserve them, the task at hand is to define new ways of preserving content that makes no sense without these constituent, dynamic aspects.

While we know how to catalog, index, and retrieve moving files, we must refine this cataloging since the elements are embedded in more readily cataloged articles. Cataloging, indexing, and retrieving the kind of content that cannot be rendered without interactive functionality are particularly vexing hurdles, especially if the content changes with every user's instantiation of that content. Dynamic electronic journals are a natural outgrowth of Internet and Web technologies. The electronic journals were born in Web environments and are meant to be rendered and displayed in current Web environments. However we preserve them, for the time being they must also be Web accessible.

In the future, it is likely that electronic material will be rendered in other digital (and perhaps even non-digital) environments. Of course, besides dynamic elements and functionalities, dynamic e-journals contain text and other intellectually significant elements.

Management of Library Collection

Information and communications technology (ICT) offers considerable potential for raising the level of collections management. It has particular applications in cataloguing and documentation and in reaching wider audiences through digital networks. Yet many institutions feel that they are lagging behind other public sector bodies in the application of technology. In some cases the problem is the lack of hardware, in others, institutions are using inappropriate software. Many also feel that they have inadequate access to the skills needed to make the most of the technology.

Resource is contributing to the development of a co-ordinated approach to digital preservation across the sector through the Digital Preservation Coalition and other collaborations. The starting point for strategic management of the cultural heritage is a better understanding of the nature and location of the various collections that make up the distributed national collection. Such understanding is also a pre-requisite for co-operation between institutions with common interests. People need to know what exists and where it is located. The process of describing and documenting collections of material is, however, far from straightforward. At present, insufficient importance is attached to conservation and collections management.

As a consequence, there is a risk that unconsidered neglect of collections will result in a loss to future generations of users. There is a particular need to raise awareness and shape attitudes among governing bodies and funding agencies More generally, Resource will work to promote a more informed public understanding of stewardship issues and how they impact upon both users and non-users of cultural heritage services. During the seventies, manual back-room activities, such as acquisition, distribution and cataloguing, were turned into computer-controlled activities. As a result, the library's traditional customers had to fundamentally reorient themselves to the new way in which bibliographic information was now becoming available, that is through an on-line public access catalogue (OPAC). This period also saw the introduction of the first local bibliographic and indexing databases, as well as various other databases.

During the second wave of library computerisation, which started in the 90s, the focus was on the deployment of computer networks providing access to remote electronic information by means of library information systems. Access to electronic information is no longer limited to so-called secondary information (catalogues, bibliographic databases). Primary information has now become electronically available as well. For instance, users will have access to the electronic full-text versions of scientific journals. Electronic textbooks and readers enable users to consult information outside the library, i.e. at the professional and private workplaces of the library's traditional customer. One very important trend is the decreasing prominence of the library's physical collection, and the corresponding increase in the importance of information reference.

The library is developing into a gateway, referring users to information irrespective of the location where that information is physically stored. A second trend is taking place in the traditional appreciation of library tasks as some kind of overhead. In the future, library tasks will be regarded as directly productive forces. It is becoming ever more difficult to distinguish between the actual provision of information and the various processes in which that information is used. A university library, for example, is connected to a university, whose primary tasks are education and research. At its most fundamental level, education is characterised by the transfer of knowledge from teacher to student. The traditional borderline between knowledge transfer through teaching on the one hand and the provision of information by the library on the other is fading fast, due to the use of information technology in education.

To a growing extent, library services are blending with the teaching process. Similar trends can be observed in the process of research and in other primary processes supported by library tasks, for example in policy-making and legal consultancy. A third trend is eroding the self-evident position of the library in the process from information production to information consumption. However, while some of the traditional library tasks are under threat, new activities also present opportunities for strengthening the library's position. In order to understand the way in which the library's activities are influenced by the implementation of new technology, we should take a look at the so-called information chain.

The role of the library is often described as one link in that chain. In the traditional information chain the main functions, i.e. the production, distribution, acquisition, and consumption of information, were always accommodated in strictly separated stages. However, the configuration of functions within the information chain has begun to change, and within this changing constellation all the parties involved are struggling to determine their positions. These developments show how important it is for those parties to innovate themselves and to experiment creatively with new roles instead of adhering to traditional patterns. Any forceful attempt to preserve the old structure will not only impede any development as such, but will also expose that structure to the increasing threat of arbitrary disintegration.

Information Retrieval

Information retrieval is not a service to be delivered exclusively by publishers. The libraries in particular have an important role as facilitators of the navigation possibilities available to the users. There are several reasons for this. Traditionally, libraries operate in close contact with their users and communicate with them in order to establish specific user needs. The invisible library could offer the following services to its users. Search facilities are subject to a number of basic user requirements, the most important of which can be summarised as follows. Users will want to be able to start the search process immediately, without first having to study complex interfaces and codes.

They are looking for information and cannot be expected to be interested in the technical structure or format of the data involved. Neither are users likely to be interested in the origin of the source (the identity of the publisher or intermediary), or in the location where the information they need is physically stored. They just want to find an answer to a particular question. During the search process, moreover, users will only want to be presented answers that are fully relevant to their question, without being swamped by thousands of articles only marginally related to the subject.

Personal alerting system is vital to provide an easily accessible information universe which the user can enter independently provided he is equipped with the proper IR tools. In addition, the user should be served by his own personal assistant, who offers packages of information tailored to the user's individual reader profile. Such assistants have already been created in self-learning software known as intelligent agents technology. These assistants, or agents, are used in the construction of a personal alerting system.

The set-up and testing of such personal alerting systems is the responsibility of support organisations, for example university libraries; their use requires no additional intermediaries. Researchers, teachers and students will all make use of this tool independently and will only require assistance from the library when they need specific instructions or are confronted with specific problems. The traditional library organisation was characterised by a decentralised structure in which individual libraries were found in the locations where teaching and research activities actually took place (mostly in the university professors' rooms).

In order to improve efficiency, to solve logistic problems and, above all, to cut costs books and magazines were relocated to central or faculty libraries. Double subscriptions were cancelled. While obviously provoking some protest from among faculty members, this operation was in many cases inevitable. Due to the advent of the Internet and electronic sources of information, the physical location of those sources has become irrelevant. From behind a PC in his or her own office, today's scientist has access to a range of sources that is incomparable to the access provided by the traditional library in the professor's lecture room. While the range of sources offers clear and major advantages, its very extensiveness also causes a number of problems.

Some of these can be obviated by IR systems and personal agents, but more tools are required; tools that help the user to create and manage his/her own limited but tailor-made collection. These tools allow the scientist to become a librarian himself, but a librarian who has no other clients. Scientists need tools to perform this role, tools that help them organise their own articles, research data, teaching material, etc.; tools which respect the preferences of their users and can deal with even the most idiosyncratic approach to building up personal collections.

It is one of the library's tasks to make such tools available. They can be described as the creation of facilities, the supply of user instructions for those facilities and the provision of assistance when problems occur, and are all consistent with user demands. Information cannot be separated from the purpose it is used for. At universities, that purpose can be found in the primary processes of education and research. This is why the university library's tasks are focused on the integration of information services in the user's primary processes. Such integration is not achieved automatically, however.

A teacher who is preparing a new online reader will need access not only to all relevant sources and search and selection tools, but also to online publishing facilities. These may be templates provided with conversion programmes which adapt the content (text, image, video) for presentation on the world wide web, or old readers already converted from the old, illegible formats to formats that enable the teacher to cut and paste selected items for use in his new reader. The library consists of information and software and has been fully integrated into the teaching process. The tasks of the library may reach beyond the efficient and effective supply of information. Researchers do not merely consume information, but also communicate intensively with their colleagues. When they read a scientific article, many researchers will want to respond, ask the author questions or give critical comments.

The integration of the library in primary processes can advance to such a degree that the library becomes altogether invisible as a separate institute. The user takes on the role of the librarian. He gains access to a vast amount of information and is provided with a set of tools and aids that will help him extract the data he needs and arrange and process it in the manner that suits him best. Library services in which libraries provide access to as much electronic information as possible and offer additional services that enable users to organise the sources of information they need for personal professional purposes. The future of the library, the 'collection' tends to be seen as a concept that will continue to play a prominent role.

The user can arrange the information sources relevant to his own professional needs into a tailor-made collection with the help of the tools presented by the library, organise those sources according to the use he expects to make of them, and integrate them into his own publications or educational programmes. These considerations do not apply to certified sources, such as freely accessible sources on the Internet. In that area, libraries will continue to be responsible for the selection of high-quality scientific material; a selection in the form of pointers, sets of references.

Far-reaching forms of cooperation among the libraries themselves are also quite conceivable. What is known in the physical world as the alignment of collection formation profiles, or priority area formation, is, understandably, only rarely successful. This concept may yield countless advantages for the virtual selection of Internet sources. The task of designating quality sources can be distributed due to the very fact that the physical location of the information is irrelevant and, hence, allows universal access. This is because this task does not involve the development of a central collection, but rather the certification of a sub-collection of information. In part, collection management is limited to measuring the frequency with which the sources are consulted and the type of use that is made of them. Related to, and indeed derived from this is the management not of the collection itself, but of various types of licenses.

Collection management refers to a distributed process of assessment of the quality of freely accessible sources on the Internet. Librarians whose careers spanned the pre- and post-1950s worlds noted a marked expansion in the scope of scholarship in America. Before World War II, academic research in America concentrated on Western culture and classical areas of science. After the war, American research horizons expanded to cover all areas of the world as well as applied and specialized fields of science. Library collections grew rapidly to house the products of this expanded research effort. In the 1950s and 60s many university librarians found themselves in the midst of a "golden age" of collection development when acquisitions funds seemed plentiful, U.S. currency was strong, and there was still room in academic library book stacks. In the mid-1980s many universities and research libraries found themselves in a period of fiscal constraint and even decline. Economic constraints affected all aspects of research library operations.

Librarians now had to balance the demands of print and digital materials, even as they sought to understand the nature and consequences of digital, networked information and the impact a new information system would have on library operations, including the budget. At the same time, scholarly publishing was also experiencing dramatic change. With fewer orders from libraries, university presses had to cut back the number of monograph titles they published, while commercial journal publishers, at least some of the largest science and technology publishers, were expanding and flourishing. Collection management librarians - and library directors - are faced with a new and uncharted environment. Libraries have much less buying power than they had a decade ago.

With fewer staff in collection management full time, many selectors and bibliographers work at collection management part time while handling a much broader range of disciplines and formats. The technical advances in digitization are truly revolutionizing the way scholarly information is published, organized, and maintained, and both the scope and extent of this change are difficult to comprehend and manage. As difficult as it was to manage a print collection, librarians now have two equally formidable formats to consider: print and digital. When digital resources were first introduced in research libraries, there was a good deal of conflict between the old and new format.

Rather than a highly decentralized system as exists today, with duplicative print collections spread across the country, digital technology has the potential to provide more centrally organized information storage and highly distributed, quick, and cost-effective access. Digital technology can also foster the integration of the various components and sources of scholarly publication. Such integration is already happening on the Web platform and through the efforts of library and scientific information services.

Issues

Libraries and universities have a stake in helping electronic publishing to succeed, and therefore have an interest in establishing secure, persistent and authoritative digital research libraries. The requirements of digital technologies will change the way most librarians work throughout research libraries. As it happens, professional librarians are uniquely qualified to take up the technological challenge. But if they do not, they will contribute to the stagnation of their own profession as well as fail in their professional responsibility to civilization.

Electronic documents, by contrast, force the preservation considerations to divide into two: the preservation of the objects, as before, but also the preservation of the information contained in those objects and which is now so easily separable from them. The primary requirement for a digital research library is that from the start it be committed to organizing, storing and providing electronic information for periods of time longer than human lives. A library is an organization, rather than a building or a collection, than the requirement for institutional commitment for electronic information to have more than a fleeting existence. The organization of libraries is already changing as electronic information increasingly becomes part of their charge.

Most research libraries have had substantial systems departments which maintain infrastructures while the librarians take on more and more digital information responsibilities. Some libraries locate the responsibility for electronic information distinctly from that for print. Most libraries are coming to see the forms as inseparable and include digital responsibilities along with artifactual responsibilities in assignments for collection development, cataloging and public service. As libraries move more into the electronic environment the historic tripartite division of libraries into public services, technical services and collection development continues functionally but in more fluid arrangements.

In addition, the need for consortial activity has become evident both for provision and preservation of digital information. People who combine bibliographic understanding, problem-solving abilities, negotiating skills and process orientation will be needed throughout libraries; such staff will take on the demanding new technical, collection and service responsibilities for long-term support of digital collections. The permanent existence of a digital research library will require assured continuity in operational funding. Almost any other library activity can survive a funding hiatus of a year or more.

Acquisitions, building maintenance, and preservation can be suspended, or an entire staff can be dispersed and a library shut down for several years, and the artifactual collections will more or less survive. But digital collections, like the online catalog, require continual maintenance if they are to survive more than a very brief interruption of power, environmental control, backup, migration and related technical care. Online catalog maintenance costs have reached a rough steady state, and the capital costs for new OPACs are decreasing relative to the capabilities provided. The catalog size will continue to increase, but catalog records are small relative to the information to which they refer.

Digital collections, however, as a proportion of the library's supply of information, will grow for the foreseeable future, and the quantity of information requiring care will become considerable. Unit costs of storage are likely to continue falling for some time, which may make the financial burden manageable. Long term funding will be required to assure long term care. Libraries and their parent institutions will need to develop new fiscal tools and use familiar fiscal tools for new purposes.

Public institutions, usually constrained to annual funding, will have particular difficulties, but existing procedures for capital or plant funding may provide precedents. One familiar technique is the endowment. It has been difficult to obtain private funding for endowments of concepts and services rather than books and mortar, but it is possible. Institutions might also build endowments out of operating funds over periods of time. Some revenue streams associated with digital research libraries may be practical.

Consortial arrangements may allow for lease or purchase of shares in a digital collection. Shorter-term access might be provided to other institutions on a usage basis. Access could be sold to certain classes of users, e.g. businesses, non-local clienteles, or specific information projects. New relations with publishers, presently difficult to perceive through the miasmic fog rising from intellectual property, might provide income for storage of electronically published materials during the copyright lifetime in which publishers collect usage fees. All these are instrumental means of accomplishing the greatest requirement, that of conscious, planned institutional commitment to preserve that part of human culture which will flower in electronic form.

The advent of electronic information will accentuate the difference between these roles as libraries take the responsibility for the preservation of information in nonartifactual forms. For the past century most research libraries have been associated with universities, and this connection seems likely to continue in the immediate future. Whatever the governance structure, an institution wishing to benefit from electronic information will have to make a conscious commitment to providing resources.

In the electronic environment, this means new longstanding financial commitments which the library and university together must identify and accomplish. The commitment will have to be clearly and publicly made if scholars and other libraries are to have confidence that a given digital collection is indeed likely to exist for the long term. It is essential that guidelines or standards be established defining what is meant by a long term commitment, and defining what electronic repositories of data can qualify to be called a digital research library. Archives serve a variety of different functions in the larger society and even within the smaller scholarly community.

Research libraries in particular serve to support education, continuous learning and research for their designated constituents. The focal points of this type of collection are intellectual artifacts generally in textual and graphic formats. An increasingly significant amount of the intellectual content is published and distributed in electronic journals. For all journals with printed versions, information about both the printed and electronic versions is available in the electronic version. All journal sites have basic descriptive information such as scope and purpose, subject coverage, and copyright statement.

Linking is a fast-changing area in e-journals and represents one of the great value-added features of electronic over paper publishing. However, links pose significant challenges in archiving. The largest application of links today is for references, allowing a user to navigate automatically from one article to a related cited article. Most publishers, however, do not simply insert static links in references. Most links today are in the form of Digital Object Identifiers (DOIs), a type of persistent link or "name" that remains valid even if the cited work moves between systems or publishers. While the majority of links found in e-journals today are for references, there is every reason to expect linking to become richer with time.

While considering the components of electronic journals which should be archived and how much of the look and feel of an e-journal should be preserved, there were concerns that costs would prohibit comprehensive archiving. It is clear that all articles, reports, columns, editorials, communications, abstracts, errata, and correspondence must be archived. It is less clear which other components should be preserved and how nontraditional components — such as links, threaded discussions, data sets, and data simulations — should be handled. Hierarchical links among volumes, issues, tables of contents, and articles were identified as important.

Auditing is particularly important for the Archive since it represents the only use of archived content while that content is in its initial dark period prior to the occurrence of a trigger event. The composition of the auditors could be drawn from domain experts, subject area librarians, faculty, and scholarly societies. It remains an open question whether domain expertise is required or practical. However, initial quality control and internal and external auditing are not sufficient to insure the viability of files over time.

Although initial quality control procedures varied, each organization maintains that actual usage is one of the best mechanisms for insuring content viability. The Harvard University Library Access Management Service (AMS) allows fine granularity of access control, down to the level of permitting access to a particular object by a particular user through the use of a particular application. This level of control is appropriate and practical to support auditing, but expensive to extend to large-scale external use.

An archive intending to restrict access to only those who have had a past subscription to the archived content would bear considerable expense to gather the required licensee information and to build and operate the appropriate access management system. Rather than pursue this option, Harvard believed that the increasingly wide-spread adoption of the "moving wall" concept in the scholarly journal environment suggested a more practical approach.

In the e-journal environment libraries are moving to an architecture which separates archiving from daily service, making archiving costs painfully apparent. Further, it is unlikely the libraries will have or need the same large-scale redundancy in e-journal archiving that they have had for paper journals. It is more likely that the operating costs of archiving will be centered in only a few places, raising obvious issues of how to spread costs fairly.

Understandably, economic issues were discussed extensively during the planning year: within Harvard, with its publisher partners, and with other institutions thinking about archiving. Beginning to understand real costs will be one of the key objectives of any implementation project. It is clear, however, that keeping costs low is enormously important; the magnitude of costs will greatly influence the outcome of the question of who is willing to share in the cost of archiving. Harvard identified some strategies for controlling costs. First, by building an archiving program over a larger digital library environment, activities (preservation monitoring), organization (computer operations), and technical infrastructure (a digital repository) already in place can be used to support the archiving activity. Second, applying smart automation to the process of adding content to the Archive can be used to reduce labor, and thus the cost, of ongoing Archive operation. Third, limiting the functionality of the Archive allows Harvard to eliminate costly development components such as subscription management systems.

Certainly Harvard would expect to contribute to the cost of archiving, but it will be difficult to convince university administrators that the institution should simply dedicate resources at this level for the common good. Some have suggested an archive should support itself, at least in part, by providing services others would pay to use based on the archived content. Harvard has proposed that funding for a sustainable archive accompany the deposit of content from the outset. The model initially proposed was that there be an explicit "archiving surcharge" publishers would charge all institutional subscribers to archived titles that would be passed on to the Archive.

The intent of the proposal was that the community that benefits from the Archive also assumes some share of the cost of archiving. Harvard's publisher partners did not want the Archive to dictate pricing policy to them, so this model was modified as follows. The publishers would pay the Archive an annual fee for archiving. They in turn could collect the required funds from any one of a number of sources including authors, sponsoring scholarly societies, or subscribers as appropriate in individual cases.

Harvard has suggested that if it chooses to cease archiving any given set of materials, this specific content of the Archive would be transferred to another archive selected by agreement between Harvard and a stakeholder community.

In addition, an amount of the remaining archiving fund proportional to the amount deposited by each publisher for those e-journal titles would be transferred to the new archiving organization. In the case where a publisher chooses to terminate its relationship with Harvard's Archive, materials that have previously been deposited will remain in the Archive, and deposit of all titles will continue until the current volumes are complete. The software and hardware environment for the Archive will rely upon existing technical infrastructure developed by the Harvard University Library over the past three years under the aegis of its Library Digital Initiative. The core component of this infrastructure is the Digital Repository Service (DRS), an Oracle-based repository for digital objects. Within the DRS, object content streams are stored along with their associated administrative and structural metadata.

The DRS, now in its second production release, currently maintains over 240,000 objects with a total size of 120 gigabytes. The DRS is responsible only for the managed preservation of the objects deposited within it; resource discovery and delivery are handled through independent systems. Digital objects are delivered out of the DRS through media type-specific delivery applications. Delivery applications are available for simple objects, those atomically composed of a single physical content stream, such as a raster image file; and complex objects, logical aggregations of intellectually or structurally related content streams, such as an electronic monograph structurally delivered in a page turning navigational environment.

The design of the Archive was conceived in relation to the OAIS reference model, with its six main archival functions: ingest, data management, archival storage, preservation, access, and administration. Large portions of the operational aspects of the Archive are amenable to automation, including areas such as publisher registration and profiling, Submission Information Package (SIP) submission, ingest validation at a syntactic level, SIP-to-AIP (Archival Information Package) transformation, archival storage deposit, preservation migration, routine reporting, and handling and responding to access requests.

This degree of automation is achievable through a strict requirement of publisher compliance to formal standards for SIPs and the definition of a small set of normative data formats. The resulting uniformity of the Archive input stream and the canonical nature of internal archive storage practices provides the opportunity to rely upon automated systems to perform routine ingest, archival storage, data management, and access functions. Through the collaborative development of community standards, there is good potential for the sharing of common infrastructure components between archiving projects and institutions.

Physically, the SIP will take the form of a three-level file system hierarchy corresponding to the e-journal title, issue, and items. The title-level directory is empty and is present only to provide a common structural parent. The issue-level directory contains a METS file encapsulating all issue-level metadata and pointers to issue-level content files and to the item-level directories, each of which in turn has a METS file containing all item-level metadata and pointers to item-level content.

Content object technical metadata stored in the METS files provides the necessary representation information to facilitate archival preservation activities and content delivery. A preliminary draft specification of the SIP is undergoing public review and comment. One of the core concepts of the Archive is the use of a common archival item-level schema for articles and "article-like" content. The design of this schema will begin with an investigation of existing common schemas, such as the ISO 12083 and the PubMedCentral Document Type Definitions (DTDs), for possible use as is or as the basis for additional development.

If a new schema should be necessary, in whole or in part, the design and documentation of it may be contracted out to an appropriate consultant and developed with coordinated input from the larger community. As will be set out in the Archive submission agreement, when practical it will be the responsibility of content providers to transform their journal content from its internal native form into compliance with the Archive's schema when the publisher has content marked up in SGML or XML.

In order to transform content to this schema, participating publishers will need a significant level of internal technical expertise or access to external technical expertise and the resources to implement the transformation workflow. It is clear that not all publishers of scholarly content will have these assets. Since digital preservation activities are performed on a type-specific basis, minimizing the number of acceptable data formats can reduce the complexity and cost of archive operations. To place this on a formal basis, the Archive will define a small set of preferred normative formats.

In general, a single normative format will be defined for each functional category of content: for example, XML for metadata, XML for full-text, TIFF for raster still images, XML/SVG for vector still images, etc. Data submitted in non-normative formats will be transformed upon ingest into an analogous normative format whenever possible without significant loss of intellectual meaning. Long-term archival preservation requires the initial capture of intellectual content at the highest possible resolution, finest possible granularity, and most abstract representation. Additional criteria for the selection of normative formats include open standards, mature and robust technology, long-term viability, prevalence of commercial grade tools, and the potential for instantiated data objects to be created as far upstream as possible in publishers' production processes.

The composition of the set of normative formats will undergo periodic review to insure they remain appropriate for archival purposes with regard to continual technological advances. The Data Management function is responsible for maintaining descriptive information about archival holdings and administrative data necessary to the internal management of the Archive. Issue and item-level descriptive metadata is received from the Ingest function.

6

Control Measures of Digital Libraries

The World Wide Web(WWW) is an effective and flexible platform for implementing digital libraries of project information. Digital libraries on the World Wide Web provide access only to their current organization and contents. This is a significant limitation. Digital libraries must be able to manage the history of documents over time, not just offer to readers the latest versions. For example, in a digital library that captures the history of an engineering project, there are documents that keep a record of design decisions made. The distributed nature of digital libraries and the variety of storage solutions that networks enable have practical advantages.

On the World Wide Web, not all electronic collections are well maintained-the degree of management of electronic collections varies considerably. Moreover, the characteristics of the Web raise many challenges for the maintainer. Collections on the Web can be extremely distributed-not only the location of the documents is distributed, but ownership is also distributed. At the moment, the Web is less like a library and more like a huge bookshelf, containing millions of documents and links to documents. This mega shelf is subject to the activities of an army of people that keep acting upon it in ways such as adding, removing, indexing, cataloguing, rearranging, modifying, and copying documents.

Additionally, all these activities tend to occur with little or no coordination, worsening the situation. Better coordination, social protocols, and institutionalized management of collection can alleviate the situation in some cases, particularly when the owner of the collection and the owners of the documents agree to coordinate their activities. The emerging digital topical libraries, while homed on the Web, are better maintained than the Web as a whole. They present a more cohesive and organized structure in order to support their patrons. Different automatic mechanisms have been devised in order to help manage the documents.

Indexing and cataloguing are considerably easier to perform than in the pre-electronic days. Nevertheless, considerable human effort is still required to monitor the changes in documents and collections. In addition to the digital library that is provided by the "owner" of the documents there are a growing number of specialized libraries with distributed ownership. In these cases librarians often are limited to working with the pointers or links to the documents. Digital documents are typically very fluid, i.e., changes are a common occurrence. Although detecting changes is easily automated, assessing the relevance of changes is not. Typically humans are needed when facing the task of relevance assessment. In fact, "relevance" is a highly abstract, contextual, and subjective concept.

Different individuals can disagree in their relevance judgment about any given change. Nevertheless, as difficult as it may be, assessing the relevance of a change is still necessary. The approach provides a way of automatically assessing the relevance of changes in the Web pages. Presentation changes are changes related to the document representation that do not reflect changes in the topic presented in the document. For instance, changes to HTML tags can modify the appearance of a Web page while it otherwise remains the same. Structural changes refer to the underlying connection of the document to other documents. Structural changes are also important to detect, as they often might not be visually perceptible.

Behavioral changes refer to modifications to the active components of a document. For Web pages this includes scripts, plug-ins and applets. The consequences of these changes are harder to predict, especially since many pages hide the script code in other files. To represent the different characteristics of a Web-based document, use a set of document signatures to infer and compute similarities between two Web pages. In the present work, the signature approach relies on identifying page features and characteristics that not only identify the Web page, but also allow quantifying the change magnitude based on a comparison with a previously computed signature.

There are some changes to Web pages that do not affect any of the previous metrics. For example, a change to an image source would not be reflected in any of the current metrics as it is not part of the text, headings, links or keywords of the document. In this case the global checksum provides a last resort to point out changes. Combining the results of the various document signatures into an single metric of change is difficult. Some Web page changes are easily perceived while others are not. Some changes might alter the visual appearance of a page while maintaining the same structure and content. Other changes might change the links while maintaining exactly the same appearance.

The specific change metrics are presented to the right of the page identification. In addition, the user can get more information on each Web page by selecting the page identification. The system will also display the page in a Web browser at the user's request. At this point the user, who might not be the same person who authored the path, might judge the page inappropriate and choose to hide the page from the viewers. Some pages are returned rather quickly, while others take longer to return. Also varying connection times means that, sometimes when a Web page seems to take too long to load, canceling the retrieval and immediately restarting the process results in the Web page being loaded faster.

Teachers have chosen pages from the Web to teach their classes and it is the participant's responsibility to check for changes. In the context of networked library services, the necessity to integrate secondary data, catalogues and primary information has been expressed quite some time ago. More specifically, librarians have brought to the fore the need to link abstracting databases with library catalogues; catalogues with primary information; abstracting databases with full-text primary information. Publishers, subscription agents, researchers and libraries are all looking into ways to create added-value by linking related information entities, as such presenting the information within a broader context estimated to be relevant to the users of the information.

The omnipresence of the World Wide Web has raised users' expectations in this regard. When using a library solution, the expectations of a net-traveler are inspired by his hyperlinked Web-experiences. To such a user, it is not comprehensible that secondary sources, catalogues and primary sources, that are logically related, are not functionally linked. Given the requirement to control the information collection, in order to be able to interlink the information, the centralized commercial solutions are restricted by the sphere of influence of the information provider.

In a consortium environment some libraries rely on the hosting authority for all their library services, making the local environment the same as the authority's. As such, integration can fully be dealt with by the authority. But in some consortia, participating libraries may host some information locally that is not relevant to the entire consortium, but still want it to be integrated with the whole.

Web Content Management

For many people in the IT community, content management simply means WEB content. The key concept in Web content management is the creation of value through a reduction in "time to web." In practice, this concept translates into more dynamic web delivery systems built on the back of a relational database tied to a template-driven workflow process that allows fewer people to create and deliver more web content. A database-driven approach to web content management opens up new possibilities within an organization to share content across units and to share in the costs of creating and maintaining digital content.

Some writers on content management have chosen to focus almost exclusively on protecting the asset value of digital objects, without regard to the purposes to which the objects may be put. From an asset management perspective, the organization of digital objects in well structured and well-documented databases is the most critical activity. The digital preservation community in libraries has tended to emphasize asset management as a key value. The present movement to specify preservation metadata requirements within the construct of the Open Archival Information System reference model is the most dramatic example of efforts define content management in terms of the archival repository. Knowledge management has traditionally suffered from the hubris of modernism: the belief that we can discover ultimate truths and organize the world according to rational principles using clever code.

Postmodern KM operates within and on the basis of existing behavior patterns, mining conversation streams and relationships automatically to incorporate structure and context into the information human users already manipulate. It fosters human intelligence and interaction rather than trying to replace them. This vision of content management suggests that librarians must reconcile the tensions between the structured and the dynamic, between "control zones" and empowerment, and between the Web that we access and the digital content that we provide. These tensions are not new or particularly interesting, except in so far as they help us extend the concept of "content" to encompass a much wider range of management responsibilities for digital content than we have heretofore chosen to consider appropriate. Increasingly, libraries are being asked or expected to step up to the challenge of acquiring, organizing, and protecting digital content that they have neither created themselves (digitization) or licensed from publishers.

Examples of new generations of digital content that are just beginning to flow into and through libraries include digital products produced and distributed or otherwise published by faculty, the output of research collaboratives, graduate student theses, the electronic records or the university's administrative offices, courseware content, and streaming audio and video resources generated from courses, conferences, and other campus activities. In the Web environment, the business community has adopted the term "knowledge management" to refer to processes that use technology to leverage human expertise and know-how to create new value for the organization. In the higher education context, knowledge management constructs are most closely tied to scholarly communication processes.

Today's library is "all digital" in the sense that all services and content are mediated via web gateways. Users begin and end their scholarly work with digital information, even if there is a considerable amount of paper in between. Without some form of digital accessibility, library resources in any format are invisible and therefore unusable. Physical browsing for all but a vocal few has become a chimera. Libraries are already in the new business of digital product development by nature of their creation of digital resources, regardless of whether creation encompasses only digitization or extends to the development of specialized aggregations of digital resources.

Libraries and archives cannot possibly assume full responsibility for preserving digital information, but rather must participate in a marketplace that itself has not come to terms with the idea of lost value. Librarians are critical players in the conception of the IT marketplace but have neither exclusive claim on content management concepts or a particularly strong share of the marketplace that is driving the development of content management tools.

Content management in the "all digital" environment within higher education can only function effectively at the corporate (i.e., university) level, even when the digital content itself is created and managed to support disciplinary or interdisciplinary scholarship. With the emergence of the World Wide Web this tool has been developed to place cited reference searching directly within the control of the user. Improved access to information is one feature of the Web, in particular through the mechanism of the Web link. The characteristic feature of commercial services on the World Wide Web is the ability to create and combine very large information resources that can be interrogated quickly, easily and efficiently.

Web technology empowers the researcher even further by enabling links from these surrogates to the original documents. Alongside various other forms of Web publishing, a number of scholarly journal publishers are implementing electronic versions of their journals, many of them using Web protocols as the basis for access to their service, whether that service is provided on subscription or on a per-article basis. Although several proposals exist for servers hosting journals from multiple publishers, at this stage in the development of electronic publishing, the majority of rights holders are establishing their own systems - many of which do not inter-link.

Cataloguing Electronic Publications

The electronic publications should be catalogued, and that they be catalogued according to existing international cataloguing standards. That electronic publications are part of the national publishing heritage and that, as such, it is appropriate to include them in the national bibliography. Because of the preservation requirements for electronic publications, it will be necessary to consider the need to record additional information than that normally required for a cataloguing record. It will be necessary, for example, to record whether a title has been migrated to another format, and, if so, when this occurred and whether there has been any loss of content or of other qualities.

There are as yet no international standards for recording this kind of information. Current indications suggest that the cataloguing of electronic publications is more time consuming than that of print publications. This may change as cataloguers become more familiar with the handling of electronic publications. International developments in metadata standards may also make it possible to collect header information in such a way as to facilitate discovery and description of on-line electronic publications. Print publications received through legal deposit are logged on arrival at the library. They are normaliy checked to ensure that they are complete and intact and are allocated a unique number so that they can be identified later. Legal deposit requires stringent record keeping. For electronic publications, the logging of receipt, checking of exterior packaging, assigning of accession numbers and claiming procedures should be the same as for print publications.

However, certain additional steps will be required for electronic publications. It will be necessary to check the publications supplied are in the preferred formats, if a format was specified in the first place. It will also be necessary to check that all the application software normally sold with the publication is deposited and that the full set of user and technical documentation is provided. The library may find that it needs not only to request the normal packaging and manuals which are sold with an electronic publication but also to request additional material which will enable the library to transfer the data from the original electronic medium onto a preservation medium.

All the documentation supplied will be a resource in its own right. It will be crucial to the long-term availability of electronic publications. Libraries are advised to do rigorous testing of electronic publications on a sample basis to ensure that they are in working order, not copy-protected and that the software supplied with them contains no computer viruses. It may be advisable to attempt to download small parts of the publication at an early stage to see whether full-scale downloading will be possible at a later stage for preservation purposes. If downloading does not appear to be possible, contact should be made with the depositor to see what provision can be made to provide access to the work for posterity.

In many libraries, print publications are sorted into categories, size being one of them. Each item is then given a shelf mark and is shelved appropriately. Shelf marks are added to the catalogue records. These processes apply to more or less all publications. However, additional processes will apply to electronic publications received through legal deposit. Storage options cannot be considered in isolation from the provision of access. A range of storage options should be considered in the context of the arrangements and agreements that are likely to emerge over conditions of use. The conditions and types of use arrived at are likely to influence the technical solutions chosen to store and archive electronic publications. Access must be provided to electronic publications received through legal deposit although in certain cases there may be a period, agreed with the copyright holder, before which access would not be permitted.

Each library should work within its own copyright and fair dealing laws but should otherwise make electronic publications as widely available as possible. In many nations, there is still a long way to go to establish an acceptable level of understanding and mutual trust between national libraries and publishers especially in so far as legal deposit and electronic transmission of published works are concerned. Libraries cannot proceed without the support of publishers and will need to demonstrate to publishers that publishers will gain from legal deposit through wide publicity of their works and also long-term care and maintenance of them.

This will most likely involve not just giving assurances that the content of publications will not be changed in any way, but also that access will only be permitted under very clear and strictly applied circumstances. Documentation will be required to describe the terms of agreement between libraries and publishers. The majority if not all libraries will not be sufficiently well endowed to be able to maintain and provide library and information services from collections of legal deposit electronic publications without additional, ear-marked funding for that purpose.

Electronic resources consist of materials that are computer-controlled, including materials that require the use of a peripheral attached to a computer; the items may or may not be used in the interactive mode. Included are two types of resources: data (information in the form of numbers, letters, graphics, images, and sound, or a combination thereof) and programs (instructions or routines for performing certain tasks including the processing of data). In addition, they may be combined to include electronic data and programs (e.g. online services, interactive multimedia). Remote access is understood to mean that no physical carrier can be handled by the user - typically, access can only be provided by use of an input-output device (e.g. a terminal) either connected to a computer system (e.g. a resource in a network) or by use of resources stored in a hard disk or other storage device.

This definition is taken as applying for the most part to resources, including interactive multimedia works, that are generally available, and includes those accessed by network or via telecommunications. Resources produced and/or generated for limited distribution, for fee on demand, or on a made-to-order basis are, however, included. A resource residing in permanent memory in a computer (ROM) is understood to be part of the device in which it is stored, and, if catalogued, would be treated as a resource requiring remote access. Characteristics of an electronic resource include:

(a) designation of the type of resource, and

(b) information on the extent of resource.

These provisions are for an electronic resource that is available by remote access which involves the use of an input-output device (e.g. a terminal) connected electronically to a computer system to access it (e.g. a resource in a network). Designation of the type of resource is mandatory. Extent of resource may be given when the information is available and the bibliographic agency desires to record it. Physical details relating to sound or colour of a resource available by remote access and accompanying material when present are given in a note. These provisions may also be given for an electronic resource that is available for local access, which is in a physical carrier such as a cassette, disk/disc, cartridge or reel designed for the user to insert into the computer or into a peripheral (e.g. CD-ROM player) attached to the computer, typically a microcomputer. The type and extent of resource area is preceded by a point, space, dash, space (. -), and each statement of extent is enclosed in one pair of parentheses (()). These designations may appear in the prescribed source of information; when they are not present in the prescribed source of information, they are supplied without brackets based on examination of the work.

When the electronic resource consists of data, the bibliographic agency may choose to identify the resource as "Electronic data" or "Data". When the electronic resource consists of a program(s), the bibliographic agency may choose to identify the resource as "Electronic program(s)" or "Program(s)" (if the general material designation is given in the bibliographic description). In the case where the designation is supplied, preference is given to a term that is currently well established, in use by both the producers and users of the particular type of program, and is mutually exclusive of other terms used as designations. When the electronic resource consists of data and program(s), the bibliographic agency may choose to identify the resource as "Electronic data and program(s)" or "Data and program(s)" (if the general material designation is given in the bibliographic description).

The terms "interactive multimedia" and "online service(s)" may be used in conjunction with these lists or else alone as resource designations. When neither of these terms nor the terms in the lists are appropriate, an appropriate designation may be supplied, qualified by the word "electronic" or else used alone if the general material designation is given in the description. In the case where the designation is supplied, preference is given to a term that is currently well established, in use by both the producers and users of the particular data resource and program(s), and is mutually exclusive of other terms used as designations.

When the data or program is incidental and not primary in the resource, it is recommended that the bibliographic agency apply the primary term. Extent of resource may be given when the information is available and the bibliographic agency desires to record it. When the resource is in a compressed form, the bibliographic agency may omit this information. Extent of resource consists of the number of files that make up the content of the data or program, adding additional measures of extent as appropriate. A statement of extent of resource is recorded in parentheses after the designation of the resource. The specific terms for extent of resource are given in the language of the bibliographic agency.

When the number of files is given, this further statement of extent is introduced with a space, colon, space. The number of bytes may be variously expressed (e.g. "megabytes", "MB", "Mbytes") but are given in the form in which they appear in the source. For a multi-part resource, the number of records and/or bytes or the number of statements and/or bytes may be given for each resource. The term "publication, production or distribution", is intended to cover all types of publication, production, distribution, issuing and release activities. These activities are distinct from the activities connected solely with the physical manufacture of the item, though both may be executed by the same person or body.

When a person or body combines the activities of publication, production, distribution, etc., with those of physical manufacture, or when it is uncertain whether the person or body is responsible for publication, production, distribution, etc., or for physical manufacture alone, the statement is treated as one relating to publication, production, distribution, etc. When more than one publisher or producer is named on the prescribed source of information, the name made more prominent by typography or, if there is no typographical distinction, the name that appears first is given.

If there is no typographical distinction and the names do not appear in sequence, the name considered most important by the bibliographic agency is given. When the name of a publisher, producer or distributor appears on the prescribed source of information in more than one language and/or script, the form of name made more prominent by typography or, if there is no typographical distinction, the form that appears first is given. If neither of these criteria applies, the linguistic form that corresponds to the language of the publication is given. The name of the manufacturer is not given as a substitute for the name of an unknown publisher, producer or distributor.

However, when a person or corporate body combines the activities of manufacturing and publication, production, or distribution, or when the responsibility is uncertain, a named manufacturer is assumed also to be the publisher or producer. When the prescribed source of information includes as an integral part of the publication or production statement an indication of the function performed by the distributor, the statement is transcribed in full.

The International Standard Serial Number (ISSN) relating to the series or sub-series is given when it is known and is transcribed in accordance with the relevant standard. The numbering of the item within a series or sub-series is given in the terms in which it appears in the item. Standard abbreviations may be used. Arabic numerals are substituted for other numerals or spelled-out numbers. When the parts of a multi-part resource within a series are numbered, the first and last numbers and/or letters are given and connected by a hyphen when the numbering is continuous.

The electronic revolution, being experienced by all organisations, offers the opportunity to re-design business processes and methods. It provides a vision of easy access to all information across all the systems in organisation and available from the wider world. All organisations, whether private or public, and individuals in their working and personal lives, need records to document their activities. Records provide evidence of business activities. Without records, people and organisations cannot prove that actions have been taken, commitments entered into or obligations carried out.

But records have a broader purpose than the immediate objective of getting business done: organisations exist within regulatory frameworks which impose various degrees of accountability for their activities. More and more, individuals expect to be able to conduct their business using electronic tools. Records are used by government administrators and business people, social watchdogs and regulators, auditors and legal professionals, and individuals in the full range of their roles, such as citizens, family members and researchers. Decision makers need records to provide precedent for subsequent decisions, to provide details of actions undertaken in case of challenge and to prove that required action was actually carried out.

Service providers need records of dealings with customers to support claims for payment and to support further service. Individuals need records to ensure their entitlements and the obligations within and between organisations and families. Records are created and used by everyone in our society. While paper still forms the most common medium for records, electronic media are replacing paper as the preferred means of conducting business transactions.

Electronic transactions are no different in nature from their paper counterparts: they need to be recorded, captured in a fixed form, maintained and made accessible as records. Electronic records need to provide the same degree of evidence of business activity, the same level of accountability and the same social resources as paper records, for the immediate and future needs of organisations, individuals and society. The role and purposes of recordkeeping in the electronic environment —electronic recordkeeping—are the same as in the paper world.

Importance of Digital Library Evaluation

Networked information systems are now an ubiquitous component of business, commerce, community, and education. Despite these advances, we have little understanding of the effectiveness of digital library systems and services in supporting these essential aspects of daily life in the 21st century. Digital libraries support specific activities in specific contexts—classroom instruction, distance learning, digital asset management, scholarship, virtual museums, and so on.

Digital libraries need to be evaluated as systems and as services to determine how useful, usable, and economical they are and whether they achieve reasonable cost-benefit ratios. Results of evaluation studies can provide strategic guidance for the design and deployment of future systems, can assist in determining whether digital libraries address the appropriate social, cultural, and economic problems, and whether they are as maintainable as possible. Consistent evaluation methods also will enable comparison between systems and services. Evaluation research can be a highly applied form of investigation, or it can test theory.

Evaluation research is particularly useful for studying aspects of communication technologies such as interactivity, adoption, use, implementation, and social impacts. Evaluation itself can be cost effective, particularly in areas of usability. Even a small amount of usability evaluation in the development of information systems can pay for itself several times over in cost savings from lost productivity. Evaluation is a general term that includes various aspects of performance measurement and assessment.

Activities include laboratory experiments, regional, national, and international surveys or quasi-experiments, time-series analyses, online monitoring of user-system interactions, observation of use, and other forms of data collection. Evaluation has a long history in fields such as computer science, education, communication, health, and criminal justice. The effectiveness of interventions such as new teaching methods, management practices, and policy can be assessed.

Digital libraries can be viewed and evaluated as interventions in these fields, drawing upon methods typically used to assess the outcomes of programs and services. In humancomputer interaction, measures include time to learn, error rates, efficiency, memorability, and satisfaction. Systems can be benchmarked for aspects of performance, using quantitative measures specific to applications, such as recall and precision measures of information retrieval. Aspects such as verification, validation, and quality assurance are based upon systems, technical and user requirements. Some useful definitions are these:

— *Quality assurance:* a planned and systematic pattern of all actions necessary to provide adequate confidence that a product (here software) conforms to established technical requirements.

— *Verification:* the process of determining whether the products of a given development phase satisfy the requirements established during the previous phase.

— *Validation:* determining the correctness of the final program or software produced from a development project with respect to user's needs and requirements.

Evaluation methods should meet accepted norms for scientific rigor in the domain of study. In the social sciences, methods should be valid (be a "true" measurement of the quality or concept under study) and reliable (the same measure should achieve the same result at multiple times). Kirk and Miller offer succinct definitions of these concepts:

— *Reliability:* the extent to which the same observational procedure in the same context yields the same information.

— *Validity:* The quality of fit between an observation and the basis on which it is made.

At least four types of evaluation are relevant to digital libraries:

— Formative evaluation begins at the initial stages of a development project to establish baselines on current operations, set goals, and determine desired outcomes. Such evaluation is usually driven by context and project-specific goals.

— Summative evaluation takes place at the end of a project to determine if the intended goals were met. Goals and outcomes must be compared to initial states, so formative evaluation generally precedes summative evaluation.

— Alterative evaluation takes place throughout a project, beginning in the earliest design and development stages. Interim stages of design are assessed in comparison to design goals and desired outcomes, and the results inform the next stages of design. Iterative approaches encourage designers to set measurable goals at the beginning of a project and provide opportunities to re-assess goals throughout the development process.

— Comparative evaluation requires standardized measures that can be compared across systems. Communities can identify and validate measures. If such measures are implemented in a consistent manner, they enable comparisons between systems. Test beds are another way to compare measures and to compare performance of different functions and algorithms.

The Workshop on Evaluation of Digital Libraries, jointly funded by the European Union and by the National Science Foundation, was preceded by many related activities in the United States, Europe, and Asia. As part of the Digital Library Initiative, DARPA and NSF funded the Dlib Test Suite and Metrics Working Group. Digital libraries are difficult to evaluate due to their richness, complexity, and variety of uses and users. During the first Digital Library Initiative, NSF funded a workshop on Social Aspects of Digital Libraries. The need for evaluation methods and metrics was among the key findings of that workshop. Saracevic also speculated that evaluation methods and models are insufficiently developed to address the complexity of digital library services.

Some progress is being made, as evidenced by a special issue of Library Trends on "Assessing Digital Library Services" and by a forthcoming book on the evaluation of digital libraries. Projects funded under the first Digital Library Initiative included some evaluation components, notably the Alexandria Digital Library Project at the University of California, Santa Barbara and DeLiver at the University of Illinois.

A recent study funded by DARPA found that developers of information systems could implement evaluation efforts successfully by sharing expertise among projects. Other U.S. entities are beginning to fund DL evaluation efforts, such as the Institute for Museum and Library Services. The Andrew W. Mellon Foundation provided funding for a workshop on evaluation frameworks for DLs of music.

In the academic library community, efforts are underway to establish metrics for networked information services. Other private foundations are beginning to fund assessments of digital information resources that people use in everyday life. The proceedings of the first two Joint Conferences on Digital Libraries include a number of papers on digital library evaluation. The efforts to date have been effective in establishing the need for evaluation of DLs, in identifying some of the areas most likely to be productive, and in demonstrating the effectiveness of small-scale evaluation efforts. Context-dependent evaluation efforts, while effective, remain hand-crafted and expensive. One of the major problems in accomplishing evaluation is the lack of expertise and resources.

Several excellent collections have been or will be created with EU funding. To maximize the benefit of this work and in collaboration with their owners, the DELOS Network of Excellence' goal is to undertake the task of promoting the creation, maintenance and operation of a Test Suite, which will make test beds available to other researchers. This action will improve the efficiency of research since the Test Suite will provide all researchers with readily available resources for testing purposes.

A generic classification and evaluation scheme for digital libraries was developed. The scheme is based upon the belief that evaluation of DLs should include a broad view of subject areas. The description scheme has four major dimensions: data/collection, system/technology, users, and usage. For each of these dimensions the major attributes are described.

Overall, the original scheme has proven to be very useful; only a few suggestions for modifications of the scheme have been received. A questionnaire about digital library test collections was created to gather input for the design of the European Digital Library Test Suite, and is being continued by setting up a DL Metalibrary. The DL

Metalibrary has now 35 entries describing possible test beds worldwide. The planned Test Suite will provide collections for comparative and quantitative experiments.

Many digital library documents are in XML format. DELOS supported the idea of creating a test bed for XML retrieval. INEX (Initiative for the Evaluation of XML Retrieval) is a coordinated effort of the University of Dortmund and the Queen Mary University of London, which received additional funding from DELOS for performing the infrastructure work of the evaluation process. As a collection, INEX uses about 12,000 journal articles from the field of computer science published by IEEE-CS during the years 1995-2001. After the call for participation in March 2002, 49 groups signed up. Finally, 25 groups were participating actively, performing retrieval for 60 topics.

The digital library community needs benchmarks for comparison between systems and services. Standards are required for DL architecture and operations if we are to achieve interoperability between systems and services. Similarly, the ability to scale DLs to full operational status, with ever- larger collections, will depend upon workable standards and interoperability. Constructing test beds is beyond the capability of individual investigators or research teams.

Test beds could be built specifically for comparing DL functions and services, as in the TREC experiments and a similar initiative in Japan for comparing cross-language information retrieval. They can also be organized as a collaboration among research groups, such as the Dlib test suite project and the DELOS Network of Excellence Working Group on Evaluation. The DELOS Evaluation Forum defined a generic classification and evaluation scheme consisting of four major dimensions each with major attributes and metrics.

Test beds and metrics are most effective when problems are well understood. However, digital libraries are a new technology that is just beginning to move from research to practice and from prototypes to operational systems and services. As DLs are implemented, people gradually adopt and adapt them as part of their information practices. These behaviors are evolving rapidly, along with the implementation of systems. Thus, now is an excellent time to be studying uses, users, and usability of digital libraries and other aspects of DL context.

Context has a variety of aspects, including goals and tasks, socio-cultural milieu, and environment, and these aspects must be considered with respect to research questions and methods. That breakout group identified 5 classes of research questions associated with context and evaluation of DLs, and suggested appropriate methods to address those questions. Evaluation of users and interfaces also must take place in a context, so that aspects such as domain, language, culture, format (text, audio, visual, etc.) can be assessed.

The breakout group on Users and Interfaces also identified research questions and methods for studying DLs in context. The latter group proposed some criteria for determining the "best" research questions and methods, such as the cost of evaluation, cost-benefit of evaluation, adaptability of methods, sharability of methods, instruments, and test beds, and validity and reliability. Both groups concluded that evaluation can serve many different goals, and that the effectiveness of evaluation metrics and methods must be goal-specific.

Methods and metrics to evaluate usability are unlikely to yield cost-benefit data and vice versa, for example. Because digital libraries serve such a rich variety of content to a such a vast array of user populations, most DL evaluation to date has been specific to a context. Methods are often handcrafted and are time consuming to develop and deploy. For example, methods used in the context of developing the capabilities and improving the life conditions of marginalized groups, such as participatory action research, can be applied to the evaluation of digital libraries. Thus, research on digital libraries in specific contexts will lead to better metrics and methods that can be applied across digital library systems and services.

7

Metadata and Digital Libraries

Libraries have always supported interactions with the fund of knowledge, interactions that come in many shapes and sizes. Libraries support scholarly communication and formal education; they also help people find facts, figures, and tax regulations. Interacting with knowledge is what lifelong learning is all about. Users of American Memory register delight when they find pictures of the town where they grew up or recognize a family member in a picture, sound recording, or letter. Genealogical research is immensely popular. Contributions to the fund of knowledge come from many sources, including individuals as amateurs.

Vast numbers of informative web pages represent personal contributions to the fund of knowledge by enthusiasts: railroad buffs; music-lovers; naval history mavens; watchers of birds, badgers, and other creatures; and many more. User communities are building domain-specific digital libraries with domain-specific metadata schemas and guidelines. This should be no surprise.

Domain-specific controlled vocabularies and abstracting and indexing services are not a new phenomenon and the full-text databases that some of these services have developed into are certainly digital libraries.

Even within the traditional cataloging community, descriptive practices vary for classes of material. Practices developed originally for cataloging books have been adapted and extended over 150 years. As Elaine Svenonius points out in her recent book, *The Intellectual Foundation of Information Organization*, these practices "have been jolted in the twentieth century by information explosions, the computer revolution, the proliferation of new media, and the drive toward universal bibliographic control. How they have withstood these jolts, where they have remained firm, where they have cracked, and where cracked how they have been repaired or still await repair is a dramatic—and instructive—history for those interested in organizing information intelligently."

For example, in response to the jolt of incorporating non-book media, the Anglo-American Cataloguing Rules have been supplemented by manuals for other classes of material: Archives, Personal Papers, and Manuscripts (APPM); Graphic Materials (GIHC); and Archival Moving Image Materials (AMIM). An archival collection of personal papers is typically cataloged in a single collection-level record. Very different descriptive and organizational practices have been developed by archivists to organize and describe collections at whatever finer level of granularity is deemed appropriate.

Varying descriptive practices have taken into account not only the observed intellectual needs of the traditional users of the resources, but also more pragmatic factors: the mission and capabilities of the traditional custodian;

economic realities (manpower and funding); technical realities (tools available to help custodial institutions prepare and users to take advantage of metadata); the pattern of updating required; and the physical nature of the artifacts themselves.

The nature of today's bibliographic systems make allowance for synergies with (or are constrained by exigencies of) inventory control and are shaped by the importance in the published literature of relationships expressed by shared author, title, and subject headings. For archivists, two of the key factors shaping practice are the importance of the integrity of a collection as a whole and the sheer impracticality of describing individual items in detail. Although catalogs in book form were replaced by card catalogs early in the twentieth century, the document form of an archival finding aid has remained useful. For museums, the importance of detailed information about provenance and the historical and creative context for individual items has led to yet another set of practices.

Many of these factors do not change simply because reproductions or surrogates can be created in digital form or when today's analogs are created in digital form. Even among the communities with preservation of the cultural record in their mission, there will continue to be heterogeneity of descriptive practice in digital libraries, and for good reason. One challenge is to identify the pragmatic factors that have changed or will inevitably change and adapt to them. Underlying principles grounded in users' needs should still guide practice.

The networked world of cyberspace and the development of advanced computational tools are shifting the balance among factors that shaped past descriptive practices. Although developed for a different purpose, the model Lawrence Lessig introduced in Code and other Laws of Cyberspace sheds light on this balance. Lessig suggests that an individual's behavior is constrained by law, architecture, market, and norms. He stresses the fundamental differences between the architecture of physical space (where distance, weight, and walls set limits) and the architecture of cyberspace (manifested in software, network equipment, and protocols).

The four factors are clearly interdependent; indeed, in response to societal norms, laws are passed to regulate architecture and the market. Turn to the business section of any newspaper, and it becomes obvious that the architecture of cyberspace is changing the market (and the overall economic environment) in which businesses, individuals, and libraries operate. Cyberspace offers new cost structures, users from new communities, users from traditional communities with new expectations, and new tools to serve those users. Clearly, understanding of the surrounding "architecture" and "market" will guide the development of future practices and systems for preparing and using metadata in digital libraries. The architecture and market for print publishing has been relatively stable and libraries are adapted for that environment. For digital libraries, the environment is likely to be in a state of change for the foreseeable future; research and experimentation will be ongoing.

In the IFLA Functional Requirements for the Bibliographic Record four objectives are listed for the bibliographic record for an entity: to enable a user to find, identify, select, and obtain access to the entity described. Elaine Svenonius suggests that it is helpful to distinguish between the objective of finding or locating a particular entity (known item) and the collocation objective, which allows a user to find sets of entities, for instance works by the same author or on the same topic. She also suggests that a navigation objective be added to reflect the wish of users to find other works related to a given work.

The Dublin Core Metadata Initiative describes the Dublin Core metadata set as facilitating discovery; this term is often applied to the process of looking for resources in a broad cross-domain universe. In a digital library, metadata may be needed to help the user not only select an item appropriate for the current purpose but also to use it. Such metadata may include structural metadata that permits navigation among components of a single intellectual "object" (for example, to skip to a particular segment of a digital sound recording) or information about terms and conditions in a machine-parsable form that can be used to limit access to authorized users.

Metadata is also required to manage content and to record information that will support future preservation activities. Metadata that leads users to resources in digital libraries (discovery, finding, collocation, navigation) and lets them choose resources for the task at hand (identification, selection). The networked world has changed the expectations of information users by removing physical constraints. In the physical world, few question the practice of storing maps or manuscripts separately from books or locating the specialists who help users access and use the resources in different areas of a library or in different libraries.

In the networked world, the digital libraries hold the potential to brings resources of many types together to the user's laboratory or desktop (or even palmtop). Some users will want first to cast a wide net as they trawl for information and then to draw it tight and precisely around the most relevant and usable resources for a particular purpose. The wide net calls for interoperability and commonality across domains and custodial communities, while assessment of fitness for a particular purpose often calls for rich and domain-specific metadata. One characteristic of a digital library is the accessibility of the content to the user.

In the traditional library, subject to the physical constraints of weight and distance, the user who selects lots of items that turn out not to be fit for the purpose at hand will incur a high cost (in effort, if not in monetary terms). If users can delve straight into the content to aid the act of selection, some metadata conventionally recorded to support selection may be less essential. Users and builders of digital libraries also recognize the potential for navigation among related items. This feature was the fundamental function underlying the initial success of the World Wide Web.

Online, citations can lead directly to cited works and works can link directly to datasets or models they describe. Reference links and thumbnail images change the architecture for research and information seeking. Users can navigate using relationships between metadata records and relationships between resources from their desktop. The functions that metadata must support may not change in a digital library, but, in the new architecture and with new tools, it seems likely that metadata practices must evolve to provide the functionality cost-effectively in the new market. Content is also accessible for building services in a digital library. Metadata or surrogates can be derived or extracted from content files.

Today, a thumbnail is essentially part of the descriptive record for an image. In the collection of negative strips from the Farm Security Administration, many of the images were never captioned; access to the uncaptioned images within American Memory is primarily through navigation. Contact sheet displays of thumbnails are ordered using the processing number sequence on the negatives (an identifier that implies chronological order, at least for negatives on a single strip).

Automatic summarization and analysis of other forms of content is an active research area. The value of including basic metadata in the header of text marked up in SGML or XML is also well recognized. Text conversion projects following the Text Encoding Initiative (TEI) guidelines often use a mapping between elements in the header section of the marked up file to fields in a MARC catalog record. In some cases, the TEI header is derived from the catalog record; in other cases, a catalog record is derived from the header. For material published in digital form, the publishing community will maintain basic bibliographic metadata for its own purposes, including promotion and business-to-business dealings with booksellers. It will be inexpensive to include it in file headers. For example, the Open eBook Publication Structure specification includes tags for "publication metadata."

In a digital library, searchable text can minimize the need for metadata (particularly when items do not merit the expense of individual cataloging). American Memory has a popular collection, American Life Histories, for which the only item-specific metadata is a title (a display string needed for result lists) and an identifier; the text itself is searched to provide intellectual access. Creators of non-text materials also recognize the value in embedding such metadata within the files. Today, cameras can record the date and time of an exposure. If there is not already a camera with built-in GPS to record location, there will be very soon. Proposals for new digital file formats, such as JPEG2000 (for images) and MPEG-7 (primarily for sound and video) include the ability to embed descriptive metadata within the file.

Metadata Models and Schemas

The educational community has been active in exploring the functional needs of educators for finding and using instructional materials. Resources are available because of economic incentives to establish and manage online learning environments and government efforts to improve education. Some information tasks call for rich metadata. For example, a teacher may be looking for material to help him explain a very specific topic in a particular class.

The teacher wants to be confident that the material makes appropriate assumptions about what the students already know, has already been used successfully in the classroom, will occupy an appropriate amount of class time, and will work on the equipment available. This level of specificity may be available in a service built by and for educators. A metadata schema for instructional resources has been developed by the IMS Global Learning Consortium, Inc., a global consortium with members from educational, commercial, and government organizations. Another area with specialized metadata needs is that of geospatial resources.

The ability to build maps dynamically or relate geospatial facts from distributed sources of information is enhanced by commonality of metadata. Such capabilities can support government tasks such as emergency management, city planning, and tracking air quality or global climate change. The Federal Geographic Data Committee has developed a Content Standard for Digital Geospatial Metadata. There is worldwide standardization activity in this area in relation to metadata schemas and to the content standards for elements.

The activity involves government, commercial and educational sectors. As with the instructional metadata schemas, the functionality required by the creator and user communities, rather than traditional libraries, is driving these activities. The Visual Resources Association has developed a two-level hierarchical model for describing objects or visual works (such as paintings, sculptures, or buildings) and images of those works. A single set of metadata elements, the VRA Core Categories 3.0, can be applied to the works and to the images. This approach follows the so-called "1-1" principle, distinguishing characteristics of the image surrogate clearly from characteristics of the work.

This principle emerged from the Dublin Core community but has provoked considerable controversy. It can not be applied in existing "flat" bibliographic systems without creating awkwardness and confusion for users through multiplicity of records and a burden on cataloging processes by requiring replication of work-level information in records for each surrogate image. A system that takes advantage of the two-level structure must allow searching across all records but present results that pull in work records automatically when a "hit" is at the image level.

The metadata schema used by the Art Museum Image Consortium (AMICO) has a similar hierarchical structure. The Visual Information Access (VIA) system at Harvard

University uses a three-level hierarchy. Although the Encoded Archival Description (EAD) standard has been used primarily for describing collections of papers and records that have not been digitized, it too provides a hierarchical structure for description at different levels. The EAD metadata structure has been used effectively as the basis for digital library services, for example at the University of California, Berkeley (and now at the California Digital Library) and Duke University.

A more complex conceptual model has been proposed by the Documentation Standards Group International Committee for Documentation of the International Council of Museums (ICOM-CIDOC). The CIDOC model is an object-oriented reference model that expresses a much more complex knowledge universe than the simple relationship of a descriptive record to a resource or even of a hierarchical structure of related descriptions and resources. It allows for descriptions not only of works, images, document, (conceptual objects) and objects (physical entities), but also of people (actors), places, and periods (time-spans).

This model will form the basis for the Cultural Materials Initiative digital library project at the Research Libraries Group. Full use of such a model will integrate gazetteers, biographical dictionaries, and encyclopedias, going well beyond the traditional use of authority records and thesauri. One example of a digital library enriched by integrating the use of reference resources such as biographical dictionaries and the Thesaurus of Geographic Names is Perseus, housed at Tufts University. In this digital library for the study of the ancient world, the books "talk" to each other. Names of places and people been identified automatically in the text and can be used as links to related information elsewhere in the corpus. This includes automated disambiguation of different places with the same name (e.g., Springfield) and of references to people who share names with places (e.g., Lincoln).

Some of these rich metadata schemas or models have great potential for enriching the interaction with knowledge for users through collocation and navigation using the relationships expressed in the models and supporting knowledge organization systems, such as gazetteers, name authority files, and thesauri. The models are, however, unfamiliar and will require new tools to implement and deploy. The web sites that present them usually have FAQ (Frequently Asked Question) pages that emphasize that most features are optional. There is plenty of evidence that, unless there is strong economic motivation, introductory guidelines and basic tools are needed before complex standards gain broad acceptance.

Part of the genius shown by Tim Berners-Lee in his original standards for the World Wide Web was the simplicity of the specifications. The conceptual model could be explained on one slide and fleshed out in three more. Implementing a server was a few lines of code; a young programmer built a graphical interface (Mosaic) as a side project and the rest is history. The other aspect of Berners-Lee's genius was the instant integration of legacy content by supporting earlier Internet protocols now seldom mentioned (gopher, wais, news). Real-world experience with the simple (e.g. HTML) has led iteratively to better understanding of which extensions to its functionality are most essential.

Complex metadata schemas present a challenge for those with valuable legacy metadata to migrate or metadata maintained in rich, but different schemas. It is relatively easy to "dumb down" metadata records from a rich schema into a simpler one, for purposes of interoperable retrieval, while still maintaining the full richness in a master system. Transforming from one rich schema to another is usually more expensive and the benefits may not be obvious to the institutions or individuals most likely to bear the cost.

At the other end of the spectrum, some digital library activities are focusing on allowing users to find resources across an information universe that spans communities, nations, types of information, and types of institution. The Dublin Core Metadata Initiative has been building consensus through a series of workshops and working group activities since March 1995. From the start this has been an international effort to develop a common core of semantics for resource description. The path has not been easy.

The Dublin Core Element Set (Simple Dublin Core) was submitted to NISO as a draft standard this year. The set has 15 elements; all elements are optional and all repeatable. The elements themselves are unlikely to be sufficient as an internal metadata schema for any particular project or application. Some proponents see the elements as the basis for a schema that can be extended by adding or refining elements; others prefer to see the set as a view of a richer, more complex description. This view can be used as a framework for mapping different element sets into a common set for indexing and searching.

The DCMI has also developed a model for extending the simple element set while maintaining the objective of interoperability. Elements can be refined. For example, Date.Created and Date.Issued are refinements of Date. Element refinements are guided by the "dumb-down" principle. If the refinement term is not recognized, it should be reasonable to treat the value of the qualified element as if it had no qualifier. This is an extremely important principle for supporting broad interoperability. The second type of qualification for Dublin Core elements is to specify an encoding scheme or controlled vocabulary.

Tom Baker describes Dublin Core as a pidgin language in a discussion of simple and qualified Dublin Core. The existence of the 15-element set has provided an important focus for other interoperability initiatives. Simple Dublin Core was recently adopted as the core metadata record format for the experimental Open Archives initiative. This initiative is testing whether a simple mechanism that allows service providers to harvest metadata records from content repositories will facilitate and stimulate the development of valuable services that draw on content from many repositories.

An initial impetus was the belief that access services could benefit from harvesting records for e-prints and other "grey" literature. Records will usually have links back to the host repository through persistent identifiers for the full content. The concept also allows the development of comprehensive search services that include significant web-accessible resources currently hidden from the "spiders" that crawl the web on behalf of search engines.

The so-called "deep web" includes the content of most digital libraries, such as American Memory, whose web presence is largely ephemeral, with records retrieved from a database in response to each search and displays generated dynamically. The Open Archives harvesting framework includes the ability to harvest records in other metadata formats.

The Open Archives initiative is based on the premise that simple records provide the first step to cross-domain discovery. Service-builders can choose to harvest records in a richer schema when available. Specifications for records marked up in the Extensible Markup Language (XML) must be made accessible for any schema used.

Cross-domain discovery is the development of a very basic profile for the Z39.50 information retrieval protocol for cross-domain discovery. This specification also supports Simple Dublin Core marked up in XML as a transfer format for records. In many ways, the stimulus for this activity is the success of the World Wide Web. People clearly find value in web search engines, whatever their shortcomings. An enormous mass of information accessible from a single search box has clear appeal; many people prefer to try several queries and skim through pages of hits than to use Boolean queries to increase precision.

The computational and linguistic tools built into commercial search engines are enhanced frequently. The architecture of cyberspace has changed the relationship between bibliographic control and access. Today, ironically, resources under good bibliographic control are likely to be less widely accessible than those simply mounted on the web. The motivation behind these simple-minded interoperability efforts is to encourage broad access to resources of value.

Genres of Digital Content

The fund of knowledge is represented by a much richer set of resources than static pages on paper, and resources beyond those traditionally found in libraries, even multi-faceted libraries like the Library of Congress. Knowledge has always been conveyed through buildings (and the archaeological sites they become), works of art, physical specimens of flora and fauna, artifacts of different cultures and lifestyles, and human memories.

Photography, sound recordings, and motion pictures have added to the fund of knowledge both in their own right as means of expression and as richer surrogates than words on paper. The digital era has added not only reproductions and analogs of older forms of information, but also new digital resources of enormous variety. Some fall into obvious categories. The broad category of datasets includes census and other survey results, gene sequences, images and other sensor data from space, geospatial information that allows maps to be generated dynamically, decades of financial statements for publicly traded corporations, directories of people and places, and structured lexical resources, such as dictionaries and thesauri.

More complex digital resources include mathematical and chemical knowledge expressed in structural forms that permit dynamic manipulation (and the software that performs or lets users perform the manipulation), interactive software for education and entertainment, and collections of re-usable "open source" software code. Digital libraries are being built to manage, serve, and support discovery of all these categories of resource.

Some of these digital libraries are extensions of traditional libraries; many have developed from other well-established activities in organizing information (for example, for collections of social science datasets). Dynamic information resources, such as the web site that delivers up-to-the minute details of event and results at the Olympic Games challenge all traditional practices for organizing and recording for posterity. However, this too could be represented as a series of snapshots of bit-patterns, a digital resource, a set of computer files.

The metadata required to support discovery and use of digital resources must clearly represent the intellectual nature and genre of the content; in a digital library, the fact that a resource can be represented by 0s and 1s is an assumption, not a useful categorization. Attempts to develop general hierarchical categorizations for genres or types of information have usually failed.

The Type working group of the Dublin Core Metadata Initiative developed, with much debate and without unanimity even in a small group, a high-level list of types (the DCMI Type Vocabulary: DCT1): Collection, Dataset, Event, Image, Interactive Resource, Service, Software, Sound, Text. MARC records can hold information about the type of a resource in several ways. Svenonius notes that there are seven different places where a "document type" can be indicated. Each element or indicator has a different set of possible values. Given the different guidelines for use and the different functions these seven elements serve, type information in MARC records has proved impossible to use uniformly within American Memory.

Type indicators in the header are excellent as triggers for systems based on MARC records. They indicate what guidelines have been applied to content fields and therefore can be used to configure appropriate displays or procedures. However, the coded values can not be incorporated into a general keyword index, and are therefore unavailable to a user as a search term as they expect. The current feeling of the Dublin Core Type working group is that some communities will develop controlled lists of terms, but agreement across communities on the important categories or even common definitions for the same terms is unlikely.

Lacking initial agreement on an acceptable "standard" typology, American Memory does not have explicit type values in all metadata records. This shortcoming means that searches limited to images may retrieve other categories of content, since the limit is actually by collection and some collections included will have text or sound as well as images. Colleagues agree that adding high-level type information consistently across the metadata records would provide more benefit for American Memory users than any other change.

Interoperability will certainly be well served if descriptive records shared or exchanged always include type information, even if all content within the repository or collection providing the data is of the same type. Based on experience with American Memory, users might be best served by the inclusion of any applicable terms from the DCT1 list and additional terms at finer levels of specificity. The user's objectives are supported not by raw metadata, but through the tools and systems that can take advantage of the metadata. In both library catalogs and digital library services, the functionality for discovery, finding, and collocating is determined not by the metadata but also by the indexes constructed for that metadata.

Different systems provide different options for configuring indexes. Public interfaces to library catalogs usually combine different metadata elements (e.g., MARC fields and subfields) into a relatively small set of indexes. For example, a keyword search by subject may find the term in any of the MARC subject fields (e.g. personal names, terms from authorized vocabularies, uncontrolled terms, genre terms, etc.). Once a record has been retrieved, elements can be labeled more specifically. Some digital libraries, including American Memory, take the same approach.

Individual elements that may be usefully distinguished (and labeled) to support the act of selection are lumped together to support discovery, finding or collocation. The University of Washington Libraries have used collection-specific element sets for their collections of digital reproductions; each set is mapped to the fifteen elements of the Dublin Core Metadata Element Set for cross-collection retrieval. Retrieved records show the specific labels.

For example, a collection of pictures of plants has a variety of fields relating to preferred soil quality and climate, whether the plant is native to the state, and other botanical details. For search purposes, these fields are all included in the Description index; on the display they are individually labeled. American Memory uses a similar approach. All descriptive notes are lumped into an overall text index; on display, a summary or abstract is usefully presented first and labeled as such. Many collections in American Memory call for unusual metadata elements, such as musical features for folk songs and descriptions of the key mechanisms in a collection of flutes.

For searching, these are all treated as notes and included in the general keyword index. For display, however, the metadata format includes tags that are ignored by the indexer, but provide labels for use in the record display. The indexing approach currently used in American Memory was developed empirically and iteratively, based on data elements usually available across heterogeneous sources and expectations of content custodians and users; it has seven primary indexes that support searching of metadata.

The developers of the Alexandria Digital Earth Prototype at the University of California, Santa Barbara have described the framework they use for querying metadata from distributed sources. Based on experience over several years of working with geo-referenced information, they chose eight search buckets. For the most basic cross-domain discovery, the developers of the Bath Profile for Z39.50 identified Author, Title, Subject, Any. The Bath Profile effort is not strictly a digital library project, but has as an aim, interoperability between library catalog systems and "other electronic resource discovery services."

The common text bucket proves invaluable when dealing with heterogeneous data and it is useful to include subject terms in this bucket. Indexing engines designed for full text will find word variants automatically, relieving users from knowing when formal subject terms use the plural form. The distinction between assigned subject terms and textual description is, nevertheless, valuable. In American Memory, it allows us to generate browse lists, which are actually static (but easily and automatically regenerated) HTML pages with "canned" searches. The subject index also permits navigation from subject terms on record displays to other records assigned the same terms.

Although American Memory indexes the primary Creator separately from the other Contributors, searching and browsing for creators and contributors is usually done together. Combining the indexes has been considered. In American Memory, the addition of roles to Creators and Contributors proves valuable, particularly for non-text materials (e.g. to distinguish composer from lyricist or illustrator of sheet music). Authorized forms for names are extremely valuable in American Memory. However, names within text are also an important access point.

The Alexandria Digital Library is designed for powerful searching by geographic location and date range. Strict machine-parsable content standards are used for those metadata elements. American Memory users would love to be able to search more effectively by date and place. For much content in American Memory, unfortunately, dates of creation for the original item are uncertain and date-ranges recorded are often so broad as to be useless for discovery. For certain collections where chronology is important, normalized dates have been generated and can be used to sort search results.

It is interesting that the Alexandria Digital Library has chosen to index date of creation/publication in the same bucket as date of coverage. In American Memory, there are many instances in which the dates are essentially equivalent. For published books and maps, the distinction is often important, but users may be interested in either or both. The Alexandria Digital Library uses special overlap and containment queries for date ranges and location. Such queries would not be efficient with a full-text engine, but American Memory users would like the capability.

Geographical location is an area in which traditional descriptive practices aimed at human-readable displays do not transfer well to digital libraries (or even support finding and collocation in traditional library catalogs). In American Memory's metadata from heterogeneous sources, location may be expressed in many ways: as an informal place-name, as a subdivision in a topical subject heading, as a traditional subject heading or a hierarchical place name. Of these, by far the most useful for manipulating automatically with simple text-based tools has been the hierarchical place name.

Users often know that they are looking for an image or for a map and would like to exclude other types of information from the start. Searching by more specific genre terms is also useful, for example for posters or cartoons. As pointed out earlier, type categories expressed in terms that users recognize should be available for limiting or searching. Controlled vocabularies are useful, but are likely to be domain-specific.

The emergence of XML (Extended Markup Language) and its widespread support as a syntax for exchanging metadata and content, particularly for e-commerce transactions and services, is stimulating the development of better tools for transforming and sharing metadata.

This, in turn is leading to support for XML from vendors of database software and text-indexing engines. It appears clear that XML will provide the syntax for metadata exchange among digital libraries in the coming years. A few examples of its adoption to support interoperability include: the Bath Profile; MPEG-7; the Open Archives Initiative; and the Federal Geographic Data Committee. XML is also being used as a syntax to represent content objects, such as the proposed Open eBook standard.

American Memory has relied heavily on common indexing of heterogeneous metadata, with different element sets and in two different digital formats (MARC communications format and an XML-like syntax for simple (Dublin Core-like) records. Migration to an XML syntax with a formal DTD or schema is anticipated.

Transformations from one XML metadata schema to another (especially from a rich one to a simpler one) can be facilitated using Extensible Stylesheet Language Transformations (XSL/T). This is just one example of the powerful XML-based tools emerging. XSL/T is already in common use for transforming finding aids marked up to the EAD standard (in XML) to HTML for display on the web.

XML also includes the ability to mix and match metadata element definitions (semantics and syntax) from other schemas (using the "namespace" feature). As the flurry of XML-related activity on the World Wide Web Consortium web site in late 2000 shows, the general acceptance of XML signals the beginning of a further period of experimentation and development. Among the unanswered questions relating to the use of XML as a syntax for metadata is how soon (or whether) there will be widespread adoption of the Resource Description Framework, an elegant modeling framework for descriptive schemas.

RDF is layered on top of XML, using a particular XML-based syntax for metadata. RDF-specific tools will be needed to take full advantage of its potential for scalable interoperability. Whether the mix-and-match potential of XML namespaces will be widely exploited also remains to be seen. In the past, text-indexing engines, relational database management systems, and SGML-based storage and retrieval systems all offered different functionality to support the finding, collocation, and discovery objectives for digital libraries.

A text-indexing engine can handle heterogeneous metadata and full text in a single system; the capabilities for matching word variants (stemming) have been invaluable for American Memory. Features standard in relational database systems, however, such as sorting by date, have been implemented by additional programming. SGML-aware systems have advantages for substantial bodies of highly structured textual content, such as books and periodicals. Recently, products in one category have found ways to integrate the capabilities of another. ORACLE now has a full text search module, CONTEXT. Some text-indexing engines can now index text stored within relational databases. All such products are announcing "support" for XML.

The other area where tools are emerging is in automated integration of thesauri and other knowledge bases to support more intelligent retrieval. Such tools can compensate for less complete metadata. These knowledge bases could also be more widely used as a resource when creating metadata. Digital libraries will benefit from network-accessible thesauri and authority files that can be queried dynamically from systems that are used to generate metadata.

OAI-Protocol for Metadata Harvesting (OAI-PMH)

OAI-Protocol for Metadata Harvesting (OAI-PMH) holds much promise for similar exchanges of metadata describing the collections of museums and other cultural heritage institutions. Materials in these types of collections often are not well indexed by commercial Web search engines. Metadata describing such holdings is hidden in databases, finding aids, and XML documents, or otherwise is not readily available to Web search systems, which typically understand little more than simple HTML.

As a result, these materials remain hard to find and out of reach for many researchers. The utility of such a metadata repository will depend on many factors, including the development of more uniform metadata authoring practices across various communities of metadata providers. Metadata is currently used primarily for a variety of local purposes, and the schemas to which collections conform have been adapted and tailored to meet local needs. Less attention has been paid to using metadata to support universal interoperability.

With the advent of OAI and similar protocols, mapping local schemas to more universally standard schemas for the support of interoperability is gaining ground. Even assuming broader and more consistent application of metadata schemas designed to support interoperability, there remains considerable work to be done in learning how best to utilize aggregations of metadata describing heterogeneous information resources.

There is a need to normalize metadata so as to enable more consistent retrieval of results from cross-collection searches. Challenges also exist for presenting search results in ways that provide appropriate contextual information for the records retrieved. As of February, 2002, the Illinois OAI-PMH project has harvested metadata from twenty-five different institutions or consortiums. The resources described range from museum artifacts such as pottery and clothing, to archival manuscript and personal paper collections, to digitized photographs and monographs. The sets of harvested metadata range in size from the largest at 900,000 records to the smallest at 23 records.

Some sites include metadata not relevant to cultural heritage mixed with more appropriate metadata. The institutions providing metadata are diverse, including academic libraries, museums, historical societies, public libraries, the Library of Congress, and special consortia such as the Colorado Digitization Project and the Alliance and Lincoln Trail Library systems in Illinois. Fourteen institutions have provided the Illinois OAI-PMH project team with snapshots of relevant metadata, in a few cases providing an entire database, which has then been made available from Illinois servers in a manner compliant with OAI-PMH.

While all of the metadata harvested from the registered OAI metadata provider sites was in the required Simple Dublin Core format (DC), metadata from the fourteen unregistered sites were given to the project in a variety of formats. These included finding aids formatted in encoded archival description (EAD), MARC format metadata describing bibliographic information, and local metadata schemas stored in HTML files, XML files, or proprietary database structures.

To enhance cross-collection searching, local metadata schemas need to be mapped to standard schemas. Even with greater adoption of standard metadata schemas like DC, there remain wide variations in the use of authoring conventions and the depth of descriptive information included when creating metadata to describe cultural heritage collections.

The Open Archives Initiative Protocol for Metadata Harvesting (OAI-PMH) is a new and still evolving protocol designed to allow institutions to share metadata easily. It is hoped that the standard can help increase the discoverability of resources by scholarly researchers. The Protocol underwent one minor revision during its first full year of experimental implementation. Version 2.0 is scheduled for release in May 2002.

The fundamental pieces of the protocol are its adherence to well-formed XML, its use of the HTTP standards for data transmission, and its requirement that metadata records shared via the OAI-PMH be made available in the DC metadata schema. One of the common challenges in setting up an OAI-PMH metadata provider service is ensuring that the metadata to be exported is mapped properly into DC.

There are fifteen DC elements: Title, Creator, Subject, Description, Publisher, Contributor, Date, Type, Format, Identifier, Source, Language, Relation, Coverage, and Rights. Any or all of these elements may be used, and all are repeatable. Because much of the existing metadata about museum and special collections was developed with limited resources, using local schemas and with local needs in mind, the process of mapping to DC can be time and resource consuming and potentially frustrating.

There is, however, a growing community of DC users and freely available tools to assist with this process. Harvesting done so far shows that metadata authoring practices differ both in the selection of DC elements used and the depth of information provided even within specific communities. As previously noted, DC elements are both optional and repeatable. These allow a significant degree of variation in the interpretation of which elements to use and how to use them when metadata are created in DC and when mapped to DC.

The Library of Congress American Memory Project, the American Museum of Natural History, the CIMI Demonstration Repository, and the Spurlock Museum to compare the use of DC elements. Within each set of sample records, calculated the percent of records that contain each of the DC elements and the average number of times an element is used in records that contain it. The usage variations are due in part to the intrinsic differences in the collections described by the metadata.

However, some variations are clearly due to different decisions made by each institution when determining how to map their metadata into DC. These variations pose a challenge when attempting to build cross-collection search services and determining what depth of detail should be shown in record display. The variations can also influence how a search engine's ranking algorithm orders the result set.

Museums began to use personal computers for tracking information about their collections using a variety of proprietary databases. The use of proprietary software not specifically designed with the museum community in mind can lead to inconsistencies in the way collections are catalogued and tracked. The descriptive elements within a locally created metadata format and the degree of completeness when classifying and cataloging the items can vary widely from one organization to another. This may have the effect of diluting the potential for discoverability as searching aggregated repositories requires some degree of predictable structure and normalization of metadata terms or concepts.

At the same time, one should not overlook the value of descriptive, locally created metadata applied to artifacts by professionals familiar with the collection and the museum. This is particularly valuable for collections used primarily by a local community of users. At the University of Illinois Spurlock Museum, FileMakerPro software is used to track the procurement, storage, stage of processing, and display of artifacts. It is also used to maintain descriptive information about the materials. The

FileMakerPro database interacts with a Web server to provide public access to a portion of the collection.

The decisions made about mapping the metadata were more time consuming than the time spent writing the scripts and manipulating the data. Here is an example of some of the decisions that were made for the cultural materials provided by Spurlock:

— *Subject:* One instance of the DC Subject element was included in each record. The decision was made to concatenate three fields from the original metadata records that could be considered equivalent to DC Subject. Colons were used to distinguish each of the three original strings that were concatenated to create the single DC Subject element. If there were not three values to concatenate, then the DC Subject filed would have two colons next to each other or a lone colon at the beginning or end of the element.

— *Date:* The Date element was qualified as DCQ date.created.

— *Coverage:* The Coverage element was qualified by appending Spurlock metadata field names to the DC element as DCQ coverage.spatial, coverage.temporal, or coverage.cultural.

— *Description:* Key words were added to the Description field values in the original metadata to clarify what was meant by the content of the Description element.

In addition to the mapping given below, 3 fixed DC Type values ("cultural," "physical object," and "original") were included in each Spurlock metadata record exported via OAI. One of the more challenging aspects of implementing the OAI protocol is mapping from metadata schemas designed to describe collections of materials (e.g., an EAD Finding Aid record) to the DC metadata schema. Finding aids may describe as many as several thousand items or folders in an archive while DC has typically been used to describe individual items (e.g., books, photographs, letters, personal journals, audio files).

Each EAD record includes metadata describing the entire collection and a "description of subordinate components" which lists the separate series, sub-series, folders and items found in the collection. Some EAD files reach hundreds of kilobytes, or even several megabytes, in size. The challenge is to allow the richness of such a large file to be exposed and made searchable alongside other records that describe a single item or a much smaller collection. Another challenge is due to the very flexible nature of the EAD standard designed to encourage participation by a large number of institutions. It is not surprising that the EAD records analyzed for the Illinois OAI-PMH project reveal many differences in tag structures and encoding patterns between institutions.

Despite these differences, the records seem to have enough consistency to make a general cross mapping between EAD and OAI-DC possible. Although the EAD Application Guidelines include two recommended mappings to DC, one for the finding aid itself (i.e. the electronic resource) and another for the resources described in the finding aid (i.e. the actual manuscripts or archives), neither mapping will generate records adequate for use in an OAI repository.

While researchers are interested in discovering the existence of actual archives or manuscripts, metadata about the finding aid itself is also necessary in order to point effectively to the source records. For this reason, a flexible approach in mapping an EAD finding aid into an OAI record is needed. This top-level record becomes a base record for the finding aid and must be as complete, accurate, and concise as possible. The base record includes a link to the source EAD file as well as references to related parts of the collection. These related parts are described in other individual records and produce for each component level found within the EAD file's description of subordinate components.

Although it is not possible to link these records to each other adequately using simple DC, a sophisticated use of qualified DC fields can produce linked records. This method will provide functional and easily searchable records. Metadata authoring practices as discussed above play important roles in determining the value of a cross-collection repository focusing on cultural heritage materials. Providing context for the metadata, normalization techniques, and developing the search engine and interface also need to be examined and explored for ways to enhance the discoverability of the collected metadata.

One real concern related to the development of cross-collection repository search tools is the context of the original artifact or digital resource. The value of information about the materials that may be found in museum collections and archives is often related to the context and the provenance of the object(s). For example, a photographic slide depicting part of a remaining wall of a basilica dating to the 4th Century would have less value if it were viewed out of the context of the architectural structure it represents. It is not good enough simply to make the slide available for viewing; it needs to be put into a proper context. Ideally, the holding institution of the artifact or digital resource will determine the appropriate context.

When the repository encounters URLs embedded within any of the metadata fields, they are mapped to the DC Identifier element. The links sometimes lead to the holding institution or organization's Web site, to the digital display of the resource's record from the holding institution or organization's database, or to an actual display of the resource itself. Given the non-persistent nature of many URLs, it is possible that providing access to them may lead to a large number of dead links over time. With regularly scheduled re-harvesting of the metadata, changes to the URLs should be reflected in the records and therefore allow to avoid excessive dead links.

For an example of a repository that has made thoughtful consideration of these efforts, consider the metadata collection contributed to the Illinois OAI-PMH project by TDC, the Teaching with Digital Content project. This project provides a searchable database of images that can be used by K-12 teachers to develop teaching modules that meet specific curriculum requirements. Partners providing metadata for the project include museums, the Illinois State Library, the Chicago Public Library and others.

All the metadata has been entered into a database in a format that meets the specific needs of the TDC project and does not conform to DC. However, the display of the records is very clean and consistent and maps well into DC for the purposes of the Illinois OAI-PMH project. With a link directly to the Teaching with Digital Content resource provided from a URL that has been mapped into the DC Identifier field, the context is easily maintained by providing more background information about the record when the user clicks on this link.

Metadata Normalization

In order to provide context internally and to enhance discoverability of metadata records in a cross-collection repository, some normalization of the metadata is desirable. That normalization can be done on several of the DC elements, including Type, Format, Coverage, and Date. Effective normalization requires to:

- Understand how the element was interpreted by metadata providers and which elements in other metadata formats were mapped to the DC element;
- Identify which - if any - vocabularies were used by data providers;
- Determine whether there is any controlled vocabulary that the project team could successfully apply to all of the data providers;
- Apply vocabulary to the metadata to augment the 'native' vocabulary;
- Build mechanisms into the search interface that would take advantage of the normalization; and
- Gauge the success of the normalization for resource discovery.
- These goals translate into a five-step process as follows.
- *Extract and analyze the element values (content)* : Each unique value was listed, along with the number of times it appeared within each individual metadata set. For example, only eleven of the twenty-five metadata providers used the Type element and that approximately 1440 different Type values appear in the entire metadata set. Some providers only use one

value, and others use over 800. The number of values seems to be dependent on whether the institutions are using a specific or general vocabulary.

The metadata providers used elements in a variety of ways. For example, the DC Date element was used for the date the digital item was created, the date the physical item was created or published, and the date an item was added to a collection. Because OAI-PMH requires use of simple DC, the qualifiers that may have explained these values further were not present. Similarly the variety and specificity or generality of controlled vocabularies also influenced the next steps in the normalization process.

Each DC element was examined to determine the focus for normalization for that particular element. While the Date element suggests a need to choose between options like 'date created' or 'date contributed' and the particular format the value is displayed in, the Type element required to focus on the range and specificity of vocabulary used.

Once the vocabulary is developed, the values in the metadata are mapped to the vocabulary terms. The actual normalization of the data is an automated process. Following the mapping, values from the vocabulary are added to each record as additional. After new records are harvested, the system compares the values of specific elements with the mapping already done and adds appropriate terms from the vocabulary where applicable. If a term that has not already been mapped appears, it is flagged and looked at by human eyes.

The last step is to provide services so that users can take advantage of the normalization process. The ability to limit searches or sort results by type of resource or to search for specific date ranges or geographic areas is each made possible by the normalization process.

Metadata Harvesting

Metadata harvesting will be an important part of the interoperability toolkit for libraries. But it is just a first step. Communities that have close affinities with libraries, such as museums and other archival institutions, have good reason to use different descriptive practices. Those practices, and the terminology used: "necessarily depend on conscious or sub-conscious assumptions about who will use it and how". A resource that is of potential use in many contexts may need to be described in several ways and using several vocabularies.

In US, the Library of Congress (LC) was an early adopter of the OAI Protocol for Metadata Harvesting to make records for some of its digitized historical collections available for integration into other services. The American Memory team was attracted by a protocol for sharing its resources that promised to be straightforward to implement with no deleterious effect on the primary users. The promise was borne out in practice; the mechanics of harvesting are working well and records for additional collections are being made available every few months.

To non-librarians, the MARC communications format, used by the Library of Congress for its catalog records, was unfamiliar and often seen as a significant hurdle. The American Memory interface was designed for users to locate individual items, not to download batches. On several occasions, LC made an entire collection (records and images) available on an "as-is" basis. Assembling batches for download and explaining what was being delivered was time-consuming, but for an entire collection and a partner with the ability to handle the metadata as it came, it was feasible. Often, what was requested was a substantial subset of a very large collection.

LC did not have the resources to do the selection or build a custom batch for download and the requesting institution did not have the capacity to receive the full collection and sift through it. Neither party had the tools or resources at hand to transform the metadata from one form to another. Many worthwhile requests for material to repurpose led to nothing because the effort involved in responding to such requests on an ad hoc basis was simply too great.

During 1996, two task forces of the newly-formed Digital Library Federation (DLF), a group of 15 research libraries engaged in projects involving digital content, met several times to consider recommendations for descriptive metadata and for an architecture to provide common access to the growing pool of resources digitized by member libraries. Both task forces found a variety of practices and local imperatives that would have to be accommodated in any shared approach.

For example, three institutions were taking different "standard" approaches to the description of photographs. At LC, the Prints and Photographs Division uses MARC records and follows Anglo-American Cataloging Rules (AACR2) supported by additional rules for describing older and unpublished visual materials. At Harvard, there was strong support, for example from the Graduate School of Art and Design, for the tiered approach represented by the Visual Resources Association's proposal for a core descriptive framework that distinguishes between records for underlying works and records for images of those works.

At the University of California, Berkeley, a commitment had been made to archival practice rather than item-level cataloging for reasons of economy;

collections of photographs would be described in archival finding aids, to be marked up in SGML (now XML) using the Encoded Archival Description Document Type Definition (DTD). Practices and technical capabilities also varied widely across university campuses; libraries could not dictate practice to academic departments doing their own digitization or creating their own digital content unless they could provide resources or services to offset the costs of compliance.

Rather than attempt to establish a single architectural design, DLF chose to start by promoting exploratory discussions, prototyping, and standards development for components that would be required in any architecture, such as authentication of users, and linking from references to cited articles. Several DLF organizations joined in a proposal to the Mellon Foundation for a project based on a pooled collection of finding aids and a common structure for complex hierarchical objects representing digitized manuscripts, photographs, and other archival objects. Out of the experience with this XML-based metadata structure has come the more general METS standard, which is now being explored by many institutions as a mechanism for encoding the structure of complex digital objects.

However, by 1999, the goal of shared access to the high-quality digital resources in the collections managed by DLF member institutions seemed no closer. Ironically, the convenience and effectiveness of the Internet search engines, such as Lycos and Google, meant that random Web pages were more conveniently available to the students and researchers these libraries served than the resources they carefully selected and cataloged. Rather than being in static HTML pages that could be indexed by the search engines, the managed resources were hidden behind a database query interface, part of the "hidden" Web.

Open Archives Initiative (OAI)

Open Archives Initiative (OAI) and its early history is well documented elsewhere. Services could be specialized, for example, by discipline or by intended audience, or comprehensive and cross-domain. The content described could be digitized historical materials as easily as e-prints. The protocol to support collaboration among organizations building collections of papers and reports deposited by authors could be applied by libraries and museums wishing to build virtual collections of cultural heritage materials. Technology for collaboration can be independent of any particular incentive to collaborate.

The enthusiasm from that first meeting led the Library of Congress to play an active role in the Open Archives Initiative. The metadata harvesting approach proposed had a great deal in common with the initially ad hoc approach LC had taken in integrating into American Memory materials digitized by institutions with awards through the LC/Ameritech competition. Based on LC's experience with the competition, many characteristics of the initiative and the harvesting protocol were immediately appealing. These included:

— the emphasis on keeping technical barriers to entry low for those with valuable resources to share through metadata;

— the recognition that requirements for interoperability should not place unacceptable loads on the primary services of institutions choosing to provide access to their content;

— a planned period of practical experimentation followed by review;

— the combination of a very generic common denominator metadata schema that would be mandatory (for purposes of basic interoperability across domains) with the ability to exchange records in more specific schemas (to satisfy specialist audiences and content owners and to support access services with richer functionality);

— the potential to integrate, for purposes of discovery, resources from libraries, museums, historical societies, and other cultural heritage institutions with a variety of descriptive traditions;

— suitability for use in any future program similar to the LC/Ameritech competition or for any organization wishing to repurpose records or content from American Memory;

— and an opportunity to make the resources digitized for American Memory more broadly available and useful, by allowing others to harvest the records conveniently and integrate them into services aimed at different audiences and taking advantage of new technological developments in information retrieval.

From a longer-term perspective, it seemed likely that a simple mechanism for metadata harvesting could provide a substantial body of metadata to support deeper collaborative exploration of interoperability. Interoperability involves agreements at several levels. In the context of the NSDL, the NSDL core integration team identified three levels of agreement needed: technical, content-related, and organizational. Costs of complying with agreements at any level inhibit adoption but without agreements the functionality that can be achieved is limited.

A simple protocol for harvesting metadata seemed to offer low-cost participation at the technical level. If a large pool of metadata records were available for harvesting, pragmatic exploration of costs and benefits of fuller agreements at the other levels could follow. Content-level agreements would cover metadata schemas and guidelines for the content and encoding of values for metadata elements. The experience with integrating the heterogeneous records for collections digitized through the LC/Ameritech competition led to some sense of what minimal normalization was necessary for metadata records to be useful in American Memory.

However, a larger "marketplace" of metadata and services established with the use of metadata harvesting might lead to broader consensus as to what is most important. Organizational agreements would cover matters such as governance of a consortium building and running a service based on metadata harvested from members.

By November 2000, with strong encouragement from Winston Tabb, the Associate Librarian for Library Services, the Library of Congress had committed itself to early implementation of the Open Archives Initiative Protocol for Metadata Harvesting (OAI-PMH) as a data provider using selected collections from American Memory as a test. The Library of Congress has been distributing catalog records since 1901, first on cards and since around 1968 in machine-readable form; making records for digitized content available for harvesting continues the tradition of adapting to new opportunities provided by new technology. Tabb also saw participation in the initiative, and other activities supported by DLF, as important for the Library of Congress, particularly in the light of criticisms of isolation in the recent report, LC21 A Digital Strategy for the Library of Congress.

The commitment was possible because the barrier to entry appeared low enough not to draw significant resources away from American Memory itself. This assessment proved true in practice. The first implementation took about 40 hours of programmer time, including analysis and testing. Mappings and conversion tools that were already used for American Memory or managed in LC's Network Development and MARC Standards Office (NDMSO) were reviewed, updated, and used to advantage. These included Perl language routines for parsing MARC records, a one-way mapping from MARC to simple Dublin Core, and a table to translate characters from the ALA character set used in LC's MARC records to UNICODE.

The first records to be made available would be those already upgraded to serve both in LC's main catalog and for indexing in American Memory. These already supported links to the content based on persistent identifiers resolved using a Handle Server, developed by the Corporation for National Research Initiatives (CNRI) and deployed at LC. Procedures for updates to American Memory could be easily extended to update the OAI data-provider service. The computer processing required to support harvesting requests was not expected to have a perceptible effect on response time for American Memory users. Also in late 2000, the DLF put out a call to members asking for lists of digital content for which they were willing to share metadata through the harvesting protocol.

At LC, this call was passed on to the custodial divisions responsible for content in American Memory described by records in the MARC format. Another mechanism to broaden access to their content was greeted enthusiastically, particularly because the links from the metadata records would bring users to the LC site, where more context for the collections would be available and users could follow leads to other related materials. At the January 2001 public release of version 1.0 of the protocol, David Woodward was able to announce that LC's data-provider service, for which he was the programmer, was up and running with records for two American Memory collections of digitized historical materials available: roughly 3,000 records for maps, and 200 records for ballroom dance instruction manuals. The records were harvestable in two formats, the full MARC records in a simple XML schema established for OAI-PMH and in unqualified Dublin Core in the XML schema.

Version 1.0 of the protocol was released in January 2001 with the expectation that there would be a period of experimentation for at least a year. Starting in September 2001, a technical committee was established with membership drawn from institutions actively using OAI-PMH to make metadata available or to harvest metadata and build a service. LC was invited to participate, not only because of its experience as an OAI data provider, but also because of the importance in the library community of MARC records as a carrier for metadata. The outcome of this process was version 2.0 of the harvesting protocol; the differences are outlined elsewhere. There are many differences in detail, but the underlying philosophy of a low barrier to entry remained. Proposals were accommodated if there was sufficient support, several through optional extension features.

LC is taking advantage of the option to provide descriptive records for "sets" of records that can be harvested as a group. Among the additions proposed but not adopted was support for distributed querying. Proponents were encouraged to participate in the activity now known as ZING (Z39.50-International Next Generation). This activity includes a number of initiatives by Z39.50 implementers to make the accumulated wisdom and functionality embodied in 20 years of experience more broadly available and lower the barriers to implementation. Simple Dublin Core was retained as a mandatory metadata format, because no other obvious candidate exists.

Version 2.0 of the OAI-PMH protocol proved as straightforward to implement at LC as the initial version. Based on experience over the first year, a revised architecture was developed to support more convenient and robust updates and additions. LC's OAI service divides records into OAI sets on the basis of Amèrican Memory collections or groups of collections. As of late 2002, there were ten sets, with one set being the aggregation of four photograph collections also available as separate sets.

The implementation of OAI-PMH is programmed in Perl, taking advantage of the popular CGI.pm library to process and respond to HTTP requests. SGML processing routines from James Clark were used to handle the character conversion. For the first version, responses to the Identify and ListSets verbs were both in static files. ListIdentifiers requests were answered from an index, stored as a file, which mapped record identifiers to sets. The OAI verbs that return records access the source files of MARC records in the standard (ISO 2709) communication format, with dynamic conversion (using Perl) to XML.

The principal change when implementing version 2.0 was to use three tables in a relational database (using MySQL) in place of the simple set-identifier index. The tables represent OAI sets, OAI items, and the set-item links that indicate set membership. Sets can be added and related information edited through a Web form. Perl is still used for the HTTP processing, querying the MySQL database, and dynamic conversion from the source MARC records. Implementation of the new version at LC took roughly 60 hours of programmer effort, including analysis and testing. It was completed during the beta-test period and in operation before the official release of the protocol in June 2002.

At NDMSO, the year leading up to the release of version 2.0 of OAI-PMH saw related developments in response to industry trends and requests from the library community. The trends included the growing adoption of XML following the stabilization of the XML schema definition language in May 2001 and the emergence of compliant software tools, the desire in libraries for a "lite" version of MARC encoded in XML, and the interest in metadata harvesting as part of the interoperability toolkit for libraries. NDMSO has developed two MARC-related XML schemata.

One of these schemata is recommended in the new OAI release as a replacement for the original oai_marc schema. This MARCXML schema can be used to encode any MARC21 record. Like oai_marc, the tagging of this "slim" schema indicates the structure of a MARC record in fields and sub-fields, allows round-trip conversion without data loss, and will not need modification with the minor changes to the MARC standard that happen routinely. In February 2003, LC's cataloging distribution service made test files available in MARCXML for evaluation and prototype development.

The second schema, known as MODS (Metadata Object Description Schema), is still at an early stage of development. Introduced in June 2002 and revised in early 2003, it is intended as a multi-purpose bibliographic element set for library applications. Unlike MARCXML, MODS includes only a subset of MARC elements and sometimes regroups them. MODS uses familiar words as element names rather than relying on MARC's numeric tags to convey semantics. In Fall 2002, LC made its OAI-harvestable records available in the MODS format in addition to MARC21 and simple Dublin Core.

These records provide richer semantics than Dublin Core and will support experimentation with the new format. The implementation uses an XSLT stylesheet to convert MARCXML records to MODS. NDMSO intends to maintain a suite of such tools for manipulating and transforming records between MARC and MODS. Implementing OAI-PMH as a data provider has had several beneficial side-effects for LC. Program code for converting records in the MARC Communications Format to an XML format can be used in many circumstances.

Experience gained with special characters has been applied in other contexts through the development of mappings among MARC 21 characters, UNICODE, and character entities for HTML and SGML. Unusual characters in LC's records have also helped harvesters test their handling of UNICODE. Having records formally validated and tested by automated transformations by harvesters picks up errors that may be hidden by local interfaces or simply not noticed. This finding is consistent with experience with the LC/Ameritech competition. When records were brought into American Memory and subjected to different indexing and display routines, errors exposed were often found to cause undetected anomalous behavior in the original system too.

The Library of Congress has registered its OAI server for American Memory collections in the central OAI registry, which means that others can harvest and re-purpose records without LC being aware of it. This is nothing new for LC. Its records are available for copying from bibliographic utilities, such as OCLC and RLG; users of Z39.50 have been able to download records directly from LC's main catalog for well over a decade. Indeed, one of the key benefits to LC from the harvesting protocol is that no special arrangements have to be made when others want to get the records and use them in another service.

LC has a particular interest in the use of its records in services with a focus on cultural heritage or humanities scholarship, and services that integrate materials from libraries, museums, historical societies and other archival institutions. The Research Libraries Group (RLG) has harvested records (in the MARC format) for several collections for integration into its cultural materials service. Dublin Core records for all collections are harvested by two services described elsewhere in this issue: OAIster at the University of Michigan and the University of Illinois-Urbana Champaign (UIUC) Cultural Heritage Repository. Records have also been harvested by the Perseus Digital Library. The mechanics of harvesting appear to be working well.

Now that records for a substantial body of cultural heritage content are easily harvestable, organizations and communities can begin to build on this base to support learning and scholarship through richer interactions with the resources accumulated in archival institutions. To achieve this will likely require communities to adopt more detailed agreements about metadata or make commitments to federated organization.

Costs associated with metadata content can be daunting. Identifying and characterizing a resource and placing it in an intellectual context is expensive. Local needs take priority and upgrading existing records on an individual basis is seldom an option. Few doubt that "better" metadata lets people find what they want more easily, but a compromise between quantity and quality is often necessary. For pictures, music, and other cultural resources that do not include full text or spoken words that can be searched, human expertise is essential to provide summaries, assign topical and genre terms, indicate where and when a work was created, or relate it to other works.

Because of the expense and investment, change in practices is inevitably slow. Most standards and formal consortial agreements allow a great deal of flexibility so that legacy records can be handled. Motivation to modify records or practices, or to develop and test more complex conversion tools, will exist only if there is obvious benefit to the unit bearing the brunt of the workload. The Library of Congress is aware that it could improve the records it makes available for harvesting in a number of ways, with more or less effort, but needs evidence or guidance from service builders to indicate which modifications would be most valuable and which irrelevant. Indications are beginning to surface. Some inferences can be drawn from an analysis from the team building the UIUC Cultural Heritage Repository and the approach to metadata normalization for that service. The section on data content in RLG's description guidelines for participants in the Cultural Materials Alliance indicates the aspects that are most significant in building their service.

The least expensive way to improve LC's records in the short term would be through modifications to the transformation from the source record into formats for harvesting. LC's current transformation from MARC to simple Dublin Core is extremely basic. Element values are copied directly without conversion to another vocabulary or encoding scheme. Where codes are converted to terms, MARC terminology is usually used, because it matches the semantics of the coding scheme. In some cases, this results in terms that do not correspond to common usage or map cleanly to categories in other metadata schemes. Issues and questions that have come up in relation to simple (unqualified) Dublin Core records include:

— *Title:* The mapping to simple Dublin Core omits all title information except from the MARC 245 field. This is on the assumption that multiple titles will be confusing for service builders (and their users) if the main title cannot be distinguished. However, significant information will be missing. For example, songs are often known by words from their first lines or choruses rather than the title on the published score. Records for works in other languages may include translated titles. Should some alternative titles be included as Description elements? Or would service builders be happy to treat the first Title element as the one to use in hits lists?

— *Date:* The value for Date is taken from the statement of publication, distribution, etc. This field is intended for human reading, and the cataloging rules provide methods to indicate uncertainty and approximation, or date ranges when the resource being described is not a single item, and even to concatenate several dates for different events. For cultural heritage materials, uncertainty about the date of creation or distribution is common. The result is that the Date element is neither easily machine-processable nor useful for sorting. Should LC consider normalizing the information it makes available in the Date element or rely on service builders to do that?

— *Description:* For American Memory materials, note fields can be very significant for discovery: they can include summary descriptions, information about provenance, or biographical details. LC has chosen to include almost all categories of notes as Description elements. Some notes may be of little value for discovery, but because the range of information included in general notes (MARC 500 field) is very broad, it is not easy to distinguish notes that are logistical or administrative from those that provide intellectual context for the resource. How valuable would it be to service builders if LC attempted to be more selective about the notes it includes in Description elements?

— *Creator/Contributor:* The current mapping uses only Creator and includes all values for MARC fields 100-111 (Main Entry Name fields) and 700-720 (Added Entry Name fields). The semantics of the distinction between main entries and added entries in MARC is not the same as the distinction between Creator and Contributor. In particular, since only one main entry name is permitted, authors beyond the first are added entries. The American Memory experience leads us to believe that a distinction based on role with relationship to the resource being described (e.g. lyricist, photographer, engraver, architect) is more significant for cultural heritage materials than either the MARC distinction or the Dublin Core distinction. Unfortunately, neither the unqualified version of Dublin Core nor the approved qualifiers can represent this distinction. Questions to service builders at UIUC and OAIster about their preferences received somewhat uncertain responses.

— *Type:* This element, which corresponds to the genre or nature of the resource, what it is rather than what it is about, is perhaps the most complex of all. Those thinking about the issue for the first time often assume that a hierarchy of genres can be established for general use. All attempts in the library community have failed, and those with experience, including the DC Type Working Group, believe that genre vocabularies will continue to be developed by communities and for specific contexts. In The Intellectual Foundation of Information Organization, a thoughtful analysis of the history of cataloging theory and practice, Elaine Svenonius (2002) pointed out: "For document types, as for general-format types, it is not possible to construct a classification that is both natural and whose categories are mutually exclusive". For historical reasons, the MARC record can hold type and genre information in several different fields and practices vary with the nature of the material. For music, genre terms have traditionally been tagged as MARC 650 fields, used primarily for topical headings. Perhaps this is because most music is not about anything, and the distinction between topic and genre has not been important. In contrast, for pictorial materials, the distinction between topic and genre is part of the code of cataloging practice and the 655 field is used for genre terms. The MARC to Dublin Core mapping converts 655 fields into Type elements. If the Dublin Core records serve primarily for cross-domain use, or to allow service-builders to filter records, perhaps there would be benefit to putting most music subjects (using a program that is more complex than a simple mapping between fields) into Type rather than Subject, and also taking steps to ensure that appropriate terms for high-level categories in other vocabularies are added as Type elements even if they do not occur explicitly in the source record.

Some of these issues will not be a problem when transforming MARC records to the MODS schema, since MODS inherits the relevant semantics from MARC. This is not a coincidence, since experience with American Memory and mappings to metadata schemes used in other communities were among the inputs to the development of MODS. Others, in particular those related to dates and genres, will continue to be a concern when transforming records from sources based on MARC records and AACR2/ISBD practices.

LC hopes there will be constructive interactions with service builders and others making metadata for cultural materials available, so that resources can be applied where the benefit will be greatest, including the development of more global support for using controlled vocabularies and matching names for people and places to authorized forms where appropriate.

One of the hopes was that a pool of metadata would support experimentation with interfaces and navigation. The interface for RLG's cultural materials service allows users to switch easily between different structural views of the current result set enabling different browsing strategies and different approaches to successive refinement of a search. Every item is represented by a thumbnail for visual browsing; explicit modeling of parent-child relationships facilitates navigation from collection records to item records and vice versa.

A rather different issue has been raised by the functionality of the Perseus Digital Library. The special features of Perseus are based primarily on full text, including the detection and highlighting of names of people and places in unstructured text so that they can function as searches for related information. In records harvested using OAI, they found that records linking back to an HTML representation of the item described seldom provide access to source SGML or XML, even when it exists.

LC has downplayed access to the SGML versions of its converted texts through American Memory because regular users were confused. Perhaps the dynamic addition of a link to the SGML version should be considered for OAI records in the MODS format. In addition to making records for more digital reproductions accessible for harvesting, OAI-PMH will play a role in other activities in which the Library of Congress is involved.

Plans are developing for two specialist gateways, one for sheet music and another for video and motion pictures. Both expect to harvest records for particular collections of records as those gateways move from the planning stage to implementation. In a very different project, OCLC, Die Deutsche Bibliothek, and LC are taking initial steps to build a Virtual International Authority File (VIAF). In the first phase, VIAF will include records for Personal Names from selected national libraries and serve the cataloging community.

8

Surfing Digital Information

Web pages and Web sites can be collected and categorized. They can be aggregated and included as parts of library collections. These libraries can take one of two forms. Web libraries can consist of native documents linked to the library, which provides access to the document but do not exercise control or ownership over the document. Web libraries can also "collect" Web documents through caching or archiving, thus creating a local electronic record on an historical Web document. Digital libraries, including Web-based collections, are redefining both the role of electronic information storage and retrieval as well as the role of traditional libraries.

Digital libraries include collections of books, journal articles, graphics, newspapers, and other material in digital format; in sum, collections of digitized content. To be a library, that collection should be organized according to some standard. There are many examples of digital libraries. On one level, the Web can be seen as an extension of and as a tool for libraries. If the Web is a tool, it is a complex tool serving to modify the information management and retrieval functions of both librarians and libraries.

The Web can be employed as a transfer and distribution mechanism for the digital and digitized collections of libraries. Web users can organize Web documents into document clusters that can be managed, searched, and accessed. These clusters or libraries have taken many forms. The vast majority of these attempt an in situ organization and categorization of Web content. Perhaps the most common are the jumppages, or Web page collections of hypertext links that point to other Web pages or Web sites with a defined content. The Web differs from the more traditional information media in several substantial ways.

The Web as a whole may not be organized to the degree that Chen might want it to meet the standard of a library, but neither is the entire corpus of print or electronic media so organized either. The Web lacks authority and quality control, but so do many print publications. Much of the Web is reminiscent of the political and religious pamphleteering so prevalent in Europe and North America over the past 200 years. There are six approaches to bring quality control to the Web. These are the programming, procedural, structuring, bibliographical, evaluative or indexed, and organizational approaches. Variations and additions to these approaches have been offered as well.

Bibliometric or Webometric approaches may provide additional quality control. These include citation analysis, link following and word counts. Others have adopted bibliometric approaches by following hypertext link trails to authoritative or substantive sites. There is no doubt that the indexes of the major search engines and directories are inadequate. The fact is do not even know how big the Web is much less how to define big.

The Web contains many documents, pages, sites, and objects. Sizing the Web has proven to be a complex and uncertain enterprise. Some Web resources are trash as is some print. But even trash (a highly subjective subject) needs at times to be classified or cataloguéed. Their other two observations are more telling. Others recognize that Web document changes are important to their bibliographic control and still others have found it necessary to modify practice in response to those changes.

Much attention has been paid to Web size and growth, as defined by server and host counts, packet traffic (MIDS) and other indicators. While we recognize both functions, we tend to concentrate more attention on the informatics of the transfer function rather than on the growth and change of the information content of the medium. That said, reasonably certain of at least two things: the Web is a big place and that it is ever-changing and ever-growing. There have been a number of approaches and proposals to categorize, index, and catalogue the Web.

Let us concede that the Web is not and is not meant to be a library any more than the authoring, publication, production, distribution, and marketing of traditional media constitute libraries. Libraries are collections of these information products, organized in some useful fashion, and made available to the appropriate client or patron pool. Perhaps not or perhaps it does not matter, for libraries can be libraries if their collections either are not universally comprehensive or if their collections do not address all points of view concerning a specific issue. In fact, no library can ever fully meet the "access to all information" test. It can also be argued that in time the Web may more likely provide access to all points of view than print because of the very ease of publication to the Web. Like other information streams, the Web can be organized, collected, and managed. Libraries, necessarily digital libraries, can be and are constructed from Web resources.

The Internet is a moving target in two ways. First, there is a constant stream of technical change and computing upgrades and improvements. New capabilities, concepts and terminology challenge the practitioner, but these are manageable. The other change is, from the perspective of managing Web content, far more profound. Web pages and Web sites undergo constant modification. These changes take two general forms. The first is existence. Both Web pages and Web sites exhibit varied longevity patterns. The second is content modification. Efforts to organize, categorize, index, or catalogue the Web all contain one inherent and fatal flaw. Before one can successfully organize Web content, one must recognize and compensate for the dynamic nature of the Web.

A Web site is removed from its server, unless it is cached or archived it is gone. It is true that the media that traditional materials are produced on deteriorate over time. It is also possible for societies to seek to eliminate whole bodies of literature either from neglect or active eradication. Conceivably, Web documents are not subject to physical deterioration but they are subject to the technological. There is an even more important difference between Web documents and traditional ones.

Moreover, when a Web document is edited or updated, the edited version replaces and erases the earlier edition. New traditional editions may update older ones but they do not erase them. Creating Web document archives and caches can solve some of these issues. A Web cache may be considered a very short term Web archive. In caching, Web documents are stored then accessed at some location closer to or faster for the end user than the original host is. Caching creates ethical, legal, as well as timeliness concerns.

Archiving raises additional problems including what to archive and how often should the archive be updated. Storage and retrieval can quickly become a major problem. The library of native documents rather than with the library of cached documents. The literature suggests for example that change and attrition effect information retrieval. Changing pages are the more frequently visited pages. The organization of Web sites may help predict document longevity.

Web pages located at the server-level domain are zero level pages, those one file removed are at the first level, and so on. This is not particularly surprising in that many zero and first level pages are navigational and will necessarily change as the Web site as a whole changes, while those pages located deeper on the file structure are more likely to be content in nature.

Web sites and Web pages undergo content change and attrition. While content and structural changes can and have been measured the limits its focus to Web site and Web page persistence. Persistence is the most fundamental form of change. Either a document exists or it does not. Both Web pages and sites manifest one of three forms of persistence behavior. They may persist of a given period of time - which is to say each time the URL is queried, the specific page addressed is accessed, it responds.

The Web page may fail to respond. Any Web page that fails to respond, but subsequently responds after one of two additional queries in a forty-eight hour period is considered present. Web page data are collected on a weekly basis. A Web page is defined here as comatose if on the sixth and subsequent weekly queries including the most recent when data were taken, that Web page failed to resolve. The term comatose is chosen purposefully, for as the data which follow demonstrate, once a Web page goes comatose, this in itself is no guarantee that a Web page will not return at some time to the same URL.

If a Web page were to return after the sixth collection period or five weeks, it would no longer be counted in subsequent assessments as comatose. Web pages that fail but return are labeled intermittent. Two forces effect library collection development from the Web. In order to provide patrons with both broad and exhaustive resources libraries will necessarily have to turn to digital and Web resources to expand and augment their collections. In the end, digital and hybrid libraries, will have to incorporate native Web documents into their collections to a degree far greater than is now the practice.

The Web and for that matter traditional publishing are in constant flux. New Web documents are constantly being added to the available resource pool, just as new print and digital materials are. This offers no original challenge to libraries. The original challenge to libraries brought by the Web lies in its ephemeral nature. Both Web pages and Web sites undergo metamorphosis, attrition, and return. Any library that seeks to incorporate Web materials into its collection must take into account this dynamic or the quality of the bibliographic representation as well as of the collection itself will rapidly erode. If indeed the half lives of Web sites and Web pages are about two years, information managers must pay attention to the process.

Document death is never trivial, for in the absence of an archive, the information contained in that document is lost. Comatoseness is not necessarily as tragic as document death in that some documents are intermittent and do return. This may not be unique to the Web, librarians have had extensive experience managing changing technology, changing media, and controlling for document demise. The document lifecycle is far more prevalent on the Web than for print; it is in fact an accepted norm. If this lifecycle is both ubiquitous and normal, those who seek to manage Web content must develop new systems and adapt old standards that specifically address it.

To manage the lifecycle, the digital library community has begun to address the dynamic and the impact that change has on the quality of collections; indexing, search, and retrieval algorithms, end user and intermediary behavior; document storage, caching, and archiving; and other related issues. There are a number of classifying digital library Web services. Users and systems need to register different types of objects, search for them, resolve references, navigate hierarchies and other types of links, decompose objects into simpler objects, enhance objects, and transform objects from one format to another.

Library web pages are focused mainly on individual libraries and the resources and services they offer. Consequently, with rare exceptions web access hosted by libraries is not designed to serve as a general entry point for the larger world of web-accessible resources. Neither are the multitude of individual library web pages equal to a single, widely known, dependable beginning place for research in the web environment. With the availability of what already numbers several dozen information.coms, one might reasonably ask whether research libraries should bother taking concerted action to get into the web information portal business.

After all, the information.coms offer a variety of different formats and approaches to finding information, and our constituencies are accustomed to using them. In addition, developing a scholars portal would undoubtedly be a complex and expensive undertaking and would require concerted action on a scale that has been difficult to achieve, let alone sustain, within the research library community. Letting a thousand flowers bloom, it turns out, has always been easier than cultivating a garden.

Conceptually, one might say that information.coms are horizontal rather than vertical information retrieval services. So except for the most straightforward types of inquiries, their ability to facilitate what the academy considers in-depth research is extremely limited. In the best of all possible web-based worlds, the subject library of the future might be conceived of as a highly customized, narrowly focused search engine adapted to the character of publications and research habits of a discipline.

Indeed, the largest drawback of all may be precisely that information.coms in general have not been designed with the particular needs of the research community in mind. Rather, for good business reasons, they appear focused on broad customer bases and the most common information-seeking activities of the general public. This may simply be a necessary condition for success with commercial enterprises.

More limited niche markets are certainly not prohibited in the commercial world, and indeed, some are beginning to appear in the education sector. At this time, however, the information.coms with an education focus are aimed more at providing content than web searching and are still able to offer only small and basic collections as gauged by research library standards.

In addition, these and other information.coms are proprietary and distinct and are themselves in some need of aggregation for portal access. For instance, while one will occasionally find information on a university web page about how to search the Internet including a listing of search engines, never will one encounter such a listing when accessing an information.com, since it would be self-destructive to promote one's competition. Thus, ironically, the information.com world, while replete with help for web information seekers, in the final analysis adds to the overall complexity of the situation.

There are other more proactively positive reasons that ARL, along with strategic partners, should undertake to build a scholars portal. One may be simply that there is arguably no other agency (or group of agencies) with the breadth of awareness, the information, the skills, and the objectivity to succeed at doing so.

This is not meant to be a grandly arrogant statement but rather to point out the unique character of the research library community: the libraries themselves, those who operate them, their not-for-profit status, and the potential resident therein for making sense of the world's largest unmanaged database, the World Wide Web. In other words, research librarians can likely create a scholars portal better than anyone else.

Perhaps less noble but still important is the growing fact that increasingly the world's business, including the business of research, is becoming web-based. Those agencies that wish to survive, let alone thrive, are busily developing new web architectures and exploring how to migrate significant portions of their business to the web environment. In the academic community, this move to the Web includes internal administrative business functions and increasingly the core functions of teaching and learning.

The potential usefulness of a scholars portal is so extraordinary that it is tempting to describe such a wonderful service that it would be practically unachievable. The following description, therefore, must be thought of as categories of possibility that may be mixed in whole or part. They are also clearly not the only possibilities. Indeed, the real work (and the fun) will consist of creating the design of the portal, deciding what to include, and determining where to begin. The scholars portal would promote the development of and provide access to the highest quality content on the Web.

Through the efforts of a myriad number of agencies the information content of the Web is growing exponentially. What is needed, however, is the addition of information content of academically sound quality. The scholars portal would facilitate the addition of high-quality material by fostering standards, searching across databases, and offering a variety of supporting tools. As a result, libraries, corporations, and many other organizations would be empowered to contribute to an accessible, distributed digital library.

The existence and efforts of scholars portal, therefore, would accelerate the growth of high-quality material and facilitate what has been referred to as the global relational research library. Such a library could contribute to a reformation in the format of scholarly publishing and usher in access to a vast and heretofore largely unusable body of original material, specialized resources for communities of scholars, and accumulated scientific data. With the growing use of asynchronous learning methodologies, there is also an increasing need for extending certain elements of traditional library public services to the Web. This is already beginning to happen through experiments with virtual reference environments. Perhaps the most ambitious test of the virtual reference environment today is the

Collaborative Digital Reference Service (CDRS) sponsored by the Library of Congress. The goal of CDRS is to provide professional reference service to users anywhere anytime by means of an international, digital network of libraries. The service will include electronic responses to questions, including document delivery, when appropriate and 24x7 virtual access to a live librarian when necessary. To accomplish this, CDRS will utilize a cooperating group of libraries around the globe in a shared enterprise.

By customizing search engines in this fashion and directing them to dependable sources of information, scholars portal would evolve increasingly "intelligent" automated systems and improve the success rate of query systems. The foundations for moving in this direction are already visible in the emerging capacities of OCLC'S Cooperative Online Resource Catalog (CORC).

With the addition of digital materials to the library's portfolio a debate about the role of the catalog has also developed. Proponents of the catalog and of libraries believe strongly that the catalog has enduring value and that it can evolve to be a useful tool for Web access, whereas critics do not foresee any role for the library catalog as a research tool for networked information. It is always humbling to learn that something you regard as a great and very contemporary problem echoes an experience from the past. In America, large libraries are getting very large. They are being run for wide constituencies on broad lines. More and more the practical American spirit is seeking for coordination and cooperation. It is by no means certain that the card form of catalog will continue indefinitely as the chief tool of library workers.

Networked Information

One of the key notions in networked information discovery and retrieval is that of federating disparate, independently maintained databases scattered about the network. Users should be able to search such constellations of databases as if they were a single, consistent, unified information resource. In order to do that, it is necessary to provide a common semantic view of the various databases involved, even though they may have radically different access points and data structures, and may be accessed through different search protocols or other query mechanisms. Traditional library catalogues or abstracting and indexing databases can clearly support queries constructed using Dublin Core data elements; thus it is possible to build a software layer that permits such databases to participate in federations that use the Dublin Core data elements. These interfaces will use mappings or crosswalks to translate from Dublin Core data elements to the actual access points in the database.

For digitized images or other materials, whether created directly in digital form or digitized from other media (e.g., special collections), full bibliographic cataloguing is particularly expensive because most of these items are unique, and libraries cannot use the system of shared copy cataloguing to control and distribute costs. User-friendliness of library information systems is important, because they are used not only by professional librarians but also by novice users.

Advanced hardware and software technologies have brought us new concepts to build user-friendly library information systems such as GUIs, multimedia user interfaces, collaboration support tools, etc. The digital library will provide us with an intellectual environment where users can interactively retrieve and read documents, books, audio-visual materials, etc. However, from a practical point of view, we cannot build such environments in one day, because not all libraries can afford high-performance computing and network facilities.

Since library information systems are data-centered, it is not easy to modify data-dependent functions or to add new information to an existing database in order to create new functions and user interfaces. The librarian is an important information resource in a library, and we cannot fully take advantage of a library without his/her help. A digital library will not necessarily be a fully automated librarian-less library, but will have to provide intelligent collaborative services of librarians. In addition to the collaborative services of librarians, the digital library will have to provide environments for group work. For example, researchers sometimes use a conference room in a library for research meetings using journals and other materials in the library. Thus, collaboration support is one of the important features that should be explored in order to build the digital library. Reference services could be carried out using conventional media such as telephone, facsimile and email.

However, these media do not offer the face-to-face communication that is quite important both for librarians and users; librarians must be able to correctly understand questions and needs of users, and users would be able to appropriately express their questions in their conversation with librarians. The library user and librarian are modeled as the participants in a conversation carried out via the system. Library materials and user materials, which may or may not be in digital form, are modeled as objects to be displayed on the terminals in front of the participants.

The librarian's desk is modeled as a display screen in front of each participant where the participants can see their partners and view the same materials. It is natural to design a library collaboration support system based on the librarian's desk metaphor. Every new technology takes a few generations to become stable, so we do not think to preserve the hardware and software necessary to read old documents.

Digital documents are particularly vulnerable, since the very pace of technical progress continuously makes the hardware and software that contain them outmoded. A Web archive must solve the technical problems facing all digital documents as well as its own unique problems. First, information must be continuously collected, since it is so ephemeral. Second, information on the Web is not discrete; it is linked. Consequently, the boundaries of the object to be preserved are ambiguous. The economic problem is acute for all archives. Since their mission is to preserve primary documents for centuries, the return on investment is very slow to emerge, and it may be intangible hence hard to measure.

Archives serve the public interest in the very long run, with immediate benefits for only a few scholars. For this reason, they tend to be small and specialized. However, a Web archive will require a large initial investment for technology, research and development, and training-and must be built to a fairly large scale if it is continuously to save the entire Web. New intellectual property laws concerning digital documents have been optimized to develop a digital economy, thus the rights of intellectual property holders are emphasized.

Copyright holders have reason for caution, because the technology is so new and the long-term implications of new laws are unknown. Although the Web is popularly regarded as a public domain resource, it is copyrighted; thus, archivists have no legal right to copy the Web. And yet it is not preservation that poses an economic threat, it is access to archives that might damage new markets. Finding a balance between preservation and access is the most urgent problem to be solved, because if today's Web is not saved it will not exist in the future. Access is a political as well as a legal problem. The answer to the access problem, like the answers to all political problems, lies in establishing a process of negotiation among interested parties.

Today, the "surface" Web contains all of the static hypertext markup language (HTML) pages that can be accessed by URLs. Some of the surface Web, especially in the commercial sector, requires passwords or encryption keys; this area might be called the "private" Web. To archive these Web pages would require permission of the owners. The private Web is often encased in security protection services that make copying and preservation doubly difficult. Beyond these problems, surface Web pages are often generated on the fly, customized on demand from databases in the "deep" or "dark" Web. The ambiguous boundaries of Web objects are also problematic because they are compounds of design elements, including texts, pictures, graphics, digital sound, movies, and code-the list expands as innovation continues.

Each of these elements has intellectual property rights attached to it, although they are rarely marked and sometimes impossible to trace. Technologies to reproduce the Web object-however defined-must be preserved, including the hardware and software necessary to access the information in an authentic context or to recreate it. This is difficult in the best of cases. Every solution changes the context of information in ways that affect its authenticity.

Magnetic storage media such as tape and discs eventually deteriorate. Moreover, hardware and software eventually become obsolete, hence very expensive to preserve and operate. A Web archive must migrate from one technical environment to another as generations of technology succeed one another. Nevertheless, under today's law such migration could be a violation of copyright law because it involves copying the signal from one medium to another. These problems are typical of those that occur in the early stages of every innovation, when getting to market quickly is more important than is perfecting the product.

Digital information products are not designed for longevity, and even if they were, it is likely they would become obsolete quickly. As a consequence, the technologies of digital preservation are complex and expensive. The problems are understood far better than are the solutions at this point, but it is already clear that a Web archive will require substantial investment in technological infrastructure and technical research and development, and that commercial entities are unlikely to lead this effort unless there is short term economic value in doing so. Both archives and libraries collect, organize, preserve, and provide access to the documentary record. The distinguishing function of archives is to preserve the integrity of documents for the long run. While the technical problem of preservation is difficult, it is well understood.

The problem of access, by contrast, involves legal and economic issues that have not yet been adequately explored. While print archives provide a useful model, the economic and legal environments surrounding print are quite different from those surrounding digital documents. Economic and legal issues cannot be separated. In 1998, the Digital Millennium Copyright Act (DMCA) gave copyright owners rights to protect their works in digital formats. The DMCA implements the 1996 WIPO Copyright Treaty and WIPO Performances and Phonograms Treaty. As a public policy, the DMCA was focused upon making the Internet safe for intellectual property. If digital information is easily moved from place to place on a network, such movement is considered to be copying and is protected by copyright.

In the digital realm, however, information may be licensed by contract rather than sold under copyright. With licenses, the provisions of the contract determine the uses that are allowed, which are unlikely to include library circulation or fair use. While printed works may also be sold with "shrink-wrap" licenses, the print market has not accepted them as readily as have markets for digital information. The fair-use doctrine allows for copying for personal educational purposes, within limits that are designed to protect information markets from damage.

The DMCA explicitly allows archives to make digital copies of print works for the purpose of preservation. To prevent illegal copying, the DMCA encourages the use of technical protection services such as encryption by making it illegal to use software to break them, and also making it illegal to develop and distribute such software. Software developers feel that this provision raises free-speech issues and perhaps property issues if it makes it illegal for the owner of a legal copy to make a backup. Print archives are permitted to collect copyrighted materials and copy them for preservation purposes. For example, it is legal to copy print materials from one medium to another as part of a migration strategy over time, but it may not be legal to do so with digital collections, or to reformat them (e.g., from CD-ROM to a hard disk). Differences between the production and distribution of printed and digital works raise additional legal issues for Web archives.

Every law ultimately relies upon the perception of citizens that it is fair. Within this general cultural approval of the legitimacy, a political consensus must be built among those with significant stakes in the issues. Often this kind of consensus begins with an agreement about a fair procedure for resolving differences; an example is the Conference on Fair Use (CONFU) process, which attempted to build a consensus that defined the Fair-Use policy. The building of a public consensus will depend in this case on developing a shared understanding of digital information.

Web pages clearly have intellectual and economic value, but thus far the new kinds of value created by Web pages, and digital information generally, have not been well described. Consumers give value to any commodity, in a sense, by sustaining markets that ultimately justify investment in innovations, but this relationship is unexpectedly novel in the case of Web pages. This information has commercial value, both enabling more customized services to be provided to the consumer, and, it is hoped, building brand loyalty and justifying advertising rates on Web pages.

The Web has grown to global scale very rapidly; it may represent the fastest diffusion of a new technology in human history. At the same time, the technology of the Web has not stopped evolving. Even now, significant evolution is occurring as, for example, new architectures replace static Web pages with customized Web pages generated on the fly. Because innovation is not linear, the development of the Web is unpredictable. For stakeholders, the best option is to participate in the new organizations that, if they do not govern the future of the Web, at least attempt to analyze and influence its direction. The Web began as software for the exchange of documents among scientists and researchers, using an Internet that was subsidized for education and research purposes.

Today the Internet is increasingly commercial, and the Web has been the subject of vigorous investment as a technology for the digital economy. The search for sustainable business models for Web business has undergone a rapid evolution, ranging from Web advertising models to banner ads, sponsorship ads, subscription models, and business to consumer (B2C) enterprises. Investment in these enterprises and technologies has slowed for the moment because there is little sense that viable economic models have been identified.

9

Information Automation

The term "automated digital library" can be used to describe a digital library where all tasks are carried out automatically. Computer programs substitute for the intellectually demanding tasks that are traditionally carried out by skilled professionals. These tasks include selection, cataloguing and indexing, seeking for information, reference services, and so on. The common theme is that these activities require considerable mental activity, the type of activity that people are skilled at and computers find difficult.

Automated digital libraries should not be confused with library automation, which uses computing to reduce routine tasks in conventional libraries. The underlying question is not whether automated digital libraries can rival conventional digital libraries today. They clearly cannot. The question is whether we can conceive of a time when they will provide an acceptable substitute. Quality of service in automated digital libraries will not come from replicating the procedures of classical librarianship.

More likely, automated libraries will provide users with equivalent services that are fundamentally different in the way that they are delivered. For example, within the foreseeable future, computer programs are unlikely to be much good at applying the Anglo American Cataloguing Rules to monographs. But cataloguing rules are a means to an end, not the end itself. They exist to provide services to users, notably information discovery.

Automatic methods for information discovery may not need traditional cataloguing rules. The criterion for evaluating the new methods is whether the users find what the information that they require. Consider the contrast between web search engines and conventional abstracting and indexing services or library catalogs. Almost everything that is best about a library catalog is done badly by a web search service. The selection of which materials to index by a web search engine relies on arbitrary considerations, the indexing records are crude at best, authority control is non-existent, and the elimination of duplicates leaves much to be desired. On the other hand, web search services are strong in ways that catalogs are weak.

While cataloguing is expensive, indexing the web is cheap. The leading web search engines index several hundred million web pages every month, more than the total number of MARC records that have ever been created. It is wrong to claim that conventional catalogs or indexes are superior because of their quality control, and it is equally wrong to claim that the web search services are superior because of their coverage and currency. The value to users depends on what the user wants to achieve. In contrast, web search services such as GoogleSM are entirely automated. The indexes are built by a team of computers with no knowledge of what they are indexing.

Google has the advantage over Medline of indexing hundreds of millions of web pages, and doing so repeatedly every month. It is quite useful for finding general information on medical topics, but it does not index the major scientific journals, its indexing records are crude, it has no understanding of medical terminology, and makes no attempt to separate sound medicine from quackery. It is a long way from being a substitute for Medline. On the other hand, consider the trade-off between Google and Inspec, which is the leading abstracting and indexing service for computing.

In many areas of computing, Google's restriction to open access web materials is relatively unimportant, since almost every significant result first appears on a web site and only later reaches the printed journals, if ever. In computing, substantially the same information is often available from several sources. Google provides a direct link to an open access version. Inspec references a formally published version, which is usually printed or online with restricted access. For example, a scientist judges a library catalog simply as a tool for information discovery, while, for a humanist, the catalog may be a bibliographic source in its own right.

Any predictions of the future value of web search engines compared with conventional abstracting and indexing services depend heavily on the publication and reading habits of people in different disciplines. The rate of progress in computing power is described by Moore's Law, that the number of transistors on a semiconductor doubles every eighteen months. This is roughly equivalent to saying that computing power increases 100-fold in 10 years or 10,000-fold in 20 years. Few people can appreciate the implications of such dramatic change, but the future of automated digital libraries is likely to depend more on brute force computing than on sophisticated algorithms. Many of the most successful methods of artificial intelligence apply simple methods to huge volumes of data.

An interesting example comes from the computer programs that play chess. The IBM system that is now equal to the world's greatest grandmasters is descended from Deep Thought, a student project at Carnegie Mellon University. The members of the Deep Thought team were not chess experts. Their breakthrough came from expertise in developing exceptionally fast hardware, which could analyze immense numbers of chess variations. Information discovery illustrates the complementary skills of computers and people. Humans are skilled at reading a few thousand words and extracting complex concepts. Faced with a billion pages (roughly the size of the web), they are helpless.

Computers can index every word in a billion pages and search the indexes for simple patterns almost instantaneously. The web search services represent the state-of-the-art in automated information discovery. Within each service lie a number of separate processes, each of which is carried out automatically, and each of which is constrained by the current state of computing. To build the indexes, a web crawler must decide which pages to index, eliminate duplicates, create a short index record for each page and add the terms found on the page to its inverted files.

To search the index, the search engine must convert the user's query to a search command, match it against the inverted files, rank the results and return them to the user. To anticipate the potential of automatic systems to rival the functionality of Medline in all disciplines, we need to examine the components of a system like Google and see how they could be improved. Moore's law predicts that computers will be 10,000 times more powerful in twenty years. With such computer power available, we know that the automatic search systems will be extremely good, even if no new algorithms are invented. For example, to decide how closely a document matches a query would seem to require human judgment, yet standard methods of information retrieval do remarkably well.

They use the power of computers to match simple patterns as a surrogate for the human ability to relate concepts. As humans, we use our understanding of language to observe that two texts are on similar topics, or to rank how closely documents match a query. Computers can estimate closeness of match by comparing word frequencies. One basic concept, developed by Gerald Salton at Cornell University about 1970, represents each document as a multi-dimensional vector and uses the angle between their vectors as a measure of the similarity of two documents. Evaluating the importance of documents would appear to be another task that requires human understanding, but Google's ranking algorithm does remarkably well entirely automatically. The idea behind this algorithm is simple.

Google ranks web pages by how many other pages link to them. It gives greater weight to links from higher-ranking pages. Calculating the ranks requires the algorithm to iterate through a matrix that has as many rows and columns as there are pages on the web, yet with modern computing and considerable ingenuity, Google performs this calculation routinely. As a result, Google is remarkably successful in presenting a user with the most important page on a topic or a well-respected overview. This algorithm was developed as part of the NSF-funded Digital Library Initiative. The Internet is an extremely important part of modern culture and contains many materials that should be preserved for future generations. Each month, a web crawler gathers every open access web page with associated images.

The Internet Archive preserves these files for the future and mounts them on computers available for scholarly research today. The Internet Archive is not perfect. Only HTML pages and images are collected, no Java applets or style sheets; the materials are dumped into a computer system with no organization or indexing; broken links are left broken; and access for scholars is rudimentary. Yet the simple fact is that without the automated approach of the Internet Archive, these materials would already have been lost. Attempts to catalog and collect web materials using skilled librarians and archivists have floundered on the scale of effort needed to do even a rudimentary job. Citation analysis is a long-standing success story of applying computers to library information. Inspired by the efforts of Eugene Garfield, the founder of Science Citation Index, there is a long tradition of using citations as bibliographic measures.

Hyperlinks are the web's equivalent to citations. Since they are already in machine-readable form, they are amenable to algorithmic analysis. Google's ranking algorithm can be seen as applying the concepts of citation analysis to the web. Hyperlinks refer to items or copies of a work, but citations normally refer to the work itself or a specific manifestation. Automatic systems are becoming capable of extracting a reference from a document and linking it to the digital object that it references. Currently, the most fully automated system for reference linking is the SFX system, created by Hebert Van de Sompel and colleagues at the University of Ghent.

Reference linking is one of the building blocks that are being used to build large-scale automated digital libraries. Metadata is one of the foundations of librarianship. There are a number of projects that extract metadata from digital objects automatically. Perhaps the most remarkable is the Informedia project, led by Howard Wactlar at Carnegie Mellon University. Informedia has the extremely ambitious goal of providing access to segments of video, such as television news, entirely automatically. Thus it includes algorithms for dividing raw video into discrete items, for generating short summaries (called "skims"), for indexing the sound track using speech recognition, for recognizing faces and for searching using methods of natural language processing. Each of these methods is a tough research topic and, not surprisingly, Informedia provides only a rough-and-ready service, but overall it is surprisingly effective.

Moreover, many of the weaknesses of Informedia could be overcome by applying huge amounts of computing power. The job of a reference librarian ranges from helping users with the mechanics of using a library to tasks that require deep intellectual understanding. The ugly term "disintermediation" is used when users perform for themselves tasks that used to be carried out with the help of a librarian. Information retrieval provides a good test case. The mechanics of searching have been almost completely assumed by computing. The current generation of scholars never experienced the tedium of reading through long lists of abstracts, searching huge card catalogs and following citations laboriously from journal to journal.

Searching a card catalog required skill. Because of the labor in creating and filing cards, only a small number of entries were provided for each work. Since few users ever mastered the complex rules for the main and supplementary headings, or the intricate filing conventions, serious users turned to reference librarians for help. Automated digital libraries can clearly help with the mechanics of searching, but information seeking is more complex. In disciplines with complex organization of information, searching for information remains a skilled task. Often, knowledge of the subject matter is paramount and the experts develop their own skills.

Computing power is much cheaper than human expertise, more so every year. When money and time are available in abundance, skilled professionals have no equal. But they are always in short supply. In the United States, the National Library of Medicine is funded by the government and provides open access to Medline, but only rich lawyers can afford to use the legal services provided by Westlaw and Lexis. Because of the cost, traditional library systems are selective. Indexing and abstracting services restrict their coverage to a carefully selected set of publications. Catalogs do not include potentially useful information from monographs, such as individual items in anthologies, subheading, captions, and so on.

There are essentially no attempts to catalog the content of web sites, below the level of the whole site. Even so, these services are very expensive. Automatic systems have no trouble with being inclusive; they have problems when they attempt to be selective. Their weakness is lack of precision. They exhibit what, in a human, would be called very poor judgment. Both ISI's Web of Science and ResearchIndex provide users with interlinked scientific documents. Web of Science is a splendid service, but its production is not fully automatic, since ISI relies on skilled personnel for election and for key parts of the input process. Because the ResearchIndex methods are automatic and are applied to raw data, ResearchIndex inevitably has errors, while the skilled staff at ISI eliminate almost all errors, but at a cost. Automated digital libraries combined with open access information on the Internet offer to provide the Model T Ford of information. Nobody would claim that the Model T Ford was a peer to the handcrafted cars of its generation, and automated digital libraries cannot approach the personal service available to the faculty of a well-endowed university.

Knowledge Management Context

In Australia, an integrated structure for the Department of Human Services (DHS) libraries was endorsed in July 2000 paving the way for new library innovations supporting a departmental knowledge management approach. During 1999 the knowledge management group of functions aligned under the management of the Director for Knowledge Management (KM), Iolanda Principe. Since this time, a Framework and Guide for Knowledge Management in the Department of Human Services was written in June 2001 and recently endorsed by the department's executive management group. This framework outlines key definitions, principles, objectives and responsibilities for KM within the department. It is designed as a practical guide for staff in the department in implementing a KM approach within their business unit while mapping out an organisation-wide approach.

This knowledge centre is a focal point for knowledge skills and the facilitation of knowledge flow within the organisation and requires the transformation of the current library and information services to fulfil this function. The DHS in South Australia is leading the way in the successful implementation of knowledge management within the public sector. The current challenge for the library within this emerging knowledge enabled department is how to further this shift and overcome the barriers identified above. There are numerous creative and innovative ways in which the library can achieve these value added services and become a re-intermediary knowledge agent.

The next challenge is to ensure that future customer participation processes enable clearer identification of knowledge worker and organisational needs and that innovative service delivery strategies are implemented to meet these needs. The balanced scorecard is one tool that will assist in this process. The DHS in South Australia has adopted the balanced scorecard as a key reporting tool for the measurement of strategic and intangible outcomes. The scorecard methodology enables the measurement of objectives that target organisational change, and, specifically, innovation and creation.

Currently, the library strongly advocates for its involvement in these processes to ensure legal deposit requirements are met and copies are available, not only within the department, but also nationally and internationally. The potential within this expanded group for further service delivery innovations and the enhancement of relationships with customers is great and an opportunity the library will take up eagerly. Specifically, the library will also be looking to expand its expertise in processes for engaging with customers through partnerships with the staff in these functional areas. The challenges and barriers have been clearly defined previously.

The library has commenced its journey, beyond its traditional library role, to support the organisation's knowledge management approach. The initiatives that have contributed to this reorientation have also been described. Libraries have experienced a strong shift in focus over the past decade towards digital formats for information resources. In a growing number of libraries, there is now an attitude that user demands will be met through digital media and electronic dissemination as much as through paper-based media.

Universities are investing to provide improved teaching and learning resources via digital media. Other institutions, including the British Library and the US Library of Congress, are developing large technical infrastructures. The implementation of technical infrastructure and the improvement of access to the digital world is seen as hugely important for regions such as Africa, which lacks overall investment in social economic growth, and Latin America, where development has been limited by the relatively lower economic status of the library. These shifts at the library or institutional level are a reflection of the macro economics of the global economy, which contains a much larger informational and digital element than ever before.

Today, many institutions have realised they must put in place information policies, services and technologies with a firmer long-term economic strategy than might previously have been considered. The business plan driving MIT's development of DSpace is one such example. DSpace is MIT Libraries' innovative institutional digital repository designed to manage, host, preserve and enable distribution of the scholarly output of MIT's faculty. There is a clear intent to roll out the DSpace model to many other institutions. Another major economic institutional issue is the long-term preservation of large documentary collections.

Almost all libraries have to think about preservation in both analogue and digital worlds. Even if they do not themselves preserve materials, they need to be sure that some institutions are doing so if they are to direct their users to them. The purchase of digital resources remains a difficult balancing act of apparently conflicting interests. Publishers want to retain and enhance profitability. Electronic availability of journals is not relieving the cost to libraries. Electronic journals are often treated as a value-added service, rather than a replacement technology.

Automatic construction of hypertexts from a collection of linear documents is one of the holy grails of the hypermedia research community. However, when a document has explicit structure, it is usually possible to produce usable hypertexts automatically. Most work in the area has concentrated on using features such as tables of contents and indexes to construct the hypermedia links. The hypertext system that we have used for these experiments has been Microcosm which has certain key advantages for acting as such an experimental workbench, not least because of the fact that it was developed at Southampton, so we have access to all its API's, but also because it supports multiple methods of locating information.

Microcosm produces hypertext applications which have a bias towards querying and information retrieval, rather than the simple "button pushing" hypertext that we have come to expect from some of the more popular authoring packages. This quality of hypertext lends itself to this application. The first method of access to the information uses the *classification information*. This is the information that that is held in the Document Management System (DMS) and is almost exactly equivalent to the information that is held in a library catalogue. It contains the position(s) within the document hierarchy that the file will be located, and it contains all the attributes, such as title, author, date of creation, physical media type and keywords.

This information is very high quality, as it provides specific information about documents, and Microcosm provides tools for traversing the subject hierarchy, and for querying the documents by attributes such as keywords. The second method of access is *hypermedia link following*. It is generally supposed that hypermedia links are manually authored in order to indicate some relationship between the two items at each end of the link. Such links are of very high value, but creating them requires considerable manual effort.

However, the Multimedia Research Group at Southampton always considered that the reduction of this effort, and the automation of link creation, was an important research issue. One of the earliest results of this research was the introduction of *generic links*, which are links with a fixed end point, but which may start at any point where the source object is located. Typically this means any place where a particular text string is located. The third method of data access is text based information retrieval.

The interface to this functionality requires the user to make a selection of text from some document, or else to type in some text, and then choose "compute links" from the menu. One of the strengths of the traditional libraries is that many large collections of books and materials in other media are catalogued with great care and attention to bibliographic detail and accuracy using standard cataloguing rules such as Anglo-American Cataloguing Rules (AACR2).

As Howard Rheingold points out 'Librarians and other specialists have a toolkit and syntax for dealing with well-known problems that people encounter in trying to make sense of large bodies of information. However even key libraries such as the Library of Congress are constantly having to review their strategies and approaches to alternative methods of cataloguing such as copy cataloguing and minimal cataloguing in order to dramatically bring down their backlogs. On-line journal abstracting databases also traditionally provide very thorough bibliographic detail created by professional graduate level staff. The combination of a variety of materials from different sources may provide a variety of classification schemes and types of subject headings. These can be added to the bundle's hierarchies.

Although at the document level the classification may not easily convey a sufficient level of separation, nevertheless it can be used in the way a library user traditionally browses a library shelf. On the World Wide Web we see subject catalogues such as the WWW Virtual Library being developed to give a useful alternative way to access a huge amount of information. At the same time Internet Yellow Pages directories, while they become obsolete fairly quickly, still sell because they provide an overview of accessible items which is not yet so easily scanned from today's computer screen. The options for locating information are varied and different ones will suit different users at different times and also the same users at different levels of understanding.

The level of a item - who it is intended for- has less frequently been emphasised in the past. It may perhaps be highlighted by a pointer such as a treatment code or a readership category, but this may become more important in the future with the enormous volumes generated by both paper and electronic publication. The catalogue entries produced by the information specialist may give a degree of rigour to the information retrieval process. However, a multimedia bundle will frequently contain documents produced by and often further modified by the authors, particularly in the academic environment, which do not have the advantage of such in-depth indexing.

One way to compensate for this might simply be to provide or point to a glossary or dictionary which helps the searchers choose their terms. The linking mechanisms of Microcosm do, in any case, give considerable help in retrieving relevant items. Free text terms used by the author are often more up to date in style and therefore more akin to the searcher's own vocabulary. The art is in balancing the effort required versus the result, particularly as terminology can change dramatically as one moves forwards or backwards in time.

The Web is complicated by the fact that only part of it is publicly accessible and by unresolved issues over rights. It is not clear, for example, that a Web site may be "harvested" for purposes of preservation without the knowledge and permission of the various rights holders. Several people in both the technical and the arts communities urged attention to "ephemera" as well as to "published" works. A number of respondents in film, television, and sound noted that again, the distinction between publication and ephemera is blurred.

Within the Web itself are emerging distinctions between the "surface" Web and the "deep" Web. E-books and e-journals download content from the Web to their respective formats and include hyperlinks to the Web for ancillary augmentation. The advent of interactive television also invites new forms of multimedia that combine resources built for the Web with those created for broadcasting in digital form. Moreover, an item that appears seamless to the user is frequently a composite document.

Formats as well understood as electronic scholarly journals are built as multimedia objects in which the constituent elements may include text, images, animation, or advertisements, each of which may be encoded in a different format. Finally, several people from the arts communities emphasized the importance of collecting the version of the object that the creator (e.g., the director of a film) considered final in the format that he or she considered final.

There are complexities to notions of "authorship"; many of these are not new to digital but are magnified by the circumstances under which digital products may be distributed and used. These complexities are related to the complicated intellectual property considerations that surround digital information. Even in a format as carefully studied as is that of electronic scholarly journals, creation and deposit can involve numerous stakeholders, and the number of interested parties multiplies in sound, television, and film, in which individuals and entities have traditionally had rights in the processes of creation and distribution. Frank Romanó points out that the e-books world is witnessing changes in traditional roles and functions; for example, writers can self-publish and thus become distributors, while software companies can behave like publishers.

The issues, which include technical obsolescence and standards, metadata, information security, and the overall architecture of the system, are by no means discrete. Several writers pointed out that the issue is not only making sure that bits survive but also ensuring the preservation of a technical environment that will permit future retrieval of the information, the work as envisioned by the author or creator, and the experience of the user. The longevity of the storage medium was a consistent concern, as was signal degradation and software obsolescence.

One technical expert urged that degradation be compared with the process by which a photograph ages. The image fades; the medium on which the image is printed also disintegrates. There are methods for error detection; however, at some point, there is concern that the integrity of the digital object is compromised. One solution is migration from one medium to another. Particularly for e-books, where so much of the design is predicated on screen size, re-creating the experience for future users implies access to the device that was intended to display the content.

The rapid obsolescence of some formats, as well as the plethora of standards, was widely considered to be a barrier both to creation and to preservation. Those who had opinions on open versus proprietary standards favored the former because they were believed to facilitate management of the archive and its content. This applies to a broad range of issues, from operating systems to markup language, compression, and fonts. Before September 11, 2001, few people consulted had strong opinions on information security, but those who did thought that it was important as a guarantor of trust.

One example that was offered was the information typically provided on copyright registration concerning the authors, who might use a pseudonym or who might wish to keep their own addresses, or the addresses of their agents, from general use. There are overlaps between this kind of information and the information included in metadata. At least one person cautioned against excessive restriction, arguing that too many restrictions inhibit accountability. Those who addressed technical issues tended to favor distributed rather than centralized systems, because the former would accommodate a high degree of "local" variation within shared protocols.

There were also calls for interoperability, which would make it possible for information to be shared across platforms and among vendors. Metadata, or "data about data," are simultaneously a standard, a management and access tool, and a feature of the system architecture. Moreover, as pointed out by Lyman in his study of archiving the Web, the metadata discussions reveal the different visions of archiving as embodied by the library and computer science communities. He writes, "The librarian tends to look at the content of the Web page as the object to be described and preserved. The computer scientist tends to look at the Web as a technology for linking information, thus looks at the Web as a system of relationships."

One of the functions of metadata, as the various schemes have evolved since 1995, is outlining the terms and conditions of use-that is, access. Few failed to identify intellectual property rights (IPR) management and fair use as key issues. The complexity of this set of issues varies across media. Some arose from unfamiliarity with the distinction that is common among traditional preservation circles in which use of rare objects, for example, can be calibrated and surrogates used in their stead. While there was near unanimity on the importance of managing intellectual property responsibly, no voices called for some version of complete lockout.

Indeed, one representative from a major company with interests in several areas thought that the most important issues were both protection of intellectual property rights and ease of use (with appropriate accommodation for potential users with special needs). There was widespread acknowledgment of the need to find a balance between the economic needs of the creators and distributors and the legitimate uses of the works, but there was a range of opinion as to what that meant. Some suggested ways to handle management of intellectual property "behind the scenes" through technological means, which could be coupled with pricing that discouraged inappropriate use.

Several people felt that existing laws were sufficient: what is required, they maintained, is appropriate enforcement. Others believed that there was a need to clarify the law. Given that the Web is an international phenomenon, attention to international law is particularly important. Several people pointed out that copyright as a mechanism, which had arisen in the context of print, had already begun to fray under the stress of its application to media other than text, and that it was becoming increasingly unwieldy.

Bibliography

Arms, William Y., *Digital Libraries*, Cambridge, MA: The MIT Press, 2000.

Blandford, Ann, and George Buchanan, "Usability of Digital Libraries: A Source of Creative Tensions with Technical Developments." *TCDL Bulletin*, Summer 2003.

Borgman, Christine L., "Digital Libraries and the Continuum of Scholarly Communication." *Journal of Documentation* 56: 412-430, July 2000

Borgman, Christine L.,"Multi-Media, Multi-Cultural, and Multi-Lingual Digital Libraries: Or How Do We Exchange Data in 400 Languages?" D-Lib Magazine, June 1997

Bishop, Ann Peterson, "Measuring Access, Use, and Success in Digital Libraries." *The Journal of Electronic Publishing* 4, no. 2, 1998.

Chowdhury, G.G., and Sudatta Chowdhury, "Digital Library Research: Major Issues and Trends." *Journal of Documentation* 55 : 409-488, September 1999

Cole, Timothy W., "Creating a Framework of Guidance for Building Good Digital Collections", First Monday 7 May 2002

Graham, Peter S., "Requirements for the Digital Research Library", *College & Research Libraries* 56 : 331-339, July 1995.

Greenstein, Daniel, "Digital Libraries and Their Challenges" *Library Trends* 49 : 290-303, Fall 2000

Harter, Stephen P., "Scholarly Communication and the Digital Library: Problems and Issues." *Journal of Digital Information,* 1, no. 1 1997

Kilker, Julian, and Geri Gay, "The Social Construction of a Digital Library: A Case Study Examining Implications for Evaluation." *Information Technology and Libraries* 17: 60-70, June 1998.

Klemperer, Katharina, and Stephen Chapman, "Digital Libraries: A Selected Resource Guide." Information Technology and Libraries 16, : 126-131, September 1997.

Lesk, Michael, "Going Digital." Scientific American 276 : 58-60, March 1997.

Lesk, Michael, "The Organization of Digital Libraries." *Science & Technology Libraries* 17, nos. 3/4 : 9-25, 1999

McKay, Sally, "Digitization in an Archival Environment." *Electronic Journal of Academic and Special Librarianship* 4, no.1, 2003

Marchionini, Gary, and Hermann Maurer., "The Roles of Digital Libraries in Teaching and Learning." Communications of the ACM 38 : 67-75, April 1995

Pope, Nolan F., "Digital Libraries: Future Potentials and Challenges." Library Hi Tech 16, nos. 3-4 : 147-155, 1998.

Smith, Terence R., "A Brief Update on the Alexandria Digital Library Project: Constructing a Digital Library for Geographically-Referenced Materials." *D-Lib Magazine,* March 1996.

Schatz, Bruce R. "Information Retrieval in Digital Libraries: Bringing Search to the Net." *Science,* 327-334, 17 January 1997

Schwartz, Candy, "Digital Libraries: An Overview." *The Journal of Academic Librarianship* 26 (November 2000): 385-393.

Shiri, Ali, "Digital Library Research: Current Developments and Trends." *Library Review* 52, no. 5 : 198-202, 2003

Waters, Donald, "Developing Digital Libraries: Four Principles for Higher Education." EDUCAUSE Review 36 : 58-59, September/October 2001

Index

Additional application services 13
Art Museum Image Consortium (AMICO) 23

Business to consumer (B2C) 284

Collaborative Digital Reference Service (CDRS) 276
Collection management 177
Computer-Aided Design (CAD) 105
Cooperative Online Resource Catalog (CORC) 276
Council on Library and Information Resources (CLIR) 45

Digital Convergence 40
Digital Libraries Initiative (DLI) 166
Digital Object Identifiers (DOIs) 183
Digital Repository Service (DRS) 186
Digital representations 162
Digital responsibilities 179
Digital Revolution 32
Document Type Definition (DTD) 153

E-journals 168
Electronic Business XML (EbXML) 15
Electronic library 2
Encoded Archival Description (EAD) 26, 153
Environmental controls 21
Extensible Markup Language (XML) 14, 53

Fault-isolated dynamic system 12

Geographic Information Systems (GIS) 105
Global Legal Information Network (GLIN) 120

Information retrieval 173
Information Technology (IT) 6
Information-seeking activities 273
Intellectual Property Conservancies (IPCs) 59

Machine-Readable Cataloging (MARC) 1
Metadata 18
Metadata Encoding and Transmission Standard (METS) 19
Microfilming initiatives 21
National Information Standards Organization (NISO) 30
National Institute of Standards

and Technology (NIST) 30
National Science Foundation (NSF) 8

Open Archival Information System (OAIS) 112

Personal information retrieval systems 1
Plagiarism 4
Policy base mechanism 13
Portable Document Format (PDF) 124
Preservation Description Information (PDI) 114
Preservation strategy 50
Preserving Access to Digital Information (PADI) 24

Reliability, Availability, and Serviceability (RAS) 11
Research Libraries Group (RLG) 23, 42
Rich Text Format (RTF) 159
Rules for Archival Description (RAD) 153

Simple Object Access Protocol (SOAP) 14
Standard General Markup Language (SGML) 14, 53
Submission Information Package (SIP) 187
Sun Microsystems 5

Tax-supported research institutions 4
Technological obsolescence 100
Text Encoding Initiative (TEI) 53
Traditional research library 3

Uniform Resource Locator (URL) 110

Virtual Learning Environment (VLE) 10

Web Services Description Language (WSDL) 15
Web-accessible resources 272
Web-enabled device 7
World Wide Web 274